• Finis Bates • Jeremy Bentham • Sarah Bernhar
James Buchanan "Diamond Jim" Brady • John R. Bri
no Cagliostro • Enrico Caruso • Leonard Casley •
us Raymond "Ty" Cobb • William Horace de Vere Col
ghlin • John Sargent Cram • Hart Crane • Frances
Jerome Herman "Dizzy" Dean • John Dee • Ferdin
Sir Arthur Conan Doyle • Doris Duke • Isadora D
Fletcher • James Vincent Forrestal • William Fra
• Clemente Giglio • Samuel Goldwyn • Waxey (Ir
(Howland Robinson) Green • Mary Louise Cecila "
nes A. Harden-Hickey • Gaylord Hauser • William
ughes • Howard Robard Hughes, Jr. • George Hull
and • Sanford Jarrell • Norman Jefferies • Al (A
rella La Guardia • T. E. (Thomas Edward) Lawrenc
Adams Locke • Huey Pierce "The Kingfish" Long •
Mannix • Marx Brothers • William Somerset Maug
izner • Edward Wortley Montagu • John Mytton •
Abraham Norton • John Humphrey Noyes • Charl
Jr. • Hesketh Pearson • Elisha Perkins • Vincenz
lolph • Grigori Efimovich Rasputin • Harry Reiche
Micheal (Harrry F. Gerguson) Romanoff • Jacob Ru
rd Shaw • Richard Brinsley Sheridan • Upton Beal
Casey" Stengel • Louis T. Stone • Eric Oswald von
ohn Taylor • Leo Taxil • Cyrus Reed Teed • Nikol
wain • Tristan Tzara • Bill Veeck • William Voight
James Marion West, Jr. • Mae West • E. J. White
lcott • Basil Zaharoff • Albert Abrams • Hans C
ssell Arundel • Delia Salter Bacon • Phineas Tayl

Lord, what fools these mortals be!

Shakespeare, *A Midsummer Night's Dream*

ZANIES

ZANIES

THE WORLD'S GREATEST ECCENTRICS

By Jay Robert Nash

NEW CENTURY PUBLISHERS, INC.

All photos not otherwise credited come from the author's collection.

Printing Code

12 13 14 15 16

Library of Congress Cataloging in Publication Data

Nash, Jay Robert.
  Zanies.

  Bibliography: p.
  Includes index.
  1. Biography–19th century. 2. Biography–
20th century. 3. Eccentrics and eccentricities–
Biography. I. Title.
CT119.N37 920'.009'03 [B] 82-2145
ISBN 0-8329-0123-7   AACR2

This book is for Neil and Vicky Nash

CONTENTS

CONTENTS

H

I

J

K

L

M

N

O

P

R

S

CONTENTS

PREFACE

Most of the world's best loved or most feared individuals have been eccentrics after one fashion or another. Their quirks, fancies, and abnormalities have usually been censored in "authorized" biographies or, at least, minimized to reflect only a wayward thought or gesture now and then that might be construed as odd but not suspicious. But, in scores of famous lives, eccentricity was a dominating factor that shaped those lives, establishing unforgettable images and often affecting the destiny of entire peoples and nations, as was the case with the profligate Grigori Rasputin, Russia's "Mad Monk."

The author has selected, from thousands of possible entries, more than two hundred of the world's greatest eccentrics for inclusion in this book, that selection based upon consistency of eccentric behavior throughout a lifetime, the impact an eccentric had upon his or her society or profession, and those who best represented the many types of eccentricity. To be sure, there is no strict gauge by which to measure an authentic eccentric, but, after a decade of studying the field, the author feels confident that he has offered up the most representative of those unpredictable, bizarre, and memorable souls who can best be called true eccentrics, a posture not of their own schemes but in and of their natural characters.

An odd trait or two did not necessarily qualify hundreds of possible entries. These included movie stars such as Ginger Rogers and Marlene Dietrich who were, at one time, addicted to bobby sox made of mink, Joan Fontaine who wore sequined-studded suspenders in 1947, Joan Bennett who sported diamond-studded spectacles one season, Mrs. William Powell who once had a stuffed velvet life-size mouse climbing up the skirt of her Sunday dress, in honor of her nickname, "Mousie." These are but faddist whims.

Then there are those with points to prove, wherein normal persons stepped briefly into eccentricity, such as Robert and Louise Loibl, who, in 1971, each ate a 10-mg capsule of DDT for breakfast over a ninety-three-day period. Loibl, an executive of a pest control firm, attempted to show that DDT, taken in small amounts, was not dangerous to humans. Their "stunt" hardly compares with the sensational exploits of flyer Douglas ("Wrong Way") Corrigan or flagpole sitter Alvin ("Shipwreck") Kelly, both of whom earned profiles in this work.

PREFACE

There were many noteworthy candidates for this book who proved to be borderline eccentrics and were therefore eliminated. To mention only a few: Mrs. Isabella Gardner, a practicing beer-drinking Buddhist who once took a stroll through Beacon Hill with an adult lion on a leash; Tulsa businessman John Zink who greeted guests by firing a revolver into the beams of his enormous office until a ricochet almost struck his secretary; Lord Berners who once dropped to all fours to bark like a dog at a Greek hotel owner accused of being a werewolf; Lord Castleton of Ireland who believed in fairies; Lord Charles Beresford who loved to throw chunks of butter at those who displeased him when dining in his private Dublin club; Lord Cloncurry who one day dyed his beard purple on a notion. Such a list is endless and could, no doubt, include any random uncle or distant aunt.

On the other hand, the true candidate for the label of eccentric is one who personifies the unswerving character of the zany. Mark Twain, the great humorist, is a classic example; his eccentricities were not only rampant but consistent throughout his lifetime, one wherein he smoked like a Soho chimney, went for days without eating, and inexplicably slept on the floor of his bathroom, to name only a *few* of his myriad quirks, albeit there is no madness discernable in his literary work.

Abnormal habits of the senses provided strong considerations in the selection of entries. The effects of alcohol upon such famous entries as John Barrymore, W.C. Fields, Squire John Mytton, John O'Hara, and Edgar Allan Poe produced both humorous and repugnant eccentricities. The gluttony of Diamond Jim Brady and Babe Ruth also falls into this category. Not to be ignored were those eccentric satyrs and nymphs whose lifelong sexual obsessions, not to mention stamina, are wonders to behold—actress Clara Bow, dancer Isadora Duncan, politician Victoria Woodhull (a prostitute who ran for the presidency in 1872), actor Charlie Chaplin, occultist Aleister Crowley, America's first free-love cult leader, John Noyes.

Money, its use and misuse, has historically created other types of eccentrics, the miser and the spendthrift, from Hetty Green to Isaac Singer, persons totally obsessed by wealth. The "health nuts"—Bernarr MacFadden, George Bernard Shaw, Upton Sinclair, to name a few—were equally obsessed with impossible diets and improbable cures, as were the quacks they believed in, eccentric medical messiahs such as Albert Abrams, John R. Brinckley, and Elisha Perkins. Two steps away from these zanies are the scientific crackpots who insisted long into the modern era that the earth was flat or hollow, such self-styled astronomers as Wilbur Voliva and John Cleves Symmes.

The medical quacks and scientific crackpots are eccentric cousins to the humbugs, those who delighted in faking newspaper stories, anthropological exhibits, and archeological discoveries that astounded and sometimes terrorized the world. Here the reader will find cunning and clever zanies such as P.T. Barnum, America's first great showman, who once exhibited a mermaid that was no more than a monkey's torso and the bottom half of a large fish; Richard Adams Locke, who reported at length how batmen were flying about the surface of the moon; George Hull, who planted the "Cardiff Giant"; and Charles Dawson, who dug up the "Piltdown Man."

Another provocative category is that of the practical joker. In these ranks the reader can marvel at the inventive escapades of Hugh Troy, the Mellon Brothers, William Cole, and Brian Hughes, to mention a few. Then there are the eccentric clowns, from the Marx Brothers to Casey Stengel, and the compulsive impersonators, from Ferdinand Demara to William Voight, who once took over an entire town in Germany with no other authority than a second-hand uniform.

Then there were the deluded religious fanatics who swayed governments (and still do) and ramrodded impossible laws into existence, some even managing to frighten the populations of the world by predicting doomsday almost to the minute, the awesome likes of Billy Sunday, William Miller, Carry Nation, Joanna Southcott, and John Dee. Hot on the heels of this group are the spiritualists, with Thomas Edison and Arthur Conan Doyle swelling their ranks, and the radically superstitious, Somerset Maugham, Enrico Caruso, Mary Roberts Rinehart (who claimed that a ghost killed her own mother), and "reincarnated" souls such as Chicago's society queen, Edith Rockefeller McCormick and the flamboyant General George Patton.

Delusion also propelled normally tranquil individuals to assume with utter belief the role of royalty or positions of absolute power that existed only in their impenetrable minds—Joshua Norton, who dubbed himself "Emperor of the United States" and was accepted as such by the indulgent citizens of San Francisco; tycoon George Francis Train, who inspired the writing of *Around the World in Eighty Days* through his incredible exploits and then bestowed upon himself the title of "Dictator of America"; and the fabulous phony, Michael Romanoff, who insisted until the day of his death that he was the son of Czar Nicholas II, heir to the throne of Russia.

But then Romanoff's eccentric behavior was entwined with criminal pursuits, as was that of the witty Wilson Mizner, the fumbling gangster Waxey Gordon, the crafty gambler Nicky Arnstein, and the enigmatic Vincenzo Peruggia, who stole the *Mona Lisa* in 1911 and kept it beneath his bed for more than two years, falling hopelessly in love with *that* smile which he later claimed almost drove him to a fine madness that demanded he burn this priceless art treasure.

It is interesting to note that, in the course of the exhaustive research on this book, the author discovered that, throughout history, America yields a preponderance of eccentrics in all fields, followed closely by England, unusual for a nationality known for a reserved nature, then France, Germany, and Russia. America's foremost position in eccentricity is undoubtedly in keeping with its historically tolerant and liberal attitudes, and the abiding concept of a nation made up of individuals, not caste systems, one where freedom of expression and action encourages, if not endorses directly, the existence of the zany, spectacular or otherwise.

Here then are those who excelled in all the ordinary human passions, ignored convention, dismissed authority, and went their own arcane ways, despite what their peers thought and society deemed proper. Many were just this side of insanity, closer to the razor's edge of brilliance than most dare go. Others lived inside of exaggerated bows and knowing winks before retreating into their own small mysteries. Some even changed the course of human events. All are eccentrics to the marrow, fascinating to any reader who has a love of the marvelous.

It is our natural curiosity that holds up the eccentric to our justifiable awe. They were and are special people, freer than most from dull tradition, from stifling custom and, as such, they stand apart from a conformist society, great objects of our wonder. Hopefully, the true eccentric, without evil intent, will remain with us, providing a constant source of humor, allowing us to puzzle his behavior, and forever calling forth from our nature that old, undying love of caprice.

ACKNOWLEDGMENTS

My deep gratitude goes to my loyal research associate, Cathy Anetsberger, who worked long, hard months in libraries and archives unearthing invaluable information for this work, along with obtaining and processing important graphics. I also wish to thank my typist and friend, Sandy Horeis, for excellent manuscript preparation.

Many friends and associates were also exceedingly helpful in providing printed material, graphics, correspondence and memorabilia—Jack Jules Klein, Jr., Leonard Des Jardins, Phil Krap, Edgar Krebs, Bill and Edie Kelly, Jerry Goldberg, Bob Howe, P. Michael O'Sullivan, Sydney Harris, Hank Oettinger, Curt Johnson, Dan McConnell, Jim and Edie McCormick, Marc and Judy Davis, Jack Conroy, Ray Peekner, Raymond Friday Locke, Bob and Linda Connelly, Bud Freeman, Arnold L. Kaye, Les Susman, Arthur von Kluge, Bruce Elliot, Michaela Touhy, George Spink, Karen Connor, Mark and Lois Jacobs.

Cinemabilia of New York City was particularly helpful in providing motion picture graphics, as was the New York Historical Society and the New York Public Library. Newspaper librarians were of particular help and my special thanks go to Lynette Francis, librarian for the San Francisco *Chronicle*; Susanna Shuster, editorial research librarian for the Los Angeles *Times*; Dorothy Frazier of the Denver *Post*; Bob Sancher of the Winstead *Evening Citizen*; the librarians of the Chicago *Tribune*, Chicago *Sun-Times*, and the New York *Times*.

Librarians and archivists throughout the United States were also of great help and these include Keven Carey of the University of Illinois Library; Melanie Dodson and Ree Dedonato of Northwestern University Library; Jerry Delaney of the Chicago Public Library; Peter Weil, microfilm, and the staff of the Newberry Library of Chicago; Pat Wilcoxon, Regenstein Library, University of Chicago; the staff of the John Crerar Library at Chicago's Illinois Institute of Technology; the staff of the San Francisco Historical Society; the Chicago Historical Society; the New York State Historical Society at Cooperstown; the New York Tourist Bureau at Latham; the History and Travel Departments of the Memphis Public Library; and Charles R. Jacobson of the Hoard Historical Museum at Fort Atkinson, Wisconsin.

I am particularly indebted to the wonderful help and guidance of my late and beloved friend, Bob Abel, a literary light that shall forever burn in my life, and his wife, Carole, the agent for this book.

ZANIES

A

Albert ABRAMS

Physician (1863–1924)

The early career of this medical messiah was undistinguished, except for the curious fact that—according to his entry in *Who's Who*—the San Francisco-born Abrams received his medical degree from the University of Heidelberg in 1882, at the age of eighteen. This statement either proves Abrams a boy genius or shows him a liar, his degree as phony as the medical cures that later made his name synonymous with flagrant quackery.

Abrams began publishing medical tracts and small books in the early 1880s, but it wasn't until 1909 that he "electrified" the medical world with his book, *Spinal Therapeutics,* in which he claimed a new method of diagnosis through "rapid percussion" of the spine. By tapping on the spine with his fingers—later he would include the abdomen—Abrams claimed he could determine any malady. Every illness possessed a "vibratory rate" according to Abrams; his tapping could produce sounds that indicated the condition of any patient.

Following up this claim with a vengeance, Dr. Abrams produced a diagnosing machine he called the "dynamizer," which was no more than a sealed box containing a maze of incomprehensible wiring. When examining patients (or suckers), Abrams merely plugged his apparatus into a wall outlet and attached a wire to the forehead of the person being examined. As part of his hocus-pocus, Abrams would prick the finger of a patient, withdraw a drop of blood, placing this on a piece of filter paper and inserting the paper into his "dynamizer." The doctor would then order the patient to strip to the waist and begin his tapping on the person's abdomen. Abrams then diagnosed the

3

patient's illness. He was careful in each examination to insist that the patient *always* face west, but he never gave any reason why facing in this direction was imperative to his examination.

It is true that the spine contains nerve fibers that do indeed "vibrate" at different rates. Abrams bent this premise to shape his own ends by claiming that his dynamizer sorted these "vibrations" from the blood, transmitting them through the patient's spine, which sent on the vibrations on many wavelengths through the patient's abdomen where Dr. Abrams was able to interpret ailments by his tapping.

Ridiculous as it may appear, Abrams was able to convince many another shrewd quack, and through these medical entrepreneurs, thousands of gullible patients, that he could not only determine every conceivable ailment known to mankind with his invention but could also, like some carnival barker, pinpoint a patient's age and even religious denomination—providing the person was a Jew, Catholic, Protestant, Methodist, Theosophist, or Seventh Day Adventist.

More inventions flowed from the fertile mind of Dr. Abrams, including the "Ocilloclast" and the "reflexophone," the first employed as a healing machine according to the spine's "vibratory" rates, the latter a device that could diagnose a patient's illness over the telephone. As a medical sideline, Abrams set himself up as a handwriting expert. Through his studies, he claimed, he could diagnose a person's illness by merely examining the subject's penmanship. This included the long-ago dead. The doctor announced to his rabid followers that he had examined the handwriting of Oscar Wilde, Edgar Allan Poe, Samuel Johnson, Henry Wadsworth Longfellow, and Samuel Pepys and discovered that all these august gentlemen had been hopeless syphilitics.

The creativity of Dr. Abrams knew no bounds; and he reasoned that he should be paid (and handsomely) for his medical labors. He began to mass produce his dynamizers, leasing them for $250 and charging $200 for his special course on their uses. The machines could never be purchased outright, and those who leased them were sworn to an oath that they would never, never look inside the boxes, which were tightly sealed.

In 1922, a committee of scientists—alarmed at Abram's wild claims—did in fact open one of the doctor's boxes where they found a maze of wiring, along with a condenser, an ohmmeter, and a rheostat, all put together without one scientific principle involved. It mattered little to Dr. Albert Abrams. By the time he died on January 13, 1924, he had amassed a fortune exceeding $2 million from leasing his miracle machines.

When the storm broke and Abrams was exposed, his methods were championed by none other than the great muckraker, Upton Sinclair (see entry), who claimed that Abrams had "made the most revolutionary discovery of this or any other age." Sinclair's support became less enthusiastic when medical authorities submitted the blood of guinea pigs and roosters for examination on Abram's machine, stating that these samples were from human beings. The reports returned insisted that the blood samples represented human females suffering from cancer, diabetes, malaria, and venereal diseases.

Abrams wrote his own medical epitaph when he compared the legitimate physician to the medical quack in a book published years earlier—a revealing insight into Abrams' own character. He had written: "The physician is only allowed to think he knows it all, but the quack, ungoverned by conscience, is permitted to know he knows it all; and with a fertile mental field for humbuggery, truth can never successfully compete with untruth."

Hans Christian ANDERSEN

Author (1805–1875)

The beloved writer of such fair tales as "The Ugly Duckling," "The Brave Tin Soldier," and "The Little Mermaid" spent most of his early years in such dire poverty that he became embittered by the time he achieved success. When riches and fame did come to Andersen, he never let the world forget his genius. He informed one and all that "he had said and done whatever Byron may have said and done!" When the applause came, Anderson reveled in it. When someone remarked that his concave chest gave him a weak appearance, he stuffed newspapers into his shirt to build up his front.

Not until Andersen was twenty-nine did he examine his need for a sexual life. When he did, he withheld (like some latter-day Jack D. Ripper in *Dr. Strangelove*) the compunction to share his sexual urges with women. "My blood is in a violent commotion," he wrote in his diary. "I feel a tremendous sensuality and I fight with myself. Is it really a sin to satisfy this powerful lust? Then may I fight it. So far I am innocent but my blood burns, when dreaming my whole being boils." Apparently, he did not submit.

And Andersen's vanity did gnaw at him forever, though he fiercely denied his posturing at every opportunity. His denials, however, were really affirmations of a vainglorious nature. In 1849, he wrote to Henriette Wulff from Sweden, stating: "I fell asleep, but was awakened by someone singing. It was the workmen from the Motala factory, who knew I was here and wanted to honor me; I felt quite glad and humble. Oh, people do not comprehend this feeling of mine! How little they know me who say I am vain."

George ANTHEIL

Composer (1900–1959)

Born in Trenton, New Jersey, Antheil took up music rather than follow in his father's footsteps as the proprietor of a shoe store. In Philadelphia, the eighteen-year-old Antheil was seen by wealthy Mrs. Edward Bok, who thought him a piano virtuoso and became his patron—paying for his tuition and expenses at the Philadelphia Conservatory of Music, where he studied with Ernest Bloch. Within a few years, Antheil was touring Europe as a concert pianist. At twenty-two he won a Guggenheim and more or less quit playing, concentrating on composition.

His reputation as the *enfant terrible* or "bad boy of music" was established in Paris where he lived on the Left Bank, above Sylvia Beach's Shakespeare & Company bookstore, in the early 1920s. He not only read (without buying) all the books he could devour from Miss Beach's bookshelves, but suggested that she would do a better business if she re-titled the books in her windows with racy, even obscene titles.

Antheil loved to prowl Paris at night and invariably found himself locked out of the small building he called home. He solved this problem by merely scaling the walls of the bookstore beneath his windows, climbing onto the Shakespeare & Company sign and pulling himself up to the small balcony fronting his apartment. Such antics were repeated even in daytime, to the amusement of passersby.

The would-be composer's appearance at this time was arresting, if not odd. "George was stocky in build," wrote Sylvia Beach in her memoirs, "had tow-colored bangs, a smashed nose, interesting but wicked-looking eyes, a big mouth and a big grin. He looked like an American high school boy of Polish origin, perhaps."

One of the first literary expatriates to influence Antheil was the eccentric poet Ezra Pound, who collaborated with Antheil in making what the composer called "mechanical" music, which involved creating noisy, discordant music rolls for player pianos. Antheil and Pound gave small concerts in hotel rooms for specially invited friends—groups of no more than ten. On one occasion, James Joyce, whose *Ulysses* had inspired Antheil (the composer claimed), attended with a group at the Salle Pleyel. He, his son Georgio, Pound, Margaret Anderson and Jane Heap, who edited *The Little Review,* Ernest Hemingway, and Djuna Barnes sat nervously staring at Antheil as he worked his way to near collapse, pretending to play the player piano, dripping with so much sweat that he had to be dried with towels during the so-called performance. At its end, everyone gave an embarrassed nod of appreciation and slunk from the room. Joyce's only remark was that he was sorry about Antheil's "pianistic contortions," later mumbling that the boy composer might hurt himself with so much physical exertion.

Antheil's magnum opus was yet to come, one of the most bizarre compositions ever performed anywhere, the *Ballet Mécanique*. The impulsive composer was much under the sway of the Dadaist cult, then popular in Paris (see Tristan Tzara entry), which gave vent to nihilism. Antheil labored for years on his ballet. He literally punched pianos to pieces while composing the score, which was essentially a monument to noise.

When the ballet was completed, Antheil implored his estranged patron, Mrs. Bok, to back the production. The wealthy woman sent a check that not only covered the expense of conductor Vladimir Golschmann and a host of

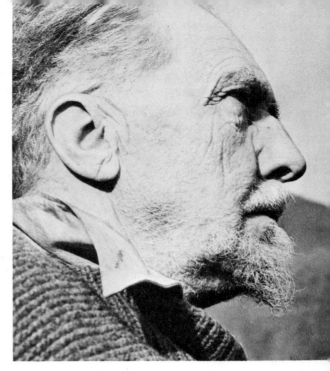

The poet Ezra Pound was one of Antheil's early, and slightly rabid, supporters.

musicians and technicians, but allowed for the rental of the Theatre des Champs Elysees, an enormous auditorium.

The 1925 production of *Ballet Méchanique* both stunned the cogniscienti of Paris and dumbfounded and shocked the audience. It demanded ten player pianos and the strangest assortment of noisemakers ever assembled for any composition—including six xylophones, electric bells, a fire siren, and actual plane propellers which (at the appropriate moment) were revved to the highest pitch so that their blasts of wind struck the audience full force.

Antheil delayed the performance, annoying the packed house, because his tuxedo (with tails) had to be repaired—a noticeable moth hole had to be sewn shut. Joyce and his wife had taken a box; T.S. Eliot was present in another box. All the major writers and painters, both native Frenchmen and expatriate Americans, were in attendance. Even royalty, such as Princess Bassiano, took choice seats. Ezra Pound purposely sat in the upper balcony to guarantee that, in the words of Sylvia Beach, "Antheil got a fair deal."

As the composition was played, the audience revolted at the horrible din emanating from the stage. Antheil, pretending to play one of the pianolas with frantic gestures, cursed his unappreciative listeners. Shrieks and groans, catcalls and demeaning hoots came from all corners of the theater. Antheil's defenders shrieked and hollered back insults at those who dared to complain. The cacaphony of the ballet was finally overpowered by the audience's roar of disapproval. Ezra Pound's voice could be heard shouting support for Antheil, and one report had it that Pound was seen hanging head downward from the railing of the top gallery. Several irate paying customers began to hurl objects toward the stage, and these were hurled back by the musicians. Others tore at their seats in frustration, uprooting the bolted legs from the floor.

"But the angry people suddenly subsided," reported Sylvia Beach, "when the plane propellers called for in the score began roaring and raised a breeze that, Stuart Gilbert says, blew the wig off the head of a man next to him and whisked it all the way to the back of the house. Men turned up their coat collars, the women drew their wraps about them; it was quite chilly."

Though the ballet proved a disaster and was universally condemned as the work of a lunatic, Antheil clung to his creation. "My ideas were the most abstract of the abstract," he wrote to Nicolas Slonimsky in 1936, and he went on to compare the *Ballet Méchanique* to the paintings of Pablo Picasso. He insisted that as a great composer (then twenty-four) he was free to do anything he wished, and this included repeating one measure "one hundred times," if he pleased, or having piano rolls silent for "sixty-two bars."

Following the performance—Mrs. Bok never saw a dime returned on her investment, nor did she attend the performance—Antheil asked his closest friends for advice on what to do next. His most ardent supporter, Ezra Pound, shrugged and told him to go on a hiking tour of Italy with his pet cat, Crazy, on his back. Antheil was disinclined to do so. After reading a book entitled *African Swamps,* which he found in Sylvia Beach's bookstore, Antheil vanished into the jungles of Africa, saying he was "in search of rhythms."

Such was the notoriety Antheil gleaned from his perplexing composition that an American publisher, Donald Friede, arranged for the *Ballet Méchanique* to be performed in Carnegie Hall in April 1927. The cream of New York society attended, believing the work to be the most avant garde composition of the day. The orchestra, assembled as before, consisted of mechanical pianos and noisemakers and gadgets, all placed in front of a tasteless drop curtain (painted by Friede) which showed "buttocksy" flappers and sugar daddies doing a wild Charleston. It was another disaster. Wrote Elizabeth Stevenson in *Babbitts and Bohemians:* "The audience never recovered from its visual shock when aural shock was added; the crowd disintegrated into helpless laughter. The musical evening concluded in a wild scene of disrepair onstage and off."

Friede tried to escape the theater unnoticed; but as he remembered in *The Mechanical Age,* he was grabbed by a hooting friend who cackled: "Too bad, Donald. You tried to make a mountain out of an Antheil!"

Not until February 20, 1954, was Antheil's monstrosity again performed, this time a shortened version conducted by Carlos Surinach at New York's Composer Forum for which the conductor as well as a weary Antheil received an ovation. The bad boy of music continued composing, producing seven symphonies, a piano concerto, and numerous other pieces, retiring to Hollywood in 1936 to work on movie scores for Paramount and Columbia studios. (He was favored by Cecil B. DeMille and wrote the scores for *The Plainsman* and *The Buccaneer,* among others.)

Though still considered an avant gardist of modern music by many—and a musical crank by an equal number—George Antheil never again received the kind of public attention his *Ballet Méchanique* produced, dying on February 12, 1959.

Poet and lecturer Matthew Arnold; no one could hear him talk.

Matthew ARNOLD

Poet, Critic (1822–1888)

Arnold, son of British educator Thomas Arnold, held the august position of professor of poetry at Oxford; he considered himself the "apostle of culture." To him the aristocracy constituted the "Barbarians" of culture and those of the bourgeoisie were nothing but "Philistines." Arnold's pessimistic, romantic poetry earned him worldwide fame. Entrepreneur James B. Pond, who grew rich promoting lecture tours (especially in America) for England's literary lights, brought the haughty Arnold to the United States.

The poet displayed his oddball behavior by appearing before large American crowds who had paid handsome prices and then refusing to speak above a whisper, if he spoke that loudly. According to Pond, Arnold's first appearance, with General U.S. Grant and his wife in attendance, utterly baffled the audience. Wrote Pond: "Matthew Arnold stepped forward, opened out his manuscript, laid it on the desk, and his lips began to move. There was not the slightest sound audible."

After some minutes, Grant turned to his wife and said: "Well, we have paid to see the British lion. We cannot hear him roar. So we'd better go home." They left the hall, but the distinguished lecturer gave them no notice. Then began a stream of people rapidly departing until the hall was empty.

Arnold's entire American tour followed suit. He gave a hundred lectures without one soul in the audience ever hearing a word from Matthew Arnold's lips, "not even those who were sitting in the front row."

Jules W. "Nicky" ARNSTEIN

Gambler (1880–date uncertain)

Born Jules W. Arndt Stein in Scandinavia, Nicky immigrated with his parents to America in 1881. He was brought up in a well-to-do home and given a fine education. He entered several businesses in his youth, becoming a contractor for a short period; but once he discovered his ability to play cards— chiefly poker—he gave up the pursuit of legitimate enterprise. For years Arnstein (newsmen contracted his name and he took no issue) supported himself handsomely be winning big stakes in games played on transatlantic lines. In 1918, this flamboyant dandy met and married the ghetto-born Follies star Fannie Brice, then twenty-one. The marriage produced two children, Frances and William, the boy named after William Fallon, a lawyer knows as The Great Mouthpiece, who defended Arnstein in a $5-million robbery charge.

Arnstein was for years considered the best-dressed gambler in New York, if not America. He was a strutting peacock who doted on purchasing clothes, spending days—sometimes whole weeks—carefully selecting his wardrobe from the best tailors and haberdashers in Manhattan. His greatest eccentricity was his devotion to his carefully appointed bathroom, where he would spend several hours pampering himself every morning. According to Gene Fowler, writing in *The Great Mouthpiece,* Arnstein's "abultionary rituals were perfectly amazing. That he had any skin left was the wonder of dermatologists." It was not unusual for Arnstein to take two or three baths in a row, scrubbing his flesh to the point where he emerged as red as a lobster.

The gambler was perhaps the most finicky eater of his profession. If any of the food he ordered to his hotel suite (he always lived in hotels, except when *visiting* his wife, Fannie Brice, in their home) was not exactly as he desired, he would order it returned to the kitchen, telling the waiters to inform the chef to "either eat it himself or give it to a worthy wanderer."

A year after marrying Fannie Bruce, Arnstein was accused of acting as the fence in a 1919 Wall Street robbery in which $5 million in negotiable stock certificates were taken. Before police could apprehend him, Arnstein fled New York and remained in hiding for two years. When reporters went to Miss Brice to tell her that her husband was charged with masterminding the stock theft, the Follies star quipped: "Nicky? Why he couldn't mastermind an electric bulb into a light socket." Her confidence in Arnstein never flagged. During her husband's two-year decampment, Fannie made famous a song entitled "My Man"—a plaintive ditty that perfectly expressed Fannie's undying devotion to Arnstein.

The wanted gambler finally engaged attorney William Fallon as his lawyer. The brilliant "mouthpiece," after arranging more than $60,000 in bail for Arnstein (through one of his clients, the notorious fixer Arnold Rothstein), allowed his client to go on a spree before surrendering. Arnstein abandoned his careful eating habits entirely in his Marmaroneck, New York hotel-hideaway and ordered an avalanche of eggs, ham, bacon—anything greasy he could imagine—thinking that he would be going to prison anyway and such fare would not be available.

When Arnstein did surrender, he and Fallon picked the most spectacular method their inventive minds could produce. They waited for New York's 1922 police parade—Arnstein idling his impressive blue Cadillac landaulet until the last company of policemen marched by—then pulled in behind the cops and proceeded as part of the parade. As Arnstein and Fallon passed the reviewing stand, half of New York's dignitaries, including the district attorney, doffed their hats to the wanted felon and his attorney, thinking them to be important police officials. With uproarious laughter, Nicky Arnstein then drove to the nearest precinct to surrender.

Since the stock theft was a federal offense, Fallon elected to have Arnstein tried in Washington, D.C., feeling that his client's flamboyant reputation in New York was sure to prejudice any jury. While in Washington, Arnstein gave magnificent parties where liquor flowed unceasingly and congressmen and entertainers kicked up their heels in wild Charlestons. Arnstein introduced an attractive blonde entertainer, Gertrude Vanderbilt, to his lawyer at one of these parties, a gesture he was later to regret with great bitterness. Fallon managed to get a hung jury during Arnstein's first trial. Arnstein gave his lawyer a huge ruby ring set in plantinum as a token of his gratitude. Fallon gave the ring to Gertrude, who promptly lost it in a cab.

Arnstein began to object to Fallon's dating the entertainer, telling him that he was neglecting preparations for his second trial. The two almost came to blows over the woman, with Fallon quitting his client. Fallon's partner, Eugene McGee (who also broke with Fallon over his quitting the case), defended Arnstein in his second trial. He lost. Upon hearing the guilty verdict, Arnstein moaned in court: "Fallon did this to me. Fallon sent me to this. God damn that woman!"

Though he received a long prison term, the dapper gambler served a mere twenty months. He was soon back with Fannie Brice; but his womanizing and carousing ruined their marriage, and the Follies star divorced Arnstein in 1927. Though down on his luck and short of funds, the gambler refused to give up his sartorial splendor, borrowing thousands of dollars to buy the best fashionable clothes. When he died, the mortician preparing his body was beside himself, not knowing which of Arnstein's two hundred elegant suits to select for the gambler's coffin appearance.

Russell ARUNDEL

Fisherman (Born 1906)

Canadian Russell Arundel, while fishing south of Wedgeport, Nova Scotia, in 1949, was blown by a storm to a small island uninhabited except for sheep and terns. Checking the charts later, Arundel discovered that he had taken

11

refuge on Outer Bald Island. It became such a favorite spot for him that he purchased the island. A short time later, Arundel published a Declaration of Independence from Canada and put together a constitution for what he called the "Principality of Outer Baldonia" (which could have easily been inspired by the Marx Brothers film *Duck Soup*).

Arundel proclaimed himself "Prince of Princes" of the Principality of Outer Baldonia and sent out official-looking letters to fellow tuna fishermen, naming them as princes. Upon local guides Arundel bestowed the rank of eight-star admirals of the Baldonian navy. The treeless fiefdom began to look more like a principality when Arundel constructed a twenty-by-thirty foot "castle" on the island with his royal flag flying from the highest tower. He issued passports and postage stamps. Further, Arundel established his own currency, based on what he termed the "tunar."

The constitution of Outer Baldonia, with its Great Seal affixed to it, along with the signature of "Russell Rex," offered a Bill of Rights to warm the cockles of the male chauvinist heart. These privileges applied to all loyal fishermen of the realm, who were given the right "to lie and be believed, the right of freedom from questions, nagging interruption, women, taxes, politics, war, monologues, cant and inhibitions." One of the main rights for Arundel's "citizens" was the right "to sleep all day and stay up all night."

Nova Scotian authorities ignored Arundel's principality. The Soviets, however, did not. Learning of Arundel's crackpot kingdom, the *Moscow Literary Gazette* denounced Arundel as a Western imperialist who had "basely exempted his subjects from the moral and ethical laws of mankind." Arundel responded with an official protest, sent to Moscow authorities on Outer Baldonia stationery. The Kremlin was disinclined to reply.

Not until 1973 did "Prince" Arundel abdicate his kingdom, turning Outer Baldonia into a bird sanctuary. The tolerant officials of Nova Scotia had no qualms with that program either.

Mary ASTOR

Actress (Born 1906)

Born in Quincy, Illinois on May 3, 1906, Mary Astor entered the film industry as a young starlet with some stage experience, having been coached by John Barrymore (see entry). The Great Profile was attracted to Astor, but their on-and-off affair was impeded by Mary's mother. She nevertheless appeared in Barrymore films, *Beau Brummel* (1923) and *Don Juan* (1926), becoming a Hollywood leading lady before she was twenty.

The auburn-haired beauty lived a tempestous private life, replete with nasty divorces and scandals that shocked America, the most lurid and highly publicized being her notorious affair with playwright George S. Kaufman. Both Mary and Kaufman were married at the time of their first encounter in 1933, when Astor was staying at the Algonquin Hotel; she was introduced to Kaufman by Miriam Hopkins and according to Mary's later statements, she "fell like a ton of bricks" for the co-author of *Once in a Lifetime, You Can't Take It With You,* and *The Man Who Came to Dinner.*

Kaufman was an unlikely physical specimen for the glamorous Mary Astor, who had been surrounded by the most handsome leading men in films. He wore thick glasses, had a scrawny physique, and was graying at forty-seven years of age. She later half-explained the attraction for the playwright when writing in *A Life on Film,* saying that what made writers, chiefly Kaufman, "attractive to me was that they all sat at a typewriter, put one word down after another, and the product was something that was of mind, while my product was simply me."

Mary, however, after attending some plays and going to dinner with Kaufman, followed by torrid love-making, began to put down words herself, one uninhibited word after another, in a blue-bound diary. This revealing document was later discovered in a bedroom drawer by Mary's husband, Dr. Franklin Thorpe, who immediately begged his wife to break off her affair with the playwright.

Mary put him off, going straight to her diary and writing: "He [Thorpe] was very badly broken up for several days, used his final weapon with me, 'I need you,' with tears...For the sake of peace and respite from all this emotionalism, I told him I would do nothing at the present. My main reason for saying that is, quite honestly, I want to be able to see George for the rest of his stay here without being upset...I want to have the last few times of completely enjoying him."

Dr. Thorpe, unable to bear his wife's continued flagrant affair, began to see several Hollywood starlets, appearing in public with these women in an awkward attempt, everyone assumed, to stir jealously, if nothing else, in his wandering actress. When the Astor–Kaufman affair continued, Thorpe had all of Mary's belongings packed—except her fabulous diary—and shipped them out of their Beverly Hill mansion. He would keep the house and their child,

Mary Astor in *Don Juan*, 1926, being leered at by John Barrymore.

Marilyn, he told his wayward wife. She could have Kaufman. He then filed for divorce.

At first Mary did not contest the divorce, then she regretted the loss of her child and filed a counter suit on July 15, 1935. Almost from the first minute of the sensational trial, Thorpe's attorneys attempted to enter into the records Mary Astor's lurid diary, as proof of adultery. The presiding judge read the diary, turning various shades of scarlet, then refused to admit the "obscene" material as evidence in the trial

In vengeance, Thorpe's lawyers released the more sensational passages to the press, and Mary Astor became the leading headline of sex scandals for the era. Readers across the nation were shocked but fascinated at the actress' candor and naked admissions, easily filling in the words replaced by blanks. Mary had written about her trysting place on 73rd Street in New York, where she and Kaufman "could be alone, and it was all very thrilling and beautiful. Once George lays down his glasses, he is *quite* a different man. His powers of recuperation are amazing, and we made love all night long...It all worked perfectly, and we shared our climax at dawn...I didn't see much of anybody else the rest of the time—we saw every show in town, had grand fun together and went frequently to 73rd Street where he fucked the living daylights out of me...One morning about 4 we had a sandwich at Reuben's, and it was just getting daylight, so we drove throught the park in an open cab, and the birds started singing, and it was a cool and dewy day and it was pretty heavenly to pet and French...right out in the open...It seems that George is hard all the time...I don't see how he does it, he is perfect."

The actress kept a score each day with Kaufman, noting the number of climaxes the playwright was able to achieve, writing "six times! Count them diary, six times!" When Kaufman visited Mary later that summer of 1933 in Beverly Hills, they resumed their fast-and-furious copulation. Mary told her diary that she "went to the Beverly Wilshire and was able to George alone...He greeted me in pajamas, and we flew into each other's arms. He was rampant in an instant, and in a few moments it was just like old times...he tore off his pajamas and I never was undressed by anyone so fast in all my life...Later we went to Vendome for lunch...then back to the hotel. It was raining and lovely. It was wonderful to fuck the entire sweet afternoon away."

The errant couple took several out-of-town trips, once traveling to Palm Springs, California, where Mary and Kaufman made love out-of-doors. The passage in Mary's diary dealing with this sexual encounter became a classic statement: "Ah, desert night—with George's body plunging into mine, naked under the stars."

Despite the thunderous revelation of Mary Astor's diary in the press, her case against Thorpe was strong. Her daughter's nurse testified that Thorpe, during his separation from Mary, had populated the Astor mansion with a bevy of Hollywood starlets, including one Norma Taylor, who ran about naked in front of Mary's child. Further, the nurse stated that she had actually seen

Mary Astor testifying in court at her sensational 1935 divorce, scandalized by her "obscene" diary which was released to the press.

Veteran actress Mary Astor, whose career remained intact despite her highly publicized sexual transgressions, is shown here in her most famous role as the scheming Brigid, with Humphrey Bogart, Peter Lorre and Sidney Greenstreet in *The Maltese Falcon;* the much-coveted "black bird" is in Bogart's clutching hands.

Thorpe in bed not only with Miss Taylor but several other showgirls, "all blondes."

After some deliberation, the court decided wholly in favor of Mary Astor, restoring her home and child to her. Officials, however, kept her diary, labeling it "pornography," and ordering it to be burned. Mary Astor's career was first thought to be ruined, but her stubborn fight for her child, all the while risking the exposure of the diary, somehow found favor with the public who continued to go to her films.

By the early 1940s, Mary Astor was still a leading lady, scoring her biggest success in John Huston's *The Maltese Falcon,* opposite Humphrey Bogart. She later went on to prove herself to be one of the finest character actresses in Hollywood, her career stretching well into the 1960s, a career that spanned almost half a century before her retirement.

B

Delia Salter BACON

Lecturer (1811–1859)

Delia was the daughter of Leonard Bacon, American Congregational minister for the First Church of New Haven, Connecticut, and a leading abolitionist. Educated in private schools, Delia became fascinated, then obsessed, with the idea that Shakespeare was not the author of those magnificent works attributed to him. The plays and verses were, Delia concluded, written by a secret group of Elizabethan scholars and writers led by Sir Francis Bacon (no relation).

In 1852 Miss Bacon announced to the public that Shakespeare was a fraud and for the last seven years of her life strove to unsuccessfully convince the world that her theory was correct. Delia painstakingly went over each major play attributed to Shakespeare, tracing the influences of Bacon, Walter Raleigh and Edmund Spenser, deciphering the works, as it were, to prove her point. Further, she announced that she was sure that inside Shakespeare's grave at Stratford on Avon were documents that would bear out her theories.

Traveling almost penniless to England, Delia haunted the tomb of the "Immortal Bard," whom she called a "vulgar illiterate." She almost convinced British authorities to violate the tomb in her mad search for the true author of Shakespeare's plays, but had second thoughts and retired to an unheated cottage to finish her opus *The Philosophy of the Plays of Shakespeare,* growing physically and mentally ill in her feverish labors.

Miss Bacon's book was finally published, but by then she was half mad and had to be confined in a mental institution. Few read or believed in her theory; even Nathaniel Hawthorne, who had written a preface to the work, thought

Delia Bacon, who drove herself mad
attempting to prove Shakespeare's plays
were frauds.

Delia's concepts dubious. (Years after her death, however, such literary lights
as Henry James and Walt Whitman wholly embraced the zany theories of Delia
Bacon.) Miss Bacon went on raving in her asylum room for several years before
a relative returned her to America where she died, a confirmed lunatic.

Phineas Taylor BARNUM

Showman (1810–1891)

When it came to extravagant entertainment in America, P.T. Barnum was
its wildest and most successful manipulator. Early in his career, Barnum
realized his ability to convince (or gull) the public to pay out good money for his
services, scant or imaginary as they might be. He was a walking billboard,
draping his massive frame with the loudest suits, the most garish cravats, the
most outrageous hats. A story of his early enterprise, apocryphal or not,
exemplifies the man's style.

Barnum alighted from a train wearing a red and yellow checked suit. A
man who had known him in boyhood approached with a look of amazement.
"You're Phineas Barnum, aren't you?"

"Right, my good man," said Barnum, brushing the dust from his vest and
fondling an expensive-looking gold watch.

"I'm Bill Jones. We were kids together."

"Wonderful memories," boomed Barnum.

"Phineas—you've prospered." The man stood before Barnum smiling
appreciation of Barnum's resplendent appearance. "How'd a fellow like you
ever get so rich?"

Barnum put a huge arm about his boyhood chum and confided: "Bill, my man. I'm in a new business, brand spanking new. It's called advertising."

"Advertising? What's that?"

"That, Bill, is selling the public on the idea of throwing away the things they need and buying the things they don't need. So far it's made me a rich man."

Barnum got richer when he began opening sideshows, culminating in his great American Museum in New York. He was, according to writer Melvyn Graham, "a genius in his way ... who made piles of gold out of piles of sawdust."

A haggler and a hoaxer, Barnum would do anything to sell the public a new exhibit—and his exhibits were probably the most unusual, if not bizarre, on record. Barnum made a habit of frequenting the Tombs Prison, visiting with warden Charles Sutton, a drinking crony, who in turn presented the showman to the worst criminals in his dungeon-like prison. Barnum was chiefly interested in murderers, knowing the public's fascination with serious crime.

On one occasion Sutton introduced Barnum to his star boarder, Albert Hicks, a mass killer who was scheduled to be hanged on Bedloe's Island. Half the city was expected to turn out in New York Harbor in boats to witness the execution. The showman wanted a death mask of Hicks and the condemned man's clothes to put on display in his museum. Knowing Hicks to be a shrewd bargainer, Barnum dickered directly with warden Sutton. The warden and the showman argued just outside Hick's cell while the killer gave them both an icy stare.

"All right," Sutton finally agreed. "You can have his clothes for $25 and I'll throw a death mask in for free!"

"Hey, now one minute, you fellows!" roared Hicks. "It's my clothes and my face you're selling. Where's mine?"

Barnum waved him down, saying: "Don't you worry about a thing, Hicks. I'm sending you two boxes of the finest cigars this afternoon."

Some hours later Hicks received the cigars and delighted in smoking them down to stubs. He was, however, extremely unhappy when he was given the clothes sent over by Barnum to replace his "murder suit."

"Look at these clothes Barnum sent," whined Hicks to warden Sutton. "This suit won't last!" Strangely enough, the killer ignored the fact that he would be dead within twenty-four hours.

Talent manager James B. Pond, who knew Barnum well, characterized him as one of the stingiest men he had ever met: "He walked from the station to his hotel rather than take a taxi. His band was composed of the cheapest musicians that could be hired. His posters were so designed that they could be changed from season to season without buying a new drawing."

Barnum once spotted an acrobat he wanted to put into one of his sideshows that traveled the country.

"A woman works with me in the act," explained the acrobat.

"Is she your wife?" inquired the showman

"No."

"Well, you must fix that. You will have to make arrangements to occupy the same berth in the sleeping car. We put four people in a section."

If Barnum could not buy an act or exhibit (for the smallest amount of money, of course), he blatantly put across a fake—which often cost him a small fortune. When the Cardiff Giant was discovered in 1889—the most spectacular of the "petrified men," a hoax perpetrated by George Hull (see entry)—Barnum attempted to buy the dubious artifact as an exhibit. When he failed to obtain the giant, he spent $2,000 having the so-called "Colorado Man" constructed out of stone, dried eggs, clay, plaster, and some human bones, all of which were baked in the form of a giant human of ancient times and "discovered" in the Rocky Mountains. Barnum put this sham on display and invited experts to prove his "petrified man" a fraud. He allowed authorities to bore into the giant at certain places where he knew human bone had been planted. At first the exhibit was accepted as genuine. Then Professor O.C. Marsh of Yale, who was instrumental in exposing the Cardiff Giant as a fake, visited Barnum's Museum. After looking over the "Colorado Man," Marsh dismissed it as a fraud, pointing out that it was too rotund to have been a fossilized human being and explaining to the press that the abdomen would have long ago collapsed.

Instead of losing face, Barnum laughed to newsmen that "the public likes to be fooled." Such crass postures earned him the title of "Prince of Humbugs." He lived up to this reputation with a vengeance. Barnum had presented one Joice Heth to the public, claiming that she was the living nurse to George Washington at 161 years of age. The woman, who was an invalid and senile, did appear to be ancient; but upon her death, an autopsy showed her to be less than eighty. Many of Barnum's exhibits and acts were genuine and great, from the giant elephant Jumbo to midget Tom Thumb and Viennese singer Jenny Lind. But that never prevented Barnum from faking when that course proved easier.

Hearing that a competitor had obtained a white elephant from Siam, Barnum painted one of his own elephants white and exhibited the animal as "The Light of Asia." When the elephant sprayed its back with water and the paint ran, Barnum yanked the exhibit. Reportedly, he shrugged off this bold chicanery too, with his classic statement: "Well, there's a sucker born every minute." This remark was also attributed to Big Mike McDonald, Chicago's first crime czar.

And the suckers flocked to Barnum's ludicrous exhibits, fakes or not, including the ridiculous Feejee Mermaid, which had been transported from Calcutta to the United States in 1817. The showman insisted it was real. The "Mermaid," it was later discovered, was a composite graft of the head and torso of a monkey and the end of a large fish.

Fakes did not matter to the showman. The only important thing to Barnum was getting crowds into his shows. He spent fortunes on advertising of all sorts to entice the public. One of his most inventive stunts was to employ a well-dressed man who would arouse the curious by placing bricks end to end

P.T. Barnum was America's first great showman, a bizarre and flamboyant character. (Library of Congress)

Singer Jenny Lind, one of Barnum's genuine acts.
(Library of Congress)

until they trailed into Barnum's Museum, where the man would collect the bricks and disappear into the theater. Those people following him down the street could not resist buying tickets and going inside to find out what the man in evening wear was all about. Once inside, the curious were side-tracked by Barnum's razzle-dazzle exhibits and acts.

So popular was Barnum's Museum that the great showman was eventually faced with a strange problem. He could not get the public to leave and make way for new crowds. He pondered this dilemma one day for hours, then leaped to his feet and raced into the museum, throwing open an exit door and bellowing to his patrons: "This way to the Egress, folks, see the greatest Egress in the world!" The customers raced pell-mell into the alleyway as Barnum unceremoniously slammed the door behind them.

John Sidney Blythe BARRYMORE

Actor (1882–1942)

He was "The Great Profile" and "The Great Lover," but John Barrymore was also the great zany, a man for whom the bizarre and the macabre were commonplace. He came to fame reluctantly, never really having a desire to act; but his family, the Drews, had long been active in the theater, and it was expected that John and his brother Lionel and sister Ethel would live their lives on the boards. According to James Robert Parish and Ronald Bowers, writing in *The MGM Stock Company*: "even if [Barrymore's] vocation was not entirely of his own choosing, his stage and screen performances, before the effects of alcohol became overpowering, were fired by far more than just technique. "He could and often did turn in inspired performances.

Barrymore's sister Ethel literally had to drag her brother on stage, insisting that he play a small part in a 1902 production of *Captain Jinks of the Horse Marines,* produced in his home town of Philadelphia. The novice actor forgot his lines almost the minute he strolled on stage, quickly ad-libbing: "I've blown up, old chap—where do we go from here?" Despite the flub, Barrymore was more than willing to take his applause at play's end. His sister remembered that "much to my surprise Jack walked out ... right to the footlights and bowed low—quite alone."

He went on bowing for the next forty years. Four years after his casual debut, Barrymore was acting in San Francisco, exactly at the time of the 1906 quake. He had already taken to drink and was wobbling down the street in evening dress, tipsy from an all-night party, when buildings began to shake and the streets broke open in yawning chasms. Through the awful carnage, Barrymore mindlessly staggered along, a bottle of champagne tucked beneath his arm, a champagne glass in his hand. The actor stumbled past the ruined Palace Hotel, in front of which sat the great Italian tenor Enrico Caruso (see entry), terrified at the calamity and crying great tears.

The two men recognized each other. Barrymore poured some of the flat champagne into his glass and lifted this in a salute to the tenor, saying in his beautiful stentorian voice: "Hello, old fellow—feeling rather dumpy about the whole thing, eh?"

Caruso stopped weeping, then began to laugh hysterically at the absurd sight of John Barrymore in his dust-covered tuxedo and scuffed patent-leather shoes. The tenor shook his head, then boomed: "You know, Mr. Barrymore, you are the only person in America—no—the only person in the world, who would dress for an earthquake!"

Ever the opportunist, Barrymore, upon sobering, quickly fled the city in real panic to Oakland where he hid out with friends. He then wrote a lengthy narrative of the disaster, his so-called "eyewitness" account (with all details fabricated), which he sold to several New York magazines for considerable amounts. He also used the disaster as an excuse not to rejoin his acting group, which was leaving on tour for Japan. Barrymore hated the Orient.

The actor's affairs were rampant and notorious. He was, for a short time, involved with Evelyn Nesbit, the New York showgirl over whom Harry K. Thaw murdered Stanford White. He married for the first time in 1910, wedding a young socialite, Katherine Corri Harris. The marriage ended in 1917. By then, Barrymore had left the stage and begun to make films, including *Raffles the Amateur Cracksman,* a title suggesting Barrymore's sexual prowess—which was becoming notorious in Hollywood. In 1920, he played the title role in *Dr. Jekyll and Mr. Hyde,* considered to be his finest film (not to mention a role that befitted his personal life).

That same year, Barrymore went back to the stage in *Richard III,* proving himself the greatest Shakespearian actor of his day. In 1922, he went on to perform *Hamlet* as it had never been acted before. Audiences and critics alike swooned with delight and praise over Barrymore's Hamlet, first in America and later in England, where the critics were the most severe in the world. It was his greatest triumph; and yet, according to Barrymore's statement years later, it was a masterpiece pickled in alcohol.

He had dallied with a British duchess, the actor claimed a few months before his death in 1942, having sex and drinking enormous amounts of champagne and brandy almost up to the hour of his London debut. "I arrived at the theater a half hour before curtain time and passed out cold in my dressing room. My man [valet] revived me as he put me into Hamlet's clothes. He whacked me with wet towels, shoved lumps of ice into me and poured pots of coffee down my gullet.

"I was the first American to play Hamlet on a London stage—and I was also the first drunk to play it on any stage in the world. I reeled out of the wings barely able to stand on my feet. The heat of the footlights made me dizzy. I had to lean on Polonius to keep from falling on my face. I had to make several unrehearsed exists in order to vomit in the wings. I returned once barely in time for my soliloquy. Unable to stand, I sprawled in a chair and recited the goddamn speech sitting down and trying to keep from blacking out.

"Mark you, I was drunk as a fiddler's bitch all through the five acts. But I missed no word of Will Shakespeare's and I missed no cue. So much I will say for myself.

"The dramatic reviews the next day were . . . marvelous. They praised me as the greatest Hamlet of the age. Every one of my drunken staggers, my exits to vomit in the wings, my reeling into a chair to recite 'To be or not to be,' were hailed as brilliant artistic interpretations of Hamlet's role."

In the same year as his success with Hamlet, Barrymore married again, this time to the writer, Michael Strange (Blanche Oelichs) who bore him a daughter, Diana (who grew up neurotic and died from an overdose of alcohol and barbiturates in 1962 following her painful autobiography *Too Much Too Soon*). His divorce followed a few years later.

The Great Profile, John Barrymore, holds Dolores Costello in his arms in a scene from *The Sea Beast*, 1925.

While filming *The Sea Beast* in 1926 (a movie based on *Moby Dick*), Barrymore fell madly in love with his co-star, Dolores Costello, whom he described as "preposterously beautiful." He married her too, in 1928; they had two children, Dolores Ethel Mae and John Jr.

By the end of the 1920s, Barrymore was drinking so heavily that he was almost unemployable. He could seldom remember his lines. His fellow actors attempted to help him, but his case seemed hopeless. Only flashes of brilliance remained. His rare stage appearances became nightmares, and he displayed an intolerance for anything that annoyed him. When one audience appeared uninterested, with several customers coughing loudly, Barrymore raced off-stage and returned to the footlights with a large fish he threw at the audience, shouting: "Busy yourselves with that, you damned walruses while the rest of us proceed with the play!" He began to live off his reputation rather than his ongoing performances, quipping: "I like to be introduced as America's foremost actor. It saves the necessity of further effort."

He was exasperating to his fellow actors. After putting up with nonsense and pranks and heavy drinking all through making *A Bill of Divorcement*, Katharine Hepburn turned on the Great Profile—who had played an escaped lunatic (her father) in the film, and played it perfectly. Said the disgusted Ms. Hepburn: "Thank God, that's the last time I will have to act with you!" Barrymore snorted a laugh and replied: "Is that what you were doing, my dear?"

Even his own family was not immune to his abuse and oddball antics. John, Ethel, and Lionel all starred for the first and only time in a film entitled *Rasputin and the Empress*. At every opportunity, John tried to vex and upstage his brother and sister. At one point during Lionel's best scene (as Rasputin), John continued to reach out and grab his arm in the middle of Lionel's most dramatic lines. Arm-grabbing was an old technique whereby an actor brought attention to himself. After several takes, Lionel stormed off the set and called

Barrymore as a menacing mentor in *Svengali*, with Marian Marsh, 1931.

Barrymore in his last years, dissolute and drunk most of the time; he is shown here with his third and last wife, actress Elaine Barrie, 1938, on board a borrowed yacht—when the ship's liquor ran out Barrymore drank from the vessel's gas tank. (Wide World)

the producer, screaming over the phone: "Will you kindly instruct Mr. John Barrymore to keep his hands off me lest at the close of this scene I will be tempted to lay one on him!"

Cameraman Charles Rosher met Barrymore when his Hollywood career was skidding drastically. Rosher lighted the once-great actor so that soft lights "smoothed away his dewlaps." They became friends, and Rosher was the only one who could persuade Barrymore to go on the set. "He was half-stiff from drink most of the time," Rosher recalled for Kevin Brownlow in *The Parade's Gone By*. "He used to get me in his dressing room to drink Napoleon brandy with him; I used to pour it surreptitiously into a flower vase."

Irving Thalberg still had faith in Barrymore's ability, and even when the actor was spending time in alcoholic "asylums" from which he periodically escaped to wreak havoc, Thalberg employed him—putting him into such great films as *Grand Hotel* and *Dinner at Eight,* in which he played, generally, himself, a man down on his luck and beyond his time. In Thalberg's ambitious flop, *Romeo and Juliet,* Barrymore was brought back to play Mercutio. By then, Barrymore was so destitute that he announced to one and all that "Irving Thalberg saved me from the breadlines." His gratitude, however, did not include abstaining from drink while performing the part. In fact he played the role of Mercutio drunk, although the performance was absolutely brilliant, so much so that after the final "cut!" of his last take was called by director George Cukor the entire cast and crew, including Cukor, broke into applause for the Great Profile. Barrymore's response was typical of him at this time. He staggered forth from the set, shouting: "Fuck the applause—who's got a drink?"

The drinking went on and on until Barrymore could find only small roles in cheap films, roles that mostly lampooned his own life. He became a public disgrace, attempting to seduce waitresses in restaurants, urinating in public, once in Earl Carroll's new nightclub and being beaten up for it. When yachting with director Tay Garnett, he was informed that they had run out of liquor.

Errol Flynn, who considered Barrymore his closest friend, was shocked into sobriety by a macabre and bizarre stunt perpetrated by a group led by Director Raoul Walsh involving Barrymore's corpse.

Barrymore drank from the ship's gas tank. He managed a fourth marriage (to Elaine Barrie) and this sadly ended in divorce in 1940. By then, Barrymore was a derelict looked after by the painter John Dekker and a few other friends. He found little work. In 1942, while rehearsing for a Rudy Vallee radio show he collapsed, moaning: "This is one time I miss my cue."

Bedridden, he refused to believe in his own end, jocularly informing a friend: "Die? I should say not, old fellow. No Barrymore would allow such a conventional thing to happen to him." He was gone on May 29, 1942.

Barrymore's end proved to be as macabre as his life had been, crowned with a bizarre gesture equal to his own zany conduct. Led by director Raoul Walsh, his friends "borrowed" his stiffened corpse and propped it up in an armchair, with a drink in one hand and a burning cigarette in the other, fixing the face with arched eyebrows over wide-staring eyes and a maniacal grin. This was done secretly in the living room of Errol Flynn's home. When Flynn entered, grief-stricken and intoxicated over the death of his closest friend, Barrymore, he took one look at the corpse grinning at him in the chair and went screaming into the night, vowing never to drink again.

Finis BATES

Lawyer (1851–1923)

More entrepreneur than lawyer, Finis Bates of Memphis, Tennessee, obtained the mummified body of a man he identified as one John St. Helen, a man, Bates insisted, who was really John Wilkes Booth. Bates told the press that St. Helen had confided his real identity to him before committing suicide in 1903. (Scores of people up to the turn of the century had confessed to being Booth and all were proved frauds.)

Bates capitalized on his sensational claim by exhibiting the mummified body of St. Helen in southwestern states, charging handsome admission prices. He later made more money by enlarging his claim in a book entitled *The Escape and Suicide of John Wilkes Booth,* a marvelous fabrication of events surrounding Lincoln's egotistical assassin.

Examined by experts, Bates' mummy did bear some physical resemblance to Booth, but the absurd claim was easily dismissed by anyone studying the recorded facts of Booth's death, at the hands of Sergeant Boston Corbett at Garrett's farm in Virginia shortly after Booth had killed Lincoln. Booth was dragged mortally wounded from a burning barn where he had been hiding, and he spoke briefly to several Union officers. His diary was taken from his body before he died in the presence of at least fifty men.

But for Finis Bates such irrefutable history was not important. He continued to make a profit from his mummy almost to the day of his death on November 29, 1923.

Jeremy BENTHAM

Philosopher (1748–1832)

Bentham was the founder of Utilitarianism, a philosophy that insisted that everything (and everyone) should serve some useful purpose. The English savant stated that "utility was the greatest good to the greatest number which is the measure of right and wrong." Bentham then proceeded to tell all good Englishmen what things would produce the greatest good for their civilization. Music was essential, claimed Bentham; and to provide music around the clock, he ordered pianos to be placed in every room of his house—including the toilet. When not playing himself, he employed musicians to lightly tap the ivories for his spiritual edification.

The rich philosopher's lifestyle was not fastidious. One biographer reported that "his apparel hung loosely about him, and consisted chiefly of a grey coat, light breeches and white woolen stockings hanging loosely about his legs; whilst his venerable locks, which floated over the collar and down his back were surmounted by a straw hat of most grotesque and indescribable shape."

Everything had its own uses, Bentham argued, including the human body—dead or alive. Burials were not only a waste of time and money but "brought the least possible happiness to the least possible number." There were sundry uses even for a good corpse. He suggested that it was wasteful to spend money planting rows of trees along the driveways leading to stately mansions. It would be much more useful to embalm the bodies of family members and erect these mummies along those same driveways so that growing children would have the benefit of viewing their ancestors each day. To that end, Bentham, at the age of twenty-one, ordered that his own body not only be embalmed and mummified in the best Egyptian tradition, but also in preparation for mummification, be dissected in the presence of his closest friends.

When Bentham went to his reward in 1832 his wishes were granted. His friends gathered to witness his dissection. A violent storm raged throughout the operation, the thunder and fierce lightning making the scene all the more macabre. One witness blithely reported that Bentham was "clothed in a nightdress," and that his face possessed "an expression of placid dignity and benevolence." The physicians performing the chore were overzealous and cut so much away that Bentham's skull later had to be replaced with a wax head. The body was embalmed, coated with copal varnish to keep out dampness, and then attired in Bentham's best suit of clothes, his favorite straw hat placed permanently upon his wax head. By his order, he was then put on display as a monument in a mahogany cabinet, which was placed in a room in London's University College—where it sits staring, cane in hand, to this day.

A century later, another eccentric British philosopher, Charles K. Ogden (see entry), insisted that "for the sake of decency" the underwear on Bentham's mummy be changed. Fresh linen was provided, and only Bentham's original outer wear remains. This ablutionary nicety would have no doubt irked the great utilitarian; one set of underwear should have been good enough for eternity.

Sarah BERNHARDT

Actress (1844–1923)

Known as the "Divine Sarah," Bernhardt was born Rosine Bernard in France; and in her heyday, she was considered to be the greatest actress in the world—performing *King Lear, Ruy Blas, Phedre* in the 1860s and 1870s. She was still going strong in 1895 when she scored a tremendous success with *L'Aiglon* and later as Hamlet. At sixty-eight, Bernhardt made the silent film *Queen Elizabeth,* and continued to be a worldwide theatrical favorite even after a leg was amputated in 1915.

As great an actress as she was, Bernhardt proved herself to be one of the most eccentric persons of any era, as well as an utterly savage woman who could physically devastate any man provoking her ire. There was nothing Bernhardt would not to do to gain attention. In 1878, when ballooning was an innovation (and a scary one at that—for many balloonists had been killed at the time), Bernhardt thought nothing of climbing into a gondola and going for a three-mile ride in the air above Paris, an act that enraged the manager of the Comédie Française where she performed.

"I have had enough of her imbecilities!" screamed the manager and promptly fined her 1,000 francs. (She made about 50,000 francs a year and spent twice that a month on her extravagant way of life, most of her debts assumed by an army of admirers.) When Bernhardt was informed of the fine, she followed her usual ritual and resigned from the theater. The fine was revoked.

All manner of violence and blood sports fascinated Bernhardt. On a rare trip to Chicago, she was shown the Stockyards; and so engrossed with the slaughtering of animals was she that the actress returned day after day to view the carnage for hours. Bernhardt somehow got the notion that the slaughtering of animals in Chicago's Stockyards would be "educational" for the ladies in her

An early newspaper sketch, circa 1890, shows the tempestuous actress Sarah Bernhardt horse-whipping Mme. Colombier for attracting one of her lovers.

visiting troupe and ordered her delicate Parisian performers to go to the Stockyards and witness the bloodshed. Her actresses fainted en masse, and several went into trauma for weeks on end.

Violence was also at the core of her many love affairs. Several duels were fought over her affections (none of them fatal). At such times, Sarah would watch her love opponents from the closed windows of a coach parked in the Bois de Boulogne, excitedly cheering her lovers on in harsh panting whispers. She herself came close to murdering several lovers. One man she physically battled to an open second-story window and pushed him out; he survived but lay in traction for months. Finding another lover with a woman, Bernhardt stormed into the bedroom well prepared to administer punishment; she carried a long buggy whip in her hands and cracked this as would an expert, horsewhipping her unfaithful lover until he fled slashed and bleeding.

Sarah's battles encompassed the press, the public, and her fellow actors. She claimed that male actors performing with her were "far more jealous than the women, and that they would stoop to greater meannesses to revenge themselves." There were times when the "Divine Sarah" would not only verbally abuse actors she thought had upstaged her, but punch, kick, and claw them. When they complained to the theater manager, they were met with the words: "Yes, she can be *trying.*"

She roared against her critics: "These *canaille!* They say that I am selfish—well, what woman is not? They say I am greedy ... indiscreet, that I am cruel and ambitious, that I pull men down and climb over their bodies on my ascent to fame!" Her ego was boundless, and she never denied that she lived only to become immortal. To Adolph Zukor, head of Paramount Studios, who produced her 1912 film, *Queen Elizabeth* (then considered to be a masterpiece), Bernhardt bubbled: "You have put the best of me in pickle for all time!" (Hollywood always held up Bernhardt as the paragon of acting, an opinion shared by almost all the great dramatic coaches in moviedom. One dramatics teacher was assigned to convert ice star Sonja Henie into an actress. After some weeks, Sonja asked the dramatics coach who was the greatest actress of all time. Without hesitation the teacher named Sarah Bernhardt. Sonja pondered the name for a moment then queried: "Could she skate?")

Perhaps Sarah's greatest love affair was conducted with the French painter Georges Clairin, who painted her both nude and clothed—and even executed an enormous canvas of Bernhardt's feet (shades of *The Horse's Mouth*). When she exploded over an imagined slight by Clairin, she went to the canvas of her "divine feet" and slashed it to pieces. She deeply loved the painter, she confided to her closest associates, but she never married him. Clairin gave her fifteen original paintings, which Sarah Bernhardt kept to her dying day, on March 25, 1923—five of the paintings were of herself.

Russell BIRDWELL

Publicist (Born 1903)

Although one-time publicity director of Selznick International Studios was not in and of himself a true eccentric, the stunts he created were masterworks of zany promotion. It was Birdwell who planted the so-called "rumor" that Clark Gable would play Rhett Butler in *Gone with the Wind*—a rumor so persistent that the public demanded the actor, which caused Louis B. Mayer of MGM to release him to Selznick (who had Birdwell plant the rumor in the first place). It was also Birdwell who came up with the gigantic talent hunt for the right actress to play Scarlett O'Hara, a hunt that generated millions of dollars in publicity for the motion picture.

Birdwell did not always work *for* Selznick. In collusion with star Carole Lombard, herself an amateur practical joker, Birdwell cajoled the city council of Los Angeles into making her mayor for a day. Lombard immediately declared a holiday. When Selznick arrived at his studio, he found the streets empty and only a single guard on hand to greet him.

Perhaps Birdwell's most bizarre stunt concerned the grave of Rudolph Valentino, the great silent film star. In 1928, to promote a short film he was producing, *The Other Side of Hollywood,* Birdwell hired a woman, dressed all in black and heavily veiled, to visit the tomb of the "Sheik," a mysterious woman mourning the loss of the great lover. It caught the public's curiosity. Was she a film star of great fame? Was she a heartbroken socialite? Or was she merely one of Valentino's loyal-beyond-the-grave fans? No one ever knew but Birdwell, who reported that she arrived each dawn on the anniversary of Valentino's death, August 3, and then departed without a word.

This particular stunt backfired. After Birdwell's stunt, a woman in black *did* begin to appear every August 3 and, ignoring the press and photographers who set watch for her, prayed a few minutes and then left wordlessly. Try as he might, Birdwell never learned her identity.

Maxwell BODENHEIM

Poet (1895–1954)

He was the most spectacular poet and/or lover of the 1920s, as well as one of the era's strangest men. Born in the small town of Hermanville, Mississippi (the hamlet has only 500 inhabitants to this day), Maxwell Bodenheim was a most unlikely prospect for the position of successful poet. His family lived in dire poverty, and Bodenheim never had a day of formal schooling. He escaped this miserable existence by falsifying his age and joining the army for four years. His military travels and influences at this time are not documented; but during his military career, Bodenheim came to a surprising decision—he would become a poet.

After completing his service in 1912, Bodenheim, for no good reason, wound up walking the streets of Chicago where he was met and befriended by journalist Ben Hecht, who introduced him to such literary figures as Margaret Anderson, editor of the avant garde magazine *Little Review,* and Harriet Monroe, publisher of *Poetry Magazine.* Hecht was later to report in his memoirs, *Child of the Century,* that the elderly but spry Miss Monroe—she died at age seventy-seven in 1936 while climbing a mountain in Peru—was the subject of much fawning by Bodenheim, an unlikely posture for the iconoclastic Bogey as he was called by friends. At one party, when Miss Monroe entered Bodenheim leapt to his feet "and bowed to her and in a voice surprisingly empty of sneer spoke to her. 'I hope you have recovered from your cold and are enjoying the blessings of a dry nose.' He smiled with what he fancied was a show of gallant interest. In reality he looked as desperate as a bank robber facing a reluctant vault .... In [her] magazine and nowhere else in the world, poetry of the sort that Bodenheim wrote was printed—and paid for."

In all his literary capers in Chicago's so-called Renaissance, Hecht counted on Bodenheim's support and got it—unflinchingly, if not without the poet's usual bizarre behavior. "Maxwell Bodenheim, in manner and appearance," wrote Hecht in his Chicago *Literary Times* (a gloriously self-indulgent periodical backed by bookseller and publisher Pascal Covici), "is the ideal lunatic. He is bowlegged and has pale green eyes. While uttering the most brilliant lines to be heard in American conversation he bares his teeth, clucks weirdly with his tongue, and beats a tattoo with his right foot. He greets an adversary's replies with horrible parrot screams. Having finished an epigram of his own he is overcome with ear-splitting guffaws."

During these innocent years, Bodenheim lived a hand-to-mouth existence, bolstered by irregular payments from small magazines printing his histrionic verse, which many claimed belonged to the Imagist movement (begun by Ezra Pound, Monroe, and others). He often collaborated with Hecht in writing plays, the most successful of which was *The Master Poisoner* in 1917 (long before Hecht joined with Charles MacArthur to create their famous plays). They also edited the Chicago *Literary Times* together, which brought Bodenheim a

Madcap poet Maxwell Bodenheim during his Chicago days.

meager but life-supporting income. Sometimes the poet received only room and board, but he did not complain. As an associate editor of the paper, he was generally allowed to attack any and all without hindrance. He enjoyed playing Hecht's henchman. On one occasion, Bodenheim reviewed an eleven-volume set of contemporary verse by established poets he loathed. His attack was so vicious it prompted Hecht to insert a headline over the review which read: "BODENHEIM RUNS AMUCK: SIX KILLED, FIVE INJURED."

Hecht was forever encouraging Bodenheim to run amuck; and to that end the two friends faked a bitter hatred for each others, casting aspersions and insults in each other's direction at will. This culminated in a literary confrontation before members of the Dill Pickle Club, which Bodenheim dubbed a "literary sewing circle." As the combatants prepared to do mortal battle on stage, a master of ceremonies announced to the eager audience that the theme of the debate was "Resolved: That People Who Attend Literary Debates Are Imbeciles!"

Hecht then strode confidently to center stage, taking his time, drinking glass after glass of water, before stating: "The affirmative rests." Bodenheim came forward, smoothing back his long blonde hair, his deep-set, piercing green eyes focusing upon the puzzled audience. He turned slowly toward Hecht, bowed, and said: "You win." So threatening did the insulted audience become that Hecht and Bodenheim were forced to flee through a side exit or face physical abuse.

Harriet Monroe not only published just about everything Bodenheim sent to *Poetry Magazine,* but invited him to speak regularly before literary groups. However, this "golden-haired youth with pale eyes and the look of a pensive Christ," succeeded in annoying and then angering most of his listeners with his invective.

At one such meeting, an irritated spectator leaped to his feet and roared: "I disagree with everything that Mr. Bodenheim has to say, and furthermore his feet stink!"

A petite dark girl rose to face Bogey's accuser—she was Minna Schein, Bodenheim's newly married wife. "You are casting a personal slur upon one of America's greatest poets," she replied, "and you, sir, are not fit to wash those feet!" (Bodenheim's best book of poetry, *Minna and Myself,* appearing in 1918, chiefly dealt with his love life and his wife.)

To be sure, Bodenheim was an unwashed genius. His suits were unkempt and soiled. His shoes were cracked and curled with sweat. He smoked a ridiculously long pipe with a blue ribbon tied in a bow about the stem. He often pretended to be people he was not. On one occasion, he darkened his skin, affected Eastern garb (including a distinguished-looking turban), and passed himself off as Moslem fakir, being so bold as to go to one of Chicago's many newspapers and sit atop an editorial desk while being interviewed, his broken-English replies delivered in a decidedly upper class dialect. Bodenheim had been drinking heavily before this masquerade, however; and when he jumped from the desk at the end of the interview, he slipped and fell forward, the turban rolling off his head and revealing the Bodenhiem blonde locks and a ring of white skin at the hairline. He was chased from the city room by howling reporters.

On another occasion, the poet, disgusted by the many poetry movements from Europe hailed in Chicago's press as earth-shattering events, became determined to point out the absurdity of such movements. Bodenheim, with Hecht's help it was suspected, dashed off an arcane manifesto announcing the Monotheme school of poetry. With great vituperation, the manifesto denounced all poets who wrote in a variety of themes and asserted that henceforth poets would be assigned to write on a single subject, that category to be assigned by the leader of the Monotheme movement, one Réne d'Or, an alleged European count who was none other than Bodenheim.

Accompanying the manifesto were five poems to demonstrate the movement's aim, poems written exclusively on the subject of bottles. A thousand copies of the manifesto and bottle poetry were sent out to editors and powerful literary lights in Chicago, along with an announcement that Count d'Or would be available for interviews at the Blackstone Hotel the following Monday.

In heavy disguise, Bodenheim prepared to meet the press at the appointed hour. According to Albert Parry, he "sat in his room from nine o'clock in the morning till midnight; he starved the whole day, fearing to miss interviewers if he went for food; but no one came or telephoned, no one printed a word about Réne d'Or and the Monotheme Manifesto."

Hecht later lampooned his friend's odd impersonation of d'Or and others in his roman à clef, *Count Bruga,* portraying Bodenheim as a satyr and loony. The satire more than rankled Bodenheim. Doug Fetherling, in his excellent *Five Lives of Ben Hecht,* was to remark that Bodenheim "was badly stung by *Count Bruga,* primarily because for years afterwards the likeness would precede him in his travels." Bogey retaliated by penning his own burlesque of Hecht in a 1931 novel called *Duke Herring.* Where Hecht's book (which was extremely popular when it was published in 1926) amused readers with its tales of the fake count, Hippolyt Bruga or Jules Ganz, Bodenheim's lampoon of Hecht (as Arturo Herring), which profiled Hecht as a money-mad pornographer who spent most of his time trying to cheat on his wife, was universally seen as a weak rejoinder in a fast-fading vendetta.

But by then Bodenheim had moved on to Greenwich Village to star as its super Bohemian; and the Hecht–Bodenheim feuds became blurry memories, as did Bogey's Chicago antics. It was while he lived in the Village (which was to be the remainder of his life) that Bodenheim established his scandalous reputation.

Alfred Kreymborg, publisher of little magazines, was one of the first to befriend Bodenheim, renting a Bank Street room for him and leading him to the Village's tea rooms, coffee shops, and saloons to meet the Eastern literati of antiestablishment bent—all of those who shared Bodenheim's nihilism, if not his cynical attitude. Said Kreymborg of Bogey at this time: "His pale eyes gave forth the insistent impression that for him life had sounded the ultimate in disillusionment. His voice, a bitter, sarcastic tinge, chanted a tireless flow of picturesque metaphors and similes."

Bodenheim's literary production increased—scores of his poems appeared in magazines and were later collected into several popular volumes; he wrote a half-dozen best-selling novels, including *Replenishing Jessica, Crazy Man,* and *Naked on Roller Skates*—novels whose titles loudly advertised Bodenheim's sex-saturated prose. Bodenheim's books created havoc with the self-styled Evangelical reformers of the age who were forever on the lookout for books to censor. *Replenishing Jessica,* like all of Bogey's works, was liberally laced with sex. (Jessica was, in Bodenheim's words, a girl "to whom the simple feat of keeping her legs crossed was a structural impossibility.") The author and his publisher, Horace Liveright, were charged with producing an indecent and obscene work. The judge in this case, however, was an admirer of Bogey's writing, thinking like many others that Bodenheim was a latter day Zola; he dismissed the charges against him and Liveright. The book was nevertheless banned in Boston and in other towns ruled by the small-minded Babbitts of the day, but that did nothing but boost the author's popularity and sales. He was a hero and a martyr to modern literature. He played the role with pomp and panache, affecting a broad-brimmed hat and a long, flowing black cape (he was to wear the latter to his final ragged days). "The Village became the palace grounds of Bohemia's King Maxwell Bodenheim," wrote John Armstrong, "and he walked surrounded by admiration."

With his fame and riches Bodenheim also increased his drinking and carousing. No longer with his wife Minna, he dallied with every naive girl who entered the Village seeking to meet the great Bogey. Of Bodenheim in this period Allen Churchill quoted one long-time Village resident in his *Improper Bohemians:* "When I came to the Village Max was a figure to be looked up to but suddenly he was a man to be avoided."

What changed the popular poet to social pariah in the more respectable quarters of the Village was his hedonistic lovelife. The poet would advance upon any woman, single or married, that caught his eye at a bar, in a restaurant, or at a party, stand close and whisper heady lines like "Your hair is like a wistful sunrise," or "Your face is an incense bowl from which a single name rises." Female victims of his amorous advances not only swooned but died. In June 1928, when Bodenheim's literary fame was at its highest, he came to disaster in the form of three women bent on the kind of tragic ends Bogey wrote about.

Gladys Loeb, a poetry-stricken eighteen-year-old living in a small room on MacDougal Street next to Bogey's lodgings was so stricken with Bodenheim that when he rebuffed her, she turned on the gas of her oven, and clutching the poet's autographed photo to her bosom, stuck her head into the stove. Her landlady smelled the gas and rushed upstairs with door-breaking police, just in time to save the lovesick lady. Gladys' father, a prominent doctor from the Bronx, was summoned. After calling Bodenheim every sort of scoundrel, Dr. Loeb took his daughter back to her ancestral home in the Bronx. Reporters mobbed Bogey some hours later. He tried to escape but was held fast by the clamoring scribes. He stuttered that Gladys had come to him with her manuscripts for criticism.

"What did you say to her after you read her work?" a reporter asked.

"I told her it was rotten," Bogey answered truthfully. "I guess that discouraged her."

Breaking away from the newsmen, Bodenheim hastily departed the Village, taking a room in a Forty-Fifth Street hotel patronized by actors. To his suite on July 22, 1928 came another literary hopeful, one Virginia Drew, a twenty-four-year-old commercial artist lugging several boxes containing un-published poems and novels. Bogey read her material and, as with the immature work of Gladys Loeb, pronounced the manuscripts inept. "It's sentimental slush," sneered Bodenheim, displaying his usual empathy for novice writers.

Virginia became hysterical. She tore at her clothes, at Bodenheim's clothes, at the hotel drapes and bedsheets; she pulled her hair, screamed, threw herself onto the floor, and kicked out a tantrum. After several hours in which she allowed herself to be soothed by Bodenheim, Virginia said in a steady voice: "If I can't write as wonderfully as you do, I will kill myself."

Panic seized Bodenheim; he was still smarting from the memory of Gladys Loeb. He begged, cajoled, and argued with the young woman for hours. When he felt that he had dissuaded her from committing suicide, Bodenheim walked her to the subway at 3 A.M. and told her to go home and "go back to commercial art."

Virginia Drew was not seen for days, and her family began to make inquiries. Her father and brother visited Bodenheim's hotel, knowing that Virginia had been seeing the poet. Bodenheim, the clerk informed the Drews, was not in. He arrived only an hour after his visitors left. When he was informed of the visit, Bodenheim began to tremble and his face went ashen. "Did they appear militant?" he asked the clerk. Then he rushed upstairs to pack. Early the next morning, Bodenheim checked out carrying a portable typewriter, his own published books, and a single bag. He left no forwarding address.

Three days later, the body of Virginia Drew washed ashore from the brown waters of the East River. Police and reporters swarmed into Bodenheim's hotel suite finding only a pair of old shoes, soiled underwear, and nine books, including *Replenishing Jessica* and a book by Robert Clairmont, *Quintillions*. Clairmont, a close friend of Bogey's, had enscribed his book thus: "To Maxwell Bodenheim, Roué of the first order, a dangerous rival in affairs of the heart. Robert Clairmont." This inscription inflamed police and newsmen. Scurrying cops sought the poet everywhere in New York. Newspapers blared his involvement with Virginia Drew's drowning. A front-page story in the New York *Times* was headlined: "BODENHEIM VANISHES AS GIRL TAKES LIFE." The story began, "A rebel against the canons of poetry and life, the poet by his absence has enmeshed himself in a case as bizarre as any of his own books."

Newsmen finally tracked Bodenheim down in Provincetown where he was hiding in a shack. Also on hand was Dr. Loeb fresh from the Bronx. His

Artist's rendition of Maxwell Bodenheim shortly before his violent death. (Sketch by Ron Myers)

daughter was again missing, and he concluded that she had gone to live with the poet. Dr. Loeb burst into Bodenheim's Provincetown shack but found him alone. Bogey talked fast and so convincingly that Dr. Loeb emerged to tell reporters that "I think we've been doing Bodenheim a great injustice."

Gladys, true to her father's suspicions, did arrive in Provincetown to see Bodenheim. A reporter recognized her and asked: "Aren't you Gladys Loeb?"

"No," Gladys snarled, "I'm Gretchen Winthrop!" She jumped into a cab, which tore off in the direction of Bodenheim's shack. Upon approaching the rundown, near-collapsing building, she spied her father and ordered the cab driver to turn around, shouting, "Step on it—there's my old man!"

The cab driver, who had been bribed by Dr. Loeb, ignored Gladys and dutifully delivered her to her father. Dr. Loeb, Gladys, *and* Bodenheim then got into the cab. The poet had hastily packed his bags and was leaving with the Loebs. On the run, he told reporters that he knew nothing about the suicide of Virginia Drew, only that she told him she planned to kill herself and that he had "argued with her until I was black in the face!"

The Loebs and Bogey argued incessantly in the cab all the way to Hyannis where Dr. Loeb ordered the cab driver to halt. Both he and Bodenheim alighted, shouting at each other in the road as the reporters trailing them roared up in commandeered cars.

"You're an irresponsible bum!" Dr. Loeb was heard to shout at the poet.

Bodenheim lifted his lion's head and roared back: "I am a genius and you are an obtuse fellow who cannot understand genius!"

Gladys interceded, and the trio continued angrily on to New York via train. Bodenheim, who feared arrest by the police over the Virginia Drew suicide, got off at Stamford (forever exiting the world of Gladys and Dr. Loeb). He hid out for days in Harlem, living in the Rose Ballroom, until police discovered him. He was taken in for questioning but was released; by then it had been determined that Virginia Drew had died at her own hand.

No sooner was Bodenheim settled once again in the Village than another tragedy exploded around his head. Aimee Cortez, an exotic dancer in the Village, put her head into a stove and turned on the gas. When her body was found, a portrait of Bodenheim had to be pried from her dead hands. Aimee had known Bodenheim for two years, but their romance had long since died; she undoubtedly chose to end her life and capitalize upon the publicity the poet had been receiving. Aimee, like Bogey, had loved the limelight. Some time later, another of Bodenheim's literary camp followers, one Dorothy Dear (that was her actual name), met an awful fate, the kind that seemed to be ever trailing in the poet's wake. As she was traveling to the Village via subway, her train derailed and crashed into another car. Dorothy Dear was killed immediately. Bodenheim's love letters to her were later found strewn over the subway tracks.

When the 1920s ended, so too ended the public's fascination with Maxwell Bodenheim. He published his last sardonic novel in 1932, but it sold little. The Village was no longer a romantic quaint place but, like most of the country, a squalid area of destitution and poverty. Bodenheim hung on, no longer a

Author Ben Hecht, Bodenheim's close and almost only friend.

celebrity but a curiosity. Within a decade, he was not only borrowing money from all his friends—Ben Hecht sent him $30 a week to live on for years—but stealing books from bookstores, as well as from the homes of his supporters. These he would resell, drinking up the meager profits. Soon he was living the awful life of the worst hobo in New York.

Toward the end of his life, Bodenheim made the San Remo bar his headquarters. He would be given a water glass brimming with gin and sit in the middle of the place raving his iconoclastic philosophy and reciting his own poetry if he could remember the lines. "I have a malady of the soul," the drunken poet would repeatedly moan to any and all who cared to listen.

In late 1953, Bodenheim took up with Ruth Fagin, a twenty-nine-year-old honor graduate from the University of Michigan. They met in a rainstorm in Washington Square. Bodenheim had an umbrella and offered to share it. From that moment on, the pair were seen sleeping in alleyways and, when luck was good, in deserted houses. When Bogey could afford the price of a flophouse, Ruth accompanied him dressed as a man. After some months, Ruth's body showed the strain of such a life; she became emaciated, her face bloodless and, when Bodenheim beat her, bruised and welted. The poet vowed he would abandon the woman who followed him about like a stray dog, but he invariably kept her at his side. She was the only loyal companion left in his miserable life, a life Bodenheim had long tired of living. On his last visit to see his friend Ben Hecht, Bodenheim croaked: "I am sick of the whole thing. I know of no sensible reason why I should not commit suicide and put an end to this whole stupid nonsense. Beauty, art, poetry—yes, I am even sick of poetry, sick of pretty words staring at me. I hate them—all the pretty words. I'd commit suicide tonight except that I am in love with my wife [He had married Ruth by this time]. She is very sick and full of suffering and she needs me."

The Bodenheims were nibbling on leftovers in the Bowery's Waldorf Cafeteria in February 1954 when they were joined by a neurotic young man, a drifter named Harold Weinberg who was in love with Ruth. When he began to whisper his affection for her, Bodenheim leaned forward and said: "Leave her alone or I'll kill you!"

"You hate me, don't you?" Weinberg shouted as he jumped to his feet.

"Of course I do," Bodenheim yelled back.

On February 7, after having been arrested several times for sleeping in the park, the Bodenheims found themselves the guests of the much-disliked Weinberg, sharing his small 85¢-a-night room on Third Avenue in the Bowery. The twenty-five-year-old Weinberg, who had served a great deal of time in mental institutions and jails, spent some of the money he had earned as a dishwasher on a bottle of whiskey. This he generously shared with the Bodenheims. After several drinks, Weinberg suddenly threw himself on Ruth, tearing at her clothes in his wild passion for her. Bodenheim dropped a book he was reading (*The Sea around Us*, by Rachel Carson) and lunged toward Weinberg. The dishwasher grabbed a revolver and shot the poet in the chest, killing him. Ruth flailed away at the killer, clawing his face. Weinberg lost the revolver in the scuffle but managed to pick up a butcher knife; and this he plunged into the woman four times, killing her.

Police arrested Weinberg a short time later; he was sent to New York's Mattewan State Hospital for the Criminally Insane for life. Friends of the Bodenheims gathered at the San Remo where Bogey's special drinking glass was ritually smashed to bits.

The couple were saved from burial in Potter's Field by contributions from writers and artists (Ben Hecht contributed $50). The legends surrounding the flamboyant Bodenheim then came with a rush. Someone vividly recalled Bogey's last night in the Village. Only hours before his murder, he had entered a Village bar and demanded free drinks—only to be turned away by a bartender unimpressed with nobly failed poets. At the bar entrance, Bodenheim struck a familiar pose, sweeping his cape about his cadaverous body and booming forth the words: "You are all unworthy of my presence, an unschooled lot—whores, pimps, and racetrack touts!"

Junius Brutus BOOTH

Actor (1796–1852)

The British-born Booth was considered one of the great figures of nineteenth-century theater in America, an actor who specialized in Shakespearian roles. He was to father actors Edwin Booth, the finest tragedian of his day, and John Wilkes Booth, who assassinated President Lincoln. Eccentricity (some called it madness) was rampant in the Booth family, particularly in Junius. He literally tore the scenery to bits when acting out his more vitriolic roles. Toward the end of his career, this once great actor drank so heavily, as was the case with John Barrymore (see entry), that he was known more widely for his capacity than for his ability to perform.

Booth's one strange passion was visiting the horrendous New York prison, The Tombs. Warden Fallon, who enjoyed entertaining visiting dignitaries, at first encouraged the flamboyant actor to visit the prison. Booth arrived, usually at dusk and close to being in an alcoholic stupor. As usual, he would be conducted along the gloomy tier of cells known as "Murderers Row."

Booth particularly enjoyed the company of a killer who was known simply as "Dave Babe." This convicted murderer, reputed to be the errant son of an Episcopal bishop, had slit the throat of the mate of the *Sarah Lavinia* in 1843. He had been convicted of piracy and murder but had been spared the gallows seven times.

It was Booth's habit to stagger into Babe's cell, with several guards looking on in amusement, and point derisively at the shackles attached to the man's feet at one end and to a large stone in the foor at the other. "Strike the fetters from that unfortunate creature!" Booth would boom. As torrents of tears coursed his cheeks, the actor would then implore the jailers to "secure me in his place!"

Guards would then soothe the emotionally upset Booth—but not before he slipped the killer a dozen expensive cigars rolled in a lace handkerchief. He would then stagger, half supported by the keepers, down Murderers Row. On one occasion, he withdrew a $20 bill from his vest pocket and handed it to a Negro prisoner who had been convicted of strangling his wife.

Warden Fallon's eyes popped at the sight of such magnaminity, and he tried to swipe the bill out of the strangler's hand. The killer was quicker and jammed the bill into his mouth, hastily attempting to swallow the money rather than turn it over to Fallon. The warden, however, was a determined man. Flinging wide the cell door, he rushed inside and began to choke his prisoner, who, preferring to breathe, coughed the bill into Fallon's cupped hand.

Fallon eventually tired of the actor's hysterics; and when Booth subsequently visited The Tombs, the warden had him locked in a cell on Murderers Row. This was grist for Booth's ever-grinding mill of drama; and on such occasions, the Shakesperian actor would moan out long soliloquies as he theatrically rattled the bars, shook chains, and made so much a nuisance of himself that even his friends—the killers in adjoining cells—cursed him. Booth would wear himself out with these tirades and eventually fall into a deep alcoholic sleep on the cell cot provided for him. Shortly before he was due at the theater for the evening's performance, two of Fallon's guards would rouse him from his torpor and literally carry him to the playhouse. The burly guards would stand by as the actor applied his make-up and dressed and then support him on either side through the wings until he emerged on stage, surprisingly ready to render a superb Richard III.

Junius Booth's youngest son, John Wilkes, as mad as his father, and the infamous assassin of President Lincoln. (Library of Congress)

Clara BOW

Actress (1905–1965)

"I never had a doll when I was a kid," recalled Clara Bow, the hottest red-headed movie queen of the silent era. "No one wanted me. My folks didn't want me because two babies had died before me and when I came along they were afraid that it would kill mother. My mother never knew a moment free from illness. I've never forgotten how she suffered. I can remember yet how white she looked as she stood over the tub scrubbing out an old red-checkered tablecloth."

Clara Bow's sad memories of the Brooklyn ghetto where she had lived somehow served as an excuse for her extravagant behavior when she was known across the country as the "It" girl of the movies. (Asked what "It" meant, writer Elinor Glyn, creator of the connotation, responded: "It is an indefinable sort of sex appeal. There are few people in the world who possess it. The only ones in Hollywood [in 1926] who do are Rex, the wild stallion, actor Tony Moreno, the Ambassador Hotel doorman and Clara Bow.")

As a sex goddess of the silent screen, Clara Bow dominated the Hollywood scene from 1925 to 1932, making "flaming youth" pictures such as *Kiss Me Again, The Plastic Age, Mantrap, Dancing Mothers, It, Wings, The Wild Party,* and *Call Her Savage,* portraying gin-gulping, Charleston-hopping flappers who lived from one wild night to the next. In real life, Clara played a similar role to the hilt.

She was discovered with her physician, Dr. William Earl Pearson, as the doctor was applying what he later termed "a love balm" to her anatomy. Mrs. Pearson promptly named the actress as correspondent in a divorce suit that cost Clara $30,000 in damages. Next came the disclosures of Clara's private secretary, Daisy DeVoe, who had kept a dossier on the "It" girl's scandalous affairs. When the actress refused to pay blackmail money for the "little black book," the secretary sold her memoirs of Clara to the sensation-seeking New York *Graphic.* The affairs listed were staggering—from Gary Cooper to Bela Lugosi, from Eddie Cantor to cowboy star Rex Bell, who later married Ms. Bow.

According to Kenneth Anger's *Hollywood Babylon,* Clara Bow "took on Trojans by the bunch. She'd play party girl to the *entire* 'Thundering Herd' [the first squad of the University of Southern California football team] during beery, brawling, gangbanging weekend parties, accommodating the fun-loving bruisers right down to the eleventh man, hulking tackle Marion Morrison [later known as John Wayne]."

Her antics became legend. She would stay up all night playing poker with her maids and chauffeur. She served beer in her patio to visiting Beverly Hills cops. She would get drunk and then go roller skating down the blocks of her exclusive suburb in the middle of the night.

Jazz Age screen siren Clara Bow as she appeared in the silent film *IT*.

Daisy DeVoe, who told all on her employer, subsequently went to prison for stealing $5,000 from Clara; but the scandals the private secretary broke about the head of the "most beautiful girl in the world" caused Paramount to terminate her contract. She fell from Hollywood grace with a thud, having several nervous breakdowns and spending many years in sanitariums. Clara Bow died a bewildered and lonely woman. Said her husband Rex Bell, who later became governor of Nevada: "If she had been Minnie Zilch instead of Clara Bow perhaps this never would have happened to her."

James Buchanan ("Diamond Jim") BRADY

Financier (1856–1917)

Brady was the epitome of the nineteenth-century American businessman, a self-made millionaire whose fortune flowed from the railroads. He sold steel railroad cars and controlled a virtual monopoly through an unusual contract that gave him one-third of all sales of the vehicles. Within a few years, Brady's bank account topped $12 million. As a traveling salesman in his early days, Brady developed an insatiable appetite for only two things—diamonds and food. He would frequent the best pawnshops, keenly aware that jewelry stores drastically marked up the price of diamonds, and bargain for what came to be the greatest single collection of gems in America. Soon he was known along Broadway in New York, or "The Great White Way," as it was then called, as "Diamond Jim." He wore diamonds everywhere on his person all the time. He glistened like a Christmas tree.

Brady would stroll down Broadway, glittering with more than twenty-five hundred diamonds and nineteen rubies that adorned his rings, watch chain, cufflinks, stickpin, shirt-studs, belt, anywhere they could be worn. Even the buttons of his coat were encrusted with diamonds. (Such a sight today on Broadway would guarantee an instant mugging, of course.) For his shirt studs, Brady ordered special designs of diamond-studded bicycles and automobiles; his cufflinks were shaped in the forms of diamond-encrusted locomotives and freight cars. There was a three-carat diamond embedded in the knob of his cane. Brady once gave Lillian Russell—the singer was the love of his life—a bicycle plated with gold and fixed with hundreds of diamonds, rubies, emeralds, and sapphires. Lillian pedaled that bike only once—along Fifth Avenue for a few blocks until she created such a traffic jam and drew such crowds that several squads of police were called to escort her and the glittering bicycle home.

Everything about Brady was excessive. His New York mansion boasted a billiard table inlaid with carnelians and lapis lazuli. He played cards with poker chips made of onyx and mother-of-pearl. Every year, Brady gave an interior decorator $750,000 to redesign his mansion, giving his priceless furniture to friends and replacing this with new furnishings worth hundreds of thousands of dollars. He overlooked nothing that surrounded him; the cows on his New Jersey farm were milked into pails thickly plated with gold.

Money was to be spent on others, according to Diamond Jim. His friends were forever receiving extravagant gifts—from jewels to huge boxes of candy (his candy bill averaged $3,000 a month). His generosity approached the ridiculous. He would hand out small diamonds to servants who pleased him. Diamond Jim also loved to give parties and had as many as fifteen parties going in one night all about New York.

An inveterate gambler, Brady went through millions, especially when playing opposite that other great plunger of the age, John "Bet-A-Million" Gates. More often he won. These two giants met in the most exclusive gambling dens of New York, Canfield's or the resplendent House of the Bronze Door.

On one occasion, Brady, Gates, and others stood at the end of the bar in the Hoffman House—a gathering place of the rich—and put up fortunes against the outcome of the 1896 presidential election between William McKinley and William Jennings Bryan. The bouncer at the Hoffman House, Big Billy Edwards, held the stakes—more than $500,000 in cash, which caused his pockets to bulge grotesquely. Every now and then, Diamond Jim excused himself, saying that he wanted to see if he could pick up more bets at the crowded bar. Returning in about fifteen minutes, Brady made staggering side bets on state-by-state returns—and Brady won and won. According to gambling historian Henry Chafetz in *Play the Devil,* Brady was really stinging Gates. "Actually, Brady went not to the bar but to the headquarters across the street where an associate of his was busily engaged calculating and working out trends and results as far as returns were telegraphed in." Diamond Jim took Gates for $200,000 that night and celebrated by devouring one of his famous dinners.

Eating was Diamond Jim's favorite pastime. Though he never touched a drop of liquor in his life, he was an out-and-out glutton. His penchant for food undoubtedly stemmed from his boyhood, spent above his stepfather's saloon in lower Manhattan. He was given little food as a child and was exposed to the lurching derelicts in his stepfather's bar, many of whom were later shanghaied through his stepfather's connivance with bestial sea captains. Brady biographer John Burke stated how Diamond Jim's stepfather "would slip knockout drops in the drinks of able-bodied patrons, and the next thing they knew they were lying half-drugged in the stinking forecastle of a tramp bound for a guano port."

Diamond Jim did drink enormous amounts of root beer, sometimes as much as 15 huge glasses before beginning a meal. His usual breakfast consisted of four scrambled eggs, a stack of wheatcakes drenched with thick syrup, a rare steak smothered in chops, grits, a bowl of fried potatoes, muffins, and several pitchers of milk to wash it all down. On other occasions, he would gulp down a gallon of orange juice before his fifteen-course meal. Following the meal he would stuff himself with a pound of chocolates.

The 250-pound Brady literally ate himself to death after Lillian Russell turned down his marriage proposal, despite the fact that he had dumped $1 million in cash in her lap. Diamond Jim was philosophical about it all, saying:

"It's fun to be a sucker—if you can afford it!" Before his death, on April 13, 1917, he tore up IOU's exceeding $250,000, telling his doctor: "If I'm gonna die, I'm gonna die, but I ain't gonna leave troube and heartache behind me." Further, the eccentric Brady left a fortune to Johns Hopkins Hospital in Baltimore, which enabled the founding of the hospital's Urological Institute.

Brady's collection of jewels—mostly diamonds, including a marvelous watch once worn by Napoleon Bonaparte, which boasted 422 pearls and 38 diamonds—was estimated at $5 million when he died. The diamonds were later removed from their settings and resold in smaller rings. According to one report: "Many a woman today, without suspecting it, is wearing a stone that once enhanced the expansive charms of Diamond Jim."

John R. BRINCKLEY

"Physician" (1885–1942)

Miracle medicines and operations guaranteeing patients total rejuvenation swept the United States during the 1920s. One of the most flagrant quacks of this period, who made millions promising eternal youth through his goat gland operation, was a self-styled doctor, John R. Brinckley, a native of Kansas. Opening his clinic in Milford, Kansas, Brinckley advertised widely that he could rejuvenate prospective patients by transplanting goat glands into any human male. Thousands of elderly men flocked to Brinckley, paying him from $750 to $1,500 per operation (the cost was higher if the glands of a very *young* goat were transplanted).

There was never any evidence that these operations lengthened the life of one patient or that the patients themselves did not have their lives shortened through the introduction of foreign matter into their bodies. Brinckley was

John R. Brinkley, notorious 1920s quack who performed thousands of goat-gland operations which he insisted would make men potent and young.

finally exposed. The license of his radio station was revoked—he had broadcast his medical messages over the airways. Undaunted, Brinckley moved to Mexico, where in the small town of Del Rio, he continued his nefarious medical practices, insisting that he could cure any prostate problem (with a medicine that was nothing more than blue dye and hydrochloric acid). At the same time, he operated a clinic in Little Rock, Arkansas, where he continued his insane transplant operations.

Brinckley ran for the office of governor of Kansas three times, almost defeating the venerable Alf Landon, such was this quack's popularity. Moreover, before his death on May 26, 1942, Brinckley became one of the biggest financial backers of American fascist organizations, donating vast sums to the Silver Shirts led by William Dudley Pelley.

Edward West ("Daddy") BROWNING

Real Estate Tycoon (1875–1934)

The American success story of Edward West Browning was in the true tradition of Horatio Alger. He had risen with hard work over the years from the position of lowly office boy to New York real estate magnate. At least, that was the business side of his story. The social side displayed one of the wackiest eccentrics ever to titillate the sensation-seeking readers of New York's gaudy tabloids. Browning not only loved the lurid publicity attending his name but sought it out—exploiting his strange fame, storing it in his own archives, and reveling in it as one might a Pulitzer Prize or a Nobel Award.

At an early age, Browning began buying property, which he would improve and then sell or rent, usually the latter. By 1915, when he married, he was a millionaire many times over. In addition to owning scores of office buildings, he gleaned more than $300,000 in annual rents from his apartments. In an early interview, the real estate tycoon summed up his success succinctly by telling a reporter: "I always show a client the sunny rooms first."

With his first taste of publicity, Browning began to manifest latent eccentricities. He took to wearing flowered waistcoats and suits of his own odd design, including one that boasted twenty pearl buttons on the sleeves. He had more than a thousand ties decorated in the most horrendous colors and patterns, each personally selected by the real estate czar. Browning was a social climber and limelighter by nature, a friend to any celebrity who cared to shake his hand, including Mayor James J. Walker.

One of Browning's friends at the time commented: "He dearly loves the spotlight and when it is turned in his direction it thrills him to the point where his balance, so evident in business dealings, becomes wholly upset. He must be seen." Given Browning's glaring and gaudy attire, which for him passed as sartorial splendor, he was indeed noted by the press—spectacularly in 1924 when his wife decamped with the family dentist. Later, when Mrs. Browning sued for divorce, the beet-faced, puffy-cheeked Browning huffed to reporters: "A dentist of all people! How can any sensible woman fall in love with a dentist, particularly with the dentist who has done her own work? The idea is preposterous!"

An indignant Mrs. Browning answered with her own salvo of accusations, claiming that her husband "always liked young girls. I don't know why he ever married. He would go with one set of girls until they were older than he fancied, then he would drop them for a younger set. The evidence on which I will base my suit has to do with his penchant for flappers."

Browning settled a large amount on his ex-wife, each taking custody of one of their two adopted daughters, Dorothy and Gloria. To eager newsmen, Browning announced that Dorothy, who was to stay with him, loved pet names as did he. "I call her Sunshine," he proclaimed. "She calls me Daddy." Thanks to the story-hunting newsmen of the 1920s, it would be Daddy Browning until the tycoon's dying day.

Less than a year after his divorce, Browning shocked New York by inserting a peculiar advertisement in the New York *Herald Tribune* which read:

ADOPTION—Pretty refined girl, about fourteen years old, wanted by aristocratic family of large wealth and highest standing; will be brought up as own child among beautiful surroundings, with every desirable luxury, opportunity, education, travel, kindness, care, love. Address with particulars and photograph.

When reporters flocked to Browning's offices at Broadway and Seventy-Second Street, Daddy greeted the clamoring scribes with a broad smile and open arms. Remembering Mrs. Browning's charges that her husband chased young girls, the reporters asked suspicious questions. Browning, his usually red face turning a deeper scarlet, maintained his fleshy smile and explained that his daughter Dorothy "wants a sister, and of course, it's up to me to find one."

It was a dream story for New York papers. Daddy Browning would escort some poor urchin into his private Emerald City. New York went crazy with the thought, thousands of down-and-out mothers dragging their daughters to Browning's spacious offices to be interviewed. Bouncing the girls on his knee,

Daddy Browning with his soon-to-be-adopted daughter, Mary Spaas, who was then allegedly sixteen. (Wide World)

48

Daddy interviewed more than twelve thousand children in two weeks, as press photographers wore out their Speed Graphics taking pictures as he caressed and pinched the desperate little applicants.

With showy pomp, Daddy Browning finally announced his selection—one Mary Spaas, a sixteen-year-old girl from Astoria who had, the tycoon stated with a tear, not a soul or a penny to call her own, a beautiful street waif who had walked dozens of miles to apply for the enviable position of sister to Dorothy Sunshine. This Cinderella story was featured on the front page of the New York *Times,* which took great editorial pains to describe the lucky winner: "The girl's cheeks are red as apples, her eyes are hazel, and her mass of light hair falls in natural curls to her shoulders. It has a golden tint when touched by the sunlight. She seems rather small for her age. She also seems rather shy."

As Daddy and Mary hurried off on a Fifth Avenue shopping spree with rioting crowds running in the wake of Browning's blue Rolls Royce, some curious reporters traveled to Astoria to investigate Cinderella's hazy background. Members of the Spaas family, neighbors, and friends all scoffed at the tale. Mary was a long way from sixteen. School and employment records proved that she was twenty-one. She had not only been a movie extra at Paramount Film Studios, located nearby, but was engaged to one Emil Vasalek, an embittered plumber who angrily stated that Mary had broken off with him to answer Daddy Browning's fairyland advertisement.

Browning hurriedly called a meeting, attended by Mary and her newly found lawyers, as well as his own legal counsel. When confronted with statements about her actual age, Mary Spaas shouted: "I'm sixteen because I want to be sixteen!" Hearing this, an embarrassed Daddy Browning raced from the scene.

The Mary Spaas hoax left the jovial Daddy unruffled and his thirst for the companionship of young girls unquenched. The duped millionaire somehow touched the hearts of millions of readers, who deluged his office with fan mail. (Before his notorious social life ceased, he would receive almost three million letters, all of which were carefully answered and filed by Browning's overworked staff.) Browning continued to receive an enormous amount of newspaper space, and he spent most of his time, when not occupied in pursuing

A thoroughly dejected Browning after the Mary Spaas fiasco, destroying letters from girls seeking to be adopted by him. (Wide World)

young females, ordering his clerks to paste down volumes of clippings in morocco-bound scrapbooks.

In the fall of 1925, Daddy hit upon the happy thought of supporting high school sororities. His emmissaries informed these sororities that Browning was more than willing to pay off their debts; provide pins, sweaters, and accouterments; and lavishly sponsor sorority dances in posh New York hotels. It must be understood, the sororities were politely informed, that Daddy expected to attend all the dances. His generous offer was accepted with alacrity by scores of sororities. The presence of this strange elderly man at dances for the very young aroused curiosity and discreet laughter.

He would arrive in his chauffeur-driven Rolls Royce and stand tuxedo-attired on the dance floor, his sheep's eyes evaluating the girls present. Though he was then fifty, Browning looked at least ten years older. His florid face changed from pink to red, and wattles gathered beneath a weak chin. Though his hair was receding, he was vain of the short curly strands. He kept a comb with him at all times and ran it through his thin locks whenever women or reporters were present.

Daddy Browning proved himself a durable if not expert ballroom dancer, fearlessly performing the Charleston and the Black Bottom, changing partners with each dance. With discreet lechery, he pinched his partners' cheeks (and sometimes a bottom). But to most, he was only a rich old rogue who footed the bills, and tolerating his antics became the custom. Daddy was a harmless old fool, the girls tittered. Nobody every took him seriously. Nobody that is, except Frances Belle Heenan, a chubby fifteen year old with an overdeveloped body, who filled Daddy's eyesight to overflowing in February 1926, when she stepped onto the dance floor of the Hotel McAlpin. On this particular Saturday night, Browning was sponsoring a dance for the Phi Lambda Tau sorority, a name he himself had selected, thinking that the name meant Pretty Little Things.

With the aid of her mother, Frances Heenan was a drop-out from Textile High. Mrs. James Heenan had been writing notes to teachers for several months in order that her fifteen-year-old flapper could stay at home and indulge her fantasies. Frances' appearance at the dance was unexpected and unwanted. She had not been invited, and she was disliked by most of the other girls. Daddy Browning was the only person to express delight when she stepped into the dance hall. He rushed forward, gushing, "You look like peaches and cream to me! I'm going to call you Peaches."

From that moment on, Browning was lost to the not-so-innocent girl from Washington Heights. Peaches had worked briefly in a department store after dropping out of school and gone on dates with older men, drinking bootleg gin and dancing at the Cotton Club and the Strand Roof. She was anything but an inexperienced adolescent. Peaches' background meant nothing to the stricken Daddy who announced to one and all that he was forever in love with the baby flapper, she of the bobbed hair and bee-stung lips. In one press interview, Daddy informed newsmen that he had talked over his marriage plans with Mrs. Heenan who approved of their engagement. "She is a lovely girl," waxed

Peaches and Daddy Browning in their brief heyday; the chin patch covers the baby flapper's acid scars. (Wide World)

Daddy when asked to describe the heart-throb of his life, "five feet, seven inches tall, weighs 145 pounds—with her dress on, of course—has blonde hair, blue eyes, and is very well matured physically."

Broadway scribe Damon Runyon, after seeing Peaches, had a much different impression: "She is a straw blonde, one of those large, patient blondes who are sometimes very impatient. She has stout legs and small feet. I hesitate to expatiate on so delicate a matter, but her legs are what the boys call piano legs. They say she is fifteen, but she is developed enough to pass anywhere for twenty."

The plump Peaches, who attended school erratically during her courtship with Daddy (being driven to classes in his peacock-blue Rolls), was unstinting in her praise of the magnanimous Mr. Browning. "He showered me with flowers," she told reporters when describing her initial courtship with Daddy, "deluged me with candy and gifts. My boyfriends were forgotten. I had glances for none save Mr. Browning, my silver-haired knight, his gentle caresses, his quiet dignity, his *savoir faire*."

The hoopla over this spring–autumn romance aroused the ire of the Society for the Prevention of Cruelty to Children, a spokesman for this watchdog group commenting: "Relations between this girl and this man must not go unheeded." In response, a shocked Daddy Browning called a press conference where he proclaimed, his face turning red, his finger running about a tight collar, that he was being victimized unjustly by the society. "I have not done anything to be ashamed of. I am not an old man seeking improper friendships with little girls. I'm a young man and I have devoted myself to business and hard work. I've helped hundreds. Why shouldn't I help little girls?"

Why not, indeed? To that end, Daddy helped himself to Peaches, marrying his overweight flapper on April 11, 1926, in Cold Spring, New York, in the home of a justice of the peace. Dozens of newsmen covered the wedding, trailing the couple to a twenty-room mansion Browning had rented in Cold Spring. (Oddly,

51

this real estate tycoon never owned a home, preferring to rent.) At the door of the mansion, Daddy turned, gave the reporters his usual foolish grin, and stated, "She will grow older and I may grow younger."

Frances had already aged considerably by then. Before the wedding, Peaches had been splashed with a vial of acid by parties unknown. Daddy Browning responded to her hysterical phone call and rushed to Peaches' Washington Heights home to administer first aid. "When I entered the room," Browning would later report, "Peaches put out her arms to me and cried, 'Daddy.' Although her mother is a trained nurse, I was surprised to find that she had done nothing for her daughter. I rushed downstairs without my hat and coat, got some sweet oil and bandages, and then returned to the injured girl." A doctor had been called at the time, but there was little he could do. For the rest of her life, Peaches would carry the corrosive marks from the acid on her chin, throat and left arm.

It was generally suspected that the girl, fearful of losing sugar Daddy Browning, spilled the acid on herself to gain the millionaire's sympathy and attention; but the plan backfired. Many of the girls in Peaches' sorority echoed this suspicion, stating that Miss Heenan intended to trap Daddy into marriage from the onset. "Here's where I get him—he likes blondes," one classmate quoted Peaches as saying after the first meeting with Browning. Another insisted that the girl was desperate to land the fun-loving Daddy, telling her that "If he doesn't call me, I'll call him."

It mattered not; Browning married his chubby flapper, scars and all. The press continued to dog the couple wherever they went. A bevy of reporters incessantly scampered after Peaches when she went shopping on Fifth Avenue, which was most every day. One thin and desperate story on Peaches being mobbed by admirers was headlined: "CROWDS TRAMPLE PEACHES."

Tiring of their Cold Springs mansion, Daddy and Peaches moved into the posh Kew Gardens Inn on Long Island, taking the Princess Suite. The move, mostly instigated by the fun-loving Peaches, would allow the couple to be closer to the nightlife delights of Manhattan. (Actually, it allowed Peaches to be closer to the expensive stores where she spent most of her time and Daddy's money.)

The honeymoon ended with an abrupt screech from Peaches on October 2, 1926, almost six months from her wedding day. Employees and guests of the Kew Gardens Inn watched bug-eyed as the fur-wrapped Peaches led a caravan of luggage carriers through the lobby. Her mother, who had been living with the Brownings, dutifully followed the procession. Like the reigning society queen she thought herself to be, the sixteen-year-old Peaches pivoted on a high heel and shouted haughtily to all present: "Money isn't everything!" With that she departed, the more than $30,000 worth of jewels, furs, gowns, and gifts showered upon her by Daddy jammed into twenty trunks.

Browning arrived hours later. He entered the vacated and utterly empty

Millionaire Daddy Browning looks on admiringly in his New York real estate office as his child–bride Peaches does an impromptu Charleston; the cup was donated by the Brownings to the winner of the World's Charleston Contest held in the Polo Grounds in 1926. (Wide World)

Princess Suite, then moaned to reporters: "They've taken everything but the radiators and the varnish on the floor!" Daddy instantly called a press conference to explain his side of the tempestuous relationship.

Then began a battle royal between Peaches and Daddy, each telling his or her "inside" story to the senstation-glutted press. Daddy told his story to clear his name of any future accusations. Peaches *sold* her story to the highest-bidding tabloid. Incredibly, the couple not only washed their dirty linen in public, but to the delight of New York readers, they scrubbed their scanties and socks.

"I was a bird in a gilded cage, but the cage wasn't so gilded," said Peaches in one of her many by-lined stories.

Charged by Peaches with indecent liberties, Daddy was quoted as saying: "My marriage to Peaches was in name only ... Yes, I annointed her back with lotions, but her mother was always there. Never has Peaches gone to sleep in my arms or in my bed." Another of Browning's statements completely contradicted this innocent posture: "Peaches talked in her sleep and I was always afraid of what I might hear as I lay beside her."

Peaches screamed back that she never slept with her elderly mate; but she also claimed that Daddy made her perform abnormal sex acts. Then she denied ever sharing any fleshy pleasures with Browning. Then she wrote under another by-line: "I had nightly relations with Daddy, except when ill."

The feud culminated in a wild court battle in White Plains—Daddy suing for separation, Peaches demanding not only a divorce, but a hefty alimony as compensation for the degrading and degenerate acts her aging satyr had demanded she perform. The five-day trial was a circus, one of the most written-about, talked-about events in the wild and reckless 1920s.

Women formed the greater part of the crushing crowds eager to see the estranged lovers, and these women—from matrons to rouge-smeared flappers—fought to gain entrance to the courtroom. They overflowed the spectator's benches and stood four deep, pressed against the walls of the courtroom. Some climbed atop radiators and windowsills to perch like vultures throughout the spectacle, eager for any morsel of sex gossip that might be dropped by the combatants. (The presiding Judge, Albert H.S. Seeger, refused to clear the courtroom of women not having seats, undoubtedly enjoying the carnival atmosphere. He merely pointed to the women on the radiators and windowsills and stated: "I warn that if anyone stands there, it is at her own risk.")

A great number of baby carriages stood unattended in the deep snow outside the courtroom, children wailing. Such lunacy did not go unnoticed by newsmen covering the trial, including Damon Runyon who summed up the farce thus: "We have the great moral spectacle in this generation of a legal hearing involving a gray-haired old wowser and a child–wife attracting more attention than the League of Nations."

When Daddy Browning arrived on the first day of the trial, he doffed his hat to newsmen on the steps of the courthouse. As he noticed photographers rushing forward, he hurriedly produced his inevitable comb and swept it

Wrapped in her ermine coat, Peaches celebrates her sixteenth birthday with husband Daddy wearing his usual foolish grin. (Wide World)

through his gray locks, smiling his foolish smile all the while. The crowd gave most of its cheering approval to Browning. Peaches, labeled a gold-digger, drew only scant applause when she appeared wearing the $12,000 sable coat Daddy had bestowed upon her. Beneath the sable was a baby blue dress. Peaches, the fashion scribes of the day were quick to point out, wore a matching blue enamel watch and a pearl choker. Her ash blonde hair slipped from a cloche hat.

On the stand, Peaches attempted to play the sophisticated but wronged young woman. However, escaping from her mouth were the typical slang expressions of the day: "So's your old man," and "Applesauce!" Her testimony more than fed the ravenous appetite of scandal-hungry crowds, readers, and newsmen. Part of her blushing statements included, "He made me run up and down in front of him naked, while he lay in bed ... If I refused he became very angry and raved ... He tried to make me a pervert on five different occasions ... He took a hold of me by the back of my neck and pushed me to the floor and said *Boo!* in a very loud voice."

Daddy Browning was an extremely peculiar man, Peaches went on, telling the court that he never tired of playing practical jokes on her, frightening her. He gave her pink teddy bears that made strange noises. When dining in their suite, Peaches insisted, she would discover that Daddy had substituted silverware that bent in the middle, placed a rubber egg on her breakfast tray, given her glasses with false bottoms. He once brought home an African honking gander that proceeded to relieve itself all over the Princess Suite of the Kew Gardens Inn. As a way of fuzzy illustration, Peaches testified that one evening Daddy "brought home a tiny white tablet which he put in the end of his cigar and when he smoked it would form a heavy snowflake and people would be amazed, but it caused me a lot of embarrassment."

Another trait, Peaches pointed out indignantly, was Daddy's penchant for

55

The infamous composograph of the Brownings in their bedroom, the gander encouraging Daddy's lecherous advance upon Peaches.

hiding behind doors and screens, then leaping out, naked, to surprise her, shouting: "Woof! Woof!" This last bit of incredible testimony inspired the New York *Graphic* to put together one of its notorious Composographs, in which the heads of the persons featured were superimposed on the bodies of ridiculously staged photographs. Daddy Browning was shown in his pajamas advancing like Tarzan upon a terrified Peaches, who covered herself with a pillow case. "Woof! Woof! Don't be a goof!" ballooned the caption from Browning's mouth. The African gander, perched on the nuptial bed, comments on the torrid scene in a caption reading: "Honk! Honk! It's the bonk!"

The sexy details of the relationship described by Peaches had women hiding their faces. The flapper claimed that Browning brought home French postcards and pornographic photos, insisting that she look at them, hoping to excite her.

"What else did he make you do?" Peaches was asked.

"He wanted me to eat breakfast with him without any clothes on."

"And did you?"

"Yes."

Women in the courtroom swooned at these remarks. Damon Runyon, the normally hard-boiled Broadway reporter, had his own cynical perspective on these antics, especially those of Peaches' mother, writing: "Your correspondent's manly cheeks are suffused with blushes as he sits down to write ... Mrs. Heenan remains the most unusual parent I have ever clapped these old orbs on. The remarkable thing to me is that she can sit in the courtroom and hear all this junk about her child without having attacks of vertigo."

Mrs. Heenan herself gave testimony, claiming that Daddy Browning was not only a lecher but a drunk, that she had witnessed his orgiastic character when she accompanied the couple on their honeymoon and lived in the Princess Suite with them.

Daddy's lawyers countered by offering Peaches' lurid diaries in court, proving that she was very much a "loose" woman, even at fifteen, before she had met her "silver-haired knight." Browning took the stand, appearing to be the victim of a con game. He shook his head sadly and lamented: "They wanted all sort of things, roadsters, Park Avenue apartments, servants. One wanted two dogs, the other three."

"Did you have any idea that your wife or mother-in-law was going to leave you?" asked Browning's lawyer.

"Not my wife."

"And your mother-in-law?"

"I-er-ah-I was hoping so."

Grinning all the while, Daddy rebuffed any suggestion that he had ordered his wife to perform abnormal sex acts. He was little more than a father figure to Peaches, he insisted, and his practical jokes were harmless. When it came to forcing his wife to cavort in the nude before him, Browning's face went beet red. "Absolutely not! Why, for one thing, the weather was always too cold for that sort of thing!" This remark raised a number of eyebrows since it was commonly known that the couple had married during a heat wave.

Daddy Browning was clearly the winner in the court battle. The public and press thought of him as a benevolent but foolish old man who had succumbed to the wiley ways of a Jazz Age Jezebel. Before he departed from White Plains, a great throng in front of the courthouse gave him three rousing cheers.

Peaches, who had not changed her dress in five days, was considered the low-life in the affair; and only a few diehards saluted her as she left the court, awarded a $350-a-week payment of temporary alimony. The court later cut her off without a penny when the divorce was finalized.

Browning retired to his press clippings and fan mail, making no more public sallies into the world of adolescent femininity. He died in 1934.

Peaches Browning, discovering that she would not immediately obtain Daddy's wealth (as his widow, she vainly claimed part of his estate at the time of his death), raced to a fat farm where she had her "piano legs" trimmed, taking off forty pounds. She then embarked on a vaudeville career to retell the seamy story of her scandalous marriage to a doddering lecher. It made her $8,000 a week for some time and provided her and her mother with comfort. She married three more times and endured three divorces in the next two decades. In 1956, at forty-six, Peaches slipped in her bathtub and died from the fall. She was interviewed a year prior to her death by a reporter from the New York *Post,* at which time the 1920s sheba attempted to explain her long-ago affair with Daddy Browning.

"Were you in love with him?" queried the reporter.

"Not at all."

"Why did you marry him?"

"I haven't the faintest idea," shrugged Peaches. "How can you account for the actions of a 15-year-old?"

Others had a very good idea, especially one of Peaches' classmates who remembered at the time of the trial what the child–bride said of her erstwhile Daddy: "You know why I married that old bozo. I married him for his jack."

George Gordon Noel BYRON

Poet (1788–1824)

Lame from birth, Lord Byron was left fatherless in 1791, but his darkly handsome looks and his romantic poetry and essays established him as one of the most sought after men of letters of his era. His closest friends were Percy and Mary Shelley; and it was Byron, vacationing with the Shelleys in Switzerland in 1816, who suggested the three have a writing contest to see who could produce the greatest horror story. To Byron's and Shelley's amazement, the shy, mild-mannered Mary won hands down with her entry—*Frankenstein*.

The poet wedded only once, to Anne Isabella Milbanke, a marriage that lasted a year. His erratic behavior and volatile temperament, along with his abiding contempt for women, wrecked the marriage. He was to have many loves, including a liaison with the tempestuous Countess Teresa Guiccoli that provided grist for his ever-churning and brilliant literary mill as he wandered restlessly through Europe, often performing daring feats to prove his manhood or to overcome his resentment at his permanent disability. He reportedly swam the Hellespont to convince himself that his lame foot did not really hamper him.

Byron's literary output was prodigious—the work of a great genius: long, romantic stories in verse that are classics today—*Childe Harold, The Bride of Abydos Manfred, Mazeppa, Cain, The Prisoner of Chillon*, and his masterpeice, *Don Juan*. Beyond his outstanding literary talent, Byron was considered the greatest lover of the nineteenth century (at least in England). Yet this handsome man of literature, in addition to having a clubfoot that caused a bad limp, was a nervous wreck who chewed his fingernails to the core, munched on tobacco, and walked about the streets of London bristling with pistols. Byron had an uncontrollable temper and would fly into a rage, his blood pressure reportedly rising twenty points, if he thought someone was staring at his deformed foot.

He enjoyed torturing women. An hour after his marriage, Byron told his wife he hated her, that he had married her out of spite, and that she would live to regret the day she first saw him. A short time later, he was smashing furniture before her in unexplained fits of rage. Next he brought his lovers into the house to taunt her. His wife raced to doctors, begging medical men to examine Byron for insanity.

Scores of young women were imported to Byron's great abbey where they, their employer, and certain guests "dressed up as monks in long black cassocks and indulged in orgies." At such times, the poet was often seen to drink wine out of a human skull.

The slender and graceful Byron was often compared with Apollo, his milky skin causing females to swoon. One female admirer stated that Byron's skin

Looking a bit stupefied by it all, Daddy Browning leaves court with his lawyers following his scandalous divorce proceedings. (Wide World)

was "like a beautiful alabaster vase lighted up from within." Unknown to most, Byron struggled madly to retain his slender form, staying on an impossible diet of one meal a day. That meal consisted of a single small potato or cupful of rice sprinkled with vinegar. He would alter this meal occasionally by taking only a handful of crackers and a glass of soda water. In addition, while exercising, he wore seven vests to sweat off the fat. Further, Byron's love life was proved mythical when one lover found his bedroom anything but a love chamber. It was cluttered with pills and potions and reeked of patent medicines. The woman fled in panic, realizing that the great lover was a hypochondriac.

Byron's nights were hideous. He took heavy doses of laudanum to suppress his gruesome nightmares. He kept two loaded pistols next to his pillow. Sometimes he would wake up screaming and gnashing his teeth. He would then grab pistols and swords and pace the floor, cursing, yelling out threats to imaginary foes. Superstitious, Byron utterly believed a gypsy fortune-teller who informed him that he would die in his thirty-seventh year. He was dead three months after turning thirty-six. Before his death, the poet insisted that his entire family was doomed by this curse, that all of his blood would die on or shortly after that fatal thirty-sixth birthday. His father had died at thirty-six. His daughter, Augusta, whose life was as unpredictable and volatile as his own, died on her thirty-sixth birthday.

C

(Joseph Balsamo) CAGLIOSTRO

Occultist (1748–1795)

The small island-nation of Sicily has been and is today one of the world's centers of black magic, hexes, sorcery, and the occult, not to mention the Mafia. No wonder! The greatest figure in the world of occult was born there in 1748. His given name was Joseph Balsamo, but it is not by this name he is known today. The world remembers this amazing, mysterious person as Cagliostro.

Joseph Balsamo was born dirt poor. His father, Peter, died three years after his birth. His destitute mother was saved from abject poverty through the kindness of a merchant brother, who supplied mother and son with enough money upon which to subsist.

Much of Joseph Balsamo's life (or Cagliostro's) is shrouded in dark mystery. It is known that Balsamo as a child associated with the worst hoodlums in Palermo. He participated in thievery and swindles. Even his uncle was not immune—Balsamo robbed him of a considerable sum. An imaginative boy, Balsamo grew bored of his petty crimes. He dreamed huge dreams of wealth and power. He was also intelligent enough to know that behind each great fortune lurked a great crime. Methodically, he plotted a grand crime upon which to base his widely planned adventures.

The sixteenth century was inundated with commonly practiced black arts. So popular were they, as Balsamo knew too well, that alchemy—the process claimed to scientifically change common metals into silver and gold—would be his perfect tool to riches.

At seventeen, Balsamo achieved a high reputation as an alchemist. He had been seen, it was reported, evoking spirits. A greed-bent goldsmith named

Marano checked even further and discovered that the Benedictine monks had taught him chemistry and medicine and that he had apprenticed in an apothecary.

Balsamo also checked on Marano and found him to be stupidly superstitious. He went to the goldsmith and stated that he knew the approximate area where a great buried treasure could be found. He would require, he stated, in addition to his considerable black magic powers, sixty ounces in pure gold.

After Balsamo performed some obvious magic tricks, Marano agreed. With the gold in his pocket, Balsamo fled to Messina where he adopted the title of Count Cagliostro. In the best show business tradition, a star was born.

Once established in Messina, Cagliostro had the good fortune to encounter a mystic named Althotas, who was always dressed in oriental garb and was usually seen walking an Albanian greyhound. Cagliostro no sooner engaged him in conversation than it was agreed that they would explore the countries of Asia and Africa together.

Cagliostro toured Africa and doted on the pyramids of Egypt. There he learned the secrets of certain sects, piecing together his interpretation of a brotherhood philosophy that was to emerge years later in Europe as Egyptian Masonry. It was singularly Cagliostro's.

On the island of Malta, Cagliostro assisted the Grand Master, Pinto, in his alchemy experiments. It was here that Althotas vanished. Cagliostro stated in his memoirs that he merely died of natural causes, but there was considerable mystery concerning Althotas' end. Some suspected Cagliostro played a part in the mystic's death.

Pinto, a wealthy ruler, supplied Cagliostro with enormous funds, which he used to travel to places where he could establish himself in high society. First he began a gambling casino of sorts, fleecing the wealthy. After some brushes with the authorities, the Count appeared in Rome and became an empiric— dispensing home remedies for the sick. By this time, Cagliostro had mastered the art of hypnotism—after meeting Franz Antoine Mesmer, creator of mesmerism. Cagliostro would, according to some accounts, merely place his hands on the sick person, place him or her into a trance, and after some hocus-pocus exhortations, reach astounding medical results.

It was during his first Rome period that Cagliostro met the beautiful Lorenza Feliciani. He married her, and they traveled throughout Europe. As Cagliostro moved through southern Europe, he established many branches of his religious sect of Egyptain Masonry. By 1772, Cagliostro's so-called wizardry of evoking spirits, healing the sick with magical fanfares and alleged feats in alchemy, caused him to be the toast of France, particularly with the aristocracy.

His masonic orders now shipped him great sums of money annually. Coupled to these were huge stipends heaped upon him by French nobility. He lived lavishly, but his wealth overflowed to the point where he gave great amounts away to the poor, winning the support of the peasants.

Cagliostro, whose patrons had enriched him and whose phony magic tricks had supported his mystical image and that of his Egyptian Masonry, now had nothing but leisure time. This he suddenly devoted to the discovery of true black magic.

His first significant find was a manuscript hidden away in an obscure London bookstall. Written by an equally obscure man, George Gaston, it contained myriad explanations of the grand mysteries and the occult. Cagliostro then submitted himself to the strange rites practiced by the celebrated Count de St. Germain.

Upon his return to Paris, Cagliostro became a court favorite. Supposedly he used his occult experience to produce phantoms in glasses of clear water, and later in mirrors. Dozens of witnesses (most probably in the occultist's employ) "saw" Cagliostro invoke spirits to appear in huge mirrors. The count himself claimed to be astonished, as he admitted to his wife Lorenza, who also assisted him on these occasions. The people of Paris adored and feared Cagliostro; however, not only did the reported images he was now able to produce begin to terrorize his mind, he admitted, but madness started to creep through his personality. With his star at its zenith (he was called the Divine Cagliostro and was on intimate terms with Louis XVI and his temperamental wife, Marie Antoinette), tragedy and fate combined against him.

Through a plot hatched by Countess de Lamotte, who was a friend and patron of Cagliostro, the queen's jeweler was swindled out of a $100,000 diamond necklace allegedly intended for the queen. Cagliostro was tried and acquitted as an accomplice to the crime, but the incident reduced his status in Paris. Both he and his wife left for Rome.

Once in Rome, Cagliostro, with Lorenza aiding him, attempted to establish a branch of his Egyptian Masonry under the nose of the Vatican. The couple performed their strange rites for only a short time before they were arrested and tried by the Inquisition.

Cagliostro was found guilty of heresy and condemned to death. His wife was sentenced to life imprisonment. It was only through Cagliostro's high political connections with certain cardinals, princes of the Church, that the pope commuted the magician's sentence to life in prison. Thus it was that the most powerful—and perhaps the richest—occultist of all times found himself in a sparsely furnished cell where he lived in misery for four years until he died in 1795.

Enrico CARUSO

Operatic Tenor (1873–1921)

Although born dirt-poor in the slums of Naples, Italy, from the moment he made his New York debut as the duke in *Rigoletto* in 1903, Enrico Caruso has been considered the greatest operatic tenor of all time (including present-day Luciano Pavarotti). His performances in *La Boheme, Pagliacci,* and other roles, coupled with his widely bought records (he was the first singer to sell a million records), made Caruso a household word. During his youth, this very same singer was told by all who knew music in Naples that his voice was weak and thin. "You can't sing," one teacher informed him. "You haven't any voice at all. It sounds like the wind in the shutters."

Only one person really believed in Caruso—his mother Anna, a peasant woman who ignored the fact that her son's voice cracked on the high notes when he sang in the church choir. Caruso later remembered that of the twenty-one children his mother bore (eighteen of whom died in infancy, mostly from malnutrition), he was the one she had picked to become a great tenor, almost willed it. His father, Marcellino Caruso, a factory mechanic, ignored his son's gift until long after the tenor had become world famous.

Caruso's mother was so poor during the singer's childhood that she paid her debts with the cheese, fruit, and olives she received from country relatives. Caruso adored her and tended to her when she became ill and later when she was invalided. He spent hours dabbing "her forehead," and fighting "an unending battle with the dirt and flies" in her bedroom. Years later, a weeping Caruso would say: "My mother went without shoes in order that I might sing." Anna Caruso begged the parish priest to aid her son in developing his voice, but the boy's practice was confined to odd hours after Caruso's father insisted he go to work in the local factory at the age of ten. Caruso's mother died at fifty, when he was thirteen; his father almost instantly remarried, his new wife being a tough, healthy woman named Maria Castaldi. Fortunately for Caruso, she too believed his voice should be developed and nagged her husband to spend a little money on training.

Not until he was twenty-one did Caruso sing himself out of the factory. His first paid performances consisted of singing in the lowly cafes of Naples; in return for his songs, he was given supper. He hired himself out as a serenader of ladies being courted, standing beneath balconies while the tone-deaf lovers who paid him stood in the dim moonlight mouthing the words to his songs, and pretending to warble themselves, á la Cyrano. When Caruso did manage to get an operatic part, he was so nervous during rehearsal that his voice cracked several times and he fled the theater in tears. Some weeks later, he worked up enough courage to take a small role in an opera, his debut, but he was obviously drunk—he had gotten tipsy to work up his nerves—and was hissed and booed from the stage. He was made an understudy; and having nothing to do, he retired each day to a small cafe where he drank himself into a stupor.

One night, the leading tenor was taken ill, and messengers were sent throughout the Neapolitan cafes to find Caruso. He was discovered in a wine shop and literally dragged to the theater, where, in a stuffy dressing room, he drunkenly climbed into his costume. When Caruso staggered onto the stage and sang a few notes, he was again hooted and jeered from the stage. Fired, he decided that he should commit suicide. He spent his last lira for a bottle of wine and began drinking. A messenger from the opera arrived that night, shaking the tenor as he sat slumped in an outdoor cafe.

"Caruso," he yelled, "Caruso, come! The people won't listen to that other tenor! They hissed him off the stage. They're shouting for you, for you!"

"For me?" said the tenor groggily. "That's silly. Why, they don't even know my name."

"Of course they don't know it," panted the messenger. "But they want you just the same. They're shouting for 'that drunkard!'"

Caruso's appearances were enjoyed by the Italian public, but the press crucified him; and he was forever afterward distrusting of all newspapermen. He refused to see critics entirely. As the singer's reputation grew, so did his fortunes, until he received as much as $1,300 a performance in New York. He made more than $2 million from his recordings, yet so scarred by his poverty in youth was Caruso that he watched every penny he ever earned. So exacting with money was the singer that he wrote down every expenditure in a small black book, a habit that became a mania (there were hundreds of these books at his death in 1921). The expenses mattered not, from the purchase of an exquisite marble statue to a tip handed a bellhop—all were written down by the tenor.

Caruso's love life was dominated by the career-minded operatic singer Ada Giachetti, with whom he had four children, only two of them surviving, Rudolfo and Enrico Jr. A headstrong, self-centered woman, Ada, who was to die in 1946 at eighty-one, ignored her children and generally Caruso, her every waking moment devoted to her own singing. The tenor was nevertheless slavishly devoted to her, even tolerating affairs and a flagrant desertion in 1908 when Ada went off with another man. She refused to marry Caruso, but she took his name after his death. Her sons were pampered by the adoring tenor who made them his legal heirs.

Caruso was not only constantly pained by his faithless lover, but plagued by manias and fears all the days of his life. One of his constant worries as a child was that Vesuvius, the smoldering volcano that looms above his home town of Naples, would erupt some day and destroy him. The mountain did

Opera singer Enrico Caruso, shown appearing in the role Pagliacci, was so superstitious that he would not travel without consulting his personal astrologer. (Library of Congress)

erupt in 1905 and 1906, with 1,844 violent explosions in one day; and Caruso, who was traveling at the time, breathed a sigh of relief at his fortunate absence. Oddly, Caruso's fear of seismic eruptions came to reality in San Francisco, where he was appearing in 1906, exactly at the time of the great quake and fire.

On the morning of April 18, the tenor was sleeping in room 622 of the Palace Hotel when the room began to shake violently. The entire suite, which had once been occupied by General William T. Sherman, began to go to pieces. A chandelier crashed to the floor, windows popped open, cracks tore through the walls, the furniture toppled and swayed, and the floor rippled like water— boards breaking away and slamming into the ceiling, chunks of which caved in on the hysterically screaming Caruso. He yelled for his valet as he madly attempted to dress.

Ignoring his priceless gems, his expensive wardrobe, and tens of thousands of dollars in his trunks, Caruso wildly tore through his belongings to find a photograph of the president of the United States. He grabbed the photo, clutching it to his chest as he wept great tears. The picture was inscribed: "To Enrico Caruso from Theodore Roosevelt." Holding only the photo, the tenor lurched about in the suite, crying to his valet to save what he could and, screaming notes higher than he had ever reached on stage, he yelled that the quake was ruining his vocal cords.

Alfred Hertz, Caruso's conductor, suddenly appeared in the suite, begging the tenor to calm himself. "You must set the example, Enrico. Everywhere people are hurt and terrified."

Caruso grabbed Hertz. "What can I do, man? We must escape!"

Hertz shook his head. "There is no escape now—you must sing. Let the people hear your voice!"

"Sing? In this?"

"Sing, Enrico." The conductor reasoned that if the tenor concentrated on his music his mind would not be filled with the fears of the disaster. Slowly, the tenor—holding Roosevelt's photo to his quaking bosom—began to sing. His voice could be heard in the devastated street below; hundreds stopped in their panic to hear that magnificent tenor. One of the guests fleeing the Palace Hotel halted and, like dozens of others, he grew calm for the moment. "It was his best and bravest performance," he later commented.

A half hour later, Caruso was led outside, his entire body quivering; and a kindly police officer placed him on a deserted horsecart in front of what was left of the Palace Hotel. To police and troopers and scurrying firemen, the sobbing Caruso held up the autographed photo of Theodore Roosevelt, thinking this to be his passport out of the disaster. He was ignored. Not until he spotted John Barrymore (see entry) stumbling down the street in a drunken state did he calm down.

A short time later, Caruso's luggage appeared, carried from the Palace Hotel by four frightened Chinese workers. The tenor believed they were stealing his belongings and quickly pulled a pistol. He pointed the weapon at the terrified Chinese, shouting: "You give me my trunk or I'll shoot! I'll shoot!"

The Chinese froze in their tracks. Before Caruso could fire, his valet rushed from the hotel to inform the tenor that the men were removing his things under orders. Caruso shrugged and pocketed the pistol. Then, with Roosevelt's photo under one arm and a sketch pad under the other, he jumped from the horsecart and began to trudge along with the citizenry escaping the flames that followed the quake. The tenor climbed Knob Hill and was last seen calmly sketching the fire that slowly ate its way through the city.

Caruso's life was in constant danger from quarters other than volcanoes and earthquakes. Criminals from his native Italy dogged his performances, sending him Black Hand notes that threatened mutilation of his vocal cords—they would kidnap him, they promised, and pour lye down his throat—unless he paid them $1,000 out of every $10,000 he earned. Caruso paid and paid. The Black Handers were stopped momentarily in New York by Caruso's good friend, Police Lieutenant Joseph Petrosino, who tracked down the sender of one Black Hand note. Petrosino broke the man's arms and then personally put him on a boat headed for Italy.

Although he had good reason to dread the Black Hand, Caruso also greatly feared what was called the "Evil Eye," an Italian superstition that encompassed all manias. He was deathly afraid to cross any bodies of water, and he never undertook a transatlantic voyage until his personal, highly paid astrologer approved of the voyage. He would not wear a new suit on Friday, walk under a ladder ever, or travel on Tuesdays and Fridays—days he considered full of danger. Caruso's penchant for cleanliness was obsessive. He changed his clothes, including his underwear, whenever he came into his home, and this might mean five or six changes a day.

The tenor also mistreated his voice to the point where his conductors and coaches went into fits of rage at his excesses. He smoked constantly in the dressing room. He gorged himself, consuming six or seven meals a day—sometimes more. Despite the protests of his advisers, he stuffed his mouth with garlic and sprayed his throat with ether, mistakenly thinking that this would strengthen his voice. Before stepping onto the stage, Caruso would signal to his valet who came forward with a large glass of whiskey that the tenor gulped down the moment before his appearance.

A few years before his death, the tenor suddenly lost all interest in the

Caruso, a self-caricature. (New York Public Library)

plaudits of the public and the millions of dollars that choked his bank accounts. He refused to open a book, saying, "Why should I read? I study from life itself." He ignored his priceless stamp and coin collections and spent melancholy months with his clippings, which he meticulously cut and pasted into scrapbooks.

In 1921, Caruso caught a cold which developed into pneumonia. For six months, the tenor fought death. Days before the end, a priest administered the last rites to the dying Caruso; the tenor however, was taking no chances. Beneath Caruso's pillow were all manner of charms and amulets to ward off evil spirits and ancient demons who might drag his soul to the wrong place.

Leonard CASLEY

Farmer (Born 1933)

In 1969, the wheat quota for Western Australia was cut drastically, a move that caused farmer Leonard Casley to protest. The well-to-do farmer accused the government of trying to turn him into a pauper. On April 21, 1970, the incensed Casley formally announced that henceforth his 18,500-acre farm was no longer a part of the Australian government. It had seceded and become the Province of Hutt River, which boasted a population of twenty.

Casley appeared at a press conference wearing white tie and tails; and using a ceremonial sword, he dubbed himself Prince Leonard. Family members and friends were soon given titles. Ignored by his own government, the farmer wrote United Nations Secretary General Kurt Waldheim, the letter written on Hutt River Province stationary and signed "Prince Leonard." Casley requested that this province be accepted by the U.N. as an observer member country. Waldheim tabled the request with a groan.

Prince Leonard nevertheless went on establishing his kingdom, setting up his own currency and stamps (the latter sold abroad as an item of the "province's" foreign trade). A national anthem was created, along with a national flag that flew over the half dozen concrete and stone buildings on Casley's estate. The government continued to ignore the new nation.

By 1975, the Province of Hutt River was drawing more than 10,000 curious tourists, mostly flown in from Perth twice a week. The airplane circled the grassy landing field as a signal to the horse-mounted Price Leonard to drive his grazing cattle off the runway. The farmer sold tourists T-shirts and wall plaques with Hutt River heraldry affixed to them. He also sold liquor to tourists; when he was fined for not having a license, Casley paid the fine and wrote an official protest to the Australian government, saying that he considered the fine "an aggressive act by a neighboring power."

The quixotic Casley continued to vex the Canberra government, tilting diplomatically with them over the years. The government finally gave out its decree: Casley was not to be addressed by his title. The official statement was clear and concise: "The Australian Government does not recognize the existence of Hutt River Province." But at this writing, Prince Leonard Casley, crackpot or not, maintains his independence.

Charles CHAPLIN

Actor (1889–1977)

He was the most beloved of film stars in America. As the little tramp of the silent cinema, Charlie Chaplin wobbled into the hearts of everyone who saw him in such classic films as *Tillie's Punctured Romance, The Tramp, The Rink, Shoulder Arms, The Kid, City Lights,* and scores of other comedies that proved him to be the greatest comedian in the world—a man who could make anyone laugh. But in his personal life, Chaplin was a wild fellow whose enormous ego and insatiable sexual appetite caused him a lifetime of suffering and finally lost him the love of the American public, a public which had made him a multimillionaire.

From the earliest beginnings in Hollywood, after migrating from British music halls, Chaplin thought of himself as a filmic giant. "I am the unusual," he once snorted to a director. "I do not need camera angles!" He was utterly irreverent, often blasphemous. To a producer thinking of making a film based

Chaplin in the 1918 short, *A Dog's Life;* the comedian would later be charged with tax evasion on the fortune he made in the movies.

on Christ in 1922, Chaplin blurted: "I want to play the role of Jesus. I'm a logical choice. I look the part. I'm a Jew. And I'm a comedian." When the Nazis later attacked Chaplin, he responded wildly with; "I am not a Jew! I am a citizen of the world!" Yet when he spoofed Hitler in *The Great Dictator,* Chaplin stated: "I made this picture for the Jews of the world."

His closest friends and associates in Hollywood found him exasperating. He demanded all the attention at parties, and when he did not receive this, he threw a tantrum and walked out, vowing never again to honor the host and hostess with his august presence. To his friend Mary Pickford, Chaplin was "that obstinate, suspicious, egocentric, maddening and loveable genius of a problem child." Producers and movie moguls generally detested Chaplin, but then again his independent genius was nettlesome to their orthodox methods. When United Artists was formed—by Chaplin, Mary Pickford, Douglas Fairbanks Sr., and D.W. Griffith—Richard Rowland growled: "The lunatics have taken charge of the asylum." He meant lunatic, Chaplin.

Chaplin's sexual preference ran to teenage girls, even at a time when such leanings, if known, would have instantly ruined his budding career. He married star-struck Mildred Harris, a sixteen-year-old actress, in 1918 after getting her pregnant. They were divorced a short time later, Mrs. Chaplin complaining that her Charlie was seeing other women. Next came sixteen-year-old Lita Gray, who had worked in Chaplin films from the age of seven. When he arranged to have her put under contract for $75 a week, Lita jumped up and down in the producer's office shouting, "Goody, goody!" When they were married in 1924, Lita was already pregnant; the union produced two sons. Two years later, Lita Gray was in court battling the little tramp, her forty-two-page complaint shocking the nation. Not only had Charlie been cruel to her, claimed Lita, but he had committed adultery with so many women during their marriage that she had lost count of his lovers. Pola Negri's name was mentioned by the gossip columnists, as were a host of others.

For that fundamentalist era, the most shocking aspect of the divorce

Comedian Charlie Chaplin in the role of the "Little Tramp," shown here in *The Paperhanger's Helper* with Edna Purviance.

proceedings, which dragged on until 1927, was Lita's charges that Chaplin had forced her to commit "abnormal, unnatural and indecent acts" and that he had threatened to kill her with a revolver, calling her "a little Mexican gold-digger" (Lita's parents were Spanish).

Charlie had wanted to end the union for months; but according to Lita, she had resisted. He entered her bedroom in their vast Hollywood mansion one night, tossing a revolver on the bed. "Here," Lita reported Chaplin as saying, "there is one way to end it all."

When she heard that Charlie was seeing a "famous actress," he reportedly snarled, "Yes, it is true and I am in love with her and I don't care who knows it. I am going to see her when I want to and whether you like it or not. I don't love you and I'm only living with you because I had to marry you."

Church groups, women's clubs, and social organizations immediately began to lobby to have Chaplin's films banned. When one women's group heard that Lita and her sons were starving because Chaplin would not support them, the well-intended ladies took up a "milk collection" for the family. Chaplin's response to this was to angrily deny that he had refused to support his family. His wife, he said, did "not want milk for the children," but wanted "to milk me!" The divorce rivaled the publicity given the Hall–Mills murder trial. Lita's charges grew; and on August 22, 1927, when she finally threatened to reveal the names of the five women her husband had simultaneously been seeing, Chaplin settled $650,000 on his child bride and created a $200,000 trust fund for his two sons.

Chaplin weathered this storm, and his films continued to be box office bonanzas throughout the 1920s. Never having taken out American citizenship, Chaplin paid no income tax on the many millions he made (although the government later demanded more than $1,000,000 in back taxes—and got it). So vain did Chaplin become during this period that he insisted that he be the first guest to be invited to any important party—and that meant the first guest to be announced. He alienated most of his friends by making a great show of his atheism, drinking heavily and then shouting out a window that "there is no God!" He was with Mary Pickford and Douglas Fairbanks Sr. at a gathering where he suddenly threw his drink into a roaring fireplace, stunning all present into silence. "There's no God!" he shouted. "If there is a God, I challenge him to strike me dead here and now!" He paused dramatically, waiting for the thunderbolt. After a few minutes he said to his disgusted friends: "You see— I'm alive. That proves it!"

"Proves what, Charlie?" asked a yawning Douglas Fairbanks.

"No God. I'm alive and *He* doesn't exist."

Fairbanks' son, Douglas Jr., would later write a short profile of the comedian. In 1931, Fairbanks never mentioned Chaplin's atheism, but he did state that his friend "likes nothing better than to be referred to as Don Juan."

Chaplin continued to enjoy a reputation as Hollywood's Don Juan throughout the 1930s, even though he was by then applying black dye to his locks; his hair had turned almost completely white during his scandalous

The great film director, D.W. Griffith, a partner with Chaplin, Mary Pickford, and Douglas Fairbanks, Sr. in the United Artists; the director found the comedian an impossible egomaniac.

divorce from Lita Gray. He was nervous and explosive, his first breakdown also coming during the Gray affair. Further, his career began to slide downhill. When Hollywood completely converted to sound in the 1930s, Chaplin clung to making silent films, his last being *Modern Times,* which introduced his lovely co-star, Paulette Goddard, who became his third wife.

No sooner had Chaplin divorced Goddard than the greatest sex scandal of his spectacular life occurred. A twenty-two-year-old starlet named Joan Barry barged into Hedda Hopper's office to tell the gossip columnist that Charlie Chaplin had gotten her pregnant and had refused to marry her. Hedda the headhunter squealed with delight; she despised Chaplin and reveled in being able to break this scandal over his haughty head. The paternity suit that ensued had Americans up in arms against the little tramp.

Joan Barry was a Brooklyn girl who had gone to Hollywood in 1940, where, instead of getting work as an actress, she took to waiting on tables to support herself. In this capacity, she met none other than millionaire oil czar J. Paul Getty, who sent her along to a party in Mexico where she in turn met agent Tim Durant, a close friend of Chaplin. Durant, Getty had told the' young woman, would further her career; the agent introduced her to the little tramp. Chaplin told her that "she had all the qualities of Maude Adams" and quickly hired her at $75 a week under an exclusive contract. She would study acting under Max Reinhardt and appear in Chaplin's next film.

After dallying with Joan for some weeks, Chaplin tired of her and told her to go away. She made a scene in his Hollywood mansion, breaking several

priceless vases. The comedian called the police and had her arrested. She received a suspended sentence and, upon leaving the courtroom, was given $100 and a bus ticket out of town. Joan Barry would not give up, however, and Chaplin caught her entering his mansion through a basement window. This time she was sentenced to thirty days in jail for vagrancy, but she spent most of that sentence in a sanatorium "because of the physical condition of the defendant."

Not until 1943 did Joan Barry file her paternity suit against the comedian, her daughter being born on October 2. By then, Chaplin had married eighteen-year-old Oona O'Neill, daughter of Eugene O'Neill. (The marriage so angered the playwright that he never spoke to or saw his daughter again, writing her one "harsh and severing" letter—O'Neill hated Chaplin and thought him a pretentious example of the worst Hollywood type.)

Chaplin was charged on several counts in the Barry paternity suit, including violation of the Mann Act, for which he was fingerprinted. He was found to be the father of Joan Barry's child, despite the fact that blood tests conclusively proved his paternity impossible. In May 1946, the courts ordered Chaplin to support the Barry child.

From then on, Chaplin's name was a mop for the gutter. During the red-baiting witch hunts of the late 1940s, he was attacked as a Left-leaning world citizen although he announced: "I am not a Communist, I am a peacemonger."

When Viennese composer and one-time Communist Hanns Eisler was about to be deported, Chaplin, along with others, protested. This caused the vituperative and vindictive columnist Westbrook Pegler to blast the little tramp unmercifully on December 3, 1947. Wrote Pegler: "This was an attempt by an alien, resident here for more than thirty-five years, guilty of a degree of moral turpitude which disqualifies him for citizenship, caught in the act of cheating the government of enormous debt for taxes, a slacker in both World Wars, although he clamored with the Communists for a second front in the latest one ... an attempt by this alien to ferment an artificial demonstration against the United States by Communists."

Right-wing John E. Rankin denounced Chaplin that year in Congress and demanded that he be deported. His films, *Monsieur Verdoux* and later *Limelight,* were shunned by a public that had once adored the comedian. Taking his millions and his wife Oona, Chaplin left the United States, ostensibly forever, moving into luxurious exile in Switzerland. He was to have seven children by Oona.

Chaplin with Claire Bloom in *Limelight,* a failure at the box office at a time when the comedian was being labeled a "red."

The much-married Chaplin (right) with producer Sam Goldwyn at his Hollywood tribute in 1972.

Chaplin did not return to the United States until 1972, when he was honored in Hollywood. After his death in 1977, Charles Chaplin, who had exercised his eccentric ego on all who knew him, was himself the subject of a bizarre prank. His body was stolen from its grave. The corpse was later found, and according to the family, no ransom was demanded.

As to the comedian's sexual prowess, Chaplin himself was modest about it all, once saying, "Like everyone else's, my sex life went in circles. Sometimes I was potent, other times disappointing."

Charles Langdon CLARKE

Journalist (1826–1909)

Charles Langdon Clarke, who wrote for the Toronto *Mail and Empire*, delighted in creating hoaxes that exposed so-called experts and authorities, particularly pompous, self-important religious and educational leaders. Clarke's most outrageous spoofing involved his coverage of the World's Fundamentalist Conference held in Toronto. He presented himself to conference officials, according to Hector Charlesworth in *Candid Chronicles,* as a reporter for the Babylon *Gazette* and the Jerusalem *Times,* periodicals he had invented. Along with these imaginary publications, Clarke created a story he claimed he had received exclusively from two scientists, Dr. Schmierkase and Dr. Butterbrod, who had made an amazing discovery in the Holy Land.

The scientists had found the remains of a whale having an unusual muscle development, one that gave its stomach a sort of trap-door opening. Clarke wrote reams on the story, then, using a phony name, submitted it to fire-eating evangelists at the convention. The religious leaders embraced the tale without question and later used the Clarke report in fire-and-brimstone speeches to "prove the story of Jonah being swallowed by the whale as a bonafide fact."

These religious speeches were accepted and seriously reviewed by the Toronto newspapers; the editors of these papers, however, were cursing Clarke the next day when the *Mail and Empire* exposed the fish tale as a fraud. The Holy Land scientists' names, said Clarke's newspaper, really meant Dr. Cottage Cheese and Dr. Bread and Butter.

Georges CLEMENCEAU

French Premier (1841–1929)

Known as "The Tiger," Clemenceau was an ardent nationalist who served two terms as premier of France (1906–1909 and 1917–1919). An uncompromising politician, Clemenceau was terrified of any crisis that might find him undressed and in bed. For decades, to prevent such unpreparedness, the politician slept fully clothed—wearing shoes, trousers, shirt, coat, and sometimes his gloves. He would change clothes when rising each morning.

Robert COATES

Actor (1772–1848)

Born in Antigua in the West Indies, Coates was a self-styled thespian who specialized in Shakespearian drama—or ruined it, as the case may be. He moved to England at the turn of the nineteenth century, where he continued to destroy the work of the immortal bard. Pryse Gordon overheard Coates rehearsing passages from Shakespeare in the coffee room of a boarding house in Bath. What Coates was uttering from *Romeo and Juliet* sounded like Shakespeare, but the text was all wrong. "I took the liberty of correcting a passage," Gordon later wrote.

Coates shrugged off Gordon's words, saying: "Aye, that is the reading, I know, for I have the play by heart, but I think I have improved upon it." Coates performed the play in Bath in February 1810, appearing in a spangled cloak of sky-blue silk, crimson pantaloons, and a white hat bedecked with feathers, with diamonds adorning his hatband, kneestraps, and the buckles on his belt and shoes. He mangled Shakespeare's play so badly that he had to retreat under a shower of orange peels.

By the time Coates reached London to perform *Romeo and Juliet,* his fame as the worst actor in history had spread, and crowds actually fought violently for theater seats, the mobs carrying "almost every conceivable throwable object." Dodging and cowering under a barrage of garbage hurled constantly from the audience, the actors barely managed their lines, but Coates himself merely brushed the objects out of the way. Upon uttering the line, "Oh, let me hence, I stand on sudden haste," he suddenly fell to the floor instead of exiting. As he crawled about, the stage manager screamed: "Come off! Come off!"

"I will come off, damn you," shouted Coates from center stage, "as soon as I find my diamond knee buckle!"

So ridiculous was this performance that a half-dozen people laughed themselves sick and required medical attention after being carried from the theater.

Coates was a rich man, and somehow he rationalized his bold theatrical appearances as the worthy pursuit of any intrepid amateur actor. He continued to face down crowds for years, despite the trauma he caused fellow actors appearing with him. So frightened of the angry audiences were the other actors that most of them froze in place on stage and rapidly spat out their lines so that they could depart and avoid being hit by garbage, sticks, even clubs. (A live clawing rooster was once thrown at Coates, but he managed to battle it to a standstill—for which he received a thunderous ovation.) "Miss FitzHenry, as Juliet," reported Edith Sitwell in her *English Eccentrics*, "became so terrified by the menacing attitude of the audience, that, shrieking, she clung to the scenery and pillars in great agitation; and could not be dislodged."

Through the years, "Romeo" Coates appeared before enraged audiences, setting a trend for bad acting (a tradition which culminated in the appearance of the Cherry Sisters, "America's Worst Act," in vaudeville; the sisters appeared in the early 1900s—protected by a huge net spread before them on stage to shield them from vegetables and eggs thrown by the audience).

To Robert Coates, audiences were boorish ruffians, but he put up with them for the sake of "the Theatre." The outrageous actor was run over and killed by a carriage in 1848 as he was fleeing a theater, a mob of angry customers in hot pursuit.

Tyrus Raymond (Ty) COBB

Baseball Player (1886–1961)

In the mostly friendly game of baseball, there existed no meaner, fiercer player than Ty Cobb. According to one sports scribe, he was "possessed of the furies." Cobb, who was to earn a seemingly insurmountable .367 lifetime batting average and election to the Baseball Hall of Fame in 1936 (he led the American League 12 times in batting and retired with 4,191 hits), began his career with the Augusta, Georgia, team in the South Atlantic League in 1902. Shortly after Cobb began playing baseball, a story dealing with his mother and father reached him, a tale that not only turned his blood cold but forever changed his personality.

Cobb's father was a traveling lecturer who lived in the country. He had returned from a lecture circuit one night, long before he was expected, and found his house locked. Noticing the window of his bedroom open, the elder Cobb retrieved a ladder from a barn and began to ascend. His wife suddenly appeared at the window with a shotgun; and not being able to see clearly in the dark and thinking him an intruder, she blew off his head. Ty Cobb was never the same after learning of the accidental killing. He became one of the most feared men on the diamond and in center field, where he played most of his career for the Detroit Tigers.

As a batter Cobb was matchless and as a runner someone to be dreaded. He purposely took the cleats from his baseball shoes and filed the screws down to needle sharpness. And just as purposely he would always stretch his singles into doubles by aiming feet-first at the legs of any second baseman stupid enough to stand his ground and receive the flesh-piercing screws. Few were. A notable exception was a rookie for the New York Yankees named Leo Durocher, but then he had been hoodwinked by the fun-loving Babe Ruth (see entry) into believing that "Cobb is all brag." Ruth told the gullible Durocher that "Cobb's an old windbag, so razz 'em a lot and you'll get him to strike out." Naively, Durocher began to insult Cobb when he came to bat, the brash young infielder calling the great hitter every derogatory name in his lexicon of abuse, which even by then was considerable. Cobb screamed back at Durocher that he would "fix him." But so unnerving was Leo "The Lip" that Cobb never got on base the entire game.

Leo "The Lip" Durocher, shown as a Chicago Cubs Manager arguing with the umpires as usual, came close to death at the hands of the violent Ty Cobb. (Wide World)

Following the game, Durocher joked about his shouting match with Cobb in the Yankee clubhouse. He took his time dressing and sauntered out, cutting through a deserted section of the stadium. Suddenly, Cobb leaped out from behind a pillar holding a shotgun, the story goes, threatening to kill the smart-aleck rookie. Fortunately for Durocher, Babe Ruth (who was always the last player out of the Yankee clubhouse) came sauntering up to the pair, and as soon as he realized Cobb's grim intent, he joked desperately with the great hitter. "The kid didn't mean it," cooed the Babe. "I put him up to it, Ty. You don't want to shoot me, do you?" Cobb slowly released the hammers on the shotgun and stalked away as Durocher looked down at his trembling hands and quaking legs. He didn't speak to the Babe for weeks after that, and he never again ribbed Cobb.

The great centerfielder never really trained during his heyday, except on booze. He was a loner, and in each city his team visited, he would make skid-row bars his home base, consuming enormous amounts of liquor—a silent, staring drinker whose tense appearance told one and all to stay clear of him. He made the mistake one dark night of paying his bar tab from a large roll of bills. As he left, four men jumped him, dragging him into a nearby alley. The muggers didn't know what they were dealing with until too late. Cobb drove one head-first into a brick wall, fracturing the attacker's skull. He beat another unconscious with a garbage can. A third responded by driving a knife into Cobb's side. The baseball player withdrew the knife from his own flesh and sent the blade into the mugger's stomach. He was busy strangling the fourth attacker when police arrived. All four attackers were in the hospital the following day, but Cobb was not. Wearing a makeshift bandage, blood seeping through his uniform, he knocked out a double and two singles.

Though Cobb invested his money wisely and became a millionaire in stocks and bonds, he remained a terrible miser all his life, paying his household help starvation wages, threatening the grocer, the laundryman, and the milkman with bodily harm unless they stopped giving him bills he thought exorbitant. (So frightened of Cobb were these service people that they cut his bills in half, insignificant as they were at the time, paying the difference themselves.) Like the penny-pinching elder Tyrone of *Long Day's Journey into Night*, Ty Cobb hated paying electric bills, allowing only a few lights in his mansion to burn. There was so little light in his house that his servants were forever stumbling around in the dark and falling down stairs (Cobb naturally

The immortal baseball player, Ty Cobb, a man also possessed of the furies. (Wide World)

refused to pay the doctor bills for these domestic accidents). Cobb finally ordered the electric company to shut off his power. Thinking himself an inventive genius, he rigged up his own system of electricity with a generator; and as a result, he almost burned down his house and incinerated the cook.

When it came to gambling, Cobb was, paradoxically, a plunger, wagering enormous amounts in Reno. Oddly, even at craps, he proved to be a long-range winner. As he grew older, living in the Lake Tahoe region, Cobb would drink all night and rave. He would suddenly have the urge to drive down to Reno; he *had* to get to the gaming tables. On such occasions, he would drive his car at breakneck speed through the snowbound mountains, oblivious to hairpin turns and death-looming gorges, racing his car madly through snowstorms.

Though Ty Cobb lived one of the most harrowing lives in American sports, he died peacefully in bed in his Atlanta, Georgia, home on July 17, 1961. The lights in his house, of course, were off at the time.

William Horace de Vere COLE

Dilettante (1879–1938)

Cole was considered by many offbeat historians to be England's greatest practical joker, at least in this century. Brother-in-law to one-time prime minister, Neville Chamberlain, the wealthy Cole loved disguises and particularly enjoyed enacting the parts of powerful Asian dignitaries. As a student at Cambridge, Cole darkened his skin and adorned himself in an exotic costume. He employed some genuine and equally exotic-looking foreigners to serve in his retinue as he passed himself off as the sultan of Zanzibar. So effective was his impersonation that the entire faculty of Cambridge turned out to honor the "sultan" at an official dinner. On another occasion, Cole dressed up as an Indian potentate; and, with his disguised friends, including Virginia Woolf, was shown in 1910 as a visiting foreign dignitary through the gigantic British battleship, H.M.S. *Dreadnaught*.

Some of Cole's impersonations produced near mayhem. He passed himself off as labor leader Ramsey MacDonald—he was almost MacDonald's doppelganger—and gave a speech to a crowd of trade unionists that was so impassioned that the laborers almost rioted. Cole's most colossal sham involved streetworkers in London, a stunt later duplicated by his American counterpart, Hugh Troy (see entry). Finding a group of street repairmen idling near Piccadilly Circus, Cole stepped forward and asked for the foreman. He was told that the foreman had not shown up. Cole immediately informed the men that he had been sent over from the "central office" to direct their labors. With that he ordered the group of workers to follow him. Two blocks away, Cole turned and shouted, "I want a ditch cut through this thoroughfare from walk to walk."

The workmen went to their labors, tearing up the street while unwitting constables directed traffic around the work site. Cole oversaw the project the entire afternoon, then ordered the men home, leaving a deep trench severing the main roadway. He never returned.

Thomas B. CONNERY

Journalist (1835–date uncertain)

Connery, who was managing editor of the New York *Herald,* was at odds with the Central Park Zoo, telling officials that conditions for the animals were unsanitary and that the wild beasts were not properly caged. When he was ignored, Connery ordered a scare story written and published in the *Herald's* November 4, 1874, edition. Five full columns blared the escape of *all* the animals of the zoo. The story luridly described, with eyewitness accounts, how tigers, panthers, lions, and other predators were racing through New York's streets devouring citizens at will; forty-nine were dead with more with two hundred injured by the time the *Herald* went to press. Most of the animals were recaptured, but twelve of the most dangerous were still roaming about looking for victims. The tail of this story explained that this was an event that *might* happen if security was not tightened at the zoo. But few got to the end of the *Herald* story. As it would be some seventy years later with Orson Welles' "Martian invasion," widespread panic broke out before the true facts were known.

The owner of the *Herald,* James Gordon Bennett, read the story and fainted in his bedroom. He refused to leave his house and ordered the windows and doors boarded up. Staff members of the *Herald,* like war correspondent George Hosmer, ran to the newspaper heavily armed, ready to hunt down the wild beasts. Said Hosmer, brandishing two revolvers in his hands as he raced into the city newsroom, "Well, here I am!"

New York residents locked themselves in their homes and inside churches. Police and troopers armed with rifles and bayonets searched frantically but vainly through the dense woods of Central Park for the prowling beasts. Rival newspapers were dumbfounded, as were city and zoo officials. No one knew about the escaped beasts.

The most embarrassing episode of Connery's wild story involved George F. Williams, city editor of the New York *Times*. Upon seeing the *Herald* story, Williams jumped into a buggy and whipped the horses wildly down Manhattan streets until he arrived at police headquarters. The irate editor raced inside and began screaming at police captains that they were showing favoritism in handing scoops to a competing newspaper. It took officials some hours to convince Williams that the *Herald* story was a fraud.

The perpetrator of this massive fright story, editor Connery, was, strangely enough, neither fired by Bennett, nor upbraided in any way. But then James Gordon Bennett was a practical man. The story had boosted circulation by 5,000 copies.

Douglas ("Wrong Way") CORRIGAN

Aviator (Born 1907)

Working at the Northrop Corporation aircraft works in Inglewood, California, as a welder, Corrigan saved most of his salary to buy a 1929 Curtis–Robin monoplane at an auction in 1932, paying $900 for the craft. From that moment, Corrigan began to plan one of the most brazen and bizarre acts in the history of modern aviation. The plane, which the young mechanic–pilot christened "Lizzy," was in terrible condition; Corrigan patched and repatched the ship so many times that in a few years little of its original surface remained.

The mechanic also busied himself by installing extra gas and oil tanks in Lizzy, one directly in front of his pilot's seat, one immediately behind, jamming himself into the cockpit so tightly that he was forced to sit bolt upright. When friends pointed out Corrigan's lack of comfort, as well as his inability to see— he had to look from the side windows to fly—the mechanic merely shrugged, saying of his ship, "It's like an alarm clock. It won't let me sleep."

In 1937, Corrigan requested permission from federal authorities to make a solo flight across the Atlantic. An agent from the Bureau of Air Commerce inspected Corrigan's much-repaired plane, then turned him down flat, snorting, "We don't authorize suicide."

Nothing would stop Corrigan from fulfilling his ambition, federal inspectors aside. In mid-July 1938, he flew Lizzy from Los Angeles to New York's Floyd Bennett Field in a nonstop twenty-seven-hour flight, an accomplishment all but ignored in the press: Howard Hughes (see entry) had just completed his spectacular three-day flight around the world and had received all the publicity.

Undaunted, Corrigan went to sleep on a cot in the hanger where he could

keep an eye on his beloved plane. Just after midnight on July 16, 1938, the thirty-one-year-old pilot rose and filled Lizzy's massive tanks with 320 gallons of gas and 16 gallons of oil.

Kenneth Behr, manager of Floyd Bennett Field, rushed into the hanger. "Corrigan, what are you doing? You're not thinking of taking off, are you? It's still dark."

"I want to take off for the West Coast now," Corrigan replied, continuing to fill the plane's tanks. "That way when I reach the desert it will be cool."

"You're not taking off in the dark," Behr ordered.

Corrigan topped off his last tank, then went to his cot. "Okay. Call me when it gets light."

Before the dawn broke, Behr found to his dismay that Corrigan's plane was being rolled out to the runway. The field manager shook his head at Corrigan's impatience to return home and ordered flares ignited along the 4,200-foot runway. Behr almost suffered a stroke as he watched Corrigan's plane lumber down the runway for 3,200 feet, the weight of its tanks holding the ship back. With less than 1,000 feet of runway remaining, "Lizzy" groaned skyward, barely clearing some trees at the end of the field.

Behr watched the plane circle the field and then, astonished, commented to one of the ground crew, "That man's crazy. He's supposed to be flying to California, but he's headed east instead of west."

Inside Lizzy's tiny cockpit, Douglas Corrigan itemized all his worldly possessions. He had a little less than $15 after spending $100 for gas and oil. He had spent 10¢ for some chocolate bars and 5¢ for an empty bottle, which he had filled with drinking water. Taped to the gas tank in front of him was an outdated map that he had torn from an old atlas hours earlier. In his hand was a small boy-scout compass he had borrowed. These crude aids were his only means of navigation. The pilot leaned out a window to get his bearings and smelled the bracing air of the Atlantic Ocean.

"Wrong Way" Corrigan arriving in New York Harbor aboard the *Manhattan,* carried from the liner on the shoulders of policemen to receive a hero's welcome for his magnificent mistake. (Wide World)

For twenty-eight hours and thirteen minutes, Douglas Corrigan vanished from the face of the earth. Late on July 17, 1938, Lizzy whined downward to make a haphazard landing at Baldonnel Airport in Dublin, Ireland, sputtering to a stop as startled airport officials raced forward.

Corrigan stepped jauntily from his plane, parts of its patched body flapping in the wind. "I've just flown from New York," the daredevil pilot announced.

"My God," said one official as he looked over the ragged Lizzy.

"In that thing?" asked another.

There was an innocent look on Corrigan's face. "Isn't this Los Angeles?"

"Los Angeles!" exclaimed an official. "This is Dublin!"

"Can you beat that," Corrigan smiled. "I guess I flew the wrong way."

The remark sparked a press barrage; and the more Corrigan repeated the statement and outlined his ridiculous story, the more publicity he received. Within weeks he was a worldwide celebrity, known as "Wrong Way Corrigan." He was taken to London, where he was photographed with United States Ambassador Joseph P. Kennedy, who greeted him with handshakes and smiles. In August, the impoverished flyer, still wearing his beat-up brown leather flying jacket, was welcomed back to the United States with a tremendous New York ticker-tape parade. He sat beaming on the back of an open touring car while thousands cheered along Fifth Avenue.

Not since Lindbergh made his epic flight eleven years earlier had the public taken a young aviator to its hero-loving heart. Even in the Depression-ridden time of 1938, Corrigan's absurd antic brought back the carelessness and dash of the lost Roaring Twenties and, for his flight of fancy, he was enriched by more than $65,000 from endorsements and appearances as a barnstormer. His

Corrigan as a test pilot for Douglas Aircraft in 1944; today he lives as a recluse in Santa Ana, California, refusing to discuss the sensational exploit that made his name a household word. (Wide World)

crazy transatlantic flight was chronicled by Hollywood in a 1939 film entitled *The Flying Irishman*. Corrigan, awkward gestures, high-piping voice and all, played himself.

Though he later became a commercial pilot, served in the Ferry Command during World War II, and unsuccessfully ran for the United States Senate from California in 1946, Corrigan never regained the fame brought about by flying the wrong way.

Corrigan settled in a Santa Ana orange grove, raised three sons (his wife Elizabeth died in 1966), and remains, at this writing, generally a recluse, refusing to grant interviews or answer fan mail. The unpredictable pilot kept his plane Lizzy in a delapidated barn on his farm property. Wrong Way Corrigan has never really admitted that he did not intend to return to his native Los Angeles in that amazing flight, but he is quoted as saying, "Well, at least I've told that story so many times that I believe it myself."

John ("Bathhouse John") COUGHLIN

Politician (1860–1938)

Chicago has always produced its share of oddball politicians, but the zaniest in its lurid history was undoubtedly "Bathhouse John" Coughlin. Born in the city's First Ward to a grocer who had migrated from Ireland in 1856, Coughlin grew up a street kid, uneducated and convinced that the only way to get ahead in the world was to take by "hook or crook," whatever was available. When he was eleven, his father's grocery store burned down with the rest of the city in the Great Chicago Fire of 1871. Years later, when friends told him that he might have owned a chain of foodstores had not the disaster wiped out his father's enterprise, Coughlin roared with laughter, bellowing, "Why, money didn't mean anything to me. I'm glad that fire came along and burned the store. Say, if not for that bonfire I might have been a rich man's son and gone to Yale—and never amounted to nothing!"

The store was rebuilt and Coughlin clerked for his father—one of a half-dozen other jobs he held down. He finally became a rubber in a Clark Street bathhouse (from which he earned his sobriquet of Bathhouse John). He met every type of person imaginable, and, reported his chroniclers Lloyd Wendt and Herman Kogan, "Young Coughlin learned that the most prominent citizen, shucked down to the skin, is much like everyone else." Through his customers, Bathhouse John learned who controlled the city and how a young, ambitious man might get ahead—with important contacts. Some of his customers liked the jovial, beefy Coughlin so much they lent him enough money—around $800—to open up his own saloon and bathhouse. A short time later, he became a Democratic precinct captain, and his road to Chicago's lusty politics was wide open.

Elected as alderman of the First Ward in 1892, Coughlin entered a city council that was perhaps the most corrupt in American political history. If an alderman sat on a committee, he could easily manage a great deal of boodle for himself—payoffs from those wanting the million-dollar city franchises that committeemen bestowed. Coughlin showed his blunt greed by telling Mayor Carter Harrison Sr., "I sure would like to get on some of them committees." He did, and he began to scoop up his graft. In tandem with Michael "Hinky Dink" Kenna, the political boss of the First Ward, Coughlin grew rich. During the Columbian Exposition of 1893, Coughlin and Kenna turned the First Ward into Chicago's red light district. The Levee, as it was called, teemed with thousands of prostitutes and hundreds of whorehouses and gambling dens, all operating around the clock, shielded by police who were fixed by Coughlin and Kenna right up to the mayor's office. (Mayor Harrison, of course, shared in the pie.)

For several decades, Coughlin's First Ward was the center of vice in Chicago, a cesspool over which the heavyset, mustachioed politician acted as feudal lord. He and Kenna established a gambling syndicate whereby a large share of the proceeds went into their coffers. Bordellos kicked back as much as a fifth of their girls' nightly earnings. One of the Coughlin runners who picked up the kickbacks was Big Jim Colosimo, later to become Chicago's first crime czar. (It was Colosimo who called in Johnny Torrio from New York's Five Points years later to help him run his underworld empire; Torrio brought in Al Capone, who started as a bouncer in 1919 in a Torrio bar and whorehouse in the First Ward.)

In addition to flagrantly grabbing boodle and graft, Coughlin· fancied himself a poet, a truly gifted genius of stunning verse. Magazines and newspapers around the country jeered at Coughlin's kitsch, but the politico wrote on undaunted. On the twenty-fifth anniversary of his first election, Bathhouse John dashed off the following, which appeared in the Chicago *Tribune:*

> In all the years I served as member from the First,
> I've never lamped a crooked dime, not e'en a weiner-wurst;
> I've heard a lot of foolish talk regarding 'easy mon'
> But I my colleagues will defend from slander's flippant tongue.

After reading his printed verse in the *Tribune,* the alderman announced to his cronies in the council chamber, "This poem is not only my first poem of the new year but it is my best!"

Reporter Jack Lait later claimed that he had acted as a mentor to the alderman and had "fixed up" some of his poetry, a remark that drew an indignant response from the poetry-proud Bathhouse John. "Nobody writes my stuff! It comes natural to me. I dash it off before I know it."

Along with Hinky Dink Kenna, Coughlin gave an annual First Ward ball, which was peopled with every prostitute, madame, pickpocket, con man, and ranking policeman on the alderman's payroll. At such times, Coughlin would entertain his rowdy guests with verses he composed for the occasion. When Hinky Dink was informed that Coughlin was about to put together a complete

Chicago alderman Bathhouse John Coughlin in action, reciting some of his verse. (Sketch by John McCutcheon)

book of verses, which would be dedicated to Kenna, Coughlin's elfin partner snarled, "If he does I'll make sure he never gets another vote!"

The bulky Bathhouse John reveled in his unofficial title of "The Poet Lariat of the First Ward"; and to prove he was up to the honor, Coughlin produced an opus he entitled "Dear Midnight of Love," a song that was to prove a monument to mawkishness. May de Sousa, daughter of a Levee district detective, was hired to sing the song in a full-scale production at Chicago's Opera House. During rehearsals, Hinky Dink Kenna sat in the back row, and when he heard his partner's song for the first time, he wheeled out of his seat shouting, "Help! Help! I need a drink!"

Coughlin helped in directing the band and chorus, and after the final rehearsal, he was lifted to the shoulders of his drunken musicians and carried jubilantly about the stage. Reporters rushed to the alderman, asking if he was going into the music field professionally. Yelled the triumphant Coughlin, "There's nothin' to it!" He could not restrain his feeling of accomplishment: "I'm certainly the best there is, the best anybody every looked at. I'm doing a stunt right here now that no alderman can touch, no alderman in the world. The orchestra's all right. The singer's all right, the song's all right, the house will be all right … Well … I ain't swelled a bit because I got it all coming to me!"

The special variety show that was to feature Coughlin's opus opened to a house jam-packed with his cronies. A chorus of fifty backed little May de Sousa when she stepped up to sing "Dear Midnight of Love." The opening ovation was so thunderous that the apprentice singer had to wait several minutes before beginning, the chorus swaying behind her:

When silence reigns supreme and midnight love forever tells
If heart's love could be seen, there kindest thoughts do dwell.
If darkness fancies gleam, true loving hearts do swell;
So far beyond a dream, true friendship never sell.

The chorus joined with May in the refrain:

Dear Midnight of Love,
Why did we meet?
Dear Midnight of Love,
Your face is so sweet.
Pure as the angels above,
Surely again we shall speak,
Loving only as doves,
Dear Midnight of Love.

More choruses and refrains went on endlessly, it seemed to newsmen present, but an audience made up of Coughlin's First Ward denizens seemed to hang on every word. At the song's end, the applause and cheering was ear splitting. Bathhouse John responded to insistent demands for his presence on stage by joining May de Sousa and the chorus. From stage center the bubbling giant waved his henchmen into silence.

Boomed Alderman Coughlin: "Gentlemen, friends, and ladies. I certainly appreciate this ovation. It is a pleasure and ambition of which every young man should be proud. I appreciate it and I know you all mean it because this is an unpartisan crowd!" He departed with awkward bows while the cheering went on for ten minutes. Hinky Dink Kenna hid in his box seat, shielding himself from view behind a huge drape where he lifted a large bottle of whiskey to his lips.

John Sargent CRAM

Philanthropist (Born 1918)

Educated at Princeton and Oxford, John Sargent Cram came from a wealthy family which had long devoted its fortunes to philanthropies. Millionaire Cram, however, refused to follow the orthodox traditions of his family. This was never more evident than in early 1962 when narcotics detectives broke into a ghetto loft in New York. Before them sprawled dozens of human derelicts, jampacking every corner of the one-time dance hall. (The place was still festooned with faded paper ceiling ornaments.)

The detectives searched every person carefully and arrested six men who possessed hypodermic needles and packets of heroin. Also taken into custody was the proprietor of the loft, a person described later by Hallowell Bowser in *Saturday Review* as "a mild, weedy-looking man who was charged with harboring drug addicts in his apartment."

The host was none other than John Sargent Cram, millionaire philanthropist. Cram explained to police that he did not know it was against the law to feed and clothe drug addicts and that he was spending about $100 a day feeding destitute persons needing help. He had rented the loft because he wanted to avoid the enormous red tape involved in setting up a charity and wanted to see his first-hand help begin immediately. "He made a point of not giving the men money, he told the police, because it only went for cheap wine."

Cram, who was known in the area as *"Papa Dio* (Father God)," was cleared of any complicity in crime after dozens of witnesses at a hearing told of his kindnesses. He left the courtroom amid wild cheers from his neighbors. The millionaire later met with the press, telling reporters, "I don't know that my work does much good, but I don't think it does any harm ... I'm quite happy, you know ... Call me eccentric. Call it my reason for being. I have no other."

Hart CRANE

Poet (1899–1932)

Born and raised in Akron, Ohio, Crane demonstrated an enormous gift as a poet at a young age, but he was also a raving alcoholic and homosexual whose death wish was as large as his talent. His father and mother were hopelessly middle class to Crane—nothing could be more middle class to the poet than a father who had invented the candy Lifesaver—and he left home and a drugstore job as soon as possible for the company of New York's literati. His poems had appeared in many little magazines, and he was well known by young writers and critics such as Waldo Frank, Yvor Winters, Sherwood Anderson, and Malcolm Cowley.

The budding critic Cowley took Crane under his wing, not only encouraging the poet to produce and finding markets for his verse, but obtaining a job for him where he and Cowley wrote advertising copy for mail-order catalogs. Crane consumed great quantities of liquor, claiming that this was the only way in which he could induce his muse to step forth. When he drank, he would sometimes vanish for days, prowling the streets for sailors to seduce. According to Cowley in *Exile's Return,* Crane "drank in Village speakeasies and Brooklyn waterfront dives; he insulted everyone within hearing or shouted that he was Christopher Marlowe; then waking after a night spent with a drunken sailor, he drank again to forget his sense of guilt."

By the mid-1920s, Crane's paranoia was rampant. He would spot an innocent-looking stranger at a nearby table in a cafe and whisper urgently to friends: "See that man staring at us? I think he's a detective." Following such

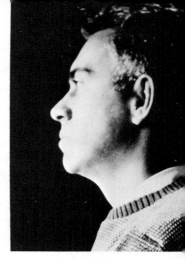

1920's poet Hart Crane, who broke his friends' furniture for inspiration.

wild observations, the poet would retire to his small room and destroy the furniture, ranting himself into a sleep produced by exhaustion. His writing was erratic, and the poetry he produced was without any distinct tradition, although the French poets served as his most lasting influences. The two volumes of poetry he finally managed to produce, *White Buildings* and *The Bridge,* are now considered minor classics.

The poet tolerated critics little. When one asked him where he could find Crane's poems, the poet replied, "Oh, behind pianos and up chimneys." On other occasions, when sodden drunk, Crane swung wildly at critics he met at parties whom he thought were making fun of his work.

The millionaire philanthropist Otto Kahn spotted some of Crane's poetry and bestowed a grant of $2,000 on him. Crane used the money to travel to Paris, where he met an equally unbalanced literary creature named Harry Crosby, scion of the great Morgan fortune, who published literary works through his Black Sun Press in Paris. (Crosby lived with his wife Caresse in total self-indulgence. He published simply to be accepted by the chic literary crowd, he dabbled in poetry; he consumed opium in great quantities; and he was a fanatical sun worshipper. Most of his waking hours he spent in bed with women other than his wife; and in 1929, he took another man's wife into a New York hotel room, shot her through the head, then killed himself. Harry Crosby was the perfect dilettante.)

Crosby asked to see some of Crane's poetry, and upon reading the verses, he advanced the poet $250 against publication. Further, the millionaire playboy invited the wild poet to his estate in Ermononville, where Crane promptly had a love affair with a visiting count before trying to seduce the Crosby chauffeur. Crane's modus operandi did not change. First he would become a happy drunk, singing and dancing. Next he would become viciously insulting. Then he would follow this with wild furniture breaking. Harry Crosby thought it amusing.

Crane would often return to Paris and go on the prowl for sailors. Such excursions had already turned his bristling hair almost completely white. After these homosexual indulgences, the poet would retire to the bistros of Montparnasse. Once, when he refused to pay his bill at the Café Select, the proprietor called the police. A wild battle ensued, with ten gendarmes finally subduing Crane and dragging him by the feet to Santé Prison where Crosby arrived to bail him out by paying an 800-franc fine. The judge told Crane that he was to drink no more while in France. Crosby immediately took him to a restaurant where he ate and got drunk. The small-press publisher told the poet that he should stay at his Paris apartment at 19 Rue de Lille, but the following morning, he regretted this generosity when he discovered that Crane had brought home a chimney-sweep who left black sooty marks from his hands everywhere on the white walls, sheets, chairs, and carpet of the guest room. Days later, when the poet appeared wearing half of the uniform of a sailor he had literally raped, Crosby took him to the White Star Line and bought him a one-way passage back to the United States.

Crane's conduct in New York in the late 1920s was identical to his actions in Paris. He started fights; he was arrested and bailed out; he drank himself into stupors and insulted all his friends; and he could produce only a little poetry after breaking furniture, usually in the homes of friends, and while listening to Ravel's *Bolero* all through the night. To one and all, Crane announced himself as the greatest living poet. In more lucid moments he would half-sarcastically state, "I practice invention to the brink of intelligibility."

His most loyal supporter, Malcolm Cowley, who (with his wife) put up with the lion's share of "The Roaring Boy's" antics, felt Crane "was a poet of ecstasy or frenzy or intoxication ... At their worst his poems are ineffective unless read ... with a drink at your elbow, the phonograph blaring and somebody shouting into your ear 'Isn't that great?' At their very best ... they have an emotional force that has not been equalled by any other American poet of our century."

In the early 1930s, Crane was able to obtain some small grants and fellowships so that he could go to Mexico to write. His companion there was Peggy Baird, a writer. While in Mexico, Crane was almost always drunk. Peggy found him sitting on the roof of his adobe house one night baying at the moon like a wild animal. The Mexicans in the neighborhood of Mixcoac were terrified of the *"loco gringo"* who would start a fight with anyone.

Crane was deathly afraid that those who had awarded him his grants would discover the facts concerning his shameful conduct. According to his

Critic Malcolm Cowley was one of Crane's foremost "sponsors" and often had second thoughts on his friendship with "the roaring boy."

biographer, Philip Horton, "His mind was so disordered by fantasies of persecution, betrayal, and guilt, that when early in July he received a telegram announcing the sudden death of his father, he suspected for a moment that it was a ruse on the part of the Guggenheim Foundation to entice him back to New York for disciplinary measures."

At Peggy Baird's urgings, Crane finally agreed to return to New York in July 1932. The couple boarded the *Orizaba* in Vera Cruz, but their sailing was anything but pleasant. Crane was drunk most of the trip and insulted the passengers. He threatened to sue the steamship line when a box of matches accidentally exploded in Peggy's hand as she was lighting a cigarette in the lounge. He threatened to beat up any ship's officer who interfered with him— and this meant his trips down to the boiler room where he attempted to seduce the coal-blackened stokers.

A night out of Havana, one of the ship's officers came to Peggy Baird and begged: "Will you give me authority to lock Mr. Crane in his cabin?" Peggy said yes, but searching crew members could not find him. He had gone to the stokers again and had been brutalized, paying the cretinous men with his ring and wallet containing his last few dollars.

The next morning he appeared in Peggy Baird's cabin, sitting on her berth and saying: "I'm not going to make it, dear. I'm utterly disgraced."

Peggy told him to put on some clean clothes, which would make him feel better.

"All right, dear. Goodbye." She turned to see him walk out and noticed for the first time that he was wearing only pajamas and a loose-fitting robe.

A half hour later, the *Orizaba's* whistles and horns began frantically tooting. The ship was sailing in circles; and from the stern of the liner crew members were wildly tossing lifesavers into the sea. Hart Crane had jumped overboard, leaping from the stern of the ship.

Peggy Baird was brought to the bridge to face a cursing captain who shouted, "Twenty-six years at sea and this happens to me for the first time!" He swore and stamped his feet as he nervously scanned the Caribbean through binoculars. He glanced at Peggy Baird, and, after a string of obscenities, he gritted, "If the propellors didn't grind him to mincemeat, then the sharks got him immediately."

Hart Crane, poet, was never seen again.

Francesca CREMONSE

Sculptor (dates uncertain)

In 1938, A French peasant, digging up his turnip patch outside of St. Etienne in Loire Province of southern France, plowed up one of the most remarkable art relics in modern history, a Venus which was missing a hand, nose, arm, and legs. Art critics flocked to inspect the rare find, pronouncing the statue a lost treasure dating from the Roman invasion of Gaul. Experts stated that the Venus was between seventeen and twenty-five hundred years old, a genuine artifact of the neo-Attican era.

President Lebrun of France signed a decree that requisitioned the Venus de Brizet, which it had been named, stipulating that the statue was a national art treasure. Experts agreed that the incredible find had enriched the nation's cultural history and placed an enormous value on the statue; some said it was priceless.

At the height of this artistic hubbub, a little-known sculptor, Francesco Cremonse, stepped forward to state that he had created the Venus and buried it in the peasant's turnip patch. The critics responded with uproarious laughter and jeers that gave way to indignant silence as Cremonse produced the statue's missing nose, hand, arm, and legs, as well as the woman who had served as the model.

The statue was no longer a national treasure. Cremonse's motive was simple. In his eccentric fashion, he had planned to expose the art critics as inept experts who could easily be duped by anyone with a modicum of talent.

Aleister CROWLEY

Occultist (1875–1947)

The two women were sitting in the open-air cafe on a beautiful spring day in Paris in 1920. One of the women was the internationally known interpretive dancer, Isadora Duncan (see entry), an eccentric in her own right. The other was her attractive companion, a sort of lady-in-waiting. A man sipping wine at the next table eyed the women intensely. There was, to Isadora's glance, something strangely familiar about him. The dancer fluttered her eyelashes at him, trying to remember.

With a quick, jerking movement, the man—short, stocky, his bloated face ravaged by years of dissipation and debauchery—gulped down his wine and threw back his chair. He stood up and placed a bowler hat squarely on his head, smoothed down an old-fashioned frock coat, and then approached the two women, his lips together in a tight smile.

He ignored the famous dancer and went directly to her beautiful young friend. He bowed slightly, his sickening smile still clinging. "How charming you are," the man grated lasciviously. "Have you ever had a serpent's kiss?"

"Why, no," the young woman said, not alarmed, for it was an age where fanciful exiles from all countries infested the Left Bank of Paris and oddness was the order of the day.

"Wonderful," drooled the man as he bent forward swiftly, taking the brunette's hand while Isadora stared, fascinated. As the strange interloper bared his two front teeth, Isadora gasped. The man's teeth were filed to razor-sharp points. He bit deeply into her companion's hand, gnashing into a tiny vein that spurted blood.

"Oh, my God! My God!" the young woman screamed before collapsing in a dead faint.

The man stepped back smiling crookedly, a small trickle of blood running from his lips. He swagged his tongue over the gore, drawing it into his mouth. He nodded quickly to Isadora, as if his brutish act had been nothing more than a usual greeting, and, before the stunned dancer could react, he strode briskly away down the boulevard Montparnasse. Isadora then ran screaming for a doctor.

The young woman recovered, even though she contracted blood poisoning from the infected wound; the man who had so ceremoniously bestowed upon her his serpent's kiss, had rubbed garlic on his fang-like teeth. Strangely, the attacker, whom Isadora finally remembered, was never apprehended. It was understood that in the bizarre expatriate circles of that permissive day one did not prosecute, let alone criticize, "The Great Beast."

He was known by many names, this sinister wristbiter. Ernest Hemingway described him as a raving maniac of the occult, calling him "the most evil man in the world" and portraying him in *A Moveable Feast* as a lonely little man whispering witchcraft to deformed and diseased women in Paris cafés—a hideous creature dressed all in black with eyes that burned like red hot pokers. He was also called "666," "Baphomet," and "Adeptus Minor" (an official title from the Rosicrucian sect, whose rituals he subverted in the creation of weird black magic rites). His real name was Aleister Crowley. Somerset Maugham (see entry) based his novel, *The Magician,* on this psychotic and satanic satyr (Maugham and Arnold Bennett shared an apartment in Paris with this mountebank at the time of the wrist-biting incident).

There was no doubt that Crowley was deranged almost all of his adult life; but given the Bohemian society that tolerated him, his form of insanity, mixed with high intelligence, made him waywardly attractive to those of similar bent. He was thought of as a gentleman sex pervert in a time when morality had been wholly discarded by what came to be labeled as "flaming youth." In their revolt against rigid Edwardian sex standards, the young came to regard Crowley as an avant gardist of some note, until finally his rampaging hedonism became overwhelmingly offensive—to the point where he was literally banished from several countries.

Born in Leamington, England, to parents of Scottish descent, Crowley inherited a vast sum—estimated to be about $400,000—at an early age. He appeared to be a solid member of a bourgeois society, despite his newly

Ernest Hemingway, at the time he met Crowley and called him "the most evil man in the world."

acquired fortune, and continued to teach mythology and anthropology at Cambridge University. In early manhood, he was content to conserve his riches and play the intellectual, busying himself with poetry. He would die with forty-five books of poetry to his credit, albeit his verses were generally more arcane than James Joyce's *Ulysses*. In addition to a self-pitying autobiography, Crowley churned out three volumes of erotica and fifteen perplexing tomes dealing with the occult and religion. His specialty in the latter field was black magic, which he termed "Magick."

One of Crowley's works is entitled *The Yi King*, known today as the *I-Ching*, which was Crowley's new translation of *The Book of Changes*. Crowley employed the pseudonym of Master Therion for this book. In 1909, at the age of thirty-four, Crowley published an edition of this work in London, calling it *Liber Trigrammaton—The Book of the Trigrams of the Permutations of the Tao with the Yin and the Yang*.

Aleister Crowley's queer credo had its center commandments from which he and his followers never strayed. "Every man and every woman is a star," was Crowley's edict. "Do what thou wilt shall be the whole of the law," he commanded. "The only sin is restriction," he decreed. In short, Aleister Crowley was a chief founder of "meism," as well as its most ardent practitioner, one who exercised a half-baked philosophy as a physical religion of violent extremes, one that displayed an utter loathing of Christianity. He became a devout pagan and emerged as such in a burst of disgusting bravado.

Coupled to Crowley's intellectual strutting was an amazing physical ability, demonstrated in mountaineering. He traveled to Mexico where he conquered Mount Popocatépetl. Crowley also made the first serious climb on the second-highest mountain in the world, K-2 in the remote Himalayas, reaching the 20,000-foot level. In 1905, he moved on to Nepal where he organized a large party to assault Mt. Kanchenjunga; five men in Crowley's expedition died in this climb.

By the turn of the century, Crowley had written and composed several hymns for the Anglican Church, two of which became minor classics. For his effort, Crowley was to be honored in a famous London club patronized by British nobility. He was to receive one of England's highest honors, one given only to knights. Upon walking gingerly into the gorgeously appointed club, Crowley spotted the distinguished members in tuxedoes waiting with broad smiles to greet him. Staring down at a priceless Chinese carpet on the floor of the club's foyer, the young composer immediately dropped his trousers, squatted, and defecated.

As the club members choked in astonishment, Crowley calmly hitched up his trousers, pointed imperviously at the grotesque feces on the expensive carpet, and said to the dumbstruck group: "Don't touch that—it's sacred!" With that, Aleister Crowley walked regally from the club and out of his role as a psalmist for the Anglican Church.

Aleister Crowley, the infamous drug-crazed occultist who shocked Europe with his free-sex communes.

This was but a forerunner of Crowley-inspired lunacies to come. By 1907, Crowley had all but put the English religious sect of Rosicrucians out of business, usurping their authority and introducing black magic stunts into their traditions and rituals. A schism ensued between Crowley's followers and the adherents of MacGregor Mathers, leader of the sect's Golden Dawn Society. Crowley insisted that the cult practice black magic exclusively where Mathers wanted the accent placed on spiritualism. According to exponents, a "classic occult battle" took place between the two. In this so-called magical warfare, reported Norman MacKenzie in *Secret Societies,* "Mathers called on the services of a vampire to destroy his former protege." Crowley later wrote that he "smote her [the vampire] with her own current of evil."

The Great Beast soon tired of the Golden Dawn rituals. (Crowley liked to be known as "666," the plate number on the mummy of a long-dead Egyptian priest, Ankh-f–khonsu, in the Cairo Museum, with whom he identified.) With the bulk of his fortune to squander, Crowley moved into his ancestral home—a gloomy, clammy castle in disrepair on the eerie moors outside Glasgow. There he lived and practiced his black magic, compelling his wife Rose and a certain whacky doctor named Mudd to perform sexual feats in his presence, and also joining them to make up a *ménage á trois* that experimented with all manner of sexual practices connected to Crowley's crazy-quilt black magic. At this time The Great Beast both gave vent to his homosexual leanings and began to indulge in hard drugs. He suddenly dismissed the much-abused Dr. Mudd for not performing on cue. The fallen disciple took the train to London, purchased a bicycle, and immediately pedaled his way to an icy suicide in the depths of the Thames. "He did not have the true calling for my Magick," Crowley later wrote.

Crowley recruited more and more women to his forlorn castle, and there, adorned in strange-looking robes similar to nuns' habits, they cavorted in candelight before the ghastly images of Satan. Stories of Crowley's cabalistic rites aroused the stolid Scottish citizenry, who demanded his banishment from the country. Eventually hounded from the castle, he began to wander about the world, going first to America. In Greenwich Village, he convinced himself he was a master artist. Crowley painted furiously for a year, his carefully selected subjects being deformed children, dwarfs, black prostitutes, and people with grotesque tattoos. He also attempted to lecture in New York, but his obscene speeches caused him to be hooted and driven from the platform beneath a shower of rotting garbage.

The ultimate dilettante, Crowley suddenly reversed himself, dedicating himself to "the art of hiking." He traveled to Burma, China, and India, hiking through these countries for years. Footsore, Crowley suddenly abandoned his cross-country exercises and returned to his one abiding obsession, black magic. Moving to the wind-swept fishing village of Cefalu on the northern shore of Sicily, Crowley established a sex cult, summoning followers from England— including Leah Faesi, his "High Priestess," whom he had met in Greenwich Village. The Great Beast purchased an estate which he called the Abbey of Themela, after the Greek word for desire. On his first night in the Abbey, Crowley gave Leah Faesi to his male followers and selected another "High Priestess," Ninette Schumway, with whom he had "ritual" intercourse as his disciples looked on.

Crowley's life in the Abbey was centered about week-long sex orgies. When pausing to hold court, The Great Beast told his non-compos-mentis followers that he could create magic strictly through certain sex acts. He could, he insisted, throw up a "cone of power" while masturbating in front of his concubines or participating in mass oral, anal, or vaginal sex. He looked upon his sex practices as a way of deliverance from troubles.

In his diaries, Crowley claimed that he had arrived destitute in America and that his first act of "sex magic" consisted of masturbating in order to bring good luck. He was successful, he claimed, in that only hours later a wealthy book collector turned up to pay him $500 for a rare tome he had brought from Scotland. Crowley went on to relate that he performed successful "sex magic" with any number of whores—rites that had enriched him almost overnight. He once required $20,000, Crowley wrote, and obtained this amount by merely having sex with a Dutch whore. He recalled his mad visions at the time of this intercourse: "The operation was excellent and vigorous, orgiastic but well-controlled. I made a mental image of the room being filled with showers and showers of big ten-dollar gold pieces, and held this very well, even in the midst of orgasm, which was lengthy.

"Though I could feel her mouth sucking up to mine, I could simultaneously SEE the gold filling the room ... We had been sniffing 171 before we began." The term "171" was Crowley's own label for cocaine. By the time of his arrival in Sicily, he was addicted not only to cocaine but to heroin. It was the latter drug that was to control his brain for the remainder of his nomadic life. Of his abundant use of cocaine, Crowley wrote: "I've had about a gram and I feel nothing but a sort of nervousness. I will go on. This is rather against my inclination, for I have a sort of despair as to its usefulness, and perhaps a trace of fear. On the other hand there is a sort of dull physical hunger for more."

Crowley instituted strict rules at the Sicilian abbey. He initiated all newcomers to his cult, male or female, by performing acrobatic sex with them. Any candidate who broke his strange rules, which changed from day to day,

Italian dictator Benito Mussolini, who angrily expelled Crowley and his hedonist minions from Italian soil.

was compelled to slash his or her forearm in retribution. Visitors to the abbey were insulted by Crowley's cultists. Some innocent passersby were invited to dine and then mescaline was secretly put into their drinks. When the visitors began to hallucinate, they were told that their visions had been brought about by Aleister Crowley's "Magick."

Crowley did possess the rare ability to hypnotize his followers, especially the young attractive females of his cult, whom he ordered to have sex with "clients" in order to finance his abbey operations. He gleaned more money by blackmailing the "clients," mostly rich old expatriates drifting about the Mediterranean.

Crowley's followers began to break at the strain of his bizarre commands. His first two wives (he had as many as fifteen) went hopelessly insane and were committed to asylums. Five of his scores of mistresses or "High Priestesses" committed suicide. The Great Beast only shrugged indifference at these deaths, stating to his diminishing cult clan that "they were unworthy of my Magick." Some of Crowley's diehard followers considered him to their mortal end as the Messiah, or at least as a mystical genius who had been brutally ignored by an unthinking world.

In 1923, when word of Crowley's wild antics reached the ears of Mussolini, the Duce ordered The Great Beast and his band expelled from Sicily. The cult, Crowley leading the way, wandered through many European lands, banished from one country after another, including Italy, Germany, and France.

By the end of World War II, Aleister Crowley was living in his native England, almost penniless, a hopeless heroin addict, his once populous cult depleted to a few ancient females—crones who begged money on the streets of Brighton in order to support their leader's drug habits. Crowley confined himself to a single room of a cheap boarding house and scratched out his mad diaries. Entered the day before his death from an overdose of heroin on December 1, 1947, his final entry read: "What an ass I am! Will heroin help me to forget it?"

Aleister Crowley's body, ravaged by decades of drug abuse and sexual perversion, was cremated.

Michael CURTIZ

Director (1888–1962)

Born in Hungary as Mihaly Kertez, the film director began his career in Hollywood with *Noah's Ark* in 1928. He was to prove himself not only one of filmdom's most durable directors but one of its most ruthless. No matter what the obstacles, Curtiz finished his pictures on time and within the budget set by his producers. This dependability made him the darling of the movie moguls—particularly Jack Warner, for whom Curtiz churned out dozens of successful pictures. Most of Curtiz' best films—eight in all—were made with Warner's superstar, Errol Flynn.

The combination of Curtiz and Flynn was box office magic, but the association of these two eccentrics proved to be an ongoing nightmare. That Flynn hated the Hungarian director above all others was blantantly obvious. Curtiz made films despite the risks to his actors; he punished them mercilessly to achieve his ends, and, in the case of *The Charge of the Light Brigade,* he irresponsibily caused the slaughter of dozens of horses—an act that brought the animal lovers of America to rise up against him and instituted a strict code against cruelty to animals followed thereafter by movie studios.

"I was to spend five miserable years with him," Flynn remembered when thinking of the brutal Curtiz, "making *Robin Hood, Charge of the Light Brigade* and many other films. In each, he tried to make all scenes so realistic that my skin didn't seem to matter to him. Nothing delighted him more than real bloodshed."

Charge of the Light Brigade was made in northern California; the background was supposed to be nineteenth-century India. All the actors, including Flynn, were dressed in thin cotton uniforms. "A cold, piercing wind, not perhaps at the freezing point, blew through you," Flynn remembered with a chill. "Meantime the hardboiled Curtiz was bundled in about three topcoats,

Flynn exercising his masterful swordplay: "Curtiz had made him take the tips off the swords."

giving orders. I didn't know enough to tell him to give me one of his topcoats, or to drop dead. He didn't care who hated him or for what." The director insisted that Flynn perform his own "horsecharge." Flynn missed death time and again in Curtiz' films, but one of his best friends was thrown from a horse during a Curtiz charge and impaled on an upturned sword. Curtiz merely shrugged at the dangers he himself established and grunted, "Moving pictures is the cruelest business in the world."

Flynn's wrath grew with each Curtiz film until he came to believe that the director was planning to kill him. In one film, Flynn's eye was almost torn out in a sword fight Curtiz was directing. "A friend came to me," Flynn remembered bitterly five years before his death, "and told me that Curtiz had made him take the tips off the swords. The last straw! I leaped up the twelve-foot parallel to get to Curtiz—I'll never know how. I grabbed Mike by the throat and began strangling him. Two men tried to pry me off. They succeeded before I killed him."

Although Curtiz never directed Flynn again, his brutal philosophy remained intact for a long time, as is demonstrated by his ruthless advice to a prop man: "If you want to become a director you must sit on top of the camera and pant like a tiger." But what reflected the real Curtiz was the explosive non sequitur he once angrily blurted: "The next time I send a dumb sonofabitch to do something, I go myself!"

D

Salvador DALI

Painter (Born 1904)

A prankster with a neurotic and unending bent for the bizarre, Salvador Dali has been called everything in the world of art from charlatan to genius. He has, since earliest childhood in Spain, nurtured and developed enough phobias and fears to add several new chapters to the history of psychiatry. He has been or still is obsessed with watches, excrement, all forms of necrophilia such as dead faces and rotting corpses, grasshoppers (which to him mean fear and his father), flies, swarms of ants, bats, and his own misshapen teeth.

Dali has had a lifelong shoe fetish; he used to steal his teacher's slipper as a boy and play with it, sometimes using it for a hat. When he was thirteen Dali turned his shoes into weapons for the pure sake of cruelty. At the time he was watching another boy, a violinist, who put down his instrument to tie his shoe in the street in front of their school. As the youth leaned over Dali kicked him so hard in the buttocks that he sent the boy flying. The ever-vicious Dali then leaped with both feet onto the boy's violin, smashing it, and then kicking and stomping the instrument until it was nothing but slivers of wood. He then fled laughing hysterically as the boy raced after him, caught him, and gave him a thrashing.

A teacher came running from the school and demanded to know why Dali had destroyed the violin.

Dali smirked: "I have just proved that painting is superior to music."

"How?" asked the incredulous teacher.

"With my shoe!"

Born to wealth on May 11, 1904 in Figueras, Catalan, Spain, Dali's christened name was Don Salvador Dali y Cusi. He was physically peculiar from early childhood, having only two top molars and retaining his two lower center baby teeth into adulthood, once described as "two grains of rice." Inside one of these baby teeth, Dali later proudly stated, was an image of "Our Lady of Lourdes."

Cruelty and abnormality consumed Dali at an early age. "As a child, I was wicked, I grew up under the shadow of evil," the artist gloated in *The Secret Life of Salvador Dali, "*and I still continue to cause suffering." He loved violence and thought to murder on occasions. At the age of five he threw a little boy off a suspension bridge outside of Figueras. The boy fell fifteen feet, landed on sharp rocks, and was almost killed. He broke a physician's glasses just as the doctor was to pierce his sister's ears when he was six. He crept up behind his ancient grandmother at age seven as she was tying her thin white hair into a chignon and cut off the knot of hair, sending the old woman into hysterics. He watched his three-year-old baby sister, Ana Maria (who grew to hate him in adulthood), crawling across the floor and then raced up to her and kicked her viciously in the head, "as though it had been a ball," he later commented.

Dali's youth was packed with self-abuse. He found a dead bat crawling with worms and jammed this horrid mess into his mouth, biting it in two (which might have served as an inspiration to G. Gordon Liddy). A bejeweled crown had been given to Dali by his grandfather and he would often force this down on his large head so that his forehead would be dented and bloodied, keeping the crown on for hours until it produced raging headaches.

Sent to study at the demanding Marist Brothers School of Figueras, Dali rebelled against classes and devised all manner of wild excuses to avoid school. He would throw himself downstairs, which later became a perverse and maschochistic pleasure for him. He would complain of "angina attacks" and cause his nose to bleed so that he could stay in bed all day and dream his dark dreams.

As a teenager Dali discovered perversity in sex. A darkly beautiful seventeen-year-old girl fell in love with him. Dali petted and necked with her, but refused to have sex, even though he purposely whipped up her desires. Dali would order the girl to sit before him with her breasts exposed for an hour each day until she begged him to fondle her and at these times he would desert her. He excited her, then caused her great depression, loving the emotional torture he could inflict. When the girl was half-mad with desire, he would tell her: "Make believe you are dead." At their last meeting, the wretched girl pleaded for sexual release; Dali yawned: "You know when I go to Madrid [to study], I won't even write to you again." Years later Dali was to state: "Unconsummated love has appeared to me since this experience to be one of my most formidable weapons."

Dali attended the School of Fine Arts in Madrid where he scoffed at those students who came from poor families. One impoverished student came to him to confide his problems which Dali had insidiously encouraged the youth to do. The student then burst into tears and asked for a loan so that he could stay in

Painter Salvador Dali with inverted umbrellas on his celebrated mustache.

school. Dali, who could have easily aided the youth, sneered: "Why don't you hang yourself, or throw yourself from the top of the tower."

As a student himself, Dali was impossible, refusing assignments and constantly arguing with faculty members. He was suspended for a year after vehemently protesting the appointment of a teacher. He was twenty-two when the university expelled him permanently from its halls. Dali, in the middle of an examination, had suddenly turned to a panel of judges and said: "I am sorry, but I am infinitely more intelligent than these three professors."

By the late 1920s, Salvador Dali had little need of a diploma. His surrealistic painting had made him the rage of Europe. Women by the score flocked to him, but he played the aloof and disinterested artist. Once, when living at Cadaques, an attractive admirer sat down next to him on the beach, putting her head on his knee. She touched his leg lovingly and suddenly Dali leaped up, shoving the girl aside, kicking her in the head and the breasts, then stomping on her until her friends dragged her screaming and bleeding away from the berserk painter.

Dali's art has been forever a subject of controversy, ridicule and marvel. His paintings are invariably smeared with his manias, phobias, fetishes, the most recurrent being crutches which have appeared over and over in Dali's surrealistic landscapes and portraits. (Asked once to explain what surrealism was, Dali snorted: "I am surrealism!") The crutch fetish dates back, again, to Dali's boyhood; he once found an old crutch in some Spanish ruins. He has used this device symbolically (and tiredly) for decades to show social and spiritual decay, weakness and corruption.

At his first success, Dali toyed with insanity as he had once played with decaying bats and dead hedgehogs in youth. He encouraged delusions, thoughts of suicide, vertigo, and compelled himself to go into laughing fits that lasted for hours. "I was trying by every possible means to go mad," he related later, "doing everything in my conscious power to welcome and help that madness which I felt clearly intended to take up its abode in my soul."

Elena Diaranoff, a Russian, who was then married to Paul Eluard, a French surrealistic poet, visited Dali with her husband in 1929. Gala, as Mrs. Eluard was called, stayed with Dali and her husband left. She was to live with the painter as a commonlaw wife until Dali officially married her in 1958.

Somehow Gala inspired the mad painter to some semblance of sanity, but it was an inspiration learned at the razor's edge. At first Dali played the clown for her, then thought to prove his love for his "Galarina" by debasing himself. Before meeting her for tea one afternoon, shortly after they had been introduced, Dali shaved his armpits and knees until they were raw and bleeding. He then coated his body with goat manure and put a red geranium behind his ear before setting off to see his sweetheart.

Within days Dali fell in love, but love for him was mingled with dementia. He took Gala to a cliff, he later recalled, and had the urge to push her off. He grabbed her by her long hair, holding her at the edge of the cliff and demanded that she tell him something, anything that would prevent him from killing her. "But tell me slowly," he gritted as he held her precariously at the cliff's edge, "looking me in the eyes, with the crudest, the most ferociously erotic words that can make both of us feel the greatest shame!"

Said Gala in a calm voice: "I want you to kill me."

Her words shocked him into tranquility; she had guessed his desire and, by uttering that secret thought, dispelled the notion. At least, that was Dali's explanation for not murdering the woman he later married and continues to live with to this day.

Dali's influence in the giddy, fickle world of art, especially in Europe where fashion and whimsy rule the galleries and salons, was potent and powerful in the 1930s. He literally dictated style and expression, yet he had his critics. The author George Orwell, whom he met, felt the painter to be repugnant, labeling him an "undesirable," and "a dirty little scoundrel ... as anti-social as a flea." The critic Malcolm Cowley later called Dali "the imp of the perverse."

Hundreds of Dali's paintings of the grotesque, the weird, the macabre, all surrounded with the theme of death, have sold for astronomical amounts. During the 1940s and 1950s Dali worked to produce surrealistic motion picture scenes in Hollywood, the most impressive being those dream sequences created for Alfred Hitchcock's *Spellbound*. Hitchcock, however, had a difficult time restraining Dali, vetoing one idea where the painter wanted to show a statue breaking to pieces and Ingrid Bergman inside, totally covered with swarms of ants.

Though a rank self-promoter and a disgusting exhibitionist, Dali's popularity has not diminished. He opened a show in 1980 in Paris which presented 436 of his works dating from 1920. The exhibit was a smashing success. Of course, Dali was on hand to instruct the critics and patrons that they were fortunate, indeed, to be able to view the works of one of the world's greatest painters. At the time the painter stated: "The difference between a madman and me is that I am not mad."He then exhibited his odd-looking mustache, waxed to bristling hard points, a mustache that has been his strange hallmark.

In the past, Dali likened his long, protruding mustache as antenna, similar to that of insects. ("The best moment is with my flies around. Then I work well.") He insisted that "my mustache is my radar. It pulls ideas out of space ... Great painters need a luxuriant mustache like mine. The points have to be just under the eyes to get the right perspective." He also pointed out the utilitarian use of his mustache, which prevented "dust from landing on my canvas or in my nose or mouth." Only once, when doing a commissioned portrait of actor Laurence Olivier, did Dali deign to shave off his "radar." At that time he commented: "I don't need vibration of antenna when I am painting materially."

Dali always thought of Dali. When asked once to name his favorite perfume, he replied: "The essence of Dali." In the August 1942 issue of *Esquire,* Dali was asked to write a self-portrait. He accepted with alacrity, making up a curious list by which all would know him. He told the world at this time that his favorite color was "absinthe green." His favorite exercise: "Riding up—but not down—in an elevator." Most admired contemporaries: "Picasso and I."

Dali never altered his opinion of himself, feeling about his work today as he did in 1965 when, at a New York showing of his paintings, he stated: "I am totally committed to science, and very knowledgable too. I am a scientific painter. That is why I am the greatest ... If you compare me with modern artists, yes, I am a genius!"

Charles DAWSON

Antiquarian (date uncertain–1916)

In 1908, part of a human skull with an ape-like jaw, along with some crude tools, was dug up by Charles Dawson, a lawyer and antiquarian, on Piltdown Common near Fletcher, in Sussex, England. Archeologists and anthropologists closely inspected the gravel pit where Dawson had made his startling discovery, but nothing beyond the skull and implements was found. The skull was enough to shock the scientific world. After seven years of study, experts determined that the discovery, labeled "Piltdown Man," was undoubtedly "the missing link" between ape and man on Darwin's chart of evolution, belonging to the Pliocene epoch. This conclusion meant that the find predated all other genuine skeletal finds in Germany, France, and Belgium—that modern man had existed for 500,000 years on earth.

Using the fragments of skull and jaw found, Dr. Smith Woodward of the British Museum reconstructed this ape-man from the fossil remains. The result was a skull with a high, steep forehead like that of modern man, with

Head and skull replicas of the notorious Piltdown Man, the colossal archaeological hoax perpetrated by Charles Dawson.

hardly any brow ridges, but the jaw indicated that the neck was more like that of an ape. From this reconstruction, scientists deduced that the Piltdown Man was a thinking, rational creature "with a brain capacity midway between the highest ape and the highest man." Professor Arthur Keith went further; his intricate studies of the fossil showed "a brain capacity slightly above that of the average modern man."

For nearly forty years, the Piltdown Man stood as one of the most important anthropological finds in history. Dawson was heralded as one of the world's most brilliant scientists, although he enjoyed his fame briefly, dying in 1916. A handsome monument in his honor was constructed in his home town, and he was referred to as the "wizard of Sussex" for decades.

This wizard's magic, however, proved to be only sleight-of-hand—in 1953, Piltdown Man was exposed as "the most elaborate and carefully prepared hoax" in the history of anthropology. The British Museum's Dr. K.P. Oakley and Doctors J.E. Weiner and W.E. LeGros Clark, both professors at Oxford, had long suspected "Piltdown Man" was a plant, an ingenious creation of Charles Dawson. Oakley, who became an expert on fluorine use during World War II, proved that bone buried in ground containing fluorine water (which was the case with the Piltdown discovery) absorbed that water at a rate that could be determined by centuries. Thus Oakley was able to positively state that the upper skull of Dawson's marvelous find was no more than 5,000 years old. Weiner and Clark experimented on the jaw of the Piltdown Man with radioactive carbon and easily proved that it belonged to a modern orangutan, not fossilized but stained. Weiner wrote a book entitled *Piltdown Forgery* in which he documented Dawson's habit of staining bones and fabricating artifacts.

When the truth was made known, scores of dithering experts who had blindly accepted Dawson's hoax mumbled excuses. It would be years before dozens of encyclopedia entries concerning the Piltdown Man were changed to conform with the facts. Dawson, however, had long since gone to his grave a scientific hero—which undoubtedly had been his goal.

Jerome Herman ("Dizzy") DEAN

Baseball Pitcher (1911–1974)

An ex-sharecropper from the Arkansas cottonfields, Jerome "Dizzy" Dean broke into professional baseball in 1932 with the St. Louis Cardinals, the team with which he would set records and earn a reputation as one of the game's all-time zanies. A great pitcher, Dean was never known as a shrewd man. He did not know the meaning of money; and after his first few weeks with the Cardinals, he was broke, having spent every dime of the handsome advance he had received.

The manager of the team came to Dean and told him that he was a spendthrift.

"What's that mean?"

"It means you're throwing away money like a crazy man. So the old man says you get only a dollar a day to spend from now on. We'll pay for your lodging."

The "old man" was owner Sam Breadon, a person Dean had never met. The pitcher, however, would never forget his name, nor would he let anyone on the team forget it. Every day, Dizzy lambasted the owner. One afternoon at batting practice, Dean was complaining loud and long about "the tightest old coot that ever drew a breath! He's plumb starvin' old Diz to death, that's for sure!"

Someone tapped Dean on the shoulder. The pitcher turned around to see an elderly man with a kindly face looking at him. "Just what's your trouble, son?"

"It's that Breadon feller," carped Dean. "He's the meanest, nickel-nursin' no-good buzzard that ever walked the earth."

"Why? Doesn't he pay you enough?"

"Hell, no! I should be gettin' two dollars a day, not the little ol' dollah he's givin' me!"

"I understand. Why don't you come to my office, son, and we'll talk it over. By the way, I'm Breadon."

As Dean strolled thoughtfully—and suddenly quiet—to the owner's office, teammates placed wagers on the time it would take before Dean was fired. Several eager players waited outside the office to witness the outcome. Within minutes the rookie pitcher barged into the outer office, grinning. "Okay, boys!" Dean shouted in great triumph. "I got the two bucks!" He waved the greenbacks over his head as if he had struck oil.

The hurler performed amazing feats on the mound (as did his brother Paul, known as "Daffy"). But Dizzy also created stunts that are forever remembered. To unnerve the opposition on a July day when the heat was soaring to the 100 degree mark, Dean suddenly ran into the dugout and emerged with a heavy woolen blanket which he threw about his shoulders. Despite the protests from umpires, he squatted on the mound and built a small fire, pretending to warm his hands. On another occasion, Dean faced a deadly hitter and completely

Dizzy Dean to Rogers Hornsby: "Kinda powerful wind blowin' out there."

Rogers Hornsby to Dizzy Dean: "That ain't what blew you in here!"

shattered his adversary's confidence by ordering everyone on his team except the catcher to sit down. He then easily struck out the batter.

He was not always in top form. Once, when pitching on the National League team in an exhibition game, he lost control, and, in the fourth inning, the opposition belted out seven consecutive hits against him. Manager Rogers Hornsby called him into the dugout, replacing him with a fresh pitcher.

Dean sat down glumly, turning to Hornsby and grunting: "Kinda powerful wind blowin' out there today, Rog."

"Yeah," nodded Hornsby, "but that ain't what blew you in here."

After his untimely retirement from baseball (caused by an injured arm in 1938), Dean became an announcer covering the Cardinals' games. His down-home style of radio sports reporting endeared him to listeners, but grammarians everywhere went into rages when listening to him.

Some of the more famous quotes from Dizzy's broadcasting: Following the breakup of some players conferring on the pitcher's mound: "An' now the players have gone back to their respectable positions." Describing the sweat dripping from players on a particularly steamy day: "The boys are covered with press-peration." After a strike that made him excited: "That, by coincidence, folks, was a strike. I don't know what 'coincidence' means, but I heard a guy use it the other day and it sure sounded mighty swell to me." Describing a diving player (tagged out): "Wow! He slud into third and he was throwed out!"

So irate did English teachers become that they petitioned the governor of the state to remove Dean from broadcasting, saying that Dizzy was corrupting the language of their students. Hearing about the petition, Dizzy answered the charges of his poor grammar with a classic remark: "A lot of people who don't say ain't, ain't eatin'."

Dizzy Dean stayed on the airways.

John DEE

Astrologer (1527–1608)

Known as "Queen Elizabeth's Merlin," Dee was undoubtedly a genius, attending Cambridge when only fifteen. From that time onward, according to

Queen Elizabeth's adviser and necromancer John Dee (right) with his assistant Edward Kelly conjuring spirits in an English graveyard.

his own schedule, Dee studied eighteen hours each day, spent two hours eating and four hours sleeping. He wrote seventy-nine books, most of which remain in manuscript to this day, in one form or other. It was Dee who first proposed the collecting of manuscripts and the establishment of a royal library, the percursor to the British Museum. A wonderful scientist whose theories in navigation vastly aided early explorers, Dee was also dedicated to witchcraft and demonology.

Though he was a close adviser and friend of Queen Elizabeth, Dee had already been branded a necromancer by Queen Mary, who had imprisoned him as "a companion of the hellhounds and a caller and a conjurer of wicked and damned spirits." The astrologer—that was his official label—was, at one time, charged with sacrificing children to the devil, but these claims were never investigated.

There is no doubt that Dee was fascinated with demonology, the practices of black magic and strange witchcraft rites. In his travels throughout Europe Dee sought out such notorious demonologista as Jean Bodin and Johan Weyer in order to discover their secrets. Moreover, Dee and his assistant, Edward Kelly, practiced all sorts of cabalistic rites by the light of the full moon in cemeteries, attempting to bring back the dead. Dee also labored for years as an alchemist to change lead and other metals into gold without success

A simple-minded man when it came to matters of the flesh, Dee was once approached by his assistant who had become passionate toward Dee's wife. Kelly told his master that he had been visited by spirits who had instructed him to sleep with Dee's wife, Jane, and that Dee should sleep with his spouse, the ghosts specifically ordering "the common and impartial using of matrimonial acts amongst any couples of us four."

When Dee's wife Jane rebelled at the wife-swapping arrangement, the astrologer admonished her for denying the spirit world; the couples then freely exchanged sexual favors. None of Dee's fancies were as harmful, however, as his prediction that the world would come to an end on St. Patrick's Day in 1842, when a flood would engulf Europe.

When that day arrived, authorities in England and in several European countries were amazed to see thousands of Dee's readers climb into boats, carrying their worldly goods and enough food and water to wait out forty days of flooding. Of course, no flood ensued. Immediately thereafter, John Dee's books suffered a sharp decline in popularity.

Ferdinand Waldo DEMARA, Jr.

Impersonator (Born 1922)

He was known as the "Great Imposter," and for Fred Demara, impersonation was a way of life, apparently a psychological compulsion that he could not resist. In his colorful career of pretension, Demara never finished high school; but through self-education, he managed to become an expert in many fields. He impersonated learned scholars and taught college-level courses until exposed. He assumed the role of a Trappist monk, and a short time later, he pretended to be a doctor in the Canadian Navy, performing brilliant surgery on injured troops during the Korean War. Not until dispatches commending him for gallant service were made public was he revealed as an imposter.

Demara became an expert penologist at Huntville Prison in Texas, dealing with hardened criminals and once prevented a prison riot in 1955. Though he was again exposed as a fraud, Demara went on to other impersonations, teaching high school in rural Maine in the late 1950s. His story was told with sensitivity in the film *The Great Imposter*.

Timothy DEXTER

Merchant (1747–1806)

Born in Malden, Massachusetts on January 22, 1747, Dexter worked as an itinerant farmer, beginning at age eight and, as a teenager, traveled to Boston where he became an apprentice leather dresser. At age twenty, with his life's savings in his pocket, all of nine dollars, Dexter walked forty miles to the thriving town of Newburyport, where Elizabeth Frothingham, a wealthy widow of thirty-one, took him into her home and subsequently into her bed as her husband.

Dexter fancied himself a shrewd businessman and, using his wife's money, he brought up small quantities of stocks at low ebb and sold them quickly as their values rose, not out of shrewdness, however. He merely aped the wealthy stock investors of the time. He did, however, manage to increase his wife's fortunes and his own to the point where he began speculating in all manner of wild ventures.

Competitors laughed at the semi-illiterate Dexter and his posturing ways, and thought to belittle him by giving him lunatic business tips. By incredible luck, these tips turned into great fortunes for Dexter. One merchant whispered in Dexter's ear that the West Indies, where colonization was booming, was sorely in need of warming pans, mittens and Bibles.

Having no concept of the torrid weather in the West Indies, Dexter bought up more than 40,000 warming pans, and an equal number of mittens and Bibles, shipping these to the West Indies. He then waited for fortune to smile on him. It grinned widely and through its teeth poured a shower of gold for the inept businessman.

When Dexter's shipments arrived in the West Indies, there was a great religious movement beginning and his Bibles were purchased at 100 percent profit. Russian trading ships visiting the West Indies ports had their agents immediately buy up the mittens to the last pair. The warming pans were at first a problem. They sat idly in a warehouse until some inventive planter discovered that, once the lids were removed, these pans made ideal skimmers with which molasses could be ladled into vats; each and every pan was sold for the highest price. These incredible sales brought Dexter an estimated $150,000, making him enormously wealthy before the beginning of the American Revolution.

Later, merchants in his town purposely sought to ruin Dexter by urging him to invest every dime he possessed in shipping coal to Newcastle, England. The unschooled Dexter, not knowing that Newcastle was the center of England's coal-mining industry, hired scores of sailing ships and filled their holds with soft Virginia coal, shipping the cargoes to England.

Instead of becoming an international laughing stock, Dexter's amazing luck held; a massive strike in Newcastle had left the mines empty and there was a shortage of coal in the area. When Dexter's ships arrived, his coal was purchased at enormous profits, making him twice as rich as he had been.

Timothy Dexter went on making investments, some of them practical, such as establishing the first manufacturing center for the making of clay pipes. He bought stock in vital toll bridges and purchased great tracts of land.

So wealthy did Dexter become that he began to think of himself as a country squire, then a member of royalty. He dubbed himself "Lord" Timothy Dexter and, emulating such men as John Hancock and Thomas Jefferson, began donating money to charities and churches, to earn himself the compliments of the community. Publicly, Dexter became a much-admired man, the business community of Newburyport especially marveling at his astounding ventures. Privately, Dexter's life became a ruin.

His daughter Nancy married a bully, one Abraham Bishop, who beat her senseless and almost crippled her before Dexter took her back into her own home. She became a hopeless drunk and later became insane. Dexter's son, Samuel, was a spendthrift. His father locked him, as an adult, in his room for weeks on end to cure his wild spending habits; yet he became an alcoholic for the remainder of his miserable life. Samuel Dexter spent most of his waking hours in the confines of his father's enormous wine cellar.

Elizabeth Frothingham Dexter was anything but a sympathetic wife. She constantly nagged her husband about his foolish ways, becoming a vicious shrew. Dexter, instead of arguing with her, pretended that she had died and her presence in his sprawling mansion was no more than that of an apparition. When visitors to his home arrived, Dexter would point to his sour-faced Elizabeth and blithely say: "This is Mrs. Dexter, the ghost that was my wife."

As he grew older, Dexter's eccentricities increased. He filled the many rooms of his mansion with clocks of all kinds; the ceaseless ticking and chiming probably helped to make his daughter go mad, his son to take to drink, and his wife to change into a monster.

Companionship and slavish devotion was needed by Dexter and to that end he hired a menagerie of weird characters, a towering giant to protect him named Burly, whom Dexter called "the dwarf," a housekeeper who shielded him from his family and, finally, a failed fishmonger named Jonathan Plummer, who thought himself a poet. It was Plummer's full-time job to write laudatory poems about his employer, Dexter, and sell these in the streets of Newburyport.

Dexter was not satisfied with his retinue of obsequious servants, and he spent thousands of dollars to turn his estate into a museum of sorts, which featured forty statues of those men he most admired, from Jefferson and Franklin to Aaron Burr, giant statues handcarved from expensive wood, the tallest of which was after his own likeness. After looking over the completed "museum," Timothy Dexter remained insecure. He wondered if he was respected enough by his neighbors. There was one way, he concluded, by which he could positively determine the true regard his community had for him; he would hold his own funeral. (This incredible event took place, of course, several years before Dexter's actual death at age fifty-nine, on October 26, 1806.)

Spending thousands, Dexter hired distinguished professors and clergymen to give eulogies at his graveside. His empty expensive casket was placed in an elegant open carriage and drawn by six thoroughbred horses. Dexter spent another fortune advertising his funeral, having expensively-printed flyers distributed to every home in the Newburyport area announcing the event.

The funeral cortege marched solemnly past Dexter's house on the appointed day and the hearse was followed by a staggering number of people, a

Timothy Dexter of Massachusetts, who made insane investments, witnessed his own funeral, and wrote the most ungrammatical book on record.

crowd estimated to be more than three thousand. Dexter watched the procession from a second-story window, beaming with pride at the homage he was being shown. He was moved to tears when he heard hundreds of the mourners wailing and weeping over his loss.

At that moment Dexter's thoughts turned to his shrewish wife Elizabeth and he went into her room to find her smirking at the procession outside. She glanced at him and called him a lunatic.

"So you can't bring yourself to cry at my funeral, ehh?" yelled Dexter. He grabbed a can and beat his wife into submission. Elizabeth Dexter did cry then, not out of remorse but out of pain.

The zenith of Dexter's eccentricities was reached when he decided to pen and publish his memoirs, a book entitled *A Pickle for the Knowning Ones, or Plain Truths in a Homespun Dress* which he paid to have published in 1802. The book, now a valuable collector's item was, from beginning to end, one long, incoherent sentence, without a single punctuation mark. The spelling was atrocious, Dexter writing out his words phonetically. The "Lord" attempted to relate all the worldly wisdom he had learned in his illustrious life.

This book was undoubtedly the most incomprehensible, ungrammatical tome in the history of publishing. Yet Dexter was proud of the work and ordered the printing of thousands of copies which were widely distributed. Few read the book and those who did ridiculed Dexter as a rich buffoon, a self-indulgent idiot who naively destroyed the English language in an expensive fit of egomania. The lack of punctuation in the memoirs was repeatedly pointed out to Dexter as the crowning point of his moronic gestures.

Dexter, in an ingenious move, answered his critics brilliantly in a revised edition of *A Pickle for the Knowing* some years later. He had the following page reproduced in the second edition:

mister printer the Nowing ones complane of my book the fust edition had no stops
I put in A Nuf here and thay may peper and solt it as they plese
,,,
,,,
::
,,,
.... !!! ....
.... !!! ....
.... ! ....
,,,
....??????????????????????????? ....

Sergei Pavlovich DIAGHILEV

Ballet Impressario (1872–1929)

As director of the Imperial Russian Ballet, Diaghilev was an absolute dictator to the members of his troupe—and this included the great dancers, Pavlova and Nijinsky (the only ballet artist ever to perform ten *entrechats*)—telling them what to wear, what to eat, when to go to sleep, and even selecting their lovers for them. He was a dandy, attiring himself in the most expensive tailor-made clothes he could order.

The son of a Russian general, Diaghilev scorned a military career early in life, taking up the piano. He proved to be an above-average pianist, and his baritone voice was suitable for opera; but he was inclined toward the dance and lobbied to take over the Imperial Ballet.

He delighted in the discovery of talent; and through him the world first heard of the painter Bakst, the choreographer Fokine, and the powerful composer Igor Stravinsky, who composed *Rite of Spring* and *Petrouchka* for Diaghilev—both of which were among his most famous productions, with Nijinsky in the leading roles. The ruthless Diaghilev considered himself "a great charlatan, a man with a great quantity of logic, but with very few principles and no real gifts."

The autocratic impresario would tolerate no interference with his direction of the ballet; and he fired anyone who displeased him at will—including the greatest ballet dancer of them all, Nijinsky. Then again, Nijinsky had been Diaghilev's lover; the impresario was flagrantly homosexual and flaunted his young men before the world, including the Russian court.

The Diaghilev–Nijinsky affair was a strange passion play, in that the dancer had met a young ballerina and fallen in love with her. At first, Diaghilev appeared to sanction the union; but later he did everything in his power to banish the young woman. He even then threatened Nijinsky's life; but Nijinsky, whose sexual attitude had changed, married his ballerina; and Diaghilev promptly fired him from the Imperial Ballet.

Romola Nijinsky, the dancer's wife, later found her husband drawing butterflies, all having his face, "and big spiders with the face of Diaghilev." Romola quoted her husband in her memoirs as saying at the time: "That is Sergei Pavlovich, and these butterflies are we, the youth of Russia, caught in his net forever."

With the coming of the Revolution, Diaghilev and thousands of other nobles and princes fled Russia. His career was ruined. He visited the Nijinskys in Paris, weeping and begging the dancer to return to him. Nijinsky refused.

Wealthy to the end of his life in 1929, Diaghilev became a homosexual predator in Paris, a true spider entrapping any young man he fancied, sometimes keeping as many as three or four males with him at all times. He was also bitter to the end about Nijinsky, cursing him at the last for giving his love and his body to a woman.

Raymond DITMARS

Naturalist (1876–1942)

Shunning a military education at West Point, Ditmars displayed at an early age a fascination for wildlife, collecting, in particular, every type of snake, preferably poisonous, he could find in the Hudson River Valley. These he secretly took home until his ancestral mansion was alive with reptiles. According to one biographer, Ditmars "bought snakes, he traded for them, he begged for them. The captain of a fruit boat gave him a boa constrictor, and he wrote to scientists in the West Indies, and traded American snakes for the reptiles that infest the jungles."

Ditmars' mother grew so alarmed at her son's live snake collection that she gave him the entire top floor of the family mansion. Terrified neighbors told newsmen about this strange collection, but instead of condemning Ditmars, the press promoted him as a novelty. Then followed a steady stream of snake charmers, circus people, and fellow viper collectors to the Ditmars' house, all begging to see the collection. Mrs. Ditmars had to order the family maid to take appointments with these strange visitors.

Tolerant though they were of their son's oddball "hobby," Ditmars' parents informed their son that he would have to provide food for his "strange pets." To that end, the snake-lover taught himself stenography and earned money for his pets by hiring himself out as a part-time secretary. To supplement food for his snakes, Ditmars traveled to New York's Chinatown where he was graciously allowed to set traps for mice and rats in the basements of Chinese restaurants, and each evening he would lug bags full of dead rodents back home to feed his vipers.

In 1899, the city decided to build a large zoo, and Ditmars was the logical choice to head the reptile house. One reporter quipped: "His mother fervently thanked God when her son moved all his rattlers and copperheads out of the house and took them to the zoo."

Within a few years, the naturalist was considered the leading authority on snakes. Later, when he became Dr. Ditmars, he took a deep interest in the behavior of monkeys. He wanted to study these creatures in an environment other than a zoo and took a half-dozen monkeys to his Scarsdale home. The animals went wild, smashing furniture, swinging from chandeliers, short-circuiting the electric wires in the Ditmars' mansion. They smeared cold cream onto the mirrors, sprinkled pickles over the carpet, smashed piano keys with a pair of old shoes, opened the drawers of a sewing machine to get at spools of thread and wound the thread throughout the house until it looked like a giant cobweb, while all the while Ditmars attempted to subdue them. He finally gave up and hurriedly called zoo keepers with nets to catch the frolicking monkeys. The eccentric Ditmars shrugged sheepishly and stated, "I was lucky that the house didn't burn up."

Sir Arthur Conan DOYLE

Author (1859–1930)

The creator of Sherlock Holmes, normally a practical man, a homebody, and a great champion of the family and the British nation, abandoned serious writing toward the end of his career, suddenly becoming a devout spiritualist.

(Over the years, Doyle had collected a vast library on spiritualism, and at his death in 1930, his estate contained more than 2,000 books and reams of notes on the subject.) Doyle's involvement led him to consult mediums, attend séances, and—indulging in his wildest fantasies—to play spiritualistic detective, looking everywhere for clues to the machinations of "the other side."

He publicly announced his beliefs, which immediately caused phalanxes of his dedicated readers to question his mental stability; sales of his books, even the immortal Holmes stories, began to drop off. Doyle persisted, stating that communion with the long-dead spirits was not only a possibility but a reality. Some of his closest friends stopped talking to him.

The author then began a world tour, lecturing on spiritualism in South Africa, Australia, even the United States. As he approached New York Harbor by ship, Doyle did have some misgivings about selling his spiritualism to Americans. He viewed his encounter with the public and press as a possible disaster: "They have a keen sense of humor, these Americans, and no subject can more easily be made humorous than this. They are intensely practical, and this would appear to them visionary. They are immersed in worldly pursuits, and this cuts right across the path of their lives. Above all they are swayed by the press, and if the press takes a flippant attitude, I have no means of getting behind it."

Doyle's message was simple. He believed that what survived after death was an etheric body, "a soul clothed in its bodily likeness," according to John Dickson Carr, one of Doyle's biographers. After death, Doyle claimed, the etheric body, the soul "clothing" the physical likeness of the real body at the best period of its earthly existence, went to another world or traveled through a series of other worlds. All of this was too much for the public to grasp; and even though Doyle was universally accorded respect, his audiences were more curious to see the great mystery writer than enthusiastic in embracing his beliefs. Many whispered that "Poor old Doyle" had gone mad.

From 1922 to 1923 Doyle traveled 50,000 miles and talked to more than a quarter of a million people. He made few converts. During the mid and late 1920s, Doyle became disillusioned—not with his spiritualistic beliefs but with a public that failed to respond to his preachings. His publishers begged him for more stories about Sherlock Holmes, but by then Doyle's only interest in life was spiritualism. When the British peerage began to criticize him, saying that he was degrading knighthood with his absurd beliefs, Doyle withdrew into semiseclusion.

After his death on July 7, 1930, the London *Times* reported: "All sincere British mediums are now sitting in the darkness, waiting for a spirit message from Sir Arthur." This was a result of Mrs. Doyle's confession that she and her husband had made a pact shortly before the author's death that he would communicate in a secret code ten days after he "passed over."

Ten thousand wealthy British spiritualists packed Albert Hall in London a week later to witness Lady Doyle receive a "spirit message" from her deceased

Sir Arthur Conan Doyle, creator of Sherlock Holmes, who believed that he could communicate from the grave.

Arthur, or so she said. Newsmen badgered her: What did the message contain? Lady Doyle smiled and replied succinctly: "Oh, it is beautiful and sweet—but private."

The universal reaction to Doyle and his spiritualistic dotage was best summed up in the attitude of Cambridge students who had once waited in vain to hear him lecture. When the distinguished author failed to show up, the students painted a large billboard and paraded across the stage, holding the billboard up to the audience. The placard said: "Sir Arthur Conan Doyle Has Failed to Materialize."

Doris DUKE

Heiress (Born 1912)

Doris Duke's father, James Buchanan Duke, was born in 1856 on a small farm outside of Durham, North Carolina. Duke and his father and brother began to grow, package, and sell tobacco on a limited basis following the Civil War (their farm was wrecked by invading Union troops, all except their small tobacco crop). Some thirty years later, Duke had bullied and bragged his way to the presidency of the giant American Tobacco Company, making himself one of the richest men in America.

A miserly man, Duke spent lavishly on himself but squeezed his employees. In 1904, he married Mrs. William McCredy, a divorcee, but he got rid of her a year later, his divorce based on adultery. Since Duke would not allow an equitable settlement, he spent the rest of his life in court battles with the first Mrs. Duke. His second wife, widow Nanaline Holt Inman, a southern belle from Macon, Georgia, who produced daughter Doris, demanded a lavish life. She hounded her husband into purchasing the Vanderbilt mansion, Rough Point, in Newport, where she attempted to outdo her wealthy neighbors by giving extravagant parties and making a pretentious display of her husband's fortune.

Duke himself was more interested in fattening his ego. He went to Trinity College and told the officials he would support the institution, but there were two conditions: They must change the name to Duke University. The college is now called Duke University. They must also bury him on campus. In 1925 when Duke went to his reward, his body was placed in a marble chapel on the campus. Outside the chapel is a bronze statue of Duke peering across beautiful college grounds named after him. The statute has a large cigar in its hand.

As in death, Duke bought everything in life he wanted. During a business meeting with competitor Pierre Lorillard, friends of Lorillard interrupted and took the financier away to "have some fun," leaving Duke to smolder and finally snort to his secretary, "Guess I'll have to go out and buy me some friends." He did.

Following Duke's death, an estate of more than $70 million (plus a private Pullman car named *Doris*) was left to his thirteen-year-old daughter Doris

Heiress Doris Duke, the Poor Little Rich Girl.

who, along with Barbara Hutton (see entry), later became known as "the poor little rich girl." Barbara had been taught to be stingy, to be zealous in her guardianship of a great fortune, and to mistrust almost everyone. But publicly she complained that being rich was a great burden. As a teenager, she was quoted as saying, "I wish I could go to a store and shop for things just as a girl." Her private convictions were another matter. "People wouldn't have money long," she told a confidant, "if they didn't ask how much things cost and then refuse to buy half of them."

Yet Doris, like her father, saw nothing wrong in self-indulgence. In 1930, with half the nation out of work, the eighteen-year-old Doris Duke debuted at a massive party where three full orchestras serenaded four hundred guests. Her half-brother, Walker Patterson Inman, had already set the pattern of family scandal that was to dog Doris. Inman sued his wife on adultery charges, claiming that the woman had been having three simultaneous affairs, favoring a con man, a crooner, and a bootlegger named Yip.

As the richest heiress in the world, Doris Duke enjoyed a youth fat with real estate—five great estates, four in the United States and one on the French Riviera. The tall blonde with the oversized jaw (which she later had "fixed" in an operation) displayed a paranoia common to the rich of her day, an era when 1930s gangs kidnapped the wealthy for enormous ransoms. Said one reporter, "She can't even go out and shop for a hat without two or three detectives armed with pistols trailing at her heels to protect her."

Her frugal habits in these years marked her as eccentric. Despite her millions, Doris dressed in common fashion and seldom wore jewelry. She carried less cash on her person than would a streetcar conductor. Designer originals were shunned by her. A week before her first marriage in 1937, Doris Duke strolled onto the sands of Palm Beach, "in a red wool bathing suit which she admitted was three years old."

Doris first married James H.R. Cromwell, who later became minister to Canada. At the time of her wedding, Doris bought a sprawling Moorish castle in Hawaii, replete with waterfalls and stone camels guarding the entrance. She was divorced in 1944. "Dee-Dee," as Doris was nicknamed by family members, next married Porfirio Rubirosa, but the playboy was sadly mistaken about the Duke millions. Only hours before the wedding, Doris' lawyers arrived with an

117

unbreakable contract stating Rubirosa was not to have one penny of the Duke fortune. The playboy gulped down several drinks then signed the contract. His spirits lifted when Doris stood at the altar and handed him an expensive gold ring. "Oh boy!" he exclaimed and handed her an inexpensive band. The couple divorced a year later.

Escaping it all, Doris and her boyfriend, John Gomez, later moved into Rudolph Valentino's gloomy Hollywood castle, Falcon's Lair. In recent years, Doris Duke has taken up her mother's interest in Newport, spending her millions on restoring the once resplendent area, a project that caused *Harper's* magazine in 1974 to comment, "The dollars Doris Duke has poured into Newport may be the best she has ever spent."

Isadora DUNCAN

Dancer (1878–1927)

The interpretive dancer, born Dora Angela Duncan, proved herself eccentric from early childhood. She and her mother moved from her birthplace of San Francisco to Chicago when she was a teenager. She had no formal training as a dancer when—billed as "The California Faun"—she performed a dance in a vaudeville show at seventeen, a dance of her own creation. Fortunately, Isadora was seen by impresario Augustin Daly, who hired her for his New York revue, sending her east to study ballet.

Isadora rebelled against the strict form of ballet and soon developed her free form of dancing, combining her own interpretive dancing usually with classical music—such as the works of Beethoven (never meant for the dance)—and often with poetry, which was spoken aloud as Isadora hopped, jumped, glided, and twisted about wearing diaphanous gowns that all but revealed her naked body. (It was reported that she danced naked in Boston, later causing the audience to riot in outrage.) The dancer sometimes wore sandals in her dances, but usually she performed barefoot.

To American audiences, Isadora Duncan was simply "a bad act," and she found universal rejection in the United States. Not until she migrated to Europe was she accepted as an artist. So popular did Isadora become that her ego soared to the point where she claimed to be the incarnation of Aphrodite. In her book *My Life,* Isadora chirped: "I belong to the Gods. My life is ruled by signs and portents which I follow to my set goals."

The dancer also followed every sexual urge that came upon her, having scores of brief affairs before establishing a semipermanent liaison with British-born Gordon Craig, a well-known set designer, in 1904. At the time, Isadora had established a school for interpretive dance at Grunewald. Craig and Isadora produced a child out of wedlock, Deirdre. Six years later, the dancer was in Paris, penniless, her lover gone off. To support herself, Isadora gave occasional performances. After one of these, she received an invitation to

118

Isadora Duncan, as a young dancer.

dine with Paris Singer, the twenty-second child of the dissolute Issac Singer (see entry) inventor of the sewing machine. In this meeting, Isadora saw her manifest destiny—she had been praying that a millionaire would take an interest in her. She and Singer began an affair that lasted three years until, in 1913, her two children, Deidre and Patrick (by Singer, also illegitimate), drowned in the Seine. (When the family chauffeur got out of the Singer limousine to crank the auto, he forgot to apply the brakes, and the car rolled into the river with the two children trapped inside.)

Grief-stricken, Isadora went off on a world tour. In Italy, she met a young artist, by whom she had a child which died in infancy. From then on, Isadora lived a nomadic existence, selecting and discarding lovers at random. Her promiscuity became an international scandal, but her interpretive dancing had set a new standard in the field. She traveled to Russia in 1921, opening a dance school which had been encouraged by the Bolsheviks, but despite its promise, the government never funded the institution, and Isadora was soon starving. She then took up with a poet, Serge Essenin, who was fifteen years younger.

The Duncan–Essenin affair was a raucous, often bloody, almost deadly union. The Russian traveled to the United States with Isadora to appear in interpretive dance performances where she danced and he read his poetry in Russian. The audiences, not understanding one word of his verse and hating the half-naked dances of the aging Isadora, booed and hissed them from the stage, often hurling garbage at them, and on some occasions, threatening to shoot "the dirty reds."

Essenin's inability to understand English (he spoke only Russian) further frustrated the poet, who was already a heavy drinker. He exploded in wild rages against Isadora, his lover and sponsor, and on several occasions made half-hearted attempts to kill her. She in turn, possessing an uncontrollable temper, thought in her most desperate moments to poison Essenin. The pair broke up before either was charged with homicide. The poet committed suicide in 1925.

By the mid-1920s, the dancer had become a curiosity, nerve-jangled, almost mindless at times, her body worn out with dissipation and sexual abuse. While staying with friends in Nice in 1927, Isadora spotted a young man

119

Isadora with her mad Russian poet–lover Serge Essenin.

sitting in a sportscar. She propositioned him on the spot, and he invited her into the car. Sitting beside the driver, Isadora threw back a long flowing red scarf tied tightly about her neck, an item typical of her flamboyant attire. The scarf, blown about in the breeze, wound itself around the spokes of the rear wheel of the car, and when the driver accelerated, Isadora's neck was snapped. She died instantly.

E

George EASTMAN
Inventor (1854–1932)

George Eastman, though he died with an estate of more than $20 million, was a man consumed by great inner fears all his life. He dreaded poverty, which was his lot as a boy and young man. He was afraid of illness, and he shunned cripples and invalids as one would the plague. And most of all Eastman feared death would find him when he was not ready for it.

The inventor, unlike Edison (see entry) and others, produced his marvelous box camera and roller film in 1888 at the age of thirty-four without the help of other craftsmen. In one swift stroke, Eastman eliminated the cumbersome glass plates calling for giant cameras, substituting a small roll of film and a lightweight portable camera, cheaply made and sold at $25 per unit. The original camera was preloaded with film, and once all the pictures were taken, the owner returned the camera and film to Eastman's Kodak firm. There the film was developed, the photos and the reloaded camera were returned to the sender. Eastman's slogan was unforgettable in his advertising campaigns: "You push the button and we do the rest!"

A man of few words, Eastman's sense of humor was terse. When asked about trademarks, in particular his hand-chosen name "Kodak," he replied: "A trademark should be short, vigorous, incapable of being mispelled to an extent that will destroy its identity; and, in order to satisfy trademark laws, it must mean nothing."

Eastman's simple box camera earned him more than $100 million. The inventor began giving away his money to charity almost as fast as he made it. In reality, the soft-spoken man with the spectacles, who preferred to spend most of his time in the study of his Rochester, New York, home instead of his factory, despised money. By the time Eastman reached his sixties, he had risked his life recklessly hunting wild and dangerous animals, from bears in Alaska to tigers in Bengal, a posture that suggested his unwillingness to grow old and possibly become enfeebled.

In the end, George Eastman cheated his enemy, death, and settled his lifelong fears. He had become ill, and to one friend he whispered in motion picture terms, "I think it's best I do a fadeout." The seventy-eight-year-old inventor, having survived untold hazards, sat down in his study and lit a cigar. After a few puffs, he scrawled out the following note:

> To my friends. My work is done.
> Why wait?
> G.E.

With that he put down the pen, removed his glasses, placed a revolver to his temple, and blew out his brains.

Thomas Alva EDISON

Inventor (1847–1931)

As the greatest inventor of the twentieth century, Thomas Edison lit up the world, made it talk on phonographs and put it in motion through his moving pictures. At the time of his death on October 18, 1931, he held more than 1,300 patents in his name. Moreover, he was a man who walked with American giants—Henry Ford, Luther Burbank, Harvey Firestone were all his personal friends. He died a millionaire, yet he never cared for money and never knew how much he had in the bank. He never thought of either food or sleep; he was the perfect workaholic. Aside from his labors as an inventor, Edison had only one other preoccupation—his undying fascination with the psychic world.

Edison was a self-made psychic who naively believed in telepathy to such an extent that he was easily hoodwinked by several charlatans, including Dr. Bert Reese, who faked his mind-reading. Ironically, the inventor was convinced of Reese's ability when the fraud employed a series of lights, a phonograph, and other creations invented by Edison himself to send and receive so-called psychic messages. Edison, thoroughly duped, wrote to his friend, Bernarr MacFadden (see entry) of the New York *Evening Graphic,* praising the phony Reese as a psychic with genuine and startling talents.

Edison himself held theories that any real psychic might question as rational, let alone sane. It was his contention that within the brain cells of the normal human were millions of submicroscopic intelligences, actual entities which the inventor likened to infinitesimal human beings; he called these entities "the little peoples." These "little peoples," according to Edison in the

Thomas Edison demonstrating one of his early model phonographs in the White House, 1878. (Wide World)

Diary and Sundry Observations of Thomas Alva Edison, were frantically busy enacting the chores assigned to them by "master entities," also submicroscopic, who "live in the fold of Broca."

One of the inventions for which Edison never applied for a patent was a secret machine he labored over to the time of his death. The apparatus was designed to eventually communicate with departed spirits, recording their images and messages. Another machine being formed in Edison's exploratory mind at the time would put humans in touch with their mental slaves, "the little peoples."

F

W.C. FIELDS

Comedian (1880–1946)

He was everybody's lovable curmudgeon, a sneaky drinker, a henpecked husband, a pompous skinflint, a bumbling schemer, an inept skirt-chaser. At least that is the image most moviegoers saw when viewing the inimitable W.C. Fields. The portrait was not far from reality, and that film image was only the tip of the Fields iceberg, broken off from a massive glacier of childhood poverty, hardship, and bitterness that would have caused most in his vagrant position to resign themselves to dedicated obscurity. Not Fields. He had the gnawing ambition to thumb his bulbous nose at the world and be paid for it, and he was, handsomely, dying a millionaire, a financial status he never dreamed he would attain.

A vast fortune was far from the mind of the boy born in Philadelphia on January 29, 1880 (according to Marquis *Who's Who,* from material submitted by Fields himself, although he may have arrived a year earlier and altered the date for arcane reasons). William Claude Dukenfield was the first of five children born to Kate Felton and James Dukenfield, a Cockney who left England for America with his parents in the 1870s; within ten years LeRoy, Walter, Elsie Mae, and Adele were born.

As the eldest, William was destined for only four years of formal schooling in Philadelphia, going to work for his father at the age of ten. He hated it. James Dukenfield sold fruit and vegetables from a horse-drawn cart to earn his

W.C. Fields (shown in a still from *The Old Fashioned Way*) began his wild career as a vagrant, then a "professional drowner," then a juggler.

meager living. It was William's job to go ahead of the cart by a block or so, shouting out what his father had to sell that day.

The imaginative William refused to advertise his father's actual wares; to him apples, tomatoes, and cabbage held no magic. So William would bellow out to customers in the street: "Pomegranates! Artichokes! Coconuts!" Every exotic fruit or vegetables he could think of spilled from his tongue. Would-be purchasers who excitedly rushed to the street to discover that James Dukenfield's cart was filled with nothing more than mundane fare would walk away grumbling. When the father discovered what his son had been advertising, he exploded, chasing the boy about the back yard of their miserable Philadelphia home. In hot pursuit of his vexing eleven-year-old offspring, Dukenfield accidentally stepped on a shovel, the end of which jumped up to slam him in the face (in the best tradition of a slapstick the boy would later employ in his acts). Stunned and enraged, the father scooped up the shovel and whacked William so hard on the shoulder that the boy was sent flying across the yard, almost knocked unconscious.

That evening William took his revenge. One report has it that William "got hold of a big box, dragged it into the house, climbed up on a chair, and balanced the box carefully on the top of the door. A few minutes later, when Father Dukenfield came in, *wham*!!—down came the box and crowned him on top of the head." Another version has William hiding in the family tool shed standing on a ladder and when his father enters, slamming the very shovel used on him over his father's head, knocking the old man senseless. No matter. The move was made and William beat a hasty departure— "he took to his heels and ran as fast and as far as his skinny, long legs would carry him. He ran so fast and so far that he never went back again."

The next time James Dukenfield saw his errant son, the boy was a man who had changed his name to W.C. Fields and become known as the greatest juggler in the world. From the moment Fields ran away from his ramshackle Philadelphia home to the point where fame slowly began to close its arms about him, the boy lived a nightmare life. First Fields lived in a large hole in the ground miles from his home, later in large crates. His friends brought him scraps of food sneaked from their own dinner plates. His blanket and shield against rain and snow was a raggedy piece of oilcloth. He took to stealing milk bottles from back porches, being bitten so many times by family pets that he shuddered forever after at the approach of any dog.

When the weather got severe, Fields begged a corner of a heatless blacksmith shop where he curled up in a rag bin. Because of these miserable lodgings, the comedian was forever grateful for laundered linen. Years later he would croak: "To this day when I climb between sheets, I *smile*. And when I get into bed and stretch out—*hot diggety*, is that a sensation!"

The hardships continued for six years, a spectacularly unhappy boyhood pockmarked by dozens of arrests for vagrancy and petty theft—of food and clothes, "survival items," he would later sneer. He became a pariah, chased daily by shopkeepers incensed at his thieving. (Fields felt that it was wise to return to a grocer or haberdasher after already stealing from him; the

Fields in *The Big Broadcast of 1938;* he worried himself sick over going broke and was a notorious drinker on and off the set.

shopkeeper would never expect the same scarecrow of a boy to come back.) During this period of stomach-shrinking vagrancy, Fields developed the lasting fear of poverty that would later make him into a miser, even with loved ones.

The boy's voice changed into a permanent rasp, which may have been caused by his continuous exposure to the elements. He began to hang around pool halls, where he meticulously learned the game and became so expert that he turned into a first-rate hustler, an experience that later stood him in great stead; his pool routines with bent-out-of-shape cuesticks would prove hilarious.

On many occasions, Fields was jumped by irate poolhall victims he had hustled. His nose was broken so many times that it became swollen and misshapen, an enormous proboscis that became a trademark in later days. He finally gave up pool hustling and got a job delivering ice. It was at this time that, whenever his hands were free, he began to juggle. He juggled chips of ice, pebbles, coins, even the small ears of corn that he fed to his horses.

Juggling became an obsession for Fields. He practiced sixteen hours each day, even when he was so sick he could not stand up without staggering about. His fingers bled from juggling, but he went on, juggling tennis balls in barns and apples in blacksmith shops. "A juggler ought to be able to juggle anything he can lift," Fields was later quoted. And so he lifted everything he could and juggled it—biscuits, cigars, candlesticks, bricks, hats, boards, eggs, canes, flatirons, and frying pans.

While delivering ice, Fields developed another habit—drinking. He would begin deliveries at 3 A.M. and stop at noontime. Then he would go to a saloon to order a nickel beer, initially not because he liked to drink but because in the 1890s every saloon offered a free lunch—all you could eat with your beer. Soon Fields began skipping the lunch. He also skipped paying the monthly $3 rent for his attic room, sleeping in the icewagon and pocketing almost all of his $20-a-month pay.

So proficient did Fields become as a juggler that he applied for a job at Plymouth Park outside of Norristown, Pennsylvania. He went on to Fortescue's

Pier in Atlantic City in 1893. By then, he had invented a technique whereby he appeared to lose the items he was tossing in the air, saving them at the last moment. To make extra money, Fields became a professional drowner, an attention-getting stunt that was guaranteed to drum up business. He would wade into the ocean, swim about for a while, then begin floundering about and screaming for help. Crowds rushed to the site to witness the rescue. At such times, Fields' employers would do a brisk business selling the crowd ice cream and hot dogs (not to mention picking a few pockets) before inveigling the curious mob into the theater where Fields would appear minutes later in his juggling act.

Fields loved performing before live audiences. He studied them as he performed, evaluating the paying customers while he went through his comedic act. He later remarked: "I like, in an audience, the fellow who roars continuously at the troubles of the character I am portraying on the stage, but he probably has a mean streak in him, and if I needed ten dollars, he'd be the last person I'd call upon. I'd go first to the old lady and old gentleman back in Row S who keep wondering what there is to laugh at."

Fields' act grew so popular that he was able to get jobs in New York, making his first major appearance at the Globe Museum on Third Avenue. His press notices were good; and the clever Fields clipped them regularly, then went to the owners demanding that his salary be raised from $35 a week to $75. They told him he was crazy. "You're crazy," he bellowed and showered them with his press clippings. He got his salary increase.

It was not until 1898 that Fields wrote to his family in Philadelphia, sending his mother some money. By then he was being billed as "The

Shown with Mae West in *My Little Chickadee*, Fields was a dedicated miser, secreting fortunes in banks under aliases; many of these deposits have never surfaced.

Distinguished Comedian," traveling throughout the country, and earning $125 a week, most of which he banked. The banking habits of W.C. Fields were in keeping with his oddball nature. Though he mistrusted banks, he opened up hundreds of accounts all over the world in the course of his travels. (According to Arthur Knight, for Fields "the most unsettling sight in the world was a bank teller with a hat on"—a promise of imminent departure that Fields later incorporated into one of his best films, *The Bank Dick.)* While in San Francisco, a friend of the comedian's was robbed, which caused Fields to rush to the nearest bank and place his "getaway money" in a safe deposit box. It was Fields abiding fear that he would be stranded somewhere without money—an incident that happened in Ohio when his troupe's business manager absconded with all the funds leaving Fields and other performers destitute. To overcome such future disasters, Fields made sure he would have money anywhere in the world he happened to visit. In his travels, he reportedly opened from two hundred to seven hundred different secret bank accounts, most of them under phony names like "Elmer Mergatroid–Haines." He attempted to keep a record of these accounts; but by the time of his death, many of his notebooks recording these deposits (perhaps as much as $750,000) were lost. In other instances, he simply forgot the crazy, on-the-spot names he had invented for himself, along with the banks he had visited. World events also affected his bank accounts; he had more than $50,000 in a Berlin bank under a bogus name which was lost when the city was gutted by bombing during World War II.

By 1901, Fields had appeared at the Palace Theater in London and performed for King Edward VII. In Paris, he appeared with a young British comic named Charlie Chaplin (see entry), long before Chaplin delighted the world in his films as the little tramp. Fields would later belch his envy of Chaplin as a comedian, even refusing to attend Hollywood parties when he discovered that Chaplin would be present. It was envy mixed with admiration, as was demonstrated once in Fields' peculiar wrath when someone compared him with the little tramp. "Chaplin!" roared Fields. "The son-of-a-bitch is a ballet dancer! He's the best ballet dancer that ever lived, and if I get a good chance I'll strangle him with my bare hands!"

Fields hit his stride as a juggling comedian in 1915, joining the Zeigfeld Follies that year at $200 a week, as well as making his first film, a short called *Pool Sharks* produced by Gaumont, a British firm in New York. In the film, Fields incorporated all the techniques he had learned over the years as a pool hustler, employing a variety of sight gags dealing with slanting tables, impossible shots, and cuesticks shaped like pretzels. But it was with Zeigfeld that Fields made his stellar reputation, becoming a star of the first order. He appeared in the Follies from 1915 to 1921, earning a top salary of $1,000 a week.

He went on to perform in successful plays like *Poppy* before going to Hollywood to enjoy greater riches and fame and make sixteen films—some of them classics. Before this period, W.C. Fields found enough time to marry Harriet Hughes, a union that produced one son, Claude. The comedian had always been leery of women, if not outright distrustful. "Women are like elephants to me," Fields once grumbled. "I like to look at them, but I wouldn't want to own one." His marriage soon went sour, and Fields spent the rest of his life estranged from Hattie Fields who became his financial nemesis. According to the comedian, she was forever making monetary demands on him, and he in turn was forever being "bled" by her. He carped but paid. Most of his correspondence with Hattie over the years was totally given over to money matters.

In his letters to Hattie, the comedian constantly complained that he was either out of work or about to be fired or let go from one show or another, which explained his inability to send her funds. Further, he was full of aches and pains from juggling, he wrote, suffering from all sorts of curious ailments, his favorite being the grippe. Later he told Hattie that his respiration was shot and that it appeared as if his career was over and he would be forced in poverty to go somewhere like Phoenix, Arizona, and "open a small store or manage a theater." This, of course, was untrue; he was paid handsomely, he had secret bank accounts everywhere, and he was in good physical health.

It was true that Fields had been mulcted by theater managers, who demanded kickbacks or so-called commissions, not to mention agents and even fellow performers bartering for the best spots on the bill. To recoup his losses in this area, Fields slept in his dressing room for years and existed on slices of pie. His career did take a slightly downward dip in the mid-1920s; but Fields magnified his troubles to the point of disaster in writing to his estranged wife, telling her he had only "worked seventeen weeks this year," or "don't believe what you read in the newspapers about actors' salaries."

Fields sent his wife regular monthly payments, plus gifts of money for son Claude, but his letters to her always carried a tinge of bitterness in having to fork money over to her. He finally arranged for her to draw a regular stipend from a bank, instructing her to "say you are Hattie Fields, that I informed you that a check would be there every week—They will then tell you to sign your name—When your signature corresponds with the one on this card you will receive $75.00 each week—go on Mondays—Do not tell them the history of your life. Just say what I have told you."

A week later, he was again meticulously explaining his bank payments to her with typical Fields sarcasm: "You will have a drawing account at the Harriman National Bank for $75.00 per week—If you fail to go to the bank for two weeks, you can draw $150—If you do not call for three weeks you can draw $225—Etc. If you do not call for a year you can draw 52 times $75.00. I hope this is lucid."

Fields was as narrow-minded about religion and a hereafter as he was about money. Hattie informed him that his son Claude was praying for his continued good fortune as an entertainer. Fields, as related in *W.C. Fields by Himself,* shot back acrimoniously: "While I appreciate the spirit in which Claude offers prayers for my success I wish he would not bother further. Prayers never bring anything ... They may bring solace to the sap, the bigot, the ignorant, the aboriginal and the lazy—But to the enlightened it is the same as asking Santa Claus to bring you something for Xmas. So please tell him to utilize his time to better advantage." The religious-minded were, in Fields' estimation, suckers; and he was ever mindful of his own words, now a classic line, "Never give a sucker an even break." (This remark is also attributed to Texas Guinan, see entry.) He stressed his antireligious bent in his will when he left instructions to endow the "W.C. Fields College for orphan white boys and girls, where no religion of any sort is to be preached. Harmony is the purpose of this thought."

The comedian's pet peeves mushroomed into enormous and nagging hatreds. He despised medical men of all kinds. "Anytime you go to a Dr. or Dentist they can find plenty wrong with you," he once told Hattie. Politicians were the scum of the earth to W.C. Fields. Elections were the worst kind of frauds: "I never vote for anyone. I always vote against." He loathed IRS and fought a lifelong battle against paying taxes.

By the time Fields began to reach his greatest heights of popularity and income in Hollywood, his drinking—he was a slow imbiber, a man who sipped constantly to retain the permanent buzz—became a humorous wink-and-nudge of moviedom. The classic story of Fields' drinking on the job involves his demands (which were met by directors) that all filming on a set stop around 10:30 A.M., so that he could retire to his dressing room and have his "breakfast," which was a thermos full of orange juice liberally laced with gin. ("I exercise extreme self-control," he once snickered to a friend. "I never have anything stronger than gin before breakfast." To another he quipped: "I must have a drink of breakfast.") Knowing exactly *what* was in the thermos, one director thought to play a joke on the comedian by substituting a thermos that contained nothing *but* orange juice. Moments after the comedian retired for his morning pick-me-up, the door of his dressing room (where he had nailed fifty hats of all varieties to the ceiling for obscure reasons) burst open and an enraged Fields leaped out and dashed onto the set, bellowing, "Somebody's been putting orange juice in my orange juice!" On another occasion, he accused his valet (who doubled as his chauffeur) of appropriating his spirits. He sat glumly holding his head in his hands on the set. "What's the matter, Bill?" asked Gregory LaCava, Fields' favorite director. Moaned Fields, "Somebody left the cork out of my lunch."

All of the comedian's close friends were heavy drinkers, if not dedicated alcoholics—John Barrymore, Gene Fowler, Errol Flynn, and his favorite producer Mark Hellinger, whose capacity for alcohol was astounding, even to such a legendary drinker as Fields. The comedian once remarked, "I got Mark Hellinger so drunk last night that it took three bellboys to put me to bed."

Another legend forever attached to the image of W.C. Fields was his overt dislike of children and animals, at least that was his permanent posture, irrespective of his private thoughts. This attitude was summed up in his unforgettable line: "Anybody who hates children and dogs *can't* be all bad!" The child that received Fields' personal wrath was boy actor Baby LeRoy. Fields resented the boy to the point where he flubbed his lines and lost his composure when on the set with the child actor. Baby LeRoy was a natural scene-stealer; and to the always paranoid Fields, the child was out to ruin him.

In frustration one day, Fields crept into Baby LeRoy's dressing room and spiked the child's morning juice with gin. An hour later, the child's head began to roll lazily upon his shoulders. His eyes became glassy, and he stumbled about like a bindlestiff on a bender. The director shouted "cut!" and ran forward to catch Baby LeRoy before he collapsed. Sneered Fields: "Walk him around, walk him around." The comedian turned to other members of the shocked cast, saying: "The kid's no trouper, no trouper at all. Tell you the truth, I think he's drunk. Disgusting display!"

The director eyed Fields suspiciously as Baby LeRoy was carried off to be revived in his dressing room. "Bill," said the director, "did you do this?"

Fields gave the director his best look of offended dignity, then squinted and rasped: "Me? But Gregory—everyone knows how much I love children!"

When it came to animals, Fields was forever complaining of their presence, particularly dogs, cats, even the swans that he himself had imported for his estate at Toluca Lake, near Burbank, California. His sprawling mansion sat on top of a hill, and his grounds sloped down to the lake where the swans frolicked. Fields threw rocks at them, claiming they were "eating up all my grass." He was later upbraided by a neighbor for shooting at the birds in the area. Holding a rifle in his hand, a straw boater at a rakish angle on his large head, a mean squint to his eyes, the slightly inebriated Fields yelled back at the neighbor over a hedge: "I'll go on shooting the little bastards until they learn to shit green!"

The cantankerous Fields always went into mortal combat on and off the screen with anyone who appeared to challenge his quirks and oddball behavior. His bantering exchanges with Mae West (see entry) in *My Little Chickadee* were legendary, as was his role as the henpecked but valiantly scheming husband in the absolute Fields classic, *It's A Gift*. Later, Fields went into radio, appearing opposite Edgar Bergen's wooden dummy, Charlie McCarthy (the program beginning on May 9, 1937). The comedian came to believe at moments that McCarthy was a real entity insulting him and he would stomp out of the studio threatening to "rent ten thousand termites to take care of that little son-of-a-bitch!" Charlie's attitude, identical to his bulbous-nosed foe's, was expressed in their long-standing feud with the classic slam: "Pink elephants take aspirin to get rid of W.C. Fields!" The comedian usually got the worst of it; but he managed to subdue his inclination to quit the "Chase and Sanborn Hour." His $6,500-a-week salary may have had something to do with his staying on the program.

As was the case in his self-styled movies, Fields walked a tightrope on the radio program, keeping advertisers biting their nails in apprehension that he would slip through something "blue" or offensive. Fields knew this and tortured the sponsors as he did producers by coming as close to the objectionable as possible. The comedian employed cuss words umbilically tied to his brand of comedy such as "drat!" for "damn," and "mother-of-pearl!" Everyone knew what he meant anyway.

Toward the end of his life, Fields enjoyed only three things—drinking with his Hollywood cronies, shooting pool or billiards, and golfing. He had made a film short on golfing which has since become a classic. The comedian was anything but a good sport. If he missed a shot, he would sometimes explode into rages that lasted an hour or break his clubs or threaten to close down a course because it was a "health hazard." Most of his close friends steered clear of the golf courses abused by W.C. Fields. That left only one easy victim to absorb his seething wrath at his poor play—the caddy.

One day on the course, Fields and another duffer were struggling through some difficult holes. They came to a water hole, and Fields, who has having a particularly "vexing day," took careful aim at the ball and drove it straight into a small lake. He swirled about, ready to unleash a string of obscenities at his fellow player, but the adversary refused to look Fields in the eye, maintaining a disinterested stare at the grass beneath his feet. The comedian frantically looked about and spotted the only available scapegoat, his caddy, a young fellow leaning casually on Fields' golf bag.

"Boy!" screamed Fields. "What's the idea of standing in back of me and getting me so nervous?" He pointed to a spot ten yards from where the caddy was standing. The caddy moved to the point indicated by Fields. The comedian put down a fresh ball, and, after his wiggles and shakes, he let loose with a powerful swing that sent the ball soaring, again straight into the lake. No sooner had the ball plopped into the water than Fields spun in a wild rage to glare at the innocent caddy. "Why in the hell are you standing over there, you nincompoop? You're in my line of vision, boy! Go stand over there!" The caddy shook his head in wonder as he walked to the point the comedian had indicated, the very same spot he had been before.

Fields eyed the caddy with out-and-out hatred. "What are you mumbling about, boy?"

"N-n-nothing, Mr. Fields," blurted the caddy in a nervous stammer. "I was only standing where you told me to."

With that, W.C. Fields roared: "Never mind what I told you! You do as I tell you!"

Heavy drinking and overwork contributed to Fields' ill health in the early forties. He was ill for several months in 1946 and finally died—in bed, between crisp clean sheets, in his Pasadena home on December 25, 1946, Christmas Day. He left an estate of about $700,000, but an equal amount was never recovered from his secret bank accounts scattered all over the world. He bequeathed $10,000 to his wife Harriet and an equal amount to his son Claude; his mistress Carlotta Monti received $25,000, along with two bottles of perfume, his Cadillac limousine, and a dictionary. Friends and relatives were awarded small sums, plus his file cabinets and some fly catchers. The rest went to charity.

The comedian was once asked, along with other notables, to write his own epitaph for *Vanity Fair* and he submitted: "I would rather be living in Philadelphia," a quote that is generally believed to be engraved on the bronze plaque at Forest Lawn Memorial Park in Glendale, California, where he is buried. It is not; the plaque contains only his name and dates of birth and death.

Death was not a dark obsession for this magnificent zany, as he lingered bed-ridden. He died the way he had lived, with a caustic quip. The actor **133**

Thomas Mitchell visited Fields shortly before he died, sitting beside the comedian's bed. Mitchell noticed a small black book jutting from the folds of the blanket.

"What's that you're reading there, Bill?" Mitchell inquired.

Fields quickly covered the book with the blanket. "Oh, nothing."

"Let me see that." Mitchell drew back the blanket. "Why, it's the Bible!" Mitchell knew all about Fields' animosity toward organized religion and his much repeated agnostic beliefs, so he found the presence of the Good Book all the more perplexing. "*You* reading the Bible, Bill?"

"Yeah," Fields sheepishly admitted.

"Why?"

Fields gave Mitchell his famous squint, curled his lips, and from the corner of his mouth escaped the line: "I was looking for loopholes!"

Horace FLETCHER

Author (1849–1919)

All of Fletcher's books were devoted to the eater and to proper digestion, which Fletcher insisted could only be brought about through thorough, in fact fanatical, mastication. In his many tomes published early in this century—*Glutton or Epicure; That Last Waif, or Social Quarantine; Fletcherism, What It Is or How I Became Young at Sixty*—Fletcher insisted that "nature will castigate those who don't masticate." In essence, the message of this eccentric was that people could eat anything they liked and that whenever they were hungry they *should* eat. The only necessity for good health, irrespective of problems with obesity, was to chew each mouthful from thirty to seventy times before swallowing.

Food must be reduced to near liquid, the author exhorted, or digestion would quickly be ruined and death would soon follow. Juices, soup, milk, liquids of any kind were to be consumed only after they had been rolled around in the mouth until thoroughly mixed with saliva. Then the liquid, as was the case with solid foods, would become a pure liquid form and would, in essence, "swallow itself."

Thousands of people followed Fletcher's oddball regimen for years until the mastication method became a common joke. Early day Fletcherites included novelist Upton Sinclair (see entry) and philosopher–psychologist William James. Years later, James, who had religiously applied the Fletcher program for three months, remarked: "I had to give it up. It nearly killed me!"

Henry FORD

Industrialist (1863–1947)

He prided himself on being a self-made man, and no American fortune was ever made by a man so insulated from the purchasing public that provided that fortune. In truth, Henry Ford, the pioneer automobile manufacturer, was

Henry Ford, at age thirty-seven, sits at the wheel of one of his brand new Model T's in 1900; he attacked the Jews, ordered his goons to beat up union leaders, and dyed his hair with rusty water. (UPI)

essentially a country bumpkin who epitomized the acerbic portrait drawn by Sinclair Lewis in *Babbitt*. In his peculiar, back-country fashion Ford was a bigot, a miser, an atavistic creature whose contribution to American industry and economy was enormous. Yet he was a shy tyrant with oddball traits that he himself suspected would bring public ridicule who therefore chose, for the most part, a life of semiseclusion.

Born near Detroit on July 30, 1863, Ford grew up a farm boy; but his mechanical aptitude soon drove him to Detroit where he worked in a machine shop, sidelining in the repair of watches. He went on to work for the Edison Illuminating Company, and, while serving Edison as a chief engineer, he began to develop his ideas about internal combustion engines, setting up a workshop in his home to construct such an engine. He built a racing car, the Ford "999," and raced it himself. Later, around the turn of the century, Ford hired crack driver Barney Oldfield to drive the racer.

Oldfield created a national sensation by winning almost every race he entered with the speedy "999," traveling at the then unheard of speed of a mile a minute. These racing achievements established the reputations of both men, Oldfield as a driver and Ford as a multimillionaire manufacturer. The two men met years later, and Ford, in his usual hesitant delivery admitted, "There's no denying it, Barney, you made me and I made you."

Oldfield, who was down on his luck at the time, whipped a cigar from his mouth and snickered, "That's true, Henry, but to be quite honest about it, you must admit that I did a better job with you than you did with me!"

Pioneer racetrack driver Barney Oldfield (shown at wheel of racer) drove Ford's first car the "999" and gave the car manufacturer his reputation.

In 1908, Ford introduced the Model T, a 20-horsepower auto later (in 1913) to be manufactured on his Detroit assembly line. Originally, the Model T sold for about $850, half the cost of a comparable car. For twenty years, this car was *the* American car; almost sixteen million of them were purchased by the public before Ford replaced it with the Model A. The "Tin Lizzie," as the Ford car was dubbed, was undoubtedly the most durable, rugged car ever produced in America, awarding its creator with profits exceeding $10 million a year. With the Model T, Ford announced that "I am going to democratize the automobile, and when I'm through everybody will be able to afford one and about everybody will have one."

In 1914, Ford further made himself into a national hero by raising the daily wage of his auto workers to $5 and reducing the work week to forty hours; he was then paying workers twice what they could get elsewhere. So popular did the industrialist become that he was convinced in the early 1920s that he could handily defeat President Harding, whose administration was then smeared with the Teapot Dome scandal (Ford had unsuccessfully run for a Michigan senate seat by them). Ford's presidential dreams faded when Harding died in office and Coolidge, a man with a pristine reputation, replaced him.

With the muscle flexing of American unions, Ford's reputation quickly changed. The industrialist hated unions and fought to keep them out of his plants. He employed an army of spies, mostly ex-convicts, who reported any worker murmuring the word "union." Not until 1941, after many bloody confrontations between Ford's goons and union workers, were his massive assembly-line factories unionized.

Beyond business, Henry Ford could easily be considered a stone-headed crackpot. Though he was thought to be a mathematical genius, Ford read books like a ten year old and had an abiding contempt for the past, once shouting, "History is the bunk!" (Oddly enough, the Ford Museum in Dearborn is devoted to American history—as Henry Ford saw it, of course.)

The industrialist's quirks were myriad. He dyed his hair with rusty water and early became a health-food fanatic, telling all who would listen that only soybeans, wheat, and carrots were necessary for long life. He was an avowed enemy of alcohol and tobacco. During Prohibition, he swore that he would close down his plants and the world would never see another Ford car "if booze ever comes back." The teetotaling Ford was as adamant about smoking. Like some berserk phrenologist, Ford announced that all criminals could be detected by simply following the trail of tobacco they left, every malefactor being "an inveterate cigarette smoker." To his credit, he was obsessed with protecting birds of all kinds. To his misjudgment, he opposed American entry into World War I, and to that end, he chartered a "peace ship" that sailed about proclaiming Ford pacifism. To his shame, his hatred for Jews led him to a rabid anti-Semitic stance in his private organ, the Dearborn *Independent*.

Ford bought the weekly *Independent* in 1918, beginning a ninety-part series of anti-Semitic articles on May 22, 1920, in which he blamed what he termed "The International Jew" for the woes of the world, claiming that the Jews were trying to take over all important areas of politics and business by fomenting wars, revolutions, and chaos—including the unionization of work- ers. As a basis for his racial complaints, Ford relied heavily on a spurious document entitled *Protocols of the Elders of Zion,* a supposedly historical work outlining the conspiracy of the Jews to control the world. Though Ford dropped his attack on Jews late in 1922 (Jews bought his cars too—quite a lot of them), he resumed his bigoted editorial stance in 1924 and 1925 with personal racial attacks on a Chicago attorney, Aaron Sapiro. The lawyer had established cooperative marketing for farmers, an act Ford saw as part of the "Jewish conspiracy."

Sapiro filed suit against Ford, who quickly settled the matter before an ugly court battle could begin. He next filed a public apology to the attorney in his *Independent* on July 27, 1927. Six months later, Ford ceased publishing his controversial newspaper, although it remained as an ugly reference tool for racial bigots over the next decade. As late as 1938, Father Charles E. Coughlin, the rabble-rousing Catholic priest who stirred up racial hatred over the radio during the 1930s—he was known as "the radio priest"—often quoted Henry Ford's anti-Semitic statements in his diatribes, saying that Ford's slurs "fit in with what's going on."

Following the public outcry against Ford for his idiotic bigotry, the industrialist retreated into less provocative pursuits, busying himself with old-fashioned dances which he attempted to foist upon a 1920s public already crazed with the wild gyrations of the Charleston and the Black Bottom. Ford's penchant ran to the Virginia Reel, and he became so active in organizing square dances that he purchased a $75,000 Stradivarius, taught himself to play "Turkey in the Straw," and not only led his own tightly organized square dances from the bandstand, but also mounted a crusade to reestablish nineteenth-century dances as a mainstream preoccupation. (Of course, Henry Ford thought that modern dances were immoral and that he was riding to the rescue of the American public by reinstituting the kind of music he thought Americans everywhere ought to support. Anything "down home" appealed to the industrialist, including poetry; the cornball verses of Edgar Guest so impressed him that he regularly awarded Guest free cars from his factory.)

Ford invited hundreds of his workers into his sprawling home to participate in his dances, which also included the minuet. He ordered his dealers to play his music in Ford showrooms across the country and encourage potential buyers to dance around the cars they thought to purchase. Ford sponsored radio shows that promoted only his brand of music. The public, however, failed to embrace Ford's music.

The tall, gangling, white-haired Ford practiced his favorite dances incessantly so that he could take to the floor and show his captive visitors exactly how it was done. One internationally known dancer, Ruth St. Denis, famed for her interpretive dances à la Isadora Duncan (see entry), was invited by Ford to one of his "performances." As the industrialist hopped about, grinning and leading a partner in a dance that easily dated from the Revolution, Miss St. Denis began to laugh hysterically, then blurted, "How awful! How awful!"

Ford was unperturbed by the jeering Ruth St. Denis. He went on swirling to his terpsichorean delight almost until the day he dropped dead, on April 7, 1947, leaving a fortune of $600 million.

James Vincent FORRESTAL

Secretary of Defense (1892–1949)

Born in New York of Irish immigrants, Forrestal was a fanatic for success—so deeply dedicated to the idea of rugged individuality that this, among his many manias, bordered on obsession. He first attended Dartmouth then transferred to Princeton, where six weeks before his graduation, he dropped out of school, an act, like so many other unpredictable moves in his life, he never explained. He later stated to his son Peter in a letter reproduced

James V. Forrestal, Secretary of Defense, brilliant, paranoid and suicidal. (Wide World)

in *The Forrestal Diaries:* "I hope you won't look up my own marks in the files [at Princeton] because they were not so hot."

Having a life-long love of the sea, Forrestal enlisted in the Navy as a common seaman at the outbreak of World War I. He later transferred to the Navy Air Corps, which stationed him in Boston; then he moved on to the office of naval operations, never seeing any action abroad. Following the Armistice, Forrestal went to work selling bonds for the investment firm of Dillon, Read. Like John P. Marquand's H.M. Pulham, Esquire, he became a man solely devoted to his work, slaving eighteen to twenty hours a day for his firm. Though he married and had three sons, Forrestal generally ignored his family. He had many affairs, but they never really put his marriage in hazard.

Forrestal rose rapidly at Dillon, Read, becoming the firm's president at the age of forty-seven. He was soon regarded in the nation's top business circles as the wonder boy of Wall Street. His abiding interest in naval matters, his reputation as a ruthless financier, and his ultra right-wing patriotism made him a good candidate for the position of undersecretary of the Navy, an appointment made by President Roosevelt. (Forrestal had been born and raised in upper New York State only twenty miles from where Roosevelt had been raised.) The position the aggressive Forrestal assumed was especially created for him by an act of Congress. He was sworn in on August 22, 1940. He later took over the position of secretary of the Navy, replacing Frank Knox, and ultimately became the nation's first secretary of defense.

Throughout Forrestal's distinguished career with the government, the man drove himself night and day. He had no time for his wife or sons and expected his boys to assume responsibility at an early age, albeit his demands were often ridiculous. At one point, Forrestal received a phone call from two of his sons, who at the time were six and eight. They were stranded at the airport in Paris. Their father, who was in London at the time, curtly informed them that "you straighten it out yourselves, then come on to London."

James Vincent Forrestal had no time for politicking or leisure. He hated making speeches, and he usually said only a few words at public functions. He hated attending social gatherings even more. The longest time he ever spent at one party—his presence was timed by onlookers—was eight minutes, long enough to shake the hands of the host and hostess, gulp a dry martini, and wave goodbye to all.

Less than a year after taking his post as secretary of the Navy in March 1945, Forrestal began writing a series of enigmatic notes in his journal and sending inexplicable memorandums to subordinates. One diary entry dealt with what Forrestal captioned "Specifications for a Presidential Candidate"; and beneath these words, he scribbled something about physical attributes, particularly "looks," "political background and experience," and "height." (Forrestal may have been measuring himself for the job; his short stature had bothered him since his college days when he was nicknamed "Runt.")

A merciless foe of communism, Forrestal began to see communists behind every tree and shrub. He felt that the communist conspiracy during the "red scare" of the late 1940s was aimed directly at him. On April 1, 1949, Forrestal wept openly and uncontrollably while being decorated with the Distinguished Service Medal by President Truman, who was extremely disturbed by Forrestal's behavior.

In the weeks following his presidential citation, Forrestal became a raving paranoid, claiming that all his phones were "bugged." Many of his friends later stated that his erratic behavior increased alarmingly in early 1949, spawned by a burglary in his Washington, D.C. home, when his wife was held at gunpoint and forced to turn over her valuables.

By early spring 1949, Forrestal told everyone that communist spies were everywhere, detailing his every move, taking his picture from hiding places, following him down Washington streets and through parks. He could not escape them. His paranoia went unchecked and unexplained. He checked into a sixteenth-floor suite at the Bethesda Naval Hospital to "rest." On May 22, 1949, Forrestal suddenly leaped from his bed and hurled himself from a window of his bedroom, falling sixteen stories to his death.

William FRAWLEY

Actor (1887–1966)

A feisty American character actor with a long history in vaudeville, Frawley broke into motion pictures in a 1933 film entitled *Moonlight and Pretzels*—brought to Hollywood sight-unseen from the New York stage by MGM. The cigar-chomping, wise-cracking Frawley (a role he usually duplicated in all his parts as drunks or incompetent cops and politicians) was ushered into the spacious offices of film magnate Irving Thalberg. The young movie tycoon took one look at Frawley and gasped.

"My God!" Thalberg pointed a trembling hand at the actor's shiny, bald dome. "You don't have a hair on your head!"

Frawley, in typical manner, jerked the cigar from his mouth and snarled: "Yeah, well, if you wanted hair why didn't you hire a lion!"

From that moment on, Frawley's sassy ways and oddball behavior made him a landmark loony in moviedom. Whenever he went on the town (which was most nights), he proved that he was one of the toughest actors in the business. Frawley would never shun a fistfight, and he loved brawls. He was also known as the most penny-pinching actor in Hollywood, an image that did not change even when he scored his greatest success in his nine-year stint on the popular *I Love Lucy* TV show (1951–1960).

Of the many stories of Frawley's strange escapades the Hollywood tramp tale epitomizes the actor's eccentric behavior. The tramp, a cunning fellow, had noticed that Frawley walked to and from work every day, a habit that saved the actor a considerable expense in cab fare. And every day for a year, the tramp waited for Frawley on the same corner, ready to deliver the same tired line in the same boozy voice, croaked to Frawley on schedule. As the bantam tugboat-like actor scurried up to him, the bum would say, as if to a stranger: "Hey, Mac. You gotta dollar?"

Frawley, never known for his generosity, looked over the sleazy bum, noticing the ragged, stained clothes, the moth-eaten hat, the sole-flapping shoes, as he had done every day for a year. Without a murmur, the actor dug into his pockets and produced a dollar, which he thrust into the bum's outstretched hand.

"Here," Frawley said in his gravel voice and hurried on. But one time, the ritual was unexpectedly changed when Frawley suddenly wheeled about and went back to the bum, who was then hurriedly pocketing the dollar. Frawley took the habitual cigar from his curled-down mouth. "Say, fella," he growled. "I wanna ask you one question."

"Yeah?" answered the bum in a surly voice.

"Every day for a year now I've been comin' past this corner and every day for a year you put the bite on me. Not for just a quarter, mind you, or even a half dollar, but a dollar, a whole dollar every damned day!"

"So?"

"So—I wanna know what the hell you do with the dollar I give you every day."

"You do, huh?" The bum curled his lips in defiance.

"Yeah, I do!" Frawley pushed his prominent jaw into the bum's face.

"Well, I'll tell you, Mac," the bum replied matter-of-factly. "I put it in my pocket and then walk down the street and up a couple of blocks to a bar I know. I put that buck on the counter and then get as drunk as I can with it. That's what I do with your dollar every day, Mac."

Frawley beamed with delight. "You know," he grinned. "I like you. I've been hit by the best con men and rollers in the business but they all got a line. Lost their carfare. Wanna eat. Need to call Buffalo, New York and talk to mom. But not you—why, you're honest, fella." The actor paused, enjoying a discovery never shared by the questing Diogenes. Then he blurted: "You know what I'm gonna do?"

"No, whatya gonna do?"

"I'm gonna buy you a drink! C'mon."

The bum at first stared in genuine amazement, then he composed himself and buttoned his suit in a dignified manner, following the cocky Frawley down the street. The actor headed for his favorite watering hole, the elegant Brown Derby, where a table was always reserved for him.

No one was more shocked than the maitre d' of the Brown Derby when he spotted Frawley entering the bistro with a smelly, unshaven, ragged bum. A headwaiter nervously showed Frawley and his unwashed friend to the actor's special booth, while Hollywood's high society gasped.

"Now, fella," said Frawley to his newfound friend, "I'm buyin' you a drink in the fanciest joint in Hollywood ... just for bein' honest with me."

The bum did not reply, maintaining his aloofness.

When the headwaiter approached to take Frawley's order, the actor said with a loud voice and great fanfare, "Two scotch and sodas."

"I'll have the same!" demanded the bum.

"Why you sonofabitch!" yelled Frawley, turning red and hitting the bum square on the jaw, knocking him cold.

To William Frawley, one of Hollywood's most entertaining oddballs, honesty was one thing; ingratitude was decidedly another.

G

Marshall B. GARDNER

Author (1854–1937)

Gardner, who worked as a foreman in a corset factory in Aurora, Illinois, published his own book, *Journey to the Earth's Interior,* in 1913. Though he vehemently denied that he based his beliefs on the theories of John Cleves Symmes (see entry), advanced a century earlier, Gardner claimed that the earth was hollow and that beneath an eight-hundred mile crust was a small sun six hundred miles in diameter which provided twenty-four hours of daylight. One could enter the inner earth, Gardner insisted, through openings at both the North and South Poles that were fourteen hundred miles wide.

All planets were of a similar construction, said Gardner, pointing to the ice caps on Mars as actual openings which at times emitted bright lights from its interior sun. This same kind of light on earth came from its inner sun, which created the *aurora borealis.*

Gardner's theories were embraced by thousands of readers, who paid considerable sums to hear him lecture, mostly in Southern states. His book became the centerpiece for a popular cult; and new and revised editions were periodically published, the most costly produced in 1920. Gardner, a heavyset man with black walrus mustache, claimed that his theories about a hollow earth were based on "solid facts ... of course it is very easy for anyone to deny all the facts of science and get up some purely private explanation of the formation of the earth," he wrote. "The man who does that is a crank."

When Admiral Richard Byrd and Floyd Bennett flew over the North Pole on May 9, 1926, on an expeditionary flight which proved there was no opening, Gardner went into retirement.

143

Frank GARNER

Jockey (1875–1928)

A splendid jockey, Garner was also the most infamous tightwad in the history of turfdom. He never tipped his grooms, he haggled fees from owners, and he went so far as to buy the cheapest saddles made. But so overwhelmed was Garner when he rode Typhoon to a slashing win during the 1897 Kentucky Derby that, losing his head in the winner's circle for the first and last time in his life, the jockey invited everyone in the racetrack community—trainers, grooms, racetract touts, and stable boys—to join him in a victory dinner.

Some hours later Garner, grown pensive and somber, was seated in one of Louisville's finest restaurants, more than a hundred ravenous guests eyeing him as he stood up. "Listen friends," he lamely announced. "This is a special occasion and I want all of you to have a good time and eat well. So all of you order something fancy and extra special."

The crowd was dumbfounded. Finally one old trainer croaked: "Aww, you order for us, Frank."

An expression of great relief flooded the jockey's face. Garner grabbed a waiter by the arm and shouted: "Bring us one hundred dollars worth of ham and eggs, fancy and extra special!"

"Colonel" Dinshah Pestanji Framji GHADIALI

"Physician" (1873–date uncertain)

Born in Bombay, Ghadiali immigrated to the United States in 1911 and became a citizen six years later. During World War I, Ghadiali served with the New York Police Reserve Air Service, refusing to accept pay for helping to patrol New York harbor. He took the title of "colonel" from this experience, a wholly invented rank.

Some time in 1920, the colonel constructed what he called the Spectro-Chrome machine, which he claimed could cure all forms of diseases and ailments, including diabetes, gonorrhea and nymphomania. All users had to do was follow Ghadiali's diets and then bathe themselves under the colored lights of his machine and they would be cured. The colonel was careful to point out that though his lights never failed, a patient could slip back into his ailment if he did not eat properly—and that meant refraining from alcohol, tea, coffee, tobacco, and meat of all kinds. It was also imperative that patients sleep with their heads pointing north. Any deviation from Ghadiali's regimen would mean failure.

The quack set up his clinic in Malaga, New Jersey; and despite his obvious crackpot theories and bogus lights, he drew thousands of desperately ill people to his machines with the flashing colored lights. So successful was Ghadiali that he went on the lecture circuit in 1925, gleaning a fortune from new suckers. He took along a teenage companion, whom he introduced to one and all as his secretary. When the couple visited Seattle to lecture, the girl went to the police and stated that the "genius scientist" had raped her. Ghadiali was prosecuted under the Mann Act and sent to the Atlanta Penitentiary for five years.

While in prison, Ghadiali angrily penned *Railroading a Citizen,* later published in two volumes. In his book, the quack claimed that he had been persecuted by Henry Ford, the Department of Justice, the KKK, Negroes, and Catholics. He also insisted not only that his teenage secretary had lied but that the girl had raped *him!*

Upon his release, the colonel returned to New Jersey to resume his Spectro-Chrome therapy, selling memberships in his so-called "Institute" for $90 apiece, herding more than ten thousand gullible people into his scheme. Members were entitled to use one of Ghadiali's fantastic machines for a few weeks to cure their universal ailments. For those wishing to study at his institute, another $250 was required.

Ghadiali's institute was finally closed down after the government proved that several persons had died while using his colored-lights machine. One witness testified that his father had been ordered by Ghadiali to stop using insulin. The father, a severe diabetic, died within a month. Although the quack was fined $20,000, he continued to open up his institute again and again until his retirement in the late 1950s.

Clemente GIGLIO

Theater Owner (1886–1943)

To promote his New York theater, Giglio hired publicist Sam Berg in early 1937, instructing the unemployed press agent that he was to "tell everyone I'm a humanitarian." When Berg inquired as to Giglio's humanitarian acts, the theater owner said that he wanted to save six young killers who had murdered a subway conductor in 1935 from the electric chair. "Why all six?" asked Berg. "Because they got a lot of friends and relatives and I'm going to offer my theater to these people to pray that the boys don't get the chair."

Berg's first move was to encourage relatives and others to write to Governor Herbert H. Lehman, begging the governor to commute the death sentences of the killers. When Giglio heard of this tactic, he upbraided Berg for not "going over the airways where they will mention my theater." He directed Berg to make sure that all future letters written on behalf of the murderers were sent to him; *he* would send them on to the governor in Albany.

"Look," Berg said, trying to reason with his crackpot employer, "why don't you get the famous Chicago lawyer, Clarence Darrow, to defend these guys?"

"Why should we get Darrow?" exploded Giglio. "I need to be on the front pages, not that guy!"

Clemente Giglio (standing) exhorting women to pray for the release of condemned killers.

Giglio finally got his front page coverage when he led more than two hundred persons rounded up by Berg to the Park Avenue residence of Governor Lehman the day before the executions were to take place. The beefy, wild-eyed theater owner ordered everyone "down on your knees—pray like hell!" A chorus of prayers followed, which the governor heard. He looked out the window to see the throng on their knees, women and children tearfully looking up to him. The governor pardoned four of the six killers.

Berg arrived in Giglio's office some days later with the press clippings mentioning the humanitarian theater owner, many of the stories running pictures of Giglio's theater and a grinning Giglio leading the prayer meeting outside the governor's home. Berg asked for his fee of $2,000.

"I'm not paying," grumbled Giglio.

"Why not?"

"You didn't get me in the newsreels!"

Berg took the flamboyant Giglio into court, where a small settlement was finally made.

Samuel GOLDWYN

Film Producer (1882–1974)

Born in Poland, Goldwyn ran away from his miserable home in Warsaw at an early age, somehow managing to travel to London. From there, the thirteen-year-old boy immigrated to the United States, where an official interpreted his unpronounceable name as Goldfish. Sam Goldfish moved to Gloversville, New York, and learned the trade of selling gloves. He became a dandy, wearing the finest clothes he could purchase on his $3-a-week salary. He was thirty before he saw his first movie, wandering into a New York theater on Herald Square. He watched a Bronco Billy Anderson western with fascination.

The story is told that Goldwyn went to the manager at the film's end, asking about the theater's operation. After listening to the man, Goldwyn blurted: "You mean you give nothing away, the customer walks out with nothing? He pays to watch a film which you keep and show over and over to new customers. What a wonderful business."

Goldwyn (he took the name of a movie company he later formed with partner Edgar Selwyn, combining both his own and Selwyn's names) went into the movie business in 1912 in partnership with his brother-in-law, Jesse Lasky, who had been a vaudeville producer, and Lasky's vaudeville director, Cecil B. DeMille, along with the established cowboy star, Dustin Farnum. The new movie producers intended to make their first film in Arizona and sent DeMille on location. He wired his partners in the East: "Flagstaff no good for our purpose. Have proceeded to California. Want authority to rent barn in place called Hollywood for 75 dollars a month."

DeMille got his approval; and not only was Goldwyn's first film, *The Squaw Man,* an enormous success, but it established Hollywood as the future capital of American motion pictures. Goldwyn's temperamental attitude, however, proved a strain on the relationship with Lasky and DeMille, particularly when Adolph Zukor also became a partner. The others bought Goldwyn out for $900,000—only a few years after he had been selling gloves for $35 a month.

Vowing never to have partners again, Goldwyn went on to great success as one of Hollywood's leading independent producers of quality movies—trusting more to his instincts than to any other factor to produce hits. He was also the best friend any writer ever had in Hollywood, insisting that "the story comes first," then the directors and actors. For an actor or actress to appear in a Goldwyn film meant reaching the top of Hollywood's star system.

Sam Goldwyn's greatest eccentricities emanated from his mouth. He garbled ideas and thoughts at every turn, providing so many non sequiturs that he became the king of malapropism in America. For years Goldwyn merely shurgged when his personally minted non sequiturs were brought up to him. Later, when he insisted on dignity, he thundered: "None of them are true. They're all made up by a bunch of comedians and pinned on me." But most of them were true.

A sample of classic Goldwynisms:

When withdrawing from the board of the Hays Office over a policy disagreement: "You can include me out!"

When calling Selznick at midnight (Goldwyn's favorite time to place phone

Producer Sam Goldwyn, the master of malapropisms.

calls): "David, you and I are in terrible trouble!" Selznick became genuinely worried, asking, "What's the matter, Sam?" The producer's response was, "You've got Gable and I want him!"

When coming upon a sundial at a Hollywood lawn party and being told how it worked: "Marvelous! What will they think of next?"

When being asked by Marion Davies why he was so depressed: "You just don't realize what life is all about until you have found yourself lying on the brink of a great abscess."

When asked to write his autobiography: "Oh, no. I can't do that—not until long after I'm dead."

When sitting down to a conference: "I had a monumental idea this morning, but I didn't like it."

When proposing a film idea to his writers: "I want to make a picture about the Russian secret police—the G.O.P."

When making conversation at a party: "Any man who goes to a psychiatrist should have his head examined."

When directing personnel on Goldwyn productions: "Our comedies are not to be laughed at!" and "Let's bring it up-to-date with some snappy nineteenth century dialog," and "I read part of it all the way through," and "For this part I want a lady—somebody that's couth," and "I can answer you in two words—impossible!" and "The trouble with these directors is they're always biting the hand that lays the golden egg," and "The publicity for this picture is sweeping the country like wildflowers."

Goldwyn was a tenacious businessman, but he sounded like a buffoon at times, telling one subordinate: "You've got to take the bull between your teeth." On another occasion, he bellowed: "In this business it's dog-eat-dog and nobody's going to eat me!"

Perhaps one of the greatest Goldwynisms involved his finest picture, *The Best Years of Our Lives*. The producer called a phalanx of newsmen together for a press conference to announce his master film achievement. Said Sam Goldwyn to the reporters: "I don't care if it doesn't make a nickel, I just want every man, woman and child in America to see it!"

Waxey (Irving Wexler) GORDON

Gangster (1892–1958)

Gordon, born Irving Wexler in New York's Hell's Kitchen, began his criminal career as a strikebreaker for Arnold Rothstein, who controlled labor racketeering in New York before Prohibition. When liquor became illegal in 1919, Gordon borrowed $175,000 from Rothstein and set himself up as a bootlegger, becoming a millionaire and a blood enemy of Dutch Schultz. He was sent to prison on tax evasion in 1933 after declaring an annual income of a little more than $8,000 when federal agents proved he paid $6,000 rent a year on a luxury Manhattan apartment and boasted a library of unopened books worth $4,000. At this time, Gordon's yearly income ranged upward of $500,000.

Mobster Waxey Gordon (alias Irving Wexler) thought himself a great judge of talent. (Wide World)

The bootlegging Gordon fancied himself a great judge of theatrical talent and spent almost all his spare time—when not out in the streets shooting it out with rival gangsters—developing his ideas for Broadway musicals, many of which he backed, losing fortunes. The shows were terrible flops, and entertainers knew they would be before they worked in a Gordon show, but the price was right. Gordon had a dozen mistresses at a time, all long-legged chorus girls he tried to make into singing or dancing stars. One of his favorite whims was to give parties after the theater closed. He would sit in the audience alone and have the complete cast perform the entire musical for his benefit, often climbing to the stage to dance crazily with the chorus line. Following the command performance, Gordon would order in catered meals and champagne, served by waiters from the best restaurants in New York.

"I can smell real talent a mile off," Gordon boasted. He would audition singers, dancers, and actors in his swanky offices then sign them to contracts. Those chosen would be sent to a Gordon club or theater to perform; but often as not, the gangster would send his clients to Hollywood to break into movies, owning a piece of their motion picture income. One such client was George Raft.

It was estimated that throughout the fabulous 1920s Gordon lavished more than $5 million on his theatrical productions and "discoveries," few of whom ever made headline status. Later in life, the self-styled impressario became philosophical about it all: "I guess most of them entertainers I promoted did stink, but I had fun doing it."

Joseph Ferdinand GOULD

Author (1889–1957)

Of all the eccentric Bohemians that have wandered through the narrow streets of Greenwich Village, the most lastingly memorable were Maxwell Bodenheim (see entry) and Joe Gould. Born in Norwood, Massachusetts, on

149

September 12, 1889, Gould was encouraged by his father, a doctor, to take up the family profession. But hard work and professional goals were far from the zany notions of Joe Gould.

Upon his graduation from Harvard in 1911, Gould drifted about the country. Then he got the notion that he was a eugenics expert, although none of his previous studies qualified him as such. He borrowed money from his mother and traveled to North Dakota where, in his own words, he "began measuring the heads of Indians. In January and February 1916 I measured the heads of five hundred Mandan Indians on the Fort Berthold Reservation, and in March and April I measured the heads of a thousand Chippewas on the Turtle Mountain Reservation, and then my money ran out. I wrote and asked my mother for more and I received a telegram from her sending me train fare and telling me to come home at once ... I really had enjoyed measuring heads."

Gould attempted to raise more funds in Boston to continue his head-measuring expeditions, but he was unsuccessful. He drifted down to New York's Greenwich Village with the idea of becoming a drama critic for one of the newspapers. Failing that, he intended to write novels, plays, essay, poetry. Others tell a different story about Gould's departure from Boston. In *Garrets and Pretenders,* Albert Parry indicated that Gould was as a literary hooligan, run out of the city for his violent attacks on authority. "Joe Gould," wrote Parry, "a freak from Harvard, tried to kick the shins of some Boston policemen, but the city did not applaud, and poor Joe migrated to New York to become a permanent fixture of Greenwich Village."

To pre-World War I Bohemians in the Village, Joe Gould presented an odd-looking appearance. He stood only five feet four inches and weighed no more than one hundred pounds. Turned down by the newspapers as a drama critic, he wound up as a glorified copy boy for police reporters, running copy from precinct stations back to the offices of the *Evening Mail*. Gould, drinking heavily, gave up the job since he found it impossible to run with head-cracking hangovers.

He began submitting essays and poems to various little magazines in the Village. His most memorable verse was short, sweet, and indicative of his lifestyle:

> In the summer
> I'm a nudist
> In the winter
> I'm a Buddhist

For years, Gould submitted material to New York magazines and newspapers, finding universal rejection. He was once asked by Burton Rascoe, book editor of the *Tribune,* to review a book on American Indians. Gould turned in a review that was hundreds of pages long and unpublishable. For a decade, Joe— by then sporting a scraggily beard—all but moved into the offices of the *Dial,* a small literary journal, pestering and nagging the editors to consider some of his essays. In despair of ever getting rid of Gould, the editor finally accepted and published one of his essays entitled "Civilization." Gould's stormy and undisciplined prose indicted the whole of modern society. To him the stock market was "a fuddy-duddy old maid's game," skyscrapers and ocean-going ships were "bric-a-brac," and the "auto [was] unnecessary." He summed up his rancor with a plea for his favorite beast of burden: "If all the perverted ingenuity which was put into making buzz-wagons [cars] had only gone into improving the breed of horses humanity would be better off."

A copy of the *Dial* carrying Gould's meandering social thoughts was bought for ten cents by a struggling writer in Fresno, California, some months later—a twenty-year-old scribe named William Saroyan. Gould's piece, Saroyan later claimed, influenced him mightily and "freed me from bothering about form." Years later, when Saroyan was an established author, he visited friends in Greenwich Village and asked if Joe Gould was still living, adding that he owed him a great debt. He was told yes, but no one ever knew where Gould was staying. Gould's usual abode for the night was a parking lot or a subway platform; by that time he had become a master bum and panhandler.

A friend stopped Gould some days later as he walked a Village street, telling him that the great Saroyan had been looking for him, that his 1929 essay had set Saroyan on his literary career. Gould merely shrugged and moved off to rummage through some garbage cans. Some days later, however, Gould appeared in his habitual ragged suit, smelling of fish and other foul odors, in front of the Hampshire House where Saroyan was staying, and demanded to see the famous author.

The doorman barred the way. "Do you know Mr. Saroyan?"

"No, but that's all right. He's a disciple of mine."

"What do you mean?" queried the puzzled doorman. "A disciple?"

"I mean that he's a literary disciple of mine. I want to ask him to buy me some teeth." Gould opened his mouth to display his toothless gums.

"Teeth? What do you mean some teeth?"

"I mean some store teeth, false teeth."

"Sure, sure. Right this way." The doorman grabbed Gould by the arm and dragged him to the street, telling him to play his jokes on someone else.

Gould eventually did meet Saroyan, but the encounter was less than rewarding for the toothless Joe. By then, everyone in the Village had learned that Gould was writing what he called "The Oral History of the World" and that for years he had been filling up school notebooks—hundreds (perhaps thousands) of notebooks that totaled nine or more million words wherein he had copied every spoken word he had heard since his arrival in the Village. Saroyan was fascinated by this project, and he could talk of nothing else when he finally met Gould. "Saroyan kept saying that he wanted to hear all about the Oral History, but I never got a chance to tell him," Gould later remembered. "I couldn't get a word in edgewise." He also didn't get any "store teeth" from Saroyan.

No matter what Gould's physical condition, he was forever lugging around a portfolio of his notebooks; and even after his death, his lovingly recorded "Oral History" was sought for possible publication—but to no avail. Only scattered fragments were ever seen, and these were thought to be nothing more

151

than the ravings of a much-glorified tramp. Writing in the New York *Sun*, Samuel Putnam stated: "The young after-1929 American ... realizes somehow, subtly, that Al Capone and the Lindbergh baby have more to do, ultimately, with literature and the literary life than all the Joe Goulds in Greenwich village."

But Greenwich Village thought of Joe Gould as its personal living relic of 1920s Bohemianism. For decades he was a fixture at almost every Village party, arriving uninvited, eating and drinking his fill, and, when drunk, stripping to the waist to display an emaciated body. At such times, he would perform his wild Indian dance, which he dubbed "The Joseph Ferdinand Gould Stomp." At other times, according to Allen Churchill in *The Improper Bohemians*, Gould "would imitate a sea gull by skipping, cawing and flapping his arms. His startling proficiency at this gained him the bar name Professor Seagull."

The other full-time Village eccentric, Maxwell Bodenheim, witnessed Gould's antics at endless parties and marveled at "his tonsured head, piebald ecclesiastical beard, and bent, shrunken frame ... like a fugitive from a medieval monastery."

Whenever he could, Gould cadged drinks and food. He was tolerated at the Minetta Tavern, where bartenders looked the other way as Gould emptied the drinks left on the bar by the patrons. He was sometimes given a free drink, but bartenders did not wish to encourage him, so the "one on the house" came usually once a month. He encouraged pretty girls to kiss his bald pate, explaining to their escorts that following this Village tradition it was customary for the escort to buy him a drink. If the drink was not forthcoming, Joe merely shrugged and pulled the stunt on the next couple. Such behavior earned Gould the reputation of being *the* Village eccentric. To his biographer, Joseph Mitchell, Gould was "nonsensical and bumptious and inquisitive and gossipy and mocking and sarcastic and scurrilous."

Indulgent restaurant owners allowed Gould into their kitchens so that he could argue the cooks into a free sandwich. His favorite eating spas in the Village were Hubert's and Stewart's, both cafeterias. Employees would see Gould coming and hide the ketchup bottles; he invariably filled up several cups of hot water and poured in the ketchup to make tomato soup. "It's the only grub I know that's free of charge," he once said.

On one occasion, a heavy-set waitress upbraided Gould for using up all the ketchup bottles in sight to make free soup.

Joe grew indignant. "This is something you people don't get through your heads—I'm not just an ordinary person. I'm Joe Gould. I'm Joe Gould the poet. I'm Joe Gould the historian. I'm Joe Gould the wild Chippewa Indian dancer. And I'm Joe Gould, the greatest authority in the world on the language of the sea gull. I do you an honor by merely coming in here, and what do you do in return but bother me about such things as ketchup!"

The heavy-set waitress glared down on the gnome-like Gould and then bellowed: "Who do you think you are, you little rat? One of these days I'm gonna pick you up by that Joe Gould beard of yours and throw you out of here."

"Try it, and it will be you and me all over the floor," responded Joe, but with little enthusiasm.

Though Joe smoked cigarette butts he found on the street, he smoked them through an elegant cigarette holder. Though Joe kept warm at night by stuffing newspapers into his threadbare suit, he would only use the New York *Times* for such purposes ("Because I'm a snob at heart"). And always he had his pride in his old-line Massachusetts heritage, booming to strangers who had offended him: "The Goulds were the Goulds when the Cabots and the Lowells were clamdiggers!"

Joe Gould was no mealy-mouthed bindlestiffed moocher to Joe Gould. He *entertained* his victims; and for that, he felt he was deserving of their patronage. Entering a Village tavern, Gould would pretend to look up a phone number but would really scan the customers, selecting a well-dressed prospect. According to Joseph Mitchell, he would approach the victim and with a flourish state: "Let me introduce myself. The name is Joseph Ferdinand Gould, a graduate of Harvard, *magna cum difficultate,* class of 1911, and chairman of the board of Weal and Woe, Incorporated. In exchange for a drink, I'll recite a poem, deliver a lecture, argue a point, or take off my shoes and imitate a seagull. I prefer gin but beer will do." He invariably received his glass of beer.

And whenever Joe Gould begged or demanded food, depending upon his disposition at the moment, he made a point of scraping up whatever breadcrumbs he could find in restaurant kitchens or on the plates left in diners and cafeterias. These crumbs he faithfully took to the birds flocking in Washington Square. Only one other activity consumed Gould's waking hours— and that was his daily entries in his "Oral History."

By 1953, Gould's health, never fair, began to fail; and he was confined in the Pilgrim State Hospital, in Brentwood, Long Island. He was becoming senile, his kidneys were failing, he suffered constant ear and stomach aches. He was plagued by bursitis, boils, chills, and severe conjunctivitis (pinkeye). The complete Bohemian lingered for four years until August 18, 1957, dying at the Pilgrim State Hospital.

Professor Seagull, the Last of the Bohemians, as the newspaper obituaries labeled Gould, was friendless at the end. Not a single person claimed his body. The Greenwich Village Lions Club finally agreed to pay for his funeral.

The massive "Oral History," which some said was secreted in Village basements or as far away as a farm in Huntington, was never located (if it ever really existed beyond a few fragments). Joe Gould felt that this enormous work would be a lasting monument to his name. He once said: "A couple of generations after I'm dead and gone the Ph.D's will start lousing through my work. Just imagine their surprise. 'Why, I be damned,' they'll say, 'this fellow was the most brilliant historian of the century.' They'll give me my due. I don't claim that all of the Oral History is first class, but some of it will live as long as the English language."

Dr. James GRAHAM

Physician (dates uncertain)

Graham, who operated as a quack in London in the 1780s, opened what he called the Temple of Health and Hymen, guaranteeing patients that he would cure all manner of nervous and sexual problems. His feature attraction was a "Celestial Bed" over which "presided" one Emma Lyons, later to become Lady Hamilton and finally mistress to Lord Nelson. Use of this bed cost 100 pounds. The bed cost 60,000 pounds, Dr. Graham claimed; and other beds in his sex clinic had set him back equal amounts. Should a customer be dissatisfied with his performance with Miss Lyons in the Celestial Bed, he could adjourn to the 50-pound-a-night Magneto-Electric bed which Graham insisted would restore any man's virility.

Authorities soon closed down Graham's glorified whorehouse and sent the quack packing.

Harry GREB

Boxer (1894–1926)

A great middleweight champion (1923–1926), Greb changed his name from Berg by spelling it backward, to avoid the then prevalent anti-Semitic feeling of boxing fans. He was known as "The Pittsburgh Windmill," because he threw whirlwind punches, hammering opponents with overhand blows that generally resulted in knockouts.

Greb had lost an eye during World War I, having it replaced with a glass orb. The fighter would often remove his eye in the middle of a fight, and,while his opponent stood motionlessly mesmerized, he would knock the man out. A strange, calculating person who avoided publicity, Greb loved to worry adversaries, calling them in the middle of the night before a fight without talking— calling repeatedly so that the opponent would be sleepless the next day (as would he).

Though a middleweight, Greb's greatest desire was to fight Jack Dempsey, then heavyweight champion of the world. To that end, Greb haunted Dempsey's training camps, jeering and taunting the champ, telling him that he'd finish Dempsey in one round. "I don't want you to have anything to do with that man," Manager Jack Kearns reportedly cautioned Dempsey. "He's nuts!"

Dempsey, however, when Kearns wasn't present, accepted a challenge from the visiting Greb to spar with him. Once inside the ring, Greb began to give Dempsey a beating. He further confounded the champion by removing his glass eye and throwing it at Dempsey. So shocked was Dempsey that he was caught flat-footed and almost knocked out by Greb, who came pounding forward after his eye. Dempsey called off the sparring match and raced into the

Heavyweight champion Jack Dempsey, shown adjusting the controls of an early day radio, feared the unorthodox Greb and his glass eye. (UPI)

clubhouse, yelling at Kearns: "I never want that Greb in my training camp again. The son-of-a-bitch threw his eye at me!"

Jack Kearns laughed: "I told you so—champ, the guy's nuts!"

"Nuts, hell!" snorted Dempsey. "He's smart—if I had a glass eye I'd throw it, too!"

Hetty (Howland Robinson) GREEN

Financier (1835–1916)

She was the world's richest woman and the shrewdest female who ever invested a dollar. She was also the strangest person, male or female, of her wealthy caste, a woman who was known as "The Witch of Wall Street." Born Henrietta Howland Robinson in New Bedford, Massachusetts, of a rich whaling and real estate family, Hetty learned early the value (or obsession) of thrift. Her Quaker relatives dressed her in second-hand clothes, and she was castigated severely if she ever spent one penny of her monthly nickel allowance. With her father's death in 1865, Hetty inherited approximately $5 million. From that moment on, she dedicated herself to becoming the richest woman in America or, she hoped, the world.

Only days after the end of the Civil War, Hetty began to buy up great quantities of government bonds, which most financiers of the day thought to be useless. Their value soared during the Reconstruction era, and Hetty added several more millions to her coffers. In 1867, she married Edward H. Green, executor of her father's estate, who was also a millionaire. Shrewd Hetty made sure that her spouse signed a contract that their fortunes would remain separate before walking to the altar. When Hetty discovered that her husband was spending money carelessly, she separated from him, actually driving him out of all the family business in 1885 and predicting that he would die a pauper. She was right; Green died in 1902 with only a gold watch and $7 to his name, albeit his miserly wife did pay for his modest lodgings at the end of his life. Hetty nevertheless complained about having to support her dying spouse: "My husband is of no use to me at all. I wish I did not have him. He is a burden to me."

155

The ever-prospering Hetty Green as she appeared in the late 1890s.

Hetty's investments centered in stocks and bonds; she also bought up railroads. By the end of her life, her real estate holdings were enormous: she owned two square miles of choice property in Chicago, along with several skyscrapers, especially in the Southwest. But most of Mrs. Green's financial coups involved lending huge amounts of money to cities and states—and to established financiers wanting short loans and willing to pay 6 percent interest or more.

Hetty could be ruthless in her business dealings. She would get her way with any banker or borrower through charm or tantrum. On one occasion, demanding that a bank return to her *all* her liquid assets that minute, a sum exceeding $1 million, she pulled at her clothes, cried, screamed, and stamped the floor, finally squatting on the floor and threatening to remain in that position until she was given her money, "right now, right away and in cash!" The banker complied and his bank failed the following day.

Mrs. Green had a sixth sense concerning money and seemed to be able to smell financial disaster days in advance. One of her female friends asked her if her accounts were safe at the Knickerbocker Trust Company, then rated the second-largest trust company in New York. Hetty, who was as niggardly in giving advice as she was in buying a newspaper, eyed the woman for a few seconds then confided: "If you have any money in that place get it out the first thing tomorrow."

Edward Henry Green, Hetty's husband, who went broke while his wife piled up millions.

"Why?" inquired the startled friend.

"The men in that bank are too good-looking," Hetty said in her usual cryptic fasion. "You mark my words."

The friend withdrew her savings the following morning. A day later, on October 21, 1907, the National Bank of Commerce announced that it would no longer accept checks from the Knickerbocker Trust Company. Some days later, the trust company closed its doors, its officers declaring the institution insolvent.

Hetty's business acumen was needle sharp, as scores of the toughest financiers in the country learned. Bird S. Coler—for years a financial officer for the city of New York, who arranged for Mrs. Green to lend the city millions of dollars over the years—claimed that Hetty "had the best banking brain of anyone I ever knew. She carried all her knowledge in her head and never depended upon memoranda. She watched the money currents so closely that when I went to ask her for a loan she often knew how much I was going to require before I opened my mouth."

Financial panics were Hetty's specialty. She could predict months in advance when and where a panic would ensue. Wrote Boyden Sparkes in *The Witch of Wall Street:* "It was then that she foreclosed her death grip on coveted real estate; it was then that her brokers found her a willing customer for the depreciated stocks and bonds of men who were being engulfed ... At such times Mrs. Green would stalk through Wall Street buying bargains. She knew what the bargains were; she knew what stocks were being sold for less than their value ... This is what she meant when she said she bought cheaply and sold dearly."

The ire in Mrs. Green never abated for competitors she felt had wronged her. Of one she threatened: "The next time I see him in front of a church I'll paste him in the face with the heel of a satin-lined slipper!" One of the executors of her many trusts, Henry Barling, mistreated her, Hetty felt, and she publicly asked God to chastise him. The results were edifying to Hetty: "I prayed that the wickedness of that executor [Barling] might be made manifest to New York, and after that prayer that executor was found stone dead in his bed!" Commented one of Hetty's critics: "Prayed Barling into his grave, nonsense! That woman literally worried him to death."

Hetty's mistreated son, Edward Howland Green, who lost a leg because of his mother's stingy nature.

The lives of Hetty's two children, Edward (born in 1868) and Sylvia (born in 1871), were lived almost on the poverty level. Hetty refused to waste money buying them new clothes. Edward was given hand-me-down clothes, and Sylvia wore her mother's ancient garments cut down to size. The daughter was later sent to a convent, where a nun's habit suited Hetty's cost-conscious mind. Sylvia would become her mother's financial adviser in Hetty's dotage, exercising the same miserly principles as her mother.

Anything modern annoyed the pernicious Mrs. Green. Cars were wild extravagances, according to Hetty, who once barked to a New York *Herald* reporter: "Jesus did not ride in automobiles—an ass was good enough for Him!" Next to modern conveniences, Hetty despised lawyers and doctors. "I had rather that my daughter should be burned at the stake," Hetty once said, "than to have to suffer what I have gone through with lawyers!" Doctors were nothing but money-grubbing quacks to Mrs. Green, men who invented illness for profit. When her son Edward injured his leg while sledding, Hetty applied her own remedies. The leg grew continuously worse, and Hetty, hating it, took Ed to Bellevue Hospital. She and her son were dressed in rags at the time; and a doctor who examined the boy thought he was a welfare case—at a time when Hetty was worth more than $50 million. When the physician asked for his small fee, Mrs. Green laughed at him and took her son out of his care before proper medical treatment was administered. She applied sand to the festering leg, but that did not stop gangrene from setting in. The boy's leg was amputated in 1887.

Attire meant nothing to Hetty Green. She wore the same black dress for twenty years—beneath which was a petticoat fitted with special pockets containing stocks, bonds, and cash amounting to millions. Hetty washed the dress every few nights but later turned that chore over to a scrub woman, informing her only to scrub the bottom of the dress and her petticoat because those were the dirtiest parts, having trailed through the dust of Wall Street. Since the scrub woman only washed a portion of the garment, Hetty paid her a fraction of what she would have received had she washed the whole garment.

Beneath her dress, Hetty wore men's underwear in the winter and provided added insulation by stuffing newspapers under her dress. She wore rubbers borrowed from a clerk in the Chemical National Bank, where she kept most of her cash and stocks and bonds. Her black gloves were torn and her fingers poked through. Her muff, also worn for twenty years, literally rotted away. Hetty would haggle with store clerks over shoes priced at $3 a pair when her stock market investments were earning $500 an hour. The most economical bargain in footwear, Hetty discovered, was fisherman's boots, which she wore into the most distinguished banking house in America.

Edward Hatch Jr. of Lord and Taylor met Hetty Green during one of her rare appearances at a social function. He was appalled at her attire, telling her, "Mrs. Green—just consider that veil through which you are looking at me. It is torn. It is faded. It looks like hell. You come down to the store some morning and I'll give you one of the best veils we have in stock."

"You will? How sweet of you."

Hetty Green, 1900, walking through New York's financial district, carrying millions beneath that long black skirt; this was the photo in which she was labeled "The Witch of Wall Street."

Hetty was at Hatch's store the first moment the clerks opened the doors the next morning. She tried on the most expensive veil Lord and Taylor had to offer, and Hatch had it charged to his own account. Delighted, Mrs. Green turned to Hatch and said: "I wonder if you have any skirts that you could let me buy at reduced rates."

Hatch nodded and led Hetty to the skirt department. There was only one skirt, returned by a customer, that was marked down to $8. "How much is this skirt?" Hetty asked in a wary voice.

Hatch quickly tore off the price tag before Hetty could see it. "Fifty cents," he lied.

Hetty Green turned her back and dug into one of the many pockets of her dress, producing a small coin purse into which she reached trembling fingers. She paid in dimes. "She never, after that day," wrote one of her many biographers, "ceased to admire Edward Hatch, Jr."

On one occasion, Hetty raced into a stable and ordered the owner, a man named Hayes, to hitch up a team of horses "and then drive her back to a place where she believed she had lost a postage stamp." The financier searched frantically through street gutters for hours while the perplexed stable owner sat by patiently watching her. Hetty's son Ed once lost a coin, and Mrs. Green and her son spent the night searching an entire block for the money, Hetty holding a lantern in her hand as she ran nervous hands over the cobblestones.

Hetty's eating habits were as bizarre as her penchant for ragged apparel. She ate in the cheapest restaurants she could find and ordered the cheapest items on the menu. Her favorite eatery in Boston was a run-down lunchroom in Pie Alley where she could buy a plate of beans for 3¢ and a slice of pie for 2¢. One wag calculated that since her income at the time was 8¢ a second she would have had to eat four pieces of pie every second in order to keep up with her earnings. A rare whim once urged Mrs. Green to give a party for her society friends. A group of people in full evening wear showed up at the cheap boarding house where she was staying. Hetty led them to another boarding house where they were served a seven-course dinner at 25¢ a plate. The party cost Mrs. Green all of $2.25.

The woman looked for economy everywhere. She would purchase a newspaper for 2¢, then after reading it have it sold again. She once provided her own empty bottle for some medicine to save 5¢. Though Hetty owned two railroads, she never traveled in the comfort of a Pullman car but sat up all night in the day coach. One boiling day in 1893, Hetty climbed into an attic where she had stored some old clothes inherited from her father. "The July sun boiled down upon the iron roof and made the attic just a trifle less hot than the outskirts of Hades," reported one chronicler. "Yet Hetty Green worked in that devastating heat for hours. Doing what? Sorting white rags from colored ones because the junk man paid a cent a pound more for white rags!"

Charles Krell, a Hoboken, New Jersey, streetcar conductor, studied an elderly woman dressed all in black when she climbed aboard his car on the morning of January 18, 1906. The woman gave him a half-dollar for her 5¢ fare. Krell studied the coin then returned it, saying: "This looks like a counterfeit to me."

"I guess you can trust me for a ride," Hetty Green told the conductor. She pointed to a mailman seated in the car. "That postman opposite can tell you my credit is good."

The mailman nodded. Clucking his tongue in disgust, Krell put a nickel from his own pocket into the coin receiver.

Two days later, Mrs. Green marched into the office of the Hoboken streetcar corporation, explaining the loan made to her by the conductor. She placed a nickel on the desk of an official, but not until she received the receipt she demanded did she lift her forefinger from the coin on the desk. A few hours earlier, Hetty Green had lent the City of New York $4.5 million in cold, hard cash.

Beyond losing money, Mrs. Green feared the tax collector most. She saw tax collectors around every corner and inside every doorway. On one occasion, while chatting with a friend in the lobby of the Waldorf Astoria, Hetty suddenly spotted a man sitting in a chair. "That man is a tax assessor," whispered Hetty to her friend. "I can tell by the way he's glancing at me." As she talked, Hetty kept glancing alternately from a clock on the wall to a streetcar transfer in her hand. She examined the time punched on the transfer then raced off to use it before it expired.

Tax collectors were on Hetty's trail to be sure, but they rarely found her. When they did, she would invariably pay $30,000 on her vast holdings. Such payments were few and far between since Hetty was the most mobile millionaire in history. She moved constantly, from one cheap boarding house— never paying more than $5 a week for the dingiest room—to another, from Manhattan to Brooklyn to Hoboken, New Jersey, always using assumed names.

She preferred Hoboken, where she mostly lived from 1895 to 1916, the year of her death. It was the New York tax collectors she feared since her fortunes were essentially made and banked in that state.

With her son and daughter boarded out most of the time, Hetty lived alone in rooming houses, fearing not only tax collectors but kidnappers and anarchists. However, she was ready for all intruders. She always rigged up a revolver, with strings attached to the footboard of her bed and to the doorknob in such a way that any unwelcome visitor forcing her door would receive a bullet in the general area of the torso. "I always sleep so," she curtly explained to one startled landlady who was almost shot coming into Hetty's room to clean up.

The only permanent address Hetty Green ever maintained was the Chemical National Bank in Manhattan. She had all her trunks and furniture stored in the enormous bank vault, along with her securities and many millions in cash. (Her ancient carriage was stored on the second floor of the bank building.) Hetty received her mail at the bank and spent several hours a day there, clipping coupons and seeing financiers who wanted loans. She would receive them as she sat on the vault floor of the bank, a dried out ham sandwich (her lunch) tucked into a pocket of her dress.

When one visitor arrived at the vault to obtain a loan on some valuable

New York's Chemical National Bank in the days when Hetty practically lived inside its vault.

gems, Hetty blurted, "I know nothing of jewels—stocks, bonds, cash invest-ments, yes, not baubles." She then proceeded to drag forth from her vault cabinet a bushel basket brimming with diamonds, rubies, emeralds, and other precious stones, explaining, "These are family gifts. I purchased not one stone. To me they are useless."

Mrs. Green came under attack in 1894 by none other than Bible-spouting William Jennings Bryan, then a congressman from Nebraska, who delivered a speech in favor of income tax and cited Hetty as a chief abuser of the system. "She owns property estimated at $60 million," thundered Bryan, "and enjoys an income which can scarcely be less than $3 million [a year], yet she lives at a cheap boarding house and only spends a few hundred dollars a year. The woman, under [the] indirect system of taxation does not pay as much toward the support of the federal government as a laboring man whose income of $500 [a year] is spent upon his family."

Hetty's response was to tell the world that though she had more money than most she was sympathetic to the laboring man. "I have always been a friend of the laboring man," said Mrs. Green, "and never a day passes but what I do something for them. Why, in a railroad accident a butcher boy was hurt and I was the first one to help him. I have got nerve. People who are honest nowadays are accused of being mad!"

Then again, Hetty did things that most thought abnormal, if not mad. Though her son Edward slaved for her interests most of his life, he received only $45 a month in salary. Her sage advice to Edward after he received his college diploma was "never speculate in Wall Street. Never maintain an office. Eat slowly. Don't stay up all night. Don't drink ice water, and keep out of draughts."

Before officially hiring Edward to work in her shadowy financial empire, the scheming Hetty devised a test for her son. She ordered him to appear at the vault of the Chemical National Bank. When he arrived she handed him a bundle, telling him to deliver it personally to her agents in Chicago. "This package contains $250,000 in bonds," Hetty informed her son.

Edward Green, who was later to take over the direction of one of his mother's Texas railroads, never forgot the assignment. "I was a young man," Green later recalled, "and stayed awake every foot of the way putting the package under the mattress in my berth and watching for robbers all night. It was with a great feeling of relief and pride that I handed the package over to those appointed to receive it in Chicago. It was opened in my presence while I waited for a receipt. The bank official burst into loud laughter. 'What do you mean telling me you have bonds here?' he asked, and then he gave me my first view of the contents of the package. Instead of bonds I saw a number of fire insurance policies, long since expired. You know, my mother ... had a very practical way of testing me out."

When later working in Texas, Edward received a telegram ordering him to perform certain duties. The wire was unsigned. An office employee questioned the identity of the sender.

"It's from my mother," Edward informed the employee.

"How do you know that, sir?"

"I know it's from Ma because it came collect."

Edward Green began to take over more and more of the responsibility for Hetty's empire as Mrs. Green began to slip into senility. She lent $1.5 million to Colonel Payne, a notorious Wall Street plunger, thinking him to be Senator Oliver Payne of Ohio. She began to rave about imaginary culprits trying to steal her fortune, to murder her in her sleep. "I've had a peck of trouble," she moaned to a friend, "and I'll tell you some of it. My son and daughter are dying by inches of nervous prostration [both were well] ... Why, ever since I began to wear long dresses schemers have been trying ... I've lots of enemies ... I tell you the devil would fear me, as many of his satellites do here."

She claimed that the directors of the Chemical National Bank, her bank, were attempting to poison her. She had lunch with the directors after demanding they give her some of the cash she had on hand, $3,900,000. "Well, there were about a dozen others at the table, set in the director's room, and the funniest thing was that there was no one else but me taken sick. I thought I was going to die. They called a physician and he said I had no fever but a terrible inflammation, and he said I probably had ptomaine poisoning. But I collected the money all right, and since then I have not made my office at the Chemical National Bank."

On her seventy-eighth birthday in November 1912, Hetty was interviewed by a reporter for the New York *Herald*. She greeted him while chewing on a large onion. "Pardon this onion I'm chewing," sputtered Hetty, "but it's the finest thing in the world for health. Perhaps that's why I live so long. I had a big tenderloin steak for breakfast, with fried potatoes, a pot of tea, and the top of a bottle of milk. I don't buy cream because it is twelve hours older than the milk. I just take off the top of the bottle of milk, set the rest in a cool place and use it for cooking."

How do you account for the color in your cheeks?" inquired the reporter.

"That's not rouge and don't you think so for a minute," snapped Hetty. "That's because I always chew a baked onion. Most people don't like the smell of onions but I find that by chewing an onion—a well-baked onion—after breakfast it kills any germs that might be in the steak or the milk and keeps my digestion fine. That piece of onion I'm chewing now will last me all day."

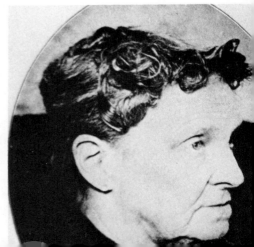

Hetty Green, the world's richest woman and the world's biggest skinflint, shown shortly before her death in 1916.

Hetty Green kept on chewing onions for four more years, until the day of her death, July 3, 1916. Nurses who had attended the eighty-one year old during her illness were ordered by Edward Green to wear street dresses. If Hetty had seen white uniforms, she would have perished in agony, knowing that expensive trained nurses were caring for her. Of the estimated $100 million left by the richest woman in the world, Edward and Sylvia Green received about $10 million each. The rest, including seven to eight thousand parcels of land, was divided among 1,478 relatives.

Hetty's last train ride was unlike any she had taken in life. Her son chartered a Pullman car, which carried her body from New York to Bellows Falls, Massachusetts, and the family plot. Defying a Quaker rule, Edward Green had the car filled with white carnations. The spirit of Hetty Green undoubtedly ranted and raved the whole trip long at such extravagance.

Mary Louise Cecilia ("Texas") GUINAN

Nightclub Hostess (1884–1933)

If there was a genuine, 24-carat character to emerge from the wild speakeasy world of the 1920s, that colorful zany was the champion wisecracker Texas Guinan, whose name came to symbolize the goofy glamour of Prohibition nightlife. Since she broke the law nightly in her many elegantly designed clubs by serving bootleg hootch, there was always an air of the illicit about Texas Guinan; but for those legions who loved her raucous madness and wit, she was an irresistible magnet of toothy and leggy excitement. She was Queen of the Nightclubs in an era that loved taunting a bad law and loved Texas even more for thumbing her nose at it with sarcastic abandon. She was as brassy as a section of saxophones, as irreverent as a bordello madam, and as frenetic as the Charleston. The woman was *alive.*

This fabulous hostess entertained her guests with gaudy shows, her low-life banter enthralling high society patrons. She was at the hub of the theater and musical world in New York. Writers like Mark Hellinger befriended her. Bon vivants like Alexander Woollcott, who called her "La Guinan," spread her fame. She became sort of a naughty national monument that had to be seen by everyone living in or visiting New York.

Jazz saxophonist Bud Freeman remembered his pilgrimage to one of Guinan's clubs to see the notorious Texas: "It was in 1929 when I went to see her review one night. I was with the Ben Pollock band and a lot of the band members went with me to see this last of the old Broadway entertainers. She was very nice to us, but then she knew about the Pollock band.

"There was a great deal of controversy about her at the time, about how she

The indefatigable Texas Guinan, Queen of the Nightclubs during the 1920s, perched atop piano, greeting customers with her famous line: "Hello, sucker!" (Wide World)

was not allowed to perform in London with her troupe and, mostly, because she had been denied this tour, there was retaliation. Ray Noble, for instance, was not allowed to bring his British band into the States—he had to come over only with his manager and hire American musicians, and I was a member of his band for a brief time because of this Guinan situation. Well, her troupe of girls was probably a little risque for London anyway ... but certainly not for Paris at the time.

"Texas, on the night I saw her, struck me as a real barrel-house babe who talked like she was a tough western cowboy. You know, in those days people weren't terribly sophisticated and they thought she was really *something* ... and I suppose she was."

Texas had begun her career with a whoop. Born and raised in Waco, Texas (ergo the sobriquet), Mary Guinan disappointed her parents, who hoped she would become a singer, by running off as a teenager to ride wild horses in a circus. Some years later, she was seen working the vaudeville circuits as a sort of western dancer and rope-twirler. By 1918, the thirty-two-year-old Texas had moved to Hollywood, where the movie industry was booming, and convinced producers to star her in several quickie westerns, including *Gun Woman* and *Little Miss Deputy*. At that time, Guinan appeared as a rough-and-tumble cowgirl with a mop of black hair and a stern look affixed to her granite-jawed face. (When taking the New York nightclub world by storm, Texas would dye her hair with peroxide like any ordinary flapper.)

Silent movies offered limited opportunities for a young woman with a voice that could be heard in the next county, a deep braying voice with the power to mesmerize any listener. Broadway had a voice where the movies were silent, and the enterprising Guinan left California in the early 1920s to establish a career as a musical singing star on the Great White Way, accompanying De Wolf Hopper to appear in a revue at the Winter Garden. Weeks later Texas went with friends to a speakeasy. According to a later interview, she found it "dull ... Someone suggested that I sing. I didn't need much coaxing. I sang all I knew, my whole damn repertoire. Then I started kidding around. First thing you know, the joint's alive. I feel fine, and everybody else in the place is having a great big wonderful time."

The big-bodied peroxide blonde, hair marcelled and cut short at the neck, her lips smeared with a blood-red lipstick, a rope of pearls dangling to her hips, her toothy smile flashing, was soon working as a hostess for the Beaux Arts, an expensive supper-club speakeasy on Fortieth Street. Her wisecracking antics— she generally insulted the customer in half-affectionate, half-sarcastic terms— soon had the nightlife elite flocking to see her.

One of these was the theatrical promoter Nils Granland, who suggested that Texas build a show around her unorthodox act. To that end, Granland first surrounded the girthsome Guinan with leggy showgirls from the Ziegfeld Follies and Earl Carroll's Vanities. "It was nothing but Tex and girls, girls, girls," Granland would later remember.

Larry Fey, a New York gangster who controlled the city's milk racket, wanted to move up in life and swim through society cream. He saw Texas perform one night and proposed they go into business together. He would back an elegant nightclub; she would lend her dynamic presence as hostess. It would appear, as with all the Fey–Guinan clubs, that Texas was the proprietor. Fey, between acts, would emerge from the shadows to make his important social and business contacts.

Guinan accepted immediately, and her fame was quickly spread by Broadway columnists who came to see her. Walter Winchell, Louis Solbe, Damon Runyon, Mark Hellinger sat stageside regularly to glean Guinan's cleaner quotes for their columns. (Hellinger would later produce a movie, *The Roaring Twenties,* that closely portrayed Texas Guinan—Gladys George superbly playing Tex opposite James Cagney, whose role was certainly based on Larry Fey; Betty Hutton also played Guinan in the movie *Red Hot and Blue*.)

The imaginative insult was Texas' specialty. She hailed patrons entering her clubs with the immortal salutation of "Hello, Sucker!" She is also credited with inventing the line, "Never give a sucker an even break!" Raucous, rowdy, sometimes profane, Texas began operating on a big-time level at the El Fey Club located on Third Street in Greenwich Village. She would later switch to the Del Fey Club, the 300 Club, the Century, the Club Intime, Club Abbey, the Rendezvous, the Argonaut, the Salon Royal, Texas Guinan's, and many others. The reason for Guinan's mobility was simple. After a police raid that caused her club to be padlocked (she also became known as "The Padlock Queen"), Texas would merely move down the block and open another club.

She created her bon mots and sobriquets where she found them. One customer, who stuffed $50 bills into the brassieres of her dancers and paid the cover charge (another of Guinan's inventions) for the entire club one night, aroused Texas' curiosity. "Say, Mister," she bellowed from the postage-stamp dance floor, "who are you?"

"I'm in dairy production," answered the big spender.

"A butter-and-egg man!" exalted the roaring hostess. The term found its way into the mainstream of American argot. A "butter-and-egg man" came to symbolize one who would spend a fortune to be entertained in the nightclub era. In a profile on the eccentric hostess, *Vanity Fair* waxed eloquent: "Out of a perambulating nightclub, an Irish wit, a knack for always landing on her feet and a genius for finding words to throw into any void, Texas Guinan of New York has emerged as a nationally known trademark for indoor fun after midnight. Her battleword is 'Curfew shall not ring tonight' and her current nightclub draws to its Musical Mornings those who know they're wise and those who are willing to get wise; the very young and the very middle-aged. With the technique of a circus 'spieler,' Miss Guinan makes her revival meetings a melting pot for Broadway and the Farm Belt ... and somehow actually rejuvenating the weary formula that all the world loves a butter-and-egg man."

The world of Texas Guinan was upside-down. She slept until 6 P.M. (always on her right side to "take it easy on my tired heart"). She ate little breakfast, then tended to personal business. She did not enter her club until a little after midnight, going backstage to gobble down a melon filled with ice cream before dressing for her revue. The Guinan clubs opened at 10 P.M., but the shows ran from midnight until 7 A.M. with Texas usually perched atop a piano, her voice raised above the din of 300 revelers, an enormous bellowing voice that could surmount any cacaphony. To "warm up" the audience, she would first liberally sprinkle insults to customers, exchange banter, and then produce a device of her own design, the kleeter–klapper, a single piece of wood split at the top, where two wooden balls were affixed. When shaken, this noise-producer created an awful din that guaranteed to break weak eardrums. Texas would throw these devices to her customers, some of them hitting patrons—which bothered her not at all. In addition, customers drinks contained swizel sticks with large wooden knobs at the ends. With these, patrons could strike against tables, glasses, and metal buckets holding champagne. The resulting uproar pierced the senses of the most sodden client. And above the clamor, Texas boomed out introductions to her acts, beginning with her Guinan Gals—no longer the statuesque Follies beauties working off-hours but a line of girls so young that most were chaperoned by their mothers, who waited backstage until the shows were over, taking their Broadway babies home at dawn. (Though many a male preyed upon these adolescent girls, Texas kept a firm rein on them and managed with cajolery, and sometimes a right cross, to keep the more lecherous patrons at bay.)

Clad in skimpy customs, the girls would go into a frantic dance number, then skip individually through the cramped table area, toying and teasing single elderly men, those selected by Guinan with a nod and a wink and sometimes a pointing finger as big spenders, butter-and-egg men. The girls would run fingers through the customers' hair, do short shimmies, and coax the sugar daddies into stuffing large bills into their scanty costumes. Should a customer prove reluctant to disgorge his money, the girls would playfully go through his pockets, taking what they found with squeals and giggles and wiggles, all under the hard-eyed direction of their den mother, Texas.

Certain customers were sacrosanct, the blue-chip suckers, Texas called them—the great stars of Broadway and motion pictures, the political sachems of New York, the newspaper columnists, and the stellar figures of the underworld. These choice clients sat at tables that were off-limits to the money-searching chorus girls. On any given night, one might see Tom Mix, the great movie cowboy star; Mae West; Ann Pennington, the dancing star of George White's popular *Scandals;* Follies stars Imogene Wilson and Frank Tinney; Al Jolson; W.C. Fields; William Fallon, the great mouthpiece of mobsters; politicians Jimmy Hines, Big Bill Dwyer and the nightlife-loving Mayor of New York, Gentleman Jimmy Walker, with Broadway dancer Betty Compton on his arm. (When later ousted from his post, Walker would divorce his wife and marry the pretty brunette, a marriage that lasted until 1941 when Betty Compton, who was twenty years younger than the fun-craving Walker, got her own divorce.)

Beyond the British royalty, the novelists, the industrial tycoons (such as Harry Sinclair of the Teapot Dome scandal who often "bought" Guinan's entire place, paying for everyone's drinks and cover charge), sitting in the dark

Cowboy superstar of the movies Tom Mix was a regular customer of Texas Guinan's spending thousands of dollars with each visit to her clubs.

corners of Texas' clubs were the real powers of New York, the sleek and evil underworld figures—Owney Madden, Dutch Schultz, Legs Diamond, Waxey Gordon, Big Frenchy DeMange. Should these men take a liking to Guinan's much-protected teenage dancers, there was little Texas could do to prevent them from whisking the girls away in their Pierce-Arrows. These men were armed, always dangerous, and they acted with impunity, with most of Mayor Walker's policemen in their wallet pockets.

Following the opening chorus number, Guinan would thunder: "Give the little girls a great big hand!" This demand also became an exclusive Guinan trademark. (Along with bad gin, the indefatigable Texas was full of quotes. The author's mother, a songstress during this time, worked briefly as a torch singer in a Guinan club, where one night she warbled out "Melancholy Baby" at the request of a rich drunk who offered her $2 at song's end. Guinan leaped forward and threw the money in the man's face, roaring, "If the sucker won't pay a fifty, kid, don't sing for a deuce!")

Actor George Raft (right) with actress Carole Lombard and Manuel Quezon, President of the Philippines, at a Paramount Studio party in 1934; Raft got his start in the Guinan clubs where he danced a wild Charleston.

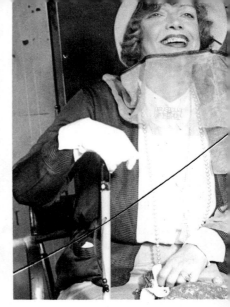

Texas Guinan grinning through a veil as she sits in a New York police station awaiting bail on the charge of violating the Prohibition Law. (Wide World)

Then the solo acts would begin. Blues and torch singers would appear for a few numbers. Then solo dancers would perform amazing acrobatic numbers. One of the most energetic of these dancers was a girl named Ruby Stevens, who later changed her name to Barbara Stanwyck. A male dancer, his slicked-downed black hair parted in the middle, performed a furious Charleston in Guinan's club. Newsman Mark Hellinger viewed this act bug-eyed, labeling it "the weirdest, maddest dance that anyone has ever seen. The customers sit in silence as he fixes his eyes on one spot and whirls. Faster, faster. It is fascinating—almost uncanny." In a crescendo, the dancer would finally fall to the floor. Guinan would holler: "Give the little guy a great big hand." George Raft would then bow, grin his soon-to-be famous smile, and hurry offstage to rush to another club—working four clubs a night in order to earn $1,000 a week. Another hoofer, a fourteen-year-old Broadway cutie named Ruby Keeler made her debut in a Guinan club, tap-dancing to Broadway musical fame before the decade was out. Three years later, she married one of the Guinan's most celebrated customers, Al Jolson.

At the end of each act, Guinan would move throughout her club shouting "Encourage her! Encourage her! Give the little girl a great big hand!" She then ordered her waiters to begin pelting customers with cardboard snowballs, and the customers would reciprocate by throwing the snowballs at each other until the entire club was alive with the white orbs caroming off the heads of customers and employees alike.

Guinan would then order her waiters—many of whom were expert pickpockets—to shout risque words to the scantily clad chorus waiting behind a diaphanous curtain (heating up the passions of the patrons) and without being asked by the customers, to refill the glasses of all, or as was mostly the case, to replace magnums of champagne in the ice-packed buckets next to tables. After all, the name of Guinan's game was getting the "sucker's money." Her prices were astronomical for that era. A fifth of scotch cost $25, as did a small bottle of champagne (a magnum was $50—$100 if the customer was drunk). Rye went for $20; gin for $15; and always there was the $25 cover charge. For those who attempted to save money by bringing their own illegal booze, Guinan provided a set-up—two not-so-clean glasses and a pitcher of water for which she charged $2. Cigarettes, which sold for 15¢ a pack then, went for $1 a pack, sold by an almost naked cigarette girl who wended her way through the tables in a hip-swinging shuffle.

Texas made no apologies about her cutthroat prices. "There's a lot of talk about how I take the customers for all they've got," she was once quoted. "It's not as bad as that, even if there aren't any charity wards in my club. The boys come here to spend, and I'm not going to disappoint them. When they drink ginger ale in my place they are drinking liquid platinum, and they like it."

Guinan was careful at this time not to mention that she served booze, but she fooled no one. Despite the fact that she paid crooked cops a fortune to stay open, her clubs were regularly raided. (One anonymous cop stated that the temperance "crackpots had to be appeased. We had to put on a show of enforcing Prohibition and since Texas Guinan was the leading star in breaking that law she was the first to be raided.")

Moreover, most of the serious raids against Guinan's clubs were conducted by some federal agent who pretended to be a customer and after being served, quickly poured the contents of his drink into a small bottle as "evidence" to be offered in court later, then arrested Texas and all her employees. (The customers, the most powerful people in New York, were politely asked to go home.) The agent, having gotten his evidence, would stand up—he usually waited for any performer to finish—and announce, "Okay everybody, stay where you are—this is a raid!"

By then Guinan was used to such events. She would nervelessly swagger up to the agent, offering her hands for handcuffs (never used on her) and bawl to her customers, "Go home, suckers—see you tomorrow night." Following Texas' instructions, her band always struck up the same tune on such occasions, a popular ditty of the day entitled "The Prisoner's Song." Guinan and company would then be led to waiting paddy wagons to be taken to the nearest precinct and booked for violating the Volstead Act. In hours, they would all be out on bail, invariably provided by gangster Larry Fey, Guinan's man, and they would almost never return for a hearing. Larry Fey and his associates owned New York's judicial benches for the most part during the 1920s.

Never missing a chance to taunt the enforcers of Prohibition, Texas wore a 24-carat necklace of padlocks, the symbol of her errant profession. She would twist the necklace impatiently before irate desk sergeants as she awaited her lawyers. Upon her release, she would huddle with Larry Fey and other financial backers and make arrangements to open a new club in the vicinity of the club just padlocked. That night, perched on a piano, Texas would regale customers with a brazen song of her own composition:

Judge Thomas said, "Tex, do you sell booze?"
I said, "Please don't be silly.
I swear to you my cellar's filled
With chocolate and vanilly."

Belle Livingstone, another hostess of upper class speakeasies and a close friend of Guinan's, was once arrested and jailed for a brief period for violating Prohibition (Texas never saw the inside of a cell). When Belle was released, Guinan had an armored car waiting at the jail to escort Livingstone back to her club in style. (Belle favored Japanese motifs in her clubs; her shoeless customers sat cross-legged on luxurious cushions gulping her bootleg hootch. Explained Belle, "I keep my clientele close to the floor—a man could get hurt falling off a barstool!")

The Padlock Queen continued to rule after-hours New York until the repeal of Prohibition. As an exclusive and eccentric product of her time, she faded when it became legal to drink liquor. Texas ceased to be a star attraction when she ceased to represent the illicit. She looked about for greener fields, returning to the movies. She had made a less than stirring film in 1929 entitled *Queen of Nightclubs,* which profiled her hectic, frolicsome career. Now, Guinan's clubs were shut down and her backer Larry Fey dead (he had been killed in 1932 by a doorman at his club, The Casa Blanca, who shot him to death because he had been refused a $5 raise). In 1933, to pick up living money, Texas appeared in the film *Broadway Thru a Keyhole.* The movie left audiences with a sour taste, reminding them of the easy-living and free-spending 1920s which seemed to mock the starving, penniless public of the Great Depression.

Texas Guinan became an anathema and she died forgotten in 1933. The 49-year-old Queen of the Nightclubs, who had earned as much as $4,000 a week, had apparently enjoyed her riches, spending as much as, if not more than, she earned, as was the tradition of the flapper era. She left an estate of $28,173.

Nubar GULBENKIAN

Financier (1896–1972)

Gulbenkian's father, Calouste, built up a gigantic fortune, ranging into the hundreds of millions of dollars, before World War I by exploiting the Mesopotamian oil fields for a consortium of German and British firms. He later took a straight 5 percent of all profits from the Iraq Petroleum Company. The elder Gulbenkian was a right-wing conservative who watched every penny; his son Nubar was a ne'er do-well who spent his family fortune like a sailor on a spree.

Like his father, Nubar kept harems in private castles and villas throughout Europe. His father once cautioned him to make sure his females were no older than seventeen; after that age, said the elder Gulbenkian, women became unmanageable. Nubar dutifully changed the inhabitants of his harems each year.

Educated at Harrow and Cambridge, Nubar all but ignored his studies, concentrating on his own investments, his race horses, and his many mistresses. It was reported that he "wore out three horses and three women a day." The playboy had a mania for Edwardian dress; and his exclusive tailors worked around the clock making morning coats, cravats, brocaded vests, striped trousers, spats, and top hats. He owned a thousand handcrafted canes and always wore gloves, sporting an orchid in his lapel.

In later life, Nubar affected a luxuriant Santa Claus beard, parted in the middle. He was chauffeured about London, his home base, in a black and gold limousine modeled after a London taxi, specially designed by the playboy because he admired that type of auto.

Gulbenkian and his father argued incessantly toward the end of Calouste's life. The elder Gulbenkian took exception to every expense run up by his son, once refusing to pay for a $4.50 chicken lunch that Nubar had ordered and eaten at his desk in the family's London office. So incensed was Nubar that he immediately filed a $10-million suit against his father. Though the case was settled out of court, more than $90,000 in legal fees for both sides were lavished upon the Gulbenkian stubbornness. Calouste never forgave his errant son for publicly embarrassing him; he left only a few million from his billion-dollar estate to Nubar.

George Ivan GURDJIEFF

Occultist (dates uncertain)

One of the world's leading crackpots, who claimed he could cure all maladies of the body and mind, Gurdjieff was a Greek born in Russia. During the 1920s, he opened an occultist therapy center outside of Paris which he loftily designated as the Institute for the Harmonious Development of Man. The towering overweight Gurdjieff presented the perfect image of the goony guru. He shaved his bald pate twice a day and grew a walrus mustache so thick that he could babble for hours without anyone seeing his lips move.

The occultist penned only one book, *All and Everything,* which supposedly dealt with Gurdjieff's many encounters with the Devil and how he had bested Satan. Most of the book is grand gobbledygook.

Patients who sought relief at the occultist's therapy center were ordered to chop trees until they collapsed of exhaustion or perform acrobatic dances so strenuous that many had to be removed to hospitals to remedy their severe muscle spasms. These were some of the Yoga-like cures invented by Gurdjieff, who claimed he had learned them from "initiates" in Eastern monastaries.

Many of the famous were attracted to the institute, including Margaret Anderson, publisher of *The Little Review,* one of the most outstanding avant garde periodicals of the 1920s. Another was British author Katherine Mansfield, who went to the self-styled guru to cure a respiratory ailment. Gurdjieff listened to Mansfield inhale and exhale for some minutes then ordered her to sleep in a cowloft, there to breathe deep of the air exhaled by the cows quartered beneath her. The author died a short time later, most agreeing that the so-called Gurdjieff "cure" had hurried her death.

Not until after World War II was the Gurdjieff institute closed down. At the time, Gurdjieff, still alive but no longer hoodwinking suckers with his exotic cures, was described by *Time* magazine as a "remarkable blend of P.T. Barnum, Rasputin, Freud, Groucho Marx and everybody's grandfather."

H

Wenceslaus HANKA

Philologist (1791–1861)

In 1817 or 1818, Hanka purportedly found some ancient manuscripts in an old Bohemian church, documents that dated from the fourteenth century and told of the original Czechoslovakian nation. These documents were used by Czech nationalists as intellectual supports for the recreation of Czechoslovakia following World War I. Thomas Masaryk, later to become the first president of Czechoslovakia, believed so ardently in Hanka's discoveries that the University of Prague refused to accredit him with a full professorship. By that time, it had been revealed that Hanka had faked his so-called discoveries. Chemicals and parchments found in Hanka's library after his death proved that he himself had created the ancient manuscripts.

James A. HARDEN-HICKEY

Author (1854–1898)

Born in San Francisco to a miner who had grown wealthy during the California gold rush, Harden-Hickey was sent to Paris by his French mother at age five in order that he be given a European education. The boy grew up on the edge of Napoleon III's resplendent court and, by the time he graduated Saint-Cyr, he had developed his own ideas of empire.

Harden-Hickey wrote many romantic novels in Paris, then became an editor of *Le Triboulet,* his own right-wing publication which supported the

175

monarchy. His vitriolic editorial stances not only brought dozens of lawsuits down on his head, but he also fought innumerable duels with those he had offended in print—he was an expert swordsman and crack shot.

Following several jaunts about the globe, Harden-Hickey met and married Anna Flagler, heiress to a great iron fortune. (He had married a French woman and divorced her years earlier.) Shortly after his marriage, and while in the throes of depression, Harden-Hickey wrote and published *Euthanasia; the Aesthetics of Suicide,* in which he not only advocated self-extinction as a noble act but listed dozens of methods to achieve an effective suicide, favoring the scores of poisons then available. The book did not sell and is now a collector's item.

The author's next move was to publicly announce that he was going to purchase the uninhabited, sixty-square mile volcanic island of Trinidad, located seven hundred miles off the coast of Brazil, not to be confused with the larger Trinidad in the British West Indies.

Next Harden-Hickey crowned himself King James I of Trinidad and gave himself the title of "baron," then sought official recognition for his barren kingdom from existing countries. Though he was universally ignored, the baron opened up his new country's chancellery on Thirty-Sixth Street in New York, where he printed up bonds and postage stamps carrying his own picture and sold these to any person gullible enough to buy, the revenues going toward the purchase of a schooner that was to take him to his island, one which he had explored years earlier in his travels.

England officially took over the island in 1895, later turning it over to Brazil. Harden-Hickey's response was to threaten to invade England with an army of mercenaries, but his plans appeared unreal even to himself after a few years of fruitless posturing as a king without an empire.

In February 1898, Harden-Hickey found himself in El Paso, Texas after having failed to sell some Mexican property; he intended to use the profits to finance an expedition to Trinidad to re-establish his sovereignty. Without funds—his wife and wealthy father-in-law ignored his pleas for money—the baron went to his hotel room and took a fatal dose of morphine, one of the drugs he had urged others to use in his long-forgotten book on suicide.

James A. Harden-Hickey, who set up his own empire, crowned himself king and planned to invade England.

Gaylord HAUSER

Nutritionist (Born 1895)

Hauser, born in Tubingen, Germany, on May 17, 1895, immigrated to the United States in 1911 and soon contracted tuberculosis of the hip. According to his own story, Chicago doctors stated that his case was hopeless; he was returned to Europe, ostensibly to die at an early age. While languishing in mountainous climes, Hauser was visited, he later claimed, by a wise old man who told him, "If you keep on eating dead foods, you certainly will die. Only living foods can make a living body." The boy abstained from meat, poultry, and fish, and ate only fresh vegetables and fruits; his condition improved dramatically.

The miracle cure Hauser claimed to have experienced led him to become the most popular self-styled arbiter of eating in America. Over the years, he produced numerous books in which he dictated to legions of followers exactly what they should and should not eat, exhorting them to consume great quantities of wheat germ, yogurt, blackstrap molasses, skim milk, and brewer's yeast. Although nutritional qualities do exist in these foods, the average human would have to consume enormous amounts of these items, far beyond normal capacities, to be able to "add five youthful years" to life, according to Hauser's dictates.

Hauser's claims were often ridiculous; he insisted that his special diets would cure menopause, baldness, insomnia, low blood pressure, and nervousness of all kinds. He even went so far as to advise those with eye troubles to throw away their glasses, asserting that a series of eye exercises would cure them and basing his beliefs on the quack theories of a notorious mountebank, Dr. William Horatio Bates. Of course, Hauser stated, it was necessary to supplement the eye exercise with his special diet of foods obtainable only through food firms such as Nu-Vege-Sal, Potassium Broth, and Swiss Kriss, among others.

Tens of thousands of food faddists followed the Hauser methods; but whether or not his diets and exercises ever helped anyone to overcome physical disabilities or illnesses is still largely in debate.

William Randolph HEARST

Newspaper Tycoon (1863–1951)

In 1859, George Hearst provided the initial fortune for his son William, a fortune scooped out of the earth at Virginia City, Nevada, where George purchased a half-interest in a mine said to be worthless for $450. It yielded a mother lode of silver; and as part of the fabulous Comstock mine, it made Hearst a millionaire. The crude, illiterate miner, whose speech was peppered with oaths, had a permanent whiskey breath and chewed tobacco every waking moment, carelessly spewing its juices onto his beard and shirtfront.

The colorful George Hearst, who later became a United States Senator from California, once leaped to his feet at a political convention to defend his illiteracy. A New York *Times* story of 1891 quoted Hearst as shouting to his adversaries: "My opponents say that I haven't the book learning that they possess. They say I can't spell. They say I spell bird, b-u-r-d. If b-u-r-d doesn't spell bird, what in hell does it spell?"

The miner seemed an unlikely spouse for the cultured and delicate Phoebe Elizabeth Apperson, but his millions undoubtedly made up for his lack of refinement. A year after their marriage, William Randolph Hearst was born, on April 29, 1863, in San Francisco where the Hearsts had settled.

Phoebe Hearst spoiled her son with her extremely possessive manner. According to W.A. Swanberg, in *Citizen Hearst,* William "was mothered, loved, pampered, praised, protected, instructed, fussed over, waited on and worried about every moment of his infant existence." When Hearst reached adulthood, he went on spoiling himself, and with a dedication unsurpassed by any American millionaire of his era.

Obsessed with power, Hearst longed to control public opinion; and to that end, he began to buy newspapers across the country until his publishing empire included thirty daily newspapers and many magazines and radio stations. In Europe, he bought enormous amounts of artwork (including whole castles), which he shipped en masse back to America to be reconstructed on his various estates. Most of the artwork he saw only once, having it packed and shipped to a gigantic warehouse in New York, where twenty employees were kept working at the staggering and ever-increasing inventory at a cost of $60,000 a year. In addition to statuary, tapestries, and paintings, the warehouse contained everything that the possessive Hearst coveted—from Eygptian mummies to cuckoo clocks.

In addition to $30 million inherited from his father, Hearst's newspapers and magazines did, during most of his lifetime, produce great profits. Moreover, the Comstock lode continued to pour millions into his pocket. Yet Hearst was a notorious spendthrift by his own admission. According to writer Gene Fowler, who was present at a dinner party at Hearst's fabulous California castle, San Simeon, "The Chief," as Hearst was called by his newspaper minions, bluntly admitted his mad spending to Henry Ford.

The ever blunt Ford looked up from his dinner plate and asked Hearst, "Have you got any money?"

Replied Hearst, "I never have any money, Mr. Ford. I always spend any money that I am to receive before I get it."

Ford shook his hand with genuine sorrow. "That's a darned shame. You ought to get yourself two or three hundred million dollars and tuck it away."

Most of Hearst's money—his personal income each year averaged $12 million—went into the construction of his fabled estate, San Simeon (now a California landmark and tourist delight). Swanberg later described the place as a "kingdom that was hermetically sealed against the republic that surrounded it." San Simeon towered on cliffs fronting the Pacific ocean; Hearst owned fifty miles of ocean frontage, property that went deep into the surrounding mountains, more than 240,000 acres. Though he spent $30 million on the estate, $1 million alone on the gardens, it was never finished.

Hearst's love of flowers was ostentatious. On a pleasure trip, Hearst, smelled daphne for the first time and fired off a wire to his chief gardner, Nigel Keep, ordering him to plant them all around the main building at San Simeon; the gardner wore out an army of landscapers, spending $12,000 on an overnight marathon of daphne planting before the Chief arrived in the morning.

The main castle of San Simeon offered dozens of enormous rooms through which Hearst wandered. Along with the other buildings on the property, it was built in Moorish fashion. The walls were adorned with Gobelin tapestries that had once hung in the most exquisite chateaux of France. Paintings by Raphael, Rembrandt, and Rubens were everywhere to be seen. The cavernous banquet hall, where Hearst dined with scores of guests each evening, was adorned with pennants high on its cathedral ceiling, with suits of armor positioned along the paneled walls, and a huge fireplace roaring at the center of the room. The entire place, according to Joseph J. Thorndike Jr., writing in *The Very Rich,* was "an interior designer's nightmare, an eclectic jumble of pieces culled from the great houses of Europe."

Oddly enough, Hearst insisted that his guests use paper napkins at lunch and always kept several ketchup bottles on the main dining-room table. As a teetotaler, he never offered his guests any spirits to drink. His mistress, Marion Davies, would sneak with her guests into the women's washroom after dinner. There they would belt down several quick drinks and spray their mouths with cologne. "That was the one place that Hearst couldn't get us," actress Carole Lombard later remembered.

Hearst also maintained a complete zoo on his property where herds of zebras, giraffes, kangaroos, and buffaloes ran wild. Caged were some of the most awesome beasts in the world—tigers, lions, panthers—and Hearst would visit the caged animals alone late at night, staring for hours as the beasts snarled and roared at him.

Hundreds of guests, usually Hollywood and press people, visited San Simeon on weekends, arriving by Hearst's private train. A spur led off the main railroad and into the San Simeon estate. Scores of servants waited dutifully on famous actors such as Charlie Chaplin and Douglas Fairbanks Sr., on tennis champion Bill Tilden, or on movie mogul Louis B. Mayer, who was one of Hearst's best friends. Hearst's picnics on his vast estate were legendary, the catered meals of caviar and other delicacies taken out to the picnic sites by trucks while the guests followed on horseback, accompanied by a full orchestra.

The power-mad Hearst amused his guests in the evening by doing clog dances and mimicking politicians and celebrities. He urged guests to challenge his encyclopedic memory, running down the names of Henry the Eighth's wives or rattling off the presidents of the United States in order. Polite applause followed the completion of these feats of memory.

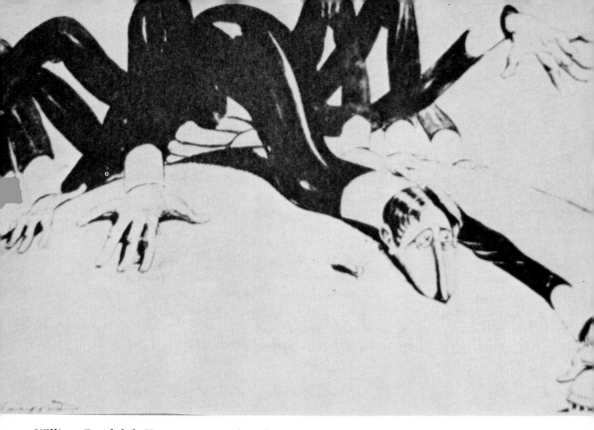

William Randolph Hearst cartooned at the turn of the century as a greedy political spider reaching out for the White House.

Though married, Hearst devoted himself to his mistress, Marion Davies, a blonde-haired, buxom actress with little acting ability whom he attempted many times to make into a star, financing many of her silent and early talking films—which lost him fortunes since most of the pictures were box-office failures. He considered her his own "creation", and many years after she had retired from the films, Hearst would spend hours in his private projection room, viewing such clinkers as *When Knighthood Was in Flower* and weeping at the scenes in which his Marion acted, or attempted to act.

Hearst built an enormous "bungalow" for Miss Davies in Southern California, but she spent most of her time in his draughty castle at San Simeon, much like the heroine in *Citizen Kane,* Orson Welles' masterpiece profile of Hearst. Welles' career was almost wrecked by the film, which is now considered one of the greatest pictures ever made. The Hearst press ignored it, refusing to take advertisements for it, and Hearst columnists villified Welles. Even the Hollywood community at the Academy Awards presentation for 1941, when the picture was nominated for eight Academy Awards, became a Hearst chorus, booing and hissing every time the film was mentioned.

Early in his career, Hearst was politically ambitious, contributing heavily to favored politicians and eagerly coveting the governorship of New York; but all his power and money could not secure him the post. He settled for his newspaper dynasty, attempting to control American morals, manners, and

This notorious sketch, a complete fabrication drawn by the noted artist Frederic Remington, appeared on all of Hearst's front pages to inflame Americans to war with Spain.

politics through his press, even attempting to affect world events. His most infamous publishing act was to provoke war between the United States and Spain over Cuba. He stirred up a witch's brew of hatred for Spain and its military commanders in Cuba to the point where the American public was in a frenzy to drive out the Spaniards, a press policy that established him as the world's leading "yellow journalist." Rival newspapers dubbed him "the wizard of ooze," but he ignored it.

Hearst sent the painter Frederic Remington to Cuba in 1896, ordering him to draw Spanish atrocities and ship these to his newspapers. Remington spent some time in Cuba, diligently looking for atrocities, and then wired Hearst: "Everything is quiet. There is no trouble here. There will be no war. I wish to return."

The Chief fired back a wire which has become a Hearst classic: "Please remain. You furnish the pictures. I'll furnish the war."

Remington did furnish sketches, notorious fabrications, one sketch showing an American woman stripped naked on board a ship in Cuban waters as Spanish secret police stood about "searching" her and leering at her nude body. Such inflammatory material soon had the citizenry crying for vengeance. Hearst got his way; following the explosion of the United States warship *Maine* in Havana Harbor, America went to war with Spain and shortly freed Cuba, as well as the Philippine Islands.

Another target of Hearst's hatred was Mexico, or its leaders. He ran a photo on the front pages of his newspapers in 1913 showing Mexican children waist-deep in water with their hands raised. The caption stated that these children had just been herded into the ocean by Mexican federales before being shot. Some weeks later, the man who took the photo, a tourist, announced that

The event that Hearst had hoped for (some claimed he helped plan it): The destruction of the American battleship, *Maine*, at Havana, on February 15, 1898. (Painting by W. Louis Sonntag, Jr.)

Newspaper tycoon William Randolph Hearst (left) leaving a Senate hearing in Washington in 1927 after admitting that he had not bothered to substantiate his press charges of theft against President Calles of Mexico.

he had asked the bathing children to put their hands up to make a better photo and that the photo was taken in British Honduras. It mattered little to Hearst, who preferred to fake his news when it served his purpose.

The Chief's abiding hatred for Communism caused him to repeatedly order phony pictures run in his newspapers showing masses of starving peasants, victims of famine and Soviet oppression; the photos were of famine victims in other countries, taken decades earlier. Any socialist leader received Hearst's venom; and in 1927, this included Mexico's socialist president, Plutarco Elias Calles. Hearst's newspapers insisted that Calles had stolen $1,250,000 from his country's treasury and used the money to bribe American senators to obtain treaties favorable to Mexico. Before a senate committee investigating the charges, Hearst boldly took the stand to state that no attempt had been made by his newspapers to substantiate the story.

At the outbreak of the Spanish Civil War, Hearst, who sided with fascist leader Franco, ran atrocity photos which were attributed to the Loyalists when in truth the actrocities had been committed by Franco's men. In the United States, Hearst lambasted FDR as a flaming liberal, backing such rabble-rousers as Father Charles E. Coughlin, the fascist-inclined "radio priest" of the 1930s, and thoroughly corrupt politicians such as Big Bill Thompson of Chicago.

Hearst was not above stealing documents for his newspapers. He was ejected from France when officials learned that he had ordered an employee to abscond with a copy of a treaty between France and Britain. Immediately upon his return to America, Hearst demanded that the Department of State file an official protest against France. (It did not.)

By the time Hearst died in 1951, his publishing empire was already on the wane, many of his newspapers having either closed down or merged with competing publications. He was then an old man, still dreaming his devastating dreams of empire.

Jemmy HIRST

Tanner (dates uncertain)

A wealthy retired Tanner, Hirst lived in Rawcliffe, England. This rotund eccentric went hunting in the 1840s by riding a wild bull, and, instead of chasing foxes, he raced after pigs "all of whom answered to their names." In addition to a valet and a housekeeper, his large country home was overrun with foxes, otters, dogs, cats, and mules. Hirst had ordered a specially large coffin constructed; and this he used as a bar, keeping whiskey inside the box and serving friends on its top slab. When Hirst died at the age of about ninety, the coffin was emptied of its alcoholic contents and he was placed inside. He had requested that he be carried to his grave by eight "old maid pallbearers," but the guinea offered each old maid in the area was not enough "to overcome the shyness habitual to the maiden state." Instead, eight widows lugged the zany to his final resting place.

Halbert Louis HOARD

Journalist, Inventor (1861–1933)

The son of the Governor of Wisconsin (William D. Hoard, 1889–91), Halbert Hoard proved himself to be one of the most eccentric newspaper editors on record during his custodianship of the Jefferson County *Union* of Fort Atkinson, Wisconsin. Fiercely anti-communist and anti-union, Hoard favored birth control but was violently against circumcision. He opposed Prohibition and argued constantly against the income tax.

Circumcision, said Hoard, diminished a woman's sexual experience. Prohibition, he insisted, did nothing more than sponsor gangsters. An habitual letter writer, Hoard once penned the following missive to Eliot Ness, leader of the federal prohibition agents battling Capone in Chicago:

Dear Mr. Ness:

I am a 100 percent wet, but I humor you for your bravery. The sooner you put those bootlegger drys where they can't vote for prohibition, the quicker we can get a repeal of the Eighteenth Amendment. I'm for you.

Sincerely,
H.L. Hoard

Born October 3, 1861 in Munnsville, New York, Hoard spent his early youth pioneering in South Dakota. He was a failure as a frontier rancher, purchasing a cattle ranch only to find out that the land held nothing but alkaline water which the cattle could not drink. He next used his land as a vast tree nursery, planting thousands of seedling walnut trees only to see them destroyed by rolling tumbleweeds in a violent sandstorm weeks later.

Hoard later wrote of these experiences in his newspaper, relating colorful western yarns, such as the frontier cafe that served $1 steaks or steaks for $1.25. Those who wisely paid the extra quarter received a sharp knife.

183

The fiery and unpredictable editor of the Jefferson County *Union*, Halbert Louis Hoard.

Hoard not only collected wild stories for his newspaper, but he encouraged every stray dog to feed at his back porch in Fort Atkinson; police arrived to tell him they would pick up every unlicensed dog within a block of his home. Hoard rushed down to city hall where he bought scores of dog licenses and thus adopted an army of canines.

The editor's personal stationary, which found its way often to the White House—he corresponded with four presidents—carried Hoard's photo and a printed line beneath stating: "A letter doesn't amount to much if you can't envision the writer."

Newly introduced female undergarments sent Hoard into an editorial rage. He despised corsets and once angrily wrote: "There is more pleasure in putting one's arm around a horse's neck than around the waist of a corseted lady." In the early 1920s the height of fashion for a female—flappers, they were called—was to wear chest-flattening brassieres. These restricting undergarments caused editor Hoard no end of frustration. Such brassieres, Hoard thundered in print, were binding and uncomfortable. Moreover, said the editor, quoting medical experts, the brassieres caused breast cancer.

Hoard's campaign against brassieres went on for for years, culminating in a petition to the United States Congress that the editor put together, somehow convincing the leading male residents of Fort Atkinson to sign their names to the following:

> We the undersigned note with alarm the increase in divorce since the Nineteenth Amendment—the woman suffrage law. We note many more women wearing breeches than before. We can stand that, but this new fad—slab-sided dressed flat in front—showing women in the fashion pictures as flat-chested as a man, we regard with jealous eyes ... We ask that the Congress of the United States do its utmost to break down these brassieres as an evil that menaces the future well-being of society.

Hoard went on railing at the new-fangled brassieres, stating that infants were being deprived of the milk of their mothers who wore the infernal undergarment and, as a result, could not produce milk.

Hoard's most outrageous ideas centered about an invention of his own, a weird looking contraption he called a "spine stimulator." In 1907, the editor thought that he was prematurely decaying. He consulted osteopaths and other medical men, then concluded that his heart needed more "food" pumped to it and this could be done by stimulating the spine. He built a machine which

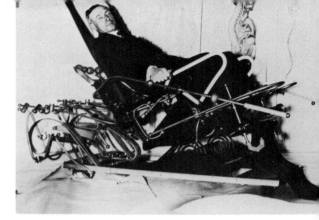

Editor Hoard in his "spine stimulator" chair, his own invention.

massaged the spine until, he said, the "proper ooze" was established to satisfy the heart's ravenous appetite. Use of his "spine stimulator," said Hoard, could cure ailments dealing with heart, stomach, bowels, and kidneys, being particularly effective in combating lumbago, rheumatism and constipation.

Several of these machines, finally labeled "curative chairs," and resembling early day electric chairs, were produced by Hoard and sold to those seeking one form of relief or another. The device, however, never caught on and only one model exists today in the Hoard Museum in Fort Atkinson. Its inventor refused to abandon its use almost to the day of his death on December 28, 1933, considering the "spine stimulator" to be the crowning achievement of a spectacular life.

J. Edgar HOOVER

FBI Director (1895–1972)

Hoover was not only the complete bureaucrat, but also the complete autocrat—a tyrannical, calculating, and utterly ruthless individual who used his position as director of the Federal Bureau of Investigation to shape public opinion, exhalt his own image and power, and intimidate American presidents for almost fifty years. Though several presidents thought to remove Hoover, they reconsidered quickly when they realized that he gathered "inside" information not only on the entire Washington political corps but on the presidents themselves. President Lyndon Johnson wanted to get rid of Hoover; but he had serious doubts about the repercussions and decided against the move, commenting in typical Johnson fashion: "I'd rather have him inside the tent pissing out, than outside pissing in." As far as Johnson was concerned, Hoover's chief function seemed to be providing spurious reports from the bureau about the sex scandals of Washington politicians—which LBJ employed as hilarious bedtime reading.

Taking over the Bureau in 1924 amidst wholesale corruption, Hoover vowed to separate the FBI from politics; instead, he turned the agency into his private barony where he ruled supreme. Any of his agents caught drinking on the job, having extramarital sex, or not adhering to Hoover's strict schedules and codes of conduct was immediately fired. The director went further.

J. Edgar Hoover in 1924, when he took over the FBI.

Anything at all that displeased him in an agent was cause for dismissal. He fired an agent for marrying a woman of Arab extraction, an act which he considered un-American. He fired an agent for wearing a tie with loud colors. He fired an agent whose handshake was "clammy."

The FBI Training Academy in Virginia was Hoover's fiefdom, which he visited regularly with the pomp of a secret police director, inspecting candidates who stood to rigid attention before him. On one occasion, Hoover spotted a trainee with a slightly mottled face. He was told that the man was a war hero; and because of the wounds received, he had undergone plastic surgery. "Get rid of him," was Hoover's decision. "He doesn't *look* like an FBI man!" With Hoover everything was appearance, the superficial images of FBI agents established by Hollywood (which he shaped as a behind-the-scenes advisor) from the "G-Man" image of the early thirties to the TV personality of Efrem Zimbalist Jr. The FBI agent, according to Hoover's dictates, wore conservative suits, white shirts, black shoes, drab ties, and a short haircut. He had to look like an eager insurance salesman, and he did. He also had to be white.

It was no secret that Hoover considered blacks inferior, physically and mentally. (His favorite radio show was "Amos 'N Andy.") For decades, the only blacks with official FBI status were his chauffeur and his office receptionist; and try as they might, presidents and attorney generals found it next to impossible to compel Hoover to hire blacks. During the Civil Rights upheaval

George "Machine Gun" Kelly, about whom Hoover lied to build the "G-Man" image.

of the mid-1960s, the director finally gave in to enormous pressure from Attorney General Robert Kennedy and hired some token blacks, but his overall racial policy remained the same. For instance, Hoover contacted the Chicago office of the FBI when Kennedy demanded blacks be added to the bureau. A black janitor was hired overnight as an agent, but his duties were confined to driving a car for the Chicago bureau chief.

The director avoided all places where he might be exposed to blacks. At the racetrack (he was a consistent $2 bettor), Hoover sat in a special box, agents surrounding him to keep away "undesirables." When in New York, Hoover always dined at the Stork Club, owned and operated by his close crony, Sherman Billingsley, also an avowed racist, whose nightclub was strictly off-limits to blacks. Here Hoover found convivial companionship with the likes of Walter Winchell (see entry), then the most powerful columnist and news broadcaster in the nation—a gossip-gulper and scandalmonger who generally acted as the director's personal PR man.

Public relations and good publicity were foremost in Hoover's mind, an around-the-clock obsession. He played to the news media and staged important arrests throughout the country for decades for the benefit of a favorable press. He was a man who lived on press clippings. Winchell was only one of Hoover's favored "journalists" allowed to accompany agents on important raids. Pulitzer-Prize winning George Bliss of the Chicago *Tribune,* who was later to commit suicide, was another.

The very word "G-Man" was invented by Hoover. He told the story in the *Tennessee Law Review* in 1946 that kidnapper-gangster George "Machine-Gun" Kelly, upon his capture in 1933, threw up trembling hands and shouted, "Don't shoot, G-Men, don't shoot!" FBI agents were nowhere near Kelly when he was apprehended. W.J. Raney of the Memphis police captured Kelly single-handedly in the kidnapper's bungalow hideout. All Kelly said was, "I've been waiting all night for you."

But the sensational gangster era was grist for Hoover's mill, and he made much of the Dillinger, Floyd, and Barker cases. Almost all the facts he provided concerning these outlaws were patently untrue. Yet he took personal credit for almost every major arrest, grandstanding himself as the nation's "gangbuster." He got rid of every agent—and there were only a few like the limelight-loving Melvin Purvis—who dared to take the spotlight away from him.

For Hoover, organized crime in the United States simply did not exist; and he denied the existence of the crime cartel almost to the day he died, concentrating on the "red menace," a life-long mania. During his oppressive reign, most of Hoover's agents spent their time keeping so-called reds under surveillance. One Chicago agent told the author that he spent almost six months observing two old men, suspected reds, playing chess every day.

Hoover demanded results from his agents, and this meant daily reports. Whether or not agents had anything to report was unimportant. The daily reports had to be filed, or agents risked being summarily dismissed. Most agents took to rewriting newspaper stories on local crime and submitting these to the Washington office. Apocryphal or not, one story concerning the submis-

President Lyndon B. Johnson, seated right, with his mother and Richard Nixon, relished Hoover's scandalous reports on Washington colleagues as bedtime reading.

sion of these reports totally reflects the awesome power Hoover wielded over his terrified agents. He received one report typed on FBI memoranda sheets so packed with words that it ran off the margins. Hoover, who spent his nightime hours reading reports, penciled in the note, "watch the borders." When the report went into the FBI hopper the next day, Hoover's notation was seen, so the story goes, and an associate director ordered agents to the Canadian and Mexican borders to keep watch for "God know's what."

Agents were regularly checked by other agents as to their social habits, friends, even the types of books and newspapers they read. More than a decade ago, the author wrote a book entitled *Dillinger: Dead or Alive?,* a highly critical account of the FBI role in the so-called apprehension of John Dillinger. The book, among a host of others over the years, was banned by Hoover; any agent reading it would risk an upbraiding if not dismissal. Agents friendly to the author stated that they secretly read the book in libraries and carried reviews of the work around in their wallets, but only read these reviews in their cars or in the semiprivacy of their own homes.

The privacy of Hoover's own home was sacrosanct. Except for Howard Hughes (see entry), he was perhaps the most secretive man in America. He had no known hobbies. He walked several blocks each day for exercise. He ate cottage cheese and peaches for lunch without variation most of his life.ime. Washington scandal-sniffers desperately went through his garbage, finding little but discarded laundry bills. The most consistent charge against Hoover— after his death—was that he was a frustrated homosexual, having a subtle liaison with his long-time associate director, Clyde Tolson (who was always at Hoover's side, even on vacation, and who inherited the bulk of Hoover's estate, almost $500,000). Of course this allegation was never proved, nor was the whispered claim that the director was murdered by an overdose of insulin ever given any credence. The director channeled whatever feeling for a fellow creature he could muster to his dogs, which, in his own words, were "the smartest and most affectionate dogs I've ever seen. Anybody would think twice before they'd commit murder because of the way those dogs bark ... The less I

The power-mad J. Edgar Hoover at the track with his eternal side-kick Clyde Tolson seated, smiling, behind him.

think of some people, the more I think of my dogs." Hoover paid regularly to maintain the graves of his departed dogs in an exclusive Washington pet cemetery.

Upon Hoover's death in 1972, the FBI underwent substantial changes, mostly in attitude. Agents no longer felt the oppressiveness of a bureaucratic tyrant who had filled their days and nights with dread, not to mention the terror Hoover's mere name instilled in the mind of the American public.

Brian G. HUGHES

Manufacturer (1849–1924)

A wealthy manufacturer of boxes, Hughes spent most of his seventy-five years on earth playing practical jokes, usually to embarrass the greedy and the pompous. He developed the habit of strolling out of Tiffany's in New York and dropping a large box that spilled hundreds of imitation gems. Hughes would chuckle with delight as passersby scrambled after the glass stones. He would purchase an expensive umbrella, hang it up in a restaurant, and watch with relish as a casual thief picked it up, scurried outside, and opened it to be engulfed by a waterfall of leaflets reading "This umbrella stolen from Brian G. Hughes."

Hughes enjoyed sending invitations under another name to infamous gate-crashers, inviting them to fabulous banquets and parties that were never held. The manufacturer purchased a small parcel of land in The Bronx with a broken-down shack on it, a monstrosity of a building occupied by an army of hoboes. This building Hughes offered free to several historical societies, stating that the premises had once housed the famous Lafayette during the Revolution. The societies leaped at the opportunity, but turned down the "honor" after inspecting the so-called "Hughes Mansion." Always eager to donate land for civic purposes, Hughes offered the aldermanic board of Brooklyn a plot of land to be turned into a park. He was lavished with praise at a special board hearing, but the gratitude turned sour when several aldermen discovered that the site for the park was no more than a two-by-eight-foot lot which had cost Hughes $35.

Like Hugh Troy and William Cole (see entries), Hughes loved disguises and spent years impersonating important officials and dignitaries, such as the Prince of Amsdam and Cyprus, bestowing honorary titles upon gullible

189

Broadway stars. The practical joker was not beyond near-criminal pursuits to humor himself. He once left empty picture frames and burglar's tools on the doorstep of the Metropolitan Museum of Art, thereby causing officials and police to frantically search the museum for missing items.

Hughes' pranks were memorable to the public, but most of all they consumed a great deal of time for a man who had nothing but money and time to spend.

Howard Robard HUGHES, Jr.

Tycoon (1905–1976)

Born on Christmas Eve 1905, Howard Hughes demonstrated a plethora of quirks and oddball inclinations from early childhood. A great deal of credit for his inexplicable phobias and fears can be given to his mother, Allene Hughes, who was forever fretting over his mental and physical condition, worrying about his weight, height, feet, teeth, digestion, bowels—anxious over his inability to befriend other boys, his supersensitivity, his nervousness. Two of Hughes biographers, Donald L. Barlett and James B. Steele commented in *Empire* that "Howard ... learned from her that the best way to attract attention or to escape unpleasant situations was to complain of illness. The slighest whimper from him would unleash a wave of smothering attention from Allene Hughes, and throughout his life he would pretend to be sick when he wanted to avoid responsibility or elicit sympathy."

At eighteen, Hughes was an orphan; but he inherited a giant fortune in the form of the enormously successful Hughes Tool Company which owned the exclusive drilling bit used by every oil rig in the world. From this simple tool, the Hughes millions flowed. The boy wonder went on to live extravagantly and secretly, forever fearful of losing his fortune or his reputation. He felt compelled to prove his courage, and time and again he set world aviation records, crashing several times only to survive miraculously. To feed an ever-bloating ego, Hughes became Hollywood's most flamboyant film producer, taking over RKO Studios and producing some of the most spectacular duds ever filmed, movies that could boast of unlimited advertising and promotion budgets and little talent.

Hughes was an extraordinary man by all standards. His phobias increased to the point of obsession over the years. He feared germs of all kinds. He was frightened of dust, yet toward the end of his life, he refused to have his rooms cleaned because he was afraid that dangerous sprays might be used. Most often he was afraid of being sent to a mental institution from which he would never escape. By his late sixties, Hughes had decided to insulate himself against the outside world; physically, he husbanded everything that he could call his own, refusing to cut his hair or fingernails, refusing to permit removal of the hypodermic needle fragments broken off in his arms, storing his urine

Millionaire Howard Hughes at the controls of his $25 million wooden flying boat, better known as the "Spruce Goose." (Wide World)

(allegedly to be examined for disease, which it wasn't), scooping up the flaking skin that fell from his to dehydrated body. Shortly before his death, Hughes ceased to eat or drink; and his weight dropped to ninety-three pounds.

Throughout his bizarre life, Hughes developed curious diets. Following his crash in Beverly Hills on July 8, 1946, while he was at the controls of his twin-engine XF–11 experimental plane (produced by Hughes Aviation), Hughes was taken to a hospital in critical condition. As he began to improve, he insisted that the only way his life could be saved was to drink enormous amounts of fresh orange juice. He ordered the hospital staff to bring oranges into his private room and cut and squeeze them in his presence so that he could make sure that the juice was fresh; he insisted that if the citrus of the orange was exposed to the air for more than thirty minutes the juice, the only ingredient that would save his life, would be useless.

Another great and persistent fear that nagged Howard Hughes every waking moment was that he would be overheard talking, even in the most casual conversations. He would sometimes go personally to Chicago to meet a contact-man who handled some minor business for him. Wearing a disguise, he would rendezvous with the contact man in a laundromat, but he would begin discussions only after the laundromat's doors had been locked to prevent patrons from entering and every machine had been turned on to cover the sound of his voice, their metallic din making his conversation all but inaudible. The contact-man dutifully nodded at Hughes' directions, even though he did not understand a word, fearing to lose his position should he ask the great man to repeat himself. The contact-man in Chicago also realized that by this time Hughes had long lapses of memory and would undoubtedly forget his directives within a few days. (This story was provided to the author by an undercover agent whose job at the time was to monitor the comings and goings of Howard Hughes in order to determine Hughes' business operations and define his holdings—a task that has proved to this day to be impossible.)

On another occasion, Hughes went to great and ridiculous lengths to guarantée secrecy in a multimillion-dollar deal, ostensibly with the Rockefellers. Hughes' behavior at the time, typically oddball, showed him to be the strangest American businessman on record. At the very least, his way of

191

conducting high finance would baffle the most perceptive negotiator. In 1954, Hughes had contacted movie mogul Spyros Skouras, telling him that he was thinking of selling all of his holdings and asking Skouras to locate a buyer. Skouras promptly called promoter William Zeckendorf, who in turn contacted Laurance Rockefeller. Both Rockefeller and Zeckendorf then flew from New York to Los Angeles to meet with Hughes.

The billionaire industrialist had left word at the Beverly Hills Hotel that Rockefeller and Zeckendorf were to follow his instructions for their ultrasecret meeting. Both men drove to an intersection not far from their hotel where they parked and waited. Next they were approached by a man wearing leisure clothes who told them to follow his car, a broken-down auto that Zeckendorf later described as "something the Okies might have used on the trek west twenty years ago."

Rockefeller and Zeckendorf were led into a slum-like area and directed to enter a building that appeared to be a flophouse, although it was guarded by neatly dressed collegiate types with short haircuts. The visitors were taken to the fourth floor, led down a long dark hallway, and then left mutely wondering as their guide knocked out a code-like rapping on a door. Hughes answered the door with a week's growth on his cheeks, wearing worn-out shoes and soiled shirt and pants. He motioned them into a sparsely furnished room and sat on the armrest of a couch, a position from which he never budged during the interview. He tapped a hearing aid to let his guests know that they had better speak loudly to make their point.

Spokesman Zeckendorf began by outlining the Hughes empire for its owner, detailing Hughes' holdings as best as he and Rockefeller knew them to be. He then offered Hughes $350 million for all his assets.

"You don't know what you're talking about," Hughes said calmly without changing his bland facial expression. He also told Zeckendorf that the offer was nowhere near "enough."

"What is enough?" pushed Zeckendorf.

"I won't tell you," replied Hughes.

"Do you want to sell?"

"Under certain circumstances."

"What circumstances?"

"If the price is right."

"What price?"

"The price you might offer me. If it is enough, I'll sell."

Zeckendorf was growing weary with the game, but he persisted as Rockefeller kept silent. "I am offering you four hundred and fifty million. Will you take it?"

"No."

"Howard," begged the perplexed Zeckendorf, "just exactly what do you want?"

"I won't tell you."

"Howard, take it or leave it, five hundred million."

"I leave it."

The visitors left the conference without further negotiations. It was later claimed that they had been suckered into an old Hughes ploy; the tycoon would appear to want to sell his empire and then discover through such weird discussions exactly what he was worth, allowing his competitors to laboriously detail holdings he himself could not properly evaluate. Such a contention is dubious at best since Hughes had weekly report sheets that broke down every penny in his estate. More likely he conducted such meetings to amuse himself and build higher an ego that was already colossal. That ego constantly fluctuated between zeniths and nadirs. Though he was one of the world's richest men, Howard Hughes was forever complaining to friends that he was lonely and depressed.

Normally shy and withdrawn, Hughes, especially during his Hollywood days as a producer, compelled himself to see as many women as possible, concentrating on actresses Billie Dove, Ida Lupino, Ginger Rogers, Ava Gardner, and Katharine Hepburn. In 1952, the tycoon became enamored of shapely Terry Moore, calling her in Germany where she was staying (and married to former football great Glenn Davis) and spending a fortune on two-hour daily phone calls. In later days, when Hughes had moved into Las Vegas, he would select women he desired in nightly casino prowls then have aides approach them and secure signed disclaimers before the women joined him. His marriage to actress Jean Peters was strange, to say the least, in that Hughes saw her almost by appointment only.

In the end, Hughes' mental disorders seized his every waking hour; he deteriorated rapidly during the 1970s until he became an utter recluse, shielded by bodyguards, fearing all manner of imaginary threats. He moved from one expensive hotel to another, occupying entire floors. Hughes ignored his many business interests, losing millions. He allowed his body to waste away, and he worried over the most petty problems. When he died in 1976, the Hughes empire was no longer his chief concern. He only thought of the millions of germs attacking his frail body. He died leaving an estate worth between $600 and $900 million.

George HULL

Merchant (1821–1902)

A successful cigar salesman, George Hull was a confirmed atheist who spent most of his spare time reading scientific books that supported Darwin's theory of evolution, plus experimenting with gases and stone, attempting to produce precious metals as the alchemists of old.

Visiting his sister in Ackerly, Iowa in 1866, Hull met a revivalist Methodist preacher named Turk, who was then staying with Hull's sister. He debated the Reverend Turk for hours on end, insisting that there had once been giants on earth. Turk said no. Hull became so indignant that the idea of creating a fake giant took root.

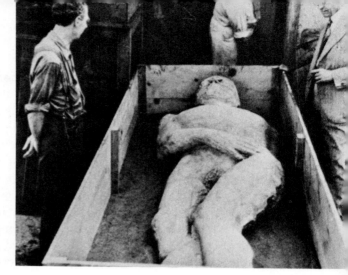

The incredible 12-foot-four-inch Cardiff Giant, George Hull's answer to an obstinate preacher.

Two years later Hull and a friend, H.B. Martin, purchased a seven-ton block of gypsum and shipped it to Chicago where, in the studio of Edward Burghardt, a marble cutter, two sculptors chiseled out a twelve-foot-four-inch form of a giant using Hull, who was on the premises for three months in late 1868, as the model. Hull refused to let the sculptors leave the studio, supplying them with beer and food until their assigned task was done.

The surface of the giant was given human pores when Hull hammered it repeatedly with a board riddled with darning needles. It was then soaked in sulphuric acid to give it a dark hue. Hull next shipped the completed giant to the farm of William C. Newell, a relative living in Cardiff, New York. The giant was buried and then "discovered" by workmen on October 16, 1889. Up to this time the giant had cost Hull $2,600, an expensive hoax, to say the least, but he expected to sell the curiosity for a fortune.

The finding of the giant sent shock waves through the press and the public. It was put on display in Syracuse, New York and great crowds, paying high ticket admissions, viewed this anthropological marvel. Once customer, O.C. Marsh, a Yale paleontologist, examined the Cardiff Giant and reported it to be "of very recent origin and a decided humbug."

Other scientists quickly came to the same conclusion and farmer Newell, under pressure from newsmen, pointed a shaky finger at his relative, George Hull, who had already sold the giant for approximately $30,000. Hull confessed to the hoax before the year was out, but that did not prevent the Cardiff Giant from becoming one of the great attractions in New York City.

P.T. Barnum (see entry) attempted to buy the Cardiff Giant, but its investors would not sell. Barnum had has own giant built and put it on display. After several successful tours about the country through the decades, the Cardiff Giant was purchased in 1948 by The Farmer's Museum in Cooperstown, New York, where it is currently on display as part of the state's history. A history that was, for a short while, wholly invented by a cigar salesman desperate to win an argument with a fire-and-brimstone preacher.

H.L. (Haroldson Lafayette) HUNT

Oilman (1889–1974)

"A man who has $200,000 is about as well off, for all practical purposes, as I am," said H.L. Hunt, who became a billionaire in the 1950s with international oil drilling. He might have added that if he followed the eccentric Hunt's lifestyle, a man did not require much more than $100 a week in salary, maybe less.

Hunt was a farm boy from Ramsey, Illinois, whose father had served in the Confederate Army. Like most self-made millionaires of this century, Hunt ran away from home, working at the age of sixteen for lumber companies and railroads. When his father died in 1911, Hunt inherited $6,000 which he used to buy a delapidated Arkansas plantation. His crops could not be sold in the agricultural panics of the 1920s, and Hunt went broke. Like thousands of others, he took to the roads, living a nomadic life until reaching El Dorado, Arkansas, in 1921. Oil had been discovered nearby only weeks earlier. Hunt by then had become a professional card player and he easily won a brand new oilwell in a furious game of five-card stud.

The oil well came in a gusher a few weeks later, and within a few years Hunt was a millionaire. With his profits, Hunt drilled more wells throughout the Southwest, but he made most of his additional millions during the late 1920s by trading oil leases—a risky business at which he was an expert. Luck was also with him; most of the wells he drilled in America (and some his firm set up in the Middle East) proved to be loaded with "black gold." By 1936, the Hunt Oil Company was the largest producer of oil and natural gas in America.

Always an unorthodox man, Hunt admired President George Washington (or at least the home Washington built) and ordered that Mount Vernon be duplicated outside of Dallas, Texas. The building was almost twice the size of the original, but after its completion, Hunt's extravagances halted abruptly. He adopted the posture of the everyday working man, sitting on his front porch during the evenings in an old rocking chair and listening to country music on a small radio. He wore cheap, well-worn clothes to his Dallas office and carried his lunch in a small brown paper bag. He drove an ancient small car between work and home. When asked why he had suddenly stopped spending money lavishly, Hunt replied that he had a dream (or fear) that he would some day wake up and be "stone broke." He made this remark when his personal fortune had already sailed beyond $1 billion.

Next to the oil business, Hunt's energies were consumed by the writing of

Billionaire H. L. Hunt and his wife singing the promotion song for Hunt's hortatory novel. (Wide World)

his opus, a novel he called *Alpaca* in which he summed up his philosophy: A citizen could vote as many times as the amount of taxes he paid. Therefore he, H.L. Hunt, could undoubtedly, under such a system, elect the president of his choice single-handedly.

Before his death on November 29, 1974, at eighty-five—he left a fortune between $2 and $3 billion, not a dime to chairty—Hunt's proudest moment was the publication of his novel, self-published, of course. The billionaire promoted the book by having his two stepdaughters stand in a bookstore window singing a little ditty of Hunt's own creation to the tune of "The Doggie in the Window." It ran:

> How much is that book in the window?
> The one which my popsy wrote.
> How much is that book in the window?
> You can buy it without signing a note.
> *Alpaca!* Fifty Cents!

John HUSTON

Director (Born 1906)

The son of the distinguished character actor Walter Huston, John Huston began his Hollywood career in 1932 by writing scripts. He went on to become a cultist director (for *The Maltese Falcon* and other Bogart classics) and then slipped into the role of actor, a part he had been playing most of his life. From Huston's earliest days, he was known as a drinking, brawling two-fisted type. He once picked a fight with Errol Flynn (or vice versa) and thought he would have an easy time of it. The two stepped to a garden lawn from a Hollywood party and went at it. Huston, who had no idea that Flynn had been an amateur boxer, found himself getting as good as he gave. (Flynn also had a little technique that surprised Huston, jumping forth with both heels onto the toes of an opponent's shoes, pinioning him, and grinding his heels into his adversary's feet.) The match ended in a bloody draw, much to Huston's surprise.

For sheer audacity, no one every approached director John Huston for filmic pranks. His first major film was the Sam Spade opus, *The Maltese Falcon,* starring Humphrey Bogart. At the time, John's father was the famous matinee idol, Walter Huston, who won an Academy Award in a subsequent John Huston epic, *The Treasure of the Sierra Madre.* When John first began shooting *The Maltese Falcon,* his famous father came to him. He asked his son for a bit part in the movie. Huston later remembered: "Dad said he wanted to appear in every film I directed, for luck."

Walter's bit part consisted of barging into Sam Spade's office in the dead of night as the mortally wounded Captain Jacobi, who delivered the fabulous Falcon to Spade. Walter Huston was never even seen in the shadows as he

Director John Huston (center), on the set of *The Maltese Falcon*, watching his father, Walter Huston, rehearsing his "bit" part; behind the camera (partially obscured) is Humphrey Bogart and Lee Patrick; "the black bird" lies on the floor, wrapped in newspapers, between the Hustons.

staggered forward; his few words were nothing more than the gutteral trickle of a dying man: "You know ... the Falcon."

To his amazement, Walter Huston received a phone call from Hal B. Wallis' secretary at his home that night. Wallis was the producer of the movie. The secretary stated that Mr. Wallis had seen the rushes of the day's shooting and stated that Mr. Huston had "overacted" in his bit part and he would have to do it again.

Huston fumed. It was an insult; he was one of the finest actors in Hollywood, in the world, and he had done the bit part without pay and for the sake of his son. "I have never overacted in my life!" Huston screamed over the phone to the secretary. But trooper that he was, Huston agreed to return the next morning and redo the scene.

Suddenly, a man's voice cut in: "Walter, this is Wallis. Hope you don't mind a retake. You were pretty bad, you know."

Huston exploded in anger. "Goddammit, I said I'd do the fool scene again, didn't I?"

Then the veteran actor heard a roar of laughter from the other end of the line. It took him a few minutes to realize that his son John was "Wallis" and that the secretary had been Mary Astor, Bogart's co-star in the movie.

In 1942, Huston was directing another Bogart thriller, *Across the Pacific,* when he received orders from the War Department to report for duty. He begged for more time, but Washington ordered him to report within twenty-four hours.

If he had to go, John Huston would leave Hollywood with one last laugh, this one on the demanding Jack Warner. Huston decided to end his shooting of *Across the Pacific* in such a manner that the movie could never be completed.

"I sat right down," he remembered, "and altered the script and set up a wild scene with Bogie trapped in Panama. Made him a prisoner of the Japanese who were out to bomb the Canal. I fixed it so his hands were tied behind him and packed the room with Japanese soldiers armed with machine guns. Outside, more armed soldiers surrounded the house.

"That night we shot it right up to the part where Bogie is hopelessly trapped. I knew there was no way in God's green world he could logically have escaped. I also knew Warner would never re-shoot the whole ending. I had them. So I waved goodbye to Bogie—and was in Washington the next morning."

Jack Warner did two things when he learned of the mess Huston left in his wake. First, he exploded, threatening death to Huston. He would personally track him down to whatever obscure point of the globe he had run.

Secondly, Warner brought in relief director Vincent Sherman. Sherman and his writers worked for days and at a great expense to get Bogie out of his dilemma. Finally, Sherman had one of the Japanese guards go berserk. A gun was miraculously placed in Bogart's hands. Freeing himself, Bogart shouted: "I'm not so easily trapped!" This scene was later modified to one guard being distracted, so that Bogie could make his move.

It didn't make much sense, but director Sherman was happy. "Listen," he explained, "If you ask me we were lucky to get that bastard out of there at all!"

In making *The Treasure of the Sierra Madre,* Huston enjoyed playing pranks on the film's Mexican bad guy bandit, Alfonso Bedoya, who made his debut in the film (the sinister-smiling, buck-toothed actor had been selected by Huston, the story goes, out of a crowd). Bedoya was more interested in food than in acting. Huston watched Bedoya literally run to the on-location kitchen every time lunchbreak was announced; the Mexican actor wolfed down several helpings as if the meal were his last on earth. The following day, Huston (with Bogart's collusive efforts) went to a prop horse on which Bedoya was to sit and spread strong glue on the saddle. The director waited to shoot Bedoya's scene just before lunch. As the actor perched in the saddle delivering his evil lines, Huston called "Cut! Lunch!" Everyone scrambled for the chow line except Bedoya, who, try as he might, could not release himself from the saddle. As he watched the rest of the cast and crew move past him with heaping plates of food, Bedoya began to weep, then sob, then wildly scream as he struggled in the glue-ridden saddle that would not give him up. Huston and Bogart strolled by eating their lunch, looking at Bedoya as if he had suddenly gone berserk. Commented Bogart to Huston, "I don't know if this new fella is right for the movie business, John."

**Actor Humphrey Bogart, Huston's close friend
and fellow prankster.**

Barbara HUTTON

Heiress (1912–1979)

As a child, Barbara Hutton, heiress of the Woolworth fortune, was estranged from her parents, who had no time for her, and reared by eccentric, if not half-mad grandfather, Frank W. Woolworth, the five-and-dime tycoon. She lived in Woolworth's Fifth Avenue mansion, built in 1901, a house that most people would consider something out of Edgar Allan Poe.

Woolworth, tone deaf as a child and frustrated at not being able to play an instrument, had installed an organ in his mansion that was played almost around the clock. Its eerie tones were heard night and day in every room of the enormous mansion, with outlets in the bedposts of Woolworth's bed and in every closet and washroom. Further, the daffy magnate had commissioned dozens of huge paintings of his musical heroes—Liszt, Beethoven, Wagner, and others—and these adorned almost every available wall. Commented Louise Tanner in *Here Today,* "A guest might have the strange experience of listening to *Die Walkurie* to an accompaniment of lightning flashes and sound effects reminiscent of roulades of thunder, while out of the half-light there slowly materialized an ectoplasmic likeness of the composer."

Little Barbara was surrounded in this Phantom-of-the-Opera atmosphere by the cackling Woolworth, his mad wife (whose mind had cracked years earlier), Woolworth's close-mouthed nurse, and Mrs. Woolworth's brutish keeper. When not living in the Woolworth mansion, Barbara stayed at private schools or in the lavish homes of relatives. She had inherited more than $50 million in her teens, as had Doris Duke (see entry), but she was shown to the public as a "Poor Little Rich Girl." Barbara aided this image with such statements as "Though I had millions of dollars, I still had no home."

She questioned herself constantly and wrote soul-searching poetry. In the end, she decided that men had been the cause of her life's unhappiness, "including my father." Barbara debuted in December 1930, the same year that saw Doris Duke's coming out party.

Barbara Hutton's debut was fancier and more expensive, a $60,000 super dance with four orchestras and Rudy Vallee singing through his megaphone. In 1931, Barbara was presented to the British court, as was Doris Duke. Unlike Doris Duke, who married only twice, Barbara Hutton began marrying men— seven in all—in 1933, when she wedded a bogus Russian count Alexis Mdivani. The phony count had played on Barbara's vanity for weeks at Newport. "He didn't dismiss my fears with a laugh the way other people did," Barbara said later, "And just told me that anybody who had as much money as I did shouldn't worry about anything." But it was money on Mdivani's mind, and he demanded of Franklyn Hutton, Barbara's father, that he receive $1 million in "royalty" for marrying his daughter.

The couple were wed in a huge cathedral in Paris. So crowded with people and flowers was the church that it took the newlyweds almost a half-hour to get from the altar to their waiting limousine. Some months later, Barbara inherited $50 million. She called herself a "princess," even though her husband's title had long been exposed as illusionry. Though counseled to live quietly and curtail spending while the world suffered through the Great Depression, Barbara spent lavishly, unthinkingly, flying an orchestra from London to Paris at a cost of $10,000 for her twenty-second birthday party. Within two years, Barbara divorced her phony count in Reno, bestowing $2 million more on the calculating foreigner and telling the press that he had cared more for the polo ponies she bought him than for her.

Then began, with a vengeance, Barbara's marrying mania. Only twenty-four hours after her divorce from Mdivani, she married Count Kurt von Haugwitz-Reventlow, a titled Dane with his own fortune, "the handsomest person I'd ever happened to see," said Barbara. With her real count and authentic title, Barbara renounced her American citizenship, which angered the American public, and moved to London where she bought the largest, swankiest mansion in Regents Park for $5 million. Ostentatiously she outfit-ted her servants in powder blue and canary yellow uniforms. She had her only child, Lance, born through a Caesarean operation.

The second marriage began to wobble when Barbara grew bored of the count's pretentious behavior. "It was always, 'I am the Count von Haugwitz-Reventlow' with Kurt. He never forgot it—until one day I said, 'Who cares? Who cares about the Count von Haugwitz-Reventlow today?'" The count cared enough to threaten Barbara that she would have "three years of hell with headlines" unless she gave him $5 million. She declined the payoff and got the scandal. The couple were finally divorced by the royal decree of King Christian of Denmark.

By then, Barbara had returned to her native country and resumed her American citizenship. Her international antics, however, had given her a notoriety repugnant to down-and-out Americans. She was attacked by a starving mob outside a New York theater, punched, kicked, and scratched—one man hissing at her, "You rich bitch! I'd like to throw acid in your face!"

A sobbing Barbara asked reporters: "Why do they hate me? There are other girls as rich, richer, almost as rich." The newsmen already knew the answer but kept silent.

The next male on the Hutton hit parade was actor Cary Grant who married Barbara in 1942 and was instantly labeled "Cash-and-Cary." This third union ended in divorce a short time later. Making no financial demands on the heiress, Grant complained only that even with all the servants scurrying about Barbara's mansion he could not get a sandwich to eat.

Prince Igor Troubetzkoy, a Lithuanian, was the next hubby, lasting from 1947 to 1951. He was dumped because Barbara considered him "the meanest man in the world." Next came Porfirio Rubirosa, who had just divorced Doris Duke. "I loved him the moment I met him," gushed Barbara in 1953 at the time of her wedding to the playboy of the Dominican Republic. During the wedding, Barbara got tipsy on champagne before she could say "I do." She swayed drunkenly before her new spouse and blubbered: "Aren't you going to kiss me now?" She pointed to a bevy of photographers. "The press has waited so long."

Renting a huge passenger plane, the couple flew to Florida for their honeymoon. A little more than two months later, Barbara's only comment on her fifth husband was, "I feel as if I'd been hit over the head." Rubirosa moaned, "It's no good. She stays in bed and reads all day. It's very boring." They were promptly divorced.

One-time tennis player Gottfried von Gramm, who had been barred from entering the United States during the 1930s on morals charges, was the next husband plucked by Barbara; the couple wed in 1955 and divorced in 1958. Philip Van Renssalaer, who was at least twenty years Barbara's junior, was her next selection. She dumped a fortune in his lap but did not marry him. Her last husband was Doan Vinh, a Vietnamese prince, whom she married in 1966, a short-lived union.

The Poor Little Rich Girl had little to say toward the end of her spectacularly eccentric life. "I won't say my previous husbands thought only of my money," she commented, "but it had a certain fascination for them." Barbara Hutton, heiress, died alone on May 11, 1979, of cardiac arrest in the penthouse of the Beverly Wilshire Hotel.

William Henry IRELAND

Hoaxer (1777–1835)

In 1795, William Ireland, then eighteen, sat down and forged Shakespearian documents and manuscripts with such great authenticity that he was able to dupe the best minds in England. Ireland "discovered" a lost play of Shakespeare, *Vortigern and Rowena,* which was promptly produced by Richard Sheridan at Drury Lane. So skillful was Ireland's imitation of Shakespeare that he quickly penned another bogus play, *Henry II,* also accepted as genuine. The boy genius was so successful at his literary hoaxing that he faked documents proving that his ancestors had not only known Shakespeare well but inherited some of the Immortal Bard's estate. (Ireland's father was a modest bookseller; his family never had any ties with Shakespeare.)

Experts such as George Chalmers and Sir James Bland Burgess examined Ireland's forgeries in the bookshop of Samuel Ireland and pronounced them authentic. Only a few Shakespearian experts such as Edmund Malone and John Kemble, the actor, were skeptical about the Ireland "discoveries." Malone began to write accusatory articles which pointed to forgery by Ireland; but the hoaxer did not confess his stupendous fakes until 1805, repeating his admission in 1832. However, Ireland later recanted his confession and insisted that the Shakespeare "discoveries" were genuine.

All of this literary *Sturm und Drang* delighted the great biographer, James Boswell, who referred to the gigantic hoax as "Ireland's sin." Wrote Andrew Lang in *Contemporary Review* (December 1883), "The joke is that after the whole conspiracy exploded, people were anxious to buy examples of the forgeries. Mr. W.H. Ireland was equal to the occasion. He actually forged his own or ... his father's forgeries, and, by thus increasing the supply, he deluged the market with sham shams, with imitations of imitations. If the accusation be correct, it is impossible not to admire the colossal impudence of Mr. W.H. Ireland."

J

Sanford JARRELL

Journalist (Born 1901)

Jarrell was a cub reporter for the New York *Herald Tribune* in the early 1920s. He had failed to develop a substantial story for the paper for several months and had botched many assignments. Knowing he was about to be fired, the cub suddenly filed a sensational story which hit the front page of the *Herald Tribune* on August 16, 1924, its headline screaming the words "NEW YORKERS DRINK SUMPTUOUSLY ON 17,000-TON FLOATING CAFE AT ANCHOR 15 MILES OFF FIRE ISLAND." The three-column story went on to describe how madcap millionaires and sex-craved flappers did wild dances on board the mystery ship while a full orchestra of Negro musicians played jazz until dawn. Liquor of all kinds flowed freely in direct violation of the then existing Prohibition laws. Drunks by the dozens were carried in stupors from the many lounges on board the liner and unceremoniously dumped into waiting speedboats that took them back to New York City.

The reporter's story stated that he had witnessed this wholesale debauchery; and although he had noted a British flag flying from the stern of the ship, there was no name on the bow. The dinner napkins, however, were monogrammed with the words "Friedrich der Grosse." Police and Coast Guard ships set out in search of the mystery booze ship but found nothing. Authorities speculated that the rum-running pleasure liner might be the *Kronprinz Wilheim,* a decommissioned German warship scheduled for the scrap heap.

The public clamored for more information, as did police and public officials in New York. Jarrell's editors demanded he follow up his sensational story. He promised to file another report within twenty-four hours. Before that time elapsed, Jarrell sent in his final dispatch to the *Herald Tribune*—his resignation, along with a written confession that he had invented the booze ship to keep his job.

Norman JEFFERIES

Publicity Agent (1866–1933)

In an effort to create interest in the exhibits of Brandenburgh's Arch Street Museum in Philadelphia, publicist Jefferies hit upon a fright scheme after reading an old book in which a mother cursed her seventh child, hoping it would be a devil. Her wish was granted—when the child was born a devil, it quickly shot up the chimney and vanished in a puff of smoke.

In late 1906, Jefferies caused several small notices to appear in rural New Jersey newspapers, reporting that "'The Jersey Devil' which has not been seen in these parts for nearly a hundred years, has again put in its appearance. Mrs. J.H. Hopkins, wife of a worthy farmer ... distinctly saw the creature near the barn on Saturday last and afterwards examined its tracks in the snow."

Further, Jefferies somehow made hoof tracks in the snow and marks to indicate where the fiend's wingtips touched down. Plaster casts of the marks were made. A representative of the Smithsonian Institution later claimed that the marks were made by a prehistoric creature, most likely a pterodactyl, which had survived in "hidden caverns and caves, deep in the interior of the earth."

Terror spread through the small towns of southern New Jersey and eastern Pennsylvania. The winged devil was reported by dozens of shocked men and hysterical women. For weeks during the terror, female workers in plants were let go early because they were too frightened to walk home alone after dark.

Newsmen gathered every piece of gossip and rumor about the beast. One report had it that "reputable citizens described in detail his horrific form, the great wings, the frenzied countenance, half human and half animal, the long tail, the eleven feet, the deadly vapors which were exhaled in a mixture of fire and smoke. The fiend was ubiquitous. He was seen all over the southern part of the state."

Reports coming from Delaware, Maryland, Pennsylvania, and even California had the Jersey Devil in each of these states at the same moment. Professor Samuel P. Langley, an aviation pioneer (after whom America's first aircraft carrier, *The Langley,* was named), was asked for an opinion. He carefully looked over the reported wingspan of the creature and said that, yes, the fiend could easily fly from coast-to-coast in a single night, which would explain the frequency of sightings at points great distances apart.

Just as the panic over the Jersey Devil reached its peak, it was reported that the monster had been captured at Hunting Park by a group of farmers. Alerted by Jefferies, photographers were on hand to take blurry photos of the devil, or what appeared to be a grotesque-looking creature, chained to a tree.

The beast was removed to Philadelphia's Arch Street Museum where it was put on display, available to all having the price of admission.

Thousands of curious customers flocked to the museum. There they saw a strange creature that appeared from behind a curtain for only moments—roaring forth and lunging as far toward the reeling audience as its cage would permit. Each group of spectators was so horrified that they ran screaming through the exits, which was exactly the plan, so that the next group of eager customers could be ushered into the museum.

The Jersey Devil in captivity, reporters quickly learned, was another Jefferies' invention. He had purchased an imported kangaroo, harnessing it with bronze wings. The animal leaped forward on cue after being prodded with a broom, Jefferies himself providing the roar of the beast through a megaphone.

As testimony to the creative imagination of Jefferies, his eccentric invention lived far beyond 1906; the "Jersey Devil" saw revivals in 1926, 1930, and 1932 when the daily newspapers and even the Associated Press reported sightings of a "flying lion," "a horrible monster," and in the last sighting, by one John McCandless of Swarthmore, Pennsylvania, a "half-man, half-beast" covered with dirt and hair. McCandless reportedly gathered a large posse and searched for the Jersey Devil for a week, a search that, of course, went on in vain.

Al (Asa Yoelson) JOLSON

Singer (1886–1950)

Born of poor parents in Russia, Jolson was never sure of his age; his parents never kept a record, he said, and he could have been born between 1882 and 1888. Some friends wanted to give him a birthday party when he became an adult, so Jolson arbitrarily selected the birthdate of May 26, 1886. According to one report, Jolson "knew it would be bad business to be born in the autumn, for actors are always broke at the beginning of a season, but they are usually feeling pretty flush in the spring, and since May is a nice, warm month, he decided to be born in May."

Jolson was undoubtedly the most popular entertainer of his day. He sang in black face, following the tradition of the old minstrel shows; and his name is forever linked with such hits as "Mammy," "Swanee" and "Rosie." He began singing at the old Winter Garden in New York, where he became an institution. He then went on to become the brightest name on Broadway through the 1920s, capping his career with the part-talking (really singing) picture, *The Jazz Singer*. Although Jolson's film career was not very successful following *The Jazz Singer*, which grossed more than $12 million in 1929 for Warner Brothers, he earned enormous sums of money, a salary of $31,250 a week for two years under one contract.

The "Mammy Singer" was later profiled in *The Jolson Story* and *Jolson Sings Again* in the late 1940s, both enormous successes; however, these films did not mention Jolson's fantastic ego. The vanity of Al Jolson was the dread of Broadway for years. He would appear on stage, sing some opening numbers, **207**

The energetically egocentric Al Jolson, extreme left, clowning about with
(left to right, seated) Douglas Fairbanks, Sr., Eddie Cantor (left to right,
standing), Mary Pickford, Ronald Coleman, and Samuel Goldwyn.

and then growl his famous line, "You ain't heard nothin' yet." The singer would
then warble himself into a state of exhaustion, sometimes going on for hours,
compelling audiences to endure marathon performances.

If customers dared to leave the nightclub or theater where he was
performing, Jolson would beg and plead with them to stay for "just one more
ditty." Sometimes he would actually weep at the sight of walkouts, other times
he would become enraged and shout angrily at departing customers, then walk
off stage and throw a tantrum, yelling at theater managers that he would never
grace their stages again. Woe to the stagehand who rang down a curtain on Al
Jolson before the singer had decided to end a performance. One stagehand did
accidentally bring down a curtain, and Jolson raced offstage and ordered the
theater manager to fire the man at once—which he did.

The singer would always arrive at the theater hours ahead of his scheduled
performance and sit for at least two hours before his dressing room mirror, first
making up his face and then going through every facial expression known to
him, as he mimed the songs he was about to sing. If anyone dared to interrupt
him at these times, Jolson threatened to walk out on the audience.

More than applause Jolson loved money, and early in his career, he insisted
upon being paid his enormous salary—in cash—*before* going on stage. Despite
a well-deserved reputation as a great entertainer, he was considered the
greediest showman on Broadway. Jolson's contracts were iron clad and entirely
favorable to the entertainer on all levels. One manager complained, "He
doesn't get a salary, it's extortion." Jolson did not spend his money; he hoarded
it and became known as mean-miserly, a man who never tipped a waiter or a
doorman.

In 1933, Jolson agreed to perform for forty weeks on the new Kraft Music
Hall radio program, demanding and getting $200,000, and this at the nadir of
the Depression. He led off his first performance with a song he had personally
chosen for the occasion: "Brother, Can You Spare A Dime?"

K

Alvin ("Shipwreck") KELLY

Flagpole Sitter (1885–1952)

Raised in New York's Hell's Kitchen, Kelly joined the Navy at an early age. By the mid-1920s, he was broke and on the bum, traveling the Midwest in search of employment. He watched a man climb a building in St. Louis as a stunt—"human flies" were then the craze—and he suddenly got the idea that sitting atop a flagpole would provide infinitely more thrills than a man edging himself up the facade of a bank. The manager of a St. Louis hotel also thought flagpole sitting might be a good idea; the stunt would attract crowds to his hotel and drum up needed business. He hired Kelly to climb the flagpole on his hotel roof and sit there as long as he could. Kelly not only drew enormous crowds to watch him sway back and forth on the pole twelve stories above the street but also set a record (seven days and one hour); he was hailed as a modern-day St. Simeon Stylites, a saintly hermit who squatted atop a pillar to do penance and preach to the heathens in the fifth century.

Within a year, Kelly was the most famous flagpole sitter in the country, prompting a national craze that had hundreds climbing flagpoles everywhere to perch like birds in the wind. Kelly, of course, had worked out a system that allowed him to retain supremacy in the field. He would be hoisted by ropes to the top of a sturdy flagpole that he had examined thoroughly in advance. Upon reaching the ball atop the flagpole, Kelly would affix to it an eight-inch, round, rubber-covered wooden seat of his own invention and plant himself. Using straps affixed to the pole, Kelly would sometimes stand up to stretch out his sore bones. When the wind blew, the flagpole sitter would jam his thumbs into holes of his specially designed seat and hold on for dear life. He sat through

209

Shipwreck Kelly standing atop the flagpole towering above New York's Hotel Belvidere in 1927. (Wide World)

Human fly Kelly has his lunch and reads a paper while atop a flagpole. (Wide World)

rain squalls and snowstorms. Once the ice formed so thickly over his legs that he had to chop it away with a hatchet.

Kelly earned extra money by allowing members of the street crowd to come to the roof of a hotel to get a better look at him; he usually charged 50¢ for the privilege of getting close to "The Luckiest Fool Alive" (Kelly's self-made title). Kelly did not prefer to carry on conversations with those standing at the base of the flagpole because "it can wear a fellow down," but he did respond to one question about his endurance by shouting, "After forty-eight hours of this, you don't mind anything!"

Kelly consumed only liquids—coffee, milk, and soup broth—sent up to him on a specially rigged series of ropes and buckets. "What about the waste?" one blunt reporter shouted up to the flagpole sitter. Kelly pointed to a small pipe that ran down the length of the flagpole to a sealed bucket. "Excess fluids go down this," he explained, his face flushing with embarrassment.

The flagpole sitter became the darling of the press. Even the haughty *New Yorker* profiled him, describing him as "etched in magnificent loneliness." The mayor of Baltimore announced that Kelly's flagpole sitting in his city represented "the old pioneer spirit of early America."

There were of course detractors, but these were few in the Roaring Twenties, an era that thrived on excess and eccentricity. One man taking an elevator in a hotel featuring Kelly's oddball performance, sneered at the pretty red-headed operator and said, "Is that damned fool still up there?" The eighteen-year-old elevator operator stopped the car abruptly, whirled about, and slapped the man's face, saying, "He's not a damn fool!" When the flagpole sitter heard of the incident, he asked to see the girl. She came to the foot of the flagpole quivering with idol worship. At Kelly's request, the girl was hoisted upward to him on ropes, and, in what is probably the strangest courtship on record, the two held hands in mid-air, falling in love instantly. They were married a short time later, and Mrs. Kelly served as first assistant to the world's leading flagpole sitter, standing loyally at the bases of flagpoles, sending up Kelly's food and cigarettes night and day. She fended off any critics with staunchly loyal statements: "Shut up! Don't you dare razz him—he's a genius and genuises know what they're doing!"

211

Kelly knew he would set records for a long time to come, and that was his life's goal. Forty-nine days—his greatest record—stood for years (Frank Perkins of Idaho would later outdo every flagpole sitter in the world by squatting above a San Jose, California, used car lot for more than a year, descending on July 4, 1976). When the 1920s ended, Kelly's flagpole sitting heyday, along with the rest of the stunt-happy era, passed from vogue as the nation settled into a spiritless Depression. But by then Kelly remembered little of the Jazz Age except wind, rain, snow, and the puzzling sight of thousands of uplifted faces staring wordlessly at him for more than twenty thousand hours of his life.

Arabella KENEALY

Author (dates uncertain)

The British writer, known widely as an antifeminist, penned a remarkable work in 1934 entitled *The Human Gyroscope* in which she insisted that all matter, from the atom to the stars in the universe, displays a male–female make-up. Southern races of the globe were feminine, according to Kenealy; those of the north were masculine. Half of the brain (the right side) was male, the other female. In summing up her astounding beliefs, the author stated: "I have ventured to base my argument upon the Gravitation of great Newton, instead of on the later Einstein theory."

Dr. William KOCH

Physician (1885–date uncertain)

An infamous quack throughout his entire career, Koch was born in Detroit and received a Ph.D. from the University of Michigan in chemisty, later taking a medical degree from Wayne University. Koch produced a vaccine he called "glyoxylide" in 1919, claiming that his discovery would cure not only cancer but tuberculosis and leprosy by making the human body so healthy that it would destroy any disease. Koch, who charged as much as $350 per injection of his miracle drug, became a rich man, his yearly earnings estimated at more than $150,000 for several decades.

Investigations into this quack's cure-all proved his miracle drug to be nothing more than distilled water, but not until 1942 did authorities prevent Koch from employing his drug. He moved to Rio de Janeiro in the 1940s and grew even richer duping incurable but desperate patients before he vanished from sight.

L

Fiorello La GUARDIA

Mayor (1882–1947)

"The Little Flower," as La Guardia was affectionately called by his supporters, was raised in western army posts, where his father was a musician. Becoming a lawyer, he entered New York politics at an early age. He served two terms as a congressman before making a bid for the post of mayor of New York, running on the Republican ticket against the popular James J. Walker and losing by a half-million votes in 1929.

The 1929 campaign was a dirty one, with much mud slung at La Guardia. Though he was known to be an utterly scrupulous man, Fiorello was accused of taking bribes from officials to present legislation favorable to certain aircraft manufacturing companies. His accuser was a U.S. Army officer. A reporter from the New York *World* entered La Guardia's office just at the moment Fiorello learned of the accusation. Flamboyant Fiorello, whose temper knew no bounds, jumped to his feet with the telephone in his hand: "You tell that officer that I say he is a lying son-of-a-bitch," he shouted through the transmitter, "and if he makes that lying charge against me I will search him out in his office in Washington or wherever he may be, and drag him out into the street and thrash him!"

Unorthodox and unpredictable, Fiorello blatantly told New Yorkers in his 1929 bid that he was a devout "wet," and that he would not send police to raid any of the more than thirty thousand speakeasies then operating in Prohibition-bound New York. The cops had more important duties, said La Guardia,

Mayor Fiorello H. La Guardia, New York City's "Little Flower."

than "snooping on respectable citizens desiring a drink." He wrote letters to corrupt administration leaders accusing them of collusion with underworld figures, especially with the loan-shark king and gambler, Arnold Rothstein, who had recently been murdered. Knowing the recipients would never disclose the nature of these letters, Fiorello made them public before mailing them.

La Guardia was unlike any politician seen in New York in this century. He was in a constant state of motion, waving his arms wildly about as he talked. He invaded neighborhoods nightly during his campaign against Mayor Walker, dancing in the street for votes and shadow-boxing an invisible opponent, Walker, as he thundered: "I've got Jimmy Walker in a corner! He can't move! He's groggy! This is a real fight! This is no time for sobbing, Jimmy! Come out and fight like a man! Come out!"

The 1929 campaign was only a warm-up. As a fusion candidate for mayor in 1933, La Guardia was swept into office by an overwhelming majority and kept in that office by a grateful citizenry for twelve years—the most eccentric (and probably the best) mayor New York ever had. La Guardia was a public mayor, and he made himself visible to the voters at every opportunity. He would unexpectedly show up at Yankee Stadium before a game, and, during the warm-ups, he would race his short, squat frame out to the mound to serve up pitches to Yankee sluggers. He became so excited while reviewing parades that he often jumped from the reviewing stand to snatch a conductor's baton and lead a band in his favorite songs, whether the band members knew the song or not.

So popular was La Guardia that FDR thought he might be a contender for the presidency. The man's style, however, gave Roosevelt second thoughts. "Of course, for President," wrote R.G. Tugwell in *The Brain Trust,* La Guardia "was just a little flamboyant." (It would be years before supporters gave up the idea of seeing The Little Flower in the White House.) William Allen White came out for La Guardia in 1937, urging the GOP to nominate Fiorello as a presidential candidate in 1940, saying: "When you have done laughing, remember how they laughed at Lincoln eighty years ago." That flamboyance was never more in evidence than when Fiorello decided to rid New York of its thousands of illegal slot machines. He personally went to dockside barges where machines had

Mayor James J. Walker, of New York, with his wife, voting in 1929, a bitter year for Fiorello La Guardia, the colorful campaigner who lost to "Beau James."

been collected, and, wielding a sledge-hammer, he smashed hundreds of these machines. It became a sport for the mayor to destroy slots.

La Guardia loved to make people laugh, and he did not care whether or not it was at his own expense. During the New York newspaper strike of 1937, La Guardia took to the airways, angry over the fact that the children of the city were deprived of vital information—the funnies—which he read to them with such animation over station WNYC that he received offers to continue as a radio personality.

La Guardia's anger was legendary. He would storm and threaten terrible retribution for any act he thought to be an injustice, and he always did it in wild style. In 1932, when he was a congressman, La Guardia became incensed at government troops routing the bonus army migrants from their shanties at Anacostia Flats near the capital in Washington. The Little Flower hurriedly scribbled a protest, then ran from his office to his reception room, slapping down the draft of a telegram he wanted sent to the White House. "What do you think of that?" he shrilled to his aide, Ernest Cuneo.

The aide carefully read the telegram aloud: "BEANS IS BETTER THAN BULLETS AND SOUP IS BETTER THAN GAS." The college-trained Cuneo politely corrected his boss, saying: "You've got to say 'Beans *are* better than bullets' or a bean *is* better than a bullet.'"

Fiorello's face grew purple with rage and he screamed at Cuneo: "The capital is in flames and *you* talk of *grammar!* Wise guy!"

La Guardia was a big man for messages from the people, asking the citizens of New York to write to him, suggesting any economic methods that might cure the Great Depression. The request met with little success. In fact, Fiorello was chagrined at the mail he received, mostly from crackpots. One letter writer claimed to have a foolproof formula for recovery and simply sent in the following:

$$\frac{MT - MW \times D}{MT}$$

La Guardia stared at this missive for almost an hour, attempting to figure it out before going into a fit-throwing rage. (Fiorello was crudely outspoken against the bankers of America, blaming them, for the most part, for the Depression. He once shouted, "The bastards broke the people's back with their usury!")

To escape the enormous pressures of his office, La Guardia developed the habit of hiding out in the homes of friends until he could collect his considerable energies and resume his responsibilities as mayor. One of his favorite hideouts was the home of his dear friend, Judge Samuel Seabury, at East Hampton. He once unconsciously answered Seabury's phone in his distinctive high-piping voice saying, "Seabury residence."

The caller undoubtedly knew who was answering but was polite enough to ask, "Is Mayor La Guardia there?"

"No," replied Fiorello.

"I must speak to Mayor La Guardia," persisted the caller.

"I told you, sir," Fiorello said, "no such person is present."

"Who is this I'm speaking to?"

Quickly adopting a British accent, the Little Flower said, "This is Judge Seabury's butler."

T.E. (Thomas Edward) LAWRENCE

Adventurer (1888–1935)

Born illegitimate in Tremadoc, Wales, Lawrence was one of five children whose father (a man named Chapman) was married to a woman who refused to divorce him. His youth was hard-scrabble among the lower middle class, but he was fortunate enough to receive a good education at Oxford, studying under Professor David Hogarth, a character who was almost as enigmatic as Lawrence. Hogarth, acting under secret government instructions, traveled to Iraq in 1910—taking Lawrence with him—ostensibly to oversee the archeological digs at Carchemish. Such an adventure for the twenty-two-year-old Lawrence was in keeping with his fantasies—he had stuffed himself with the legends of medieval knights and the glories of the crusades as a child.

Hogarth's scientific excursion was a ruse; along with the astute Lawrence, he really went to Carchemish to spy on the building of the Berlin–Baghdad Railway which the Turks were constructing. (This episode was later used as the premise for the motion picture *Five Graves to Cairo.*) Here Lawrence met a teenage boy, Dahoum (also called Salim Ahmed), who became his inseparable companion and, many whispered later, his lover. Lawrence's *Seven Pillars of Wisdom,* the story of his life in the Arab wars, was dedicated to "S.A.," along with a love poem—a dedication apparently intended for Salim Ahmed.

Historians have argued over Lawrence's homosexuality for decades. There is every indication that he was a latent homosexual, for he shunned women and

Lawrence of Arabia, mysterious, masochistic, a death-seeker. (Wide World)

thought heterosexual love disgusting. He did loosely propose to Janet Laurie, a childhood sweetheart, in 1909, but nothing came of the affair. His brother maintained that Lawrence was merely a purist who lived a monk-like life for the sake of intellectuality. Irrespective of his sexual bent, the adventurer was unquestionably a disturbed person with a passionate love of self. He was also an inveterate liar who found it impossible to tell a truth when fabrication was easier. Charlotte Shaw, the wife of playwright George Bernard Shaw and Lawrence's close friend, once exploded at the mere mention of Lawrence's name, shouting, "He's such an infernal liar!" In the guise of hardening himself against the rigors of life, moreover, Lawrence endured pain and physical agony time and again to the point where he enjoyed the pain and became an out-and-out masochist. (Toward the end of his life, Lawrence hired a young man to beat him over the bare back with birch branches to "toughen" him up.)

By the time World War I broke out, Hogarth and Lawrence had already sent vital intelligence to British authorities. Lawrence was sent to Cairo as an officer, where he continued his intelligence work in 1914. Two years later, he was sent to see Prince Faisal and organize Arab resistance to the Turks, who had aligned themselves with Germany. The Arab revolt against the Turks was vital to British interests in the Middle East, for England had committed the bulk of its troops to the European war and counted on the natives to hold down the strong Turkish forces, keeping them away from Cairo and the Suez Canal.

Lawrence had studied well the customs and thinking of the Arabs. To convince them of his loyalty to their cause of independence, he donned Arab garb, living with them and like them. He was accepted as "El Aurens," leading the tribes in open warfare against the Turks, attacking strongholds, and blowing up trains. A visiting journalist, Lowell Thomas, heard of the daring young British officer leading the ragamuffin Arab legions and visited Law-

T. E. Lawrence in the Royal Air Force as an enlisted man, using the alias of Shaw. (Wide World)

rence. He became the adventurer's most ardent admirer, not only promoting the Arab cause in dispatches and pictures but making a superhero out of the reserved, close-mouthed Lawrence. Thomas would later earn more than $1 million from his stories about the British officer, chiefly from his best-selling book, *With Lawrence in Arabia.*

The Robin Hood image served Lawrence well; by focusing attention on the forgotten Arab campaign, it enabled him to raise funds to keep the revolt alive and obtain needed ammunition. Lawrence bought Arab loyalty chiefly with great amounts of gold, which he distributed to poverty-stricken tribesmen. When addressing Arab leaders, the adventurer bought their support by promosing them total independence once the war was won, a promise he knew to be a lie. (This side of Lawrence was basically ignored in the Peter O'Toole movie, *Lawrence of Arabia.*)

By 1917, Lawrence had grown moody and despondent. His closest friend Dahoum had died of disease. He also underwent a horrid experience when briefly captured by the Turks in November, being sodomized brutally before he was able to make his escape. His nerves were shattered, and he broke down after being recalled to Cairo.

Following the war, Lawrence served briefly under Winston Churchill in the colonial office; then he cut himself off entirely from the government, going into seclusion to escape his fame. He became so paranoid about being recognized that he took to wearing disguises and using false names. Many later claimed that this was no more than a manifestation of the guilt he felt for betraying the Arabs. Following the Paris Peace Conference of 1919, the Arabs fell under British and French domination instead of being granted their promised independence.

Using the name John Ross, Lawrence enlisted in the tank corps; he switched in 1924 to the RAF, working as a mechanic under the name T.E. Shaw, having taken the name of the playwright, George Bernard Shaw. For ten years, Lawrence lived in his obscure RAF capacity while the world wondered what happened to the "Uncrowned Prince of Mecca."

In his last years, Lawrence fell in love with speed. He worked on high-speed launches, which he raced madly, and helped to design hover craft. Upon his release from the military, Lawrence began a motocycle trip through the English countryside. He loved to race motorcycles at their full capacities. On his way to Clouds Hill from Bovington, England, on the overcast morning of May 19, 1935, the forty-seven-year-old Lawrence was gunning his Brough motorcycle at its top speed of 38 MPH.

Police Corporal Catchpole, bicycling in the opposite direction, saw the goggled Lawrence race toward him, his motor bike sputtering. Just ahead, the great adventurer momentarily disappeared from view as he and his bike went into a dip in the road. A black van going the other way sped past Catchpole and also went downward into the hollow of the road and out of sight.

Moments later, Catchpole slammed his bicycle to a halt and gaped at Lawrence's motorcycle as it emerged riderless from the hollow at full throttle. When the policeman examined the bike, he found that it was stuck in second gear. In the hollow of the road was T.E. Lawrence, smashed beyond recognition. He had overtaken a boy on a bicycle, swerved to avoid hitting him, and gone square into the other lane where the oncoming van knocked him from his bike—which continued on its own up the hill.

Oddly, Lawrence was not immediately identified. True to his custom of anonymity, he had been traveling under the assumed name of Thomas Edward Shaw. Only minutes before his death trip, Lawrence had sent a message to a friend, Henry Williamson. The cryptic wire read: "LUNCH TUESDAY ... WET FINE ... COTTAGE ONE MILE NORTH BOVINGTON CAMP. SHAW."

Lawrence had recently written a poem for his friend Lord Carlow, a bit of doggerel that grimly foretold his own violent end. It read:

In speed we hurl ourselves beyond the body;
Our bodies cannot scale the heavens except in a fume of petrol.
Bones. Blood. Flesh. All pressed inward together.

Charles Godfrey LELAND

Author (1824–1903)

After a distinguished newspaper career as the editor of the New York *Times* and the Philadelphia Evening *Bulletin,* Leland discovered the "Shelta" language, once employed by Celtic thinkers. Though an American citizen, he lived most of his later years in England and Italy, writing under the nom de plume of Hans Breitmann. The last book issued under this pseudonym, *The Alternate Sex,* was published posthumously in 1904. Unlike anything he had ever written before, the book put forth the theory that there was a "homosexual center" of the brain.

The subconcious part of the mind, Leland insisted, was always the opposite gender to the physically conscious person. The author had absolute proof of this weird claim, he stated. In all of his dreams, Leland stated, he saw himself as a woman. This proved his theory beyond a doubt.

Anne de ("Ninon") LENCLOS

Courtesan (1616–1705)

Her father was a pimp who trained his daughter Anne, later infamously known as Ninon, to become a successful courtesan. Ninon went further, assuming the much-earned title of the "teacher of love"; her name was on the lips of every sophisticated Parisian of the seventeenth century. Ninon's parents died before her twentieth birthday. Her inheritance, plus some shrewd investments, provided the young woman with a comfortable living, but Ninon wanted more. Establishing herself as a courtesan of high fashion, Ninon began to receive scores of well-paying lovers, selecting her bed partners from the nobility.

Not only was Ninon sensationally acrobatic in the bed chamber, as most of her satisfied clients proudly boasted, but she quoted poetry and exemplified the most delightful manners. She was above all else a lady of quality, and she may have inspired the notoriously obscene literary work by that name. Counts and dukes flocked to her. Even the august Cardinal Richelieu (see entry) lusted after Ninon, offering 50,000 crowns for a night with her. The courtesan disdainfully rejected the cardinal, turning him over to one of her pupils, Marion Delorme; by then Ninon had become so famous a sex partner that she instructed other courtesans on sex techniques.

Ninon was full of sage advice, telling her eager students that "one requires a hundred times more spirit in order to love properly than to command armies." She lavished praise on her clients, all of whom, she stated ardently, she loved deeply. A typical letter, changed a bit for different customers, gushed: "Love, I feel thy divine fury!...Today a new sun rises for me; everything is animated, everything seems to speak to me of my passion!"

The beautiful Ninon could be critical as well as laudatory, criticizing her bed partners in public. Of one inadequate aristocrat she stated, He "has a soul of boiled beef, a body of damp paper, with a heart like a pumpkin—fricasseed in snow."

So successful did Ninon become that she opened up a school for sex education in Paris to which most of France's nobility subscribed; sons of aristocrats were sent to her to learn the vagaries and intricacies of fleshy pleasures. Ninon actually conducted classes filled with youthful males, performing with one after another. She later tutored nobly born women in the ways of "fashionable" sex.

On one occasion, a female student asked Ninon, "How large should a woman's breast be to attract a lover?"

220   "Large enough to fill the hand of an honest man," replied the arbiter of sex.

Ninon lived to be ninety, dying a rich woman and much respected by the amorously inclined French. Her life, however, was not without excruciating agony; a young nobleman fell in love with her when she was middle-aged but learned that she was his mother through a liaison of her youth. The young man fell on his sword in the garden of Ninon's sumptuous villa as the famous courtesan looked on in horror.

John Llewellyn LEWIS

Labor Leader (1880–1965)

The fire-eating president of the United Mine Workers from 1920 to 1960 was undoubtedly the most colorful labor leader in American history, a truly great leader but a colossal egotist, flamboyant grandstander, and mumble-minded wordsmith who fairly dumbfounded his listeners, be they uneducated workers or presidents of the United States. He was one of the most colorful speakers on the labor front, and he reveled in his ability to dazzle a crowd. On one occasion Lewis thundered: "It ill behooves one [referring to President Franklin D. Roosevelt] who has supped at labor's table and who has been sheltered in labor's house to curse with equal favor and fine impartiality both labor and its adversaries when they become locked in deadly embrace."

Aggressive with strike tactics, Lewis was eternally at odds with business and government leaders and always embroiled in endless court battles. When winning, he was jovial and friendly—a giant of a man with eyebrows so bushy that they all but hid his eyes and a mane of thick hair that flew in all directions as he expressed himself with wild physical gyrations. When suffering setbacks, Lewis was as petulant as a little boy deprived of candy. He would first pout and sulk, then actually throw temper tantrums that left his office a shambles. In 1936, his union contributed $500,000 to FDR's presidential campaign; Lewis expected to be nominated to a post in Roosevelt's advisory council on labor. When he was ignored, he turned with hostility on Roosevelt and his administration.

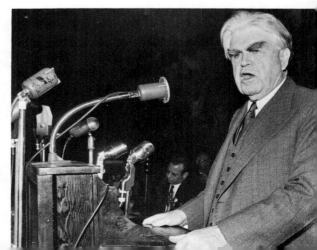

The colorful labor leader John L. Lewis delivering one of his many unforgettable speeches. (Wide World)

Lewis once rose from a bargaining table to scrutinize his opponents then roared, "Good day, gentlemen. We trust that time, as it shrinks your purse, may modify your niggardly and anti-social propensities."

When describing conditions in Depression-ridden West Virginia, where his miners were suffering, Lewis told a group of mine operators, "There, the shanties lean over as if intoxicated by the smoke fumes of the mine dumps. But the more pretentious ones boast a porch, with the bannisters broken here and there, presenting the aspect of a snaggle-toothed child. Some of the windows are wide open to flies, which can feast nearby on garbage and answer the family dinner call in double-quick time."

Once, when accused of self-aggrandizement, the titan of labor whirled about, towering over his accuser and making the face of an angry lion, and snarled, "He who tooteth not his own horn, the same shall not be tooted!"

Richard Adams LOCKE

Journalist (1800–1871)

With circulation of the penny-a-copy New York *Sun* flagging in August 1835, editorialist Richard Adams Locke was given the assignment of coming up with something to boost sales. His brainchild was a series that would prove to be the most sensational ever published in American newspaper history. In that far-away day of public gullibility, Locke hit upon the happy notion that scientists had discovered life on our moon—not merely life as it was known in 1835 but exotic, fearsome life that would both fascinate and frighten the pants off the everyday reader.

Locke's series began with a report by Sir John Herschel, a distinguished British astronomer whose powerful telescope was situated at the Cape of Good Hope. Herschel's accounts, first serialized in the *Sun* on August 28, 1835, had originally appeared in the Edinburgh *Journal of Science*. Of course, neither Herschel nor the Edinburgh Journal ever existed.

The so-called scientific report revealed the existence of winged creatures flying about the moon's surface, creatures that were half man and half bat. "We counted three parties of these creatures, of twelve and fifteen in each, walking erect towards a small wood," Locke quoted Herschel as he peered through his mythical telescope. "Certainly they were like human beings, for their wings had now disappeared and their attitude in walking was both erect and dignified.

"About half of the first party had passed beyond our canvas, but of all the others we had a perfectly distinct and deliberate view. They averaged four feet in height, were covered, except on the face, with short and glossy copper-colored hair, and had wings composed of a thin membrane, without hair, lying snugly upon their backs from the top of the shoulders to the calves of the legs.

"The face, which was of a yellowish flesh color, was a slight improvement upon that of the large orangutan...so much so that but for their long wings, Lieutenant Drummond said they would look as well on a parade ground as some of the old cockney militia. The hair on the head was a darker color than that of the body, closely curled but apparently not woolly and arranged in two curious semicircles over the temples of the forehead. Their feet could only be seen as they were alternately lifted in walking; but from what we could see of them in so transient a view they appeared thin and very protuberant at the heal.

"We could perceive that their wings possessed great expansion and were similar in structure to those of the bat, being a semi-transparent membrane expanded in curvilineal divisions by means of straight radii, united at the back by the dorsal integuments. But what astonished us most was the circumstances of this membrane being continued from the shoulders to the legs, united all the way down, though gradually decreasing in width. The wings seemed completely under the command of volition, for those of the creatures whom we saw bathing in the water spread them instantly to their full width, waved them as ducks do theirs to shake off the water, and then as instantly closed them again in a compact form."

The series shot the *Sun*'s circulation to the largest in New York City. The public clamored for more, and Locke spewed out one absurd "scientific revelation" after another. Scientists, however, were suspicious from the start; no telescope in the world at that time was powerful enough to pick up detail on the moon, and they knew it. A contingent of Yale University professors invaded the *Sun*'s offices, demanding to see the original reports of the alleged *Journal of Science*. They were stalled by *Sun* publisher Benjamin Day. Meanwhile, the frantic competing newspapers, unable to find a copy of Herschel's reports, cribbed heavily from Locke's zany prose and put out their own stories of the "moonmen."

Not until September 16, 1835, did Day confess that the entire series was a hoax, proudly adding that the series had boosted the *Sun*'s circulation by almost 20,000 readers. The competing New York newspapers were thoroughly humiliated, vowing venomous wrath on Day, Locke, and the spurious but successful *Sun*.

Even more ridiculous was the response of clergymen throughout the East Coast, who not knowing the "moonmen" story was a hoax, wrote scores of letters to Sir John Herschel in care of the *Sun,* asking the astronomer if he knew of any method whereby Gospel messages could be transmitted to those heathen creatures flitting about on the moon.

Huey Pierce ("The Kingfish") LONG

U.S. Politician (1893–1935)

Known as "The Kingfish" to his slavish followers in Louisiana, Long had a political career that could easily be compared with Adolf Hitler's. He was a dynamic and thoroughly unscrupulous politician, the epitome of the redneck rabble rouser who would stop at nothing to keep power and gain more. An egomaniac, Long thought he might some day be president, a delusion shared by his armies of political hacks and gun-toting supporters, not to mention his murderous phalanxes of bodyguards.

Born to a large sharecropping family outside Winnfield, Louisiana, Long attended Shreveport High School but dropped out. He took a crash course in law at Tulane University, only seven months, and passed a special examination for admission to the bar. He was admitted to practice in 1915.

A few years earlier, Long had gotten involved in a bloody shoot-out in Shreveport. Rose McConnell, his sweetheart, provided his alibi, testifying that Long had been with her at a theater on the night of the shooting, showing ticket stubs as evidence. (Long married Rose following her testimony.) Long was cleared, but this was only the first in a long line of violent incidents in his traumatic career.

As an attorney, Long grew wealthy, buying up (some said stealing) oil stock or accepting shares in oil wells as fees for his services. In 1923, Huey ran for the governorship of Louisiana and lost. Four years later, he won. Then began the reign of Huey Long, a period of terror, intimidation, and corruption never equaled in American history.

Long ran Louisiana as his private fiefdom, taxing business and the wealthy to build modern roads and buildings. He called it his "Share the Wealth" program, but the miserably poor constituents who backed him never saw a dime. The Kingfish surrounded himself with a private army of machine-gun-carrying thugs.

Impulsive, violent, and carnal, Long did as he pleased, attending wild sex parties in New Orleans where he orchestrated activities. His drunken revels and womanizing were only whispered scandals, since for the most part, Huey controlled the press of his state. The fact that Long was a satyr was nevertheless firmly established by the stream of women, mostly high-paid prostitutes, who went in and out of his office at the state capital.

Long's quirks were not confined to his insatiable lust. He disliked jazz and most modern music and developed the habit of storming bandstands to break instruments, usually violins, over the heads of band leaders. He loved to roar down his state's highways in his armor-plated limousine, flanked by dozens of

In this artist's rendition, "Kingfish" Huey Long flees down a corridor of the Louisiana capitol building, wounded, as his goons kill Dr. Carl Austin Weiss, Long's assassin.

motorcycles carrying his hand-picked goons, driving traffic off the road. (Years later, his antics would be profiled in books like Robert Penn Warren's *All the King's Men* and motion pictures such as Frank Capra's *Mr. Smith Goes to Washington*.)

In 1930, Long sought to increase his power by running for the United States Senate. He won by a narrow margin—his illiterate supporters were beginning to rightly suspect that he was nothing more than a demagogue. By then, Huey had been exposed as corrupt and murderous, charged with ordering one of his henchmen to kill a state senator who opposed his dictatorial ways.

Long's violent career came to an end on September 8, 1935, when he was assassinated by a mild-mannered physician, Dr. Carl Austin Weiss, who stepped from behind a granite pillar of the capitol building and fired two shots into Long, whose bodyguards immediately let loose a fusilade of bullets, sixty of which slammed into Weiss, killing him on the spot. (Weiss' motives for shooting Long remain hazy to this day; the best explanation is that he sought vengeance for Long's slanderous attack on his father-in-law, the much respected Judge Benjamin Pavy.)

The Kingfish died the following day, September 9, 1935, perplexed by the attack and whispering to an aide: "Why would anyone want to shoot me?"

Count Felix von LUCKNER

Adventurer (1890–1966)

Von Luckner was a man out of his own time, addicted to the tales of medieval knights and sagas of chivalry, which he attempted to duplicate in his own life at every turn. A young man at the time of World War I, the adventurous count proved himself eccentric by any standard when he refused to serve in any branch of the military except the German Navy, and only in the capacity of captain of a ship. Preposterous, cried the German admirals. Not at all, answered von Luckner. *He* would provide his own ship, his privately owned sloop, *Seeadler,* which he would arm at his own expense. Rebuffed, the count pestered the Kaiser with numerous petitions until an exasperated Wilhelm made him a captain, asking that he never again be bothered by "this mad Prussian."

Von Luckner in the disguise of a Norwegian fisherman when he eluded the British blockade during World War I. (Historisches Bildarchiv Handke, Bad Berneck)

225

Von Luckner frolicking in the surf of Mopelia during the 1930s, when he pretended to be a tourist but was desperately trying to remember where he had hidden his wartime loot.

In 1916, von Luckner ran the English blockade with his fast-sailing *Seeadler.* Armed only with two 105-mm guns, the quick little motor and sailing ship attacked and sank eleven Allied merchant vessels as it aimed itself like an arrow toward the South Seas.

Von Luckner showed himself to be an odd creature by ignoring Teutonic customs and behavior. He loved disguises and had on board a large wardrobe of custom-made costumes and uniforms into which he changed several times each day. His chivalrous attitude toward prisoners taken from the ships he sank was contrary to the stern conduct of almost all other German skippers seahawking the shipping lanes. Captive survivors had the run of his ship and were never confined to quarters. It was von Luckner's gallant practice periodically to present flowers to female "guests" on board his ship. The count ordered his small band to play "Tipperary" and "There's a Long, Long Trail" after dinner for the benefit of his British prisoners.

Before the bizarre voyages of the *Seeadler* ended, von Luckner, knowing Allied warships were drawing near, made sure that most of the survivors were put aboard the French bark, *Cambronne,* which was permitted to sail to its destination unmolested. In his many sea encounters, Lieutenant von Luckner had taken the time to rifle the strongboxes of each ship before he scuttled it. By the end of several months, the German captain had looted more than $5 million in gold, jewels, currency, which he secreted on board the *Seeadler.*

In August 1917, while anchored in the peaceful harbor of Mopelia Island in the Society (Tahitian) Islands, his luck ran out. The *Seeadler* wound up on a coral reef, high and dry after one of von Luckner's officers ran the ship aground. (The mate was drunk; von Luckner allowed his men spirits at all hours.) With only one other man to help him. von Luckner dragged his huge captain's chest, loaded with loot, onto the reef. From there, the two men towed it into a small lagoon, and at a spot known only to von Luckner (the other man mysteriously died later), placed it on an underwater shelf.

The sixty-five crewmen of the *Seeadler,* plus three captive crews and the ship's unpredictable captain disappeared after the war. But von Luckner came back. "When I returned on my yacht to Mopelia in 1938," the count later wrote, "for a sentimental visit, I was watched by the islanders from arrival to departure and therefore I made no attempt to recover this loot."

Von Luckner died penniless in Sweden in 1966 without ever retrieving his spoils, estimated to be worth about $5 million. Though several attempts have been made to swim through the six-knot current in the small lagoon, the treasure remains hidden.

Commented the dashing von Luckner in the late 1940s, "Looking for [the treasure] is better than having it!"

M

Charles MacARTHUR

Playwright (1895–1956)

Born in Scranton, Pennyslvania on November 5, 1895, Charles MacArthur was educated at the Wilson Memorial Academy in Nyack, New York before leaving home at an early age to join the 1st Illinois Cavalry and be sent to Mexico on a punitive expedition against Pancho Villa in 1916. Upon his return to Chicago, MacArthur went to work as a reporter for the Chicago *Herald Examiner,* and later worked for the Chicago *Tribune.* He met Ben Hecht in Chicago and the two newsmen eventually produced *The Front Page,* the classic story of Chicago's wild and wanton journalism of the early 1920s.

MacArthur was to produce several plays with Hecht, including *Twentieth Century* and *Ladies and Gentlemen.* He and Hecht also united to write some of the most entertaining film scripts ever produced in Hollywood. MacArthur married Carol Frink in 1917 and divorced her in 1928; that same year he married the actress Helen Hayes. The writer met Miss Hayes at a New York theater party, the story goes, spotting the petite blonde while eating from a bag of peanuts. He approached her and offered her some peanuts, saying: "I wish they were emeralds."

From his earliest days in Chicago, MacArthur proved himself an eccentric. He was a brawler, a drinker, a lover of nightlife and sinister characters; his loose friendship with gangster Dion O'Bannion vexed his editors no end. O'Bannion would find Charlie in some gin mill and, before dawn, drive his favorite reporter home, aiming his flivver along the sidewalks of Chicago instead of on the streets.

MacArthur loved to visit condemned men in Chicago's Old Criminal Courts Building on Dearborn and Illinois Streets. He would sit for hours on the other side of the bars of a death cell, playing poker with those to be hanged at dawn. He invariably won every penny the prisoner possessed before the hapless miscreant was led to the gallows. He and Hecht once thought to revive a hanged man after learning of a local quack's claim that he could revive the dead with special serums. The experiment failed and MacArthur and Hecht were almost jailed for attempting to steal a corpse. "It would have made a helluva story had it worked," MacArthur later mused.

On another occasion, MacArthur asked convicted murderer Carl Otto Wanderer to read an attack on his newspaper editor from the gallows. Wanderer happily agreed, but found it impossible to read from the newsman's script; he was led to the gallows with his hands strapped to his sides. Instead Wanderer thought to edify the on-looking and disappointed MacArthur by singing a tune entitled "Dear Ol' Pal O' Mine." After Wanderer fell through the trap, MacArthur said to his friend Hecht: "You know, Ben, that son-of-a-bitch should have been a song-plugger!"

Hollywood provided MacArthur with an enormous playground where he and Hecht amused themselves at the considerable expense of the movie moguls. David O. Selznick thought Hecht and MacArthur were the greatest screenplay writers alive, but was forever quarreling with them over their scripts. Selznick had the writers to dinner at his estate one night with the producer's brother, Myron, in attendance. Myron Selznick was the most influential talent agent in Hollywood then and was the representative for MacArthur and Hecht.

The foursome began drinking heavily after dinner, Selznick criticizing a recent Hecht–MacArthur script which was being written for him. Myron took his brother's side, a rare stance. The writers hurled insults at the producer. Selznick, who considered himself an expert boxer, challenged the writers to back up their verbal abuse with fists. MacArthur, whose saloon sluggery was legendary, jumped to his feet. Selznick removed his glasses, which rendered him almost blind, and rushed toward MacArthur. He grabbed the nearest figure and knocked him out. He had floored the wrong man, his brother Myron.

Hecht and MacArthur were habitual pranksters. They discovered that David Selznick had the habit of waking at midday. The first thing the mogul did was to throw open the double doors leading to his patio and make a running dive into his swimming pool. Selznick would swim the length of the pool and back before getting dressed and ready for work. In the dead of night, the two writers had several gallons of gluey gelatin secretly poured into Selznick's pool and showed up the next day to view the fun.

On schedule, they watched as the great David O. Selznick pulled back the glass doors of his house and run to the pool, diving head first into the jello-like water. Still groggy with sleep, the film tycoon did not at first notice that he was swimming frantically and getting nowhere. He was all but stuck in the giant aspic.

His impish writers let out a roar from behind the bushes where they had been hiding when they heard Selznick yell for help. A janitor finally had to pull him out of the gooey mess with a rake.

Selznick was not the only target of Hecht and MacArthur's highly humorous and sometimes costly jokes. The two writers were extremely lazy and hated producers who pounded on their bungalow door (all writers had special bungalows on the studio lots in those days).

To ward off Louis B. Mayer, who was a specialist in annoying his writers, Hecht and MacArthur devised a particularly devilish scheme. It was well known to them that Mayer could not stand to look at anyone who was deformed in any way, one of the tycoon's many peculiarities. So the writers advertised for and hired a deformed person whose affliction was sometimes termed as being a "pinhead." They positioned this pathetic person at the entrance of their bungalow.

The first time Louis B. Mayer burst through their door and got a wide-eyed look at the writer's new secretary, he began to quake with anxiety, finally escaping out the door never to bother the writers again.

On another occasion, Hecht and MacArthur were writing a western script for Mayer which the magnate was constantly changing. It so unnerved Hecht and MacArthur that they sought serious revenge. The two went to one of Mayer's largest lots where thousands of Sioux Indians were living. The entire tribe had been brought to Hollywood by Mayer for the filming of the epic western.

Through an interpreter, Hecht and MacArthur told the Sioux Indians from their box-top perches that the real reason Mayer had brought them to Hollywood was to steal their lands in the Dakotas while they were away! Once they got the message, the Indians went berserk and tore wildly through Mayer's expensive sets, setting fire to backdrops, and ripping scenery to pieces. The result was several thousand dollars in damage.

Mayer never learned why this carnage was wreaked upon his sets. "I'll never understand what made those Indians act up that way," he said to MacArthur shortly after the rampage.

"Yeah," MacArthur replied innocently. "They're sure strange, those Red Devils."

The writers' most elaborate prank was played on Adolph Zukor, head of Paramount Studios. Zukor's birthday parties were the social events of Hollywood and at one of them Hecht and MacArthur gave Zukor a present he would never forget.

Without Zukor's knowledge, the two writers had written, directed and produced an insane movie called "More Soup." It starred Ben Hecht as a bumbling waiter and MacArthur as a drunken scriptwriter. No one ever saw this movie except Zukor and his birthday party guests.

It was an exclusive birthday gift from the writers to their boss. He was overwhelmed and delighted. Zukor stated it was the most novel gift he had ever received.

Playwright Charles MacArthur with his wife Helen
Hayes, relaxing at their Nyack, New York home.

"You like it, chief?" MacArthur asked Zukor.

"I love it. Tremendous." Zukor was almost in tears.

Then Charles MacArthur handed him a bill for the movie he and Hecht
had produced. (The total was almost $100,000!)

Zukor went MacArthur one better ... he paid the bill.

Bernarr MacFADDEN

Physical Culturist, Publisher (1868–1955)

A practitioner of naturopathy (a European cult believing in nature as a
cure-all), Bernarr MacFadden, who lived to be eighty-seven, was the epitome of
the "health nut." He carried his beliefs to the extreme when authoring a five-
volume work entitled *The Encyclopedia of Physical Culture* in 1912. In this
work, MacFadden stated that all major diseases, including polio, cancer, and
Bright's disease, could be cured by simple diets, water therapy, and modest
exercises. One diet called for nothing more than grapes which, MacFadden
insisted, would eradicate any cancer in the system.

MacFadden later established himself as an expert on eyesight, recom-
mending eyeball bathing and massage to improve vision. The physical
culturalist produced eight children, six of whom were females. He insisted that
children are usually of the opposite sex from that of the parent with the
strongest virility and deepest passions. This, of course, explained why he had
sired a preponderance of females.

Health nut and eccentric newspaper publisher, Bernarr
MacFadden.

So dedicated to his beliefs was MacFadden, that when he contracted jaundice he refused all medical help and trusted to a three-day fast which undoubtedly brought about his death on October 12, 1955. Throughout his lifetime, MacFadden attempted to convert the American public to his way of thinking and, to that end, established a group of magazines and a daily newspaper in New York as propaganda tools. He proved himself to be the most unpredictable and bizarre publisher in the 1920s and 1930s. In one publication he exhorted young men to shun females who wore modern shoe apparel. "If you are looking for future happiness," he warned, "avoid girls who wear high heels." Such heels, MacFadden stated, "devitalized" the wearers, impeding their ability to conduct proper sex, not to mention the damage such togs might bring to unborn children.

True Story Magazine, a popular periodical published by MacFadden before World War I, warned young women to be watchful of random flirtations and promiscuous sex. One of the headlines above a typical MacFadden story read:

The Rise of Liz O' The Lane
The Life Story of a Girl
Who Wouldn't Stay Down
She Wanted to Be Clean

Another read;

Black Eyed Susan's Story
Keep to the Right
The Right Will Keep to You,
Her Motto

Still another:

When May Changed Her Mind
She Found Other Girls Might
Be Sometimes be Right After All

Years later when sales appeared to dip for *True Story,* the ever commercial MacFadden did a complete turnabout, running as the lead piece in his December 1920 issue a cover story entitled:

Why I'm Glad
I Left My
Husband

MacFadden and his editors of the New York *Evening Graphic* aimed for mass public response and hit all-time lows, faking front page photos purporting to show celebrities in the news in intimate settings, such as the infamous "composographs" employed to detail the perverse lovelife of Edward "Daddy" Browning (see entry) and his child–flapper bride, Peaches.

The composograph was never more blatantly used than at the time of Rudolph Valentino's death. The Great Lover of the silent screen took ill in mid-

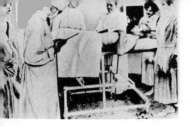

Left, one of MacFadden's fake composographs purportedly showing Valentino on the operating table just before his untimely death. Right, an absurd but effective composograph showing Valentino in Heaven with Enrico Caruso.

August 1926 while on a trip to New York. The "sheik" was rushed to surgery; operating physicians removed a near-bursting appendix, and also found two perforated gastric ulcers. Within days Valentino developed pneumonia, pleurisy and peritonitis. He died on August 23, 1926 and women across the land went into frenzied mourning. New York's Campbell Funeral Home was mobbed long before the body was put on display in one of the most disgusting ghoulish revels ever held.

MacFadden lost no time, sending two photographers to the funeral home. One of the photographers posed in the empty casket Valentino was to occupy while the other took his photo. When this shot was developed, a head-shot of Valentino was superimposed on the front page of the *Evening Graphic* the next day, purporting to show The Great Lover lying in state (long before his body ever arrived).

The tabloid, at MacFadden's direction, fed on the hysteria lingering for weeks after Valentino's death. The *Graphic* published several more "composographs" which ran on its front pages and showed how Valentino *might* have looked on the operating table and, after his demise, portrayed the Great Lover as seen by a medium, standing somewhere in Heaven with no less a personality than Enrico Caruso looking down upon scores of dead souls clambering up the steps of Heaven.

When criticized for such publishing outrages, Bernarr MacFadden scowled, then turned to one accuser and bellowed: "What's the harm in telling the public the truth as you see it? I ask you, sir?"

William Francis MANNIX

Journalist (1873–date uncertain)

One of the most colorful newsmen in American history was William Mannix, whose consistent fabrication of stories earned him the reputation of the profession's leading prankster. Early in life, Mannix, to earn extra money, began submitting celebrity lists to New York newspapers, describing the stellar personalities visiting the posh summer resorts in upstate New York. His services were dismissed when a sharp-eyed editor realized that some of the personalities allegedly frolicking in the Adirondack mountains had been dead for several years.

Undaunted, the always inventive Mannix next advertised himself as a lecturer on Demon Rum and, as a reformed alcoholic, he was paid handsome sums to deliver diatribes against liquor throughout the villages and hamlets of New York State. Tiring of his battles against John Barleycorn, Mannix traveled to Cuba where he became a correspondent for the *Army and Navy Journal,* and the Washington *Star.* According to Charles H. Brown, writing in *The Correspondent's War,* Mannix was expelled from Cuba because "he had violated regulations forbidding contact with insurgents by interviewing Salvador Cisneros, president of the Cuban Republic the insurgents had formed." The truth was that Mannix had, like most of the journalists then in Cuba, fabricated atrocity stories. Mannix's stories, however, were so blatantly faked that incensed Spanish authorities frog-marched him at bayonet point to a boat leaving for the states.

So widely did Mannix spread the story of his expulsion that members in the United States Congress debated his case. A decade later, Mannix was working for the Philadelphia *Press,* but was fired after fabricating another story that brought a $1 million libel suit against the newspaper. The errant newsman looked about for greener fields and was soon on a boat headed for Hawaii where, in November 1911, he obtained a job as a reporter with the Honolulu *Advertiser,* using faked recommendations from clergymen in the United States. By then Mannix's name was so umbilically tied to journalistic fraud that he was compelled to go to work for the *Advertiser* under the alias of William G. Leonard.

Mannix lived well, so well that his newspaper salary proved insufficient for a lifestyle fat with wine and women. He forged his publisher's signature to a small check, was discovered, and was given a year in jail. The journalist looked upon imprisonment as another opportunity to meditate and produce what he considered "lasting literature." To that end he asked that visiting friends bring him historical writings about China. Hawaii's Governor Walter Francis Frear sympathized with Mannix's plight and, at the journalist's request, sent him a new typewriter. The Governor and Mannix's friends, of course, had no way of knowing that they were contributing to one of the great literary hoaxes of the era.

After careful study of Chinese history, Mannix wrote the *Memoirs of Li Hung Chang,* a Chinese statesman who had earned an international reputation. So authentic did the memoirs read that, among others, it was endorsed by John W. Foster, one-time secretary of state under President Harrison, and a diplomat who had met the real Li Hung Chang in 1897 at a peace conference. The publisher of the faked memoirs, Houghton-Mifflin, had a best seller for years. Not until 1923 was the literary fraud discovered; at the time E.B. Drew, a scholar and former official of the Imperial Chinese Customs, found discrepancies in the book that led to its exposure as a Mannix hoax.

Mannix had used an alias when authoring the memoirs. Houghton-Mifflin's editors grew suspicious in 1916. Using another alias, Mannix answered mail from the publisher by offering to track down the true author of the *Memoirs of Li Hung Chang.* This, of course, would mean traveling to China at considerable expense. What the charlatan really proposed was that he be paid to look for himself. One report had it that the gulled publishers did advance Mannix money for this very purpose. Mannix spent the cash by establishing the bogus Pacific Associated Press, which, for years, reaped profits by syndicating fake news stories and interviews with world famous personalities, especially Chinese celebrities who were next to impossible to track down, and whose stories were thus equally impossible to verify.

MARX BROTHERS

Comedians Chico (Leonard: 1887–1961)

Harpo (Adolph: 1888–1964)

Groucho (Julius: 1890–1977)

A great cult now, the Marx Brothers brought a special brand of comedy to the American stage and later to films, sort of a smiling nihilism that said between puns, quips, gags, and assorted kitsch: "Who's the sucker—we're actually getting paid for doing this." Born in New York to Sam and Minnie Marx, the brothers, along with Gummo, and the youngest, Zeppo, went into show business at their mother's insistence and with the help of their talented uncle, Al Shean, of vaudeville's Gallagher and Shean fame.

The uncle sketched out their first acts and the boys, never enthusiastic about the entertainment business until they proved to be successful, proceeded to butcher their lines, insult audiences, and create general mayhem to keep up their own interest in their early shows.

The first born, Chico, was an inveterate gambler all of his life, a craps player, and a long-shot artist at the races. He was once sent to retrieve his father's suit from the cleaners and, when returning home, spotted a crap game in an alleyway. He stopped in for a few rolls and promptly lost his father's pants. A born mimic, Chico avoided beatings from ethnic gangs by adopting Irish, Italian, and German accents as he walked through various neighborhoods. The Italian accent was to serve him through his long and lustrous career, permanently affixed to his role as Chico.

Early in the brothers' career, Chico was the business manager for the group, but he spent the money the boys made almost the very hour he would receive it from a theater manager, losing it, naturally, in impossible wagers. He was able later to put together fabulous deals for the group, but he never managed to hold on to the money, which prompted his playwright friend George S. Kaufman to consider Chico "an odd combination of business acumen and financial idiocy."

Harpo and Groucho, after years of seeing their brother broke, and fearing he would die a pauper, refused to sign any more movie deals until Chico agreed to give up half his salary to the family money manager. Only through such drastic measures did the brothers keep Chico from the poorhouse, or so they later claimed.

A strain of the mischievous, the oddball, even the macabre, ran through the humor of all the Marx Brothers. None of them ever liked to admit that they were in show business. When Chico was once asked by a neighbor what he did for a living, the Marx brother replied that he was a smuggler. "Nothing serious," he added, "just Mexicans." To further perplex and perhaps frighten his neighbor, Chico appeared hours later with a Mexican gardener, offering to sell him "cheap."

Groucho, whenever out with his wife, Ruth, and children, was not always recognized without his greasepaint mustache. When his wife urged him to identify himself to a headwaiter in order to be promptly seated, Groucho would state: "Do you know us? We're the Jacksons. I'm Sam Jackson [his favorite alias], this is Mrs. Sam Jackson, and these are the little Jacksons." Marx and his family would then continue to wait in line while the headwaiter ignored them. Invariably, after they were seated, Mrs. Marx would ask Groucho why he didn't give his correct identity. At that point, Marx would summon the headwaiter and say something to the effect that "I should have told you who I *really* am—I'm Joe Schwartz, this is Mrs. Joe Schwartz and these are the little Schwartzes."

Harpo was the natural clown of the troupe, a man who enjoyed making faces, wearing costumes and cavorting in public or private, possessing a child-like quality of innocence which undoubtedly endeared him, more than the other brothers, to the literati of New York in the 1920s at the time of the Marx Brothers' first theatrical success. Actually, it was the critic Alexander Woollcott (see entry) who discovered the brothers. He was given an assignment to review *I'll Say She Is,* their first legitimate (if it could be called that) play which opened at New York's Casino Theater on May 19, 1924. Woollcott literally fell into the aisle—he said in his review—laughing at the antics of these zanies. He encouraged all of New York to see the clowns and their careers were magically established.

Woollcott took Harpo under his wing and introduced him to Heywood Bruan, George S. Kaufman, Robert Benchley, the whole crowd of Algonquin Round Table fame. Harpo became Woollcott's eternal companion in croquet, but he always lost to the critic, undoubtedly by choice, since Woollcott would throw violent tantrums if he were beaten. Many times Harpo was seen to weep after Woollcott who, enraged at Marx' good play, would slam Harpo's ball into the shrubbery.

Harpo, however, got even. Woollcott invited him to sit in one night at the famous Saturday night poker game held at the Algonquin. The smiling Marx brother promptly won a reported $30,000, although the comedian later claimed that "it was only a few thousand." And most of it was Alexander Woollcott's money.

Groucho shunned the limelight when off-stage or off-camera, preferring to be a homebody. He read incessantly—all manner of books, periodicals, and scripts—and, while his brothers enjoyed the nightlife, he worked on the act. (Groucho accepted his brothers' wild ways, especially Chico's, once stating: "There are three things my brother Chico is always on—a phone, a horse, or a broad.") Groucho's own peculiarities were itemized by his son Arthur Marx in *Life with Groucho.* When eating, the youngest of the trio insisted that his **235**

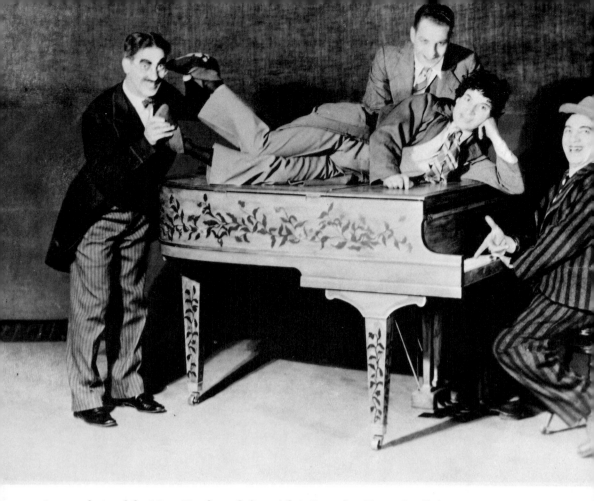

A rare photo of the Marx Brothers (left to right), Groucho, Harpo (reclining on piano), Gummo, a rare appearance, and Chico, at the piano in the stage version of *Animal Crackers*. (Note: Harpo is wearing a dark red wig which he later exchanged for a blonde rug of curls.)

dining room be as brightly lit as a movie set. He could not tolerate having courses served separately and constantly changed his mind about what kind of food was healthy and what was not, first warning his children that a particular food was dangerous to eat and, a week later, encouraging them to eat that very food.

It was probably just as well that the acerbic Groucho did not go out much. When he did, especially in Hollywood, his irreverant ways created havoc. He once lifted a large hat from the head of Greta Garbo to see who she was, and then snorted: "Excuse me. I just thought you were a fellow I once knew in Pittsburgh."

All the Marx Brothers were irreverent toward their plays and films. They ad-libbed and changed the material so frequently that the original story seldom remained. George S. Kaufman visited the theater where his play, *Animal Crackers,* was enjoying a long run. He had written it with Morris Ryskind especially for the Marx Brothers. As the playwright was talking in the back of the theater with Ryskind, during the play, Kaufman suddenly and excitedly held up his hand and said: "Excuse me, Morris, but I think I just heard one of the original lines!"

Art Fisher, a monologist appearing on the same bill with the Marx Brothers early in their careers gave them their names, but as far as Groucho was concerned, "it didn't help the act at all." The act consisted chiefly of wild slapstick at first, then wild patter between Groucho, the smoothie who played to the sophisticates in the audience, and Chico, the dumb-but-street-wise straight man. Harpo had no lines, but compensated by wearing a red (later yellow) wig with a mass of curls, honking a horn or employing noisemakers to make his whacky presence known, and dropping thousands of items, from forks to steaming cups of coffee, from his baggy sleeves. Harpo was always the favorite of children.

For relief, Chico, an inventive musician, played the piano. Harpo, to contribute to the act, took up the harp, learned how to play the instrument in two weeks, and worked it into the act. Whenever it came time for his brothers to play their instruments, Groucho would rush to stage center, or, when later in films, stare glumly into the camera, and pipe: "They're gonna play now, folks, so go and get your popcorn!"

Harpo enjoyed being Harpo everywhere. When Groucho got married, his capricious brother moved all around the church *inside* of an enormous plant, making it appear that the plant was moving on its own. When the Kaufman–Hart comedy, *The Man Who Came To Dinner,* was premiered, Harpo, who had no part, suddenly appeared everywhere on stage, honking his horn, and working his other many noisemakers so that the playwrights, who were playing their own leads, would be at ease. He succeeded in relaxing Kaufman

The three mad schemers scheming in *At the Circus;* Chico gambled, Harpo played with the literati, and Groucho stayed at home and out of trouble, sometimes.

and Hart, but the audience heard only a few lines filtering through his incessant racket.

The brothers are best remembered for their film classics, *The Coconuts, Animal Crackers, Duck Soup, Horsefeathers* (written especially for them by S.J. Perleman), and *Monkey Business,* all vintage Marx Brothers comedies. Their MGM films, *A Night At The Opera* and *A Day at the Races,* though great money makers, were not pure Marx Brothers vehicles.

Harpo and Chico retired for the most part with their last film *Love Happy,* in 1950. Groucho, however, began a whole new and lucrative career with the radio program, *You Bet Your Life,* in October 1947. So successful was the program that it later became a television standard.

Then Groucho's penchant for work was always stronger than that of Harpo or Chico. He was, according to his son Arthur, in constant fear of going broke and dying in the poorhouse. This phobia may have begun in 1929 when Groucho lost about $250,000 in the Stock Exchange Crash, a traumatic experience that forever left the Marx brother in doubt about his financial future.

At the time the Marx brother hurriedly met with his lawyer Morris Ernst, according to Margaret Case Harriman, writing in *The Vicious Circle,* Groucho nervously showed Ernst his investment list while stocks were crashing by the second.

Ernst pointed to one of Groucho's stocks on the list. It had fallen from 122 to 2. "Where did you get this recommendation?"

"From Bernard Baruch," replied Groucho, telling the truth.

Ernst pointed to another stock which had, just that dismal day in 1929, dropped from 130 to 1. "How about this one?"

"From Gerard Swope himself!"

Suddenly Ernst grabbed the list and held it closer. One stock which Groucho had purchased at 31 had only dropped a point and still stood defiantly at 30. "For God's sake," Ernst said, some confidence returning to his voice. "Where did you get *that* tip?"

"Oh, *that,*" sighed Groucho. "I got that one from a wardrobe woman in the Shubert Theater in Chicago."

Following World War II, Groucho convinced his business agent, Salwyn Shufro, to accompany him to the visitor's gallery of the New York Stock Exchange. Marx leaned over the railing smoking his cigar and disdainfully flicking ashes on the stockbrokers scurrying about on the main floor. He then began to sing, his voice rising in volume until he was blaring "When Irish Eyes Are Smiling."

The trading suddenly ceased as all eyes turned upward at Groucho who was not wearing his mustache and was not recognized. Marx continued to sing at the top of his voice.

Groucho pitching woo on the witness stand in *At the Circus;* he used aliases in public to bedevil his wife.

"Please, Groucho," begged Shufro. "I'm afraid they don't appreciate clowning in the Stock Exchange."

Marx ignored his business adviser and went on with his song, shouting it rather than singing it.

The sergeant-at-arms yelled up from the floor of the Exchange: "Quiet, you lunatic! Or I'll call the police!"

Marx leaned even further over the railing and snarled out his wonderful lines of revenge: "Listen, you crooks—you wiped me out of two hundred and fifty thousand dollars in 1929! For that kind of dough, I think I'm entitled to sing if I want to!"

William Somerset MAUGHAM

Author (1874–1965)

After Maugham's mother died early in his life, the author was raised by a series of nannies under the supervision of an uncle who was the vicar of Whitestable, England. He attended St. Thomas' Medical School in London and later practiced as a doctor, but his gift was always as a writer. Maugham's novels, *The Moon and Sixpence, Of Human Bondage, The Magician* (based on the bizarre Aleister Crowley, see entry), *Cakes and Ale, The Painted Veil,* and *The Razor's Edge* earned for him a high place in world literature. His short story, *Miss Thompson* (the story of the south seas slattern Sadie Thompson), earned for him more than a half-million dollars through stage and film versions.

Though he was considered one of the world's great voices in literature, Maugham was a strange and secretive creature, who stammered at the slightest criticism of his work before going into a screaming frenzy. He was superstitious and an avowed atheist, but repeatedly stated in his notebooks that he would probably call on God whenever he felt his life threatened, which he did. The author denied the existence of God following a night of deep prayer in which Maugham begged God to cure him of his awful stammering when he was a youth (much the same way his hero in *Of Human Bondage*, Phillip Carey, prayed to God to miraculously cure his clubfoot). When awakening Maugham looked into a mirror and spoke. He stammered as before. There was no God, he concluded.

Maugham was secretive about his superstitions, but it was evident that he believed deeply in fortune or fate and to that end ordered that "the evil eye"—a Moorish sign—be carved over the entranceway to his Villa Mauresque on the Riviera at Cap Ferrat. The same sign was stamped on the bindings of his books, family plate, stationary, playing cards, even etched above the marble fireplace of his study. The author, when questioned about his obsession with this "evil eye," merely smiled knowingly and said: "It brings luck."

240

When it came to women, Maugham experienced bad luck all the way. His first sexual encounter occurred when he was practicing medicine in London. Young doctor Maugham picked up a prostitute and, by his own admission, was infected with gonorrhea. By the time he had discarded the medical profession and had become a successful playwright, Maugham met a blue-eyed blonde actress who became his mistress; he never identified this beauty except by her first name, Nan. The woman was sexually disloyal to Maugham, but he accepted her promiscuity. "I knew that all my friends had been to bed with her," he later commented. "There was no vice in her. It just happened that she enjoyed copulation and took it for granted that when she dined with a man sexual congress would follow." Maugham literally chased the actress to Chicago where she was to appear in a play, begging her to accept his ring, imploring her to marry him. She rejected him out-of-hand and, a few weeks later, married an earl.

In 1913 the wealthy Maugham met Gwendolen Syrie Barnado Wellcome at a party. The darkly attractive woman was then married to an American millionaire, but was separated. Her income from her husband was restricted, so she went after Maugham who foolishly supported her in grand style. Unknown to the author at the time, Syrie was also carrying on an affair with another man, Gordon Selfridge, who was also paying her bills.

Mrs. Wellcome became pregnant and decided that Maugham was the father; he was, after all, single and Selfridge was a married man. Henry Wellcome, who had not yet obtained his divorce from Syrie, publicly accused his wife of having a child out of wedlock and named the author as correspondent. Maugham went into virtual hiding, but then he heard that Syrie had taken veronal tablets. Syrie's near suicide frightened the author into marrying her, which had been her intention all along.

The marriage proved disasterous. A daughter was born, Liza, later Lady John Hope. Syrie continued her love affairs, flaunting her lovers in Maugham's face. (She was undoubtedly the prototype for the scheming Mildred in *Of Human Bondage*.) Not until 1927 did the couple divorce with Syrie receiving $1 million as a settlement. Maugham's daughter, in 1962, sued him for half that much when he attempted to sell some of his paintings, works that Liza claimed to be rightfully hers.

"It's an act of ingratitude!" yelled Maugham. "My daughter has never cared a ha'penny for me!"

After lengthy court battles, Liza was not only awarded a share of the sale of the paintings, $280,000, but received more than $1 million from Maugham's estate, plus a share of all his future royalties; Maugham had attempted to cut her out of his will and make his secretary–companion, Alan Searle, who was with him from 1945 on, as his only heir.

Maugham's attitude toward women in general was, for most of his life, negative, often vicious. Some stated that this was understandable, given his experiences with assorted vixens; others claimed that the author had undergone a change of sexual attitude, giving his affections wholly to men.

Much of Maugham's venom about women was spent in his writings. At one time he wrote: "No man in his heart is quite so cynical as a well-bred woman." He took delight in hearing that the once great beauty Lily Langtry haunted New York music halls at the age of sixty, her beauty and body gone to flab, and how she paid men fifty cents a dance to twirl her about the floor. "...she, who once had had the crowned heads of Europe at her feet, felt no shame about it," he wrote.

Toward the end of his life, Maugham had surrounded himself exclusively with male companions. Before this withdrawn and deeply resentful man died at age ninety-one on December 16, 1965, in Nice, France, he carped: "I was never what is known as a 'ladies man.' I didn't have the looks or disposition, or, I might add, the time to play at it. In my company I found most women uncomfortable and somewhat contentious, somehow sensing that I found them transparent and was quite aware of all their grubby little tricks. I think that most women went to bed with me out of curiosity, or accepted me as a temporary lover to maintain their standard of copulating only with the well-known and well-to-do gentlemen, or for personal gain."

Edith Rockefeller McCORMICK

Society Queen (1872–1932)

Daughter of John D. Rockefeller, Edith Rockefeller was raised with more than one silver spoon. Privately tutored, she grew up shielded by her father's millions from unpleasant realities. She lived and died a woman of immense wealth without a moment's discomfort, if all reports are to be believed.

Marrying Harold Fowler McCormick, a scion of the reaper fortune, in 1895, Edith proceeded to set herself up as the reigning society queen of Chicago, a title which she bought with her millions and that of her husband, vying with local runners-up to that title in purchasing the largest mansions, the biggest estates, and accumulating a staggering amount of rare gems.

Edith McCormick demanded that her husband bestow upon her priceless jewelry each year. Harold McCormick dutifully gave her a rope of pearls worth $2 million. He followed this up by presenting his wife with a $1 million emerald necklace. The next year he offered her another necklace made up of 1,657 diamonds, price unknown.

Mrs. McCormick believed in strict regimen at home. She only spoke to her servants through a secretary and insisted that *four* butlers wait on her at breakfast, whether she ate or not. Even her own children, when they became adults, had to make an appointment to see her.

Mrs. McCormick decided to have lavish parties on the spur of the moment and, within a week or so, preparations would be hurriedly made for the arrival

Chicago's fabulously rich Edith Rockefeller McCormick; her children saw her by appointment only.

of several hundred guests. She liked costume parties and would designate exactly *what* kind of costumes her guests should wear, irrespective of what her guests might have to pay for such tailor-made costumes.

Edith divorced McCormick in 1921 when he began to run around with a failed opera diva, the eccentric Ganna Walska (see entry). (It was Walska who served as Orson Welles' prototype for the singer in his film *Citizen Kane*.) Harold McCormick was undoubtedly as zany as his wife and girlfriend. When Walska insisted that he somehow improve his virility, McCormick underwent an experimental operation by the notorious European quack, Serge Veronoff, whereby he received a monkey glad transplant. The operation only served to shorten McCormick's life and not at all satisfy Ganna Walska.

Mrs. Edith McCormick spent the last fifteen years of her life living abroad and contributing to various charities and music foundations. Toward the end of her life she fanatically believed that she was the reincarnation of another great lady from bygone days—the mother of Egyptian King Tutankhamen. And no one dared to openly doubt her.

MELLON BROTHERS

Industrialists (Andrew: 1855–1937)

(Richard: 1851–1933)

The Mellon Brothers achieved fame and riches in their long lifetimes, Andrew William Mellon holding the post of United States Secretary of the Treasury (1921–31) and Richard heading up the powerful Mellon Industries. Both brothers were multimillionaires and philanthropists. They were recognized as two of America's foremost business leaders, their wealth derived from the family banking fortune in Pittsburgh. Through them the Mellon Fund and

Industrial and banking tycoons Andrew and Richard Mellon (second and third from left when they received citations from the American Institute of Chemists for their charitable acts in 1931); both Mellon brothers were incurable practical jokers.

philanthropic foundations were established. The National Gallery of Art came into existence through benefactions from Andrew Mellon.

Yet these two ultraconservative, withdrawn, and tight-lipped brothers privately practiced unending practical jokes, which they played on each other until they were well into their eighties. So dogged was Richard B. Mellon about practical joking that the eighty-two-year-old played out his hand right to his death on December 1, 1933.

Confined to his mansion at 6500 Fifth Avenue in Pittsburgh, the dying multimillionaire looked from his immense four-poster bed to the members of his family standing nearby. One of these was his distinguished brother, Andrew William Mellon.

Richard raised a bony arm, motioning feebly for Andrew to draw closer. Andrew Mellon moved to the side of the bed.

"Closer," the pneumonia-ridden Richard gasped.

The Mellon brother moved closer still, leaning over his brother's prostate form. Richard Mellon, using up his last ounce of strength, again raised his arm and brushed Andrew's shoulder, his final breath hissing out the words: "last tag." With that, the tycoon died, and left his brother Andrew permanently "it."

William MILLER

Religious Prophet (1782–1849)

This one-time Vermont farmer, justice of the peace and deputy sheriff was born in Pittsfield, Massachusetts on February 15, 1782. After serving as a captain in the War of 1812, Miller slowly became a militant fundamentalist, preaching as a licensed Baptist clergyman that Christ would soon be returning to earth. Not only would Christ return, Miller began to tell his anxious flock, but the world would come to an end on April 3, 1843; this revelation had come to him, he stated, after long and exhaustive day of study of the Book of Daniel.

Miller began warning his followers of this momentous event as early as 1831. When shooting stars were seen two years later, Miller informed the public and press alike that these heavenly movements confirmed his prediction. The New York *Herald,* always in search of the sensational for its columns, sent several reporters to interview the prophet of doom and gave his prediction widespread play in its pages. How would the earth end on April 3, 1843, Miller was asked. "By fire," came his terse reply. He added that the dead would be taken to heaven before the living. This incredible comment, when published, caused religious fanatics to commit suicide by the hundreds. Worse, other rabid followers of Miller's zany beliefs murdered their family members in order to give them prominent positions in that long queue before heaven's gates.

At the designated hour, Miller and thousands of his followers gathered in wailing prayer upon hilltops all over New England, chiefly in Vermont. As the sun set on one small village a piercing sound was heard that caused the multitude to shriek and scream for mercy, but the heavens did not split nor did fire engulf the earth. The sound the fanatics heard was that of a pranksterish youth ineptly blowing a bugle in a shabby imitation of Gabriel. Several minor injuries occurred when followers attempted to soar heavenward on makeshift wings and accomplished nothing more than falling from hilltops. Miller remained undisturbed and set a new date for the world's end, July 7, 1843.

Up to that date Miller grew prosperous by selling "ascension robes" to his followers who dug thousands of family graves and sat in these hollowed plots of earth on the Day of Judgment, only to discover that it was another false alarm. Miller, without explanation, set a new date for Armageddon, March 21, 1844, which gave him enough time to organize more than a half-million adherants to his newly founded Adventist Church, of which he became the president, amassing great wealth through his lectures and the sale of his ascension robes and bibles.

When the world did not end on March 21, 1844, Miller moved up the date to October 22 of that year. This time the throngs so long patient for Judgment Day rebelled when their numbers were not burned to a crisp by heavenly fire. Miller was jeered and hooted from his place on the hilltop and, like the multitudes fleeing the Biblical Tower of Babel, Millerites went their separate ways to set up scores of different religious sects, the most powerful of which became the Seventh-Day Adventists, intact to this day.

Prophet William Miller, who predicted the end of the world—many times.

Miller ignored his departing flock of disbelievers and continued to enrich himself through his myriad of lectures and through the sale of his doomsday items. He died in Hampton, Vermont on December 29, 1849, insisting on his deathbed that, even though his calculations might have been slightly in error, the death of the Earth would soon follow his own.

Wilson MIZNER

Entrepreneur (1876–1933)

Adventurer and raconteur, Wilson Mizner came from a family which practiced stern religion. He and his two brothers moved to Guatemala in 1889 with their father, Lansing Bond Mizner, a minister intent upon converting the heathens. Returning to the United States, Mizner studied at Santa Clara College from 1892 to 1894, but was always yielding to his wanderlust, which got the better of him in 1897 when he went off to Alaska as an employee of the Alaska Fur Company. His real reason for going to the frozen northlands was to hunt for riches in the newly discovered gold fields of the Klondike; in fact, Mizner was among the first dozen men into the fabulous region where he won and lost fortunes.

He soon gave up prospecting and busied himself with gambling and con games which invariably got him into trouble. Mizner, however, had no difficulty in defending himself against the brawny types in Fairbanks and other boom towns. By his mid-twenties, he stood six-foot-four and weighed almost 250 pounds. His enormous head was covered with an iron–gray mane that reminded one and all of a lion.

Down on his luck in Fairbanks, Mizner was near to starving. Prices in the boomtown were astronomical. One egg, uncooked, sold for $5. A bowl of bear soup was $10. Fortunately for the young scapegrace, he had befriended a waiter who was later to become a movie theater mogul, Sid Grauman (of Grauman's Chinese Theater in Hollywood fame).

Grauman worked his own con game. He cut the pockets out of his trousers and replaced these with wide-necked hot water bottles. When carrying bowls of the precious soup down a long, dark corridor from the kitchen to the dining room, Grauman would pour some of the soup into his pocket. When the hot water bottles were full, Grauman would step out into an alleyway where dozens of men were gathered to sell his stolen soup for $5 a bowl. He also fed a starving Wilson Mizner on credit. Grauman, however, was not one to encourage prolonged dependancy upon his generous nature; he firmly suggested that Mizner get himself a routine. Wilson decided to play the old Badger Game.

After taking a waitress on a date (she paid), Mizner suggested compromising some gold-dust-laden miner. The waitress, also down on her luck, agreed. The two selected a prospector who had just hit it rich and the attractive waitress soon inveigled the miner back to her makeshift cabin to spend the night.

Mizner went to his favorite bar to wait the appropriate time before storming the cabin. The bartender on duty drew him aside, saying: "I know what you and that dame are planning. You'd better watch out."

"Whaddya mean?" asked Mizner, pretending the innocent.

"Look, that dame's a no-good whore, don't you know? I'm your pal, so I'm telling you she's got a swinging door for a conscience. She'll two-time you, so watch out."

"How do you know all this?" Mizner asked.

"I'll tell you how—that dame is gonna pretend she's your wife. You show up at her cabin and find her with the old miner and play the outraged husband. You threaten to shoot 'em both. He pays you off with the dust—and he's got plenty of it—and you and the dame retire. Only one thing wrong—"

"What's that?"

"The dame came to me and told me the whole story. Only she tells me that she will split the boodle with me if I leave you to the old man's shotgun. Imagine? I'm supposed to run off with her and the gold and ditch you, my pal!"

Mizner gave the bartender a quizzical look. "Why didn't you take the deal?"

The bartender patted Wilson's hand, giving him a broad smile. "I don't like her—in fact I don't like women at all. I like you."

Mizner sheepishly muttered his thanks and then proceeded to the cabin through knee-high snow. He did not have a pistol with which to menace the miner, but brought along the next best thing, a can of tomatoes which he wrapped in newspaper so that it appeared to be a pack of dynamite commonly used by the local miners. As he burst through the door, Mizner shouted: "Oh God, my wife!" He stood in the shadowy cabin peering down at the miner and the waitress who were suddenly petrified in their naked glory. "I'm going to blow you both to Hades!" screamed the indignant Mizner. With that he lit a match and prepared to light his fake dynamite.

Grabbing his parka and pants, the miner dove frantically into his clothes, babbling: "It's all a mistake, sir, all a mistake, please believe me! The lady never told me she was married!"

"Prepare to meet your maker," yelled Mizner at his theatrical best, moving the match closer to his lethal-looking package. "We're all going up together!"

"I swear to God I didn't know she was your wife!" bellowed the frenzied miner as he stumbled about, trying to slip into his pants and boots. "I'll make it all right, believe me."

The match in Mizner's hand moved dangerously close to the package. "God will take me to his bosom," he intoned, "and you know where he'll send you two sinners!"

In a final desperate gesture, the miner tossed his gold belt to Mizner. "Take it—there's fifty thousand worth of dust in that." He began to rush past Wilson. "You can find a new woman, a good woman, with that kind of money."

Mizner continued to curse and swear as the miner rushed wildly into the snowy night, slamming the door, his voice trailing the words, "don't light that fuse, mister, don't light that fuse!"

Crushing the match, Mizner put the gold belt around his waist. He tipped his hat at the waitress who was still in bed. "I'll see you around, babe."

The woman jumped from the bed, yelling: "Hey, wait a minute, buster! Where's my share?"

Mizner tossed the can of tomatoes onto the bed, snorting: "That just got me fifty thousand dollars. See what it can do for you." He raced from the cabin as the woman hurled the can and any other objects she could grab at his fleeing form.

Whenever Wilson Mizner was pressed for funds he could always invent some sort of short con to refill his empty coffers. Requiring funds once in Atlantic City, Mizner befriended some high rollers, men who would bet on anything. He engineered this group out onto the beach which was littered with colorful small tents which protected bathers from the hot sun.

Mizner stopped, seeing an enormous pair of feet protruding from one of the tents. "I've never seen such feet on a human," he said. "I wonder how tall that fellow is?"

"Got to be six-foot-two," one of the plungers guessed.

"More than that," replied another.

Mizner proposed a large wager as to the height of the man beneath the beach tent. Everyone bet that the bather was well over six feet, every one but Mizner who said rubbing his chin thoughtfully: "Something tells me that that man is no more than five feet in height."

When the tent flap was thrown back the gamblers gasped to see a dwarf who suddenly stood up to a height of no more than four-and-a-half feet. Mizner collected several thousand dollars and walked away humming. He later gave the dwarf—a carnival character he had recruited for the purpose of the scam—part of the profits. Mizner felt no qualms in mulcting the gullible rich and was credited (along with several others) with the quip, "Never give a sucker an even break."

Mizner and his brother Addison found suckers by the tens of thousands during the Florida land boom in 1925. Addison had been a society architect who, for reasons of ill health, moved to Florida in 1918. Within a few years speculators moved into southern Florida and created the great land boom, Mizner being one of the most active. Addison Mizner created a wonderful hodge-podge type of architecture for his Florida buildings. In *The Legendary Mizners,* Alva Johnston described Addison's architecture as being the "Bastard–Spanish–Moorish–Romanesque–Gothic–Renaissance–Bull Market–Damn-the-Expense Style," although the Spanish motiff dominated. Addison Mizner became a millionaire designing mansions for the nouveau rich. He established Mizner Industries, Inc., and asked his brother Wilson to join him in selling more and more lots to the phalanxes of northerners pouring into Miami.

Wilson journeyed from New York to help his brother create an ostentatious subdivision which they called Boca Raton ("Rat's Mouth"), located south of

Palm Beach. Competitors called the Mizner subdivision "Beaucoup Rotten," yet thousands of the estimated 2,500,000 persons flooding into the area in 1925 purchased impossible lots from the Mizner brothers.

With most of the real land gone, Wilson Mizner took to selling lots that were underwater but were visible at low tide, and only at these times did Wilson conduct his sales. Naturally when the customer returned to find his property beneath rolling ocean waves, warrants were sworn out for the capricious Wilson. One irate client brought Mizner into court, telling the judge that Wilson had sold him a tract of land which Mizner guaranteed would produce exotic and profitable crops. "He said I would be able to grow nuts," wailed the sucker, "and I can't grow a damn thing because my land is under-water."

Mizner drew himself up to his full impressive height and said to the judge: "Your honor, I think this man is deaf. I told him that if he bought my property he would *go* nuts. Look at him. I think he already has." The case was dismissed.

The witty con man was again brought into court on another charge, but angered the judge by his disdainful conduct. "Are you trying to show contempt of court?" inquired the judge as he leaned menacingly toward Mizner.

"No, your honor," replied Wilson softly. "I'm trying to conceal it."

Mizner proved himself a master of concealing information that might damage opportunities. On one occasion when he had moved to California, he applied for a large life insurance policy. When asked by an inspecting physician for a urine sample, Mizner deferred, stating he would return the next day with the sample. The con man fretted for hours, knowing that his years of dissipation, from the Klondike to China, would produce a less than desirable urine sample. As he pondered his problem he spotted a young and healthy-looking actress of his acquaintance strolling down a Los Angeles street.

Approaching the actress, Mizner explained his dilemma. He asked her to "stand in" for him, promising her a free trip to Europe once he obtained the large insurance policy. The actress agreed and provided Wilson with the required sample which he rushed back to his doctor's office.

Within a week Mizner was approached by the same actress as he sat in a cafe. "Well," she said impatiently, "when can I leave for Europe?"

"Europe! Are you kidding?" replied a sour-faced Mizner. "Honey, you couldn't tinkle your way to Catalina. It may interest you to know that the laboratory report came back on that sample, and I'm *pregnant!*"

For the most part Wilson Mizner idolized women, young and old, ugly and beautiful, preferably the latter. Mizner was dining one night with Lionel Barrymore in a posh San Francisco restaurant when an elderly but attractive woman passed his table and, recognizing him, gave him a warm hello. Mizner asked the woman to join him and Barrymore and she did. Wilson introduced her as one Molly Danford, explaining to Barrymore that Mrs. Danford owned a great deal of property in San Francisco, including one of the largest mansions on Knob Hill where she had entertained judges, bankers, even the governor.

"Your brother John spent many happy days in my house on the hill," said

Mrs. Danford to Lionel. She went on to tell him that she had just purchased through her broker large sections of real estate in Hollywood which she had never visited. "I understand it's the sin capital of the world. Is that not true, Mr. Barrymore?"

Barrymore assured Mrs. Danford that the wild acts of a few had given Hollywood undeserved notoriety. The elegantly attired lady then said goodnight to Mizner and Barrymore.

The actor was more than impressed with Mrs. Danford and thought of seeing her again. "Tell me, Wilson," asked Barrymore. "Is the lady married?"

"I should say so," replied Mizner. "She's married to her work."

"What *is* her work?"

"Why, she owns the biggest whorehouse in San Francisco!"

It was the kind of trick ending to conversations in which Wilson Mizner delighted. He was good at trick endings, as was his friend Willian Sydney Porter, the famous short story writer who wrote under the name of "O. Henry." Porter and Mizner roomed together in New York just after the turn of the century. Both men were broke, but Mizner always found a way to keep them in high cuisine. The pair lunched at Sherry's one early afternoon at Mizner's insistence. After gorging themselves on a seven-course meal, Mizner borrowed a pen from a waiter and began to write on the back of the restaurant's large menu. When he finished he told the waiter: "I think we owe you about thirty dollars for that excellent meal. I've written a story on your menu." He handed it back to the dumbfounded waiter, ordering him to "take it to the address I've written down. The editor will give you fifty dollars for the story. Take care of our bill and keep the change."

The waiter looked over the story quickly, then said: "But you haven't signed the story, sir. Without a signature I won't receive the money."

Mizner looked at Porter who, according to the story Wilson Mizner told, gave him a nod and said: "Sign it." Mizner signed the story "O. Henry."

The enterprising Mizner never revealed the title of the O. Henry story, but insisted to his final hour that it was published as a genuine O. Henry story all the same and appeared in every collection of his work. The story, of course, had the usual O. Henry trick ending, which was also a specialty of Wilson Mizner's. Since it is well-known that all the stories published under the O. Henry byline were not written by Porter, one might wonder at how many stories with trick endings attributed to O. Henry were actually written by the sagacious Mizner.

Porter remained Mizner's idol long after the author's death in 1910. He was forever championing the work of his one-time roommate and went into a rage any time someone had the affrontery to compare himself with O. Henry.

When the writer Jim Tully publicly stated that he was a much better writer than Porter, he received a searing blast from Wilson Mizner that scarred Tully's memory for the rest of his life. "You digger in the garbage of literature!" wrote Mizner. "You impudent red-headed cur! You porter in the bawdy house of words ... You low rat ... You befouler of the great dead. You slime of the underworld. You shady reprehensible rogue. You a better writer than O. Henry! Why, you couldn't sign his tax receipts! You're as illiterate as a

The bizarre hustler and wit, Wilson Mizner, shown with fellow zany, Texas Guinan.

publisher. If you had a Roman nose you'd be a courtesan ... you damned brainless jazzer of decent English!"

It was undoubtedly Mizner's friendship with Porter that steered him into writing down what his quipster's mind naturally produced. Mizner was considered one of the cleverest slinger of bon mots of his era. It was Mizner who stated that "when you steal from one author it's plagiarism; if you steal from many, it's research." He also advised men to "treat a whore like a lady and a lady like a whore," and counseled the soon-to-be-successful of the world to "always be pleasant to the people you meet on the way up. They are always the people you meet on the way down." When news reached Mizner one day in 1910 that Stanley Ketchel, the great middleweight champion he had once managed, had been shot to death in Missouri over a woman, Mizner reportedly said through great tears: "Have someone start counting over that kid—he'll get up on the count of nine!"

Mizner employed his wits to write some clever dramas that were not only produced in New York and Chicago, but became financial hits. These included *The Only Law, The Deep Purple,* and *The Greyhound.* He later moved to Hollywood to write for films, although he hated the town, saying that "Hollywood is a sewer with service from the Ritz Carlton." A variant on that quip appeared in the October 1927 *Photoplay Magazine;* Mizner was asked how he found the film capital. "The joint is as dead as a New York nightclub," said Mizner. "I though it was going to be a delightful trip through a sewer in a glass-bottomed boat."

At first Mizner had difficulty selling his scripts to producers. B.P. Shulberg was particularly stubborn in accepting any script Wilson brought him. He tossed several Mizner stories back at the author, telling him that "they're no good, nobody would pay to see such stories." Mizner showed up at Shulberg's office for the fifth time in one week, handing over another story treatment. Shulberg read the story, then shoved it back to Mizner in his usual manner, droning: "Nobody would pay to see such a story."

"Oh, yeah?" sneered Mizner. "I thought you'd say that. It's a synopsis of my play *Deep Purple,* which ran for two years on Broadway."

251

Even more difficult a customer for Mizner stories was Jack Warner of Warner Brothers Studios. So many times did Warner reject Mizner that Wilson grew to despise the producer. Warner eventually did hire Mizner to write screenplays, but insulted the writer at every opportunity (Warner hated writers, calling them all "lazy bums"). Mizner never missed a chance to lambast his boss. "Jack Warner has oilcloth pockets," he once stated, "so that he can steal soup." He was undoubtedly remembering his friend Sid Grauman at the time. On another occasion Mizner complained that "working for Warner Brothers is like screwing a porcupine—it's one hundred pricks against one."

Jack Warner suddenly got it into his head that he wanted Mizner to "write an epic for the studio, a very big epic," and sent Wilson off to create, without specifying what kind of epic he desired. Some days later Mizner buttonholed Warner, asking: "What kind of an epic do you want? A western? The Crusades? Pirates? What?"

Warner merely shrugged and sauntered into his office.

Weeks went by and finally Jack Warner remembered his assignment to Mizner. He got him on the studio phone, shouting: "Where's that goddamned epic you're getting paid big money to write?"

"Epics take time," replied Mizner.

More weeks went by until an irate Jack Warner summoned Mizner to his office, demanding that he bring the completed script for the epic with him. Mizner showed up some hours later carrying an enormous package which he dropped with a resounding thud on Warner's desk. "Here you go—probably the biggest epic Warners will ever produce, a cast of tens of thousands." Without another word Wilson Mizner abruptly left the office (and the studio).

After he had gone Jack Warner laboriously untied the large package to find a copy of the New York Telephone Directory.

Mizner's bizarre sense of humor remained sharp and steady to the day of his death, on April 3, 1933. A priest was summoned by family members. Mizner came out of a coma momentarily to see the clergyman sitting at his bedside.

"I'm sure you'll want to talk to me," the priest said to the dying man.

Wilson Mizner gave him a weak grin. His large, bulbous eyes twinkled, and he quipped with his dying breath: "Why should I talk to you … I've just been talking to your boss."

Edward Wortley MONTAGU

Aristocrat (1712–1776)

Montagu was a mad marrying man who wedded on whim. During the course of his worldwide traveling, Montagu, an immensely wealthy British nobleman, married (and discarded) scores of females from washerwomen who might catch his eye while on their knees scrubbing his lodgings, to high-born ladies in France, Italy, England, and Turkey.

The man was eccentric in many ways. He once insisted that the Vatican make his daughter a nun in spite of the fact that he and his family practiced a different religion. Montagu spent most of his time studying languages and flitting about the known world.

Always bizarre in his appearance, Montagu adorned himself with diamonds, down to his shoebuckles. In Paris he had an iron wig fashioned after his own design and wore this monstrosity to all social functions. When not wearing his iron wig, Montagu sported Turkish garb and even wore a turban while studying in his house and also while sleeping. In a day when all high-born Englishmen went clean-shaven, Montagu grew a wild-looking beard and allowed his hair to grow down over his shoulders.

Though he was undoubtedly one of the world's leading bigamists, Montagu avoided prosecution by wedding women in many countries and towns and then hurriedly departing after consummating the marriage. It was estimated that when Montagu died in Padua in April 1776 he left more than 100 widows.

John MYTTON

Aristocrat (1796–1834)

Born to the estate of Halston, near Shrewsbury on September 30, 1796, Squire John Mytton was orphaned at age two and his early years were glutted with self-indulgence, encouraged by a retinue of rather cretinous servants who allowed the child to satisfy his every whim. By his late teens, Mytton proved himself to be one of the great English eccentrics, if not a fat footnote in the history of alcoholism, consuming eight bottles of port every day before embarking upon his "duties." (When port was not available he drank cologne.)

Mytton's "duties" included punishing himself for being born into enormous wealth. He would go hunting wearing only a few rags to protect himself against the ravages of winter and, on more than one occasion, gamekeepers on his sprawling estate were blushingly startled to see their squire stalking ducks, gun in hand, without a stitch of clothes, plodding naked through knee-deep snow.

The Squire simply loved to wreck his own carriages, driving them wildly through the pigpens of neighboring farms and over piled timber; he would tear along village streets, directing his horses to smash through outdoor tables laden with goods and foodstuffs, and even drove headlong into a large shop window once because the proprietor had not been prompt in a delivery a week earlier.

"Mango, the King of Pickles," was the sobriquet bestowed upon Mytton by his friends, what few of them remained after enduring the Squire's fancies.

Mytton did not fancy his riches; during the last fifteen years of his life he literally threw away more than a half-million pounds (perhaps more than $10 million today). Much of his fortune was spent to maintain his great stables where dozens of thoroughbred horses were kept, along with hundreds of foxhounds in scores of kennels about his estate. He made dozens of tailors rich, ordering hundreds of trousers, waistcoats and coats, many of which he never wore.

Carelessness made up for much of his financial ruination. One night Mytton was returning home in his carriage and suddenly decided to count about five thousand pounds, all in paper notes, which he had somehow managed not to throw away gambling. He fell asleep in the open carriage and a sudden and violent wind swept the pound notes from his hands, whirling them across the countryside. For weeks afterward, farmers and village folk found the notes and spent most of their time either searching for more of the windswept money or squandering what they had found in local pubs.

One evening while preparing for bed, with two male servants in attendance, Mytton suddenly began to hiccup. "Damn this hiccup," he roared, and then recalled how fire had cured the evils of Troy, Persepolis, Rome, and even London. With that he grabbed a lighted candle at his bedside and shouted: "I will frighten it away!" He put the flame to his own thin cotton nightshirt which quickly blazed up so that he was enveloped in flames. His terrified servants sprang forward and tore away the blazing garment from Mytton's flesh. Although he was badly burned, he stood triumphant before his servants, saying: "The hiccup is gone, by God!" And with that he hurled himself into bed. Weeks passed before Mytton's burns healed, but during that time he showed the festering sores to anyone he encountered as if these were badges of courage.

A womanizer and an habitual drunk by the time he was thirty, Squire Mytton was forever being attacked by thieves who knew that he carried vast sums on his person. One night, when the Squire reeled drunkenly from a whorehouse, a gang of thieves grabbed him by the arm and attempted to drag him into an alleyway to rob him. Almost at the same moment another gang appeared and grabbed Mytton's other arm, thinking to drag the Squire to another dark spot to relieve him of his purse. A madcap tug-of-war ensued, with each gang of ruffians pulling the Squire by the arms in opposite directions. Mytton, however, was a large man possessing enormous strength, and he resolved to stand his ground, somehow managing to pull *both* gangs toward him and fling them to the cobblestones, all the while bellowing for the constables who finally came on the run and captured some of the robbers.

Mytton's wife left him when he refused to pay his enormous debts. His fortune wasted, the Squire fled to Calais, France, but soon had creditors on his trail there. Returning to England, Mytton was thrown into King's Bench Prison. When released, he again ran up enormous debts and lived the last few years of his life in debtor's prisons, eventually dying of delirium tremens at age thirty-eight.

N

Bronko NAGURSKI

Football Player (Born 1908)

"He's the only man I ever saw who ran his own interference," said Steve Owen, the coach of the Giants, in according kudos to the most devilish opposing fullback he ever encountered, one hard-charging, unstoppable Bronko Nagurski, whose football spurs and fame were won while playing for George Halas' powerhouse Bears of the 1930s.

Following a sterling college football record at the University of Minnesota, this son of Ukranian immigrants (he was christened "Bronko") was selected by George Halas to be the team's workhorse, a job from which he never flinched but in fact, relished, especially in crunching through opposing lines where he might have the opportunity to break legs and arms (an attitude later reflected by fullback Jim Taylor of the Green Bay Packers who was quoted once as saying, "I love to hear the sounds of breaking bones!").

Nagurski seldom lifted his head when hitting the line after taking a handoff and crashing his 230-pound, six-foot-two inch frame into waiting adversaries. He once explained his unorthodox posture by saying that he did not want to see the fear in the eyes of opponents and thus "melt with sympathy." His blind running often led to injuries, usually inflicted upon others. He smashed through the line in a Packer–Bear game once, and ran pell-mell over Packer tacklers for thirty-five yards to a touchdown, taking the last three defenders with him as he finally crashed into the end zone. The last three defenders were carried from the field on stretchers.

Only once did Nagurski's inexplicable blind running backfire. He and Clark Hinkle, the giant Green Bay fullback, fought a wild battle against each

Bronko Nagurski of the Chicago Bears working out in Wrigley Field, 1943; he always led with his head. (Wide World)

other (this in the days when players were on the field for sixty minutes, playing both offense and defense). Nagurski, attempting another head-on-the-chest run, was hit by Hinkle's full force, the other fullback driving his head upward into Bronko's down-turned face. Nagurski was led from the field with a bloody, broken nose.

In that same year, 1933, Nagurski ploughed into the end zone of Wrigley Field and kept going, right into the well-known brick wall which is still in back of home plate in this baseball stadium. He hit the wall with such force that he put a large hole in the structure, one that required repair by a bevy of bricklayers.

The legendary fullback was never more the human dynamo than in a game between the Bears and the Washington Redskins. The Redskins put up a stiff, bruising resistance to Nagurski, stopping him for the most part through fifty minutes of play. Going into a huddle, the enraged Nagurski roared to his quarterback: "Gimme that ball. This time I'm not going to be stopped by any of them Skins—they better look out for themselves!"

Taking the handoff on the Redskin thirty-yard line, Nagurski churned forward, his head down as usual. He charged through the Redskin line like a rushing locomotive, crushed the secondary, and, without looking up, plunged onward directly toward the safety, hitting the last defender with such force that the entire stadium winced at the crunching sound of the crash. Nagurski kept going, even though his way was clear to the goal line, as if a host of tacklers awaited him, still not looking up. He slammed into the goal post, caromed off, then ploughed onward for another thirty yards until he smashed into a steel and concrete wall.

Wobbly legged and with a dazed look in his eyes, Bronko barely made it to the Bears bench on the sideline. He sat down, removed his headgear and rubbed his enormous cranium, moaning: "Gosh, but that last guy sure hit me hard!"

Carry Amelia (Moore Gloyd) NATION

Social Reformer (1846–1911)

Born in central Kentucky on November 25, 1846, Carry (her name was entered into the family Bible that way) was the daughter of a planter, George Moore, who moved the family to Texas and then to Belton, Missouri where the Moore's finally settled. Where Carry's father was almost illiterate, her mother, brother, and sister were decidedly unbalanced. Mrs. Moore believed she was Queen Victoria and insisted that whenever she went for a ride that servants ride before her carriage as escorts and that footmen be in constant attendance. She was finally committed to an institution where she died. Carry's brother and sister also died in asylums.

From sixteen to nineteen Carry was left to herself, shunted from relatives living in Texas and Missouri. At this time she developed what she later termed a permanent "consumption of the bowels," but the life-lasting illness was undoubtedly imaginary.

At twenty-one Carry met and married a Civil War veteran named Charles Gloyd, who was a physician. Dr. Gloyd had seen so much butchery during the war that it had made of him an alcoholic, or so he later claimed. Carry felt that she could cure her husband by "arguing him out of it." Whenever Gloyd was in his cups Carry would let loose a blasting diatribe on the evils of drink. The doctor's response was to stagger immediately to his Masonic lodge where he took refuge and continued to swill rotgut liquor.

Somehow the couple managed to produce a daughter, Charlien, but Gloyd never saw the child age beyond six months. He died of delirium tremens. To support Gloyd's elderly mother and her child, Carry took in laundry and became a dressmaker. The burden was too much and when she met David Nation, a preacher, she promptly married him, hoping that he would support her family. Nation could barely support himself, having failed miserably at preaching and farming. He became a lawyer and failed at that, too.

Nation's failure as a preacher was not completely his fault. Carry would sit in the front pew during services and, while he was delivering a sermon, loudly correct his grammar. On more than one occasion Carry rose before her husband had completed his Sunday text and shouted: "That will be enough for today, David!" With that she would march from church, nonplussed members of the congregation following her, so that her husband was left to talk to an empty church.

By the age of forty-five, Carry was running a boarding house in Medicine Lodge, Kansas. When not performing her usual back-breaking chores in the house, Carry could be found at the headquarters of the Women's Christian Temperance Union. The philosophy of the WTCU fit Carry's thinking perfectly in its crusade against alcohol and tobacco. In 1891 Carry was elected to the WTCU post of county chairman. She used her position not only to stamp out the use of liquor in her local area, but to advance the cause of women's suffrage, along with punishing at every opportunity men in general, whom she disliked as a whole, if not detested.

Her father had been weak, as was her second husband. Her first husband, the rum-guzzling Dr. Gloyd, was ever present in her avenging thoughts. Not only had Gloyd imbibed alcohol but had been a dedicated user of tobacco. She had written at the time of her terrible union with Gloyd: "I believe that, on the whole, tobacco has done more harm than intoxicating drinks. The tobacco habits is followed by thirst for drink. The face of the smoker has lost the scintillations of intellect and soul. The odor of his [Gloyd's] person is vile, his blood is poisoned ... Prussic acid is the only poison that is worse ... Tobacco users transmit nervous diseases, epilepsy, weakened constitutions, depraved appetites and deformities of all kinds to their offspring ... Deterioration of the race is upon us ... The tobacco user can never be the father of a healthy child. [Her own daughter Charlien was sickly all of her life.] Therefore he is dangerous for a woman to have as a husband. If I were a young woman, I would say to the men who use tobacco and who would wish to converse with me: 'Use the telephone; come no closer. I would as soon kiss a spittoon as to kiss such a mouth.'"

Though Kansas was a "dry" state in the 1890s, saloons operated around the clock in almost every town, Medicine Lodge being no exception. At first Carry wrote blistering letters complaining of the liquor violations to the sheriff of Barber County, then to the attorney general and the governor. When these officials ignored her, Carry Nation, in 1899, along with the local Baptist minister's wife, moved a portable harmonium into the streets of Medicine Lodge, praying and singing hymns outside the various saloons for the salvation of those poor sinners ruining their livers at the bars.

Carry also kept a black book into which she wrote the names of not only the town's heavy drinkers, but the saloon owners. She denounced these gentlemen in church, and at public meetings, and later in the very streets of the town, pointing her accusing finger and screeching: "Maker of drunkards and widows! Rum-soaked rummy! Friend of the Devil!"

When this ploy did not appear to stem the flow of liquor, Carry marched into the mouth of hell—the very saloons themselves, to denounce proprietor and patrons alike. As time passed, she was followed in these sallies by most of the women in the town. The ploy began to take effect, and soon the taverns began to close, one by one, until not a single "joint" was open. When Carry learned that the local druggist, one O.L. Day, was receiving secret whiskey shipments, she stormed into the store wielding a sledgehammer. (Mrs. Nation was a big woman, almost six feet in height and weighed about 175 pounds.) Setting her square jaw, Carry swung a mighty blow at the whiskey keg she found in Day's back room, smashing it to pieces. The mouth-gaping druggist packed his belonging the next day and left Medicine Lodge forever.

This triumph brought accolades from her fellow WTCU members at the next meeting. But the champion modestly waved away the applause, telling her

The irrepressible Carry Nation, the dread of every bartender in America. (Library Congress)

crusading sisters that she was nothing more than "a bulldog, running along at the feet of Jesus, barking at what He doesn't like!" (Physically, Carry *did* resemble a bulldog, having scraggily gray hair, and a pudgy, furrowed face fixed with a permanent scowl.)

A miracle of sorts was not long in coming to Carry Nation. On the evening of June 6, 1900, a date she recorded with solemnity in her memoirs, Carry sat in the peace of her own home and opened a Bible. She flipped the pages and picked at random a quote from Isiah (60:1): "Arise, shine; for thy light is come, and the glory of the Lord is risen upon thee."

Carry thought long and hard about this Biblical passage as she prepared for bed. (One historian, J.C. Furnes, writing in *The Life and Times of the Late Demon Rum,* stated that Mrs. Nation made *special* preparations for bed that night, expecting to receive a direct message from on-high that would clarify the scripture she had earlier found. "... she had a spell of praying ... in sackcloth and ashes," wrote Furnes, "literally donning a gunnysack and sprinkling ashes on her graying head.") Just before dawn, a thunderous voice filled her bedroom, Carry later insisted, commanding her to "go to Kiowa!" With that she leaped from her bed, hurriedly dressed and ate breakfast, then filled a buggy with what she later called her "smashers"—rocks, bricks, bottles, short iron bars which she wrapped in newspapers so that her booze-gulping adversaries would not grow suspicious. Lashing her horse, Carry flew off in the direction of Kiowa, Kansas, a wide-open town a little more than ten miles away.

Kiowa boasted some of the most notorious saloons in the county and was a hotbed for bootleggers and distributors of alcohol. The first target was a large tavern owned by a man named Dobson. Carry smashed through the swinging doors of his establishment. She spotted the culprit at the bar. "Dobson," Carry intoned, "I told you last spring to close this place, and you didn't do it. Now, I have come with another remonstrance. Get out of the way! I don't want to strike you, but I am going to break up this den of vice." She began to hurl her bricks, and rocks, smashing mirrors, glasses and whiskey bottles to pieces. The men inside the saloon stood petrified as Carry then walked out and up the street to another saloon. Here, running out of "smashers," she used the balls on a pool table to demolish the place. This saloon destroyed, the one-woman cyclone whirled off to destroy yet a third bar before she was dragged to the street by several deputies and threatened with jail.

"Send me to jail?" Carry sneered. "For destroying an illegal place?

Knowing the vixen had the law on her side, the deputies brushed Carry off and put her in her buggy, sending her out of town. But this, the residents of Kiowa ruefully predicted, was only the beginning.

Carry waited and planned for many months, carefully selecting her next target. On December 27, 1900, at exactly 9:45 A.M., the determined woman found herself descending the red-carpeted stairs of the posh Carey Hotel in Wichita, going to the huge basement bar, considered to be the finest saloon in the state. For a moment the gaudy glare of the saloon mesmerized and shocked her. She stared at the $1,500 plate glass mirror behind the bar surrounded by twinkling lights. Her eyes drifted to a nearby wall and popped at the sight of an enormous canvas, entitled *Cleopatra at the Roman Bath*, the very essence of obscenity in Carry's glaring eyes.

With several bricks tucked under one arm (still wrapped in newspaper) and a cane and iron rod tied together under the other, she strode to the bar. "Young man," she sternly asked the bartender, "what are you doing in this pit of hell?"

The bartender smirked and said: "I'm sorry, madam, but we don't serve women."

Carry went berserk. "Serve *me*? Do you think I'd drink that poison brewed in hell?" She nervously wagged a bony finger at the Cleopatra painting. "Remove that image of naked Jezebel!"

"What?"

"Take that filthy picture down and close this murder mill!"

"Lady, maybe you *do* need a drink after all." The bartender poured Carry a shotglass full of whiskey and inched it toward her.

"Glory to God!" shrieked Mrs. Nation. "Peace on earth, good will to men!" With that she began to hurl her bricks, smashing holes in the ornate bar mirror, reducing it to shards. She drove the cane and rod into the painting and tore it to pieces, whirling like a dervish as she moved through the saloon. The men dashed for the exits or hid beneath tables as she ran wildly along the bar, smashing glasses with the rod, and then behind the bar, to demolish every bottle of liquor she could locate. Running out of objects to smash, Carry began to turn over tables and slash chairs. When a Wichita detective arrived, summoned by the frantic owners, he found Carry attempting to dismantle the heavy cherrywood bar with a spitoon.

"Madam," the cop politely informed the raging Mrs. Nation, "I must arrest you for defacing property."

"Defacing?" came Carry's wail. "I am defacing nothing—I am destroying!"

She was taken to jail and locked inside a cell. This is what she had expected and what she had desired. It fit the mad scheme that boiled in her mind. News of the wild woman spread through Wichita and soon newsmen were scurrying for the jail to interview her and take her photo. Stated John Kobler in *Ardent Spirits*: "Carry, serene in her martyrdom, happily knelt on the stone flagging of her cell, Bible in hand, while a news photographer clicked away. So posed, she became one of the most familiar front-page figures of the era."

This was a scene to be repeated over and over again through the decade; the martyred Carry locked behind bars for "attending to the Lord's business." She would invariably began to sing loud hymns and create every manner of distrubance. Later, her followers would arrive outside the jail and begin chanting and praying for their "saint's" release. Commented Gerald W. Johnson in *The Lunatic Fringe*: "Upon a tankful of drunks already on the verge

A caricature of Carry Nation with hatchet, after destroying her "enemy"—a saloon.

of the heebie-jeebies, the effect may be more easily imagined than described. Often the street outside would be filled with frenzied women ... kneeling in the roadway to the disruption of traffic."

So unnerved would the jailors become that, at the height of the prayerful caterwauling, they would dive for the phones and call the mayor, the governor, anyone who had the authority to release the wild Mrs. Nation.

Her trial after the Carey Hotel incident was attended by many WTCU adherents. The charges were dismissed and Carry was quickly sent on her way. Instead of returning home as her husband begged, Carry immediately went to two more Wichita saloons and destroyed them, this time using a hatchet. She attempted to return to the Carey Hotel bar, but a squad of burly detectives barred her way. Turning to the mob of females who had followed her, Carry held aloft the new symbol of her crusade, a bright and gleaming hatchet. Shouted Mrs. Nation: "Smash! Smash! For Jesus' sake, smash!" It became Carry's rallying call to arms.

Yet not all in the WTCU and womens' suffrage movements flocked to Carry's colors. Stated one WTCU leader: "While we cannot advise the use of force ... we are wide awake to the fact that Mrs. Nation's hatchet has done more to frighten the liquor sellers and awaken the sleeping consciences of Kansas voters than the entire official force of the state has heretofore done." When Carry's crusade became particularly destructive in the month's to come, many of her followers fell away, one spokeswoman stating: "More harm than good must always result from lawless methods."

Despite the loss of some support, Carry and her most fanatic followers continued to conduct "hatchetation,"—a word of her own coinage—through the land. She moved on to the bars and saloons of Topeka, Des Moines, St. Louis, Chicago, Cincinnati, Atlantic City, Philadelphia, leading more than fifty wild and mirror-breaking, bottle-smashing raids, chopping out her very physical brand of temperance.

Amazonian in strength, Carry tore into bars with "the might of hosts," performing awesome feats—she once tore a huge cash register from its wall

Some of Carry's disciples practicing "hatchetation."

mountings and hurled this the length of a saloon where it crashed through a wall. With her bare hands Carry ripped open a mommoth icebox containing liquor, unhinging the doors and hurling them aside to get at "the enemy."

Though she was arrested scores of times, Carry always got off with a small fine, the charge against her invariably being a misdemeanor. Nothing could persuade her to cease her crusade to rid the country of alcohol. She visited almost every major city to do battle, saving New York for the last. She arrived there on August 28, 1901 and stayed only six hours on the island of Manhattan. The minute she alighted from a train, Carry raced to the offices of Police Commissioner Murphy. She strode into his offices unannounced with a two-foot hatchet strapped to the girdle beneath her linen jacket.

Murphy did not need to be told who the interloper was; he had been warned that Carry Nation was on her way. He watched her nervously as she sat down heavily in a chair opposite his desk.

"Don't you think New York is a terrible place?" asked Carry.

"I don't think anything of the kind," replied Murphy.

"Well, it is," Carry instructed him. "It's full of hellholes and murder factories!"

Murphy summoned his courage and barked back: "Stop right there! I don't want to listen to you or hear that kind of talk in this place."

"You won't listen to me? Why, I came here on purpose to discuss these matters with you. Do you mean to tell me that you won't discuss these murder shops, these hellholes, these sinks of depravity in New York?"

"That's just what I mean."

"Now, now, now. I want to know why the saloons are permitted to open on Sundays."

"I won't discuss the matter with you," huffed Murphy.

Seeing that her frontal attack was failing, Carry tried a gentler approach. She placed a pudgy hand on Commissioner Murphy's arm which he angrily brushed away. "I only came here to do New York good," cooed Carry. "I want to do good for humanity. I want to do something for you."

Murphy was then in a seething Irish rage over Mrs. Nation's patronizing manner. "You don't know what you're talking about!" he roared. "Go back to Kansas! If you want to do something, why don't you do it for your husband?"

Carry's voice was low when answering, "I have no husband now. I suppose you know all about that." (David Nation had divorced Carry only months earlier on grounds of desertion.)

Murphy grinned. "Oh, yes. All I have to say is that I congratulate Mr. Nation. He ought to be a happy man now."

"I insist we talk about these New York hellholes. It's your duty—"

"I won't sit here and be lectured!" shouted Murphy. 'I don't want to talk to you. You are not in your right mind."

"Do you think I am crazy?" Mrs. Nation shouted.

"Yes, I do," Murphy replied in a solemn voice.

"You say, then, just what those wicked, riotous, rum-soaked, bedeviled Republicans in Kansas City say. They say that when they know that forty hellholes are closed in Topeka!"

The Commissioner suddenly appeared nervous, apprehensive, as if Mrs. Nation might reach beneath her linen jacket for the hatchet and begin chopping up his desk. He motioned for a detective named Linden to take the wild woman away.

Carry quickly told Murphy: "No, father, be calm. I want to talk to you without quarreling."

Murphy was weakening. "*Please,* don't call me father."

"I *will* call you father. You are old enough to be my father. I'm only fifty-four and you are at least eighty, and I'll call you father anyway. Now, father, do you think a little 'hatchetation' would do a lot of good in New York?"

The Commissioner went back to shouting: "If you violate the law, I'll have you locked up!"

Detective Linden began to walk toward Mrs. Nation, hands outstretched, preparing to yank her from her chair. Carry saw the cop out of the corner of her eye and jumped up, telling Murphy: "Now, father, we could have had a nice long talk if you didn't quarrel with me. We will all [of us] have to give an account of our stewardship—remember that." She turned her back on Murphy and began to march from his office.

Sputtering, Murphy stood up, shaking his fist at Mrs. Nation, yelling: "Don't you tell me how I can get into Heaven, madam, don't you dare tell—"

But she was gone, passing into the outer office where she glared at Deputy Commissioner William Devery who was hiding behind a door; he had positioned himself thusly so that he could overhear Mrs. Nation's conversation without being seen. "Did you get an earful?" growled Carry to Devery. Next she spotted a detective smoking a cigarette. She boldly faced the man, jerked the cigarette from his mouth, and screamed: "Horrid, nasty man! Don't you know that your fate will be an eternal smoking?"

Carry's manager stood meekly in an outer hallway. Mrs. Nation walked up to him with new instructions: "Now take me to see John L. Sullivan. He once said some mean things about me!" (Sullivan was once quoted as saying that if

Carry Nation "comes into my place, I'll throw her down the sewer!" Oddly enough, Sullivan later took the pledge and gave up liquor completely.)

The manager obediently escorted Mrs. Nation to the Forty-Second Street saloon once owned and operated by the heavyweight champion. The saloon was closed, but Carry had learned that the Great John L. was still living on the second story. She sent a messenger up the stairs to fetch the boxer.

Sullivan answered the door sleepily. "What is it? Can't you see I'm getting my winks?"

"There's a woman waiting downstairs to see you champ."

Sullivan's eyes lit up. "Yeah? What's her name?"

"Carry Nation."

"That woman!" Sullivan slammed the door shut, bolting it. He shouted to the messenger through the door: "Not on your life! Tell her I'm sick in bed!"

So terrified of a visit from Carry Nation was Acting Mayor Guggenheim that he ordered special guards to patrol the entranceways to City Hall and his office, telling the guards to "arrest that woman on sight if she tries to hatchet her way in here."

But Mrs. Nation had no time to visit Mayor Guggenheim; she was off to catch a train to Ohio to begin her fabulous lecture tour, a tour that would last ten years and make her a household word, as well as a small fortune. (She would also greatly profit from the sale of hatchets, sold as souvenirs at her lectures.)

Mrs. Nation also appeared in several theatrical productions laced with temperance propaganda. One of these extravaganzas was entitled *Ten Nights In a Barroom* (later retitled *Hatchetation*), produced in 1903, and provided a scene where Carry destroyed a saloon, chopping the set to pieces. (The temperance leader's name went up in lights thirty years later when a loosely dramatized biography, *Carry Nation,* was produced at the Biltmore Theatre in New York on October 30, 1932 and had a short run, a production notable only in that Mildred Natwick and Joshua Logan played minor roles.) Carry ended her theatrical days in a shabby manner, delivering harangues no one cared to listen to at the end of burlesque shows.

She continued to make headlines when she tried to scream and threaten her way into the White House to lecture President Theodore Roosevelt for smoking cigarettes. She never got on the White House lawn, but it was later rumored that Teddy had a nervous time waiting for her to be turned back.

Mrs. Nation kept at it by making an occasional raid on a saloon, her last being an attack on a tavern in Butte, Montana in 1910. She finally settled again in Kansas, publishing a weekly newspaper, *The Smasher's Mail,* in which she wrote a hortatory column against demon rum which she called "Letters from Hell." When the newspaper folded for lack of support, Carry stated: "The paper accomplished this much—that the public could see that I was not insane."

But what Carry Nation feared the most in life, that she would slip into the insanity that possessed her mother, sister, brother, and daughter, happened on January 11, 1911 while she was delivering a lecture at Eureka Springs,

Arkansas. Her normally free-flowing invective suddenly came to a halt. She stared blankly at the audience for some minutes. Then, shaking her head, she began to stagger offstage, weeping.

She was taken home to Kansas and placed in Leavenworth's Evergreen Hospital. For five months her mind let in shadows until all was dark and silent. Carry Nation died in her padded cell on June 9, 1911.

Florence NIGHTINGALE

Nurse (1820–1910)

Known the world over as "The Lady of the Lamp," Florence Nightingale is rightfully credited as the founder of modern nursing. She was also a strange, withdrawn woman of many quirks who endured one of the most prolonged death agonies on record. At the age of sixteen, Florence claimed to have heard the voice of God tell her to take up nursing. This she did, training in Germany, then later opening the Institute for the Care of the Sick Gentlewoman in London.

At the outbreak of the Crimean War in 1854, Florence, using the influence her high-born family could bring to bear, was placed in charge of a contingent of thirty-four nurses and sent to Turkey where she established field hospitals at Scutari and Balaklava; it was at Balaklava where the famous "Charge of the Light Brigade" took place.

Discovering many of her nurses to be either drunks or whores, Florence sent most of them back to England and permitted no one in the wards except herself after 8 P.M. (She made her nightly rounds holding aloft a flaming lamp, thus the sobriquet.) Through her new hygienic techniques, the great nurse was able to save thousands of lives, but she also exposed herself to myriad diseases, many of which she contracted, including various fevers and dysentery. She developed rheumatism and arthirtis from her exhausting labors in the wards. After one illness she lost all her hair.

Florence returned to London to found the Nightingale School and Home for training nurses at St. Thomas' Hospital in 1860. By then she had been so close to death on several occasions that she had given detailed instructions for her funeral. She did not die, however, for another fifty years. During that time she was bedridden for several years, then, in the last twenty-one years of her life, she gradually went blind, then deaf, then lost the use of her voice. The great nurse finally died on August 13, 1910.

Miss Nightingale's quirks were almost as numerous as her illnesses. She was often overheard talking to herself, using different voices, as if holding conversations with several imaginary persons at one time. It was claimed that she forbade other nurses from visiting the Crimean wards at night, not to curb promiscuity but so that she could baptize the mortally wounded without detection. It was known that she kept her pet owl in her pocket wherever she went and when the bird finally died, she had it stuffed and continued to carry it about.

Joshua Abraham NORTON

Merchant, "Emperor of the United States" (1819–1880)

Joshua Norton was born to a Jewish farmer on February 4, 1819 outside of London, a city he was never to know. His father took his family to South Africa to pioneer a homestead when he was two. John Norton was one of a few which founded Algoa Bay (now Port Elizabeth). He soon gave up farming to establish a profitable general store where Joshua worked until he was twenty. Joshua was then sent on commercial voyages aboard ships in which his father had part ownership.

Norton was thirty when his father died, leaving him the family fortune. He spent his inheritance in several losing ventures before making a considerable sum, about $40,000, in Brazilian transactions. Hearing of the gold strike in California, he sailed aboard the steamer *Franzika* to San Francisco, arriving on November 23, 1849.

San Francisco was then not a city, but a sprawling camp of rickety buildings and muddy streets. Norton, however, saw that it was a natural port and that it would someday become a thriving community. In *Tales of San Francisco*, Samuel Dickson quoted the young merchant as saying upon his arrival "I shall stay here until I have seen this village grow to be one of the world's greatest and most beautiful cities." He was told that the brawling camp town was no place for an upstanding businessman to seek his fortune. "Someday the men will come back from the hills," replied Norton, "multiplied a thousand times." He put up a small office building, hanging out a shingle which read: "J.A.Norton, Merchant."

Emperor Norton I, circa 1869, enjoying his bicycle, a gift from the citizens of San Francisco. (Photo by "Helios")

He invested his $40,000 wisely, buying up land cheap and selling it at high rates. Using the practices learned from his father, Norton also became the business agent for several mercantile operations and a broker who shrewdly invested for others. He amassed a fortune, more than $250,000 by 1853, dealing in high-demand goods such as coffee, tea, coal, flour, beef, and rice. Norton generally held on to his goods until the price was driven sky-high, then unloaded at the top dollar.

San Francisco's business community marveled at young Norton's success. Bankers and shipowners nodded respectfully to him on the street. He was thought of as the wisest businessman in the booming city and the most important investors sought his advice. He was called an empire builder and many took to calling him "emperor." The salutation became commonplace. It was "how are you, emperor?" when he passed on the street.

Always cordial and well-mannered, Norton would smile and reply: "Fine, making money as usual, but don't call me emperor, please. This is a great country and its strength is in its democracy."

The undoing of "emperor" Norton was rice. A shortage of rice had caused it to shoot from 4¢ to 32¢ a pound. Norton knew that the Chinese had banned the exporting of rice from their homeland. Such a scarcity could only guarantee enormous profits to the person who cornered the rice market.

Norton began to buy up every grain of rice in San Francisco, as well as the few shipments that periodically arrived. He did not, however, think that nations other than China would begin to import rice to San Francisco. When several cargo ships arrived loaded with rice Norton went broke trying to buy up the cargoes. Further adding to his woes was a great fire which destroyed hundreds of wooden buildings in the downtown district, including his own. He was ruined; not only did Norton lose every penny he had, but he was $50,000 in debt.

Disgraced, Norton took on menial jobs to support himself, but his lack of enthusiasm and constant daydreamings (some said his business losses left him in a permanent daze) caused his dismissal from one job after another. He finally wound up clerking in a Chinese warehouse. Soon he disappeared from this position and from the public eye entirely.

On September 16, 1854, a curious-looking gentleman entered the editorial offices of the San Francisco *Call*. He was dressed in a comic-opera uniform, a dark blue army officer's uniform with golden epaulets, a red sash and a tarnished sword dangling from his short, squat frame. The man's face was darkly and heavily bearded and on his head sat a tall beaver hat with a brass clip which held three bright feathers. The visitor's pants were blue with yellow stripes down the outside seams, pants such as an admiral might wear. (The costume, it was later learned had been donated by the commanding general at the Presidio.)

This strangely attired creature quietly placed a formal-looking document upon the desk of the *Call's* editor. In a low voice the visitor stated: "It is my request that you print this decree in your next edition." He then turned on his heel and marched from the newspaper office.

The editor carefully read the document, then, wag that he must have been, broadly smiled as he ordered a copy boy to rush the decree to the composing room. The next day the *Call* ran the following on its front page without editorial comment:

At the preemptory request and desire of a large majority of the citizens of these United States, I, Joshua Norton, formerly of Algoa Bay, Cape of Good Hope, and now for the last nine years and ten months of San Francisco, California, declare and proclaim myself Emperor of these United States; and in virtue of the authority thereby in me vested, do hereby order and direct the representatives of the different States of the Union to assemble in Musical Hall, of this city, on the 1st day of February next, then and there to make such alterations in the existing laws of the Union as may ameliorate the evils under which the country is laboring, and thereby cause confidence to exist, both at home and abroad, in our stability and integrity.

NORTON I,
Emperor of the United States
and Protector of Mexico

Readers of the *Call* found the decree as amusing as had the newspaper's editor and the populace, remembering the disasters endured by Joshua Norton, merely felt that his mind had slipped. A few said he was "deranged" or "demented," but for the most part the citizens of San Francisco—an extremely colorful populace in and of itself with its streets teeming with pirates, prostitutes, miners, highwaymen, con artists, along with the more upstanding residents—were inclined to humor their emperor, even pay him good-natured allegiance. From that moment on, Norton I became as firm a fixture in San Francisco as would the Golden Gate Bridge in the following century.

Emperor Norton's appearance on the streets of San Francisco became an accustomed sight. His admiring subjects bestowed gifts upon him from time to time, including new boots, a colorful Chinese umbrella to keep out the rain and hot sun, a magnificent walking stick. Although legislators from the Union failed to appear at Musical Hall to mend the nation's errant ways, at Norton's directive, his authority went undiminished with the *Call* continuing to publish his decrees without comment.

All of Norton's decrees voiced his concern for the public welfare and the integrity of the United States, sentiments which endeared rather than alienated his San Francisco "subjects" to him. Reacting to widespread "fraud and corruption" in the land, Norton's second proclamation, following his first by only a month, advocated stern measures: "We do hereby abolish Congress and it is hereby abolished." When no response was forthcoming from Washington, Norton issued another decree: "We do hereby Order and Direct Major General [Winfield] Scott, the Commander-in-Chief of our Armies, immediately on receipt of this, our Decree, to proceed with suitable force and clear the halls of Congress ... we, Norton I, by the grace of God and the national will, emperor of the thirty-three states and the multitude of territories of the United States, do hereby dissolve the Republic of the United States of North America." Norton also dissolved both the Democratic and Republican parties, but suggested that

Emperor Norton I, dining free—as usual—at a San Francisco buffet as his camp-following dogs Bummer and Lazarus look on hopefully.

the governors of the states stay in their posts until a national convention would establish a new order under the emperor. The convention would take place at San Francisco's Musical Hall on February 1, 1860, but the building burned down a week before the scheduled meeting so Norton was spared the embarrassment of being ignored by his unresponsive political minions.

To provide a suitable emperor's salary, Norton I issued "Bonds of the Empire," and these were sold to citizens for nominal amounts, usually 50¢ each. Residents happily paid the price, knowing that the emperor paid 50¢ a night (he refused to rent by the week or month) for his lodgings at a boarding house on Commercial Street where he lived for seventeen years. Any extra money accumulated by the emperor invariably went as dues to the Occidental Lodge of Masons, where Norton was a much-respected member.

Norton's single room was spartan in its decor, having a cot, a bare table and chair, a worn-out carpet and a wash stand. Dozens of pegs held a great number of hats and caps. A small portrait of the Empress Eugenie of France was on one wall.

Norton's necessities were cheerfully provided by all manner of merchants and businessmen. He ate and drank free in all the restaurants and taverns in the city. His clothes were washed and mended free by a Chinese laundry near his lodgings. The emperor's evening meal was generally a full-course supper and taken in the best eateries in San Francisco. At such times waiters fawned over Norton and, playing the part of the finicky emperor, Norton had no qualms in returning food that was not prepared to his liking. Waiters who were slow or indifferent to his majesty received a royal scolding.

Naturally, the emperor rode free on all public conveyances, and if he saw a conductor being rude to customers, Norton would properly chastise the offender. Those who did not possess the fare for streetcars were often "guests of the Empire," when Norton was present, much to the chagrin of over-indulgent conductors.

"When Norton's uniforms wore out," wrote Joan Parker in *American Heritage*, "a public subscription bought him a new one. On a similar occasion the board of supervisors voted city funds. Tailors who made and contributed uniforms proudly announced themselves on window cards 'by appointment to His Majesty.'"

No social event, be it a lodge meeting or a high-society party, was ever complete without the presence of Norton I. He was even invited to address political gatherings, both Democratic and Republican. The emperor graciously did appear at all functions to which he was invited, but he never overstayed his welcome, leaving within a few minutes of his arrival. He was always courteous to guests and complimentary to hosts. San Francisco loved its emperor and, for the most part, paid him homage.

Visiting local banks and other financial institutions, Norton would present a banker with tax assessments, sometimes running into the hundreds of dollars. The financial leaders heard him out patiently—many of these gentlemen had known Norton earlier when he was a prosperous merchant— and would then pay something "on account," usually $1. Norton accepted the reduced levies with grace and went off to assess other businessmen and merchants.

In his daily travels about the city, Norton was invariably accompanied by two dogs, one named Bummer, the other called Lazurus. Though these dogs were not really the property of the emperor, they slavishly followed him about, no doubt inspired by his liberal handouts from the free lunch counters he visited. Bummer, a Newfoundland dog with a white stripe, had become the toast of San Francisco in 1861 when, following the excavating of the old Blue Wing Saloon, he slew an army of rats while the citizenry cheered him on. He regularly patrolled Montgomery Street thereafter, following in Norton's footsteps, to be fed at saloons and restaurants where the emperor regularly stopped.

The other dog, Lazurus, got his name after surviving a terrible fight with a pack of wild dogs; he was, in the words of Mark Twain (see entry), Bummer's "obsequious vassal," since it was Bummer who saved Lazurus by driving off the other dogs. From that moment on Lazurus followed Bummer everwhere and Bummer followed the emperor. (When both these dogs were later killed, Bummer stomped to death by a drunken miner, Lazurus poisoned by a prostitute who found him pesky, Twain wrote stirring obituaries for both animals.)

Norton enjoyed the dutiful attention the dogs gave him; he permitted them to follow him on Saturdays into the Synagogue Emanu-El, where he was a member in good standing. He would sit in the first row of the balcony with the two dogs sleeping at his feet. So as not to offend the Christian community in San Francisco, Norton I made it a ritual to attend all churches, selecting a different church to visit each Sunday.

No theater opened a new show without Norton I sitting in the balcony's first row. In fact, there were always three tickets waiting for the emperor and his two dogs at the box office. Space was also permanently reserved at the Mechanic's Library for Norton and his dogs; here the emperor would read books and newspapers avariciously while Bummer and Lazurus dozed at his feet. Sometimes he would play chess with local experts and almost always win.

From 1855 to 1880, Norton I made his presence felt at all levels of San Francisco society. He gave innumerable lectures and, though his audiences often failed to understand him, he was accorded respectful silence during his talks. On one occasion, Norton addressed a large crowd at a discussion on free love. Following several speakers, Norton stood up and told the audience that eighty-two percent of all children were destroyed in the United States shortly after their births. His way of explaining this unheard-of phenomenon was cryptic, to say the least. Said Norton I: "Take twenty-five miles of land. Let it rain on that land twenty-four hours. Then turn every one of those drops of water into a baby. How many babies will there be?" When no one in the audience could answer what Norton thought to be a simple question, the emperor stormed from the meeting hall, disgusted with the ignorance of his subjects.

In later years, Norton attended several meetings of the National Women's Suffrage Association, many of which he thoroughly disrupted by taking over the podium and declaring: "Go home, all you women, clean your houses and raise your children. Leave the lawmaking to men who know how to make laws."

When mob violence erupted against Orientals in the city, Norton came to the rescue of "these poor downtrodden Chinese people." Hoodlums attempted to take over one meeting concerned with a rash of lynchings in San Francisco. A free-for-all broke out, but the mob was hammered into silence by Norton I who pounded the podium with his grapevine cane. First the rioters laughed at the absurd-looking man, but their chuckles gave way to silence as the emperor led the entire group in reciting the Lord's Prayer. The rioters filed from the hall in solemn silence.

Even the legislators in Sacramento, the state capital, paid respect to Norton. He would travel by rail to the city and take a seat reserved for him in the visitor's gallery of the Senate. He often addressed an attentive assembly. Once outside the capitol building Norton encountered a candidate for the Senate who was imploring a hooting crowd to vote for him. The emperor walked to the man and placed a fatherly arm about him, telling him: "You need not speak to these ruffians further. I hereby appoint you a state senator."

Norton busied himself more and more with the problems of politics, even taking a world view. He thought that the United States and England should be bonded together more firmly and, to that end, sent a wire to President Lincoln, urging him to wed that august widow, Victoria, Queen of England. A wire came back from Washington which stated that Mr. Lincoln would take the emperor's suggestion under close advisement. Wires to other crown heads of Europe were also sent by Norton, where he would outline programs to prevent war and improve the lot of their subjects. Kindly telegraph operators would compose responses from kings and queens in which they promised to follow the constructive dictates of Norton I; the emperor cherished these wires and kept them in his room until his dying day.

Christmas in San Francsico was improved, at least for the children, through a scheme of the emperor's. He wanted an enormous Christmas tree erected in Union Square and this was to be lighted for the benefit of the city's children. The city fathers nodded agreement and San Francisco's first outdoor Christmas tree was put up, establishing a tradition that exists to this day, one begun by Norton I. The emperor's ideas were often thought of as the whims of a lunatic, but many of them not only proved sound, but prophetic. It was Norton who first suggested the construction of the San Francisco Bay Bridge to join San Francisco and Oakland. It was the emperor's overall blueprint that was subsequently adopted when the bridge was built decades later.

Few of Norton's edicts went unheeded and fewer still were those who did not pay him honor and minor tribute. Those who ignored, or worse still, refused to acknowledge his rank, were chastised by the authorities. One day, while traveling on a Central Pacific train to Sacramento, Norton entered the dining car and ordered a sumptuous meal. After being served, he paid with his own oddly printed script. The waiter took one look at Norton's self-styled currency and refused to honor it.

Norton flew into a rage; he pounded the table with his cane and shouted: "How dare you outrage the person of the emperor! I will revoke this railroad's franchise when arriving in Sacramento!" When officials of the railroad later heard of the incident they promptly issued Norton I a lifetime pass good on all trains, along with free dining car service.

A few years later, on January 21, 1867, Norton I endured the unthinkable. A new policeman unfamiliar with his status in San Francisco, discovered the emperor strolling through his domain and arrested him on charges of vagrancy.

"I, sir, am no vagrant," replied an indignant Norton. "I possess five dollars." He withdrew the money and showed it to the officer.

"In that outfit," sneered the cop, "you're a nut. I'm charging you with insanity." With that the officer collared Norton I and dragged him to the nearest police station. Hearing that the emperor had been arrested, the Chief of Police hurried to the station and personally escorted Norton from his cell, profusely apologizing for "the mistake and insult visited upon your majesty's person." The local press published broadsides against the perpetrator of the outrage, quickly pointing out the many virtues of the emperor. Said the *Alta:* "Since he has worn the imperial purple [Norton] has shed no blood, robbed nobody, and despoiled the country of no one, which is more than can be said of any of his fellows in that line."

From that moment on, Norton was treated with great courtesy by all officers in San Francisco. The city would have it no other way. In fact, when an authentic monarch, Dom Pedro II of Brazil, visited San Francisco nine years later, city fathers, with great fanfare, introduced the Brazilian monarch to San Francisco's reigning emperor. Dom Pedro was quietly told of Norton's true identity, but the king nevertheless treated Norton as an equal.

In his declining years Norton I took on the image of a city landmark, a living historical monument of colorful San Francisco, and all who knew him saw him as the embodiment of the bustling metropolis. The writer Robert Louis Stevenson wrote of the strange-looking monarch in his novel *The Wrecker,* published in 1892: "Of all our visitors, I believe I preferred Emperor Norton; the very mention of whose name reminds me I am doing scanty justice to the folks of San Francisco. In what other city would a harmless madman who supposed himself emperor of the two Americas have been so fostered and encouraged? Where else would even the people of the streets have respected the poor soul's illusion? Where else would bankers and merchants have received his visits, cashed his cheques, and submitted to his small assessments? Where else would he have been suffered to attend and address the exhibition of days of schools and colleges? Where else in God's green earth, [would he] have taken his pick of restaurants, ransacked the bill of fare, and departed scathless?"

On the night of January 8, 1880, Emperor Norton I, dressed in his full uniform, his sword at his side, stepped from his rooming house and began walking to a civic meeting. The sixty-two-year-old monarch reached the hall and collapsed on the steps. By the time passersby rushed him to a hospital, Norton I was dead.

In tribute to America's first and only emperor, the San Francisco *Chronicle* announced to its readers the following day: "LE ROI EST MORT." Mourned the *Morning Call:* "He is dead and no citizen of San Francisco could have been taken away who would be more generally missed."

Norton lay in state for several days, dressed in a new uniform purchased by the city fathers. More than 30,000 citizens filed past his funeral bier to pay their respects before the emperor was buried in the Masonic Cemetery. In 1934 the expanding city overran the old cemetery and the bodies there were removed to Woodlawn Cemetery, including the remains of the long dead monarch.

The people of San Francisco, however, had not forgotten him. A new granite monument was erected over his majesty's final resting place. It read, without quotes around the inscription:

NORTON I, EMPEROR OF THE UNITED STATES, PROTECTOR OF MEXICO, JOSHUA A. NORTON, 1819–1880

John Humphrey NOYES

Social Reformer (1811–1886)

Born in Brattleboro, Vermont, on September 3, 1811, Noyes graduated from Dartmouth in 1830 and went on to study at the Theological Seminary at

Andover, Massachusetts and then the Divinity School at Yale. It was while studying at Yale that Noyes began to conceive and express notions that outraged faculty members and frightened the local inhabitants. He organized a small group of religious dissidents and openly preached that Christ had come back to earth in 70 A.D., with the Fall of Jerusalem. Noyes stated that he had "discovered" Christ's real meaning in returning to earth, that He expected "moral perfection" in all his followers.

Noyes, in his opposition to Calvinistic teachings, organized a free church which advocated free love. Such radical beliefs soon caused his expulsion from Yale. Further, he was denied a license to preach because of his bizarre beliefs. Undaunted, the radical Noyes moved to Putney, Vermont in 1836; here the religious fanatic—he called himself a "social reformer"—established a burgeoning community of free love and promiscuity which Noyes labeled the Putney Corporation of Perfectionists.

So notorious was the Putney group that, by 1848, members, chiefly Noyes, were placed under constant surveillance by local constables. Officers broke into a home one night and found Noyes in bed with *several* married women. He was arrested and charged with adultery. Noyes jumped his bail and fled to Oneida Creek, New York. His rabid disciples decamped Vermont en masse and followed him.

Noyes and his followers firmly established their community at Oneida Creek, where all property was communally owned— "Bible Communism," Noyes called it. No one owned each other either, the leader insisted, and everyone was instructed to literally "love all other members equally." The most serious sin,any of Noyes' congregation could commit was upholding marital fidelity, which the leader branded a "sin of selfishness." Any sexual liaisons desired by any male or female in the community was not only sanctioned, but encouraged at all times.

Paradoxically, Noyes strictly enforced regulations dealing with his much-advocated free love. Birth control was strictly enforced, a system of eugenic laws which Noyes termed "stirpiculture," whereby the community's "future stock" was controlled and organized, a racial experiment that Adolf Hitler could have later pointed to with pride had he known of it. Noyes outlined his eugenic laws in a pamphlet entitled *Male Continence* (later praised by Havelock Ellis), emphasizing for the first time in American print, the separation of sexual pleasure and the bearing of children.

Noyes stated that such separation was best achieved through what he termed *coitus reservatus*, whereby the male, exercising enormous willpower, denied himself orgasm. Sex, Noyes instructed, must be conducted at a slow and quiet motion on the part of the male and, once the woman achieved climax, the male was to come to a gradual halt, a sort of grinding down motion. The religious leader actually instructed couples in his sex therapy, directing movements and positions.

Following this copulation credo, Noyes stated, would conserve the energy of the male, increase virility and prolong life. (Many advocates and cults would spring from this bizarre belief, the chief disciple being a female physician,   **275**

Alice Bunker Stockam, an Ohio Quaker and early-day woman suffragette who advanced "social purity" beliefs based on Noyes' work, summarizing her theories in her book *Karezza,* published in 1896.)

Promiscuity was organized at every social level in the Oneida Creek community. Older women indoctrinated young boys in the sexual practices of the leader. When girls were considered of age (usually at sixteen), older men undertook to instruct them in the ways of the "religious sex." To eliminate the "idolatrous love of mother and child," Noyes ordered all children to be placed at an early age in the homes of foster parents.

Each Sunday the large community would assemble at Noyes' church and all wrongdoing having occurred during the week was set right, not by punishments but by public criticism—"mutual criticism," Noyes termed it. At such times those members who had insisted upon acting as parents to their natural children, those women or men who had shunned sex with other members demanding coition, were thoroughly denounced and shamed.

Local New York authorities ignored the strange doings at Oneida Creek and for thirty years the free sex cult thrived and grew. By the late 1870s, the community began to split into angry factions. When Noyes' life was threatened, the leader fled to Canada where he continued to publish a plethora of sex pamphlets until his death at Niagara Falls on April 13, 1886.

The free love community at Oneida Creek slowly succumbed to outside social pressures and, by the turn of the century, had given up its radical sex practices, turning to the lucrative manufacturing of steel hunting traps and the plating of silver which later developed into the world famous Community Plate industry.

O

Charles K. OGDEN

Scholar (1889–1957)

Considered to be one of the most eccentric personalities of the Academy in this century, Ogden lived in the college area of Cambridge, England. He supported himself through four small bookstores which specialized in rare tomes, mostly supplied to American libraries, and acted as a sort of philosophical analyst to visiting millionaires in search of intellectual identities. His manner of dress was decidedly weird. He wore suede shoes with square toes and donned flannel shirts with the collar so wide that he could, without unbuttoning the shirt, reach downward through the collar to scratch his chest, which he did at all times despite the presence of decorum-minded members of royalty and businessmen.

The scholar owned a vast and expensive wardrobe, contributed to Ogden, claimed the British editor Kingsley Martin, by an American millionaire grateful for being infused with Ogden's philosophy. Visitors to Ogden's Alice in Wonderland home, and this in a day when most men wore hats, were perplexed to see in the foyer a hat rack placed high over a staircase, so high that it was out of reach to any wanting to hang up a hat. Two hats were permanently affixed to the hat rack, a straw boater and a bowler. "Often it was a long time," wrote Nigel Dennis, "before his visitors realized the hats were made to fit the undersized heads of a nonexistent breed, midway between men and midget."

The bespectacled "Og," as he was known to friends, contributed essays to philosophical journals under the pseudonymn of "Adeline Moore," but was best known for his creation of a new English language which Ogden boiled down to

850 simple words, a language which he expected would revolutionize international communication. It didn't.

Ogden's inventive mind created all sorts of intellectual games to amuse his guests, but mostly to amuse himself. One exercise he called "on and off," where players wrote down all the famous persons they could remember, names ending in on and off. The names were then checked against the encyclopedia. Only those names *not included* scored points. "My best score to date," Ogden once beamed, "including Rachimaninoff and Carry Nation, is twenty."

The scholar's most bizarre behavior involved noise. As a staunch member of the Anti-Noise League, Ogden was downright fanatic in preventing street cries and traffic racket. He would not tolerate such noises and found a unique way in which to prevent unwelcome sounds from penetrating his abode. He collected dozens of clocks which chimed, ticked and rang. Further, he would turn up a half dozen radios full blast until his home rocked with noise, *his* noise. And inside his privately created din, Charles K. Ogden would labor through the nights, working on his new language, compiling bibilographies, penning philosophical essays, stopping his labors only at dawn when he ordered his dinner—when everyone else was having breakfast—a routine that never varied in forty years until his death in 1957.

And no one, absolutely no one, ever complained about *Ogden's* noise.

John O'HARA

Author (1905–1970)

One of the most popular authors of American novels, O'Hara concentrated on producing social history and is best remembered for works such as *Appointment in Samarra, Butterfield 8, Ten North Frederick,* and *From the Terrace.* He had a penchant for accenting styles, brands and logos, from Chevas Regal scotch to Rolls Royce autos, all the trappings that he thought gave one status. (This writing technique was a double-edged sword, a gimmick whereby the reader of his day identified quickly with current fads and styles, but one that also aged and dated O'Hara's material for a new generation of readers.)

Vain, egotistical and pompous, O'Hara's sole purpose for becoming a writer appears to have been a way of achieving status. He loved honors, awards and kudos of any sort; he sought them out, lobbying for honorary degrees from Harvard, Yale and other Eastern establishment centers of learning. He was a rabid social climber and status-clinger which may have been caused by the backward posture of his home town, Pottsville, Pennsylvania, a mining center, where he was born on January 31, 1905.

A heavy drinker all his life, liquor brought John O'Hara's uncontrollable temper to the surface and also brought him notoriety, self-recrimination, and

Author John O'Hara, drinker, brawler and victim of midgets. (Wide World)

physical pain. As a youth O'Hara began drinking in local Pottsville bars. When his father, a country doctor who made house calls religiously, first discovered his son in an alcoholic state, he exploded. Dr. Patrick Henry O'Hara, John's father, had a volatile nature that surpassed even his son's. Dr. O'Hara, once finding young John in a boozy stupor, began to beat the youth until he bled. He finished the beating by smashing a large, heavy chair over his son's head, and might have hospitalized John, or worse, had it not been for the intercession of Mrs. O'Hara.

O'Hara attended Fordham Prep School, where drinking constantly interferred with his studies. He later claimed that the school's curriculum bored him; he spent most of his time drawing cartoons at his desk. He later attended Niagara University Prep School at Niagara, New York, where he excelled in English literature. O'Hara had been selected as valedictorian. The night before commencement, in June 1924, O'Hara and two other youths went to the local bars and returned to the school at dawn so drunk they could hardly walk. O'Hara was seen to wobble toward his dormitory by most of the parents and faculty assembling for the exercises. He was sent home in disgrace; his honors taken from him, his diploma withheld.

During the 1920s O'Hara busied himself by writing for newspapers, beginning with the Pottsville *Journal* where he got a job, through his father's influence, as a reporter. He spent most of his spare time drinking and collecting empty gin bottles. O'Hara put together a list of the town's most ardent teetotalers and temperance leaders and, late at night, he would sneak up to the homes of these anti-liquor crusaders and line their porches with the empty gin bottles.

At first the iconoclastic O'Hara rebelled at any decorum demanded of him. If he was invited to a formal dinner or dance he would appear in filthy, unpressed clothes. He was regularly thrown out of the Schuylkill Country Club for drinking and brawling. Yet O'Hara's impression of his own qualities as a writer went undiminished; in fact he thought of himself as one of the world's most gifted scribes, informing his father that he would be listed in *Who's Who* before he reached the age of thirty, to which his father reportedly replied: "The way you're going you won't be alive by the time you're thirty!" He also stated in a piece written for the *Journal* that he would some day win "a Pulitzer Prize, and if I ever get to it, I intend to write the Great American Novel." He was not to realize the first ambition, although he was given the National Book Award for *Ten North Frederick;* only one of his novels, his first, *Appointment in Samarra,* approaches greatness, according to most critics.

O'Hara traveled to New York in 1928 with less then twenty dollars in his pocket, going to work for the New York *Herald Tribune.* He later worked for *Time* and *The New Yorker.* The budding writer spent most of his leisure hours inside of speakeasies, dating a different girl every night. O'Hara's promiscuity often lead to his contracting venereal disease and he spent a good deal of time enduring painful gonorrhea. He somehow managed to get married three times.

After O'Hara's books began to be published, the highly publicized author—mostly through his own efforts—not only increased his drinking but established a reputation as a mean drunk, a truculent imbiber who would insult anyone within listening range, and answer the mildest challenge with his fists.

Anything violent appealed to O'Hara. One night, when drinking in Costello's, a Third Avenue bar in New York, O'Hara showed his new blackthorn walking stick to Ernest Hemingway. Holding up the stick, Hemingway bet O'Hara that he could break the stick over his own head. O'Hara made the bet. Hemingway promptly raised the strong stick over his head and broke it. O'Hara gladly paid Hemingway $50.

Whether at "21" or the Stork Club, John O'Hara was always testy, even when not drinking. According to his biographer, Frank MacShane, "once at the Stork Club he refused to pay the bill because he and his guests were placed at the wrong table."

O'Hara and his friend John Steinbeck were drinking in a New York bar one night when O'Hara began to argue with a midget sitting next to him. Another midget came out of the washroom and sat on the other side of the author. When the first midget snarled an insult at O'Hara, the author raised his arm, as if to strike. With that, both midgets pushed him backward on his high bar stool so that he crashed to the floor. The midgets jumped on him and battered him mercilessly until the bartender rushed forward and grabbed O'Hara, escorting him to the door. Steinbeck watched the entire incident without interfering.

When working in Hollywood as a screenwriter, O'Hara's conduct was as outlandish as it had been in New York. He terrorized Chasen's, the Brown Derby, all of the better restaurants and saloons in the movie capital. At private parties he was close to being lethal. He attended several gatherings at Robert Benchley's lodgings in the fabulous "Garden of Allah" and proved himself obnoxious. At one party, O'Hara, thoroughly drunk, grabbed several women, then held a young starlet by the throat so tightly that Benchley thought the writer might choke her. The host pulled O'Hara away and the novelist knocked Benchley's cigar from his mouth.

O'Hara, sobering the next day, called Benchley to apologize. The humorist, according to his son Nathaniel, as quoted by MacShane, replied: "Look, John, please don't apologize to me. You're a shit and everyone knows you're a shit, and people ask you out in spite of it."

Jazz was a private love of John O'Hara's, although he seldom remained sober enough when in a jazz club to hear the music or even recognize the performing artists he had come to see. Following World War II, O'Hara entered a small jazz club to hear his favorite jazz saxophonist, Bud Freeman. He was already drunk by the time he was shown to a table. After several more drinks, O'Hara began to tell the world that he was the greatest living writer. When a couple sitting nearby asked him to lower his voice, O'Hara kicked their table, upsetting their drinks.

A heavyset waiter came over and asked O'Hara to quiet down. The writer kicked him in the shin so hard, the waiter doubled up in screaming pain which brought over a heavyset bouncer. Before the bouncer could open his mouth, O'Hara also a massive man, jumped up and smashed the bouncer in the face, knocking him to the floor.

"This, of course, brought my set to an abrupt halt," Freeman told the author. "Manager, waiters and assorted hoods who owned that dive were preparing to rush O'Hara. I stopped them, saying: 'Look, this is John O'Hara, the famous novelist.' One of the hoods snarled: 'Ah, who'd know anyone like dat?' I persisted, telling the goons: 'We're friends, I can handle him, I can take care of him. He'll listen to me.' A hoodlum said, 'all right, go ahead, calm that madman down.' So I put my arm around O'Hara and said, 'John, it's me, your pal Bud Freeman, take it easy.' He looked at me for the longest time and then a grin spread across his face as he embraced me, saying: 'Bud—Jesus Christ, it's good to see you! Where you working now?'"

O'Hara's drinking, many claimed, was prompted by lack of critical recognition. Even though he was an immensely popular success and his books—many of which were made into films—had brought him great riches, he yearned vainly for the distinguished prizes of literature. When his friend Steinbeck won the Nobel Award, O'Hara wired his congratulations but added that he should have received the award himself.

He would feel that way, embittered and resentful, until his death on April 11, 1970 in Princeton, New Jersey.

P

Phillippus Aureolus PARACELSUS

Physician (1493–1541)

Born in Switzerland as Theophrastus Bombastus von Hohenheim, Paracelsus was the son of an improverished physician and a woman bonded to a nunnery; his mother, a confirmed manic depressive, later committed suicide by leaping from a bridge. As a youth, Paracelsus—he took the name at age seventeen to signify his superiority in medicine to the famous Roman doctor, Celsus—learned what he could of his father's profession. He then studied chemistry, becoming fascinated with minerals.

Paracelsus' education was skimpy and, perhaps, in part, fabricated. While still in his teens, he left home, visiting many European universities where he studied briefly. He later claimed that he had earned a medical degree in Italy, but no records verified a diploma. Moreover, Paracelsus refused to provide documentation that qualified him to teach at several universities, but he was so persuasive with officials that he was usually allowed to conduct classes.

Academic education held little interest for this self-styled genius. His attitude on this matter was summed up thusly: "Universities do not teach all things, so a doctor must seek out old wives, gypsies, sorcerers, wandering tribes, old robbers, and such outlaws and take lessons from them." Whatever lessons the physician did learn brought him to conclude that minerals could mightily affect diseases. Thus, he began to prescribe mineral water and other chemicals for internal use—the first to do so—to remedy ailments. He was also the first to apply homeopathic plant remedies, as well as diagnose tuberculosis, silicosis and congenital syphilis. Paracelsus is generally recognized today as the father of pharmaceutics.

The brilliant surgeon and chemist was also a raving eccentric whose day-to-day actions were wholly unpredictable. Instead of wearing the traditional fur-trimmed red robes of the physician, Paracelsus walked about in the rags of a beggar. When he was observed to lecture in the stained apron of the alchemist—Paracelsus believed for most of his life that it was possible to change lead into gold—his superiors criticized him, ordering him to wear clothes suitable to his station in life. Paracelsus' answer was to buy an expensive suit of clothes, gilttering with jewels, but he wore this finery for months on end, never removing his clothes, sleeping in them, until his body odor was so overpowering that students and faculty shunned him.

Paracelsus defied the custom of lecturing in Latin and delivered all his talks in German. When teaching at the university in Basel, he collected most of the standard works on medicine and, since he disagreed with the tenets of those books, built a huge bonfire and burned the tomes in front of his shocked students.

The strange doctor abstained from all sensual pleasures until he was twenty-five, when he discovered how to drink wine. From that time until his death, Paracelsus consumed all manner of spirits, challenging peasants in pubs to match him drink for drink. According to one of his biographers, he "drank them under the table, now and then putting his finger in his mouth like a swine."

Women had no part in the physician's life. He did not seek out female companionship and when he was approached by women of the street, he fled screaming to his lodgings. (Paracelsus was at no time in life the least bit physically attractive, becoming bald and fat by his early thirties.) It was claimed that the doctor was castrated by thieves during his wanderings as a youth. Another story has it that Paracelsus castrated himself so that he would not be bothered with carnal desires that might interfere with his intense medical work.

Wherever the physician went he wore a great sword that dragged and clanked on the ground. He wore this sword to bed every night for the last twenty years of his life, as he did his boots and spurs. The sword was never unsheathed and not until Paracelsus' death was it learned that the sword had a hollow pommel in which the physician kept his most cherished drug, laudenum, his own opiate-based pharmaceutical creation. Also found in the doctor's home in Salzburg shortly after his death were elaborate drawings he had made in his attic, thousands of astrological signs, occult figures and characters that the physician felt aided him in his war against the world's maladies.

George Smith PATTON

General (1885–1945)

Born in Gabriel, California on November 11, 1885, Patton attended the Virginia Military Institute and graduated from West Point in 1909. He was a cavalry officer whose verve and invention soon earned attention from superiors. He accompanied General John Pershing as his aide-de-camp on the punitive expedition into Mexico against Pancho Villa in 1916–17. It was at this time that Patton first displayed incredible courage and amazing eccentricity.

After crossing into Mexico, Pershing sent his aide Patton on a special mission to accept the surrender of one of Villa's officers, General Julio Cardenas. Patton went (with six troopers) to a ranch twenty-some miles distant from Pershing's field headquarters, driving a Dodge touring car.

Upon his arrival at the ranch Patton was greeted by the Villista general and two followers with bullets. All three Villistas mounted horses in their attempt to escape. Patton jumped from the Dodge and whipped out his pistol, standing in the middle of an open yard and firing at the fleeing Mexicans, like some latter-day Wyatt Earp. He shot all three from their horses.

Cardenas, wounded, lay on the ground, trying to reload his pistol. Patton, whose sense of chivalry was exaggerated to say the least, stood patiently nearby, allowing the Mexican general to reload and fire at him before returning fire. After some moments, Cardenas managed to reload; he aimed his weapon at Patton from a prone position and exchanged shots with the American lieutenant. Patton's aim—he was a crack shot—was true. Cardenas received a bullet square in the heart. Patton went unscathed.

Hours after this wild west show, Patton arrived back at Pershing's headquarters. He sauntered into Pershing's tent and asked his chief if he would like to take a photo with him and the captured Mexicans. Pershing stepped outside to see Patton rush to his Dodge touring car and pose before a photographer who had already, at the lieutenant's insistence, set up a huge camera. On the bonnet of the Dodge, Patton had carefully arranged the bodies of General Cardenas and his bodyguards. He had strapped them to the car like prized hunting trophies.

Pershing took one look at the macabre scene and then curtly told his aide-de-camp that he was disinclined to take such a photo. Patton merely shrugged and ordered the photographer to snap the picture.

Such bizarre behavior became the hallmark of Patton's career. He proved himself to be a remarkable officer and a great military leader, but his fearless conduct was prompted by a vainglorious and foolhardy nature. During World War I, Patton led reckless charges through no-man's-land. Though most of his troops were usually killed or wounded at the time of these over-the-top bayonet

attacks, Patton went uninjured time after time. These experiences undoubtedly caused him to believe that he was immune to harm and, through the years, he repeatedly tested this idea by recklessly placing himself in extreme danger.

It was Major George S. Patton who, in 1932, led the charge of troopers that cleared the Bonus Army Marchers from Anacostia Flats in Washington, D.C. He personally torched the shacks the marchers had set up. One of these clapboard structures was the shabby home of Joseph Angelina, a World War I veteran who had saved Patton's life in the trenches fourteen years earlier.

Patton's exploits as a general during World War II were nothing less than spectacular. He led his tank divisions successfully against Rommel in the deserts of North Africa and mounted the invasion of Sicily, conducting a breakneck campaign on that island that led to the first major surrender of German forces to American troops during the war. It was at this time, however, that Patton, who hated malingerers, slapped a shell-shocked soldier in a field hospital, calling him a coward, an act that brought worldwide criticism and a rebuke from General Eisenhower. (He was ordered to publicly apologize for the slapping, which he did, before his own massed troops.)

As commander of the Third Army in Europe, Patton's lightning thrusts through France and Germany helped to bring the war to a swift conclusion. His heroic race to save American troops surrounded in the town of Bastogne made him a military legend.

General Patton believed all his life that God had devined his destiny, that he was born to lead great armies, and that he was invincible. Further, he believed that he was the reincarnation of soldiers from bygone ages and that he had fought as a Greek warrior against Cyrus of Persia, as a trooper of Alexander the Great during the siege of Tyre, as a bodyguard to Julius Caesar in Gaul, as an armored knight killed at the battle of Crecy during the Hundred Years' War, and as a marshal of Napoleon Bonaparte "who laughed at death and numbers." All this before he became General George S. Patton, who, alone, was more than enough for the world to handle.

Patton was killed in an automobile accident in Germany on December 21, 1945. (Rumors had it that Patton was murdered by American officials who thought that he might bring about a war with Russia through his meddling.) He is buried at the American Military Cemetery in Hamm, Luxenbourg. None of his former selves are identified on his white stone cross.

Hesketh PEARSON

Biographer (1887–1964)

The British biographer of Dickens and a host of other historical giants, Pearson produced a strange tome entitled *Whispering Gallery* which purported

The flamboyant General George S. Patton, shown here in Sicily in 1943, his ivory-handled pistol on hip; he believed he was the reincarnation of many soldiers from ancient wars.

to reveal the behind-the-scenes activities of the world's leading statesmen. The book, published in the United States and in England simultaneously, did not carry Pearson's byline. The anonymously published work revealed double-dealings and secret agreements at the top of the world power structure before World War I. One chapter was devoted to a top secret meeting between Kaiser Wilheim II of Germany and his cousin, King Edward VII of Britain. Wilhelm, at the time of this meeting, outlined in detail—the book claimed—his complete plan for the conquest of Europe. Edward, knowing of this sinister ambition, did nothing.

The book received widespread criticism, especially from those living diplomats and members of royalty who were privy to the movements of those exposed in *Whispering Gallery*. When the book was universally denounced as a fraud, the publishers demanded that Pearson admit to authorship, which he did reluctantly. Pearson also admitted that the book, which was called in by the publisher, was a complete fraud, but he never explained his motive for producing such an outrageous hoax.

Elisha PERKINS

Physician (1742–1799)

Perkins was not only America's first great quack, but he so instrinsically believed in his hocus-pocus remedies that it brought about his own death. Born in Norwich, Connecticut on January 27, 1742, Perkins attended Yale, studying medicine. He moved to Plainfield at the age of twenty and married Sarah Douglas. The union produced ten children.

The doctor's career was uneventful until he turned forty. He then announced to the world that he had made an amazing discovery: Dr. Elisha Perkins could draw diseases and ailments and pain from bodies by simply passing over the afflicted areas a metal device of his own creation. He worked furiously to design a U-shaped piece of metal, with three-inch long prongs. One prong was reportedly made of platinum, iron and silver, the other of zinc, copper and gold. He would later, in 1796, patent this device which was called the Perkins Patented Metallic Tractor.

Perkins treated all manner of illnesses, numbering among his patients such luminaries as George Washington and Chief Justice Oliver Ellsworth. He sold his "tractors" by the score and became a wealthy squire. Hundreds of testimonials were collected by Perkins from lawyers, doctors, politicians, and leading educators, all claiming that his device had not only relieved pain and suffering but actually saved lives that, before the application of "Perkinism," were deemed terminal.

These testimonials were later published by one of the doctor's offsprings, Benjamin Douglas Perkins, who also became a physician and continued to use and sell tractors into the nineteenth century, even when he knew that the devices were useless.

Dr. Elisha Perkins, on the other hand, was a bit unbalanced and believed to the day of his death that he had invented a miracle gadget. No serious physician, however, thought of "Perkinism" as anything other than a medical scam. Perkins began to receive open criticism from his fellow doctors by the mid-1790s and, when Perkins refused to admit his "tractors" were specious, the Connecticut Medical Society—a society which Perkins himself had founded in 1792—expelled him from the ranks in 1798.

The following year Perkins learned of a serious outbreak of yellow fever in New York and was again inspired to produce a miracle cure; he put together a concoction of vinegar and muriate of soda and, after accumulating barrels of this "drug," led a caravan of horse-drawn wagons into New York to save the city.

Perkins promptly contracted yellow fever while administering his quack medicine and died on September 6, 1799.

Vincenzo PERUGGIA

Thief (1881–1927)

The most famous portrait ever painted in the history of art is undoubtedly Leonardo Da Vinci's *Mona Lisa (La Gioconda)*. The painting was commissioned by Francis I of France, who gave Da Vinci 4,000 gold florins for the work, and when it was completed, the French king hung the painting in his bathroom. The masterwork was later displayed in Italian galleries, removed in a raid by Napoleon Bonaparte and placed in the emperor's bedroom, later becoming a permanent and prized possession of the majestic Louvre in Paris.

Millions flocked through the years to visit the Salon Carré in the Louvre to view the lovely woman with her mysterious and haunting smile, a smile that received enormous amounts of press over the decades. Even Sigmund Freud wrote a paper attempting to explain the curious smile, vaguely claiming that Da Vinci had painted it in memory of his mother who had dominated him in life and continued to do so in his masterpiece.

By 1911 the painting was estimated to be worth more than $5 million (today it is priceless). Small acts of vandalism during the summer of 1910

Vincenzo Peruggia, who stole the *Mona Lisa* for the honor of Italy.

caused worried curators at the Louvre to put many of the museum's valuable oil paintings behind glass as a way of providing protection beyond the guards who moved through the Louvre's halls and salons. The institution of the glass caused protests from Parisian art lovers who claimed that such measures made the paintings appear to be behind shop windows that obscured true sight of the masterworks. Further, some gossiped, the glass panels had been installed to cover the fact that the curators had substituted copies of the paintings and had removed the originals for safekeeping. Some went so far as to accuse curators of selling the originals secretly for their private gain and putting up the glass panes to shroud inept duplicates. None of these accusations were true. The original paintings remained behind the glass panels.

Criticism, however, continued, with hundreds of art lovers protesting with picket lines and petitions to have the glass removed. To point out the absurdity of using the glass panels, one man, novelist Roland Dorgeles, went so far as to appear in the Louvre one morning and shave himself in the reflection of a glassed-in Rembrandt. (He was removed by churlish guards, the lather still patching his jaw.)

The first publicly stated suggestion that the *Mona Lisa* could be stolen had appeared in print a year earlier, in July 1910, when *Le Cri de Paris* printed a satiric article claiming that art thieves, knowing the glass would make a duplicate undetectable, had stolen the original Da Vinci, sold it to an American millionaire, and had substituted a copy painted by an old woman living in London. In response to this jibe, Theophile Homolle, France's director of national museums, snorted: "You might just as well pretend that one could steal the towers of the cathedral of Notre Dame."

Such an impossibility became reality on the morning of August 22, 1911. Louis Beroud, a painter, walked into the Salon Carré, intending to sketch a model primping before the *Mona Lisa,* using the glass covering the painting as a mirror. He stood alone in the gallery—no guard was present—and stared at a wall he knew by heart, stared and blinked amazement. The place usually occupied by the Da Vinci, between Titian's *Allegory of Alfonso d'Avalos* and Correggio's *Mystical Marriage of St. Catherine,* was empty, except for the four iron pegs that held the *Mona Lisa.* Beroud asked a head guard as to the painting's whereabouts and was told that the *Mona Lisa* was undoubtedly in the photography annex where copies were made. The painter waited until noon and then asked the guard to check with the photographic section of the Louvre. The photographers had not seen the painting. Within minutes dozens of guards and officials raced through the museum in a frantic search. The police and special detectives from the Sûreté were called in. Visitors in the museum were seized and strip-searched in private rooms, then let go with apologies. A policeman walked down a spiral staircase that led into a museum courtyard facing the Seine. Beneath the staircase he found the pane of glass that had covered the *Mona Lisa* and its frame. The authorities had no choice but to announce shamefacedly that the Louvre's great prize, the *Mona Lisa,* had been stolen. ·

The *Mona Lisa,* which was almost burned on the whim of the man who took it and hid it beneath his bed for two years.

The news of the world was swept from the front pages of Paris newspapers which headlined the theft, using words such as "Unimaginable" and "Impossible." Germans in the city were arrested and held as suspects since at the time there was a very real threat of war with Germany concerning Morocco. An indignant German journalist, speaking for his country's diplomats, insisted that the whole affair was a ruse concocted by the French government to sidestep French chicanery in the Moroccan crisis.

L'illustration, a popular magazine, offered a 40,000-franc reward to anyone who returned the painting to its offices. The magazine was quick to point out that no questions would be asked and that the person collecting the reward would remain anonymous. Further, the periodical offered an additional 10,000-franc reward to anyone who would provide information leading to the return of the *Mona Lisa.*

The French newspapers soon followed suit. The Paris *Journal* offered 50,000 francs. *Le Matin* begged any clairvoyant who could envision the painting's whereabouts to contact government officials. As the weeks and months dragged on without results, suspicious characters carrying rectangular packages were regularly arrested and searched on the boulevards of Paris, in train stations, all over France, in cities and villages, and particularly at French ports. Painters were especially suspect and many, including Pablo Picasso, were taken in for questioning. When police learned that the poet Guillaume Apollinaire had a particular affection for the *Mona Lisa,* he was arrested and grilled unmercifully. In the end, not a clue to the great painting's whereabouts was discovered.

More than two years after the *Mona Lisa* had vanished, a wealthy Florentine art dealer, Alfredo Geri, patronized by Eleanora Duse and other illustrious art lovers, placed an advertisement in several Italian newspapers. The ad, run in the fall of 1913, read, in part, that "a buyer at good prices of art objects of every sort" was looking for work to display in an upcoming exhibition.

On November 29, 1913, Geri received a letter dated from Paris. The writer, identifying himself only as "Leonard," stated that he was in possession of the *Mona Lisa* and that he would restore this great treasure to the country where it belonged, Italy, for a price. The art dealer thought the writer was either a crackpot or an amateur collector who had purchased a cheap copy of the masterwork. Geri nevertheless wrote back to a post office box in the Place de la Republique, stating that he was too busy to come to Paris to inspect the painting but if the writer wished to visit him in Florence he would then look at the painting. If it was, indeed, the authentic *Mona Lisa* he would pay any price for it.

A wire arrived, telling Geri that Leonard would visit him in his office on December 10, 1913. As a precaution, Geri asked Giovanni Poggi, director of the famous Uffizi Gallery in Florence, to be on hand when the stranger arrived, just in case "the man was not crazy and indeed did possess the real *Mona Lisa*." At 3:15 P.M. on the appointed day a thin man in his thirties with a heavy black mustache and sleepy eyes appeared. Geri introduced "Leonard" to Poggi.

The young man gaped in shock, then grabbed Poggi's hand and said: "I am honored to shake the hand of the man to whom the art of Florence has been entrusted."

Geri then nervously asked if they could see the painting. Leonard readily agreed and led the two men to a small hotel, the Tripoli-Italia, taking them to a little room on the third floor. He locked the door once they were inside. Geri stuck his trembling hands into his pockets as he anxiously watched Leonard go to his bed. From Geri's later testimony, Leonard "drew out from under his bed a trunk of white wood that was full of wretched objects: broken shoes, a mangled hat, a pair of pliers, plastering tools, a smock, some paint brushes, and even a mandolin. He threw them onto the floor in the middle of the room. Then, from under a false bottom in the box he took out an object wrapped in red silk. He placed it on the bed and to our astonished eyes, the divine 'Gioconda' appeared, intact and marvelously preserved. We took it to the window to compare it with a photograph we had brought with us. Poggi examined it and there was no doubt that the painting was authentic. The Louvre's catalogue number and stamp on the back of it matched with the photograph."

Poggi and Geri, delighted that the masterwork had surfaced, shook Leonard's hand, congratulating him. Poggi then stated that the painting should be removed to the Uffizi Gallery where it could be better examined. Geri added that Leonard would be amply rewarded for returning the painting. (According to Geri, Leonard had originally asked for 500,000 lire, about $100,000 at that time.) Leonard, wrapping the painting in the piece of silk and putting it under his arm, nodded his approval and the trio left for the Uffizi. As they were leaving the hotel, the concierge rushed forward, blocking the entranceway. She had not received her rent and she wanted to know what Leonard was removing from his lodgings.

"It's only a picture that we are taking to the Uffizi Gallery," replied Leonard laconically.

The concierge then recognized Poggi and bowed, allowing the three men to pass. "Ah!" laughed Geri later. "If the guardians of the Louvre had had the same curiosity, never would the 'Gioconda' have come to Florence."

After depositing the painting with Poggi at the Uffizi, Leonard inquired about his reward for "returning 'La Gioconda' to Italy" and "righting the wrong committed by that thief, Napoleon." He was told to return to his hotel and wait, which he did.

More experts were called and examined the painting which had all of its known marks, cracks and smudges. It was authentic. News of the recovery was sent to the press of the world immediately and Poggi made preparations to put the Da Vinci portrait on display at his own gallery, even though he knew it would later be returned to the Louvre.

Hours later police swarmed into Leonard's hotel room as he was packing his white box, arresting him. He made no move to resist and went quietly with the Florence chief of police and several detectives. He had registered under the name of Vincenzo Leonardo, but it was soon learned that his real name was Vincenzo Peruggia (sometimes spelled Perugia), born in Dumenza, a village near Como in northern Italy. He was taken to jail where he was asked why he had stolen the *Mona Lisa*. "For the glory of Italy and in vengeance against the sins of Napoleon Bonaparte," was his answer. He was a housepainter by trade, he explained, and that he had worked briefly at the Louvre before taking other employment. When one detective called him a thief, Peruggia shouted: "I am no thief—I am a patriot!" He went on to state that, while working at the Louvre, he had been shocked to see the scores of Italian masterpieces on display in the French museum. National pride had motivated his theft of the greatest of these Italian masterpieces.

The art world sighed with relief when hearing the news of the painting's recovery. It was quite unharmed except for two small scratches made in Peruggia's tool box. The painting was put on display at the Uffizi and tens of thousands fought to see it, causing riots where hundreds of police had to club back the more ardent art lovers.

Hundreds also jammed the courtroom in Florence on June 14, 1914 to witness the trial of Vincenzo Peruggia, who calmly faced a tribunal charging him with the theft of the *Mona Lisa*. The housepainter told the court how he first saw the painting in 1908 and again in 1909 when he worked at the Louvre. He was also part of the crew that had put the *Mona Lisa* under glass in January 1911. Peruggia explained that the painting had captivated him and, having fallen under its spell, he felt compelled to steal it, to return it to Italy, of course, its rightful owner.

Not so, countered the prosecution. Peruggia was an out-and-out criminal. The prosecutor pointed out that the accused had been arrested in Macon, France for an attempted robbery on June 24, 1908 and in Paris on February 9, 1909 for illegal possession of firearms, and had served short prison terms for both offenses.

Though uneducated, Peruggia gave moving and eloquent testimony on his own behalf. He went on claiming that he was "outraged" by the fact that the painting was held captive on foreign soil, that he vowed early in 1911 that he would return it to his native Italy. "I had only to choose an opportune moment," Peruggia admitted, "and a mere twist would put the picture in my hands. The idea took possession of me and I decided to take the step. One morning [August 21, 1911] I joined my fellow decorators at the Louvre, exchanged a few words with them and quietly stole away. I was wearing the same long white workman's blouse as they did and attracted no attention and was asked no questions. I entered the salon in which the picture was hung. The salon was deserted. In a moment I had taken it from the wall. I carried it to the staircase, took off the frame and slipped the painting under my blouse. It was all done in a few seconds."

French police officials later admitted that Peruggia certainly had been a suspect at the time of the disappearance of the painting and that they had thoroughly searched his room in Paris, but found nothing. The painting, of course, was sitting in the false bottom of the white box all during the search. Peruggia's frank and naive attitude, they added, also disarmed their suspicions. The same officials then stated that they had recently searched the Paris room and had found Peruggia's diary. One entry, under a date in 1910, listed art dealers and collectors in the United States, Italy and Germany, Americans such as Andrew Carnegie, John D. Rockefeller, and J.P. Morgan. Alfredo Geri was also listed among Italian collectors. Since these entries, police maintained, were made ten months before the theft of the *Mona Lisa,* it was obvious that the housepainter intended to steal the painting for the money it would bring and not for the honor and glory of Italy.

Peruggia persisted in his patriotic motives, and also told the court that the painting itself had held him spellbound. "I shall never forget the evening after I carried the picture home," he said, almost in tears. "I locked myself in my room in Paris and took the picture from a drawer. I stood bewitched before 'La Gioconda'. I fell victim to her smile and feasted my eyes on my treasure every evening, discovering each time new beauty and perversity in her. I fell in love with her."

"If you loved her so much why did you try to sell her?" sneered the prosecutor.

"I was anxious to ensure a comfortable old age for my parents. Besides that, I felt I must take myself away from the influence of that haunting smile. I sometimes wondered in those two and a half years whether or not I had not better burn the picture, fearing that I should go mad."

The prosecution demanded a three-year sentence, but the tribunal, after an hour's deliberation, sentenced Peruggia to one year and fifteen days. He left the courtroom handcuffed.

A spectator shouted to the pale, thin man, whose head was bowed: "What are you thinking?"

"But..." he answered slowly, "it could have been worse."

It became popular to psychoanalyze Peruggia and his motives for the theft.

The London *Times* wryly stated: "All is well that ends well, save for Vincenzo, who is still bewildered at finding his pains rewarded by prison and is convinced of an honorable release. What were really his motives, it would be hard to say. *Mona Lisa,* who might tell, only wears her enigmatic smile. After all, perhaps, the story was one of simple enchantment and Vincenzo, who has shared a garrett with *Mona Lisa* for two years, is not so much to be pitied."

The courts, however, did take pity on Peruggia and shortened his sentence to seven months, following appeals by his lawyers. He moved back to his home town where he married a cousin. He served with distinction in the Italian army during World War I, then moved with his wife to Paris where he opened a hardware store, dying in 1927.

Vincenzo Peruggia's amazing theft was not without its aftereffects. The hotel where he had stayed in Florence changed its name to La Gioconda. His home town of Dumenza honored him as a national hero. And there lurked the devastating possibility that many multimillionaires the world over had been bilked in colossal *Mona Lisa* swindles. One lengthy report was that during the painting's absence from the Louvre, a clever group of sophisticated art forgers had made many copies of the painting and had sold these for fabulous fortunes to wealthy persons who thought they were buying the stolen *Mona Lisa* and were content, like Peruggia, to never admit to possession or allow another to view the masterpiece, greedily ecstatic at owning the painting under any circumstances. Even today, the story goes, these copies are sold and resold at enormous prices that would have astounded the bold housepainter who thought of himself as Italy's greatest hero.

Samuel Andrew PETERS

Clergyman (1735–1826)

Born in Hebron, Connecticut on November 30, 1735, Peters graduated from Yale in 1757 and was ordained a deacon and priest of the Anglican Church in 1759. A Tory to the bone, Peters protested loudly the activities of revolution-aries as the rector of the Anglican Church in Hebron, Connecticut (1760–74). In 1774 he and his rectory were twice attacked by mobs under the banner of the Sons of Liberty. Peters fled to England where he stayed throughout the Revolution.

Peters was elected bishop of Vermont in 1794 while still in England, but was prevented from taking office since Parliament had prohibited the Arch-bishop of Canterbury from consecrating American bishops. While in England Peters proved his eccentric behavior by writing several specious historical accounts about America, the most notorious being his *General History of Connecticut,* published in 1781.

The clergyman fabricated historical events to the point of absurdity, describing a caterpillar invasion along the Connecticut River, the insects eating everything in a path three miles wide and two miles long, devastating 100 square miles. Peters stated that the caterpillars were more than two inches long, had red throats and white thorny bodies. He also detailed an attack of giant bullfrogs that destroyed the town of Windham in 1758 with such precision that readers of his history—Peters did include many factual and verifiable events and personalities—came to believe that the preposterous tales were true.

Peters returned to the United States in 1805 and was hailed as a literary genius. He drew a comfortable income from his books, hoaxes that they were, until his death in New York City on April 19, 1826.

Edgar Allan POE

Author (1809–1849)

He was America's first Bohemian, not by choice but through circumstances, a brooding, melancholy genius whose poems and tales of terror captivated readers worldwide after his death. It was death and all its morbid, morose trappings that obsessed Edgar Allan Poe; a life-long fascination that ruined his social life, destroyed domestic relationships, led him to drink and drugs, and hurried his own terrible end.

Born in Boston on January 19, 1809, Poe's mother, Elizabeth Arnold, and his father, David Poe, were actors. Elizabeth, born in England, was an accomplished actress; her husband David was only a mediocre player and, by an early age, an habitual drunk. The couple produced three children, William, Edgar and Rosalie, who were regularly abandoned when their parents played theater dates or attended parties and visited the more genteel saloons.

Poe's father, who was consumptive, deserted his wife in 1810 and Elizabeth Poe, depleted of funds, went to Richmond, Virginia with her three children. Unable to find employment, Elizabeth literally starved to death on December 18, 1811; Edgar and his brother and sister were taken in by a kindly tobacco exporter, the wealthy John Allan, and his wife. The Allan's were charitable toward the children but aloof, Allan refusing to adopt the Poe offspring. He nevertheless did rename the middle child Edgar Allan Poe.

Edgar's older brother William, who was said to possess great poetic talents, was rejected in a love affair and took to drink before going off to sea and later dying at age twenty-six in a brawl with other sailors. Rosalie, the youngest of the Poe children, was retarded and spent most of her adult years in a Washingpon, D.C. asylum where she died at age sixty-four.

Poe remained with the Allans, living in Richmond. He would spend hours staring at the ruins of the Broad Street Theater, where his mother had had her greatest theatrical successes; the theater had burned down and the black shell had been allowed to remain. Seventy persons, the cream of Richmond society,

The tortured author, Edgar Allan Poe.

had lost their lives in the theater when it blazed up on December 26, 1811, a calamity that was discussed for years by a shocked public. Next door to the theater was the Indian Queen Tavern, which Poe as a child passed every day on his way to school. He knew that all of his mother's friends and members of her troupe had gathered here to drink themselves into stupors while she lay dying. Poe had a morbid fascination with taverns for the remainder of his life.

These early day traumas were heightened when Poe, as a boy, met Mrs. Helen Stannard, the mother of a classmate, who was kind to him. He attached himself to her, confiding to her his boyish fears and enthusiasms. When she died prematurely, Poe's grief was insurmountable. He could not tolerate the thought of the woman lying alone in her tomb. Each night for months, young Poe slipped from his bed, dressed, and stole from the Allan house to go to the graveyard where he entered Helen Stannard's tomb to talk to her dead spirit and keep vigil against the unknown. As Lorine Pruette was to write in *The Literary Imagination:* "His broodings in the darkened cemetery by the tomb of the one person he felt had understood him must have laid a foundation for much that was weird and abnormal in his after life." (Poe's lyrical poem "To

297

Helen" was inspired by Mrs. Stannard, along with the haunting, chilling visions of women returning from the dead in later works such as "Ligeia" and the grim revival of Lady Madeleine in "The Fall of the House of Usher.")

In 1815, the Allans left to live in England, staying for five years. At this time Poe studied in Stoke–Newington, a suburb of London, at a classical academy under Dr. Bransby who thought of him as a "quick and clever boy ... [He] would have been a very good boy if he had not been spoiled by his parents who allowed him an extravagant amount of pocket money, which enabled him to get into all manner of mischief." The trouble was drink, for Poe, even though not eleven, had taken a liking to spirits and began consuming large amounts of wine. Though Poe was showered with money, fine clothes and all manner of creature comforts, he later claimed that his adoptive parents gave him no affection.

Returning to Richmond, Poe entered a wealthy preparatory school, but his classmates made his life miserable for him by sneering at his ancestral past, pointing out that his mother was nothing but an actress, his father a drunk, and that an uncle, Samuel Poe, who lived in Baltimore, tottered between eccentricity and lunacy. Poe could point with some pride to his paternal grandfather, David Poe, who had been a major in the Revolution, but this meant little to the status-conscious snobs who vexed the boy.

The youth was self-willed and capricious, although a good student. Poe, however, had a mean streak. He loved to frighten neighborhood girls, leaping out from behind bushes as they passed and even hurling live snakes at them, vipers he had laboriously trapped.

On February 14, 1826, Poe entered the University of Virginia, where he spent most of his time gambling and drinking. He would take one drink, usually gulping it down to achieve instant stimulation rather than savor the taste, and this would produce an euphoric state. It took little to get Edgar Allan Poe drunk, and his one-drink habit would continue throughout his life. He was a miserable gambler, taking foolish risks at cards and dice and invariably losing. His debts mounted up to the point where he owed more than $2,000 by the time he left the university on December 15, 1826. Since his Scotch stepfather adamantly refused to pay these debts, Poe quit the University of Virginia.

Allan offered Poe a job in his offices, telling the youth that he required discipline. Poe worked at a dull paper-shuffling job for a few weeks then, in the dead of night, he packed his bags and ran away to Boston, the town of his birth. The flight of Poe to Boston was prompted not so much by the monotonous position with his stepfather, but by the fact that his sweetheart, Sarah Elmira Royster, had rejected him and married another.

In Boston, Poe met a printer and convinced him to publish a slim volume of verse he had worked on in college, although some of the poems were written when he was twelve. The published book, *Tamerlane and Other Poems,* did not sell and Poe, near-to-starving, joined the army as a private, using the alias, Edgar A. Perry. He was then nineteen. Within a year he had distinguished himself with such exemplary conduct that he was promoted to sergeant–major.

He was honorably discharged and, after his stepfather secured an appointment, he entered West Point as a cadet.

Poe excelled in his studies at West Point, but rebelled against military duties and resigned within five months of his arrival. When his resignation was refused, Poe made a spectacle of himself on parade and broke every imaginable rule, including being drunk at roll call. He was promptly court-martialed and dishonorably discharged on March 6, 1831.

This last act of rebellion caused Allan to disown his stepson, telling him never to contact him again. Without family support, Poe moved to Baltimore to live with his aunt, Mrs. Maria Clemm, who mothered and comforted him as had Mrs. Stannard. He was given a room and encouraged to write. Poe produced several stories at this time, from 1831 to 1834, publishing "Metzengerstein" and four other stories in the Philadelphia *Saturday Courier*. His "MS Found in a Bottle" won a $50 prize from the Baltimore *Saturday Visitor*.

It was during these years that Poe also wandered widely from Mrs. Clemm's home, his travels unrecorded, always returning to his aunt and her daughter, Virginia—the consumptive cousin Poe was later to marry. Poe later claimed that he had gone to Europe at this time, to Greece and even to St. Petersburg, Russia where he had been imprisoned. These travels have always been attributed to Poe's wild and reckless imagination and most literary historians consider these journeys mythical. Yet, an odd and strong reference to Poe's alleged Russian trip, exists in the narrative of V. Piast, an upstanding literary historian and poet known for his veracity. Piast had reported in *Vstrechi* (*Meetings,* published in Moscow, 1929), that *Ochrana* detectives, during the chaos of the March 1917 revolution, had burned the archives housed in the Kazanskaya precinct station in St. Petersburg. These archives, Piast wrote, included "among other documents, as I succeeded in learning later, a thing of fabulous value to the history of world literature—a document confirming the truth of that which has been, since the beginning of the twentieth century, considered a legend—the protocol of the arrest on the street, in the beginning of the 1830s, of an American citizen, Edgar Allan Poe."

John Allan died in 1834 and left Poe nothing. This embittered the budding author who grew more morose and began drinking heavily. He openly denied the existence of God, placing his belief entirely in himself. At one point he wrote: "My whole nature utterly *revolts* at the idea that there is any Being in the Universe superior to *myself.*"

To support himself, Poe took a job in 1835 as Assistant Editor of the *Southern Literary Messenger* in which he published such stories as *Berenice* and *Hans Pfaal,* following these bizarre tales with *The Narrative of A. Gordon Pym.* The following year he married his cousin, thirteen-year-old Virginia Clemm, a sickly child. Then began a nomadic life as Poe moved Virginia and Mrs. Clemm first to New York, then to Philadelphia.

Like John Ruskin (see entry), Poe's association with women was ethereal, not sexual. He wished to worship women through idealized visions, never as flesh-and-blood creatures. There is every possibility that he never consummated his marriage with Virginia Clemm. (Marriage for Poe, on a normal basis, was too harsh a reality.) He hated the present with its oppressive poverty, its day-to-day struggle to survive starvation, that hideous fate that had consumed his mother. He would later write to the New England poet James Russell Lowell: "My life has been *whim*—impulse—passion—a longing for solitude—a scorn of all things present, in an earnest desire for the future."

Poe, after several editorial jobs, began freelancing as a journalist in 1842, but much of what he wrote was fiction which he passed off as factual reporting. These specious stories appeared, for the most part, in the New York *Sun* which specialized in sensational stories like the impossible report on bat creatures observed on the moon fabricated by Richard Adams Locke (see entry). Poe faked one fantastic piece on mesmerism which he entitled "The Facts in the Case of M. Valdemar." Another Poe hoax was headlined in the *Sun* on April 14, 1844: "Astounding News by Express via Norfolk; the Atlantic Crossed in 3 Days; Signal Triumph of Mr. Monck's Flying Machine." Poe had reported that Monck and eight companions had flown the ocean in a balloon in 3 days, landing near Charleston, South Carolina. The story was proved a fake in a few days, but by then the *Sun,* as usual, had enlarged its circulation by thousands.

The writer's real fiction became more and more macabre, his characters deeply sinister and forbidding, although his collected stories—*Tales of the Grotesque, Arabesque*—were brilliantly conceived and written. Though he was known as a book critic and poet in his day, he is best remembered for his chilling tales of horror, "William Wilson," "Murders in the Rue Morgue" (one of the first detective stories in America, based upon the career of Vidocq, the French inspector of the Sûreté), "The Pit and the Pendulum," "The Tell-Tale Heart," "The Gold Bug," "The Purloined Letter," to name a few. His masterful poem "The Raven" is a classic tale of fear.

The strangest story Poe ever wrote was "The Mystery of Marie Roget," which he set in Paris, although the gruesome tale was based upon the murder of pretty Mary Cecilia Rogers, who was mysteriously strangled to death on July 28, 1841. Poe had known the girl, stopping to buy tobacco by the snuff and cigar stand at 319 Broadway in New York where she worked. Poe, even though he was married at the time, dated Mary Rogers, taking her to dinner, sitting in private booths. Following her murder, Poe wrote a series of articles in which he suggested that the police check to see if the dead girl was pregnant, also hinting that she had been killed by an abortionist. Police did check and discovered that Mary Rogers was, indeed, pregnant and her body showed the signs of an abortion. Poe, who was a suspect for a short time, used the case to write America's first thriller, one that established him as a teller of great horror tales. But by then, Poe himself was living a life of horror.

The writer consumed great quantities of liquor, drinking himself into alcoholic stupors that would last for days. His production slowed down and he tried to write under the influence of alcohol and drugs—laudenum and opium, forcing his pet cat at such times to sit on his shoulder. He came to believe in phrenology, a bogus science that claimed to be able to determine a person's morality and intelligence by the shape of the head.

By 1847 Virginia Clemm Poe, who had been invalided for years, was overcome with consumption. Poe was then so poor that he could not afford proper medical attention. Her only warmth as she shivered herself to death on the night of January 30, 1847 on a bare bed was Poe's threadbare army coat. Poe wore this same coat to her funeral the following day. He commemorated his wife's death with the famous poem, "Annabel Lee."

The two years following Virginia's death, Poe's last, brought a nightmare existence to the writer. He drank constantly and was seen haunting graveyards and morgues. He consumed all manner of known drugs and had screaming fits that Mrs. Clemm and his other female admirers could not suppress. To save himself, Poe took a temperance pledge and began to give lectures against the evils of drink. It had wrecked his life and his career, he told grim-faced audiences.

Privately, Poe went to doctors who examined him for mental disturbances. One physician reported that he had a lesion on the brain. (This was later thought to represent syphilis, although this condition was never verified.)

Poe seemed to rally in 1849. He met his boyhood sweetheart Sarah Royster Shelton, then a widow, at a lecture he gave in Richmond, and became engaged to her. It appeared that he might salvage his life after all. He received $1,500 for a series of temperance lectures delivered in Richmond before leaving for Philadelphia to see a friend, John Sartain, a printer. Poe appeared at Sartain's engraving shop "looking pale and haggard, with a wild and frightened expression in his eyes." He told Sartain that he was being persecuted, that

The Schuylkill River, in Poe's time, where the writer thought to drown himself.

"hellish demons in human forms" were on his trail to waylay and murder him.

"He said it would be difficult for me to believe what he had to tell, or that such things were possible in this nineteenth century," Sartain later recalled. Poe stated that on the train coming to Philadelphia, he overheard some men seated behind him plotting to kill him, "and then throw him off the platform of the car."

The plotters, Poe insisted, spoke so low that it would have been impossible for any normal person to hear their sinister words but he, Poe, had such acute hearing, that he picked up every word.

Sartain replied gently: "This scare is a creation of your own fancy. What interest could those people have in taking your life at such great risk to themselves?"

"It was for revenge," Poe said in an ominous voice.

"Revenge for what?"

"Well ... woman trouble."

Sartain managed to change the subject, but Poe further alarmed the printer with "an idea of self-destruction, and his words clearly indicated this tendency."

Poe was silent for a long period then blurted to Sartain: "If this mustache of mine were removed I should not be so readily recognized. Will you lend me a razor, that I may shave it off?"

Sartain said that because he never shaved he had no such implement available, a lie. He said he had a scissors and Poe, trapped by his own excuse, was forced to allow the printer to remove his mustache with the scissors.

That evening Sartain made Poe tea and some food in the back of his shop, then offered him a bed. Poe, listless, suddenly headed for the door.

"Where are you going?" asked the apprehensive Sartain.

"To the Schuylkill [River]," answered Poe.

"A good idea," Sartain said, "a pleasant walk in the moonlight. I think I'll join you."

Poe shrugged and the pair left after the writer slipped off his shoes which he said hurt him and replaced them with the printer's slippers. On the way to the river, Poe asked that several personal effects of his be given to Mrs. Clemm, in the event of his death. When they got to the river Schuylkill, Poe began to talk wildly about ghosts and prisons. They stood close to the water and Sartain tried desperately "to hold him in conversation."

As he peered downward at the inky waters, Poe spoke in a deliberate voice, relating the most fantastic imaginings as fact. "I was confined in a cell at Moyamensing Prison [in Philadelphia]," he told Sartain in a steady voice, "and through my grated window was visible the battlemented granite tower. On the topmost stone of the parapet, between the embrasures, stood perched against the dark sky a young female brightly radiant, like silver dipped in light, either in herself or in her environment, so that the cross-bar shadows thrown from my window were distinct on the opposite wall. From this position, remote as it was, she addressed to me a series of questions in words not loud but distinct, and I dared not fail to hear and make apt response. Had I failed once either to hear or to make pertinent answer, the consequences to me would have been something fearful; but my sense of hearing is wonderfully acute, so that I passed safely through this ordeal, which was a snare to catch me."

Poe went on to state that jailors came to his cell and threatened torture. They offered him a scalding drink, which he declined. Then Poe told Sartain that the jailors had brought his "mother," Mrs. Clemm, into his cell, "to blast my sight by seeing them first saw off her feet at the ankles, then her legs to the knees, her thighs at the hips," and so on. At this point Poe went into a convulsion that lasted several minutes. He sat down.

Sartain asked him how he came to be in Moyamensing Prison.

"I was suspected of trying to pass a fifty-dollar counterfeit note."

Sartain later learned that Poe had been arrested for drunkenness and had been taken to court, not to the Philadelphia prison. He was recognized by a member of the court who told the judge: "Why this is Poe, the poet." He was fined a small amount and sent on his way.

That night the printer walked Poe back to his quarters and, as the writer slept fitfully on his narrow bed, Sartain sat watching him, stretched out nearby on three chairs. Poe appeared calm in the morning. "He saw that he had come out of a dream," Sartain remembered. Poe left for New York.

The writer appeared in Baltimore on September 28, 1849, then vanished. The story of his disappearance is as horror-filled as his own tales. He was reportedly seized by an electioneering band of thugs—the October 3 election was hotly contested—and drugged, then taken from poll to poll as a "repeater," voting fraudulently many times under assumed names.

Doctors were summoned to a Baltimore tavern on October 3 to attend a derelict who was raving in a closed booth. He was penniless, in a drugged or drunken state, and he wore shabby clothes. It was Edgar Allan Poe. He was taken to the hospital and for four days he raved deliriously to phantoms and ghosts that he claimed flitted in and out of the room. Several doctors heard Poe repeatedly say in brief moments of lucidity: "My best friend is the one who would blow out my brains!"

On October 7, 1849, Poe half sat up in bed, looked about the hospital room and said, "Lord, help my poor soul." He fell back on the pillow dead. He was forty.

Edgar Allan Poe was not respected in his own time. It was years before his works achieved high status in American literature. His peers, including Charles Dickens, who did not like him personally after their first meeting, attempted to get his British publishers to print Poe's works. (Dickens also contributed $1,000 to Mrs. Clemm's upkeep following Poe's death.)

One last goulish indignity remained for the author of horror stories. He was exhumed in November 1875 and given a new grave and larger headstone (his old one merely gave the lot number "80"). On that cold windswept occasion, Walt Whitman joined the crowd to commemorate the reburial. Members in the crowd took away pieces of Poe's rotting coffin for souvenirs after gaping at his remains, one of them remarking that the poet's "skull was in excellent condition ... the teeth were perfect and white as pearl."

Ten years later Virginia Clemm Poe joined her husband in his final resting place at Westminster Presbyterian Cemetery in Baltimore. She had been exhumed years earlier after developers unearthed her remains. William Gill, a friend and admirer of Poe's, had kept Virginia's bones in a box beneath his bed until she was reburied with her husband.

Poe's head in relief and a stone raven were etched on his gravestone erected in 1875. The epitaph engraved thereupon was apt: "Quoth the Raven nevermore."

George PSALMANAZAR

Linguist (1679–1763)

Arriving in London from France in 1703, an exotic and decidedly Oriental-looking foreigner who called himself George Psalmanazar established the "Formosan Institute," which taught the upper class of the city the customs, habits and language of Formosa (today's Taiwan). The foreigner who, of course, was an imposter, invented the Formosan language, along with the most outlandish claims to native customs on the island, including the eating of raw meat, particularly cannibalizing the flesh of condemned prisoners. Psalmanazar went on to insist that his fellow Formosans murdered thousands of boys under the age of ten each year, carved out their hearts and burned these gruesome items as offerings each year to propitiate the gods.

The linguist died a rich man, but before his end he admitted that all of his statements, including his widely read book, *The Historical and Geographical Description of Formosa,* published in 1704, were complete fabrications.

R

John RANDOLPH

United States Senator (1773–1833)

For all of its bizarre, unpredictable, venal and outright zany members of Congress, no representative ever matched the antics and viper-like tongue of John Randolph, or Randolph of Roanoke (Virginia), as he was popularly called. He served, on and off, for thirty years in the House of Representatives (1799–1829), until he was elected a U.S. Senator from Virginia (1825–27), proving himself to be an arch-conservative who voted *against* more legislation in his long tenure than *for,* often casting his negative vote merely to be contrary. He opposed President Madison and northern Democrats on all issues as a matter of southern principle. He opposed the War of 1812, even when British troops were violating American soil. He led the fight against the Missouri Compromise and became the chief advocate for state's rights, establishing the position the Confederacy would take twenty-eight years after his death.

A strange disease, never specified by Randolph (probably a form of scarlet fever), attacked the politician at age nineteen, which left him beardless and altered his voice so that when he spoke he sounded like a choir boy with a soprano voice. His appearance and the sound of his voice caused him to be publicly lampooned, but those who made fun of him felt his wrath. He was expert with pistol and sword and fought many successful duels with those who sought to belittle him.

Randolph bragged that he was the greatest horseman in America and to prove it, he once rode nonstop on an 1,800-mile trip that ended in Savannah, Georgia, killing several horses in the process. He also preferred his hound dogs

305

The bizarre congressman, later United States Senator, John Randolph. (Library of Congress)

to human company, bringing his dogs into the chambers of Congress where they would sleep at his feet under his desk.

A Jeffersonian Republican to the marrow in his early days in Congress, Randolph hated the very idea of democracy. He once jumped up in the House to yell: "I am an aristocrat! I love liberty, I hate equality!" When bored or annoyed, Randolph would slap the top of his congressional desk loudly with one of the many riding crops he carried everywhere. Other members of Congress pretended to ignore him, but were secretly fearful that he would attack them with these crops; he had a habit of striking the Congressional page boys on the backside with them, administering stinging blows, if they did not do his bidding promptly.

In 1803, without being urged and with no gossip to cause his announcement, Randolph suddenly rose in the House and told everyone present that he had fathered an illegitimate child and would tolerate no libel on the matter, *if* the subject were ever brought up. Stunned congressmen later whispered that Randolph had lied in order to prove his manhood, but none dared openly challenge the man who was, even then, thought to be slightly unbalanced.

Randolph had proved his courage years earlier. The rich Virginia planter—he owned vast tracks of land in and around Roanoke and claimed to be a descendent of Pocahontas—had declared openly in 1799, when he was first elected to the House at age twenty-six, that the American Army was made up of uniformed "ragamuffins" and "mercenaries." In response, two Marine Corps officers, seeing him at a theater one night, forced their way into his box, seeking redress for Randolph's aspersions against the American military. They yanked at his cape and insulted him, trying to goad him into a fight. Randolph suddenly stood up to his full and imposing height—he stood six-foot-three—and glared at the men with such a look of wrath that they fled in terror before he could raise his riding crop. "You're nothing but puppies!" he called after the fleeing officers. For this affront, Randolph insisted that then President Adams render him a personal apology.

Once, when a member of Congress obliquely referred to Randolph's apparent lack of manliness, the Virginian lashed back with: "You pride yourself with an animal faculty in respect to which the Negro is your equal and the jackass infinitely your superior!" On another occasion, when hearing that Edward Livingston, a political rival, had maligned him, Randolph yelled out in the congressional chamber that Livingston "shines and stinks like rotten mackerel by moonlight!"

Never, Randolph gritted, would he vote for the admission of a new state beyond the original thirteen states. Inclusion of new states, he decreed, would destroy the sovereignty of the Union as it was founded. "Asking one of the States to surrender part of her sovereignty," he shrilled, "is like asking a lady to surrender part of her chastity!"

Anything that smacked of world politics found instant and vitriolic opposition from Randolph, the dedicated isolationist. When members of Congress urged the construction of a powerful navy, Randolph rose to shout in his piping voice: "What! Shall this great mammoth of the American forest leave his native element and plunge into the water in a mad contest with the shark? Let him beware that his proboscis is not bitten off..."

"The Greast Irreconcilable," as Randolph came to be known, fought the Missouri Compromise with tooth and nail, urging the southern states to secede rather than give up slavery on any level; he was a slaveholder. During these debates Randolph was so excited that he could hold nothing on his stomach for days, except gruel and crackers.

Randolph, who later went hopelessly mad and spent his remaining years racing horses to death on his Roanoke estate, thought only of the state of Virginia. All else in America was of no interest to him, an attitude which prompted the poet John Greenleaf Whittier to write this verse concerning Randolph of Roanoke:

> Too honest or too proud to feign
> A love he never cherished,
> Beyond Virginia's border line
> His patriotism perished.

A silhouette of Senator Randolph at his Roanoke, Virginia estate, where he later went mad. (Library of Congress)

Grigori Efimovich RASPUTIN

Mystic (1872–1916)

The "Mad Monk of Russia" was born Grigori Efimovich Novyky in the Siberian town of Pokrovskoye some time in 1872. He grew to be a strapping peasant with hypnotic powers and a sexual charisma that no Russian noblewoman, if certain accounts are to be believed, could resist once he had ingratiated himself to the Imperial Family. As a young man Rasputin joined a heretical sect called the Khlysty, a sect of flagellants who not only beat themselves bloody each night for sins real or imagined, but, as part of their pagan rites, partook of all-night orgies in which couples interchanged sexually at random.

Leading the beatings, wild, naked dances, and taking on more sex partners each night than any other member of the sect, was Rasputin, whose stamina and sexual appetite qualified him as one of the world's foremost satyrs. His very name, given to him by fellow members, signified his sexual prowess in that it meant "debauchee." Rasputin, at the time, was married and had young children, but he nevertheless led the Khlysty cultists in their wild revels each night, forcing his wife to join in the orgies, foisting her naked upon other male members while he sought out the prettiest of the females present.

While ploughing a field one day, Rasputin later claimed, he had a blinding vision of the Virgin Mary and she instructed him to go throughout the land preaching his brand of sexual religion. In truth, Rasputin fled his home town, abandoning his wife and three children because he was under investigation by the local police and orthodox priests outraged at the conduct of the Khlysty.

For several years Rasputin traveled nomadically through Russia, calling himself a *starets,* a self-appointed holy man who claimed to heal the sick and one who practiced the strangest type of baptism known to any religion. Rasputin would enter a town and call a meeting of the ignorant, illiterate peasants, making sure the local priest was absent from the community at the time. He would then proceed to baptize the entire village in his own inimitable fashion, leading the naive populace to the river where he would quickly baptize the males, children and older females. He would then announce that to make the young women "clean of spirit," they would have to undergo the pleasures of the flesh with a holy man, namely himself.

The innocent peasant males, fathers, brothers, and husbands, would stand idly by at these times and watch as their young women—Rasputin was careful to select the prettiest for his sexual blessings—joined the monk in the public baths or river and under his coitional rituals. The spreading of Rasputin's sexual religion produced countless children strewn, all direct offsprings of the monk, from western Siberia to European Russia. On occasions, he would return home to describe in detail his experiences. His blue-eyed wife, Praskovia, submitted completely to Rasputin's lifestyle, believing that his promiscuity was divined by God. Even his daughter, Maria, came to believe that her father's satyrism was heavensent and she later wrote a book glorifying

The mad monk, Grigori Rasputin, at about the time he entered St. Petersburg, Russia.

his every act, including his wholesale orgies with dozens of women, detailing these exploits as high religious rites.

Wrote Maria: "His female devotees ... were drawn to the worship of his phallus, endowing it with mystical qualities as well as sexual ones, for it was an extraordinary member indeed, measuring a good 13 inches when fully erect ... As their passions were aroused, there was a tendency to forget the ritualistic aspect ... and the participants would fall into a general orgy."

Thousands of Russian peasants came to sing the praises of "Father Gregori, our savior," and his reputation spread across the land to St. Petersburg, to which Rasputin traveled in 1903. At the time he was fleeing police in several cities and towns who intended to arrest him at the request of the Russian Orthodox Church, which had condemned him as a heretic; the Khlysty had already been wiped out by this time, its members disbanded.

Fortunately for the mad monk, the flighty and idle noblewomen of St. Petersburg thought him a novelty and invited him into their homes so that he could lecture them on spiritual matters. The first grand palace Rasputin entered was that of the Countess Ignatiev, who was close to the Empress. It was later reported that Rasputin raped the countess and several other noblewomen who attended that first meeting, along with several female servants. The women later gossiped that they had "undergone sexual salvation" at Rasputin's hands. Moreover, they had been hypnotized, they said, by this incredible mystic.

The man who entered high Russian society in 1903 was anything but physically attractive. His best biographer, René Fulop-Miller, described the monk at this time as "ungainly ... coarse ... and ugly ... His big head was covered with unkempt brown hair, carelessly parted in the middle and flowing in long strands over his neck. On his high forehead a dark patch was visible, the scar of a wound. His broad, pock-marked nose stood out from his face, and his thin pale lips were hidden by a limp, untidy mustache. His weatherbeaten, sunburned skin was wrinkled and seamed in deep folds, his eyes were hidden under his projecting eyebrows, the right eye disfigured by a yellow blotch. The whole face was overgrown by a dishevelled light brown beard."

Rasputin's body stench was overpowering. He ate with his hands and his beard was matted with food that rotted in the hairs for weeks on end. He would sometimes go for months without washing his hands or face, claiming that taking baths was hedonistic, the devil's work, that humans must smell like the animals of the woods to keep their "natural order of the flesh," whatever that meant. Rasputin's terrible body odor, however, did not diminish the numbers of high born Russian females who flocked to his filthy apartment to undergo his "baptism of the flesh." In fact, his bizarre behavior only served to whet their appetites.

When invited to the grand palaces of the nobles, Rasputin always excused himself from the large halls, preferring small rooms where he could gather the females about him. He would then go into a wild dance, gazing intensely at those women he wished "to baptize." They were mesmerized rank upon rank and fell prey to his lustful grabs and caresses. "Soon a wide circle of women from all classes of society," reported a biographer, "ranging from ladies of the highest rank down to servant maids, peasant women, and seamstresses, looked on Rasputin as a higher, divine being."

The Empress Alexandra first heard of Rasputin's name from a mystic named Feofan, an ordained priest who had tried, at the Empress' request, to aid her hemophiliac son, Alexis, only heir to the Romanoff throne. Alexis suffered painful and seemingly unstoppable hemorrhaging at the slightest fall. If he merely brushed a sharp-edged table he would begin to bleed. The Empress had tried every known remedy, and had consulted with hundreds of specialists. Nothing seemed to help her son's condition. In desperation she turned to mysticism, consulting many wandering religious zealots. None were able to stop her son's bleeding.

Father Feofan also tried to help the boy but failed. He was sent away, but before he departed the Royal Palace at Tsarkoe Selo, outside St. Petersburg, Feofan mentioned Rasputin's name, saying that he was reported to be the greatest healer in Russia. When Alexandra consulted with Countess Ignatiev, she was told that, indeed, the *starets* was a worker of miracles. She herself had witnessed marvelous healings in her own home, the countess exclaimed, performed by none other than this very Rasputin. The countess neglected to mention the orgies she and her noble-born sisters had joined in with the wild-looking monk.

Rasputin was sent for, arriving at the Royal Palace in November 1905. On the night of his first visit, Rasputin took pains to bathe and wash his face. He wore a clean black robe called a caftan. He said nothing as he was led toward the Czar's study. At the study door he suddenly turned and glared at his guide,

The Czar and Czarina of Russia shown as Rasputin's puppets in this political cartoon.

Россійскій
Царствующій
домъ.

a noble-born woman, and snarled: "What are *you* gaping at?" He then spun about, putting on his best face, the one with the wide and pleasant smile, and rushed into the study where the Czar and his consort waited to greet him. Instead of kissing their hands, as was the custom, Rasputin boldly walked up to the royal couple and kissed them paternally on the forehead.

Ironically, it was only a matter of minutes before attendants came rushing from the nursery to report that Alexis had had another accident and was bleeding. Frantic, the Empress begged Rasputin to do what he could for the child. "Certainly, certainly," the monk replied and was led to the nursery.

Entering Alexis' room, Rasputin fell to his knees in a dark corner. He prayed incoherently as the royal couple fidgeted, listening to their son moan in agony in his bed at the far side of the room. Rasputin was suddenly on his feet, moving quickly about the room, blowing out all the candles except one which he held in his hand, carrying it to the foot of the boy's bed. He held the candle to his own face, close to his eyes and made the sign of the cross as the boy stared at him. Rasputin undoubtedly hypnotized Alexis, and, while he was in a trance, sat on his bed, introducing himself as "your friend, the best friend you have in this world." He began to gently caress the child's arms and legs, including an area that was bleeding, saying all the while: "Now, don't be afraid, Alesha, everything is all right again ... Look, Alesha, look, I have driven all your horrid pains away." He continued his massage, stroking the boy from head to foot. "Nothing will hurt you anymore, and tomorrow you will be well again. Then you will see what jolly games we will have together!"

The bleeding stopped. Rasputin had performed his miracle.

Alexis grew completely dependent upon Rasputin in the months and years to follow, listening spellbound to the monk's wild stories of life in Siberia. Whenever the heir to the throne began to bleed Rasputin was called, and he soon hypnotized the impressionable child to the point where he could actually control the hemorrhaging.

For this inestimable service Rasputin was, at first, allowed the freedom of the palace and given any amount of money he desired. But it was power Rasputin wanted and he got it. Nicholas II and Alexandra became his willing pawns as he proved to be the only one who could keep their son alive. When he entered the palace it was the royal couple who gratefully kissed *his* hand.

Gradually, insidiously, as was his style, Rasputin worked his way into affairs of state, first making suggestions, then demanding that the Czar do his bidding. He was generally obeyed. Whenever the Czar proved critical of Rasputin, the monk would simply blackmail him into submission. Following one of these confrontations, the monk returned to his luxuriously appointed office—apartment to laughingly boast of his conquest to his assembled harem. "Well, I went straight in," he bragged. "I saw at once that Mama [the Empress] was angry and defiant, while Papa [Nicholas] was striding up and down the room whistling. But, after I had bullied them both a little, they soon saw reason! I had only to threaten that I would go back to Siberia and abandon them and their child to disaster, and they immediately gave in to me in everything." He held up his fist and said: "Between these fingers I hold the Russian Empire!"

The office–apartment where Rasputin lived was guarded night and day by Imperial cossack troops, lest some one attempt to injure the monk; he had received many threats against his life after he became what he termed "the czar above the czar." He dispensed political favors to any and all, but for great fees; all paid in gold at his insistence. Some of his fees for obtaining appointments through the Czar—bestowing estates, granting franchises— were not for cash. He traded in flesh. If he knew that a certain nobleman or merchant had a particularly good-looking daughter or wife, he would demand that these women be sent to him for "spiritual guidance."

Incredible as it seemed, most males seeking his favors through the throne readily agreed, escorting their women to the mad monk's apartments and waiting until he had finished his assignations with them. Sometimes there was a waiting line of *several dozen* women, sitting patiently in Rasputin's outer chambers, preparing themselves to partake of sex with the *starets*. Often as not, Rasputin would call a half-dozen women in at a time, ordering them to disrobe immediately— "sinners ashamed of their bodies wear clothing" —and then join him in a room that was really one large bed. The female visitors had heard of the monk's overhwelming body odor by this time and took the precaution of literally bathing in perfume so that their scents would overpower his. Said Prince Felix Yusupov, who hated Rasputin and was the eventual ringleader in a successful conspiracy to murder the monk: "His office smelled like that of a French whorehouse, so thick was it with the scent of perfume. No wonder! He had made of our women whores, low and disgusting creatures, tainted by his awful disease." The last remark referred to Rasputin's having permanent gonnorhea after his nonstop sexual liaisons, or worse, syphilis, a disease many claimed that had made him insane.

The Russian secret police assigned an around-the-clock surveillance on Rasputin and his every guest was noted, including their gifts to the monk, from gold to the number of wine bottles and tins of caviar they carted into his apartments in huge baskets. Rasputin was followed everywhere. Agents watched as he was driven to the estate of Madame Karavia where he frolicked

Rasputin with the Empress in his apartments; Alexis sits next to the monk, his supposed savior; Grand Duchess Anastasia stands behind the Empress.

with the women of the house, got drunk, then ran outside and leaped upon a horse, stark naked, and raced about the palace, drinking wine from a bottle. Rasputin went to the train station one night and entered the compartment of a departing countess, agents noted, having the train wait until he had ravished her repeatedly.

The police reports on Rasputin's nocturnal activities, which amounted to huge volumes after several years, were revealing, to say the least. Here are but a few:

"On the night of 17th to 18th January Maria Gill, the wife of a Captain in the 145th Regiment, slept at Rasputin's."

"26th January. This evening a ball took place at Rasputin's in honor of some persons who had been released from prison, at which behavior was very indecorous. The guests sang and danced till morning."

"16th March. About 1 A.M. eight men and women called on Rasputin and stayed till three. The whole company sang and danced: when they were all drunk, they left the house accompanied by Rasputin."

"3rd April. About 1 A.M. Rasputin brought an unknown woman back to the house; she spent the night with him."

"11th May. Rasputin brought a prostitute back to the flat and locked her in his rooms; the servants, however, afterward let her out."

"On the night of 25th to 26th November Varvarova, the actress, slept at Rasputin's."

On one blustering cold February night, police noted that more than forty women, from 8 P.M. to dawn, visited the monk, some staying no more than fifteen minutes. They were the wives of diplomats and generals, noblewomen, actresses, street whores, maids and even a cook from the Royal Palace. The monk slept with them all, according to the police report, and all left his apartments in happy moods.

Even the Empress, accompanied by her four daughters, visited the monk at his office—apartments, but on these occasions Rasputin was on his good behavior. These visits, however, prompted the leading religious zealot of the day, Iliodor, to denounce Rasputin, a man he had originally sponsored during Rasputin's first visits to St. Petersburg, defending the *starets* against the accusations of orthodox church leaders.

Iliodor obtained the police reports of Rasputin's scandalous behavior and published a reviling pamphlet entitled "The Holy Devil," in which he detailed the monk's intolerable transgressions, labeling Rasputin as "the curse" on the throne of Russia. Further, Iliodor blatantly stated that Rasputin and the Empress were having constant illicit sex, and that Rasputin was undoubtedly enjoying the sexual favors of the four Grand Duchesses. For this libel, Iliodor was banished. Rasputin saw to that.

Like Joseph Balsamo, the notorious Cagliostro (see entry) who once said "I can afflict as well as heal," Rasputin would tolerate no interference with his private or public policies. If a man did not turn over his wife or daughter to him, he was criticized by the monk to the Czar and his fortunes fell. If a diplomat or general took issue with Rasputin, the monk would hold a conference with the

A composite photo showing Czar Nicholas II with his adviser, Rasputin, at his side, originally published in an underground Bolshevik newspaper.

Czar, instructing him to either imprison or banish the offending person, and this was almost always done.

Enemies of the mad monk began to increase in number. First, reports of the monk's behavior—actual rapes of high-born women—were registered with the police. The police threw away these reports or ignored them. Next, members of the court went to the Empress and even Nicholas with stories of Rasputin's excesses, but the royal couple refused to believe the tales. Their beloved "friend" was a saint, they insisted, maligned and slandered because of his divine mission on earth and because he "had the ear of God."

Opponents concluded that more direct action was necessary and assassination began to be plotted in early 1913. The conspirators, however, talked too much and the plot was overheard by one of Rasputin's spies, Sinitsin by name, who warned the monk. The plotters were arrested and jailed.

Iliodor and others then formed a "Committee of Action," and decided that the instrument of their wrath would be a demented creature, Kionia Guseva, a morbidly neuroitic prostitute who was dying of syphilis. She was easily persuaded to right Rasputin's "vicious deeds" by murdering the monk. To that end, she waited outside the monk's quarters. On June 28, 1914, Rasputin appeared in the street to collect a letter from the Empress.

Kionia Guseva ran forward to the *starets,* begging for alms. As the monk reached into his robe for his purse, the prostitute produced a long knife and plunged it to the hilt into Rasputin's abdomen. As he fell forward, Guseva screamed: "I have killed the anti-Christ!" She ran shrieking down the street. Rasputin steadied himself, placing his hand tightly over the bloody wound, staggering into his apartments. A doctor was called and an operation was performed as Rasputin lay on his dining room table. He was saved. The would-be assassin, Guseva, was put into an asylum for life.

While Rasputin recovered, Czar Nicholas led his country into World War I, an act the monk later claimed he would have prevented had he not been hospitalized. Several more plots against Rasputin's life were still-born over the next two years as Russia bled to death in the trenches of the Eastern Front. Rasputin had then little control of the Czar, who was invariably close to the front directing his troops.

The mad monk went on directing policy in Russia during the Czar's absence, having a complete hold upon the Empress through his hypnotic care of Alexis. Prince Felix Yusupov, however, vowed that he would kill the monk and rid his country of "a vile cancer" or perish in the attempt. He and a close-knit group of nobles inveigled Rasputin to his palace on the night of December 29, 1916. As bait the prince used his beautiful wife, Irene, whom he knew the monk coveted greatly. Rasputin arrived drunk and was shown to an empty banquet hall. Yusupov told him that he was late, that the guests had already eaten and departed.

"I don't care about the guests," Rasputin said. "Where is your wife?"

Yusupov told the monk that she would join him shortly, and offered him some cakes and wine, both of which were laced with enough poison to kill a regiment. Rasputin ate an entire tray full of cakes and drank three bottles of the wine while the prince sat in shock. Yusupov finally got tired of waiting for the cyanide to kill his "superhuman monster" and suddenly rushed Rasputin, driving a dagger into him a dozen times until the monk fell to the floor bleeding from his wounds. The prince summoned his co-conspirators and they tied the monk in ropes. Suddenly Rasputin jumped up, breaking his bonds and lurching toward the petrified prince. Yusupov managed to draw his pistol and he emptied this into Rasputin as the monk lunged for him. Finally stilled, the monk was tied with chains and then dragged to the Neva River. The conspirators cut a hole in the ice and dumped the monk's body into it.

Two days later Rasputin's bloated body was found on the river bank. He had somehow survived the poison, the stabbings and the bullets. He had almost survived the frozen waters of the river, but his incredible strength had finally given out just as he managed to punch a hole in the ice and surface. His lungs were filled with water and he was officially listed as having drowned.

A political cartoon picturing Rasputin holding aloft the Czar as his plaything.

Great numbers of Russians, peasants and high-born alike, mourned Rasputin's death. The Empress went into shock. Yusupov and his wife left the country before they could be arrested. (They settled down in New York, the prince dying in 1967.)

A large chapel was built on the royal estate outside of St. Petersburg and into this went Rasputin's body. However, the Romanoffs were toppled two years later and executed, and the monk's chapel was destroyed by revolutionaires. His remains were dragged from his casket and soaked in kerosene, then burned.

Harry REICHENBACH

Publicist (1881–1949)

Beginning with the silent films, Reichenbach promoted motion pictures with the energies of a whirling dervish, or, some later claimed, a mania that could only be found in a lunatic asylum. It was Harry Reichenbach who was assigned to promote the first Tarzan movie, *Tarzan of the Apes,* produced in 1918 and starring Elmo Lincoln. Reichenbach hired a live ape and ordered the beast dressed in a specially tailored tuxedo, releasing the ape in New York Hotel lobbies. He got his publicity for the film and several bills for damaged furniture.

Two years later, Reichenbach promoted *The Return of Tarzan* by smuggling a lion into the suite of a New York hotel occupied by a wild-haired pianist who kept ordering twenty pounds of raw meat at mealtime. Reichenbach however, made sure that reporters heard of this unusual hotel guest and the live lion scampering about. The newsmen arrived at the hotel to find that the guest has registered as T.R.Zan.

When Elinor Glyn's cheap novel, *Three Weeks,* was made into a film, Reichenbach brought the book's racy sections to the attention of postal authorities who promptly banned it from the mails. The attending publicity not only made the film a box office hit but caused the book to become a best seller.

Reichenbach's all-time stunt, as related in his posthumously published autobiography, *Phantom Fame,* was to promote a banal painting from deserved obscurity to world notoriety. The promoter was passing a small art gallery in Brooklyn one day in 1912 when he spotted a painting of a nude rising from the sea; the picture was entitled *September Morn* and had been painted by an unknown French artist named Paul Emile Chabas (1869–1937).

More to vex New York's self-appointed censor, Anthony Comstock, than to reap any personal rewards, Reichenbach spent about fifty dollars hiring a group of unwashed street youths to stand in front of the art gallery window. He then made an anonymous phone call to Comstock who arrived an hour later to witness the children gawking, gaping and making lewd and obscene remarks and gestures before the painting. Comstock publicly denounced *September Morn* as a perverse work of art designed to corrupt the minds of youth. He insisted that the gallery owner and the artist be arrested, which they were.

317

The dealer and artist were acquitted of "contributing to the delinquency of minors." The resulting publicity created by Reichenbach made *September Morn* household words. Chabas made quick arrangements to have copies of the painting run off and more than seven million were eagerly purchased by an alerted public. The portrait of the naked woman rising from the sea was duplicated on umbrellas, calendars, even tattoos.

Chabas revealed before his death that the model for *September Morn* had been a penniless sixteen-year-old waif he had found in a Paris garret. By the time of Chabas' statement in 1937, the year of his death, the model had married a wealthy French businessman and had had three children. He refused to identify her.

Harry Reichenbach, who had brought fame to the painting and its creator, didn't care to know who the model was; he had, without compensation, proved he could promote a third-rate painting to a "modern classic" and that was reward enough.

Robert REIDT

Evangelist (1891–date uncertain)

Friday the thirteenth has always loomed ominous in the minds of the superstitious, but none took that date more seriously in 1925 than a self-styled evangelist and Bronx house painter, Robert Reidt. The unschooled Reidt had read with obsession the news stories concerning a California girl named Margaret Rowan who had claimed that the Archangel Gabriel had appeared to her in a vision and announced that the end of the world would occur at midnight, February 13, 1925, a Friday.

Reidt, using his life savings, placed ads in Manhattan newspapers, asking followers to join him on a rural hilltop on the appointed hour. Scores of the faithful appeared wearing white robes, which had been especially designed by Reidt for the event. Newsmen also appeared and, seconds before the predicted end of the world, began to take photos of Reidt and his followers who were shouting to Gabriel with arms akimbo.

When the hour of doom passed, Reidt angrily pointed to the photographers and yelled: " You ruined it with the flashbulbs from your cameras!"

Armand Jean du Plessis duc de RICHELIEU

Catholic Prelate (1585–1642)

Epileptic and unpredictable, the famous Cardinal Richelieu of France was not only the leader of the Catholic Church in his country, but a powerful, statesman, a minister of King Louis XIII. He led the court intrigues, meddled in overall European diplomacy and foreign courts and took sides during the Thirty Years' War, even against his own country, France, his actions cloaked in secrecy, of course.

Richelieu became so powerful that no king—not even the Pope—dared to criticize him, and he flaunted his power, often endorsing Protestant movements and more often shielding and harboring those who had been branded heretics, such as Tommaso Campenella. When Louis XIII mustered the courage to mildly criticize his minister for his more outrageous policies, Richelieu tongue-lashed his sovereign into silence.

The Cardinal's personal conduct was appalling. He dallied with the king's mistresses and had an ever-flowing number of courtesans streaming into his private chambers. The most beautiful prostitute of Paris, however, Anne Lenclos ("Ninon," see entry), refused his overtures, even after he offered her a fortune to spend one night with him. Richelieu indulged himself at every turn with the pleasures of the flesh, conducting long drinking and eating bouts with aides, then swearing off spirits and food for extended periods of time when he would rigorously diet, along with conducting peculiar exercises, such as leaping over furniture hours on end.

As he grew older, the prelate ordered the kidnapping of political enemies, who were held captive and tortured in his palace. As Founder of the French Academy, Richelieu dictated France's intellectual and scientific posture for years.

The man knew no loyalties. His rise to power was arranged by the regent, Marie de Medici, but when he became chief minister to Louis XIII in 1624, Richelieu not only reversed her pro-Hapsburg policy but had her exiled in 1630. From that point on he ruled France as an absolute dictator until his death in 1642, taxing the people to the point of exhaustion and then depleting the national treasury with his wild expenditures. He became the most unpopular man in France.

Richelieu left more than 1.5 million livres to the crown, and enriched several nephews and nieces. One nephew was left his enormous library, but only on the condition, the Cardinal's will stipulated, that 400 livres a year be paid to a cleaning woman who was to dust the books daily.

Mary Roberts RINEHART

Author (1876–1958)

One of the most popular mystery writers in America for decades (*The Circular Staircase, The Man in Lower Ten,* adapted as a successful play, *The Bat,* in 1920), Mary Roberts Rinehart was a practical woman with a hard-headed business sense that brought her great wealth. But she began to succumb to her own overactive imagination shortly after World War I. The mystery writer and her husband, Dr. Stanley Marshall Rinehart, moved into a luxurious Washington, D.C. apartment. Mrs. Rinehart was the toast of the town, having won the Pershing Medal for bravery for her exploits as a war correspondent. Many of the sixty novels she was to write in her long lifetime were already published and her fans numbered in the millions. She was successful, wealthy and content. And then she began to hear and see things that she attributed to an actual haunting.

The Rineharts went to bed early, exhausted after moving into their new apartment on that first day. As was her custom, Mrs. Rinehart read a book in bed. Some hours later she switched off the reading light and a moment later, she insisted, "something raced through the bedroom." It was as if "a huge dark curtain had been drawn across the room." It was the beginning of what Mrs. Rinehart would later term her "special haunting."

The following day the writer questioned employees of the apartment building and was told, she later claimed, that a politician had died in her apartment and "was haunting the apartment as well as his old office on Capital Hill."

In the weeks that followed, Mrs. Rinehart insisted that her "personal ghost" vexed and terrified her. Her maid came to her rooms at odd hours, bringing her coffee and food when she had not been summoned. There were knocks at the door, and when answered, no one was there. Curtains fluttered, drapes closed across windows without being touched, cold drafts swept the apartment rooms.

The author kept locking her door, but every time she checked the door it was unlocked. Her alarm clock mysteriously appeared time after time in the middle of her bedroom floor. She continually heard dishes and books crash to the floors in the other rooms, but, when checking, found nothing broken or out-of-order. Then Mrs. Rinehart began to find dead birds and bats in the hallways and closets. Her bull terrier took to snarling viciously as if "some unseen thing had advanced upon him." The dog's hairs on his neck would bristle as he leaped frantically into the writer's lap. All these inexplicable events, Mrs. Rinehart swore to her closest friends, were actually happening to her.

Tappings, scrapings, furniture moving without the aid of human hands were further manifestations of the ghost's presence, according to the writer. The haunting came to a halt after the death of Mrs. Rinehart's elderly mother. The ghost, Mrs. Rinehart always claimed, directly brought about the death of the invalided Cornelia Gilleland Roberts, her mother.

Mrs. Roberts had suffered a stroke and was paralyzed. So helpless was the woman that she had to be carried to her bath. The Rinehart maid was preparing the old woman's bath one night when she heard the doorbell ring. Turning on the bath water, the maid went to answer the door. No one was there. The bath water, meanwhile, became searing hot. When the maid returned to the bathroom she looked at the tub and then went screaming hysterically into the night. Mrs. Roberts was in the tub, dead, scalding hot water swirling about her. She died from the shock, Mary Roberts Rinehart always claimed, pointing out the fact that the woman was completely helpless and could not have gotten into the tub from the bedroom by herself. The writer had an answer to the mystery—the ghost did it.

Matthew (Lord Rokeby) ROBINSON

Hermit (1712–1800)

The son of Septimus Robinson, an aide to King George II of England, Robinson was later made Lord Rokeby of Mount Morris in Kent, and by early manhood, he was known far and wide as an eccentric hermit who would rather commune with nature than converse with human beings. When Rokeby did talk to people he shouted so loudly that listeners fled holding their ears.

Disdaining all human company, Rokeby built a small hut near Hythe, right on the beach. He grew to love the water so much that he spent almost every waking moment, from dawn until dusk, in the sea. According to his biographer, Dame Edith Sitwell, Rokeby would stay in the water "until he fainted and had to be withdrawn forcibly from the water."

When the waters of the ocean grew too cold, Rokeby, with liveried servants standing by for hours, soaked himself in an outdoor bath of his own construction. The bathwaters were warmed only by the sun's rays. When hungry, Rokeby called for his servants, ordering them to throw food to him while he stood chin-high in the bathwater. Visitors, aristocratic and common, were asked to stand next to the bath and conduct their business with the splashing gentleman. Commented one offended noble: "I shall never to able to stand the joke of a gentleman's bathing with a roast loin of veal floating at his elbows."

Rokeby let his beard grow the full length of his body and continued to shun the comfort of houses. In the winter he did take refuge in his hut, but kept the windows wide open. He refused to take medicine of any kind and when he once fell ill, he threatened to disinherit a nephew if he called a doctor; he felt that all physicians were "butchers."

Despite his Trojan existence, Rokeby lived to be eighty-eight, dying in December, 1800.

Michael (Harry F. Gerguson) ROMANOFF

Restaurateur "Prince" (1892–1971)

He was known as the fabulous phony, a charlatan and a mountebank who both amused and befuddled America for decades, and he claimed with ardent insistence that he was none other than His Imperial Highness Prince Michael

The bogus "Prince" Michael Romanoff in the 1930s.

Alexandrovitch Dimitry Obelensky Romanoff, Prince of all the Russias and the only surviving son of Czar Nicholas II. He was born, according to varied reports, Harry F. Gerguson (or Gaygusson) in Russia, New York, Ohio or Illinois. Most of the reports about Romanoff were issued by himself to confuse law enforcement officials and immigration authorities. All of them were inventive lies.

It is known that Romanoff had lived as a foster son in the home of F. L. McDavid, a New York banker, and was later taken in by Gordon Russell, a congressman from Texas. Romanoff had been orphaned at an early age and had somehow managed to place himself with well-to-do Americans. Even as a youth, Romanoff could not tell the truth, claiming that he was the descendant of Russian royalty. Following the Czar's death in 1918, when the entire Romanoff family was exterminated at Ekaterinberg, Russia, and knowing that the dead Imperial Family could not refute him, Romanoff claimed to be the Czar's son, an absurd claim but one that was believed by hundreds, perhaps thousands of naive suckers who fell victim to the "Prince's" schemes.

Romanoff was a master of disguises and prided himself in his impersonations. He once estimated that he had employed more than fifty aliases during the 1920s and 1930s, his heyday as a compromising gigolo, imposter, and passer of bogus checks.

One of Romanoffs more daring impersonations was that of a history professor exiled from Russia. He actually convinced authorities at Harvard, who allowed him to conduct classes, that he was a learned Russian scholar whose qualifying papers and diplomas had been destroyed during the Russian Revolution. Also as a Romanoff Prince, the imposter arranged for the sale of various art works in American museums and galleries that had been at one time or other the possessions of the Imperial Family. These art treasures were rightfully his to sell, said Romanoff, as he was the sole survivor of that tragic family.

After traveling to Europe—Romanoff invariably sailed on luxury liners as a stowaway—the Prince wound up in Southern California in the early 1920s. Here he pretended to be a visiting European film director and actually signed with *several* studios to make films, receiving, of course, hefty advances before disappearing. He bilked several English actors, including C. Aubrey Smith, who advanced him money thinking him to be a Captain Reginald Chitterin, late of the British Army and down on his luck.

The Los Angeles *Examiner* exposed Romanoff in 1927 and he fled east; his trail could be followed by the phony checks he left in his wake from hotel to hotel. Arriving in New York, the charlatan stowed away on the *De Grasse*. The first evening out the bogus prince found himself in the grand salon, dressed in a tuxedo and meeting dignitaries at the captain's table where he had been hastily seated with apologies for having been overlooked as an important passenger. He spent the voyage in the stateroom of a wealthy woman he met that night. The dapper, mustachioed Romanoff, who stood only five-feet-three-inches, was a great womanizer, and females, young and old (but always rich, at the prince's insistence), found him irresistible.

Arriving in Paris in 1928, Romanoff went to his favorite watering hole, The Ritz Bar. The manager took one look at him and raced forward, angrily waving a heavy bar tab Romanoff had run up and failed to pay in 1922, and shouting: "You won't get a drink here, in fact you are not welcome in this establishment, until this bill is settled, and I mean immediately!"

Romanoff politely took the bill, examining it carefully. Then, with gloved hands, he tore it to pieces and flung it haughtily on the bar, ordering a magnum of champagne from the bartender.

"Are you insane?" screamed the manager. "What about the bill?"

Romanoff gave the manager a sideways glance of annoyance and lied in his stentorian voice: "*You* are obviously unaware, sir, that all bills in France are invalid after a period of five years. The bill was dated 1922 and this is 1928. You see how it is?"

Nonplussed, the manager shrugged and accepted Romanoff's statement, thinking him to be a legal expert on French law. With that the prince ran up another bill for hundreds of dollars and signed the tab, having no intentions of ever paying, of course.

After mulcting a small fortune from several attractive widows on the Riviera, Romanoff headed back to America. Even though he could have afforded deluxe accomodations, he stowed away on an American ship and was not discovered as a nonpaying passenger until the vessel arrived in New York Harbor. As Romanoff was heading for the gangplank to disembark, ship's officers blocked his path, confronting him with his illegal passage.

"Excuse me, sir," said one officer, "but would you tell us what your cabin number was on this trip?"

Romanoff brushed aside the officer and began walking down the gang-plank, saying imperiously over his shoulder: "The entire ship is my cabin!"

Going to the West Coast in 1931, Romanoff took on another identity, passing himself off as the famous illustrator, Rockwell Kent. He visited bookstores, signing the guest registers as Kent, and was introduced to authors and publishers as the illustrator. He was feted and partied as Kent and, oddly enough, Kent's own books enjoyed a rebirth. The real Kent later stated: "My books have never had such a run in California before." Kent was less enthusiastic about Romanoff's) impersonation when he discovered that the prince, in Kent's name, had contracted to illustrate a book, for which Romanoff received a sizeable advance. Kent, nevertheless, did perform the illustrations after the pleading publisher stated that he had already widely advertised Kent as the artist for the book.

By that time, late 1932, Romanoff was back in New York where he was picked up by immigration authorities claiming that he had no record of American citizenship. While the records were checked, Romanoff was kept at Ellis Island. The imposter, however, charmed authorities into letting him return to his Manhattan apartment to retrieve his clothes, under guard, of course. When the prince and his plainclothes guard arrived in New York, Romanoff easily convinced his companion to accompany him to several speakeasies. "I wish to say farewell to my friends," Romanoff told the guard, "as I believe my departure from this wonderful city is imminent."

The pair made the rounds of speakeasies, the guard enjoying himself to the point where he merely shrugged when Romanoff told him that he was stepping outside for a moment, explaining that "I've neglected to pay our cabdriver, old boy." With that, he vanished.

Some days later Romanoff called immigration officials to tell them "I have not been murdered and am in good health. Don't worry about me." He had no intention of giving himself up. Authorities, incensed at being made to look ridiculous, assigned more than 100 federal agents to track down the bogus prince. He was found in a speakeasy some weeks later and was taken back to Ellis Island, still clinging to a champagne glass and a bottle of Mumm's.

Following a hearing, Romanoff was sent back to France where he was imprisoned for using an American passport that belonged to a U.S. diplomat. Released in 1933, Romanoff managed to return to America. He immediately assumed new roles to perpetrate lucrative frauds. As "Prince Romanoff," the imposter seduced a wealthy, attractive married woman, Mrs. Wilma E. Gould of New York, whose husband sued for divorce, naming Romanoff as correspondent. Mrs. Gould brought a half-million dollar conspiracy suit against her husband, after learning that her brother-in-law, Congressman Norman Gould, had hired Romanoff to compromise her in the old badger game. (Mrs. Gould was subsequently awarded $25,000.)

Romanoff went on with his con games, undaunted. He convinced college officials in Virginia that he was an esteemed historian, one John William Adams, a full professor, and was permitted to teach classes. He also impersonated politicians in Washington, D.C. and financiers in New York.

By 1939 Michael Romanoff was so well known that he had worn out his imposter routines. His Hollywood friends, Humphrey Bogart and Robert Benchley, convinced him to reform and suggested, that since he was the perfect host, had great charm and impeccable manners, he would do well with a restaurant in Hollywood. Financiers Joseph Schenck and John Hay Whitney, at Benchley's urging, put up the money for the swanky restaurant which was named Romanoffs'.

The restaurant became a Hollywood landmark. The fabulous phony, who finally took out American citizenship, accumulated greater riches through his restaurant than all his impersonations and scams had managed to produce. He also became a celebrity in his own right, and made cameo appearances in several Hollywood films, including *The Arch of Triumph* and *A Guide for the Married Man*. One impersonation he refused to discard was that of being of the blood royal and to this day many of his customers continue to believe that they had been guided to their booths by none other than the last of the Romanoffs, Prince Michael himself.

Jacob RUPPERT, Jr.

Baseball Club Owner (1867–1939)

The colorful New York brewery magnate and owner of the powerful New York Yankees during the days of Ruth and Gehrig was, in reality, fairly ignorant of his players' ability and of baseball in general. Coupled to that, the Colonel—he had been given an honorary title which he insisted everyone use in addressing him—befuddled most everything his managers, chiefly Miller Huggins, told him regarding the team.

Once in St. Petersburg, while watching his famous "Murderer's Row" — Ruth, Gehrig, Lazzeri, Meusel—the colonel noticed that his sluggers were striking out or merely hitting weak singles.

"What's going on with my team here, Miller," Ruppert asked Huggins. "The boys are not hitting the ball. Are they finished as players?"

"No, no," laughed Huggins. "Don't worry, Colonel. Right now *the pitchers are ahead of the hitters*. Happens every spring."

Some days later Ruppert was joined in the stands by a competing club owner who witnessed the weak hitting of the Yankees. "Looks like old age has overtaken your players, Colonel" the club owner snorted. "A sad end to a great team."

"Aww," the colonel said with a wave of the hand, "my players are all right. You must understand that *the pitchers are now ahead of the catchers*."

Another story concerned Ruppert's blind faith in new prospects for his club, but it was a faith tempered with monetary apprehension. One of the colonel's scouts, Paul Krichell, told Ruppert that he had discovered a young ballplayer with great potential and upstanding character; in fact the hopeful was a practicing preacher.

Ruppert nodded and signed an advance check for $1,000 for the player, telling Krichell to have the boy report to one of the farm clubs. Weeks went by and the youth failed to appear at the club. A frantic search was made to locate the rookie, but he had utterly vanished.

The colonel angrily called in his scout Krichell, telling him: "It's all your fault. You give this fellow $1,000 of my hard-earned cash and he doesn't show up. And this fellow is a preacher, even. So what do I get for my money? Can you tell me that?"

Krichell replied cautiously: "Well, colonel, there's the good will, and *you know* that the boy who took your thousand dollars will sure be praying for you."

Money was the colonel's worry, even though he had millions. He spent most of his time close to his investments—his brewery and at his ballpark, Yankee Stadium, seldom missing a game. His star hurler was Waite Hoyt, one of the great pitchers of all time, and Ruppert, who called him "Hoyts," paid particular

The colorful Colonel Jacob Ruppert of the New York Yankees; he knew about money, not baseball.

attention to the pitcher's performances, even though he rarely understood the finer points of the hurler's qualities.

Once, when the Yankee's won a doubleheader, Ruppert bounded into the clubhouse to congratulate Joe Bush, who had won his game 15–2 and Hoyt, 2–1. Old Jake lavished praise on Bush while Hoyt waited expectantly for his kudos. Finally the colonel turned to the pitcher and said sadly: "Hoyts, why the blazes can't you win your games, fifteen to two like Joe here?"

Hoyt was constantly plaguing the colonel for much deserved raises. This often led to hotly exchanged words, Ruppert always emerging triumphant. After winning a number of games, Hoyt went with grim determination to Jake Ruppert's brewery one day, resolved to getting the raise that had so long eluded him. Ruppert, knowing the reason for Hoyt's visit, kept his star pitcher waiting for more than an hour in the outer office. When the colonel finally did appear he found Hoyt, having nothing else to do, studying the pictures on the walls of the outer office.

"Ah, my dear Hoyts," beamed the colonel, "I see you are looking over my wonderful pictures, huh?" He put a fatherly arm about the pitcher and began an inventory of the graphics on the wall. "That one is of the Ruppert Building which cost me $3,500,000. This one is of my estate, which went for $1,500,000. These pictures here are all of my splendid brewery which I would not sell for less than $6 million. And there—there is my prized possession, Yankee Stadium which I would not sell for $5 million!"

"Yes, colonel, that's interesting," said the peevish Hoyt, "but I think we should talk about my contract for next year and that raise we have been discussing. I had a very good season and I think we should talk about that raise right now."

Suddenly Ruppert withdrew his arm from the pitcher's shoulder, appearing to be offended and hurt. "Hoyts, my boy—a raise? You players are all alike, and I thought you were—well, I treat you like my own son."

"Let's talk about the raise, colonel," Hoyt said defiantly.

"What do you think, Hoyts," Ruppert said, putting his hands indignantly on his hips, "That I'm a millionaire?"

John RUSKIN

Critic (1819–1900)

England's stellar art critic during the Victorian era, Ruskin was also a universal scholar whose vast knowledge expressed in brilliant essays in the fields of architecture, nature, society and economics made him one of the leading intellectuals of his day. He was also a master poet so respected that, upon the death of Tennyson, Prime Minister Gladstone wanted to make Ruskin the Poet Laureate of England, but was persuaded against the move since it was well-known privately that John Ruskin had by then become mentally unbalanced.

That there was insanity in Ruskin's family was evident from the actions of his ancestors; his grandfather, an Edinburgh grocer, lived a wild life before moving to Bowerswell, near Perth, where he went insane and killed himself in 1817, two years before Ruskin's birth.

A manic depressive, Ruskin's mind began to slowly deteriorate at middle age. Critic Kenneth Clark wrote that at one time "his attack of mania lasted about six weeks. After his recovery he accepted, with perfect candor, the fact that he had been mad, and seems rather to have enjoyed describing his symptoms to his friends..." Coupled to his manias, Ruskin suffered as a celebate, who had many women in his life but never performed the sex act. He was also what psychiatrists term a nympholeptic, one wholly entranced with young girls who have not reached puberty. Beyond that, the poet masturbated excessively—he called it "a suicide committed daily"—and, as a result, was overcome with remorse and self-recrimination.

Born on February 18, 1819 near London, Ruskin's parents were cousins (such in-breeding, some later stated, planted the seeds of insanity in Ruskin). He was educated at Oxford and, since his father was a wealthy sherry merchant, he was able to travel extensively through Europe in style, observing various architectural fashions and, particularly, the painting of the period. His first major work, *Modern Painters* (in five volumes), championed the much-

Critic John Ruskin in 1865.

327

A Ruskin portrait of his wife Euphemia; he refused to consummate their marriage.

abused landscape artist, John Turner. Ruskin went on to write definitive works in architecture, poetry, economics, botany, ornithology and geology, proving himself to be one of the great minds of the nineteenth century.

At seventeen Ruskin fell in love with Adele Domecq, the teenage daughter of his father's business partner in Spain. He could not bring himself to propose marriage and went off to study at Oxford instead, his unrequited love for the darkly beautiful Adele driving him to fits of hypochondria and despair. In April, 1847 Ruskin married a nineteen-year-old Scottish girl named Euphemia Gray, whom he had known when she was a small girl. Effie Gray Ruskin was informed on her wedding night by her twenty-nine-year-old genius husband that he wished to remain a virgin and that he wanted to refrain from having sex for six years. Angry, Effie nevertheless agreed to this strange pact. The real reason Ruskin did not consummate his marriage, it was later stated, was because he was shocked to see his wife disrobe and display pubic hair; he believed that women, up to that moment, possessed bald-pated pubes as he had seen on female statues.

Said Kenneth Clark in *Ruskin Today:* "He had a boyish notion of femininity, half kitten, half fairy queen, and when confronted with the real thing he shrank back in horror ... Since his wife was not the fairy kitten which he had anticipated, he could not be bothered with her. She became simply a nuisance." Effie had the marriage annulled in 1854. She later married John Everett Millais, a protege of Ruskin's. While still married to Effie, Ruskin himself encouraged his wife to see Millais, and hopefully have an affair which would relieve him of his duties as a husband.

In 1858 Ruskin fell in love with a beautiful ten-year-old girl named Rose La Touche, who had been sent to the intellectual by her mother to be tutored. (Mrs. La Touche herself was then genuinely in love with Ruskin.) Ruskin vowed secretly that he would marry his beautiful Rose when she became of age. He waited seven years; by then Rose's mother had become embittered by Ruskin's rejection of her and had turned Rosie against the intellectual.

Ruskin's elusive love, Rose La Touche, shown in a portrait he did of her as a teenager.

Further, Effie, hearing that Rosie might marry Ruskin in spite of her parent's objections, wrote the girl a letter in which she stated that her former husband was either impotent or a latent homosexual (albeit those terms were not employed in that genteel era). "He is quite unnatural," wrote the vengeful Effie to Rosie, "and in that one thing all the rest is embraced."

Rosie continued to hold out against Ruskin's marriage proposals, taunting and tantalizing him, until she was twenty-six. At that time, Rosie La Touche grew steadily ill. As a last act of vengeance, Rosie sent Ruskin a letter stating that she would see him only if he told her he loved her more than God. Ruskin did not reply and Rosie died on May 26, 1875.

Ruskin had increasing bouts of madness following Rosie's death and blamed his parents for his disasterous lovelife, writing them accusatory letters. "You fed me effeminately," he wrote to them, and "thwarted in me the earnest fire and passion in life!"

Ruskin's self-portrait, a distorted image of a tortured man.

Ruskin (left) shown in old age
with Henry Acland, 1893.

Ruskin went off to a girls' school, Winnington, where he regressed to the point of playing games with the little girls, acting as one of their number, becoming a dedicated nympholeptic, admitting offhandedly that he was incapable of relations with mature women.

As he grew older, Ruskin addressed everyone as "darling" and manifested effeminate movements and manner of speech. His mind began to fail in the early 1880s and, during one of his lectures, he began to sputter incoherently, making what the shocked audience easily interpreted as obscene gestures. He was escorted from the podium by attendants.

In the last eleven years of his life, John Ruskin lived in a silent coma, shut off from the world by his own desire, fondling his memories of nymphs until his death on January 20, 1900.

George Herman ("Babe") RUTH

Baseball Player (1895–1948)

One of the most beloved and unforgettable figures in American baseball was George Herman Ruth, top slugger for the New York Yankees in the 1920s, home run hitter supreme (until Henry Aaron topped Ruth's 714 lifetime HRs in 1974). He was known to millions of fans as "Babe," "The Bambino," and "The Sultan of Swat." During his spectacular career he established great records, first as a pitcher with the Boston Red Sox, then as a powerhouse hitter for the Yankees. "He came out of a tree," said pitcher Waite Hoyt of his friend Ruth. "He wasn't human."

Between 1914 and 1934 Ruth earned more than $1 million and the building of Yankee Stadium in the Bronx was certainly prompted by the enormous crowds he drew, which caused the stadium to be dubbed "The House That Ruth Built." (He had, however, nothing to do with the candy bar, Baby Ruth, which was named after President Grover Cleveland's daughter Ruth; when Babe

George Herman "Babe" Ruth, great ballplayer and eccentric, shown just after he left the Boston Red Sox and joined the Yankees (and before the famous pin-stripe uniform went into effect).

attempted to market something called Babe Ruth's Home Run Candy, the Curtiss Candy Corporation successfully blocked the enterprise on patent violations.)

An orphan, Ruth was raised in a Baltimore semicorrectional school. He lived a hard, bitter life as a youth, but somehow managed to retain an innocence that endeared him to almost all who met him. Sports writers lionized him, competitors bowed to him, and children loved him. Until 1974 when Aaron topped his career home run record, Ruth owned the record books as the only man to ever hit fifty or more home runs four times, forty or more home runs thirteen times, and two home runs in a game seventy-three times. Even when he was old, fat and through in 1935, Babe Ruth, as a magnificent swansong in one of this final games, smashed three home runs out of the ballpark.

Ruth's feats in the ballpark were the stuff of legends. Once, when the Yankees were playing the Washington Senators he drove a line shot home run through the legs of pitcher Hod Lisenbee. Then there is the "called shot" where Ruth, almost out on strikes, stepped out of the batter's box in Wrigley Field on October 1, 1932 in a World Series and pointed to center field, to tell the world where he would place the next pitch and then smacking the ball for a home run in center field. At least most sports writers, from Paul Gallico to Grantland Rice, insisted this happened: Chicago pitcher Charlie Root who served up the homerun ball, denied it, but the denial was in his best interest.

Charley Root, the Chicago Cubs pitcher against whom Ruth batted his classic "called" home run in 1932; Root insisted that Ruth never picked his shot, but the rest of the world disagreed.

Judge Kenesaw Mountain Landis, the powerful baseball czar who could do nothing for the Babe when he was suspended for threatening to beat up Manager Miller Huggins.

Off the field, Ruth, married twice and having two daughters, was a rampaging bull, a drinker who broke all the rules ever invented for a ballplayer, a womanizer whose sexual appetite was insatiable. For most of his stupendous career, Ruth was overweight. He loved to eat and the fare mattered little. He would eat just about anything and at all hours. He once began to satisfy his gargantuan appetite during a ball game, downing in the dugout two sandwiches, nine hot dogs, and six bottles of soda. He finished this "snack" by gnawing on an apple. Before the end of the game Ruth collapsed and was taken to the hospital with "the belly ache heard "round the world." When he recovered, Ruth said: "I knew I shouldn't of eaten that apple!"

Ruth was always in trouble with his managers and particularly hated being bossed about by the diminutive Miller Huggins, whom he once threatened to beat up. Huggins suspended him. Ruth went to Judge Kenesaw Mountain Landis, who was the first commissioner of baseball, but Landis could not or would not order Huggins to revoke the suspension or the accompanying fine of several thousand dollars until he apologized.

It was weeks before Ruth worked up enough nerve to make the apology, but Huggins stalled him until *he,* Huggins, was ready to hear the apology and take back the errant ball player. Ruth's temper had nothing to do with his break with teammate and fellow slugger Lou Gehrig; they had been friends for years, but their wives, especially Gehrig's domineering mother—who once criticized Ruth's wife for not dressing her children properly—led to the ruination of their deep friendship. (Ruth nevertheless warmed the hearts of the baseball world when he embraced "The Iron Man" in 1939 during Gehrig's farewell appearance in Yankee Stadium; Gehrig was by then stricken with an incurable disease.)

333

The Babe in his declining years with the Yankees, flanked by manager Joe McCarthy and Ruth's best friend, Lou "The Iron Man" Gehrig, before Mama Gehrig destroyed their friendship. (UPI)

The limelight was Ruth's favorite place and he seldom missed an opportunity to appear at a public function. He agreed to meet visiting Queen Marie of Romania during her tour of the United States, but he overslept. Christy Walsh, the Yankee manager finally woke Ruth up. "What's the matter with you, Babe," yelled Walsh over the phone. "Did you forget that you're supposed to meet the Queen of Romania this morning? Everybody's down here at City Hall waiting for you!"

"*You* meet her," grumbled Ruth in his sleepy, raspy voice. "Them foreign dames give me a pain."

Ruth was a disaster at remembering names. On a coast-to-coast radio show he substituted "Duke Ellington" for the "Duke of Wellington." Bandleader Paul Whiteman asked Babe to introduce him to members of the Yankee team. Ruth obliged by taking Whiteman down the bench, introducing all the great players to Whiteman, calling them all by the nicknames Ruth gave to his fellow players. "This is Rabbit Ears, here's Horseface, this is Applehead, Whiffy,

Muttonchops, Big Mouth," etc. Though Whiteman had shaken hands with every member of the team he hadn't learned one of their true names.

Like Ty Cobb (see entry), Ruth was a great imbiber. He could consume endless amounts of alcohol and still play the next day without a jangled nerve, smacking out home runs as if swatting mosquitoes. During his drinking bouts he was liable to do anything he thought amusing. He got drunk with slugger Al Simmons one night in 1930 and went to see the legendary Bix Biederbecke in his hotel room. Jazz saxophonist Bud Freeman was on hand to witness, horrified, as Ruth playfully grabbed Simmons around the neck and held him out the window, twelve stories high, as Babe casually conversed with the stuttering jazzmen.

Among the Babe's many eccentricities was his deep belief that deformed persons were good luck charms if they crossed his path before a game. He once bumped into a dwarf with a hunchback while racing, late, into Yankee Stadium and had a magnificent day. For the rest of that season, 1928, Ruth hired a hunchback to cross his path at all home games, he would rub the man's back and then run inside the stadium, feeling that "the luckies" were with him.

His luck ran out in 1948 when cancer struck him down and killed him. Ruth was not told that he was slowly dying from cancer. He undoubtedly knew. Yet when the venerable Connie Mack came to visit him in the hospital, Ruth displayed his usual off-handed humor, cracking: "Hello, Mr. Mack—the termites have got me!"

Unpredictable and wild, unschooled and yet full of street wisdom, Babe Ruth went to his grave as one of the most loved celebrities in the history of sport. In the words of Paul Gallico, writing in his memorable *Farewell to Sport:* "Ruth will always be one of the great success stories, the fairy tale come true— From Rags to Riches, or the Orphan Who Made Good. It is one of the favorite fables of our democracy, and when it comes to life as it sometimes does in startling places, we are inclined to regard the lucky character as more royal than royalty ... [His] was the gift of being able to deliver where there was something important at stake, when it meant the most, when the greatest number of eyes were upon him ... just as Ruth hit his home run for the sick boy the day he promised to do so."

S

Russell SAGE

Financier (1816–1906)

Born and bred on a New York farm, Sage began work early as an errand boy in his brother's grocery. He later became a clerk and then a salesman, acquiring several stores until he established himself as a wholesale grocer, becoming enormously wealthy. Sage moved into Wall Street in 1863 where he made millions in stocks and bonds.

Sage later bought railroads and vast real estate, but he seldom spent his money. Though not as mean a miser as Hetty Green (see entry), the tycoon seldom spent a dime when it was unnecessary. For years he wore a single $10 suit and rode trolley cars to work, eating only an apple for lunch or a bowl of penny soup.

When Sage died, his widow, Margaret Olivia Slocum Sage (1828–1918), spent every waking moment giving his money to charity.

George Bernard SHAW

Playwright (1856–1950)

Witty, acerbic, prudish, iconoclastic—all of these terms perfectly suit the dramatist and social reformer, George Bernard Shaw, whose eccentricities, real

e quirkish and great British playwright George Bernard Shaw, who called Americans oobs" and feared germs, doctors and operations. (Wide World) or manufactured, were rampant. The Irish-born playwright produced hortatory works that were masterpieces in spite of his preachiness—*Arms and the Man, Caesar and Cleopatra, Man and Superman, Major Barbara, Pygmalion,* and many others.

A dedicated curmudgeon, Shaw took great delight in insulting his peers, including fellow members of the intellectual Fabian Society, founded in 1883. He had little regard for women after being seduced by a nymphomaniac, one Jenny Paterson, at age twenty-nine. He refused all sex for fifteen years thereafter, until marrying in 1898, wedding Charlotte Payne-Townsend, an heiress, and even then he spent most of his honeymoon ignoring his bride and writing a play.

Shaw was an unswerving vegetarian, which he later insisted was solely responsible for his long life; he ate the produce of his own garden and, much to the constant vexation of his cooks, oversaw the preparation of all his own meals. The playwright was also a fanatic about germs, stipulating that no germs could be airborne, but were produced in sick body cells inherent from one generation to another. Epidemics, Shaw said, came mostly from laundries where handkerchiefs from diseased people infected the clothes of healthy persons. Shaw's laundry was done on his own premises.

The playwright bitterly opposed most hospital operations including Caesarean births, removal of appendix and tonsils, vaccination and vivisection. In addition to being a health fanatic, Shaw loved to deliver G.B.S. insults which he thought helped his prestige as a lovable crank—lovable he was not—and promote his work. It was Shaw who was oddly selected to speak to America on the first trans-Atlantic telephone call. He said: "Hello, America—how are all you boobs?"

Many of Shaw's plays were made into films, all of which, upon viewing, he hated, but then he hated Hollywood with a deep passion, thinking that the heads of the great studios were idiots. When Samuel Goldwyn (see entry) offered Shaw an enormous salary to write film scripts, the playwright scoffed: "The trouble, Mr. Goldwyn, is that you are only interested in art—and I am only interested in money."

Despite his hatred for Hollywood, Shaw appeared before the cameras in 1928 for the first time to introduce one of his filmed plays, an appearance that prompted the American playwright, Sherwood Anderson, to comment: "Satirists should be heard and not seen."

When Shaw appeared in New York in 1933, he took particular delight in ridiculing the American public, telling reporters that the only salvation for the United States was for its politicians to rip up the Constitution. He spent most of his time in Manhattan driving about the city in taxicabs, ogling skyscrapers.

The playwright's own impossible temper was his final undoing. In 1950 Shaw was playing croquet with friends in England. Always a bad sport, Shaw missed a shot, and angrily kicked the croquet ball so hard that he slipped and fell, dislocating a hip. Complications set in and the great crank died on November 2.

Richard Brinsley SHERIDAN

Playwright (1751–1816)

The brilliant Irish-born dramatist produced an amazing body of work by the age of twenty-eight, six major, highly polished plays that made him famous and rich, including such productions as *The School for Scandal* and *The Rivals*. In 1779, the twenty-eight-year-old playwright woke up one morning and instantly decided that he would write no more. When asked by friends why he had come to this decision, Sheridan merely shrugged and said: "It is a good idea to quit." He never wrote again, and never gave a reason for his inexplicable decision.

Upton Beall SINCLAIR

Author (1878–1968)

With more than eighty-odd books to his credit, the crusading muckraker, Upton Sinclair, is best remembered for his exposé of Chicago meatpacking firms, *The Jungle,* which was read by a shocked President Theodore Roosevelt and led to the establishment of the Pure Food and Drug Act of 1906. "I aimed at the public's heart," Sinclair later lamented when referring to *The Jungle,* "and hit its stomach." He would later win the Pulitzer Prize for another novel, *Dragon's Teeth,* in 1943, but his fame would never exceed that which *The Jungle* produced.

Sinclair, when not churning out books, occupied most of his time championing quack remedies, and weird cure-all machines that most sane persons would disavow in a moment. He believed that fasting could remedy any ailment, and wrote in *The Fasting Cure* (1911) that if one starved oneself all manner of deadly diseases could be overcome, including syphilis, cancer, liver ailments, tuberculosis, asthma, colds, Bright's Disease and locomotor-ataxia.

In another work, Sinclair stated that physicians were wrong to prevent prolonged fasting: "I would not like to guess just what percentage of dying people in our hospitals might be saved if the doctors would withdraw all food from them!"

Author Upton Sinclair, who believed starvation was a cure-all, shown here broadcasting a speech during his 1934 campaign for the governorship of California.

Sinclair also gave his utter belief to occult fakers, supporting clairvoyant crackpots and séance stuntmen who claimed to produce spirits from "the other side."

The prolific author, after various enterprises that failed, ran as a Democrat for the governorship of California in 1934, a bitter campaign that ended in his defeat. After that, Sinclair became reclusive, continuing to turn out novels and nonfiction works almost to his death in 1968.

Isaac Merrit SINGER

Inventor (1811–1875)

The first all-American product to sell widely to a world market, even predating the harvester, was the sewing machine as invented by an unschooled mechanic, Isaac Singer. Actually, Singer did not invent the sewing machine, but refined it to a low-cost product and, in doing so, made a fabulous fortune which he spent like a wastrel on a spree. Other models had existed in one cumbersome form or another since the late eighteenth century. Yet Singer's modification and his iron-clad patents gave him a virtual monopoly on sewing machines.

Singer was born in Oswego, New York on October 27, 1811, the son of a millwright. Leaving home in his early teens, Singer labored as an unskilled worker in many New England manufacturing plants. He was, however, always tinkering with new gadgets and, by 1839, he had developed a rock-drilling machine. Ten years later he invented a wood and metal carving machine. Even though he held patents on these inventions, Singer made little money and was compelled to continue working as a mechanic. In that capacity at a Boston plant, he was asked to repair a Lerow and Blodgett sewing machine. Singer spent two days refining the product so that it could perform continuous stitching, developing what amounted to a new machine. A year later Singer, with the aid of Edward Clark, a New York lawyer, secured a patent on the machine and his fortune, along with Clark's, was permanently established.

In 1851, Singer marketed his sewing machine by employing unusual business practices, a "buy now, pay later" credit system of purchase that swept the country and caused the sale of more than 100,000 of his sewing machines inside of a few years. By 1854 Singer and Clark had monopolized the industry. The Clark family took over direction of the I.M. Singer Company in 1863, when Isaac retired to his fleshpot pleasures.

A natural-born actor, Singer, once he came into his great wealth, was fond of posing in public, showing off his expensive attire and jewels. He even dabbled with the stage, giving performances where he told little jokes, an act on the Chautauqua circuit that would be known in the next century as that of a stand-up (and third-rate) comic. "Why is a Singer Sewing Machine like a kiss?," he would ask his audience while stroking his luxuriant beard. "Because it *seams* so good!"

Singer built an ostentacious mansion on Fifth Avenue, where he resided with his wife and many children. He ordered the construction of a strange vehicle, a two-ton canary yellow carriage that could accommodate thirty-one passengers with a nursery at the rear and seats for a small orchestra. (Singer liked music when he traveled.) It took nine horses to pull this monstrosity up and down the streets of Manhattan.

Called a "vulgar brute" by his partner's wife, Singer spent his last twelve years on earth pleasuring himself with sex. He was a veritable satyr, having several mistresses before divorcing his wife. Along with the mistresses was a host of illegitimate children Singer refused to adopt or support. One of his concubines, Mary Ann Sponsler, finally sued, telling her sordid story to the press. Other mistresses came forward demanding child support. Singer quickly divorced his wife and raced off to England with one Katherine McGonigal, the younger sister of Mary McGonigal, who had also been one of Singer's women in New York.

Once in England, Singer built a fabulous mansion at Torquay on the Channel coast. He quickly got rid of Kate McGonigal and married Isabella Boyer, with whom he settled down. The old profligate died on July 23, 1875 at Torquay, but not before siring a total of twenty-five children—the number may have been higher—eight of whom were legitimate. His legitimate offsprings inherited his enormous wealth and, of the lot, Paris Singer, named after the city in which he was born, became the most celebrated.

Paris Singer kept up family tradition by having numerous affairs with attractive women, the most famous being the dancer Isadora Duncan (see entry). He later joined Addison and Wilson Mizner (see entry) in creating the Florida land boom around Palm Beach during the mid-1920s.

Joanna SOUTHCOTT

Religious Leader (1750–1814)

An unschooled, illiterate farm girl living in Devonshire, England, Joanna Southcott always nurtured ideas that she had been devined to establish a new religion. In 1792, Joanna announced to the world that she had the gift of prophecy. Further, she predicted, on the morning of October 19, 1814, a miracle would occur in the skies over England. She quoted the following scripture (from Revelation 12:1–2): "And there appeared a great wonder in heaven; a woman clothed with the sun, and the moon under her feet, and upon her head a crown of twelve stars: And she being with child cried, travailing in birth, and pained to be delivered."

When asked to identify the woman scheduled to appear in the heavens,

Joanna said that it was she, inferring that she would appear as part of the Deity. Southcott's strange prophecy was ballyhooed by William Sharp, who acted as her advance man whenever she was to speak. The seeress not only spoke, but collected great amounts of money as way of donations.

In the following three decades the woman penned dozens of incoherent and illiterate manuscripts in which she made a number of prophecies. She also kept a "treasure box" in which, she said, were the answers to problems the world would face in centuries to come. Tens of thousands of followers came to believe in Joanna as they waited expectantly for the heavenly miracle to occur at the appointed hour in 1814.

The miracle, however, did not materialize on October 19, 1814, even though an ailing Joanna prolonged her life for the event. When she died ten days after the date of her unfulfilled prophecy, hordes of followers disowned her.

Gertrude STEIN

Author (1874–1946)

Born to wealth, Gertrude Stein studied psychology under William James at Radcliffe College and later studied brain anatomy at Johns Hopkins University. In 1903, Miss Stein took up permanent residency in Paris, making her address, 27 Rue de Fleurus, into a famous salon. Like her brother Leo, Gertrude considered herself a master arbiter of art and began buying up works of the impressionists and other artists, including Pablo Picasso, before these artists were known worldwide. Her purchases were made cheaply and the scores of paintings that adorned the walls of her salon served as her annuity, or so she thought.

Stein was a pioneer in stream-of-consciousness writing, aiming for concreteness and extreme simplicity of diction. Her works, however, proved to be confusing and obtuse, purposely so, in that she went out of her way to avoid punctuation and generally ignored syntax. Many of her works—*The Making of Americans, Lucy Church, Amiably,* and *Tender Buttons* are almost unreadable.

Author Gertrude Stein, a master of the insensible.

Stein shown with her secretary and lifelong lesbian lover, Alice B. Toklas.

The most popular work Stein penned was a gossipy tome about her fellow Paris expatriates, cleverly entitled *The Autobiography of Alice B. Toklas,* Miss Toklas (1877–1967) being Stein's secretary, lifelong companion and lesbian lover. The sexual liaison between Gertrude and Alice was well known, even in the 1920s, when Stein's salon thrived with visiting artists and writers whom she "discovered," including Hemingway, Matisse, Braque, Picasso, and Juan Gris. The two women, dowdy and repulsive of figure and face, were inseparable. They had lovers' quarrels constantly in front of their patrons and proteges, and often excused themselves in the middle of a tea or social gathering they were hosting to retire to a back room where, oblivious to their guests, they would make up in loud lovemaking. (This last report was later rendered by none other than Ernest Hemingway.)

Stein is best remembered for her famous line: "A rose is a rose is a rose is a rose," which signified, of course, the blossoming of that particular flower. She is also credited with the profound remark, "you are all a lost generation," which Hemingway employed as a prefatory statement to his novel, *The Sun Also Rises.* The real circumstances under which Miss Stein made the remark, however, are considerably less than profound. She was visiting a garage with Hemingway, inquiring when her auto would be repaired. The garage owner merely shrugged and pointed to two mechanics asleep beneath her car, an empty bottle of wine nearby. Stein merely shook her head and carped, "you are all a lost generation," much the same way one might say "you are thoroughly useless bums."

An intellectual and physical oddity for her day with her short cropped hair, constant stare and bullying manners, Gertrude Stein went to her death in 1946 thinking she had left a great literary estate and would be remembered as one of the foremost judges of modern art. In truth she is read little today and her selection of art was a case of having the luck and money to purchase the work of a talented crop of new and destitute painters, obtaining great art treasures more out of whimsy than knowledge.

Alice B. Toklas, following Gertrude's death, was left only a small amount of cash, the Stein family denied her Gertrude's art collection and the woman died impoverished in 1967.

Charles Dillon ("Casey") STENGEL

Baseball Manager (1890–1975)

Hall of Fame member Stengel played, coached and managed on seventeen professional baseball teams during his long and colorful career. He was one of the game's most unforgettable characters, a clown prince of the sport who never failed to amuse the public and astound his players with unpredictable behavior.

Stengel was a salty talker, too. Once, when playing for the Giants in an exhibition game down south, Stengel put on an amazing display, hitting three home runs and making spectacular catches in the field. The game, however, did not stimulate him, as the crowd numbered only a few hundred.

That night Stengel attended a banquet in the town where, as the guest of honor, he was asked to speak. Casey stomped to the podium and peered out at the enormous crowd in the dining hall. Then he said: "Ladies and gentlemen, it's nice to see so many of you here tonight—but where were you bums this afternoon?"

He was also rough on players, especially the group of oddities that made up the Brooklyn Dodgers in the days when he coached third base. He once signaled Tony Cuccinello to round second, stretching a comfortable double into a triple. Though there was plenty of time, Cuccinello seemed to trot into third

Casey Stengel, the colorful manager who spent fifty years clowning in baseball, shown as the Yankee manager in 1949 and in 1959. (Wide World)

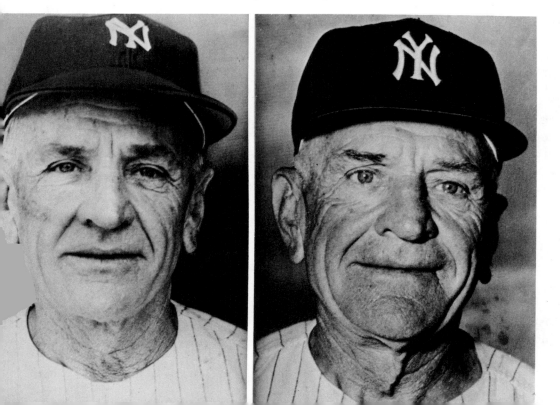

base where he was promptly tagged out. Stengel went berserk, yelling at the player and grabbing Cuccinello around the throat. "You bum!" roared Casey. "How come you came into base like that—why didn't you slide like I learned you?"

Cuccinello shook loose and looked at the red-faced Stengel with a hurt expression. "I couldn't do it, Casey. I would have busted all the cigars in my pocket!"

When Stengel was announced as the new manager of the New York Yankees, he gathered together his favorite camp-followers at Toots Shor's, which was also his favorite watering hole. The cronies wined and dined at Casey's expense, then began to figure the odds for the coming season, each writing on the tablecloth the number of games they expected Stengel's team to win.

"Well, Casey," one friend chirped, "I can't see your team doing any less than winning the pennant. I mean, look at the tablecloth, it's all here in black-and-white!"

When the group adjourned, Casey hung back, then carefully removed the tablecloth and folded it neatly before slipping it under his arm. He started for the door with a great smile on his face.

Toots Shor, seeing all this, rushed forward, shouting: "You crumbum, Stengel! Who do you think you are?" (Toots was a rabid Giants fan.) "You can't come into my joint and steal tableclothes, even if you are the new manager of the Yankees. Now hand it over."

Stengel continued to grin, holding the tablecloth for dear life and heading for the door. Over his shoulder he said sweetly to Toots: "I've got to have this one—I just won my first major league pennant on it!"

Winning was of the essence to Mr. Stengel, no matter the cost, even his own skull. When managing the Dodgers one year Casey was beaned accidentally on the head in practice before a game, as pitcher Frenchy Bordagaray was warming up. At first Stengel thought to take a bat to the wild-throwing pitcher, but realized he needed Bordagaray's arm that day. His pitcher won and Stengel gladly forgot about the beaning. Bordagaray did not.

Bordagaray walked up to the feisty Stengel in the clubhouse and said in a serious voice: "You know, Casey, I think I can keep on winning if I can hit you on the head every day for luck."

Louis T. STONE

Journalist (1875–1933)

In 1895, a cub reporter working for the small town *Evening Citizen* in Winstead, Connecticut needed $150 to pay a pressing debt. There was no way out of it for Louis T. Stone. The only way he figured he could obtain such an astronomical amount in that day was to invent a big news story for a large metropolitan daily newspaper in New York City.

His fabricated story sold, and then it got to be such a habit for Stone to create his own spectacular news for money that he became known as the Winstead Liar.

Some of the more famous Winstead Liar stories which were published in respected newspapers across the country were: A tree on which baked apples grew; a farmer who picked his hens for market with a vacuum cleaner; a rooster that stopped a train; a deaf and dumb pig; a three-legged bullfrog; a hen that laid a red, white and blue egg on July 4; a Plymouth Rock hen that hopped off a railroad engine's cowcatcher when "Plymouth" was called, and left an egg in payment for her ride; a cow that grazed in a horseradish patch and gave burning milk; a cat with a harelip that whistled "Yankee Doodle"; a man who painted a spider on his bald head to keep the flies away.

Stone became so famous for his tall yarns that he rose in national prestige. His own townspeople of Winstead loved their fame and rewarded Stone, who had become the managing editor of his newspaper by 1933. After his death that year on March 13th, the town put a roadsign outside the city limits that greeted visitors with these words:

"Winstead, founded in 1779, has been put on the map by the ingenious and queer stories that emanate from this town and which are printed all over the country, thanks to L.T. Stone."

William Ashley ("Billy") SUNDAY

Evangelist (1863–1935)

The American public had never seen anything like him. He was a mortal storm raging against the Devil, alcohol, foreigners, modernism, tobacco, immoral women, slang, cabarets, motion pictures, anything that might tempt the human soul. He was Billy Sunday, the greatest evangelist to ever stir up the sawdust trail of revival meetings. And from 1896 to 1917 he spoke to an estimated 100,000,000 people, converting one percent of them to his calling, all before the existence of radio, TV, or any other form of mass communication.

Sunday was born in Ames, Iowa on November 19, 1863; his father died in the Civil War a week after his birth and his mother soon followed her husband to the grave. Little Billy was raised an orphan, but graduated from high school in Nevada, Iowa. During his summers, Sunday played baseball constantly, joining a local team. Sunday was fast, perhaps the fastest outfielder Cap Anson had ever seen. The manager of the Chicago Whitestockings hired the fleet-footed youngster after seeing him play for the Marshalltown, Iowa team. Sunday told Anson that he had developed his speed as a member of the local volunteer fire department while running to catch up with the horse-drawn fire wagon as it roared from the stationhouse. He had also worked as an errand boy, farmhand, hotel clerk, even an undertaker's assistant. Ball playing was just another job, but one where he could have fun, the youth told his new employer.

A weak hitter, Sunday more than made up his deficiency with a bat by his superb fielding and running. He played professional ball from 1883 to 1890, as a member of the Chicago, Pittsburgh, and Philadelphia teams. As a base stealer, Billy Sunday was unequalled; in one season alone he stole ninety-five bases, a record that stood until Ty Cobb (see entry) topped it in 1915.

As was the case with most early-day ballplayers, young Billy spent most of his leisure hours off the field either drinking or gambling. It was a dissolute but demanding life which the ballplayer seemed to embrace wholeheartedly. Just how and when Sunday's conversion to the Bible trail took place is still in doubt. Billy told many stories concerning his abrupt spiritual transformation.

He met a beautiful girl from the Jefferson Park Presbyterian Christian Endeavor at a social gathering in Chicago, Sunday once said, falling in love with her. Quite naturally, she would have nothing to do with a ne'er-do-well ballplayer who drank whiskey, chewed tobacco, played pool, rolled dice and, worst of all, was rumored to have visited houses of ill repute. The girl's rejection of him set his mind to thinking of the better life.

Then there was the story Sunday told of how he was playing in a crucial championship series between Chicago and Detroit in 1886. "It was the last half of the ninth inning," Billy recalled for rapt revival audiences. "Two men were out and Detroit, with Charley Bennet at bat, had one man on second and another on third. He had two strikes on him and three balls called, when he fell on a ball with terrific force. It started for the clubhouse. Benches had been placed in the field for spectators and, as I saw the ball sailing through my section of the air, I realized that it was going over the crowd and I called, 'Get out of the way!' The crowd opened and as I ran and leaped those benches, I said one of the swiftest prayers that was ever offered. It was 'Lord, if You ever helped

Ex-baseball player turned evangelist, Billy Sunday calls "out" to sinners. (UPI)

a mortal man, help me get that ball!'" Sunday caught the ball and made up his mind that he would serve the Lord thereafter.

A more down-to-earth story had Billy drunk one afternoon, sitting with his fellow ballplayers in a Chicago gutter. A Salvation Army band at this time marched down the street, its members singing gospel songs. So stirring did Sunday find the music that he immediately renounced his wicked ways, reportedly standing up on wobbly legs and telling his friends: "I'm finished with this life. I'm going to Jesus Christ. We've come to a parting of the ways."

"Aww, sit down you rube," said one of the ballplayers.

"You're right," said Billy staunchly. "I am a rube, and I'm going to stay a rube."

This conversation was not wasted on Sunday. Years later he would hurl himself at an audience, introducing himself as "a rube of the rubes, a hayseed of the hayseeds." At first there were no audiences. Billy went to the YMCA, working as an assistant secretary in the Chicago office. In this capacity Sunday met an ancient evangelist named J. Wilbur Chapman, who used him as an advance agent.

It was Billy's job to go ahead of Chapman into small towns, and distribute leaflets and paste papers on walls that heralded the arrival of the evangelist. And in this way Sunday learned the business of revivalism—half prayer meeting, half vaudeville—held beneath a circus tent, the aisles coated with sawdust. When Chapman grew too old to make his circuit rounds, a group of ministers asked the energetic Billy to replace him.

At first Billy approached his job with a stiff collar and a somber sermon which yielded few conversions and brought scant crowds to his tent. Then Billy began to liven up his show, becoming absolutely athletic on the stage and before the podium. His gyrations and gymnastics startled and stunned his audiences and he salted his sermons with tough street talk, harangues that bruised the mass ego of the crowd. Before long he became a preaching wonder, drawing thousands to his meetings. He would begin like a gathering storm on

Billy about to make his famous "slide for souls."

the plains until he was a veritable tornado tearing up the stage which he stomped and kicked and pounded. He broke chairs for emphasis, pretending the furniture to be the skin of the Devil. He smashed podiums. As he sweated forth, he ripped off his suitcoat, then his vest, until he was down to an open-collared shirt dripping with perspiration.

Next would come his wild impersonations of wicked humans. He would prance peacock proud across the stage imitating a society matron more concerned with jewels, furs and plumes than with her "immortal soul." He would slow his gait to the mincing steps of what Billy called the "phony liberal preachers" who allowed their flocks to wander into perdition. He would next stagger wildly about the stage pretending to be drunk and convincing all that he was a sickening, wobbly-legged dipsomaniac for moments, falling to his knees with a thud to vomit (offstage) before his astounded audience. He was then the banker smoking the cigar, the farmer chewing the plug until, gasping and hacking and coughing from the health-destroying tobacco, he gagged and spat.

Suddenly himself again, Billy pointed out the Devil, right up there on the stage with him. "See the blackguard, folks, the foul-smelling cloven-hoofed creature from the fires? This is how we take care of bozos like him." And with that Sunday would begin to shadow-box an invisible Satan, landing power-house blows as he traversed the stage and back until knocking down the beast and stomping on his chest. "See what I mean, folks? You *can* knock him out—he'll go down!"

And always, the highlight, the crescendo of his crouching, bobbing, jumping and weaving performance was the famous baseball slide. Sunday would begin at one end of the stage, shouting his message all the while that a sinner was always trying to slide into heaven as a player would slide into home plate. Then he would slide almost the entire length of the stage—boards greased to aid his movement—only to be called "Out!" by God "You're out, mister! You can't slide under the pearly gates—you walk in or you don't win the ball game!"

Billy's performances at revival meetings were athletic and exhausting, often causing women in the audience to faint and men to crow like roosters. (UPI)

Thousands flocked to see Sunday week after week. From 1904 to 1907, Billy Sunday seemed to convert all of America, with four to five thousand stepping forth each week to be "claimed by God," taking the temperance pledge against not only liquor, but tobacco and lustful ways.

As Sunday's success swelled, he became enormously rich through "gifts" from his flock, a millionaire before World War I. Yet he never relaxed, never let up. He was always moving as if in the throes of some strange cabalistic rite or St. Vitus Dance. He never let up on his audiences either. Billy would spot a man in the audience who looked to him to be a heavy drinker. He would point in the general direction of the man and shout that "a man who drinks is a dirty, low-down, whiskey-soaked, foul-mouthed, bull-necked hypocrite!" Invariably the guilty party would shoot from his seat wailing and rush forward to be saved.

Most often, Sunday would indict the entire audience, shouting his motto: "Get right with God! The church needs men who will fight, not weasel-eyed, four-flushing, mushy-fisted, hog-joweled, pussy-footing, jelly-spined, sponge-columned Christians!"

And always he laced his rousing verbal attacks with baseball images. "Oh, Lord, give us some coaches out at this Tabernacle so that people can be brought home to you. Some of them are dying on second and third base, Lord, and we don't want that!" If the crowd held back when it came time to take up the collection, Sunday would silence the chorus that always sang at this time, and moan and groan: "Lord, there are a lot of people who step up to the collection plate and fan. What we need now for Your church is home runs!" If Billy spotted any parishioners he thought were cheapskates, he would shout: "Take a stand there, and get into the game!"

He had his detractors, mostly sophisticated newsmen and writers, living in the large cities such as H.L. Mencken and poet Carl Sandburg. It was Sandburg who once attacked the ever-bouncing Billy with: "You slimy bunkshooter ... I like to watch a good four-flusher work, but not when he starts people puking and calling for doctors." The poet was referring to the many hundreds in Sunday's audiences who became so emotionally drained by his performances that they swooned, fainted, or grew ill.

The evangelist knew how to handle critics, thundering his answer from the podium. "Lord," he would intone, his arms akimbo, his eyes raised heavenward, "there are always people sitting in the grandstand and calling the batter a mutt!"

He had an answer to any challenge and a quick one. At one meeting, Billy was badly frightening his audience with hot images of fires that awaited below for sinners. The jam-packed tent was utterly silent except for the sound of his voice booming: "Beware the wrath to come! I warn you sinners who do not find the path of righteousness that there will be weeping and wailing and gnashing of teeth!"

An ancient crone rose slowly to her feet, startling the preacher with her piercing scream: "I ain't got no teeth!"

The normally gentle poet Carl Sandburg was incensed by Billy Sunday's wild revival meetings, calling the evangelist a "slimy bunkshooter."

"Fear not, madam," soothed Billy Sunday. "Teeth will be furnished for one and all!"

On another occasion, Sunday was in the middle of an impassioned address when a loud voice interrupted him with the question: "Who was Cain's wife?"

For a moment Sunday paused, amazed at the audacity of someone severing his eloquence. Then he snapped back: "Oh, I know you atheists, and I say to you that the desire for knowledge is worthy of praise but, my good man, I also want to warn you—don't risk damnation by seeking to know too much about other men's wives!"

When America entered World War I, Billy, who had been an avowed pacifist, suddenly did a complete turnaround. The Kaiser, he prayed fervently before a crowd of thousands, should "go to hell with the rest of them!" He also told an enormous throng that every able-bodied man should enlist, then prayed to heaven that God "strike down in his tracks" any draft dodgers or slackers.

With the coming of the Eighteenth Amendment, Sunday's temperance caused appeared vindicated. Prohibition was the law of the land and he and the Dry forces had won. On the day the new law went into effect, July 16, 1920, Billy Sunday called together 10,000 followers in Norfolk, Virginia where he held a mock funeral for Old John Barlycorn, gleefully sending the deposed "despoiler of man's brain and soul" to his grave in a twenty-foot casket strapped to a horse-drawn carriage.

Wailed the triumphant Billy: "Goodbye, John. You were God's worst enemy. You were Hell's best friend ... The reign of tears is over." Then he turned to the host and wept as he said: "The slums will soon only be a memory. We will turn our prisons into factories and our jails into storehouses and corncribs. Men will walk upright now, women will smile, and the children will laugh. Hell will be forever for rent."

Prohibition had just the opposite effect, bringing with it the worst reign of debauchery and wholesale killing known in America to that time. The 1920s produced the flapper and the flask, the Charleston and high skirts; everything and anything modern was good. Billy Sunday was history, a has-been still sputtering about motherhood, virtue and America. By 1928, the man who had once swayed millions by his earthy oratory was back to preaching at county fairs, drawing only a few of the faithful. Billy shunned the big cities, but made a surprise appearance in Detroit that year. Despite expensive advance hoopla announcing the evangelist's coming, few seemed to care. Sunday himself showed up in the offices of the Detroit *News,* begging for some publicity.

An editor called one of his photographers to his desk telling him: "Show this guy out to the alley and take his picture."

"Who is he?" inquired the photographer.

"One of those religious nuts—used to be a ball player."

Billy Sunday died seven years later on November 6, 1935 at Winona Lake, Indiana.

John Cleves SYMMES

Army Captain (1780–1829)

Symmes, born in New Jersey, had illustrious relatives, including Judge John Symmes, who served in the Continental Congress and helped to found the city of Cincinnati. At twenty-two, Symmes joined the army as a private and soon earned promotion. During the War of 1812, his distinguished gallantry and leadership in three separate battles, where he led bayonet charges, earned him his captain's bars.

Staying in the army after the war, Symmes served in frontier posts along the Mississippi. He resigned his commission in 1816 and set up a trading center at St. Louis, which was then in the Missouri Territory. Here Symmes married a widow and adopted her six children. The union produced four more children.

To while away the hours, Symmes purchased a large telescope and spent hours each night studying the sky. He began to read every available book on the subject of astronomy. The rings around Saturn fascinated Symmes and after long examinations of this planet he came to a startling conclusion: "The principles of concentric spheres or hollow planets does exist." He applied that theory against the make-up of the earth itself, coming to believe that the earth had five concentric spheres, one inside the other, with openings at the poles that were several thousand miles in diameter.

He rejected Newton's idea of gravity, believing that gravity had been created by an "aerial elastic fluid [which] creates a *pushing* instead of a *pulling power.*" Rotating formless matter, he also came to believe, took on the dimensions of spheres ..." therefore a nebular mass in rotation, as our earth during its formation, will not assume the form of a solid sphere, but rather of a hollow one." He reinforced his logic by pointing to other hollow objects such as bone and human hair.

So consumed with his new-found belief was Symmes that, as a man of action, he made his wonderful discovery known to the world on April 10, 1818, mailing out hundreds of flyers to members of the United States Congress and scientists throughout Europe and America.

Said Symmes' circular:

> I declare that the earth is hollow, habitable within; containing a number of solid, concentric spheres, one within the other, and that it is open at the pole twelve or sixteen degrees. I pledge my life in support of this truth, and am ready to explore the hollow if the world will support and aid me in the undertaking. John Cleve Symmes of Ohio, Late Captain of Infantry.
>
> N.B. I have ready for the press a treatise on the principles of Matter, wherein I show proof of the above proposition, account for

Captain John Cleves Symmes, who "knew" that the earth was hollow and urged an expedition to the worlds inside our world.

various phenomena, and disclose Dr. Darwin's "Golden Secret." My terms are the patronage of this and the new world, I dedicate to my wife and her ten children ... I ask one hundred brave companions, well equipped to start from Siberia in the fall season, with reindeer and sledges, on the ice of the frozen sea; I engage we find a warm and rich land, stocked with thrifty vegetables and animals, if not men, on reaching one degree northward of latitude 82; we will return in the succeeding spring. J.C.S.

To allay what fears the scientific community might have for his possible lunacy, Symmes took the precaution of also sending with his circulars a recent medical report verifying him as sane. Only the Russians and certain Congressmen in the United States responded favorably to Symmes' fantastic proposal. Yet no offers of direct financial support were forthcoming. Symmes decided to campaign for his idea, moving his large family to Kentucky where he wrote numerous articles regarding the openings at *both* poles, North and South. He inundated newspapers with his pieces and several published his work so that within a few years the outlandish theory was being referred to as the Symmes Hole Theory, one that began to gather adherants, even distinguished men like Kentucky Congressman Richard Johnson. Further, Symmes took to the lecture trail, going to Cincinnati and other large towns in the Ohio River area to convince the public first-hand that other worlds existed inside the earth. He became specific, alarmingly so, during his discourses, insisting that "the shell of the earth is about one thousand miles thick, and the edges of this shell at the openings are called verges, and measure, from the regular concavity within to the regular convexity without, about fifteen hundred miles."

Proof of his theory was everywhere, argued Symmes. The bright twilight of the Arctic areas proved his case. "This twilight, coming from the north," he stated, "may be caused by the sun's rays thrown into the interior through the southern opening, which by two refractions from the inner concave surface, would pass out at the north over the verge, and produce there this strong twilight." Then there was the migration of birds and animals to consider, said Symmes. "There is a land beyond the frozen Arctic belt, withir some beasts, fowls and fish go to at the approach of winter and whence they return in the spring sleek and fat."

Attacks against Symmes began subtly in 1820 when a novel, *Symzonia; A Voyage of Discovery,* authored by one Captain Adam Seaborn, lampooned the captain's theory. *The American Quarterly Review* later satirized Symmes by stating that men living inside the earth could weigh no more than eight ounces. "It would be one of the advantages of these inner men," smirked the magazine, "that they might fly through the air, with great ease, by the aid of a lady's fan."

Supporters attempted to ride to the rescue. Congressman Johnson actually petitioned Congress to finance an expedition to Symmes' holes in 1822 and 1823, but the idea was rejected or put aside as "unsound" and "unscientific." This governmental decision did not dissuade a rich doctor named Watson from financing a private expedition in October 1829 when two ships, the *Annawan* and the *Seraph,* set sail from New York, bound for the Symmes hole at the South Pole. The expedition was a disaster. Varied accounts reported that the ships abandoned the search when running into heavy seas, or landed at the South Pole but search parties were lost in snowstorms, or the captains and mates were overpowered by fearful, mutinous crews who turned to piracy along the coast of Chile. It was known in fact, however, that neither of the ships reached the South Pole.

The ardent Symmes never had the opportunity to lead his own expedition. He was badly injured in a fall from a lecture stage in Canada and was carted home to Ohio where he died in the arms of his family on May 29, 1849. The captain's theory, however, did not die with him. Several disciples penned books expanding upon the belief in a hollow earth. James McBride published a strongly supportive work in 1826 entitled *Symmes' Theory of Concentric Spheres.* Almost thirty years following his father's death, Americus Vespucius Symmes published another pro-Symmes book in 1878. Wrote Americus: "A hollow earth, habitable within, would result in a great saving of stuff," thus reasoning that God, being a frugal Entity, would not waste matter by creating solid planets.

Although Symmes' fabulous idea was eventually proven false after several arctic expeditions successfully reached the North and South Poles, the good captain did serve to inspire a host of fiction writers to produce marvelous stories based upon his notions: Edgar Allan Poe's "MS Found in a Bottle," and the unfinished *Narrative of Arthur Gordon Pym* by the same author, and of course, the granddaddy of the inner earth stories, Jules Verne's *Journey to the Center of the Earth.*

Stanislaus SZUKALSKI

Sculptor (1896–date uncertain)

Szukalski, born in Poland, was a gifted but strange sculptor who traveled to Chicago following World War I to make his reputation. Renting a cheap loft, the artist fairly wrecked the building by attempting to get a ten-ton marble block lifted to his third-floor garret. He had to knock out an outside wall to

A fragment of Szukalski's massive "Prometheus Bound."

finally have workmen swing the enormous block of marble into the room using pulleys. As soon as it rested on the floor, the marble block crashed downward three floors, fortunately killing none of the occupants on the lower floors.

Szukalski, however, continued to work with huge pieces of granite and marble, chipping out his creations eighteen hours a day. One day in 1922, Ben Hecht, a celebrated Chicago newsman, discovered Szukalski and invited several art critics to view his work in the artist's walk-up studio.

One of the art critics carried a walking cane and, as he inspected an enormous Venus executed by Szukalski, he poked and jabbed at the statue, commenting: "That's nice ... That's fine."

"Excuse me," Stanislaus said, stepping up to the critic. He snatched the cane from the startled critic. "One does not poke the art of Szukalski." He broke the cane over his knee.

"Who do you think you are?" cried the offended critic.

"The greatest artist in the world," responded Szukalski in a calm voice, and, with that, grabbed the critic by the collar and the seat of the pants and ran him over to the long flight of stairs leading downward, hurling him into the air. Fortunately the critic was only bruised in his long fall, but Ben Hecht never again invited critics to appraise Szukalski's work.

Sculptor Stanislaus Szukalski, who had the habit of throwing critics down stairs.

Tiring of Chicago, Szukalski returned to his native Poland where, after a few years, his works were suddenly acclaimed as great national treasures. He was commissioned to put up statues all over Poland and did so, only to see these monumental works destroyed by the Nazis at the beginning of World War II. Following the war, Stanislaus Szukalski, a forgotten artist, moved to southern California where he worked as a ceramicist, until vanishing.

T

Leo TAXIL

Author (1851–1913)

Taxil hated Freemasons and enlisted all in France who would share his abhorrence for this secret society. He organized an anti-Mason group called the Society of Free Thinkers and then went on to attack both the Masons and the Vatican, penning a libelous biography which he called *The Secret Amours of Pius IX*. He was brought to court and fined 65,000 francs, but he succeeded in getting the indictment quashed through powerful friends. Taxil then went on to author another spurious book, *The Scandalous History of the Maid of Orleans*.

The Frenchman saved most of his venom for the Masonic Order, authoring a series of books which purported to reveal the secret Masonic rites, quoting so-called eyewitnesses who had seen the Masons invoke the Devil in ceremonies akin to the Black Mass.

Not until April, 1897 did the irresponsible Taxil confess that he had invented all the "findings" in his books, but, he said to a throng of incensed Catholic clergymen in Paris, he was vastly aided in his endeavors by a gullible clergy who accepted his wild statements about the Masons. With that Leo Taxil fled the meeting hall, laughing hysterically.

John TAYLOR

Publisher (1824–1897)

Taylor ran a small publishing firm in London and was given to publishing books with eccentric theories, the most colossal of these being *The Great*

Pyramid: Why Was it Built? And Who Built It?, which Taylor also authored. For arcane reasons, Taylor believed that the Great Pyramid was not constructed by the Egyptians at all, but by an Israelite whose actions were directed personally by God. And Taylor named the architect—Noah. The author reasoned that if Noah could build the Ark, he was certainly capable of putting up the Great Pyramid.

For further proof, Taylor offered involved mathematical equations known only to the Creator of the Universe (and supposedly Mr. Taylor), mathematical equations that corresponded with the pyramid, such as the sacred cubit mentioned repeatedly in the Bible.

Taylor's work was not widely accepted and his book did poorly with the reading public. He did, however, inspire a host of other crackpot pyramidologists who wrote and published scores of books on the subject which further clouded the true identity of the pyramid's designer.

Cyrus Reed TEED

Alchemist (1839–1908)

Born in rural New York, Teed served as a corpsman in the Union Army during the Civil War. He later attended Eclectic Medical College in Utica, New York, studying herb remedies. A few years later, Teed set up a medical laboratory of sorts in Utica, but, instead of seeking remedies to ailments, he busied himself with alchemy, positive that he could change lead into gold.

During one of his experiments, Teed later related, he suddenly heard the voice of a ghostly woman. This apparition told him that he had evolved through many famous personalities in the past and that now he was ready to assume his most important role as a human; he was to be a scientific messiah who would explain, simply and directly, the makeup of the cosmos.

Explanations of our universe simply poured from Teed thereafter. He wrote and published his "learned visions" in a book he called *The Cellular Cosmogony* under the name of Koresh (Hebrew for Cyrus).

Teed told the world that the universe was egg-shaped; the stars, sun, moon, planets, our own green earth were all *inside* this egg which had seventeen layers and was 100 miles thick in density. We could not see the shell because of the thick atmosphere, Teed insisted. The planets really didn't exist as actual bodies but were "mercurial discs floating between the laminae of the metallic planes." Other than our sun, and the earth, of course, all heavenly bodies detailed from Copernicus to Teed's time, were nothing more than reflections.

Teed, who insisted he be called Koresh following the publication of this book, moved to Chicago sometime in the mid-1880s where he gave many lectures concerning the cosmos, winning a huge audience and several thousand followers who supported the Koreshan Unity, sort of an unaccredited university where Teed taught his theories to devoted students who, in turn, spread his grand philosophy. The organization subsequently issued a monthly publication entitled *The Flaming Sword,* which attempted to convert unbelievers to Koresh's point of view.

With visions of empire spreading in his ever-imaginative brain, Teed–Koresh moved to Florida, buying some land near Fort Meyers and establishing the town of Estero in the mid-1890s, a center for his cult which the founder boasted would shortly be populated by no less than ten million people and become the capital of the earth. Less than two hundred souls dwelled in Estero and most left in 1908 when their distinguished leader was killed in a brawl with law officers.

The reason for the departure of Koresh's dedicated followers was not due to the manner of Teed's demise. He had repeatedly stated that within a few days of his death he would rise like Lazurus and ascend to heaven, taking all of the faithful with him. The disciples patiently waited for Teed–Koresh to resurrect himself, but his body putrified within days and he was buried by court order. There would be no mass ascension into heaven.

A few of Teed's diehard followers lingered in Florida and some remained in Chicago, continuing to publish Koresh's beliefs until the late 1940s, when the sect at last disbanded.

Nikola TESLA

Inventor (1856–1943)

The Croatian inventor proved himself a genius at an early age, as a pioneer in the field of high-tension electricity, creating scores of electrical devices including the transformer—the Tesla Coil—and alternating current motors. Immigrating to the United States in 1884, Tesla was a University of Prague graduate and had studied in Paris. He went to work for Thomas Edison (see entry), another brilliant and eccentric inventor, but Edison used him in secondary capacities, discouraging Tesla's concepts about alternating currents by telling him that "it's just a waste of time. Nobody will use it, ever. It's too dangerous. An alternating current, high-voltage wire gets loose and it could kill a man as quick as a bolt of lightning. Direct current is safe."

Tesla ignored Edison and went off on his own to develop his ideas, founding the Tesla Electric Company. He invented dynamos and motors employing alternating currents for Westinghouse and these were used to light the magnificent World's Fair pavillions in Chicago in 1893. Tesla later used his talents to harness the power of Niagara Falls.

Though a recognized genius in his own time, Nikola Tesla grew exceedingly paranoid just before World War I, withdrawing to his laboratory and refusing to see even old friends. He was overheard by his assistants to murmur to himself; he seemed preoccupied with his boyhood. (In his early youth, Tesla's brother Dane was mysteriously killed and Nikola thought for years that his parents suspected him of secretly murdering his brother.)

The scientist would fly into a rage if Edison's name was ever mentioned and refused to have any devices in his house or laboratory bearing the Edison

The brilliant scientist Nikola Tesla, shown in 1935, who grew to hate his one-time employer, Thomas Edison, ran away from friends and concentrated his energies on destroying mankind.

label. He felt that Edison had suppressed his achievements at every turn. He was once asked to attend a dinner sponsored by the Institute of Electrical Engineers, at which time he was to receive the Edison Merit of Achievement Award. Tesla adamantly refused to attend the dinner, saying: "Every time the Institute awards an Edison medal, Edison is glorified more than the recipient. If I had the money to spend for such nonsense, I would gladly pay to have a Tesla medal awarded to Mr. Edison." Though he later agreed to attend the ceremonies, he vanished at the last minute and was later found by friends feeding the pigeons near the New York Public Library.

As the years flitted by, Tesla became more and more uncommunicative, a lonely strange-looking old man whose phobias became his abiding passions. He feared contamination from all sources and, for this reason, refused to shake anyone's hand or touch any round surfaces such as pearls or billiard balls. He gave up all thought of inventing devices to aid man and became entranced with creating a machine that would photograph thoughts on the retina of the eye so that he could "read his enemies' minds," according to his biographer, John H. O'Neill, writing in *The Prodigal Genius.*

Tesla's only joy in life was feeding the pigeons in New York parks. At such times, if anyone spoke to him, he would scurry away, frightened, suspicious that he was being either watched or stalked by killers. Murder must have been much on Nikola Tesla's mind at the end. Before his death in 1943, he labored each day to the point of exhaustion on an elaborate machine he thankfully never completed—a death ray.

Mrs. Virginia ("Bridey Murphy") TIGHE

Housewife (Born 1922)

It began as a purely amateur experiment by an amateur hypnotist, one Morey Bernstein, a businessman in Pueblo, Colorado who visited the Tighe home one November night in 1952. With Mr. Tighe and his own wife looking on, Bernstein hypnotized Mrs. Tighe as she lay on the couch. He asked her innocuous questions, then asked that she recall her earliest experiences from memory. Mrs. Tighe's responses indicated that she could remember events almost to the womb. Bernstein asked for more, if the woman could recall anything *before* birth, beyond conception.

Mrs. Tighe's response, after a few minutes, from her deep trance, shocked all present, it was later reported. She told her hypnotist that she remembered scratching the paint from her iron bed as a child and that her name was "Bridey Murphy." (Why Bernstein was shocked at this response, since he was probing with the obvious intention of establishing a previous identity in Mrs. Tighe, has never been explained.)

There was more, much more. Mrs. Tighe went on to state that, as her other, former self, the elusive Bridey, she was born on December 20, 1798. Her father, Duncan Murphy, was a barrister, her mother a housewife who kept a trim home in County Cork, Ireland. She was a red-headed colleen who married one Sean Joseph MacCarthy at age seventeen, then moved with her husband, who was also a lawyer, to Belfast, where she settled down, living a fairly comfortable and happy life until the age of sixty-six, when she accidentally fell down some stairs and died.

Bernstein took his amazing findings to William Barker, the editor of the Sunday supplement of the Denver *Post*. Barker serialized the hypnotic findings under the title of "The Strange Search for Bridey Murphy," on September 12, 19, and 26, 1954. The reincarnation story shocked Denver readers and received so much public attention that Bernstein promptly sat down and wrote a bestseller, *The Search for Bridey Murphy,* published by Doubleday in 1956. Scores of newspapers syndicated the story and it was condensed by *True* magazine. A long-playing record of part of Mrs. Tighe's six-stage recital while in a trance was issued at $5.95 and sold in the tens of thousands.

Bridey Murphy became the national rage with four major songs immediately issued on the case, one being a rock-and-roll oddity that began with the words: "Bridey Murphy did the rock'n'roll a hundred years ago." There were reports of people all over the country committing suicide to see if they could discover their own reincarnations.

The craze went on month after month. Then the serious investigations began, prefaced by statements from learned psychiatrists who doubted the methods employed by Bernstein in producing reliable statements from his subject. *Life* magazine conducted an investigation of the case and reported, after having consulted experts on Irish lore, that Bridey's house in Cork never existed, records of her parents and her husband were nonexistent and, specifically, Bridey Murphy never scratched paint from an iron bed as a child since iron beds did not arrive in Ireland until 1850, when Bridey would have been a middle-aged woman.

Sparked by *Life,* several newspapers took up the hunt in earnest, not to verify Mrs. Tighe's incredible story but to expose it as a fraud. The Chicago *American* scooped competitors by sending investigative reporters into Chicago neighborhoods where Mrs. Tighe had lived as a child. With the aid of Reverend Wally White, who knew Virginia as a child, they found the actual Bridey Murphy in the living form of one Mrs. Anthony Corkell, a widow with seven children. Virginia had lived across the street from Mrs. Corkell in a basement apartment and had visited the Corkell household regularly, reporters discovered. As a child, Virginia had listened with fascination to Mrs. Corkell's tales of Ireland. Mrs. Corkell's maiden name was the giveaway—it was Bridie (spelled with an "ie") Murphy.

Virginia had danced Irish jigs as a child, taught to her by Mrs. Corkell—as in Cork, the country where Virginia had said she had grown up as Bridey. (One of the shocking revelations in Bernstein's book was where Mrs. Tighe, supposedly in a trance, performed an Irish jig.)

Old Chicago friends of Virginia came forward to state that it was no wonder that Mrs. Tighe remembered having flaming red hair as Bridey; she had dyed her own hair red when she was a child. The name of Bridey's husband, Sean Joseph Brian MacCarthy, was now easy to explain, newsmen wrote. One of the Corkell boys Virginia liked as a child was named John, "Sean" in Gaelic. Brian, it was later discovered, was the middle name of Mrs. Tighe's husband. That left Joseph MacCarthy, or Joe McCarthy, the flamboyant junior senator from the state of Wisconsin who was, at the time of Bridey's so-called emergence, the most controversial political figure in America.

Informants from Wisconsin explained that Mrs. Tighe had been born in Madison in a wooden frame house that was almost identical to that which Bridey described as her own in Ireland. Moreover, Virginia's mother was named Kathleen, as was Bridey's mother. Further, Mrs. Tighe's sister had fallen down some stairs in the Wisconsin house in an accident identical to that which Bridey claimed had killed her.

The search for Bridey Murphy ceased abruptly. Morey Bernstein and Mrs. Virginia Tighe had little or nothing more to say. Those who owned one of the more than 170,000 copies of Bernstein's book possessed a collectors item—as a laughable oddity, even though dedicated reincarnationists continued to support the flimsy tale.

It was kindly concluded that Mrs. Virginia Tighe had done nothing more than relate her childhood experiences, construing these, with Bernstein's aid, to be a report from "the other side." As one account of the day stated: "It would have been the simplest thing in the world for Bernstein to have checked on Virginia's past, but then, of course, he wouldn't have had his book."

Sofya TOLSTOY

Countess (1845–1919)

Sofya Tolstoy was a child bride, marrying the great Count Leo Tolstoy in 1862 when only seventeen. Like Tolstoy, she had been born to great wealth and

Count Leo Tolstoy, shortly before his tragic death, prompted by his fiery wife Sofya.

expected her life to be one of luxury and leisure. Tolstoy, author of the magnificent novels, *War and Peace, Anna Karenina,* and a plethora of writings that filled more than 100 volumes before his death on October 28, 1910 at age eighty-two, at first wrote love stories for his young, beautiful wife. As the marriage deepened—the couple producing several children—Sofya Tolstoy began to admire her husband less and less, even though he was thought of as a saint in his old age. The love between them turned to biting, lasting hatred, so vicious that it brought about Tolstoy's death.

As a member of the Russian aristocracy, Tolstoy had lived through a dissolute and violent youth, "a dirty, vicious life," he once labeled it, where he wallowed in drinking, whoring, duelling, and even murder. He was a snob and a tyrant as a young man, mistreating the many servants who worked his vast estate and forty-two-room mansion at Yasnaya Polyana. By the time Tolstoy was thirty-four and had married his beautiful, dark-haired Sofya, he had begun to mellow, to regard his life up to then as wasted, and to begin to make amends. Humanity crept ever larger into his writings. By the time Tolstoy reached his seventies, he had given up the ways of the aristocrat, exchanging fine clothes for a peasant's smock. Though he had servants, he insisted upon making his own bed and cleaning his own room. He ate at a bare table from a wooden bowl, using a wooden spoon.

This transformation caused Sofya to seeth with indignation and rage. She insisted that the old lifestyle be upheld—she loved luxury, fame, the plaudits of society, money and titles, everything her husband had renounced. Worse, Sofya hated her daughter Sasha, her husband's favorite child, and was consumed with jealousy to the point where she drove the daughter from the house. Moments later, so full of wrath for Sasha was Sofya Tolstoy that she ran into her husband's room and shot the girl's picture with an air rifle, almost hitting Tolstoy who was laboring at his writing.

The woman hated Tolstoy's friends and insulted most visitors who came to pay homage to Russia's greatest living writer. When she learned that Tolstoy had turned over all his future royalties to the Russian people, Sofya went into fits of anger, shrieking, pulling her hair, smashing vases and pictures.

On these fierce occasions which increased in regularity, Tolstoy would attempt to restrain his wife, rebuking her. Sofya, in turn, would then throw herself to the floor in an hysterical fit, roll about with a bottle of opium to her lips, screaming: "I will kill myself, I swear it! I will throw myself down the well!" The great writer would then attempt to soothe her, but she would soon return to her incessant scolding and nagging, chasing Tolstoy into his room where he had to bolt the door to escape her shrewish tongue.

Finally, on the night of October 21, 1910, Tolstoy was unable to bear Sofya another hour. He watched her go through his diary when she thought he was sleeping. Getting dressed he fled, lightly clad, into the cold darkness, not really knowing where he was going, his daughter Sasha at his side. He boarded a train to run away, oblivious to destination. Feeling a chill, the writer disembarked at a small stop, Astopovo, where he developed pneumonia and was taken to the stationmaster's room. "Where to go?" he mumbled, "where to go? The farthest possible."

Hearing that her husband was dying, Sofya took a special train to the small waystation. She emerged spitting wrath at her daughter Sasha, screaming: "I had to come running out here on a train that cost five hundred rubles!"

From the stationmaster's room Tolstoy heard his wife yell. He groaned to a friend who stood guard at the door: "You understand if she wants to see me I can't refuse, but I know the encounter will be fatal for me."

Sofya was asked to wait in a train car parked on a siding. Shasha told her mother that Tolstoy did not want to see her.

"Does he know I tried to drown myself?"

"Yes," answered Sasha, a smile on her face, feeling it a great victory that her mother was to be denied visiting her father on his deathbed. Sofya was kept out of the stationmaster's room until Tolstoy passed into a coma. Before doing so, Tolstoy rambled and raved to his children who were present: "Seek ... Keep seeking ... I am still composing. I am writing. Each thing moves on smoothly to the next." His last coherent words were: "The truth ... I care a great deal ... How they ... "

When the great author began to die, Sofya was called into the room. (Only minutes before he had said: "A great deal has fallen upon Sofya.") She knelt at his bedside, kissing him on the forehead. "Forgive me, forgive me," she wept. He never heard her.

Sofya Tolstoy lived nine years beyond her husband's death, dying inside a depression that had not ceased since the scene in the stationmaster's room. On November 4, 1919, she looked up from her own deathbed and said to the daughter she had once hated enough to murder: "Sasha, forgive me. I don't know what was going on inside of me in those days."

George Francis TRAIN

Financier (1829–1904)

Orphaned at age four after a Yellow Fever epidemic in New Orleans killed his parents, George Train was raised by a maternal grandmother in Waltham, Massachusetts. With a cursory education, Train went to work as a youth in a grocery store in Cambridgeport, then bullied his relative, Enoch Train, into giving him a position with his shipping firm. Train's ingenuity and shrewd business sense soon earned him a partnership in Train and Company.

Train argued old Enoch into building a modern fleet of ships and opened up several new lines of importing and exporting, including illicit opium traffic with which he dabbled on the side, making tens of thousands of dollars. He later began his own firm in Australia and grew rich.

Forever restless, Train began to invest heavily in railroads and real estate, and had a large hand in developing the transcontinental railroad, generally responsible for putting together the Credit Mobilier of America which funded the enormous project. At thirty-one, Train had arrived in high American society; he and his wife were among those attending Lincoln's inaugural ball. Ten years later, grown listless and discontent with his ever-increasing fortune, Train suddenly decided that he should be President of the United States and was seriously backed by large numbers of Republican bigwigs as a legitimate candidate for the nomination. In the summer of 1870, Train's latent streak of eccentricity got the better of him; he completely abandoned his political candidacy and set off on a trip around the world, leaving New York and traveling on the Union Pacific, the very line he had helped to create. After giving many speeches in California—few of them politically oriented, mostly having to do with Train's notions of how Union generals should have conducted the Civil War—the financier took a clipper to Japan on August 1. From there Train took a ship to India, then France. His whirlwind trip was widely publicized.

Novelist Jules Verne read of Train's exploits, actually traveling around the world in less than three months (Train did return to New York within that time), an incredible speed for that day of steam locomotives and sailing vessels and it was Train's fantastic exploit that spurred the writer to pen his most popular novel, *Around the World in Eighty Days*. The book was serialized in dozens of newspapers and magazines throughout the world and sold tens of thousands of copies in several languages during its first year of publication.

The role model for the book's hero, George Train, was too busy to read the book; he had joined French revolutionaries marching to overthrow France's president, Leon Gambetta, and was named head of the Communist movement, although he turned this position down. Train was expelled from France for his involvement with the violent Communards.

He settled in England where he introduced a trolley car system in several

George Francis Train, who went around the world in less than eighty days and inspired the writing of the Jules Verne classic.

cities, and went on to publish a magazine expressing the American expatriate point of view, a publication that made him unpopular with the British upper class since Train advocated the establishment of a democracy in England.

By 1872 the flamboyant financier had re-settled in New York City and was championing Victoria Woodhull (see entry), who had also been a candidate for the presidency as a suffragette. Miss Woodhull and her sister Tennessee Claffin had been arrested and placed in prison on charges of obscenity. The women had exposed the sex life of Henry Ward Beecher, a high-handed reformer who had exposed Miss Woodhull as having been a prostitute. In Train's defense of the women—published in his own newspaper, *The Train Lique*—he had quoted every passage in the Bible dealing with sex and this, in turn, caused his arrest. He was thrown into prison and later given a sanity hearing; he was released, labeled "a lunatic by judicial decree."

The stigma was too much to bear. Train angrily assumed the role of a public eccentric, calling himself "The Great American Crank," and went out of his way to prove himself as having the nature of a dedicated zany. He became an eater of peanuts, stating that this nourishment, coupled only with fresh fruits and vegetables, would guarantee a lifespan of, at least, 150 years. When old friends approached him, Train pulled his hand away refusing to shake, saying "I have adopted the Chinese custom of salutation," and would then shake hands with himself. Later, he refused to speak to friends entirely, but deigned to communicate with them on the street by writing on pads of paper. When pressed for an explanation of such conduct, Train smiled and told the inquisitor that he was "saving up my psychic powers."

The financier held press conferences at which time he announced that he was running for Dictator of America and henceforth the country would have to use a new calendar of his own invention, one beginning with the date of his birth. Train, nevertheless, continued to give lectures and earn additional money by writing newspaper articles in which he proposed legislation and inventions that would "aid mankind." He also published a weekly newspaper, *Train's Penny Magazine,* which few read but provided enough income for the recluse to pay his no more than $3-a-week living expenses, as set down in his own strict budget.

Train's lectures were rambling, almost incoherent affairs, but he drew large crowds and earned as much as $100 for each appearance. He gave a performance rather than a talk, moving and gesticulating wildly about the stage, his long white hair swirling, his long black cape flowing, as he thundered forth his ever-changing credos. At one appearance in San Francisco, Train was confronted by Norton I (see entry), a fellow eccentric who had declared himself Emperor of the United States. Norton retired with Train to a small room in a boarding house and there argued about who really should control the American continent, Dictator Train or Emperor Norton. Train grew tired of Norton's badgering and ran him out of his room.

The crackpot financier busied himself to the end of his days by completing his somewhat confused and fiercely posturing autobiography entitled *My Life in Many States and In Foreign Lands,* which was later published by D. Appleton. Also, to the day of his death, on January 19, 1904, George Train grumbled about not having received the proper recognition in life, especially when it came to Jules Verne's most popular novel, *Around the World in Eighty Days.* Complained Train: "He [Verne] stole my thunder. I'm Phileas Fogg. But I have beaten Fogg out of sight. What put the notion into my head? Well, I'm possessed of great psychic force ... I have lived fast. I have ever been an advocate of speed. I was born into a slow world, and I wished to oil the wheels and gear, so that the machine would spin faster and, withal, to better purposes."

Following the death of the imminent eccentric, the brain of George Francis Train was removed and examined. It was enormous, in fact it weighed 1,525 grams, a brain heavier than Daniel Webster's on a list of 100 famous people; such strange lists were popular in Train's day, an era where the most eccentric person could slip by censorship and make millions before society closed in with sanity hearings.

B. TRAVEN

Author (date uncertain–1969)

Known throughout the world as a major novelist, particularly as the creator of *The Treasure of Sierra Madre,* a classic study in human greed, and later a memorable Humphrey Bogart movie, B. Traven was undoubtedly the most enigmatic scribe of modern times. No one, including his agent, Hal Croves, knew who the man really was or where he came from, if, in fact, Hal Croves was not Traven himself.

Nothing of a documented past for Traven has ever been found, although it is claimed that Traven was really a German actor and writer named Ret Marut, who published a violently antiregime magazine in Munich, a propaganda organ for the Spartakus group opposing World War I, German nationalism, and the military dictatorship of Kaiser Wilhelm II. Experts claim that the reason why Marut was never executed for treason was that he was the illegitimate son of the mad Kaiser, a statement later supported then denied by

Rosa Elena Lujan, a Mexican woman who was married to Hal Croves, and who insisted that Croves was Traven and her real husband.

Marut, one story has it, was abducted by German secret police and held for trial but managed to escape and vanish, surfacing in the mid-1920s in Mexico as Hal Croves, who said he was Traven's cousin and literary representative, selling the author's books which established him as a world writer. Croves, however, kept journalists away from Traven, explaining that the author hated publicity and would never grant an interview. A dogged reporter, Luis Spota, however, found Croves in Acapulco where he had lived since the early 1930s and, after interviewing the agent, accused *him* of being Traven, Croves ordered the reporter from his house, yelling that he was not Traven, so fierce a denial that the writer concluded that he was correct.

Oddly enough, when John Huston made *Treasure of Sierra Madre* into a film in 1948, he asked Croves to contact his author, hoping that Traven would be on hand as an adviser during the on-location shooting in Mexico. Croves appeared instead of Traven, saying that he had Traven's complete authority to represent him and interpret his novel for the director as he, Croves, saw fit. Huston had his suspicions about the man from the beginning. Croves avoided all publicity and, whenever snapshot cameras were present, he excused himself. Huston did manage to take one photo of Croves and later showed this to the star of the film, Humphrey Bogart.

"Do you know who this little fellow is?" the director asked Bogart.

"Sure—don't you?" replied the actor. "It's Traven, the author of the book."

"How do you know that?"

"He told me."

Croves later denied any such admission. When he died in 1969, Rosa Lujan came forward to state that she was married to Croves and that he was B. Traven after all and, further, Traven was Ret Marut, errant offspring of the Kaiser. Later she stated that her reclusive husband was really Berick Traven Torsvan, a farmer's son born near Chicago sometime around 1890, but no records substantiate this claim.

The true identity of B. Traven, novelist, will probably never be known, which, of course, is the way he wanted it. When repeatedly asked for background information by the publicity department of his publisher, the mysterious writer wrote back: "In my books you will find my whole personality."

Hugh TROY

Illustrator (1906–1964)

The greatest practical joker in American history without question was a mild-mannered innocuous looking gentleman named Hugh Troy, son of a

Cornell University professor. Troy was born in Ithaca, New York. Following his graduation from Cornell, Troy became a book illustrator in New York City and spent almost every leisure moment trying to think up spectacular practical jokes; he was so successful that he easily matched the eccentric antics of his British counterpart, William Horace de Vere Cole (see entry).

Troy had already established a lifelong pattern of practical joking when in college. He once plucked a roadside sign stating "Jesus Saves" and decorated an Ithaca Bank with the placard late at night for the benefit of startled depositors arriving the next morning. Discovering that a friend had an unusual waste basket, one made from the actual foot of a rhinoceros, Troy used the basket to make tracks across a snow field and on to a frozen reservoir, ending them at a large break in the ice. Zoologists in Ithaca were baffled and had to report that, indeed, the rhino tracks were authentic. A frantic search of nearby zoos failed to report the disappearance of a runaway rhino. Citizens in the area later complained that their water tasted of rhinoceros.

The joker's antics in New York City were on a grander scale. A theater owner refused to refund Troy's money after the joker complained of seeing a bad movie. Troy's response was to go to the theater the next evening, carrying a jar filled with moths. He released the moths in the middle of the feature and they instantly fluttered upward to the light from the projection machine, covering the window of the operator's box and blotting out the picture.

In the mid-1930s Troy became fascinated with the public's reaction to exhibits, particularly those spectators pretentiously fawning over art. When the Museum of Modern Art opened a Van Gogh exhibit, Troy smuggled his own work of art into the hall, a mock-up of an ear made up of chipped beef in a little glass case, placing this gruesome artifact on a table with a sign that read: "This was the ear which Vincent van Gogh cut off and sent to his mistress, a French prostitute, December 24, 1888." Minutes later the whispering art patrons suddenly mobbed the table, ignoring van Gogh's paintings while Troy stood by gloating; he had felt that the spectators had visited the museum only out of curiosity for van Gogh's sensational background and had proved it by their morbid fascination with his severed ear. (The ear was subsequently removed after curators discovered the hoax.)

Buying a bench like those used in New York City's parks, Troy took his purchase to Central Park. When a policeman approached, Troy suddenly got up from his bench and picked it up, carrying it away. Naturally, he was immediately arrested for stealing city property. Red-faced cops at the station, however, released him with apologies after Troy produced his bill of sale. He pulled this stunt so much that, after a half-dozen arrests, officers aware of the hoax, merely waved at him as he carried his bench about.

Troy's most colossal practical joke was a large-scale operation, involving several of his college chums from Cornell. He and four others placed wooden horses along a half block of Fifth Avenue and then, using jackhammers, began to tear up the street. Police cooperated by diverting traffic from the busy work site. The sweating, filthy crew broke for lunch, going to a swanky Fifth Avenue restaurant, and then resumed their work. Laboring until 5 P.M., the crew, Troy directing their efforts, quit for the day, leaving the wooden horses and a half block of choice city roadway in rubble. They did not return and it was several days before authorities realized without a chuckle that they had been victimized by a bizarre practical joker.

During World War II Troy joined the air force, serving as a captain. Part of his duties involved processing what he thought to be an unnecessary amount of paper work, reports on everything from the use of garbage cans to toilet paper at his South Pacific base. To show the absurdity of such useless paper shuffling, Troy began to submit reports to Washington which detailed the effectiveness of flypaper being used in mess halls and barracks, giving the number of flies found dead on each strip of flypaper every day. Washington officials receiving these reports, instead of questioning the sanity of Captain Troy, demanded that other units also submit flypaper reports, a bureaucratic move Troy had anticipated and predicted. Zany or not, Hugh Troy proved himself a great judge of human character, even though he did go to great lengths to drive home his point.

Mark (Samuel Langhorne Clemens) TWAIN

Author (1835–1910)

The much loved author of *Tom Sawyer* and *Huckleberry Finn,* along with a great number of other wholly American novels that fix him as a literary giant, Twain employed his boyhood adventures in Hannibal, Missouri, his birthplace, to create his finest work, stories that dealt chiefly with life along the Mississippi River. He traveled the country widely, first as a pilot for the Mississippi riverboats during the golden age of the paddlewheelers, then as a frontier journalist, before going east to Connecticut to produce his great books.

As an old man Twain gave vent to anti-Christian, anti-democratic philosophies that earned for him a reputation as a lovable curmudgeon rather than the image of the fearsome iconoclast. His early down-home works had so firmly fixed his image of country sage that no amount of fulmination and fury could undo what his countrymen already and intrinsically believed him to be. Twain, however, throughout his life, was superstitious and a prankster, and when the story suited his needs, an outrageous fabricator.

In 1865 Twain wrote his first fabulous short story, "The Celebrated Jumping Frog of Calaveras County" for the San Francisco *Call*. The tale was outlandish and humorous, the kind of story that reflected Twain's sense of the sardonic and the whimsical. In actual life Twain sought out individuals as outrageous as those portrayed in his fiction. He championed the deluded Joshua Norton (see entry) of San Francisco who had proclaimed himself Emperor of the United States. He favored any bold man. He loved to tell the story of his encounter with a notorious bandit.

Left, Mark Twain at the time he was a river-boat pilot on the Mississippi.

Right, Twain shown writing at his desk, "inventing" newspaper stories in Carson City, Nevada.

Twain, then an established author visiting his native Missouri, entered a small dry goods store. A tall, bearded man wearing a brace of pistols, turned away from the counter with his purchase and began to leave. He took one look at the famous writer and said: "You're Mark Twain, the author, aren't you?"

Twain smiled around his pipe, admitting his identity.

"You're the best in your business, Mr. Twain, and I'm the best in mine." The tall man began to walk toward the door.

"What *is* your business?" inquired Twain.

"I rob trains," the pistol-packing man said, not losing a step.

"You what?"

The tall man turned at the doorway of the store and smiled widely at the humorist. "I rob trains, Mr. Twain—I'm Jesse James!"

Anything new or modern fascinated Twain. He was the first American author to buy a typewriter—a Remington I for $125 in 1874—and submit a completed manuscript, *Life on the Mississippi,* in typewritten form, although he complained that he was only able to type nineteen words a minute on the machine.

Twain also loved fads and strange sciences, becoming a vociferous advocate of palmistry, believing that a person's history and future could actually be determined from reading the creases of flesh in the palm of the hand. When it came to doctors, medicines and hospitals, however, Twain showed that he relied upon old wive's remedies and some out-and-out crackpot cures. He believed that starvation would cure most anything and claimed to have fasted for days to rid himself of a cold or a fever. "A little starvation," he once wrote, "can do more for the average sick man than can the best medicines and the best doctors … I mean total abstention from food…"

With the coming of linotype machines, Twain invested heavily in typesetting and printing, even becoming his own publisher, putting out *Huckleberry Finn* under his own imprint, and selling 500,000 copies of the novel. He went on to publish other books, notably the *Memoirs* of U.S. Grant, which sold more than 300,000 copies at $9 a set, but he almost went broke by giving the bulk of the profits to the President's widow. In fact, Twain was so much in debt from his publishing ventures that he dissolved his firm in 1894 and embarked on a four-year gruelling lecture tour to pay off the publishing bills he had accumulated.

Such disastrous enterprises never worried Twain. He was supremely self-confident and knew early in his writing career that he could always count on his wits to extricate himself from financial problems. Desperate for a story, Twain kept his job on a small newspaper in Carson City, Nevada by inventing an awful murder. He reported that a rancher went berserk and slaughtered his wife, who fought back savagely, slashing out with a large knife before half her head was taken off. The humorist had written that the killer rode wildly into Carson City "with his throat cut from ear to ear and bearing in his hand the reeking scalp from which the warm, smoking blood was dripping." It was the kind of reckless copy the local residents craved, even though the killing never occurred.

While working in Nevada, Twain took up the game of billiards and became a superb amateur at the game. He thought that he was an expert and bragged that few men alive were talented enough to beat him. One man challenged him in a pool hall, saying: "Pardner, I'll tell you what I'll do for you. I'm afraid your skill may not match mine so I'll just play you left-handed."

"That made me mad," Twain later reported, "and I thought I'd better give the churl a lesson." Twain raised his original bet with the challenger and then stood idly by, without ever getting a chance to shoot, angrily chalking his cue as he watched his opponent win without missing.

Twain paid the bet, then commented: "If you're that good with your left hand, how well would you do shooting right-handed?"

"Well, maybe not so good," replied the stranger. "After all, I *am* left-handed."

Twain was also an outdoors person who loved to hunt and fish. He habitually bragged about his prowess as a hunter and fisherman and, at least once, his strutting ways almost brought about his arrest. Returning from the

Twain in old age when he believed in fortune-telling, phrenology, and that he would die with the return of Halley's Comet, which he did, in 1910.

An original illustration for Twain's first important story, "The Celebrated Jumping Frog of Calaveras County."

Mark Twain on the lecture circuit; he was forced to this four-year task to pay off enormous debts incurred as a self-publisher.

Maine woods after having spent three weeks fishing, Twain relaxed in the lounge car of a train heading for New York. Sitting next to Twain was a sour-faced little man who he engaged in conversation.

"Been in the woods, have you?" asked the little man.

"Have I been in the woods! Let me tell you something. It may be a closed season for fishing here in Maine, but I have a couple hundred pounds of the finest rock bass you ever saw iced down in the baggage car. By the way—who are you, sir?"

"I'm the State Game Warden," replied the sour-faced man, wearing a new look, one of menace. "Who are you?"

The humorist thought fast. "Well, I'll be perfectly truthful, warden" said Twain, almost choking on his cigar. "I'm the biggest damned liar in these whole United States!" Apochyphal or not, the story reflects Twain at his shifty best.

Whatever Mark Twain was, his death, in 1910, brought to an end one of the world's most wonderful humorists. Twain's end was predicted by himself. He was born with the appearance of Halley's Comet, in 1835, and always believed that he would die when the comet once again appeared, in 1910. Mark Twain died on time, according to his own schedule.

Tristan TZARA

Poet (1896–1963)

Small, dark and born into wealth, Tristan Tzara, a Swiss poet of limited talent, is best remembered today as the founder of the wacky art movement, Dada, the mother of surrealism, or rather the ogre that gave birth to a literary artistic movement questionable to this day. The twenty-year-old Tzara, already a rich dilettante living in Zurich, became a lounge lizard, sitting out World War I in neutral Switzerland with other artists such as Hans Arp. One night in 1916, Tzara, adjusting his monocle and smoothing down his vest, stood up haughtily in the Cafe Voltaire and shouted for silence. He marched to the middle of a dance floor and produced a French dictionary, holding it aloft and screaming: "I am about to begin a new movement, the greatest and the last movement on earth." He opened the dictionary and, produced a pen knife, jabbing the blade into an open page. He peered downward to see the point meeting the word "Dada" (meaning "hobbyhorse"). The name of our new and glorious movement," announced Tzara, "which is against all movements, will be called Dada."

The new movement was denial of everything and everybody, a nihilistic movement that, at its core, was Tzara's so-called philosophy, nothing more than bizarre outrageous thoughts and actions, gobbldygook stretched to its zenith. Tzara, Arp and other poets and writers began issuing senseless manifestos and small literary publications which carried inane and incomprehensible poems and essays.

Tzara and other pranksters in the anti-movement arrived in Paris late in 1919 and immediately began preparations for an all-out assault on public sensibility. The result, on January 23, 1920, was a performance of sorts, featuring Tzara, Andre Salmon, Andre Breton and several other French writers and poets who had recklessly joined the Dadaist Movement, perhaps out of the rage and confusion left by World War I. Tzara was the star performer, wearing a mask and reading a newspaper article he called a poem while one account reported, he was continuously "accompanied by an inferno of bells and rattles. The audience of course could stand no more and began whistling and booing."

Painter Marcel Duchamp who reveled in Tristan Tzara's Dada Movement, allowing patrons to attack his works with hand-axes.

French painters flocked to the Dada Movement, including Francis Picabia and Marcel Duchamp, who both displayed paintings at subsequent Dada exhibits at which time some hand-axes were handed to stunned art patrons who were told that they could attack the works of art if they pleased. The Movement increased noisily and without pattern. On February 5, 1920 the Dadaists held another performance at the Salon des Independents. Thirty-eight persons read manifestos, as many as ten at once, making it impossible to understand a single word. One of the manifestos read:

No more painters, no more writers, no more musicians, no more sculptors, no more religions, no more republicans, no more royalists, no more imperialists, no more anarchists, no more socialists, no more Bolsheviks, no more politicians, no more proletarians, no more democrats, no more armies, no more police, no more nations, no more of these idiocies, no more, no more, NOTHING, NOTHING, NOTHING. Thus we hope that the novelty which will be the same thing as what we no longer want will come into being less rotten, less immediately GROTESQUE!

The audience reaction was rage. They felt they had been cheated in the first place when it had been announced that the film star Charlie Chaplin (see entry) would be present to render a manifesto. "Although we denied the rumor," Tzara later stipulated, "there was one reporter who followed me everywhere. He thought that the celebrated actor was up to some new stunt and was planning a surprise entrance." A man named Buisson, who hawked newspapers at Metro exits, gave the final speech, a baffling muddle on the future of art but, before he finished, the audience was hurling coins at the performers and they had to retreat under the barrage. Later audiences would get into the mood of Dada by bringing all manner of food, preferring raw eggs to hurl at the raving Dadaists. "Enough! Enough!" members of the audience at one Dada exposition cried and left the hall, tearing out some of the seats which were bolted to the floor, burning these in front of the theater.

In a performance at the Salle Gaveau, the audience outdid the Dadaists in weird behavior. An old man, after listening to some of the manifestos, went berserk and sexually attacked three young women. He was carried out, screaming passionate cries. A pregnant woman gave birth in the fifth row. Flashlight powder was set off and many thought the theater was on fire, dozens racing toward the exits, trampling each other.

Some days later the Dadaists struck again, with Tzara, Picabia, Louis Aragon and Andre Breton delivering manifestos while noisemakers and firecrackers were employed by friends offstage to drown out their voices. Three thousand workers and intellectuals were so agitated by this performance that they began to storm the stage, shouting that they would execute "the madmen." Raymond Duncan, a half-crazy eccentric who walked about Paris in the costume of Socrates, and who had brought all the pupils of his school to this performance, leaped up on the stage and soothed the enraged members of the audience, thus preventing bloodshed.

The performances of madness increased. Thousands jammed another French theater in May. Twelve hundred were turned away. "There were three spectators for every seat," said Tzara. "It was suffocating. Enthusiastic members of the audience had brought musical instruments to interrupt us. The enemies of the Dada threw down from the balconies copies of an anti-Dada paper called *Non* in which we were described as lunatics." The Dadaists hurled their own publications, *391, Cannibale,* the bulletin *Dada,* at the audience. Philippe Soupalt, a leading Dadaist, shouted from the stage: "You are all idiots! You deserve to be presidents of the Dadaist Movement!"

Dada was again re-defined as being "against the high cost of living," and "Dada is a virgin microbe." Three short plays were enacted. One play, by Tzara, was described by its author as "a boxing match with words. The characters, confined in sacks and trunks, recite their parts without moving, and one can easily imagine the effect this produced—performed in a greenish light—on the already excited public. It was impossible to hear a single word of the play."

This was followed by a Dada festival at the Salle Gaveau where, Tzara remembered, "the scandal was also great. For the first time in the history of the world, people threw at us not only eggs, salads and pennies, but beefsteaks as well. It was a very great success."

One critic, of the phalanxes who hated Dada, reviewed a Dada exhibition of paintings, which was accompanied by a performance. "With characteristic bad taste," wrote the critic d'Esparbes, "the Dadas, have now resorted to terrorism. The stage was in the cellar, and all the lights in the shop were out; groans rose from a trap door. Another joker hidden behind a wardrobe insulted the persons present ... the Dadas, without ties and wearing white gloves passed back and forth ... Andre Breton chewed up matches, Ribemont-Dessaignes kept screaming: 'It's raining on a skull,' Aragon caterwauled, Philippe Soupault played hide-and-seek with Tzara, while Benjamin Peret and Caharchoune shook hands ever other minute. On the doorstep, Jacques Rigaut counted aloud the automobiles and the pearls of the lady visitors."

The idiotic movement spread through Germany, Italy and Australia, with more than a half-million Dada books purchased within a year. By 1922, however, most of the serious painters and writers, who had had their hour of pranksterism, decided to lend themselves to more serious enterprises. Tzara, the founder, persisted in his maniacal movement almost to the day of his death in 1963, a curious little man, dapper and arrogant to the end, who had created havoc and chaos in the literary and artistic worlds of Europe on a whim.

V

William Louis VEECK

Baseball Club Owner (Born 1914)

He has been known as the "Clown Prince of Baseball," and to others, Bill Veeck (as in "wreck"), was a tough competitor, sometimes an abusive antagonist, but always and forever a showman who habitually brought great entertainment to his fans and vitality to sagging teams he took under his wing. The sports executive, born in Chicago on February 9, 1914, began his career with the Chicago Cubs, working as the team's secretary and treasurer from 1933 to 1941 when he joined with Charley Grimm in buying the weak Milwaukee Brewers team with a $100,000 investment.

It was during his years with the Brewers, 1941 to 1945, that Veeck instituted zany entertainment at the ball park, stunts, devices and outright buffoonery to entice crowds into the park. He hired a six-piece band to play before and after the games and he and Grimm, who managed the club, would join the band to play, respectively, the flute and the banjo.

Besides regular entertainment built around the flagging team, Veeck invented myriad stunts and promotion ideas. He held sort of a lottery where one spectator won a spectacular item at each game, sometimes a 300-pound block of ice, sometimes pigeons (without cages, although winners managed to hold onto the birds throughout the game), once even an ancient swaybacked horse. The gimmicks worked and the Brewers drew 200,000 more fans the first year Veeck took over than in 1940.

Veeck's partner in the Brewers gamble, Charley Grimm.

A youthful Bill Veeck (shown with Harry Graebiner, Vice President of the Chicago White Sox) as the new owner of the Milwaukee Brewers.

A gentle and subtle man, Veeck's sense of humor has never failed him, even when it came to his stubborn attire. He never wore a necktie in his life, preferring sportshirts and, even on the most formal of occasions, a sportshirt with a sportcoat. One story told of Veeck's traditional garb has him invited to a white tie affair where he was to be the guest of honor. He arrived wearing his sportshirt and jacket. Hundreds of men in tuxedoes looked disapprovingly in his direction, grumbling about his appearance.

Veeck sat unperturbed at the speakers' table and was finally called upon to give his acceptance talk. He studied the mass of guests bedecked in their finery, paying particular attention to the gentlemen in tuxedoes and white ties. He gave them a wide grin and then infected the crowd with his humor when he said: "Well, folks, this is the first time I ever saw 1200 waiters for one lone customer!"

The colorful owner went on to take control of the Cleveland Indians, who became champions under his reign, the St. Louis Browns, and the Chicago White Sox, before leaving the game in 1980. His was a world of never-ending promotions and stunts that had fans gossiping and returning for more. He invented exploding scoreboards that sparkled and popped and banged whenever his team scored. He created special days for everyone from grandmothers to plumbers. He offered flagpole sitters and auto races. But his most outrageous stunt occurred on August 19, 1951, when his Browns were playing the Detroit Tigers. The impresario sent to bat on that day one Eddie Gaedel, a twenty-six-year-old midget (who stood three feet seven inches), as a pinch hitter. Gaedel, who wore the number 1/8, utterly baffled the Detroit pitcher who walked him. The Browns fans loved the stunt and it became a classic baseball tale. (Gaedel, who died in 1961, was the only midget ever to play in a major league game.)

Bill Veeck, who brought stunts and stimulation to baseball, in 1978 with Hank Greenberg.

Veeck's criticism of his fellow club owners was unstinting; he never cared for the company of these individuals, most of whom were stuffy and arrogant. "My friends are the fans," Veeck was fond of saying, "not the owners. Dignity isn't my suit of clothes."

And the fans rewarded the grand old hustler by turning out in droves whenever his teams played, whether they won or lost. They had fun at the ball park. Bill Veeck saw to that.

William VOIGHT

Shoemaker (date uncertain–1914)

One of the most spectacular frauds in German history began on the morning of October 16, 1906 in the small town of Kopenick, six miles outside Berlin. The Berlin train stopped at the town and an aged Captain of Prussian Guards got off. He commandeered some marching soldiers nearby, and then marched from the station in rigid step, the captain in the lead, to Kopenick's Town Hall.

The precise officer stationed a guard at each entrance to the Town Hall, instructing his troopers that no one was to enter or leave the building unless he personally gave his permission. He then led his soldiers into the office of Dr. Langerhans', the town's burgomeister.

Langerhans' stared, puzzled, from his desk. "What do you want, captain?"

"You. You're under arrest."

"For what?"

"The authorities in Berlin will tell you all about it."

"Where's your warrant, captain?"

The captain pointed to the rifle-carrying troops behind him. "These men are my warrant. Hurry up, now, you're going to Berlin as my prisoner."

At this point Dr. Langerhans' wife entered the office along with the town's Inspector of Police. The captain ordered the Inspector to "get your men and station them in the town square in the event there is a disturbance." The Inspector saluted smartly and did as he was ordered. Dr. Langerhans told his weeping wife that it was all a mistake, that authorities in Berlin would soon clear up the matter. She insisted, however, in accompanying her husband and the captain relented, telling one of his troopers to have two closed carriages brought around to the rear entrance of Town Hall. The captain then went to the office of the Treasurer, placing him, too, under arrest.

Just as the Treasurer was being led down a hall to join Dr. Langerhans and his wife, a deputy police chief from a nearby village appeared. Seeing a crowd assembled before Town Hall he slapped back the rifle of a guard at the door and rushed inside. "What's going on here?" inquired the police chief of the Captain of the Prussian Guards.

The Captain drew the chief aside, saying: "There have been irregularities in the finances of this town. The burgomeister and the treasurer are suspected and their arrest has been ordered. They are being taken to Berlin for questioning. You will go to the Town Square and help keep order." The police chief looked hard at the Captain standing stiffly in his uniform and then snapped to attention, going to the square to do as ordered.

Ordering the Treasurer back into his office, the Captain told him to "fix your books before departing. You will turn over all the money you have on hand."

"I can't do that," protested the Treasurer.

"Why not?"

"I cannot turn over money unless the burgomeister orders it."

The Captain gave the quaking Treasurer a withering glance and said in a commanding voice: "The burgomeister is under arrest! I am now the highest authority in Kopenick! Is that understood?"

Nodding, the Treasurer obediently turned over approximately 4,000 marks (about $300), all the cash that was in the town vaults. He was then ushered into a waiting carriage to join the Langerhans' and, with a sergeant in charge, driven off to military headquarters in Berlin. The Captain of the Prussian Guards ordered the rest of his troops to return to their barracks. He then disappeared.

The Langerhans' and the Treasurer were greeted at military headquarters by police and military officers perplexed at their presence. They were passed from one office to another until reaching the Berlin Police Chief and the Adjutant-General, Count Moltke, and not until that time did the highest civil authorities realize that the Captain of Kopenick, as he was later known, was an audacious and colossal fraud.

The news of the bold swindle leaked to the press and newspapers across Germany had a field day with a story they thought hilarious. "They will all lie on their bellies before a uniform," jeered one editorial.

Nine days later, on October 25, 1906, the imposter was apprehended. He was William Voight, his twenty-seven-year police record showed, a petty criminal who worked mainly as a shoemaker. He admitted that he got the idea for the swindle after seeing the resplendent uniform in a shop window. He had used his life savings to buy it. Then he traveled to Kopenick and, seeing the soldiers marching in the street, merely stepped forward and ordered them to follow him to the Town Hall. Voight, though lacking a formal education, was a shrewd judge of the German character at the time, one that was instantly survile and slavish to anyone wearing a uniform. His uniform carried the insignia of a captain, which made him all the more a figure of authority.

The crime was taken lightly and Voight received a minimum sentence of four years which was reduced to twenty months by the Kaiser himself, who apparently thought the caper amusing. Upon his release, Voight found himself famous; he was immediately offered vaudeville contracts and happily appeared on stage wearing his officer's uniform and retelling his fabulous story. Voight traveled to England and the United States and earned a comfortable, if not a handsome income from his extraordinary escapade. A 1932 motion picture, *Der Hauptmann von Kopenick,* was based on Voight's exploit, starring Max Adalbert. Voight died, cherishing his notoriety, in 1914, only months before his native Germany launched World War I.

Wilbur Glenn VOLIVA

Clergyman (1870–1942)

As a clergyman, Wilbur Voliva was a tyrant, a bigot, and one of the most extraordinary crackpots to ever control the moral and mental destinies of thousands of disciples in the strange city of Zion, Illinois, forty-some miles north of Chicago. Voliva, ordained in 1889, became the assistant to John Alexander Dowie at the turn of the century. Dowie, a faith-healer from Scotland, founded a severe religious sect known as The Christian Apostolic Church in Zion in 1895. Within ten years Voliva had forcibly removed Dowie from his office, banishing him from the position of "General Overseer" of the community. From 1905 to 1935 Voliva ran things in Zion and, as he saw fit, through his spiritual impulses.

A strict fundamentalist, Voliva made it an offense to drink alcohol or smoke tobacco in Zion. It was also forbidden to hum, whistle or stay outdoors beyond 10 P.M., and that meant adults of all ages. No store was allowed to sell bacon, ham or oysters and cosmetics of any kind were taboo. Certain female clothing was proscribed, such as high heels, bathing suits, short dresses. Any female, irrespective of her religious affiliation, caught breaking these rules was immediately arrested and heavily fined, if not jailed. Under Voliva's fascist-like regime, Zion became a closed city with the most fanatical Blue Laws on record.

Moreover, the overweight, bald Voliva insisted that each and every member of his tyrannized flock believe, as he did, that the world was flat. The General Overseer stated repeatedly that the earth was shaped like a flapjack or a stove lid. When it was pointed out to him that the world had been circumnavigated many times since Magellan, the religious elder snorted derision, saying that the North Pole was at the center of the earth and that the South Pole was spread around the base.

Voliva offered $5,000 to anyone who could prove that the earth was round and his own travels around the globe to give lectures on his dogma proved nothing to the elder; he had merely traveled in a circle on the flat earth, he explained. He went on to point out that ships did not fall off the edge of the earth because there was an enormous ice wall to prevent such mishaps. Beyond the wall was a long drop-off to Hell and beneath Hell was a lower area where dwelled departed spirits of a race that predated Adam and Eve.

What about the stars? Voliva shurgged, saying that they were very small flapjack-like bodies, much smaller than earth, that rotated about our planet. The moon was lighted from within he said, and the sun was only a stone's throw from the earth. "The idea of a sun millions of miles in diameter," Voliva once thundered, "and 91,000,000 miles away is silly. The sun is only thirty-two miles across and not more than 3,000 miles from the earth. It stands to reason it must be so. God made the sun to light the earth, and therefore must have placed it close to the task it was designed to do. What would you think of a man who built a house in Zion and put the lamp to light it in Kenosha, Wisconsin?"

And the elder did not stop at mere statements. In a 1930 edition of *Leaves of Healing,* the sect's propaganda sheet, Voliva reproduced a photograph taken of Lake Winnebago, Wisconsin. The caption beneath the photo of the lake pinpointed a Voliva "truth". Said the caption: "ANYONE CAN GO TO OSHKOSH AND SEE THIS SIGHT FOR THEMSELVES ANY CLEAR DAY. With a good pair of binoculars one can see small objects on the opposite shore, proving beyond any doubt that the surface of the lake is a plane, or a horizontal line ... The scientific value of this picture is enormous."

Voliva's astronomy was upheld by his followers as an extension of the only true fundamentalism. All others who called themselves astronomers were, in the elder's considered opinion, "poor, ignorant, conceited fools." Voliva bragged: "I can lick to smithereens any man in the world in a mental battle. I have never met any professor or student who knew a millionth as much on any subject as I do." When once challenged in court, Voliva screamed: "Every man who fights me goes under. Mark what I say! The graveyard is full of fellows who tried to down Voliva!"

The religious fanatic promised the press that he would soon embark on a flat-earth journey to Europe and Asia, and evangelize every living soul. When not lecturing on his flat earth beliefs, Voliva took careful scientific pains to predict the end of the world, first selecting 1923, then various years up to 1935, when he began to lose control of his flock. None of his predictions even brought a severe storm from Lake Michigan.

In 1935 other religious leaders moved into Zion and began to steal Voliva's thunder. Then his parishioners, who were eager to throw off his yoke of three decades, deserted him. The elder suddenly announced that he was retiring, but would live to see the age of 120 years. "My diet proves it," he explained, and then told the world, flat or otherwise, that he had been existing on nothing but Brazil nuts and buttermilk most of his life, and would go on doing that for sixty more years. Wilbur Voliva's predictions about his own life expectancy, as well as that of the earth's, were again wrong. He perished October 11, 1942, at age seventy-two.

Erich Oswald VON STROHEIM

Motion Picture Director (1885–1957)

Born Hans Carl Maria von Nordenwall in Vienna, Austria on September 22, 1885, von Stroheim was the son of a Jewish merchant from Geiwitz in Prussian Silesia. His mother was born and raised in Prague. This unforgettable flamboyant, nonconforming tyrant of a film director has always been thought of as a member of Prussian aristocracy. Yet von Stroheim played that part all of his life until he undoubtedly came to believe that such a highborn military station was genuinely his.

There was authentic background to some extent to support von Stroheim's peacock posture. He apparently graduated from the Austrian Imperial Military Academy in 1902, serving briefly as an officer of the elite palace guards where he witnessed the dying splendors of Emperor Franz Josef's court. He appeared in the United States some time in either 1906 or 1909, reports vary, even von Stroheim's. For a while he worked for magazines and newspapers as a writer, then wrote a play, *The Pinnacle,* which was not produced. He went to Hollywood some time in late 1913 and began appearing as an extra and then performing bit parts in several films, doubling as a directorial assistant to the great D.W. Griffith on several films. It was from "the master," as von Stroheim always called Griffith, that he learned the fine art of directing films, albeit von Stroheim always had his own quirks and fancies that later deepened into disastrous habits that might have wrecked several studios had he not been removed.

Von Stroheim's first break came during World War I, when his knowledge of Prussian military codes and manners made of him a film adviser. Following the war, von Stroheim's career collapsed; the mere mention of German officers was box office poison. Broke and desperate, von Stroheim decided to risk

Von Stroheim's mentor, the great director D.W. Griffith, at camera
during a screen test of A. Barton Hepburn.

everything by forcing himself upon the whimsical head of Universal Studios,
Carl Laemmle. He walked to the mogul's estate and pounded on the front door
of Laemmle's mansion.

A butler opened the door and told von Stroheim that Laemmle was dining.
"I only want to see him for ten minutes," said von Stroheim.

Laemmel came to the door, saying: "Who wants to see me for ten minutes?"

With disarming European manners, von Stroheim introduced himself and
told the mogul that he had brought his play for him to read, and that if the play
were to be made into a film, Laemmle would not only reap a fortune but would
be thought of as the industry's artistic leader. "Uncle Carl" invited von
Stroheim inside, but warned him he could only spare ten minutes, that he had
an appointment. Both men talked about the project until dawn when Laemmle
amazingly agreed to not only allow von Stroheim to direct his play, but also
write the film script and star in the movie. There was one point of discontent
registered by Laemmel; he did not like von Stroheim's title, *The Pinnacle*.
"What means this word 'pinnacle?'" asked Uncle Carl. "The public won't know
what it is about. There are more blind husbands about than there are
pinnacles, so we'll call it 'Blind Husbands.'"

Blind Husbands not only brought a box office bonanza to Universal, but critical acclaim which established von Stroheim as one of the finest directors in the medium. He also became one of the most insufferable men in the industry, his success serving as a catalyst to unleash an ego-maniacal nature that soon terrorized the film community, especially the moguls who invested in his pictures.

Von Stroheim's art as a director was wholly different from the one-dimensional portraits drawn by most American directors at the time, and his constant theme was usually centered about his favorite obsession, the love triangle. The director's technique was decidedly Germanic, dark, brooding scenes with a mobile camera allowing for close-ups, the accent on the sensual which bordered on the sexually perverse. Von Stroheim, in almost all his films, had a penchant for the human mouth and his actors were invariably directed to create oral images, sticking anything into the mouth that might suggest pleasures of the flesh, from fingers to long-stemmed pipes.

The director made quick use of his new status, launching expensive new film projects that firmly established him in the early 1920s as the dominant film director in Hollywood (rivaled only by Cecil B. deMille). The films gushed forth—*The Devil's Passkey* (1919) *Foolish Wives* (1921), *Greed* (1923), *The Merry Widow* (1925), *The Wedding March,* (1926–28), with the director often playing in his own films the part he had created for himself in real life, the high-born Prussian officer with tight collar, bull neck, and unswerving purpose.

A fanatic for realism, von Stroheim ran up incredible costs during his productions. Real champagne and caviar were served to his actors in dining room scenes. He spent fortunes on duplicating the exact uniforms of certain German regiments, and was upbraided by front office brass on one occasion for ordering silk underwear for his imperial guard, monogrammed with the guard's insignia. He was called into the office of Irving Thalberg, the young, brilliant new head of Universal's production department, to explain the underwear.

"It must be done," von Stroheim demanded. "The public, of course, will not see the underwear, but the actors must *know* they are wearing authentic Prussian undergarments!"

He insisted on full orchestras being present to play off camera for his dancing actors, even though these were the days of silent film. On one occasion he insisted that giant bells be purchased to gong across a lake, ignoring the fact that the viewing audience would never hear them. In one scene he rented at great expense thousands of pigeons which were to fly in from the Pacific off Monterey, where von Stroheim was shooting on-location. Each time the birds were released, the Pacific winds blew them inland, spoiling the shot.

Von Stroheim's demand for realism became excessive and when a scene called for a bordello to be portrayed, the set was closed, even to the studio heads. The "authenticity" of this and similar scenes caused Hollywood to be labeled a "sin capital." Yet the director ignored all cautions, partaking of the scandalous orgy scenes with relish. Wrote Norman Zierold in *The Moguls:* "On one occasion, von Stroheim entered so gaily into the sport of things that he passed out even as he was directing his cameraman."

Irving Thalberg, who was later considered to be the boy wonder of Hollywood and would serve as the role model in F. Scott Fitzgerald's *The Last Tycoon,* found von Stroheim to be the greatest thorn in his side; but he did not shrink from confronting the arrogant and hostile director with his extravagant costs. When von Stroheim began to stretch the shooting of *Foolish Wives* into its second year, the twenty-one-year-old Thalberg went to the location where the director was working and took him aside, saying: "I have seen all the film, and you have all you need for the picture. I want you to stop shooting."

Von Stroheim, who had by then become a prima donna, sneered contemptuously at Thalberg, whom he considered an upstart, and snorted: "I am not finished as yet."

"Yes, you have," replied Thalberg quietly but emphatically. "You have spent all the money this firm can afford, and I won't allow you to spend more."

The director slapped a riding crop against his side and then growled: "If you were not my superior, I would smash you in the face." With that von Stroheim turned his back on Thalberg and marched off.

Foolish Wives, however, became an enormous financial success, Universal's biggest to date, so von Stroheim was kept on in all his savage glory. He began to think, however, that Thalberg and other studio heads were spying on him, watching every penny he spent on his new and fourth film, *Merry-Go-Round,* reporting the presence of every attractive starlet he interviewed in his private office. "Carl Laemmel had all his relatives from Laupheim," the director later recalled with a sour face. "Most of them were unable to do anything—you took them whether you liked them or not. Some were nice, others were arrogant bastards. The first script girl I had was a niece, and a spy for the front office. If I had caught her spying, I would have thrashed her; but oddly enough—I don't know whether it was my looks or my uniform—she didn't squeal."

At Thalberg's order, von Stroheim was finally removed from *Merry-Go-Round* as the film's director. He left Universal hurling insults in all directions, stating that he would go to another studio that appreciated his talents. He went to the Goldwyn company, but strangely enough, Thalberg also moved to this studio and was again forced to face the volatile director who was shooting a new film, *Greed,* based on the Frank Norris novel, *McTeague.* There is no doubt that *Greed* was von Stroheim's masterpiece, even in its truncated version of present day, a character study in human avarice that has not been matched.

Again the director insisted on perfect reality for every scene, shooting on location and exhausting his stars, Gibson Gowland, Zasu Pitts, and Jean Hersholt. One of the locations called for in the novel was Death Valley, but, to save money and wear and tear on the cast, the front office strongly suggested to von Stroheim that he shoot the scenes on dunes near Hollywood. The director exploded, saying that he would take the entire crew to Death Valley or die in the effort.

"We were the only white people who had penetrated into the lowest point on earth since the days of the pioneers," von Stroheim later boasted. "We worked in 142 degrees Fahrenheit in the shade, and no shade. I believe the results I achieved through the actual heat and the physical strain were worth the trouble we had all gone to."

The film as it stood upon completion was gigantic, forty-two reels, which would, as von Stroheim casually explained, require audiences to take lunch and dinner breaks while watching it. *Greed* cost almost a half-million dollars, an enormous budget for those silent picture days. As it was, the film could not be released. Thalberg ordered von Stroheim to cut it down and, after much arguing and complaining, the director edited the film down to twenty-four reels. Thalberg ordered him to cut it down to ten reels, and von Stroheim exploded, yelling: "You are cutting out my soul!"

The film was eventually, under Thalberg's direction, cut down to twelve reels and released without a proper advertising budget. It failed at the box office and von Stroheim looked upon its treatment by Thalberg as a deliberate act of vicious sabotage, and, in this instance, he may have been right. The director was beside himself with rage and vowed that he would never look at *Greed* as it was released to the public. In 1933 he gave in but wept through the entire film which he considered "butchered." Von Stroheim later commented: "When ten years later I saw the film myself, it was like seeing a corpse in a graveyard."

The director's last great damn-the-expense fling was *The Merry Widow,* for MGM. Again Thalberg, his nemesis, was in charge of production. Von Stroheim gave out several interview's before the making of this film, just to let everyone know who was in complete charge. "They call me hateful," he told one interviewer, "and say I talk to my people as if they were dogs, that I am in truth a typical pre-war German. But I know what I am doing. It is my method. I must undermine this surface of acquired false technique and bring out the real feeling that is like a kernel beneath a girl's superficial charm. I glower at them. Never in their lives have they been spoken to as roughly as by me. I crush them, beat them down with satire, with harsh words, with scorn. They are ready to quit. Then I get at the real soul and guide its natural unfoldment."

All of these remarks were aimed at Von Stroheim's new star, Mae Murray, whom he considered "artificial, self-conscious, and full of cuteyisms." He intended to break her, remold her, use her and discard her. Von Stroheim played his cameras mostly on the male star, John Gilbert, and the sinister Prussian rake portrayed by Roy D'Arcy, concentrating on orgies and revels and every low and debasing scene that would portray European aristocracy, which von Stroheim really hated, as perverse and decadent. He created scenes for Mae Murray that tended to downgrade, if not degrade her role. He antagonized her at every opportunity, once saying to the cameraman shooting her love scene with Gilbert, as he ostentatiously turned his back on the set: "Tell me when it's over."

Miss Murray thought the entire film was obscene, that von Stroheim concentrated on every sexual innuendo and catered to fetishes and abnormal

The macabre Erich von Stroheim, directing Maud George in *The Wedding March*, 1926.

foreplay. Mae finally went to Thalberg in a rage, screaming: "That madman is making a filthy picture! All this business of a dirty old man kissing girls' feet and drooling over a closet of women's shoes! It's repulsive!"

Thalberg did look at the rushes and saw that the director was up to his old tricks, indulging himself in excessively wasteful scenes, one of which was a long, long pan shot of a closet filled with hundreds of pairs of women's shoes, the very scene that had incensed Mae Murray. Thalberg called von Stroheim into his office and demanded that the director explain the closet scene.

"But you don't *understand,*" wailed von Stroheim, "the man has a foot fetish!"

"*He* may have a *foot* fetish, Mr. von Stroheim," said Thalberg politely, "but *you* have a *footage* fetish."

The director finished the picture and was asked to visit with Louis B. Mayer, the unpredictable, hot-headed studio chief, a man who considered himself a maker of "family pictures." Although Mayer was notorious for his casting couch seductions of starlets, he revered marriage and motherhood. He had listened to Mae Murray's charges that *The Merry Widow* was a "filthy picture made by a dirty Hun."

Sitting in Mayers' office, von Stroheim smoked from a long cigarette holder, blowing smoke rings disdainfully above the mogul's head. Mayer told him that he did not care for the way women were portrayed in *The Merry Widow,* that the film seemed to degrade womankind.

"All women are whores anyway," snapped von Stroheim.

Mayer's eyes popped. "What did you say?"

"I said, all women are whores."

A short, squat man, Mayer knew how to use his fists; he had knocked Charlie Chaplin (see entry) to the floor when the comedian had made sexual advances to one of his budding female stars. Mayer stood up and moved around his desk to face von Stroheim. "You have a mother?" Mayer asked.

Von Stroheim looked up contemptuously at the mogul and sneered: "Of course."

"And you still say that?"

"Yes."

"Why, you filthy Hun!" roared Mayer, repeating Mae Murray's indictment, and then struck out a savage blow, his fist hitting von Stroheim's considerable jaw squarely, and sending him to the floor. Mayer than grabbed the thoroughly deflated director by the seat of the pants and the back of his neck and ran him out of his office, tossing his hat and cane after him. Von Stroheim was finished at MGM, and with most other studios. His incredible excesses had ruined what was probably a brilliant career.

After directing a few more less-than-memorable films, von Stroheim drifted back to acting, playing dissolute aristocrats and during World War II, more Prussian officers, including that of Rommel in *Five Graves to Cairo,* directed by Billy Wilder. (Wilder would later direct von Stroehim as a caricature of himself in *Sunset Boulevard.*) Though in his decline, von Stroheim still thought of himself as the only great director Hollywood ever had—after D.W. Griffith—and his arrogance was intact to his last days.

Wilder would later recall: "When I first saw von Stroheim at the wardrobe tests for his role as Rommel, I clicked my heels and said: 'Isn't it ridiculous, little me directing you? You were always ten years ahead of your time.'"

"Twenty," retorted Erich von Stroheim.

W

George E. ("Rube") WADDELL

Baseball Pitcher (1876–1914)

A giant of a man, Waddell was one of the great pitchers in baseball history, a Hall of Fame legend who made his reputation with Connie Mack's Philadelphia Athletics. He was also one of the zaniest hurlers in the sport, an adult with the mind of a child, and whose boyish impulses were obeyed anytime and everywhere. Waddell loved horse-drawn fire engines, and whenever one raced by the ball park, Waddell would run after it, even if he happened to be on the mound pitching at the time. He would simply drop the ball and run to the nearest exit or even scale the small wooden fences bordering the outfield in those days. At such times, Connie Mack, normally a mild-mannered, soft-spoken gentleman, would go into a state of apoplexy. But Mack never gave up on his great pitching star.

Rube loved to consume alcohol almost as much as he enjoyed racing after clanging fire engines. His intake increased so drastically one year that Mack decided that he had to take action. He brought Waddell into his office and sat him down before his desk, giving him a lecture on the terrible effects caused by liquor. "It will ruin you, Rube," he said. "I've never seen a ballplayer who was good enough to drink and stay in the big leagues. And now I'm going to prove how bad alcohol can be, a little demonstration of what that rotten stuff can do to your insides."

With that, Mack produced a bottle of whiskey and a shot glass, filling the glass and then taking a long worm which he had in a can on the desk. "Watch closely, Rube," said Connie Mack. "Keep your eye on this worm." He dropped it into the shotglass containing the whiskey. The worm struggled vainly, twisting and turning until it floated limp and dead in the whiskey.

Mack spread out his hands in explanation. "Well—that ought to speak for itself. Doesn't it?"

"It sure does, Mr. Mack," replied the awed Rube.

"Okay, Rube, my boy, now tell me what it means?"

"It means, Mr. Mack, that you're getting rid of my worries."

"What?"

Rube nodded in the direction of the dead worm. "It's good to know that a drinking man ain't ever gonna have to worry about worms in his stomach."

Waddell, like many in that early baseball era, made extra money off-season by appearing in vaudeville skits, but his awkward gestures and reckless ways almost proved disastrous to one road show. Appearing in an opus entitled *The Stain of Guilt,* Waddell was supposed to rescue a lady in a burning building on stage but, in his reckless dash into the door of the set, he smashed the facade so hard that the set began to collapse, almost setting the theater on fire.

The pitcher was forever putting himself in peril, mostly through his heavy drinking. One night he adjourned to a hotel room with some of his teammates, enjoying a party that almost ended in his premature death. The morning following the party Waddell woke up in a hospital bed, bandages covering most of his body. Every bone in his body ached. Painfully, he turned his head to see his teammate Ossie Schreck standing next to the bed, studying him.

Moaned Waddell: "What the Hell happened to me? Last thing I remember is being in a hotel room with you and the boys, having fun."

"Rube, you got the idea, all of a sudden, that you could fly, and one of the fellows said you couldn't. And you got mad and opened a window. Then, like lightning, out you went, like a bird, straight out of a second-story window."

"My God, Ossie," said Waddell, "I could have killed myself. Why didn't you stop me?"

"Stop you? Hell, no! I bet a hundred bucks you could do it!"

Ganna WALSKA

Opera Singer (1887–1963)

The Polish opera singer was more predator than performing artist and her ridiculous career was almost nonexistent. But Ganna Walska did inspire one who knew of her strange saga, Orson Welles, into using her as a role model for the inept singer profiled in his marvelous movie *Citizen Kane.*

The oddball diva made her debut in *Fedora* with the Havana Opera Company in 1917, a first appearance in opera that was also her last. She had no voice at all and the audience knew it, responding with an avalanche of boos, hisses and a shower of rotten eggs and vegetables. (It was later gossiped that

The **tempestuous** and **gold-digging** opera singer Ganna Walska with her equally eccentric millionaire husband, Harold Fowler McCormick.

Ganna had used her wiles on the opera company's manager to arrange for her debut.)

By 1920 the enterprising Ganna appeared in Chicago, dripping jewels and furs given to her by a recent and departed admirer. It was at this time she met the gullible and incredibly rich Harold Fowler McCormick, the eccentric son of Cyrus McCormick, inventor of the reaper. Though he was then married to Edith Rockefeller McCormick (see entry), Harold became enamored of the sultry Polish siren and began visiting her in her hotel suite where she sang for him. McCormick, no judge of singing, thought Ganna's voice to be the most exquisite he had ever heard. She told him she was not appreciated. He told her that he would take good care of her career, make her the star she should be. He and his wife Edith were the chief sponsors of the Chicago Opera Company.

McCormick's liaison with the vamping Ganna led to his divorce; he married Madame Walska and proceeded to make her another Amelia Galli-Curci, or so he thought. It all worked according to the diva's devious plan. Said one society columnist: "She clearly marked him [McCormick] as her prey and meant to devour him. Worse, he was crazy to be devoured. I've no idea of how many of his millions she managed to swallow too, during the years they spent together. Besides what he gave her in cash, jewels and real estate, he was forever hiring halls for his wife, subsidizing opera companies, making up ill-advised attempts to bolster up a mythical talent."

No matter the preparations, Ganna Walska never appeared in any of the extravaganzas her husband planned for her; she knew better than that. Her closest shave with exposure was Leon Cavallo's *Zaza*, in which she was to sing the lead, opening in Chicago on December 21, 1920.

Ganna seldom rehearsed with the company and when she did make an appearance her voice was so weak that director Pietro Cimini could not hear her. The director finally begged: "Madame, please sing in your natural voice."

This was the opportunity the scheming diva had looked for; she exploded in a burst of wild temperment, on cue. "Pig!" she shouted at Cimini. "You would ruin my performance?" She stomped off, warning the company's officials that "I am packing my bags! At the end of the season you will be packing yours!"

Walska departed for Europe, McCormick chasing after her to explain that it was all a mistake. He would provide a new opera company, anything she wanted. She told him that she was through with singing—no one appreciated her wonderful talents and golden voice. Moreover, she informed the fawning

The crackpot doctor, Serge Voronoff, who transplanted monkey glands into Harold McCormick in an attempt to improve the millionaire's love life with Ganna Walska. (UPI)

McCormick, she was through with him, unless he could find a way to improve her lackluster sex life. He was inadequate for her needs, she said.

Desperate, McCormick contacted a weird physician and notorious medical charlatan, Dr. Serge Voronoff, in Paris. Voronoff had long claimed that he could rejuvenate any man of any age by a simple operation—the transplanting of monkey glands. McCormick paid Voronoff a large fee for the operation, but it failed to produce the drive demanded by Ganna who sent the sheepish tycoon away, keeping his money and jewels, living like a monarch in a Santa Barbara mansion until the end of her days. Upon her death, obituary writers were in a quandry to discover what roles Ganna had performed as a "famous opera singer." Her real role, of course, had been that of a wild gold-digger, and she had played that part to the hilt.

Charles WATERTON

Naturalist (1782–1865)

Perhaps one of the greatest eccentrics of all time, Waterton did not strive to present an unorthodox and unpredictable nature. For him the abnormal was normal, the whimsical, real and the bizarre, mundane. Born into wealth, Waterton's untitled parents owned a great manor house, Walton Hall, in Yorkshire England. They sent their son to Stonyhurst College where Jesuit teachers imbued Waterton with a sense of discovery, encouraging him to develop his considerable talents in natural history.

His formal education completed, Waterton sailed for British Guinana in 1804 to oversee some of his family's vast estates. While in South America he began to explore the jungles, fascinated with the wild interior tribes. He somehow became convinced that *curare,* the poison into which tribesmen dipped their blowgun darts, would cure hydrophobia and other strange ills. He went in search of the poison and other weird remedies he had heard natives talk about. Waterton was equally interested in snake venom and took every opportunity to capture the most exotic vipers.

Natives woke him early one morning to report a behemoth phython slithering near his hut. Waterton raced outside and, while his native bearers held the snake's head to the ground with a forked branch, the naturalist leaped upon the tail, binding it to the head with his suspenders. He took the huge snake back to his hut in a knotted sack and went to sleep with the serpent wriggling about in the sack beneath his bed.

Everywhere Waterton journeyed in South America, even in the most savage Brazilian wilds, he went barefoot, stopping every now and then to cut away insects with a clasp knife, and cutting stones which had become embedded in his bare feet, along with bad pieces of flesh. He staunchly maintained that no man could properly climb a tree wearing boots and proved his ability by shinning up trees with great speed and hopping up and down on one foot along the tops of high walls, feats he continued well into his eighties.

No adventure was too preposterous for Waterton, as he confirmed in his hilarious *Wanderings Through South America,* published in 1825, a document of his travels which the naturalist intended to be taken seriously. He related how his guides deserted him when he was trying to capture a crocodile. Determined to study the specimen, Waterton jumped on the beast's back on a river bank. Wrote Waterton: "I saw that he was in a state of fear and perturbation. I instantly ... sprang up and jumped on his back, turning half round as I vaulted, so that I gained my seat in a right position. I immediately seized his forelegs, and, by main force, twisted them on his back, where they served me for a bridle ... It was the first and last time I was ever on a cayman's back."

The naturalist became entranced with stories he heard from natives about vampire bats. These creatures would attack small domestic animals and suck the blood from them until they died. Waterton wondered if the bats would also attack humans, and resolved to have one of the creatures bite him and drain some of his blood. To that end he traveled alone to huge caves where the bats were reportedly housed and went to sleep in a hammock which he placed nearby, dangling his bare toes as bait to the vampire bats. He was unsuccessful in provoking the creatures to his bidding, even though he rubbed his toes with animal blood as a lure.

During a brief visit to the east coast of the United States, Waterton sprained his ankle while walking barefoot near Niagara Falls. He remembered how he had affected a speedy cure of an earlier sprain by placing his foot beneath a water pump and decided that the pressure of the falls would cure his current sprain twice as fast. "As I held my leg under the fall, I tried to meditate on the immense difference there was betwixt a house pump and this tremendous cascade of nature ... but the magnitude of the subject was too overwhelming and I was obliged to drop it."

Before returning to his ancestral estate, the naturalist married a seventeen-year-old granddaughter of a Guiana Indian princess, taking her to Paris where he attempted to teach her the fine craft of taxidermy. The girl, however, could not adjust to life outside her native jungles and died within a year of her marriage. Waterton, broken-hearted, resolved never to marry again. He returned to Walton Hall, converting the entire estate to an animal shelter and bird sanctuary, fencing in three square miles with an eight-foot wall and patrolling the area each day against poachers.

Waterton's bird sanctuary was unusual to say the least. He took in the kind of birds that are usually shot on sight—magpies, carrion crows and buzzards. He argued that these birds were discriminated against and deserved a resting place where humans could not get at them. Further, Waterton became one of the world's leading taxidermists and would tolerate no bureaucratic interference with his work.

One of Waterton's cargoes of South American birds was delayed by over-efficient British custom officials. The naturalist vowed revenge. He disemboweled and preserved a howler monkey, dressed it in a tailor-made suit, and gave it the face of the British Chief of Customs. He next placed this grotesque creation in the reception hall of the London Club to which the Chief of Customs belonged.

There was one creature in England that Waterton sought strictly to kill, black rats. He informed any who cared to listen that these rats were really "foreigners who had been smuggled into England by Hanoverian Protestants," and, as a devout Catholic, it was his duty to exterminate them.

Home life for Waterton at Walton Hall was as spartan as his life in South America had been. He slept on the bare floor of his room, using a beam of wood for a pillow, much like that used as an executioner's block. He wore loose clothes and no coat, even in the coldest winters. Invariably he got up in the middle of the night to say his prayers in his private chapel, then returned for a few hours sleep, rising at 4 A.M. to begin his work.

Guests invited to Walton Hall never knew what to expect from the naturalist. Often as not he would hide behind the tapestries in the entrance hall and when his visitors entered and went to hang up their coats, he would make snarling sounds like some wild animal, then pounce forward, crouched on all fours, sinking his teeth deep into their ankles.

Such bizarre greetings were only opening numbers for Waterton. He would resume a natural stance and carry on normal conversation at dinner, then announce that the back of his head itched. He would then proceed to scratch his head by lifting his foot and scratching with his naked right toe. Waterton's behavior really startled none of his friends; they expected it and loved him in spite of his eccentricities. And he never failed to amaze his friends.

One friend later wrote: "He would come out to welcome me in slippers ... and prove his pleasure by actually dancing down the whole length of the broad flagged walk, occasionally throwing one of his loose slippers from his foot high in the air, and expertly catching it in his hand in its descent. The wetness of the flagstones never constituted any impediment with Mr. Waterton, even when he was approaching his 80th year."

John Gottlieb WENDEL

Real Estate Tycoon (1847–1914)

"Buy, but never sell New York real estate." This was the credo of the strangest family of millionaires in America, set down by old John Wendel, a one-time partner of John Jacob Astor. Wendel proved his point by merely sitting still and allowing the city of New York to grow up around him. His son carried on the tradition as did John Gottlieb Wendel, the most eccentric of the family, and, perhaps the shrewdest investor of the lot.

The Wendel mansion, built in 1856, on Thirty-Ninth Street and Fifth Avenue, was a vast, towering structure, five-floors high with spiral staircases and no elevator, and with forty spacious but sparsely furnished rooms. For years, the building that housed one generation of Wendels after another was boarded up at the entranceway, servants and family members using a rear door. None of the doors had bells. Here dwelled members of the richest family in Manhattan, most of them eccentric, some of them mad.

Zinc bathtubs and marble washstands were used in the mansion; gas lamps were used everywhere, since the Wendels believed that electricity was not only expensive but was hard on the eyes. There were no radios or dumb-waiters in the building. The family lived in the past and refused to have any modern conveniences, even an auto. They walked most everywhere, but occasionally they had a 166-year-old carriage rolled out from the garage where two horses were kept and, even in the 1930s, rode this ancient contraption through the streets.

There was no phone in the mansion until two days before the death of the last of the Wendels, Ella Virginia von Echtzel Wendel, and that was only installed so that a nurse could call for an ambulance, if needed. Though the family hated the mere thought of liquor, thousands of bottles of wine and champagne were found in the cellar of the Wendel mansion when it was being demolished. It had not been touched in so many decades that it had all turned to vinegar.

John Gottlieb Wendel exercised the strangest business procedures in New York real estate dealings. A broker took Wendel to the corner of Broadway and Liberty streets, where the Westinghouse Building was later to be, and offered the tycoon the property for $750,000. Wendel excused himself, telling the broker he would return to the site within fifteen minutes. He reappeared in twelve minutes and began counting out the payment in cash.

"But I can't carry that amount of money," complained the broker.

"Young man," said John Gottlieb Wendel, "the Wendel terms are cash, nothing but hard cash. Take it or leave it."

The broker took it.

Wendel would never permit any liquor in the buildings he rented or leased and once held up a million-dollar lease until he received a written agreement that no more than a pint of alcohol in the first-aid kit and medicine cabinet would be kept in the building for emergencies. He also opposed any signs on his buildings, saying that "they might fall down sometime and hurt someone." He was also violently against having any wire in or around his property.

A branch of the National Republican Club strung a wire that passed over some Wendel property. John G. Wendel marched into the Club an hour later, threatening to thrash everyone in sight with his cane, and yelling: "That wire must come down!"

"Why?" questioned one of the officers of the Club.

"It might hurt a bird in flight, that's why!"

Wendel was a man who watched his pennies, as well as signs and wires. He saw no reason to buy an extensive wardrobe, even though he was worth more than $100 million. He purchased a suit shortly after the Civil War and had all his suits tailored after the exact design of that original suit. He refused to wear any fabric that had been dyed. His black suit and black coat were made of wool, but ordered from a firm in Scotland that provided the wool especially shorn from black sheep. Wendell habitaully carried an umbrella every day of his life, rain or shine, summer or winter. He wore only one straw hat summer after summer, until it went to pieces and he reluctantly purchased a new one. His derby, which he wore all his life, was preserved for decades with black varnish, applied twice a year at Wendel's specific order. He also had varnish applied to the lapels of his overcoat to preserve that garment, too.

No one was ever invited to the Wendel mansion as guests. John G. Wendel, on rare occasions, did invite business associates to lunch and these were extremely formal affairs in archconservative restaurants. At such times Wendel sent out invitations which he wrote completely in Latin. Lunch guests would arrive to discover that their host had already ordered for them—the special.

Germ conscious to the point of a mania, Wendel was convinced that all diseases were contracted through the feet and, to prevent illness, he ordered the soles of his two pair of shoes to be made of gutta percha not less than an inch in thickness. In this way he was insulated against the deadly germs on the ground attempting to get at his feet.

The shoes didn't help. Wendel died in 1914 when the germs got to him. He left seven strange spinster sisters, all in mortal fear of getting married, something Wendel had warned them about. Men were evil and calculating, he had told them. They would only steal the family fortune, he had cautioned them. This was Wendel's real fear, that his enormous family holdings would be divided among strangers.

The sisters remained faithful to their brother's wishes, except for Rebecca, who married but not until she was sixty years of age. Georgianna was the only sister to rebel against her family's rigid code, having a secret lover then giving him up in mortal fear, she said, of family reprisals, a fear that blossomed into a persecution mania that drove her to an insane asylum, where she died. Josephine removed herself from the Manhattan mansion, going to live in one of the Wendel country houses, her only companions being the family servants. "The pitiful part of it," wrote one scribe, "is that she dreamed that the house was filled with noisy, happy children, and used to talk and play with them. She imagined that people came to see her and she used to have her servants set six places at the dinner table. As each course was served, she would change places, pretending that she was all of the guests in turn."

The last sister to die was Ella Wendel, who stayed on in the great house with only her servants and a French poodle, Tobey, to keep her company. Ella locked all the rooms, except her bedroom, the dining room, a large room upstairs, and the servants' quarters. She ordered that the shutters be permanently locked. She could not bear to enter any of the other rooms where she and her sisters had once spent their lonely childhood.

Tobey, the poodle, was treated as a human, having his own four-poster bed, an exact replica of his mistress' bed. He ate in the dining room each night, served at a brass table covered with a velvet cloth.

When Ella died in 1932 she left a family fortune that had dwindled from $100 million to $36 million. She also died believing that she did not have a living relative in the world. Less than a month after her death, 2,312 possible heirs to the real estate fortune put in claims, more claimants for a single estate than any other in the history of the United States. The German Consulate filed a blanket claim representing 400 Wendels in Germany. Hundreds more were filed from Czechoslovakia. The state of Tennessee produced 290 claimants. One dogged claimant, Thomas Patrick Morris from Scotland, insisted that he was the only son of John Gottlieb Wendel, who, Morris said, married his mother secretly. He produced a marriage certificate and a will. Both of these documents, it was later proved, were forged and Morris was sent to jail for fraud.

Ironically, John Gottlieb Wendel had never executed a will, saying that he "didn't want any damned lawyer making money out of my property." In the end, his decision proved expensive; more than 250 lawyers collected handsome fees in the mad scramble for the Wendel millions.

James Marion WEST, Jr.

Oil Tycoon (1903–1957)

The Hollywood image of the wildcatting Texas oilman turned millionaire, from *Boomtown* to *Giant,* is largely mythical. Most of the Texas oil men who brought in the gushers and fortunes lived, and continue to live, low-profile lives, forsaking the pillared mansions and limousines, driving, most likely, a pickup truck to the bank or office. There was one notable eccentric exception, James Marion West, Jr., who lived up to all the legends and created a host of his own.

West was known as "Silver Dollar Jim," because he carried pockets sagging with silver dollars which he would toss like confetti on the streets of Houston during rush hour just to see the mad scramble he could create. West kept a fleet of thirty cars in top running order, mostly Cadillacs, at a downtown garage and would drive about Houston all night long, talking with the foremen at his many oil rigs over one of four phones installed in the dashes of his cars. The autos were also equipped with police band radios so that Jim could listen in to important calls and respond to major crimes; he was a Texas Ranger and wore a Ranger's badge encrusted with diamonds.

Silver Dollar Jim's cars were also four-wheel arsenals, equipped with shotguns, 30-30 rifles, submachineguns, and cannisters of tear gas. In addition, Ranger West wore a .45 on his hip in a gold-plated holster hanging from a belt studded with gems and centered with a gold-plated buckle engraved with western scenes.

The citizens of Houston thought nothing of seeing West race behind a squad car en route to a robbery or homicide. At such times West would toss silver dollars to the crowds gathering at the curb. There is no record of Silver Dollar Jim ever apprehending a criminal, let alone shooting it out with an armed thief, but it was gossiped that the self-styled lawman–tycoon accidently shot one of his policeman friends on a routine burglary call.

West's wild antics came to a halt after the oilman sprayed some jeering teenagers with tear gas. They had the nerve to make fun of his ten-gallon hat and diamond-studded badge. Parents of the children made such an uproar that West put his guns and cars in storage and stayed home to increase his already heavy drinking, undoubtedly the cause of his death in 1957, a rather ignomious and lonely end for a man who once stated that "I'd like to go down fighting the bad guys."

Mae WEST

Actress (1892–1980)

No other actress in this century was more endowed with physical attributes and less acting ability than the incomparable Mae West, now a cherished cult figure whose blatant sexual postures of the 1920s and 1930s now seem dated and amateurish, if not outright embarrassing. She thought of herself as "different," even as a child.

Born to John and Matilda West on August 17, 1892 in Brooklyn, Mae stated in 1934 that her younger brother, John, and sister Beverly, were unruly but she was only "sulky and stubborn. My mother insisted upon my having my own way. 'Let her go; she's different,' my mother would tell my father."

Her mother was addicted to vaudeville and took young Mae to the theater at every opportunity. By the time she was five, Mae was imitating Eddie Foy, Bert Williams, and all the other Broadway stars. Two years later she took singing and dancing lessons and by age fifteen she was acting as a straight lady to a comic. She got her first break in 1911 when she appeared in a review called *A la Broadway* as a featured chorus girl. She received her first mention from the New York *Times* which commented that "a girl named Mae West, hitherto unknown, pleased by her grotesquerie and snappy way of singing and dancing."

For the next fifteen years Mae appeared in mostly unsuccessful musicals

The strange Hollywood sex siren, Mae West, as *Klondike Annie*.

402

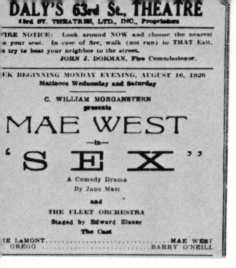

DALY'S 63rd St. THEATRE

63rd ST. THEATRES, LTD., INC., Proprietors

FIRE NOTICE: Look around NOW and choose the nearest
to your seat. In case of fire, walk (not run) to THAT Exit.
4 try to beat your neighbor to the street.
JOHN J. DORMAN, Fire Commissioner.

WEEK BEGINNING MONDAY EVENING, AUGUST 16, 1926
Matinees Wednesday and Saturday

C. WILLIAM MORGANSTERN
presents

MAE WEST
—in—
'S E X'

A Comedy Drama
By Jane Mast
and
THE FLEET ORCHESTRA
Staged by Edward Elsner
The Cast

IE LaMONT.................................MAE WEST
. GREGG.............................BARRY O'NEILL

The program of Mae West's own low-down play, *Sex*.

and some offbeat dramas, her notices fair to poor. She sought to salvage a sagging career by shocking Broadway with a play of her own called *Sex* in 1926. She wrote this opus, which portrayed a group of prostitutes servicing sailors in a Montreal bordello under the *nom de plume* of Jane Mast. It was crude, awkward, and gauche with as much gutter languange as Mae could pass off as dialog. It was a smash hit, running 385 performances, in spite of universal condemnation from the press and a later close-down by police, who jailed the author and star.

The play opened on April 26, 1926. Two days later *Variety,* which invariably offered up the kindest reviews, soundly damned it. Said its reviewer: "Mae West ... has broken the fetters and does as she pleases here. After three hours of this play's nasty, infantile, amateurish, and vicious dialog, after watching its various actors do their stuff badly, one really has a feeling of gratefulness for any repression that may have toned down her vaudeville songs in the past." The New York *Times,* four days later, tersely slammed *Sex* as being "a crude, inept play, cheaply produced and poorly acted." Yet the house was full every night until the evening of February 21, 1927 when police raided the theater and closed it down, arresting and jailing Mae West and her principal actors and charging them with corrupting the morals of youth.

Mae and her producer, Jim Timothy, were fined $500 each and given ten-

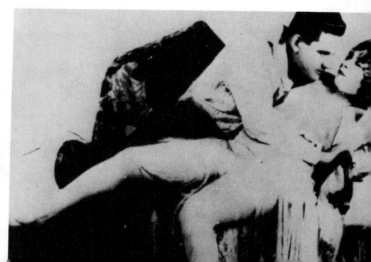

Mae, who was once called a female impersonator, is shown here with actor Warren Sterling in a "scandalous" scene from *Sex*.

day sentences in the work house. The actress merely gave a sneer that was to become famous to newsmen, and sauntered defiantly off to Welfare Island to serve out her sentence. She was released two days early for good behavior. Upon her release, Mae again gave authorities headaches by quickly writing and producing a play called *The Drag*, a sordid little drama about homosexuals, and it was from this production that Mae earned her lifelong support of homosexuals, who thought of her as their champion.

She was later quoted as saying of homosexuals: 'They're crazy about me 'cause I give 'em a chance to play. My characterization is sexy and with humor and they like to imitate me, the things I say, the way I say 'em, the way I move. It's easy for them to imitate me 'cause the gestures are exaggerated, flamboyant, *sexy*, and that's what they wanna look like, feel like, and I've stood up for 'em.."

Mae's image of a voluptuous figure with an enormous bosom crammed into tight fitting dresses took on new dimensions and captured new audiences after she signed with Paramount Pictures in 1932 and began to make films. She swept into Hollywood like a grand diva, with expensive luggage, dogs, a limousine, and dripping diamonds. "I'm not a little girl from a little town makin' good in a big town," Mae told newsman when she arrived in Hollywood. "I'm a big girl from a big town makin' good in a little town!"

Mae moved her body like a large snake in front of cameras, grinding out her films—*Night after Night, She Done Him Wrong, Diamond Lil* (a smash hit that made $2 million in three months), *I'm No Angel, Belle of the Nineties* (the title was changed from *It Ain't No Sin* to appease censors), *Klondike Annie* to her final Paramount film, *Every Day's a Holiday* in 1938. Mae ever burlesqued herself in the W.C. Fields vehicle (see entry), *My Little Chickadee,* in 1940, but she hated that film because Fields dominated the script which he deigned to write with her, and also dominated every scene he played with her. He was mean, cantakerous and often insulting to her, she later claimed, but she put up with it, managing to complete the film "without belting the old jerk!" Mae returned to the screen only once—following her film, *The Heat's On,* for Columbia in 1943—when she appeared in the grotesque *Myra Breckinridge,* in another caricature of herself, wearing the skin-tight dresses and the famous blonde wig she wore for decades in all of her films.

Cary Grant, Mae's favorite leading man.

Whether playing opposite Cary Grant or Randolph Scott, Mae's role was that of the vamp, seducing the innocent young man and rendering lines like "Come on up and see me some time," or, to a gangster, "Is that a gun in your pocket, or are you just happy to see me?" The more suggestive the line the better Mae played it. In a way she burlesqued sex in such a hokey manner that she somehow managed to make it repulsive, if not distasteful, and she positively defied the censors and church members who conducted vigorous crusades against her throughout her career. The censors finally managed to succeed, after Mae appeared in a rather innocuous skit with Edgar Bergen and Charlie McCarthy, the witty wooden dummy, in a 1937 radio show sponsored by Chase & Sanborn Coffee. The following dialog is what spelled Mae West's doom:

Mae: Why don't you come up ... home with me now, honey? I'll let you play in my wood pile.

Charlie: Well, I'm not feeling so well tonight. I've been feeling nervous lately. I think I'm gonna have a nervous breakdown. Whuuup! There I go.

Mae: So, good-time Charlie's gonna play hard to get. Well, you can't kid me. You're afraid of women. Your Casanova stuff is just a front, a false front.

Charlie: Not so loud, Mae, not so loud! All my girlfriends are listening.

Mae: Oh yeah? You're all wood and a yard long.

Charlie: Yeah.

Mae: You weren't so nervous and backward when you came up to see me at my apartment. In fact, you didn't need any encouragement to kiss me.

Charlie: Did I do that?

Mae: Why, you certainly did. I got marks to prove it ... and splinters, too.

Protests over this show, led by church elders and women's social groups, flooded NBC's offices. Some of the responses were quoted as saying that the radio show was "profane ... dirty ... obscene." It was later concluded that the show should not have been aired on a Sunday. The hubbub reached epic proportions and the sponsor publicly apologized to listeners the next Sunday. Hollywood studio heads bent over backward to convince everyone that they had nothing to do with the radio skit and disavowed Mae West, as did NBC. She was all but finished as an entertainer and was never again to appear on radio, came the edict of the bosses.

Mae, at right with her mother kissing her and her sister Beverly looking glumly on, goes cheerfully off to jail after being convicted of "corrupting the morals of youth" with her play, *Sex*.

Salvador Dali's surrealistic interpretation of sexpot Mae West.

Mae West, from then on, was labeled everything from a tramp to a female impersonator, a sex joke on the lowest level. Yet her personal life was anything but scandalous, at least in public. She attended prizefights, an abiding passion, with her manager, Jim Timothy, but seldom went to Hollywood parties. In the early 1940s she was sued by a Milwaukee man, who claimed that he had married Mae years earlier and she had never divorced him. Mae settled with him out-of-court.

In her later years, the sex goddess gave interviews from her golden shell bed in Hollywood, and then wrote her memoirs, lurid tales of marathon sex she claimed to have had with dozens of men, many at the same time, one long-distance young man providing her with fifteen hours of nonstop lovemaking, undoubtedly a sexual endurance record. Was it all true?, the press wanted to know. Said Mae, before her death on November 22, 1980: "I do all my best work in bed."

E.J. ("Stroller") WHITE

Editor (date uncertain–1933)

White traveled as a young man to Alaska in the late 1890s, following the herd of miners to the gold fields. But, instead of panning for nuggets, White established his own newspaper, *Stroller's Weekly,* in Juneau, a publication that dealt with anything but facts. The initial financing for his paper came from selling job printing, or rather bogus stationary, such as that which listed the Sour Dough Hotel at 1322 Icicle Lane, Juneau.

White churned out absurd tales for years which miners clipped and sent to awed relatives in the lower forty-eight states. One story dealt with "ice-worm cocktails," reportedly a drink served at local bars which included a frozen worm dropped into any drink, free of charge. Those brave enough to consume the drink were given a second snort, also free of charge. The worms, White later admitted, were strips of cooked spaghetti which had been put on ice.

The most outrageous story White ever printed was turned in by his lone reporter, Casey Moran, who dashed into the newspaper office one day waving an affidavit he said had been signed by an Indian chief. The Indian's statement reported the discovery of a "house as big as a white man's town built in a big canoe." This amazing find, insisted Moran in his story, was none other than Noah's Ark, which the chief had stumbled upon while climbing Mt. Koyukuk. The story was picked up by the wire services and sent to every daily newspaper in America and Europe, hundreds of them using the entire ridiculous account.

Lewis Robert ("Hack") WILSON

Baseball Player (1901–1948)

He was called The Million Dollar Slugger from the Five-and-Ten-Cent Store, after he was purchased from the Giants in 1926 by the Chicago Cubs for a paltry $5,000. He was Lewis Robert Wilson, known to Chicago fans as "Hack," because his powerful, squat figure was similar to that of a strong man named Hackenschmidt.

Wilson's best professional years were with the Cubs where he proved himself a great outfielder with a strong arm and an even stronger bat that, for six seasons, 1926–31, produced 190 home runs and scores of hits; Wilson's best year, 1930, produced the long-standing National League record of 56 home runs.

Great as he was on the field, Wilson was a night-owl, a boozer, and a headache to manager Joe McCarthy. The manager had a little trick that unnerved the top Cub slugger to no end. After a brief conversation in the dugout before each game, McCarthy would suddenly snarl to Wilson: "And I *know* you were in Martha's speakeasy last night—stay out of there, Hack, or you'll be paying out some heavy fines for breaking regulations."

Wilson would make his rounds that night, careful to stay out of Martha's, spending his time, money and energy in another dive. But no matter what

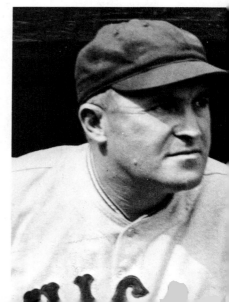

Joe McCarthy to Hack Wilson: "Stay out of those speakeasies!" (UPI)

nightspot Wilson happened to be in, McCarthy uncannily pinpointed that speakeasy the next day before the game, every day.

Wilson went to his friend, pitcher Perce "Pat" Malone, rubbing his jaw and whining: "I can't understand it, Pat. McCarthy knows where I go every night. I know he ain't got anyone following me, because I take lots and lots of cabs and go around in circles before I pick out a joint, and the best detective in the world couldn't be on my tail after all of that. Yet, every time I step into the dugout before the game, he's on to me, and tells me to my face where I was the night before. It's driving me nuts, and I ain't having any fun."

Malone thought for a moment than asked: "What does Joe say to you first off?"

"He asks me for a match. You know he's never got a light for that cigar of his."

Malone began to laugh, then blurted: "You dummy! He's reading the names of the joints off the matches you give him, probably the ones you pick up from the bars the night before."

"Why, that sneak," Hack said. "I'll fix him tomorrow."

The next day McCarthy approached Wilson with his cigar butt jutting from his jaw. "Hey, Hack," said the manager. "Got a match?"

Wilson jumped up, ready. "Sure, Mac." He handed the manager a book of matches. McCarthy studied the book of matches for a moment, turning them over a few times, noting that they were blank. Wilson grinned widely and said: "*Now* tell me where I was last night!"

On one occasion it was impossible for Wilson to make excuses. He had been arrested for violating the Volstead Act in a speakeasy raid. Only through the efforts of William Veeck (see entry) of the Cubs front office was the slugger released before being booked. McCarthy was waiting for the sheepish Wilson in the dugout the next day. "What happened to you last night, Mr. Wilson?" inquired McCarthy.

Wilson thought fast, then stated: "Well, Mac, it's like this. Me and the wife

Hack Wilson to Joe McCarthy: "Now tell me where I was last night." (UPI)

take in a movie, see, and I says to her, 'Let's get a couple of sandwiches and a couple of bottles of beer and go home and listen to the radio.' So we go by this speakeasy I heard about. We push the button and all of a sudden there's a million cops behind me, pushing me *into* the place!"

The story was so contrived that McCarthy broke into howling laughter while Hack Wilson stood blinking through a deadpan face. "I don't think it's funny, Mac," said the slugger. "My God, we was *abducted!*"

Walter WINCHELL

Journalist (1897–1972)

Once Walter Winchell's column and radio show held more than fifty million Americans captive. He began his radio show with the memorable words: "Hello, Mr. and Mrs. North and South America and all the ships at sea," and those areas, too, formed the geography of his vast audience. He was the most powerful journalist in the nation for thirty years, his terse and his terrifying words were syndicated in over 1,000 daily newspapers. Friend, foe and stranger alike were ripped apart in Winchell's column and he never apologized. Confronted, WW would only shrug and casually blurt: "I'm a shitheel."

Winchell accumulated gigantic powers, so vast and so influential that he could destroy reputations in a single sentence in his column or on his radio programs (or make a career overnight which was less likely to happen). Winchell's was the power of the press at its zenith, and he used it ruthlessly to destroy whole populations, including, eventually, himself.

A product of Hell's Kitchen in New York, Winchell came from a poverty-stricken home where he and his brother Al were raised in a haphazard fashion. His father was a drinker and gambler who was never able to support his family. His mother worked odd jobs and barely managed food and rent. Young Walter felt financial oppression from the beginning; so acutely did he resent his poverty that he saved almost every dime he earned, never investing in anything. When he retired in 1968 he had millions locked away in bank vaults. Before his retirement, Winchell delighted in showing the heavy ring of keys in his pockets that opened the strongboxes holding his cash.

The power-mad newsman Walter Winchell, on the air in 1935.

410

FBI Director J. Edgar Hoover, one of Winchell's best friends and fellow habitue of the Stork Club.

The millions were far off in 1910 when Winchell entered vaudeville as a slightly talented soft-shoe dancer, singer, and teller of bad jokes. He claimed that he began his career with George Jessel, but Jessel always denied the assertion. Walter and Al Winchell, along with another boy, Jack Wiener, sang in orchestra pits as The Imperial Trio. (Underage boys could not then legally appear on the stage.) When the act folded, Winchell stayed in Vaudeville, teaming up with a pretty dance partner, Rita Greene, whom he married. By 1922, Winchell was more interested in reporting gossipy items to the *Vaudeville News* (which paid him $25 a week) than wearing out his feet on the stage. In a few years the carrot-eating eccentric publisher of the New York *Evening Graphic,* Bernarr MacFadden (see entry), hired Winchell as a daily columnist. He soon went with the Hearst papers for $500 a week to write a syndicated column that appeared in the New York *Mirror.* Winchell had arrived, and he reveled in his new position of power as he took the bows along Broadway then The Great White Way at its glittering height, awash with millionaires, statuesque chorus girls, and racketeers.

Suddenly, Winchell was all things to all people. He wept in print over heart-breaking Broadway stories. One tear-jerker profiled a chorus girl down on her luck, locked from her room after the hotel detective called to pretend he was a producer with a part for her, in order to entice her out of her lodgings. And when Walter wept, the nation wept. When Walter laughed, the American public roared. When Walter hated, Americans almost everywhere joined forces with him.

The columnist's private life was never mentioned in his reports. The public, he undoubtedly thought, would never have understood his obsession for gangsters, rascists, leggy chorus girls and a nightlife which he ruled as an absolute tyrant. One of Winchell's closest friends during the late 1920s was a vicious underworld killer and bootlegger, Owney Madden. Winchell and Madden would stroll down Broadway with Madden's bullet-proof, sixteen-cylinder touring car trailing behind. When they tired, Madden would signal the chauffeur to drive up and then gangster and columnist would roar off to a penthouse party. During the day, Madden would take Winchell to the races and place $1000 bets for him.

Winchell, in turn, would plant items in his column that made gang chief Owney look more like a respectable citizen than the killer he was. Winchell was rewarded by inside tips on underworld events; Madden went so far as to

411

present Winchell with a $2,000 roadster. The inside underworld tips Winchell received allowed him to miraculously scoop all rival newspapers. He reported that Mad Dog Coll would be executed in a phone booth, in oblique terms, twenty-four hours before the gangster was actually slain as WW had predicted. It was Winchell who, in 1939, arranged for Louis "Lepke" Buchalter, then the most wanted man in America as head of Murder, Inc., to turn himself in to Winchell and his friend J. Edgar Hoover (see entry) on a New York street. The columnist would later accept the surrender of garment district killer Bernard Macri for which the Damon Runyon Cancer Fund, begun by Winchell, collected a $25,000 reward.

Winchell's power grew when he began his coast-to-coast radio gossip show. At first he was nervous on the air, arriving for his debut breathless, sweating and red-faced. He sat down before the microphone and hurriedly studied his notes. He unbelted his pants, pulling down the zipper as his legs began to pump rapidly. A studio official came forward and asked if anything was the matter.

"I have to go to the washroom," Winchell snapped, not looking up from his notes.

"You still have a few minutes before we go on the air," advised the official.

"No, thanks," replied Winchell. "It'll be better this way—my voice will have a sound urgency."

Later Winchell used his radio show to carry out his personal vendettas. On one occasion he called all those who elected his enemies in Congress "damned fools," but he was not reprimanded by the FCC. He attacked Mayor Bill O'Dwyer of New York for breaking a policeman to the ranks—the cop was a friend of the columnist—and insisted that the patrolman be restored to the rank of sergeant. This was to be done immediately warned Winchell, or the Mayor would not be welcome in the columnist's favorite watering hole, The Stork Club. O'Dwyer restored the cop to sergeant.

The Stork Club was owned and operated by Sherman Billingsley, who had a record of arrests and had once served a prison sentence. The club owner once bragged of killing a man in Oklahoma, but such talk never bothered Winchell, who took his reserved seat at table number fifty in the Stork's Cub Room (celebrities only) every night, often accompanied by FBI Director J. Edgar Hoover. Billingsley ran his bistro almost as a private club, telling one and all it was reserved for "nice people," and he meant white people only. He once refused to seat the great black dancer Josephine Baker and her party, turning them away with a smile. Winchell took no notice.

When Sugar Ray Robinson, then welterweight champion, won a large purse and donated it to Winchell's Runyon Fund, the columnist asked what he could do for him.

Said Robinson: "I'd like to go to the Stork Club."

Winchell winced. "Ask me anything but that," he pleaded. "Billingsley doesn't want your people in the Stork and if he did or said something to embarrass you, I'd have to end a friendship of twenty years."

Robinson did not go to the Stork Club, but Winchell continued to take his

Winchell, who kept millions in cash in safe deposit boxes, is shown here testifying on behalf of Senator Joseph McCarthy in 1954. (Wide World)

table nightly, receiving a host of New York press agents who would grovel before him, begging for space in his column for their clients and Winchell, playing the potentate of the press, would either nod or shake his head, and either make or break a man's career. If a press agent ever dared to give him a fake lead or old news he was immediately put on WW's "Drop Dead" list, which meant that none of the press agent's news items would appear for at least six months, maybe never.

Several press agents literally starved while waiting for such Winchell bans to lift. On the other hand, if a press agent gave Winchell top-notch items, he was rewarded with dozens of plugs for his clients which could and did make many of them millionaires.

The powerful portrait Winchell drew in his heyday would later be used to thinly present him in a Broadway play entitled *Blessed Event,* subsequently made into a Warner Brothers film, which portrayed Winchell as a god-like figure who rode to the rescue of a pregnant chorus girl. Just the opposite was the profile rendered Winchell in the devastating *Sweet Smell of Success,* which showed a Winchell-like tyrant for what he was—possessive, ego-maniacal and ruthless, even when dealing with his own family.

The columnist, however, was not all-powerful. Many stood up to him, some being creatures of his own gossipy world. Westbrook Pegler labeled Winchell "a gent's room journalist." Ed Sullivan, appearing on the Barry Gray Show once, stated that "Winchell has developed into a small-time Hitler ... He has capitalized on the big lie." When Winchell met Sullivan following the show he demanded an apology. Sullivan grabbed him by the lapels of his expensive suit and shouted: "Apologize to you? You son-of-a-bitch ... if you say one more word, I'll take you downstairs and stick your head in the toilet!"

Winchell insulted Congressman Martin Dies once and the two slugged it out over a coast-to-coast show for fifteen minutes. Dies' assault was vicious and personal. Winchell, by then an old hand at "reading" public sensibility, answered cooly by simply declaring his principles. The confrontation contributed mightily to the loss of Dies' Washington position.

When it came to Senator Joseph McCarthy of Wisconsin, however, Winchell was disgracefully ardent in his support of the witch-hunting demogogue. Then again, McCarthy was being encouraged secretly by Hoover to "get the reds" and Hoover was one of Winchell's closest friends.

The number of Winchell's enemies mounted over the years. Singer Al

Jolson, who once punched the columnist in the nose, put Winchell on *his* "Drop Dead" list. Actress Ethel Barrymore hated the man and asked friends: "why is he allowed to live?" The Schuberts, the powerful theater-chain owners, barred Winchell from their halls for life after receiving bad reviews from him. The columnist countered this move by going to Harpo Marx's (see entry) apartment one night and donning a disguise—a wild wig, a hunchback made of a rubber mat, a set of false whiskers, and a suit of shabby clothes—in order to sneak past guards at a Schubert theater to review a play.

By the 1960s Winchell's hand was played out. In 1968 his columns were appearing in only 100 newspapers. His voice was long gone from radio. The quick magic he had been able to produce through contacts no longer existed. The columnist's personal life by then was also a shambles. His adopted daughter, Gloria, died of pneumonia. His daughter Walda had grown to hate him when he interferred with an early marriage; Winchell had disapproved of her producer husband and reportedly arranged, through his powerful Washington friends, to have the producer sent to jail on income tax evasion.

In that same devastating year for Winchell, his son, Walter, Jr., walked into his garage and blew out his brains. He was then thirty-three and had never managed to accept the role of the great columnist's son. With that suicide, Walter Winchell retired. The man who had been wholly infatuated with himself no longer cared about power. In the words of New York *Times* writer Alden Whitman, "The more powerful he became, the harder his basic sense of insecurity drove him to further displays of omnipotence. And the more lax he became in digging up his own items. Ultimately he was hand-fed by a covey of flacks, fawned upon by those who sought status through him."

The staccato-voiced columnist died on February 20, 1972, with few alive to mourn his passing. It would not have mattered to the eccentric newsman. Years earlier he had boasted to the world that he would take his bows a century later: "One hundred years from now I'll be the only newspaperman of this era they'll remember."

Victoria Claflin Martin WOODHULL

Free Love Exponent (1838–1927)

She was named after Queen Victoria, but she was just the opposite of that refined and remote British sovereign. Victoria Claflin Woodhull was a bogus clairvoyant, a swindler, and a prostitute. She also ran for the Presidency in 1872 (representing the Equal Rights Party) and at one time, almost took complete charge of the Woman's Suffrage movement, coming to head-to-head combat with the venerable Susan B. Anthony.

Victoria Woodhull, prostitute, clairvoyant and candidate for the United States presidency, shown in 1872.

Victoria's father, Reuben Buckman Claflin, sired ten children, of which Victoria was the seventh. He was shiftless and irresponsible by nature. He was also a crook who set fire to his own wood mill and then attempted to collect insurance money on a policy he had taken out only weeks before the blaze. His awkward swindle in 1849 was so obvious to the townsfolk of Homer, Ohio that Claflin and his family were run out of the community. Roxanna Claflin, Victoria's zany mother, did not really mind. She was only concerned with contacting spirits of the dead, fortune-telling, and developing her ability to put gullible patrons who staggered into her shabby salon into a trance, using the dubious techniques advanced by Friedrich Mesmer.

The Claflin family lived a nomadic life, moving from one small Ohio town to another, surviving on the income Roxanna produced through her séances and, when the Claflin daughters were grown, whatever money could be gleaned through prostitution. In 1853, Victoria met a handsome drunk, Dr. Canning Woodhull, marrying him after a short love affair. The marriage was shaky from the start, the alcoholic Woodhull spending his wedding night in a whorehouse. Victoria, however, had a soft spot for her errant husband and tolerated his dissolute character; in fact, she would take care of the drunkard throughout his miserable life.

The union bore two children, Byron, who suffered brain damage after falling from a second-story window, and Zulu Maud, a daughter who was blindly faithful to her mother no matter what scandals she later perpetrated. The Claflin–Woodhull brood moved to Cincinnati where the women continued their clairvoyant readings, enticing wealthy men who came to their séances into bed at a higher price than fortune-telling could yield. Tennessee Claflin, Victoria's beautiful younger sister, took to blackmailing her clients and the family had to leave town quickly, under the threat of a mass lynching.

During a tour of the midwest, Victoria met and took up with James Harvey

Blood, a married man attracted to Victoria's free love theories. They began living as commonlaw husband and wife, even though Canning Woodhull continued to share Victoria's bed. The crazy spiritualistic road show, *BLOOD IN TOW,* finally settled in Pittsburgh. It was while living here that Victoria claimed she saw a ghost wearing a Greek tunic, the apparition identifying itself as the spirit of Demosthenes and directing her to go to New York to seek her fortune. The family moved to Manhattan, to 17 Great Jones Street in Manhattan, an address specifically mentioned by the ghost, Victoria later claimed. It was from this address that Victoria launched her campaign to become rich and famous, rich first, famous later.

Using her strumpet sister as bait, Victoria managed an introduction to the lecherous Cornelius Vanderbilt in 1868. Commodore Vanderbilt, then the wealthiest man in America, was obsessed by two things—sex with pretty young women, and any kind of spiritual healing that would prolong the life of his much-abused body. Tennessee Claflin *and* Victoria more than satisfied the Commodore's sexual needs; Victoria read the tycoon's future and predicted a long, long life.

In return for such extraordinary favors, Vanderbilt gave Victoria large amounts of cash and, more importantly, tips on stock investments. He confided to her that his opponents, Big Jim Fisk and Jay Gould, were trying to corner the gold market and that she should buy all the stock she could. Victoria bought low and sold when the gold market peaked, receiving $160 a share, and thus making her fortune which later grew to almost $1 million, fed by Victoria's brokerage firm and her shrewd investments. (Her prostituting sister Tennessee, who died in 1923 after marrying into British aristocracy, earned at least half that amount.)

With her wealth secure, Victoria turned to more important matters. She

Victoria Woodhull sought to destroy the powerful religious leader, Henry Ward Beecher (shown here), but instead was ruined by Beecher's followers, including his sister, Harriet Beecher Stowe, author of *Uncle Tom's Cabin.*

began to give lectures on equal rights for women, enlarging her ambitions with a public announcement on April 2, 1870, when she declared for the Presidency of the United States. "While others argued the equality of woman with man," said Victoria, "I proved it by successfully engaging in business ... I therefore claim the right to speak for the unenfranchised women of the country, and believing as I do that the prejudices which still exist in the popular mind against women in public life will soon disappear, I now announce myself as candidate for the Presidency."

A year later Victoria addressed members of Congress in Washington, urging them to support her candidacy. They were polite, but few committed themselves. The powerful leaders of the National Women's Suffrage Association were present at this speech, and they did urge Victoria to continue her campaign, even though they held back a full endorsement.

The soothsaying prostitute had achieved the heights. Her wait-and-see supporters now included Susan B. Anthony, Elizabeth Cady Stanton, Isabella Beecher Hooker, and Paulina Wright Davis. When the Association's first convention was held on May 11, 1871, Victoria was one of the featured speakers, electrifying her audience with: "If the very next Congress refuses women all the legitimate results of citizenship, we shall proceed to call another convention expressly to frame a new constitution and to erect a new government ... We mean treason; we mean secession, and on a thousand times greater scale than was that of the South. We are plotting revolution; we will overthrow this bogus Republic and plant a government of righteousness in its stead."

Members to the convention responded with great enthusiasm, hundreds of them asking Victoria to lead their movement, as well as run for the Presidency. This put her at odds with the real power behind the movement, Susan B. Anthony, who then felt that Victoria wanted to take over Women's Suffrage in order to gain support for her Presidential candidacy, and she was right. Anthony was aided, however, when an enormous scandal broke out about Victoria Woodhull's head, one of her own making.

Feeling that the leaders of the movement opposed her because of her tainted background, which was secretly known by Anthony and others, Victoria struck a blow against the most powerful reformer in the land—Henry Ward Beecher, who had been carrying on a secret love affair with the wife of Theodore Tilton, his protege. Victoria, who had learned of this scandal from Elizabeth Cady Staton, revealed the facts publicly, also stating that Beecher, a liberal-minded preacher, had had many affairs. (Victoria herself would later admit to having slept with *both* Beecher and Tilton.) Using her own weekly newspaper, published in tandem with her sister Tennessee, *Woodhull & Claflin's Weekly,* Victoria printed every lurid detail of the Beecher scandal, adding that the preacher was "a poltroon, a coward and a sneak."

Though Beecher refused to sue, his heavy-handed reformer friend, Anthony Comstock, brought charges of obscenity against the sisters. Both were arrested and, on and off, spent six months in jail before being pronounced "now guilty." Victoria's past, however, branded her as unacceptable in the minds of most voters. She had already lost the race to take over Women's Suffrage, storming into Steinway Hall and demanding that the delegates follow her to *her* rented hall, the Apollo. Susan B. Anthony successfully blocked her efforts in a face-to-face showdown as the two women stood in the main aisle of the hall. "Nothing that this person has said," announced Anthony to the swarms of delegates, "will be recorded in the minutes. The convention will now adjourn to meet at eleven o'clock in *this* hall."

About six hundred delegates defected to Victoria's convention, where she was endorsed for her Presidential candidacy, but the free-lover knew that she had lost the major support of the Women's Suffrage movement. The thirty-four-year-old candidate, the first to run for the American presidency, received only a few thousand votes. Her platform, which included free love, short skirts, magnetic healing, birth control, simple divorce laws, vegetarianism and a world government, was soundly rejected by a conservative populace.

Victoria Woodhull, still under pressure from Comstock and others for continuing to live with two men, for libeling Beecher, and for daring to run for the presidency, decided to retreat to England where she lived out her life comfortably and alone, except for the companionship of her sister and daughter.

Fearing in her old age that her bed was her coffin, Victoria refused to sleep anyplace but in her rocking chair. She would not touch another human, thinking to avoid germs and infection. Her only pleasure was having her chauffeur drive her limousine at high speeds along English country roads in afternoon outings. Her love of speed proved her existence and prolonged her life, she said cryptically. Victoria Woodhull died at age eighty-nine, finally slowed to a crawl, on June 20, 1927.

Alexander WOOLLCOTT

Critic (1887–1943)

Though he appeared to be nothing more than a plump, apple-cheeked man with owlish eyes, Alexander Woollcott, drama critic for the New York *Times* and other newspapers, and the "Town Crier" of the airways, was without question, the most savage wit to ever devastate a literary gathering or a play production. Woollcott served in the ambulance corps during World War I, then wrote the newly born *Stars and Stripes* which was edited by Franklin Pierce Adams, the legendary "F.P.A." Adams and Woollcott would remain friends all the days of their lives, even though Woollcott was a trying person, by choice, not accident.

It was Alexander Woollcott who began the famous Round Table in New York's Algonquin Hotel, which flourished during the Jazz Age, and boasted on any given day the likes of Heywood Broun, Robert Benchley, James Thurber, Marc Connely, George Kaufman, F.P.A., Dorothy Parker, Frank Ward O'Malley, Harold Ross, the founder of the *New Yorker* magazine, and a host of other

Critic Alexander Woollcott, loved by his friends, in
spite of the terrors he brought to them.

literary lights. Woollcott's choice of a hotel for a historic meeting place was
simple; he discovered that the Algonquin served home-made apple pie for
lunch.

Woollcott always thought of himself as the best-read, best-informed person
in the world. He would tolerate no superior attitudes but his own. Once, when
Gertrude Stein visited New York, she had the audacity to correct Woollcott. He
thundered back at her: "Madam, you are undoubtedly unaware of the fact that
in New York I am never contradicted!"

Harold Ross and his wife took two interconnecting brownstone houses on
West 47th Street, sharing the buildings with bachelor Woollcott. Though they
loved the critic dearly, they regretted their move myriad times. Woollcott
developed the habit of returning from the theater to tell the Ross's about a play
he reviewed that night. It became a wearisome routine and the Ross's thought
to end it one night when they heard Woollcott's cab pull up outside their
building at the regular time. They quickly raced through their apartment,
turning off all the lights and diving for the bed, yanking the bed covers over
them, even though they were fully dressed. They reasoned that Woollcott would
not bother them if he thought them asleep. Minutes later they heard the heavy
footfalls of their friend. He entered their apartment, turning on lights as he
moved, then stomped into the bedroom, sitting down heavily on the edge of
their bed. "You're not fooling anyone," said the critic. "I saw all the lights go
out when I pulled up." He began to relate the values and failures of that night's
play while the Ross's stared at each other in disgust.

If the Ross's decided to give a party, Woollcott insisted upon blue-penciling
their invitation list. If the Ross's balked at such high-handedness, Woollcott
would stalk off to his own apartment grumbling and later, when the party was
in full swing, return to invite all present whom he thought friends to *his*
apartment for a party.

The critic was impossible at games. He loved poker but if he lost he would
throw his cards, knock down chips and sometimes kick over the table like a
child throwing a tantrum. When in such moods he might turn on old friends

419

and insult them with acid barbs. Once when George Kaufman, who was Jewish, bested him in a poker game, Woollcott screamed: "Shut up, you Christ-killer!"

He was equally a terror at croquet. If he missed a shot he was liable to hurl his mallet at anyone standing nearby. Most often he would pick up the balls and throw them into the woods, saying to an opponent—usually Harpo Marx—"Let's see if you can hit the goddamned thing from there!"

When not ravaging infant play productions, or writing for the *New Yorker,* or working on his radio scripts for the Town Crier program, Woollcott retreated to his island home at Bomoseen, Vermont, where he had a large house that could accommodate a dozen guests, and a beautiful beach and boating area. Woollcott enjoyed having his friends visit him at this tranquil island and played the warm host on most occasions.

Once, when Dorothy Parker was flat broke, Woollcott took her to Bomoseen, telling her that she could stay as long as she pleased and not to worry about expenses. After a few weeks at Bomoseen, Woollcott looked up from his morning newspaper and said to Mrs. Parker: '"Say, isn't it about time you were leaving?"

"On what?" said the impoverished guest.

Woollcott bought her a train ticket back to New York—coach—and handed her $2.50 in cold hard cash.

On another occasion, a dozen distinguished guests assembled at Woollcott's breakfast table inside his sprawling house at Bomoseen. The host was nowhere to be seen. Woollcott suddenly appeared in his slippers, pajamas and bathrobe. With a flourish he walked to the head of the table and sat down, ordering the cook with a wave of the hand to bring on his usual massive breakfast. The guests waited expectantly for Woollcott's witty good morning salutation. He looked at them with a great smile and stated: "I've just had the most wonderful bowel movement in my life. Let me tell you about it..."

Z

Basil ZAHAROFF

Munitions Tycoon (1849–1936)

He was called "Mystery Man of Europe" and was responsible, one way or another, for the death of millions of people. He died as rich as the fabled Count of Monte Cristo. He was Basil Zaharoff, whose life is still shrouded in shadows to this day.

One report has it that Zaharoff was born in Constantinople, another places his birth in Smyrna, another Athens. The place is not certain; neither is the man. He had all the records of his youth and early manhood destroyed or stolen to cover his trail against the prying eyes of any biographer. It was stated that Zaharoff, who became the king of world munitions, had murdered several people in pursuit of riches, inside international intrigue, a policeman in Ankara, a secret agent in Russia. (Though Eric Amblier always emphatically denied that his protagonist in *A Coffin for Demitrios* was based on Zaharoff, the similarity is striking.)

Zaharoff, as a young man, began selling arms and ammunition to the highest bidder, playing off one country against another, concentrating his efforts in the volatile Levant and in the Balkans. He moved to Greece and began whipping up public hatred for the Turks, hiring orators to harangue crowds about the Turkish menace. At the height of the war fever he created, Zaharoff appeared as an avenging angel to the Greek government, providing them with much needed weaponry to defend themselves against the Turks. He also sold the Greeks, at this time, the first submarine to be used in warfare.

Basil Zaharoff with his wife, a woman he waited forty-eight years to marry.

Immediately after reaping a fortune from this giant sale, Zaharoff raced off to the Turks. "Look what the Greeks are doing," he told Turkish leaders. "They are preparing to wipe you off the face of the earth." The Turks bought tons of war equipment and two submarines. Zaharoff grew rich from wars. He sold guns to both Russia and Japan during the Russian–Japanese war. He sold bullets to Spain that were used in the Spanish–American war to kill Rough Riders. World War I was Zaharoff's biggest bonanza. By 1914, he owned controlling interest in munitions firms in Italy, Germany, France, Russia and England, all of the major combatants, and he sold to both sides, becoming a billionaire. He was a regular visitor to every war office in every major country for five decades. To keep his missions secret, Zaharoff employed several doubles, men who looked exactly like him and were paid fortunes to appear publicly in Monte Carlo, Madrid or London when he wished to travel unseen to some other country.

Not once, from birth to old age, did Zaharoff allow a photo to be taken of him. Only in his dotage were photographers permitted near him. He never gave an interview and no matter how many scathing, libelous attacks upon him were printed, he remained silent.

The mystery man's one and only love was a duchess he met on a train traveling from Paris to Athens. She was then seventeen and he was about twenty-six. The girl was then married to a lunatic aristocrat. Zaharoff told her that he did not mind; he would wait. He waited, content with love letters and short meetings in parks, for forty-eight years, finally marrying the duchess in 1924, a year after her husband died in an insane asylum. He was then seventy-four and she was sixty-five.

Uneducated, Zaharoff taught himself to speak and write fourteen languages. Once arrested as a common thief in London in 1896 (an uncle claimed that he was stealing goods from a family-owned import-export firm, but the charges were dropped), Zaharoff was honored thirty years later by being

A political cartoon depicting munitions czar Basil Zaharoff pinning flags on countries where he instigated wars to sell his war materials.

knighted by the King of England. About the same time, Oxford University bestowed upon him the title of Doctor of Civil Law.

More than $1 million in rewards stood waiting for anyone who would murder Basil Zaharoff, yet he survived dozens of would-be assassins, although many of his doubles were reportedly killed. Perhaps the assassins were looking in the wrong areas for the man who is said to be responsible for the deaths of fifty million men in the wars he helped bring about. They might have gone to the zoos, as did their prey.

Zaharoff spent most of his leisure time in the great zoos of Europe, quietly feeding the animals. To any passerby he appeared to be nothing more than an old man whiling away his last years, not one of the richest men in the world, who made his billions from mass murder.

APPENDIX

BIBLIOGRAPHY

The exhaustive research for this book was done in libraries and archives throughout the United States, along with being taken from the author's own files and a personal library of 50,000 books. When possible, correspondence and interviews were employed to obtain additional information. Moreover, hundreds of newspapers and periodicals throughout the world were consulted, specific dates too numerous to cite herein. Some of the most helpful published sources follow.

BOOKS

A

Abrams, Albert. *Spondylotherapy*. San Francisco: Philopolis Press, 1912.

Adams, Franklin P. *The Diary of Our Own Samuel Pepys*. (2 vols.). New York: Simon & Schuster, 1935.

Adams, Samuel Hopkins. *A. Woollcott, His Life and His World*. New York: Reynal & Hitchcock, 1945.

Adamson, Joe. *Groucho, Harpo, Chico and Sometimes Zeppo*. New York: Simon & Schuster, 1973.

Ade, George. *The Old-Time Saloon*. New York: Ray Long & Richard Smith, 1931.

Allen, Frederick Lewis. *Only Yesterday, An Informal History of the Nineteen-Twenties*. New York: Harper & Bros., 1931.

——. *The Lords of Creation*. New York: Harper & Bros., 1935.

——. *Since Yesterday*. New York: Harper & Bros., 1940.

——. *The Big Change*. Ney York: Harper & Bros., 1952.

Allen, Hervey, *Isafel, The Life and Times of Edgar Allan Poe*. (2 vols.). New York: George H. Doran, 1927.

Allen, Lee. *One Hundred Years of Baseball*. New York: Bartholomew House, 1950.

Allsop, Kenneth. *The Bootleggers*. London: Hutchinson, 1961.

Altick, Richard D. *Lives and Letters*. New York: Ray Long and Richards Smith, 1931.

——. *The National League Story*. New York: Hill & Wang, 1961.

American Heritage, Special Issue "The 1920s," August, 1965.

Amory, Cleveland. *The Last Resorts*. New York: Harper & Bros., 1948.

——. *Who Killed Society?* New York: Harper & Bros., 1960.

——, and Bradlee, Frederic (eds.) *Vanity Fair, A Cavalcade of the 1920s and 1930s*. New York: The Viking Press, 1960.

Anderson, Margaret. *My Thirty Year's War*. New York: Covici-Friede, 1930.

Angly, Edward. *Oh Yeah?* New York: Viking Press, 1931.

BIBLIOGRAPHY

Antheil, George. *Bad Boy of Music.* Garden City, New York: Doubleday, Doran, 1945.

Arens, Egmont. *The Little Book of Greenwich Village.* New York: Published by author, 1918.

Asbury, Herbert. *Carry Nation.* New York: Knopf, 1929.

——. *Gem of the Prairie.* New York: Knopf, 1940.

——. *The Great Illusion, An Informal History of Prohibition.* New York: Doubleday, 1950.

Astor, Mary. *A Life on Film.* New York: Delacorte Press, 1967.

Atkin, Ronald. *Revolution! Mexico, 1910–20.* New York: John Day, 1970.

Atkinson, Brooks. *Broadway Scrapbook.* New York: Theatre Arts, 1947.

——. *Broadway.* New York: Macmillan, 1970.

B

Bacon, Delia. *The Philosophy of the Plays of Shakespeare Unfolded.* London: Groombridge and Sons, 1857.

Bacon, Theodore. *Delia Bacon.* Boston: Houghton, Mifflin & Co., 1888.

Bailey, James Osler. *Pilgrims through Space and Time.* New York: Scribner, 1912.

Baker, Leonard. *Back to Back.* New York: Macmillan, 1967.

Baragwanath, John. *A Good Time Was Had.* New York: Appleton-Century-Crofts, 1962.

Barber, Rowland. *Harpo Speaks!* New York: Bernard Geis, 1961.

Barlett, Donald L., and Steele, James B. *Empire, The Life, Legend and Madness of Howard Hughes.* New York: W.W. Norton, 1979.

Barnum, P.T. *Life of P.T. Barnum.* Buffalo: The Courier Company, 1888.

Barrett, James Wyman, *Joseph Pulitzer and His World.* New York: Vanguard, 1941.

Barrett, Marvin. *The Jazz Age.* New York: Putnam, 1959.

Barrymore, Ethel. *Memories.* New York: Harper & Bros., 1955.

Bates, Ernest, and Carlson, Oliver. *Hearst, Lord of San Simeon.* New York: Viking Press, 1936.

Bates, Finis. *The Escape and Suicide of John Wilkes Booth.* Naperville, Illinois: J.L. Nichols & Co., 1907.

Beach, Sylvia. *Shakespeare and Company.* New York: Harcourt, Brace and Co., 1959.

Beard, Charles A., and Mary R. *A Basic History of the United States.* New York: New Home Library, 1944.

Beecher, Henry Ward. *Lectures to Young Men on Various Important Subjects.* Boston: Jewett, 1846.

Beer, Thomas. *The Mauve Decade.* New York: Knopf, 1926.

Benchley, Nathaniel. *Robert Benchley, A Biography.* New York: McGraw-Hill, 1955.

Bendiner, Robert. *Just Around the Corner, A Highly Selective History of the 30's.* New York: Harper & Row, 1967.

Bernstein, Morey. *The Search for Bridey Murphy.* Garden City, New York: Doubleday, 1956.

Berton, Mme. Pierre. *The Real Sarah Bernhardt.* New York: Boni and Liveright, 1924.

Billington, Ray Allen. *The Protestant Crusade, 1800–1860.* New York: Macmillan, 1938.

Bishop, Jim. *The Mark Hellinger Story.* Englewood Cliffs, New Jersey: Prentice-Hall, 1952.

Bode, Carl. *The American Lyceum.* New York: Oxford Univ. Press, 1956.

Bolitho, William. *Twelve Against the Gods.* New York: Simon & Schuster, 1929.

Brace, Charles Loring. *The Dangerous Classes of New York.* New York: Wynkoop & Hallanbeck, 1872.

Brackett, Charles. *Entirely Surrounded.* New York: Knopf, 1934.

Brinnin, John Malcolm. *The Third Rose, Gertrude Stein and Her World.* Boston: Little Brown, 1959.

Brooks, Van Wyck. *Days of the Phoenix: The 1920s I Remember.* New York: Dutton, 1957.

Broun, Heywood, and Leech, Margaret. *Anthony Comstock.* New York: Albert & Charles Boni, 1927.

——. *It Seems to Me, 1925–1935.* New York: Harcourt, Brace, 1935.

Brown, Charles H. *The Correspondents' War.* New York: Scribner, 1967.

Brown, John Mason. *Two on the Aisle.* New York: Norton, 1938.

——. *The Worlds of Robert E. Sherwood.* New York: Harper & Row, 1962.

Brown, Susan Jenkins. *Robber Rocks, Letters and Memories of Hart Crane.* Middletown, Connecticut: Wesleyan Univ. Press, 1968.

Brown, T. Allston. *History of the American Stage.* New York: Dick and Fitzgerald, 1870.

Brownlow, Kevin. *The Parade's Gone By.* New York: Knopf, 1969.

BIBLIOGRAPHY

Bunner, H.C. *The Bowery and Bohemia.* New York: Scribner, 1906.

C

Cairns, William B. *A History of American Literature.* New York: Oxford, 1930.

Capra, Frank. *The Name Above the Title.* New York: Macmillan, 1971.

Carr, John Dickson. *The Life of Sir Arthur Conan Doyle.* New York: Harper & Bros., 1949.

Carryl, Guy W. *Zut and Other Parisians.* Boston: Houghton-Mifflin, 1903.

Carse, Robert. *Rum Row.* New York: Holt, Rinehart & Winston, 1959.

Carson, Gerald. *Cornflake Crusade.* New York: Rinehart, 1957.

Case, Frank. *Tales of a Wayward Inn.* New York: Frederick A. Stokes, 1938.

——. *Feeding the Lions.* New York: The Greystone Press, 1942.

Chambers, Julius. *The Book of New York.* New York: The Book of New York Co., 1912.

Chambers, Robert W. *In the Quarter.* Chicago: F.T. Neely, 1894.

Chapin, Anna Alice. *Greenwich Village.* New York: Dodd, Mead, 1917.

Chase, Stuart. *Prosperity: Fact or Myth.* New York: Boni, 1929.

Churchill, Allen. *The Improper Bohemians.* New York: Dutton, 1959.

——. *Park Row.* New York: Holt, Rinehart & Winston, 1959.

——. *The Year the World Went Mad.* New York: Crowell, 1960.

Clark, Kenneth. *Ruskin Today.* New York: Holt, Rinehart & Winston, 1964.

Clark, Tom. *The World of Damon Runyon.* New York: Harper & Row, 1978.

Clegg, Charles, and Emrich, Duncan. *The Lucius Beebe Reader.* Garden City, New York: Doubleday, 1967.

Coats, Peter, and Niklaus, Thelma. *The Little Fellow.* London: Paul Elek, 1951.

Cobb, Irvin S. *Exit Laughing.* Indianapolis: Bobbs-Merrill, 1941.

Coblentz, Edmond D. *William Randolph Hearst: A Portrait in His Own Words.* New York: Simon & Schuster, 1952.

Colvin, D. Leigh. *Prohibition in the United States.* New York: Doran, 1926.

Cooke, Bob (ed.). *Wake Up the Echoes.* New York: Hanover House, 1956.

Cowles, Fleur. *The Case of Salvador Dali.* Boston: Little, Brown & Company, 1959.

Cowley, Malcolm. *Exile's Return.* New York: Viking, 1951.

Craven, Avery, Johnson, Walter and Dunn, F. Roger. *A Documentary History of the American People*. Boston: Ginn and Co., 1951.

Creamer, Robert W. *Babe*. New York: Simon & Schuster, 1974.

Creel, George. *How We Advertised America*. New York: Harper & Bros., 1960.

D

Dabney, Virginius. *Dry Messiah*. New York: Knopf, 1949.

Dali, Salvador. *Diary of a Genius*. Garden City, New York: Doubleday, 1965.

Daniels, Josephus. *The Wilson Era: Years of Peace*. Chapel Hill, North Carolina: Univ. North Carolina Press, 1944.

Davenport, Guiles. *Zaharoff, High Priest of War*. Boston: Lothrop, Lee and Shepard, 1934.

Davis, Richard Harding. *Real Soldiers of Fortune*. New York: Scribner, 1912.

Davis, Robert H., and Maurice, Arthur B. *The Caliph of Bagdad*. New York: D. Appleton, 1931.

DeKay, Charles. *The Bohemian*. New York: Scribner, 1878.

Dell, Floyd. *Love in Greenwich Village*. New York: Doran, 1926.

Dempsey, Jack, with Considine, Bob and Slocum, Bill. *Dempsey*. New York: Simon & Schuster, 1960.

Deschner, Donald. *The Films of W.C. Fields*. New York: Citadel Press, 1966.

Dexter, Timothy. *A Pickle for the Knowing Ones, or Plain Truths in a Homespun Dress*. Newburyport, Massachusetts: Published by author, 1802.

Dickson, Samuel. *Tales of San Francisco*. Stanford, California: Stanford Univ. Press, 1957.

Donnelly, Ignatius. *The Great Cryptogram*. London: R.S. Peale & Co., 1888.

Dorr, Rheta Childe. *Susan B. Anthony*. New York: Frederick A. Stokes, 1928.

Drennan, Robert (ed.). *The Algonquin Wits*. New York: Citadel Press, 1968.

Duncan, Isadora. *My Life*. New York: Boni & Liveright, 1927.

Durso, Joe. *Casey: The Life and Legend of Charles Dillon Stengel*. Englewood Cliffs, New Jersey: Prentice-Hall, 1967.

E

Early, Mary Dawn. *Stars of the Twenties*. New York: Viking Press, 1975.

Edwards, Clarence E. *Bohemian San Francisco*. San Francisco: Paul Elder & Co., 1914.

BIBLIOGRAPHY

Einstein, Charles. *The Fireside Book of Baseball.* (vol. 2). New York: Simon & Schuster, 1958.

Ellis, Edward Robb. *A Nation in Torment.* New York: Coward-McCann, 1970.

Ellis, Jack D. *Georges Clemenceau.* Kansas City: The Regents Press, 1980.

Engelbrecht, H.C., and Hanighen, F.C. *Merchants of Death.* New York: Dodd, Mead, 1934.

Erskine, Helen Worden. *Out of this World.* New York: Putnam, 1953.

F

Farnsworth, Marjorie. *The Ziegfeld Follies.* New York: Putnam, 1956.

Farr, Finis. *Fair Enough: The Life of Westbrook Pegler.* New Rochelle, New York: Arlington House, 1975.

Farrar, Mrs. John. *Recollections of Seventy Years.* Boston: Tichnor & Fields, 1866.

Fetherling, Doug. *The Five Lives of Ben Hecht.* Toronto: Lester & Orpen, 1977.

Fields, W.C. *By Himself.* Englewood Cliffs, New Jersey: Prentice-Hall, 1973.

Finler, Joel W. *Stroheim.* Berkeley, California: Univ. California Press, 1968.

Fleischer, Nat. *Jack Dempsey.* New Rochelle, New York: Arlington House, 1972.

Ford, James L. *Bohemia Invaded.* New York: Frederick A. Stokes, 1895.

——. *Forty-Odd Years in the Literary Shop.* New York: Dutton, 1921.

Fosdick, Gertrude Christian. *Out of Bohemia, A Story of Paris Student Life.* New York: Geo. H. Richmond & Co., 1894.

Fowler, Gene. *The Great Mouthpiece.* New York: Blue Ribbon Books, 1931.

——. *Good Night, Sweet Prince, The Life and Times of John Barrymore.* New York: Viking, 1944.

Frank, Waldo. *The Rediscovery of America.* New York: Duell, Sloan and Pearce, 1947.

Freccero, John. *Dante.* Englewood Cliffs, New Jersey: Prentice-Hall, 1965.

Friede, Donald. *The Mechanical Angel.* New York: Knopf, 1948.

Fulop-Miller, René. *Rasputin, The Holy Devil.* Garden City, New York: Garden City Publishing Co., 1927.

Furnas, J.C. *The Late Demon Rum.* New York: Putnam, 1965.

G

Galbraith, John K. *The Great Crash, 1929.* Boston: Houghton-Mifflin, 1954.

Gallico, Paul. *Farewell to Sport*. New York: Knopf, 1938.

Gardner, Martin. *Fads and Fallacies*. New York: Dover, 1957.

Garnett, David. *The Golden Echo*. New York: Harcourt, Brace, 1954.

Garnett, Tay. *Light Your Torches and Pull Up Your Tights*. New Rochelle, New York: Arlington House, 1973.

Ghadiali, Dishah Pestauji Framji. *Railroading a Citizen*. Malaga, New Jersey: Spectro-Crome Institute, 1926.

Gill, Brendan. *Here at the New Yorker*. New York: Random House, 1975.

Gissing, George. *New Grub Street*. New York: Modern Library, 1926.

Glaspbell, Susan. *The Road to the Temple*. London: E. Benn, Ltd. 1926.

Goldman, Eric F. *Rendezvous with Destiny: A History of American Reform*. New York: Knopf, 1952.

Gomez de la Serna, Ramon. *Dali*. New York: William Morrow & Co., 1979.

Gordon, Ruth. *Myself Among Others*. New York: Atheneum, 1970.

Gould, Thomas R. *The Tragedian*. New York: Benjamin Blom, Inc., 1971.

Graham, Sheilah. *The Garden of Allah*. New York: Crown, 1970.

Grant, Jane. *Ross, The New Yorker and Me*. New York: Reynal-Morrow, 1968.

Green, Abel, and Laurie, Joe. *Show Biz From Vaude to Video*. Garden City, New York: Garden City Books, 1952.

Griffin, Bulkey S. (ed.). *Offbeat History*. New York: World Publishing Co., 1967.

Griffith, Richard. *The Movie Stars*. Garden City, New York: Doubleday, 1970.

Gunn, T. Butler. *The Physiology of New York Boarding Houses*. New York: Mason Bros., 1957.

Gurdjieff, George Ivan. *All and Everything*. London: Rutledge and K. Paul, 1950.

H

Hansen, Harry. *Midwest Portraits, A Book of Memories and Friendships*. New York: Harcourt, Brace, 1923.

Hemingway, Ernest. *A Moveable Feast*. New York: Scribner, 1964.

Hapgood, Hutchins. *Types from City Streets*. New York: Funk and Wagnalls, 1910.

Harriman, Margaret Case. *The Vicious Circle*. New York: Rinehart & Co., 1951.

Harrison, Harry P. *Culture Under Canvas*. New York: Hastings House, 1958.

Hart, Moss. *Act One*. New York: Random House, 1959.

Hawthorne, Nathaniel. *Our Old Home*. Boston: Houghton, 1863.

BIBLIOGRAPHY

Haynes, William. *Men, Money and Molecules*. Garden City, New York: Doubleday, Doran, 1936.

Hecht, Ben. *A Child of the Century*. New York: Simon & Schuster, 1954.

——. *Charlie, The Improbable Life and Times of Charles MacArthur*. New York: Harper & Bros., 1957.

——. *Gaily, Gaily*. Garden City, New York: Doubleday, 1963.

Henderson, Yandell. *A New Deal in Liquor*. New York: Doubleday, Doran, 1934.

Hibben, Paxton. *Henry Ward Beecher*. New York: The Press of the Readers Club, 1942.

Higham, Charles. *The Adventures of Conan Doyle*. New York: W.W. Norton, 1976.

Hoffman, Frederick J. *The Twenties*. New York: Viking Press, 1955.

Hohenberg, John. *Foreign Correspondence: The Great Reporters and Their Times*. New York: Columbia Univ. Press, 1964.

Holbrook, Stewart H. *Lost Men of American History*. New York: MacMillan, 1936.

Honan, Park. *Matthew Arnold, A Life*. New York: McGraw-Hill, 1981.

Hoogenboom, Ari, and Hoogenboom, Olive (eds.). *The Gilded Age*. Englewood Cliffs, New Jersey: Prentice-Hall, 1967.

Horan, James D. *The Desperate Years*. New York: Crown, 1962.

Horton, Philip. *Hart Crane*. New York: W.W. Norton, 1937.

Howard, John Tasker and Bellows, George Kent. *Music in America*. New York: Crowell, 1957.

Howells, William Dean. *Literary Friends and Acquaintances*. New York: Harper and Bros., 1900.

——. *Years of My Youth*. New York: Harper & Bros., 1916.

Hoyt, Edwin P. *Gentleman Broadway*. Boston: Little, Brown, 1964.

——. *Alexander Woollcott: The Man Who Came To Dinner*. New York: Abelard-Schuman, 1968.

Huddleston, Sisley. *Paris Salons, Cafés, Studios*. Philadelphia: Lippincott, 1928.

——. *Back to Montparnasse, Glimpses of Broadway in Bohemia*. Philadelphia: Lippincott, 1931.

Huff, Theodore. *Charlie Chaplin*. New York: Abelard-Schuman, Ltd., 1951.

Hutchens, John K. (ed.) *The American Twenties: A Literary Panorama*. Philadelphia: Lippincott, 1952.

Hyndman, H.M. *Clemenceau, The Man and His Time.* New York: Frederick A. Stokes Company, 1930.

I

Irwin, Will. *Highlights of Manhattan.* New York: The Century Co., 1927.

J

Jacobs, Lewis. *Rise of the American Film.* New York: Harcourt, Brace, 1939.

Jessel, George. *So Help Me.* New York: Random House, 1943.

Joad, C.E.M. *The Babbitt Warren.* New York: Harper & Bros., 1927.

Johnson, Gerald. *The Lunatic Fringe.* Philadelphia: Lippincott, 1957.

Johnston, Alva. *The Legendary Mizners.* New York: Farrar, Straus & Young, 1953.

Josephson, Matthew. *Portrait of the Artist as American.* New York: Harcourt, Brace, 1930.

——. *Edison.* New York: McGraw-Hill, 1959.

K

Kahn, E.J., Jr. *The World of Swope.* New York: Simon & Schuster, 1965.

Karolevitz, Robert F. *Newspapering in the Old West.* New York: Bonanza, 1965.

Kaufman, Beatrice and Hennessey, Joseph. *The Letters of Alexander Woollcott.* Garden City, New York: Garden City Publishing Co., 1944.

Keats, John. *You Might As Well Live.* New York: Simon & Schuster, 1970.

Keller, Allan. *The Spanish American War.* New York: Hawthorn, 1969.

Kemp, Harry. *Tramping on Life.* New York: Boni & Liveright, 1922.

——. *More Miles.* New York: Boni & Liveright, 1926.

Kipling, Rudyard. *American Notes.* New York: G. Munro's, 1896.

Kirchwey, Freda (ed.). *Our Changing Morality.* New York: Boni, 1924.

Klurfeld, Herman. *Winchell, His Life and Times.* New York: Praeger, 1976.

Knoles, George Harmon. *The Jazz Age Revisited.* Stanford, California: Stanford: Univ. Press, 1955.

Knowles, Horace (ed.). *Gentlemen, Scholars and Scoundrels.* New York: Harper's, 1959.

BIBLIOGRAPHY

Kobler, John. *Ardent Spirits*. New York: Putnam, 1973.

Kobre, Sidney. *The Yellow Press and Gilded Age Journalism*. Miami: Florida State Univ., 1964.

Kohut, Rebekah. *As I Know Them*. Garden City, New York: Doubleday Page, 1929.

Kramer, Dale. *Ross and the New Yorker*. Garden City, New York: Doubleday, 1951.

Krout, John Allen. *The Origins of Prohibition*. New York: Knopf, 1925.

Krutch, Joseph Wood. *Edgar Allan Poe, A Study in Genius*. New York: Knopf, 1926.

Kuenster, John. *From Cobb to "Catfish."* Chicago: Rand McNally, 1975.

L

Lake, Carlton. *In Quest of Dali*. Toronto: Longmans, 1969.

Lambert, Gavin. *On Cukor*. New York: Putnam, 1972.

Lane, Allen Stanley. *Emperor Norton*. Caldwell, Idaho: The Caxton Printers, Ltd., 1939.

Lee, Henry. *How Dry We Were*. Englewood Cliffs, New Jersey: Prentice-Hall, 1963.

Leech, Margaret. *In The Days of McKinley*. New York: Harper & Bros., 1959.

LeGalliene, Richard. *The Romantic '90s*. New York: Simon and Schuster, 1949.

Leland, Charles Godfrey. *Memoires*. New York: D. Appleton, 1893.

Leuchtenberg, William E. *Perils of Prosperity. 1914–1932*. Chicago: Univ. Chicago Press, 1958.

Levant, Oscar. *A Smattering of Ignorance*. New York: Doubleday, Doran, 1940.

Lewinsohn, Richard. *The Mystery Man of Europe, Sir Basil Zaharoff*. Philadelphia: Lippincott, 1929.

Lewis, Mildred and Lewis, Milton. *Famous Modern Newspaper Writers*. New York: Dodd, Mead, 1962.

Lewis, Oscar, and Hall, Carroll D. *Bonanza Inn*. New York: Knopf, 1939.

Lieb, Fred. *Baseball As I Have Known It*. New York: Coward, McCann and Geoghegan, 1977.

———. *The Story of the World Series*. New York: Putnam, 1949.

Link, Arthur. *American Epoch*. New York: Knopf, 1935.

Livingston, Bernard. *Their Turf: America's Horsey Set And Its Princely Dynasties*. New York: Arbor House, 1973.

Livingston, Belle. *Belle of Bohemia*. New York: Barse & Co., n.d.

Loeb, Harold. *The Way It Was*. New York: Criterion, 1959.

London, Jack. *John Barleycorn*. New York: The Century Co., 1913.

Lueders, Edward. *Carl Van Vechten and the Twenties*. Albuquerque, New Mexico: Univ. New Mexico Press, 1955.

Luhan, Mabel Dodge. *Lorenzo in Taos*. New York: Knopf, 1932.

Luthin, Reinhard H. *American Demagogues: Twentieth Century*. Boston: Beacon Press, 1954.

Lutz, Alma. *Susan B. Anthony*. Boston: Beacon Press, 1959.

Lynch, Denis Tilden. *Criminals and Politicians*. New York: Macmillan, 1932.

M

MacFadden, Bernarr. *The Encyclopedia of Physical Culture*. New York: MacFadden Book Co., 1931.

MacKenzie, Norman. *Secret Societies*. New York: Holt, Rinehart, & Winston, 1967.

MacShane,Frank. *John O'Hara*. New York: Dutton, 1980.

Marquand, J.P. *Lord Timothy Dexter of Newburyport*. New York: Milton, Balh & Co., 1925.

Martin, Frederick Townsend. *Things I Remember*. New York: John Lane, 1913.

Marx, Arthur. *Life with Groucho*. New York: Simon & Schuster, 1954.

Marx, Groucho. *The Groucho Letters*. New York: Simon & Schuster, 1967.

Marx, Harpo with Barbarer, Rowland. *Harpo Speaks!* Bernard Geis Associates, 1961.

Masson, Thomas L. *In Tune With the Finite*. New York: The Century Co., 1928.

Matlaw, Ralph E. (ed.) *Tolstoy*. (Twentieth Century Views Series). Englewood Cliffs, New Jersey: Prentice-Hall, 1967.

Matz, Mary Jane. *The Many Lives of Otto Kahn*. New York: Macmillan, 1963.

May, Henry F. *The End of American Innocence*. New York: Knopf, 1959.

McBride, James. *Symmes' Theories of Concentric Spheres*. Cincinnati: Morgan, Lodge & Fisher, 1826.

McCormick, Donald. *Peddler of Death, The Life and Times of Sir Basil Zaharoff*. New York: Holt, Rinehart and Winston, 1965.

McCullogh, Hugh. *Men and Measures of Half a Century*. New York: Scribner, 1889.

BIBLIOGRAPHY

McLoughlin, William G., Jr. *Billy Sunday Was His Real Name*. Chicago: Univ. of Chicago Press, 1955.

Meltzer, Milton. *Mark Twain Himself*. New York: Thomas Y. Crowell, 1970.

Menard, Wilmon. *Somerset Maugham*. Los Angeles: Sherbourne Press, Inc., 1965.

Mencken, H.L. *A Book of Prefaces*. New York: Knopf, 1917.

Merz, Charles. *The Dry Decade*. Garden City, New York: Doubleday, Doran, 1931.

Mezzrow, Milton "Mezz," and Wolfe, Bernard. *Really the Blues*. New York: Random House, 1946.

Mitgang, Herbert. *The Man Who Rode the Tiger*. Philadelphia: Lippincott, 1963.

Mitchell, Joseph. *Joe Gould's Secret*. New York: Viking, 1965.

Morgan, H. Wayne. *America's Road to Empire*. New York: John Wiley & Sons, 1965.

Morley, Sheridan. *A Talent to Amuse*. Garden City, New York: Doubleday, 1969.

Morris, Lloyd. *Postscript to Yesterday*. New York: Random House, 1947.

——. *Incredible New York:* New York: Random House, 1951.

Morrow, W.C. *Bohemian Paris of Today*. Philadelphia: Lippincott, 1900.

Mott, Frank Luther. *Golden Multitudes*. New York: Macmillan, 1947.

Muddiman, Bernard. *Men of the Nineties*. New York: Putnam, 1921.

Murger, Henri. *The Latin Quarter*. New York: Doubleday, Page, 1901.

Murrell, William. *History of American Graphic Humor: 1865–1938*. New York: Macmillan, 1938.

Mussey, J.B. (ed.). *The Cream of the Jesters*. New York: Albert and Charles Boni, 1931.

N

Nadeau, Maurice. *The History of Surrealism*. New York: Macmillan 1965.

Nash, Jay Robert. *Dillinger: Dead or Alive?* Chicago: Regnery, 1970.

——. *Citizen Hoover, A Critical Study of the Life And Times of J. Edgar Hoover and His FBI*. Chicago: Nelson-Hall, 1972.

——. *Bloodletters and Badmen, A Narrative Encyclopedia of American Criminals from the Pilgrims to the Present*. New York: M. Evans, 1973.

——. *Hustlers and Con Men, An Anecdotal History of the Con Men and His Games*. New York: M. Evans, 1976.

——. *Darkest Hours, A Narrative Encyclopedia of World-Wide Disasters From Ancient Times to the Present.* Chicago: Nelson-Hall, 1976.

——. *Among the Missing, An Anecdotal History of Missing Persons from 1800 to the Present.* New York: Simon & Shuster, 1978.

——. *Murder, America, Homicide in the United States From the Revolution to the Present.* New York: Simon & Schuster, 1980.

——. *Almanac of World Crime.* Garden City, New York: Doubleday, 1981.

——. *Look for the Woman.* New York: M. Evans, 1981.

——. *People to See, An Anecdotal History of Chicago's Makers and Breakers.* Piscataway, New Jersey: New Century Publishers, 1981.

Nation, Carry. *The Use and Need of the Life of Carry A. Nation.* Topeka, Kansas: F.M. Steves, 1905.

Neugroschel, Joachim. *Conversations with Dali.* New York: Dutton, 1969.

Nevins, Allan. *The United States in a Chaotic World: A Chronicle of International Affairs, 1918–1933.* New Haven, Connecticut: Yale Univ. Press, 1950.

Nijinsky, Romola. *Nijinsky.* New York: Simon & Schuster, 1934.

Nordon, Pierre. *Conan Doyle.* New York: Holt, Rinehart and Winston, 1964.

O

O'Connor, Harvey. *Mellon's Millions.* New York: John Day, 1933.

O'Connor, Richard. *Heywood Broun.* New York: Putnam, 1975.

O'Neal, John Joseph. *The Prodigal Genius.* New York: I. Washburn, Inc., 1944.

O'Reilly, John Boyle. *In Bohemia.* Boston: Pilot Publishing Co., 1886.

P

Packer, Vin. *Sudden Endings.* Garden City, New York: Doubleday, 1964.

Parish, James Robert, and Bowers, Ronald L. *The MGM Stock Company.* New Rochelle, New York: Arlington House, 1973.

Parry, Albert. *Garrets and Pretenders, A History of Bohemianism in America.* New York: Dover Publications, 1960.

Pearson, Edmund. *Books in Red and Black.* New York: The Macmillan Co., 1923.

Pearson, Hesketh. *The Whispering Gallery.* London: John Lane: The Bodley Head, Ltd., 1926.

Phillips, Cabell. *The 1940s.* New York: Macmillan, 1975.

BIBLIOGRAPHY

——. From *The Crash to the Blitz, 1929–39, The New York Times Chronicle of American Life*. New York: Macmillan, 1969.

Piast, V. *Vstrechi*. Moscow: Federatziz Publishing House, 1929.

Poole, Ernest. *The Harbor*. New York: Macmillan, 1919.

Pond, J.B. *Eccentricities of Genius*. London: Chatto & Windus, 1901.

Porte, Joel. *The Romance in America*. Middletown, Connecticut: Wesleyan Univ. Press, 1969.

Pumpelly, Raphael. *Across America and Asia*. New York: Leypoldt and Holt, 1870.

R

Ransome, Arthur. *Bohemia in London*. New York: Dodd, Mead, 1907.

Rascoe, Burton. *Before I Forget*. Garden City, New York: Doubleday, 1937.

——. *We Were Interrupted*. Garden City, New York: Doubleday, 1947.

Rawcliffe, D.H *Illusions and Delusions of the Supernatural and the Occult*. New York: Dover, 1959.

Reichler, Joe (ed.). *The Game and the Glory*. Englewood Cliffs, New Jersey: Prentice-Hall, 1976.

Regan, Robert. *Poe*. (Twentieth Century Views Series). Englewood Cliffs, New Jersey: Prentice-Hall, 1967.

Reimer, William. *The East Side Cafés of New York*. New York: N.p., 1903.

Reumert, Elith. *Hans Andersen The Man*. Detroit: Tower Books, 1971.

Rice, Damon. *Seasons Past*. New York, Praeger, 1976.

Rice, Grantland. *The Tumult and the Shouting, My Life in Sport*. Cranbury, New Jersey: Barnes, 1954.

Robbins, Russel Hope. *The Encyclopedia of Witchcraft and Demonology*. New York: Crown, 1965.

Rogers, Agnes. *I Remember Distinctly*. New York: Harper & Bros., 1947.

Rosenfeld, Paul. *By Way of Art*. New York: Coward-McCann, 1928.

Ross, Ishbel. *Ladies of the Press*. New York: Harper & Bros., 1936.

Rothstein, John. *A Pot of Paint*. New York: Covici-Friede, 1929.

Rothenstein, William. *Men and Memories*. (2 vols.). New York: Coward-McCann, 1931, 1932.

Ruitenbeek, Hendrik (ed.). *The Literary Imagination*. Chicago: Quadrangle, 1965.

S

Sann, Paul. *The Lawless Decade.* New York: Crown, 1960.

Sargent, Nathan. *Public Men and Events.* Philadelphia: Lippincott, 1875.

Schlesinger, Arthur M. *The American as Reformer.* Cambridge, Massachusetts: Harvard Univ. Press, 1951.

Scott, Arthur L. *Mark Twain at Large.* Chicago: Regnery 1969.

Seitz, Don C. *Uncommon Americans.* Indianapolis: The Bobbs Merrill Co., 1925.

Seldes, Gilbert. *The Stammering Century.* New York: John Day, 1928.

——. *The Years of the Locust.* Boston: Little, Brown, 1933.

——. *The Lively Arts.* New York: Sagamore Press, 1957.

Seymour, Harold. *Baseball, The Golden Age.* New York: Oxford Univ. Press, 1971.

Shaw, Arnold. *The Street That Never Slept.* New York: Coward-McCann, 1971.

Siegfried, Andre. *America Comes of Age.* New York: Harcourt, Brace, 1927.

Sinclair, Andrew. *Prohibition: The Era of Excess.* Boston: Little, Brown., 1962.

Sinclair, Upton. *Money Writers.* Chicago: Boni, 1927.

Sitwell, Edith. *English Eccentrics.* New York: Vanguard Press, 1957.

Sitwell, Osbert. *Laughter in the Next Room.* Boston: Little, Brown, 1948.

Slossen, Preston William. *The Great Crusade and After, 1914–1928.* New York: Macmillan, 1930.

Smith, H. Allen. *The Life and Legend of Gene Fowler.* New York: Morrow, 1977.

Smith, Alphonso C. *Edgar Allan Poe.* Indianapolis: Bobbs-Merrill, 1921.

Smith, Alson J. *Chicago's Left Bank.* Chicago: Regnery, 1953.

Smith, Anthony. *The Newspaper, An International History.* London: Thames and Hudson, 1979.

Smith, Arthur D. *John Jacob Astor.* Philadelphia: Lippincott, 1951.

Smith, Mrs. Samuel Harrison. *The First Forty Years of Washington Society.* New York: Scribner, 1906.

Smith, Mrs. E. Vale. *History of Newburyport.* Boston: Press of Damrell & Moore, 1854.

Sobel, Louis. *Along the Broadway Beat.* New York: Avon, 1951.

Soule, George. *Prosperity Decade: From War to Depression, 1917–1929.* New York: Rinehart, 1947.

BIBLIOGRAPHY

Sparkes, Boyden, and Moore, Samuel Taylor. *The Witch of Wall Street*. Garden City, New York: Doubleday, Doran & Co., 1935.

Spigelglass, Leonard. *Hello, Hollywood*. Garden City, New York: Doubleday, 1962.

Spink, J.G. Taylor. *Judge Landis and Twenty-five Years of Baseball*. New York: Crowell, 1947.

Stahl, John. *Growing with the West*. New York: Longmans, Green, 1921.

Stevenson, Elizabeth. *Babbitts & Bohemians*. New York: Macmillan, 1967.

Stein, Gertrude. *The Autobiography of Alice B. Toklas*. New York: Random House, 1933.

Stewart, John T. *The Deacon Wore Spats*. New York: Holt, Rinehart, and Winston, 1965.

Stirling, Monica. *The Life and Times of Hans Christian Andersen*. New York: Harcourt, Brace & World, 1965.

Stoddard, Charles Warren. *Exits and Entrances*. Boston: Lothrup, 1903.

Stowe, Lyman Beecher. *Saints, Sinners and Beechers*. Indianapolis: Bobbs-Merrill, 1934.

Stevenson, Robert Louis. *The Wrecker*. New York: Scribner, 1892.

Sullivan, Mark. *Our Times*. (6 vols.). New York: Scribner, 1926, 1927, 1930, 1932, 1933, 1935.

Swanberg, W.A. *Citizen Hearst*. New York: Scribner, 1961.

Symons, Arthur. *Colour Studies in Paris*. New York: Dutton, 1918.

Symmes, John Cleves. *The Symmes Theory of Concentric Spheres*. Louisville: Bradley & Gilbert, 1878.

T

Taper, Bernard (ed.) *Mark Twain's San Francisco*. New York: McGraw-Hill, 1963.

Taylor, Bayard. *The Echo Club*. Boston: Osgood, 1876.

Taylor, Dwight. *Joy Ride*. New York: Putnam, 1959.

Tebbel, John. *The Life and Good Times of W.R. Hearst*. New York: Dutton, 1952.

———. *The Compact History of the American Newspapers*. New York: Hawthorn, 1969.

Teichmann, Hoard. *Smart Aleck, The Wit, World and Life of Alexander Woollcott*. New York: William Morrow, 1976.

Thayer, George. *The War Business*. New York: Simon & Schuster, 1969.

Thomas, Bob. *Thalberg*. Garden City, New York: Doubleday, 1969.

——. *Winchell*. Garden City, New York: Doubleday, 1971.

Thomas, Lowell. *With Lawrence in Arabia*. Garden City, New York: Garden City Publishing Co., 1931.

Thompson, Slason. *Way Back When*. Chicago: A. Kroch, 1931.

Thorndike, Joseph J., Jr. *The Very Rich*. New York: Crown, 1976.

Thornton, Willis. *The Nine Lives of Citizen Train*. New York: Greenburg, 1948.

Tietjans, Eunice. *The World at My Shoulder*. New York: Macmillan, 1938.

Towne, Charles Hanson. *This New York of Mine*. New York: Cosmopolitan Book Corp., 1931.

Train, George Francis. *My Life in Many States and in Foreign Lands*. New York: D. Appleton, 1902.

Trevelyan, G.M. *History of England*. (vol. III). New York: Doubleday, 1953.

Trollope, Francis. *Domestic Manners of Americans*. New York: Dodd, Mead, 1901.

Troyat, Henri. *Tolstoy*. Garden City, New York: Doubleday, 1967.

Tugwell, R.G. *The Brain Trust*. New York: The Viking Press, 1968.

Turkin, Hy, and Thompson, S.C. *The Official Encyclopedia of Baseball*. New York: A.S. Barnes, 1951.

Tuska, Jon. *The Films of Mae West*. Secaucus, New Jersey: Citadel Press, 1973.

Tyler, Parker, *Chaplin*. Vanguard Press, 1948.

W

Walker, Alexander. *The Celluloid Sacrifice, Aspects of Sex in The Movies*. New York: Hawthorn, 1966.

Walker, Stanley. *The Night Club Era*. New York: Frederick A. Stokes, 1933.

Walsh, Raoul. *Each Man in His Time*. New York: Farrar, Straus and Giroux, 1974.

Washburne, Claude C. *Pages from the Book of Paris*. Boston: Houghton-Mifflin, 1910.

Waterton, Charles. *Wanderings Through South America*. London: J. Mawman, 1825.

Weber, Brom. *The Letters of Hart Crane*. Berkeley, California: Univ. California Press, 1965.

Wechter, Dixon. *The Age of the Great Depression*. New York: Macmillan, 1948.

BIBLIOGRAPHY

Weiner, Ed. *The Damon Runyon Story*. New York: McKay, 1948.

Weinstein, Gregory. *The Ardent Eighties*. New York: International Press, 1928.

Wendt, Lloyd and Kogan, Herman. *Bosses in Lusty Chicago*. Bloomington, Indiana: Indiana Univ. Press, 1967.

Wheeler, John. *I've Got News For You*. New York: Dutton, 1961.

Wicksteed, Philip H., and Gardner, Edmund G. *Dante and Giovanni del Virgilio*. London: Archibald Constable & Co., 1902.

Wilson, Edmund. *Axel's Castle*. New York: Scribner, 1931.

——. *The Shores of Light: A Literary Chronicle of The 20's and 30's*. New York: Farrar, Straus & Young, 1952.

——. *The American Earthquake: A Documentary of the Twenties and Thirties*. New York: Doubleday, 1958.

Wilson, G.W. *The Eccentric Mirror*. London: James Cundee, 1893.

Winter, William. *Old Friends*. New York: Moffat, Yard & Co., 1909.

Wlaschin, Ken. *The Illustrated Encyclopedia of The World's Great Movie Stars*. New York: Bonanza Books, 1979.

Wolff, Geoffrey. *Black Sun*. New York: Random House, 1976.

Y

Young, Art. *On My Way*. New York: Liveright, 1928.

Young, James Harvey. *The Toadstool Millionaires*. Princeton, New Jersey: Princeton Univ. Press, 1961.

Z

Zeckendorf, William, with McCreary, Edward. *Zeckendorf*. New York: Holt, Rinehart and Winston, 1970.

Zierold, Norman. *The Moguls*. New York: Coward-McCann, 1969.

——. *Sex Goddesses of the Silent Screen*. Chicago: Regnery, 1973.

Zinn, Howard. *La Guardia in Congress*. Ithaca, New York: Cornell University Press, 1959.

Zolotow, Maurice. *It Takes All Kinds*. New York: Random House, 1946.

PERIODICALS

A

"American Credulity." *The Outlook*, December 2, 1910.

Angoff, Charles. "The Tone of the Twenties." *Literary Review*, Vol. 4, No. 1, Autumn, 1960.

"At the White House, at the Ritz." *Time*, January 9, 1938.

Austin, Mary. "The Town that Doesn't Want a Chautauqua." *New Republic*, July 7, 1926.

——. "George Sterling at Carmel." *American Mercury*, May 1927.

"The Awkward Age, Curse or Blessing?" *Modern Screen*, March 1949.

B

"Bad Boy of Baseball." *Newsweek*, May 17, 1951.

Bainbridge, John. "Toots Shor." *The New Yorker* (series), November 11, 18, 25, 1950.

Baird, Peggy. "The Last Days of Hart Crane." *Venture*, Vol. 3, No. 1, 1961.

Baldwin, Charles Sears. "Bohemia." *Dial*, June 1926.

Barnes, Cela. "An Editor Looks at Early Day Kansas." *Kansas State Historical Society Quarterly*. Summer, 1960.

Barrows, Samuel J. "The Temperance Tidal Wave." *Outlook*, July 4, 11, 1908.

Beatty, Jerome. "A Boy Who Began at the Top." *American Magazine*, April, 1932.

Bence-Jones, Mark. "Irish Eccentrics." *Vogue*, October 1, 1964.

Bernstein, Jeremy. "Out of My Mind." *American Scholar*, Winter 1977.

Birnbaum, Lucille. "Behaviorism in the 1920s." *American Quarterly*, Spring 1955.

Bowser, Hallowell. "The Long Shrill Cry." *Saturday Review*, January 27, 1962.

Boyd, Ernest. "A Midwestern Portrait." *Bookman*, May 1924.

Brown, Carleton. "Confidence Games." *Life*, August 1, 1946.

BIBLIOGRAPHY

Brown, Joe David. "A Kind Word for Drink." *Saturday Evening Post*, May 25, 1963.

C

Chesterton, G.K. "The Spirit of the Age in Literature." *Bookman*, October 1930.

"Chicago as Seen by Herself." *McClure's Magazine*, May 1907.

"Chicago's Fabulous Collectors." *Life*, October 17, 1952.

"Chicago's Trials with 'Grand Opera'." *Literary Digest*, February 21, 1925.

Churchill, Judith Chase. "Right Out of This World." *Good Housekeeping*, July 1947.

Cobb, Irvin S. "Twixt the Bluff and the Sound, Improbable People of an Impossible Land." *Saturday Evening Post*, July 28, 1917.

Collins, J.H. "If Anyone Leaves You Money—Beware!" *Pictorial Review*, January 1927.

Cort, David. "The Order of Absurdity, Ha!" *Nation*, September 28, 1957.

Cowley, Malcolm. "The Flight of the Bonus Army." *New Republic*, August 17, 1932.

——. "The Imp of the Perverse." *New Republic*, January 18, 1943.

Crossley, Stella. "Florida Cashes in her Chips." *The Nation*, July 7, 1926.

Crowley, Karl A. "How Gullible Is the Public?" *Scribner's Magazine*, August 1935.

D

"Dali, Gala and Molah." *Newsweek*, December 27, 1965.

"The Dali News." *Time*, January 5, 1959.

Day, Holman. "Does Prohibition Pay?" *Appleton's*, August, 1908.

"Dazzling Parties Introduce Debs." *Literary Digest*, January 16, 1937.

Decker, Karl. "Why and How the Mona Lisa Was Stolen." *Saturday Evening Post*, July 25, 1932.

Deen, Rosemary, F. "Antique Disease." *Commonweal*, February 28, 1958.

Dell, Floyd. "Mona Lisa and the Wheelbarrow." *Harper's Weekly*, July 14, 1914.

Dennis, Nigel. "Treasury of Eccentrics." *Life* Magazine, December 2, 1957.

De Schell, Emilie Ruck. "Is Feminine Bohemianism a Failure?" *Arena*, July 1898.

Duff, Gilfond. "Americans We Like: Congressman La Guardia." *The Nation,* March 21, 1928.

Durrell, Lawrence. "In Praise of Lunatics." *Holiday,* August, 1962.

E

"Election of a Queen." *Newsweek,* December 28, 1953.

Eliot, Charles Warren. "A Study of American Liquor Laws." *Atlantic Monthly,* February 1897.

Ellison, E. Jerome. "Fabulous Frauds." *Reader's Digest,* September, 1936.

"England's Darlings." *Time.* December 30, 1957.

"English Eccentrics." *Horizon,* Winter 1972.

F

Fadiman, Clifton. "Party of One." *Holiday,* December 1956.

Falkowski, Ed. "Guido Bruno—Romantic Ghost." *Bookman,* April 1929.

Fischer, John. "The Easy Chair." *Harper's Magazine.* December 1974.

Fishback, Margaret. "Little Women of the World." *Atlantic Monthly,* March 1940.

"Florida Disaster." *The Survey,* December 15, 1926.

"The Ford Reich." *The Nation,* May 4, 1940.

G

"Girl Guide at the World's Fair." *Life,* May 22, 1939.

Gleason, Arthur H. "Promoters and Their Spending Money." *Colliers,* March 2, 1912.

Graham, Melvyn. "Quirks They Had." *Good Housekeeping,* May 1940.

Grainger, Boine. "Patchin Place." *Plaintalk,* November 1927.

"The Great Debutante Parties of the Century." *Town and Country,* June 1965.

H

Hamburger, Philip. "The Crier." *The New Yorker,* January 20, 1945.

Hinchman, Walter S. "Footpath and Highway." *Forum,* July 1929.

BIBLIOGRAPHY

Holbrook, Stewart. "From Cotillions to Supper Dances." *New York Times Magazine*, May 6, 1964.

Hoover, J. Edgar. "Bankruptcy Frauds." *Journal of Criminal Law and Criminology*, March–April, 1933.

———. "White Slave Traffic." *Journal of Criminal Law and Criminology*. July–August, 1933.

———. "How Safe is Your Daughter?" *American Magazine*, July 1947.

Hughes, Robert. "Howard Hughes—Record Breaker." *Liberty Magazine*, February 6, 1937.

"Hustler's Return." *Newsweek*, December 22, 1975.

I

"Imaginative Crooks." *Literary Digest*, February 7, 1914.

Irwin, Will. "The First Ward Ball." *Collier's*, February 6, 1909.

"It's a Small World." *Pictorial Review*, August 1936.

"It's What's Happening." *Newsweek*, April 25, 1966.

J

"Jefferson County Union Editor's Causes, Outspokenness Made Lively Reading." *Wisconsin Then and Now*, May 1974.

Jolas, Eugene. "Transition: an Epilogue." *American Mercury*, June 1931.

K

Katz, Donald R. "Mad Money." *Feature Magazine*, February 1979.

Kennedy, John B. "Lords of the Loop." *Collier's*, April 3, 1926.

Kraft, Joseph. "J. Edgar Hoover, The Complete Bureaucrat." *Commentary*, February 1965.

L

Landesco, John. "The Criminal Underworld of Chicago in the Eighties and Nineties." *Journal of the American Institute of Criminal Law and Criminology*, May–June, 1934, March–April, 1935.

Lardner, John. "Washington Eyes a Millionaire." *Newsweek*, August 29, 1955.

"The Law of Kenesaw." *Newsweek*, December 6, 1943.

"Leonardo da Vinci and His Two Masterworks." *Ladies Home Journal*, January 1910.

Lewis, Sinclair. "Hobohemia, A Story of Greenwich Village." *Saturday Evening Post*, April 7, 1917.

Littlefield, Walter. "The Two Mona Lisas." *Century Magazine*, February 1914.

"A Long History of Hoaxes." *Time*, March 4, 1974.

Loth, David. "A Look at Famous Swindlers." *American Legion Magazine*, August 1969.

Loving, Rush, Jr. "The View From Inside Hughes Tool." *Fortune*, December 1973.

M

Marcossen, Isaac, F. "The 'Easy' Rich." *Collier's*, April 16, 1914.

Maxwell, Elsa. "Society, What's Left of It." *Ladies Home Journal*, March 1939.

McDermott, Jack. "The Man Who Died on Time." *Life*, January 18, 1960.

Mitgang, Herbert. "The Downfall of Jimmy Walker." *Atlantic Monthly*, October 1962.

"Model T. Tycoon." *Time*, March 9, 1941.

"Mona Lisa's Return." *Literary Digest*, January 3, 1914.

"Mona Lisa's Smile." *The Outlook*, December 27, 1913.

Munson, Gorham. "The Birthday of the Twenties." *Literary Review*, Autumn, 1954.

Murphy, Charles J.V. "The Blowup at Hughes Aircraft." *Fortune*, February 1954.

——, and Wise, T.A. "The Problem of Howard Hughes." *Fortune*, January 1959.

N

Nash, Jay Robert. "Heyday! Chicago's Golden Era of Journalism." *Mankind Magazine*, October 1972.

Nathan, George Jean. "The Mermaid and the Farmer." *Harper's Weekly*, May 29, 1911.

Navasky, Victor S. "His Majesty's Secret Society." *Antioch Review*, November 3, 1971.

"New Ford, New Fight." *Business Week*, February 1, 1933.

Newport, Helen. "Dinner on Fifth Avenue." *Reader's Digest*, September 1936.

"Night Clubs." *Vogue*, March 1, 1934.

BIBLIOGRAPHY

O

"Of Arms and Automobiles." *Fortune*, December 1940.

O'Neill, Paul. "The Little Queen Hollywood Deserved." *Life*, June 4, 1965.

Oppenheim, James. "The Story of the Seven Arts." *American Mercury*, June 1930.

P

Parker, Joan. "Emperor Norton I." *American Heritage*, December 1976.

Pinney, Harvey. "The Radio Pastor of Dearborn." *The Nation*, October 9, 1937.

"A Plea for Eccentrics." *The Christian Century*, February 5, 1958.

"Prince of Hutt River." *Time Magazine*, June 16, 1975.

Pringle, Henry F. "Movie Magician." *Collier's*, March 19, 1932.

"Purge and Pistol." *Time*, October 11, 1937.

"Portrait of Mona Lisa." *Art World*, May 1917.

R

"The Reality of Salvador Dali." *Newsweek*, December 3, 1945.

"The Recovery of the Mona Lisa." *The Independent*, December 25, 1913.

Reilly, Joseph J. "A Keltic Poe." *Catholic World*, March 1920.

Rice, Grantland. "All American Makers." *Collier's*, December 6, 1941.

"River Rouge Revolt." *The Nation*, April 12, 1941.

Rogers, Will. "Bacon and Beans and Limousines." *Survey*, November 15, 1931.

Rosenblatt, Roger. "Eccentrics." *New Republic*, April 29, 1978.

S

"The Sad State of Eccentricity." *Time*, March 14, 1969.

San Severino, Bernardo Quaranta. "The Case of the Mona Lisa." *Bookman*, November 1911.

"The Search for Scarlett O'Hara." *Time*, March 28, 1938.

Seldes, Gilbert. "That Was Woollcott Speaking." *Esquire*, July 1937.

"The Servant Problem." *Fortune*, March 1938.

Shary, Dore. "I Remember Hughes." *Time*, May 2, 1976.

Shelby, Gertrude M. "Florida Frenzy." *Harper's Magazine,* January 1926.

Sitwell, Osbert. "New York in the Twenties." *Atlantic Monthly,* February 1962.

"The Smile of the Mona Lisa as Explained by Freud." *Current Opinion.* January 1917.

"The Soft Watch and the Beady Eye." *Time,* March 3, 1980.

"The Startling Theft of a Priceless Painting." *Harper's Weekly,* September 9, 1911.

Stoddard, Charles Warren. "Ada Clare, The Queen of Bohemia." *National Magazine,* September 1905.

T

Teall, Gardner, "Art." *World Today,* October 1911.

Tenenbaum, Samuel. "Eccentric Literature." *American Mercury,* September 1945.

"Tivoli's Victorian Man." *Time,* October 28, 1974.

"The Tribe of Barnum." *The Nation,* March 20, 1913.

"23 Men vs. Henry Ford." *Time,* February 4, 1941.

U

"U.S. Deb." *Fortune,* December 1938.

V

Vanderbilt, Amy. "The Poor Vanderbilts." *American Mercury,* February 1941.

Villard, Henry S. "Florida Aftermath." *The Nation,* June 6, 1928.

W

"White Elephant." *Time,* January 17, 1940.

White, Lee Strout. "Farewell, My Lovely." *Reader's Digest,* July 1936.

"Will the Theft of the Mona Lisa Help the Louvre?" *Review of Reviews,* October 1911.

Wilson, Edmund. "15 Beech Street." *New Republic,* June 29, 1927.

Wise, T.A. "The Bankers and the Spook." *Fortune,* March 1961.

BIBLIOGRAPHY

Wood, Clement. "The Story of Greenwich Village." *Haldeman-Julius Quarterly,* October 1926.

Y

"Yankee Doodle Salon." *Fortune,* December 1937.

Yoder, Robert M., and Kearns, James S. "Boy Magnate." *Saturday Evening Post,* August 28, 1943.

"The Younger Social Set." *Scribner's Magazine,* January 1936.

NEWSPAPERS

Anchorage *Daily News, Times;* Arizona *Republic;* Arkansas *Gazette;* Army and Navy *Journal;* Atlanta *Constitution, Journal;* Atlantic City *Press;* Baltimore *Patriot, Saturday Visitor, Sun;* Bangor *Times;* Baton Rouge *Advocate, Gazette;* Boston *Evening Post, Evening Traveller, Globe;* Chicago *American, Commercial Advertiser, Daily News, Democrat, Evening Journal, Herald Examiner* and *Examiner, Inter-Ocean, Journal, Record-Herald* and *Herald, Republican, Sun, Sun-Times, Times, Tribune;* Cincinnati *Enquirer;* Cleveland *Plain Dealer;* Dallas *Times-Herald;* Dearborn (Michigan) *Independent;* Denver *Post;* Detroit *Free Press, News;* Edmonton (Canada) *Journal;* Fairbanks (Alaska) *Daily News-Miner;* Florida *Herald;* Galveston *Post;* Hartford *Courant;* Honolulu *Advertiser;* Houston *Chronicle, Post;* Indianapolis *News, Star;* Jefferson County (Wisconsin) *Union;* Kansas City *Star, Times;* Kodiak (Alaska) *Bear, Mirror;* London (England) *Daily News, Evening Post, Gazette, Globe, Standard, Times;* Los Angeles *Examiner, Herald-Examiner, Times;* Manchester (England) *Guardian;* Milwaukee *Journal, Sentinel;* Minneapolis *Tribune;* Montreal (Canada) *Gazette, Star;* New Haven *Register;* New Orleans *Bulletin, Daily Crescent, Picayune, Times-Picayune;* New York *American, Call, Daily Graphic, Daily News, Evening Graphic, Evening Journal, Herald, Herald-Tribune, Mercury, Mirror, Post, Press, Sun, Times, Tribune, Vaudeville News, World, World-Telegram;* Paris (France) *Herald;* Philadelphia *Daily News, Evening Bulletin, Inquirer, Press, Saturday Courier;* Providence *Journal;* St. Louis *Globe Democrat, Post-Dispatch;* San Francisco *Alta, Call, Call-Bulletin, Chronicle, Examiner;* Toronto (Canada) *Mail and Empire, Star, Telegram;* Washington *Post, Star;* Wilmington *Courier;* Winstead (Connecticut) *Evening Citizen.*

INDEX

Numbers in italics indicate pages on which photographs appear.

INDEX

INDEX